My Falkland Days

Rex Hunt

To Jim Graham

With best wishes,

Rex Hunt

David & Charles

To Kelpers . . . and all who stood by them
in their hour of need.

British Library Cataloguing in Publication Data

Hunt, Rex
  My Falkland Days.
  1. Falkland Islands. Governors, history – Biographies
  I. Title
  997'.11

  ISBN 0-7153-9087-2

Typeset by XL Publishing Services   Nairn
and printed in Great Britain
by Billing and Sons   Worcester
for David & Charles
Brunel House   Newton Abbot   Devon

Contents

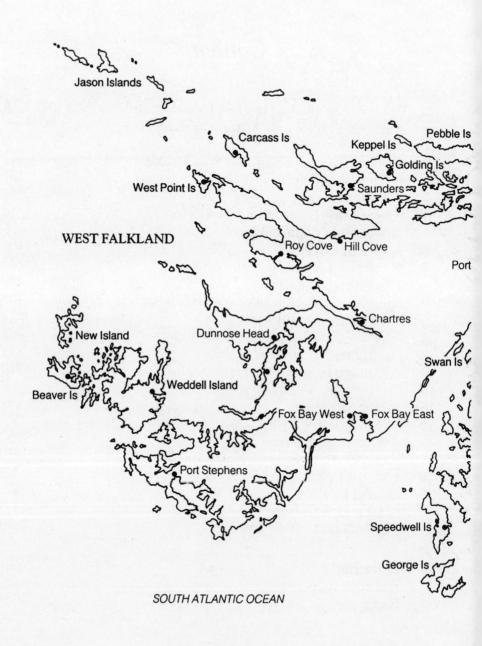

Jason Islands

Carcass Is

Keppel Is

Pebble Is

Golding Is

West Point Is

Saunders

WEST FALKLAND

Roy Cove   Hill Cove

Port

Chartres

New Island

Dunnose Head

Swan Is

Beaver Is

Weddell Island

Fox Bay West   Fox Bay East

Port Stephens

Speedwell Is

George Is

SOUTH ATLANTIC OCEAN

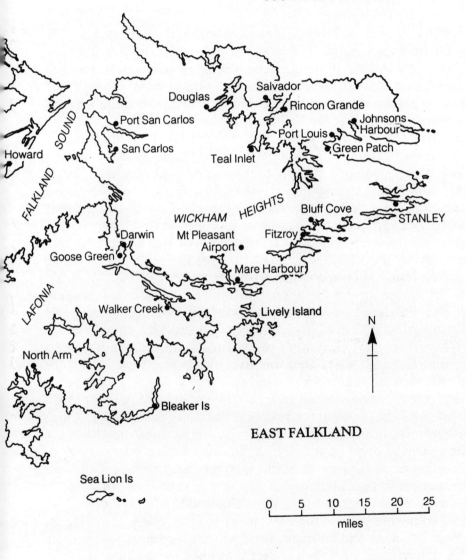

FALKLAND ISLANDS

SOUTH ATLANTIC OCEAN

Douglas

Salvador

Rincon Grande

Port San Carlos

Johnsons Harbour

Port Louis

San Carlos

Green Patch

Howard

FALKLAND SOUND

Teal Inlet

WICKHAM HEIGHTS

Bluff Cove

STANLEY

Darwin

Mt Pleasant Airport

Fitzroy

Goose Green

Mare Harbour

LAFONIA

Walker Creek

Lively Island

N

North Arm

Bleaker Is

EAST FALKLAND

Sea Lion Is

0   5   10   15   20   25
miles

Foreword

By the Rt Hon Lord Shackleton KG, PC, OBE

People have, at least, a vague idea as to where the Falkland Islands are. Dr Johnson described them in the eighteenth century as 'bleak and barren'. 'A land destined to be a bone of contention amongst nations', said Darwin, when he visited them in 1833. Darwin was right and Dr Johnson was wrong. Most people tend to believe Dr Johnson and think that the Falklands are covered in snow. There is, certainly, some snow in winter and occasionally some in summer, but it never lies long. I remember looking across Stanley harbour at the rocks gleaming gold in the sunshine and revelling in the clear, unpolluted atmosphere. It can fairly be described, because of the wind, as a chilly place, but it is not chilly enough to prevent strawberries and raspberries growing out of doors.

Another misunderstanding is revealed whenever people talk about giving the Falklands 'back' to Argentina. They can never be given back, because they were never Argentine. At least one Argentine professor agrees with the international lawyers that the Falklands are British and the people are totally and indistinguishably British. It is hardly surprising that they have no love for Argentina. They were the victims of a sudden undeclared war and, although there were no atrocities, some were locked up and others were taken away – no one knew where at the time. Many feared that they might suffer the fate of many Argentines who disappeared during military rule and were never heard of again. Furthermore, the Islanders could never forgive the Argentines for telling them to drive on the right-hand side of the road!

But this book is more than the story of the occupation and the liberation, it is also the story of life in the Falklands both before the invasion and afterwards. It is about the life of the kelpers (those who were born in the Falklands) in their lonely homesteads, of their devotion and courage, their warmth and hospitality, their independence and pride in the fact that until the conflict they had never been subsidised from Britain. It also reflects the positive

6

advantages of living in such a sparsely-populated country with wide vistas and a unique wildlife.

Although the Falklands enjoy a vigorous democracy, the population of about two thousand is too small to have independence. It has, therefore, to be a colony. Today colonialism is a dirty word, but there is no doubt that British Colonial Officers always served the people with dedication and devotion, administering British justice with fairness and impartiality. Rex Hunt is an old-fashioned but modern-minded servant of the Crown in the great tradition of the British Colonial Service. He and his Chief Secretary, Dick Baker (later the Governor of St Helena), are almost extinct species!

This is a most unusual book, through whose pages shine the humanity and warmth of Rex, his wife, Mavis, and those who worked with them.

SHACKLETON
December 1989

Author's Preface
and Acknowledgements

Old men forget: yet all shall be forgot,
But he'll remember, with advantages,
What feats he did that day.

Henry V

The important thing to remember is that there has to be
a preparedness to make sacrifices for what is right: and to
accept that there are principles, ideas and people that are
worth dying for.

Major-General Sir Jeremy Moore KCB OBE MC

This book is based upon a scrappy diary, which I have been in
the habit of keeping off and on since childhood. It started with
terse entries like 'Saw 2 Ansons, 1 Hudson, 1 Spitfire' (I was
a keen aircraft spotter during the Second World War) and grew
naturally with me. In the Falkland Islands, I usually scribbled it in
the early morning, before tackling my in-tray. It was not intended
to be source material for a book, but merely to remind me of the
things that I had done the day before, and the things that I had left
undone. Also, writing down the names of people that I had met
helped me to remember them. It was not a diary in the classical
sense: I had no illusions of emulating Samuel Pepys or Harold
Nicolson. It served a useful purpose, however, in opening the sluice
gates through which the memory poured — or, more accurately,
trickled, because the words took a long time to come down from
the brain and out through the fingers. But old men forget and the
memory plays tricks, so I apologise in advance for any inaccuracies
or omissions that may upset the reader.

Had it not been for Galtieri's folly, I doubt whether this book
would have found a publisher. There was little world interest in
the Falkland Islands before 1982. Since then, many thousands of
words have been written about them. Most of the publications to

8

date have naturally concentrated upon the conflict itself and it is perhaps still too soon to put it into its true historical perspective, though I should mention one wider effect that was immediately apparent: our standing went up in the world. In the words of one of President Reagan's advisers: 'The United Kingdom responded swiftly with a quiet, grim professionalism which made us all walk a little taller, our shoulders a little farther back and with an admiring eye on the Union Jack.'[1]

I have tried to show in a personal account how the war affected life in the Falkland Islands. Despite all the publicity that they have received since 1982, there are still many misconceptions and misunderstandings about the Islands and their doughty inhabitants. If this book does even a little to clear these away, it will have been well worth while.

I could not have written it without the constant encouragement and support of my wife, Mavis, who not only typed and retyped the manuscript, but also had the patience to listen to me reading it aloud in bed and corrected me on a number of points, for all of which I am indeed grateful. I would like to thank Velma Malcolm and Michael Brown for checking the manuscript, Jack Bishop and Verna Hurt for photocopying it and Lyn Blake, Joan Spruce, Alison Bleaney and many other friends in the Falkland Islands for their patience and kindness in answering my countless questions. My thanks are also due to Records Branch of Library and Records Department, the Foreign and Commonwealth Office, for their help, the Ministry of Defence for permission to use certain Crown Copyright photographs, Express Newspapers plc, Cindy Buxton, Annie Price and Steve Whitley, whose names appear under the photographs that they kindly allowed me to use.

I would also like to place on record my deep appreciation of Lord Shackleton for doing me the honour of contributing the Foreword.

The dedication includes, of course, all the members of the Task Force, whose heroic deeds in regaining the Islands have already been well documented. For those who paid the ultimate sacrifice, Falkland Islanders will be everlastingly grateful. The dedication also includes the members of Naval Party 8901 who were with me on the night of the invasion and who would have fought to the last man had I so commanded. It is a sad fact of war that decorations are more often awarded for success than for bravery.

Finally, kelpers would not forgive me for ending this Preface without giving special thanks to Margaret Thatcher, who stood by them in 1982 and has given them her unwavering support ever since. In the House of Commons on the day after the invasion, she summed up what it was all about:

> They are few in number, but they have the right to live in peace, to choose their own way of life and to determine their own allegiance.

May it be forever thus.

R.M.H.
1989

Notes
1. Mr Edwin Meese, the Lord Mountbatten Memorial Lecture, 4 May 1983.

1

'A Tranquil but Absorbing Way of Life'

I was serving in Kuala Lumpur when the Foreign and Common-wealth Office first suggested to me the post of Governor of the Falkland Islands. It was towards the end of 1979 and my wife, Mavis, and I were enjoying a full life in the sun with a cosmopoli-tan circle of British, Malay and Chinese friends and living in one of the best houses in Her Majesty's Diplomatic Service. As Com-mercial Counsellor and subsequently Deputy High Commissioner, my main job for the past four years had been to promote British trade and business interests in Malaysia. This involved travelling extensively, from Penang to East Malaysia (Sarawak and Sabah), which had been our home for three absorbing years during Indonesian confrontation. We both greatly enjoyed the Far East and were confirmed 'tropical birds', having served for twenty-two of the last twenty-seven years in Africa or South-East Asia; but our tour was coming to an end and we knew that we should shortly have to move on.

As a colonial officer at heart, I was thrilled at the prospect of the Falkland Islands. It had been the ambition of most young District Officers in the Colonial Service one day to become Governor; but my generation was too late – or so I had thought until now. There was no doubt about my own feelings, but I was not so sure about Mavis's. Whatever the good points of the Falkland Islands, they were certainly neither tropical nor cosmopolitan. On the day the FCO telegram arrived, I made the mistake of going home early – my usual routine was to dash in at the last minute for a quick bath and change before our first evening engagement. 'You're early, aren't you?' Mavis inquired, looking at me suspiciously. 'So what's our next posting – Ulan Bator?' 'Er – no – ', I said, hesitantly, 'the Falkland Islands.' Not a flicker of surprise, or dismay, come to that. We walked onto the verandah, stretched out in the wicker armchairs so redolent of the British Raj and watched the local troop of monkeys swinging homeward. Our five acres of jungle provided one of their main routes through Kuala Lumpur.

11

'Shall I get the globe and . . .?'

'I know where they are', said Mavis sharply. Then, more softly, 'You want to go, don't you?'

'Yes.'

'Then I want to go, too.'

How lucky, I thought (not for the first time), to have an understanding wife.

There was no literature about the Falkland Islands in Kuala Lumpur. The British Council had a 16mm cine film on South Georgia, which we watched with interest. It contained spectacular shots of Shackleton's ship *Endurance* breaking up in the ice, but was hardly the best introduction to the Falkland Islands.

We left Kuala Lumpur with great sadness and treated ourselves to a flight home on Concorde from Singapore. On arrival in London, the FCO told me that my appointment had been confirmed. It was quite a mouthful: Governor and Commander-in-Chief of the Falkland Islands and their Dependencies and Vice-Admiral of the same, and High Commissioner of the British Antarctic Territory. The formal recommendation had gone to Buckingham Palace and we were to be informed later of the date of our audience with the Queen. I was to take up my new post about the end of January. We read up all we could about the Falkland Islands, discarded tropical clothing and stocked up with winter woollies. The FCO was as usual helpful in arranging briefings and providing background material, though the 'Post Report' for Stanley was out-of-date and it was interesting to see the quaint way in which this august establishment treated colonial governors. There was a special section to look after the heads of our overseas missions called, appropriately enough, 'Heads of Mission Section'. I went there with a few personal queries to be politely informed that the Heads of Mission Section did not deal with heads of colonial missions; they were the responsibility of the Colonial Service Unit of Hong Kong and General Department. There I found a most helpful Mrs Eileen Gregory, who had run the unit for years; but it did seem a curious repository for the rump of the old and once great Colonial Office.

Our reading on the Falkland Islands dispelled many previously held misconceptions. First, we had not realised that they were no further south of the equator than London was north. We had imagined them in the barren wastes, covered in snow all winter, no summer to speak of and lots of wind. It was pleasantly surprising to discover that the records showed more hours of sunshine and fewer inches of rainfall a year than Kew Gardens. The temperature rarely fell below -3°C (27°F) in Stanley and snow did not settle for long. The wind provided the chill factor, blowing at an average of 16 knots throughout the year and tending to be stronger in the summer than the winter. And, of course, without the Gulf Stream, the sea temperature was lower than the waters around Britain. In general, however, the Falklands enjoyed a temperate, maritime climate without extremes. This cheered up Mavis no end.

Secondly, we had not appreciated the size of the Islands. Looking at them on the map, two little dots off the southern tip of South America, we had pictured them the size of Jersey and Guernsey. We now read that the land area amounted to 4,700 square miles, almost the size of Northern Ireland, over half the size of Wales, and that there were over three hundred islands, scattered around a much greater expanse of water. More significantly, they were separated from the mainland – Argentina – by over two hundred miles of open Atlantic Ocean. For an area of that size, it seemed incredible that, at the last census, the population was a mere 1,813 (the highest number recorded had been 2,392, in 1931). How ironic, I thought, to reach the pinnacle of my colonial career and be responsible for fewer people than at the start when, as Assistant District Commissioner in Uganda, I had been responsible for over 100,000 souls. It was an interesting reflection on the decline of the British Empire over the same period.

Our third misconception concerned the ownership of the Islands. Like most British people of our generation, we had been taught colonial history at school and knew that the Falkland Islands, along with many other parts of the globe at that time, were marked red on the map; but they warranted scarcely a mention in the history books. The only relevant bit of history that I could recall was the Battle of the Falklands, 1914, when Admiral Sturdee had routed Admiral von Spee's naval squadron; but that had been in a book on the First World War, not on British colonial history. We were totally ignorant of the origins of the sovereignty dispute with Argentina and assumed that there was merit on both sides. In this I suspect that we were no different from the vast majority of our fellow countrymen. In marked contrast, there was probably not a single Argentine who did not know the 'Malvinas' story (Argentine version) off by heart. Peron had seen to that by dissemination in schools and constant repetition in the media, following Herr Goebbels' principle that, if you said something long and loud enough, people would believe it.

The more we read, the more we realised that, on all the normal grounds for claiming sovereignty, Britain had the stronger claim. I was sceptical, therefore, about the so-called leaseback solution, which amounted to ceding titular sovereignty of the Islands to Argentina but receiving them back immediately on a long lease, during which British government, law, institutions and the English language would prevail and Islanders would continue to live their lives undisturbed by the Argentines. Some drew, a distinction between sovereignty of territory and sovereignty of people, and between Islanders' interests and their wishes. I doubted whether such esoteric doctrines would find favour with the Islanders and, although I had not yet met any of them, I could imagine their reaction to leaseback. I was uneasy about the whole concept. It seemed to me that both Anthony Williams, our new Ambassador to Argentina, and I were in for a difficult time: how could he improve relations with Argentina without a solution to the very problem that had bedevilled those relations for so long, and how could I persuade the Islanders against their wishes that leaseback was in their best long-term interests?

Subsequent discussions in the FCO increased my unease. The then Permanent Under Secretary, Sir Michael Palliser, emphasised that my first task was to win the confidence of the Islanders. Yes, indeed; but my second was left unsaid. For a decade or more the Islanders had suspected 'the Foreign Office' of trying to get rid of them. To win their confidence, I should have to convince them that there was no question of a 'sell-out' against their wishes.

As well as the FCO, I had useful meetings with my future Foreign Secretary, Mr Francis Pym, who was then Secretary of State for Defence, and the then Commandant-General of the Royal Marines, Lieutenant-General Richards, who explained to me the 'trip-wire' role of Naval Party 8901. This was the odd name given to the forty-three Royal Marines who garrisoned the Falkland Islands. Neither of us suspected then that they would be called upon to fulfil that role two years later. The First Sea Lord, Sir Henry Leach, and Lady Leach entertained Mavis and me to lunch and I paid my first visit to Northwood to meet the then Commander-in-Chief, Fleet, Sir James Eberle. I also met, and struck up a firm friendship with, Captain Nick Barker, who was shortly to take command of HMS *Endurance*. As a result, I had every confidence in the support I could expect from the Royal Navy and the Royal Marines.

The highlights of our stay in London were two visits to Buckingham Palace. The first was to receive my CMG and, by a remarkable coincidence, at the same investiture was an old RAF friend, Peter Latham, to receive his CB. He and I had trained together and in 1948 had shared a room on the same squadron in Germany. Frustrated at flying so little at the time, we had agonised over staying in the RAF or going back to university. Eventually, I had decided to leave and Peter to stay. Seeing him again after all those years, and hearing of all the fast jets he had flown while I had been driving a desk, I could not suppress a tinge of regret.

Our second visit to the Palace was even more memorable. The Queen receives all newly arrived heads of foreign missions accredited to the Court of St James and also grants an audience to newly appointed heads of her overseas missions. Mavis and I waited in an outer room while the new German Ambassador, accompanied by a large entourage, presented his credentials. Then we were ushered in to find the Queen standing on her own. Our audience passed all too quickly and we withdrew with the Queen's parting good wishes to the Falkland Islanders as yet another ambassador's entourage assembled in the outer room.

Later that day, I went to Sackville Street to collect my uniform from those most traditional of English tailors, Hogg and Johnstone. They had been making colonial governors' uniforms for almost as long as the British Empire existed and, as our colonies diminished, so they lavished more care on the few remaining. By now, there were only three full ceremonial uniforms left: Hong Kong, Bermuda and the Falkland Islands. The other remaining colonies were in the tropics and required only the lighter tropical uniform (Hong Kong and Bermuda had both). As mine was reverently unveiled, tailors with tape measures over their shoulders and pins in their lapels emerged from the honeycomb of cubicles and watched with as much pride as if it had been the latest Dior creation. I had previously pronounced myself satisfied except for the feathers on my hat. Mr Johnstone himself had been harder to please. He was a perfectionist and had insisted upon minor alterations which had escaped my notice. But he had advised against taking the red and white feathers out of their special container. The fewer occasions on which they were removed, he said, the longer they would keep their shape. He explained that it was a simple matter of inserting a central bolt into the hole at the top of the hat and tightening a butterfly nut inside. Being singularly stupid in these matters, I said that nevertheless I should like to try on the hat, feathers and all. To Mr Johnstone's dismay, we discovered that, in order to screw the feathers down firmly, I would have needed a half-inch hole in my head.[1] Poor Mr Johnstone was most apologetic and took the feathers away to have the bolt shortened. As he left, one of his assistants muttered, 'I thought governors had wooden heads.'

After a last meeting with Nicholas Ridley, the Minister responsible for the Falkland Islands, we left Gatwick in the good care of British Caledonian on the first leg of our journey to the Falkland Islands. My ceremonial sword caused a fuss as it was designated an offensive weapon and had to travel by hand of pilot. The flight took about four hours to Las Palmas, seven to Rio-de-Janeiro and five to Buenos Aires, with a stop at Sao Paulo. We were met at Buenos Aires by Richard Gozney, the personable young First Secretary on the Falkland Islands desk in our Embassy, and driven to the Ambassador's residence. It was almost an hour's drive and gave us our first glimpse of Buenos Aires. Mediterranean in atmosphere and architecture, I was intrigued by the cobblestones, which Richard explained had been brought over from England as ballast in British ships coming to load with beef. Hedwig Williams, Anthony's Austrian-born wife, gave us our first taste of the famed Argentine beefsteak that evening, and we were not disappointed.

During the next two days, I met Embassy staff and several British businessmen, but no Argentine minister or official. Not recognising our sovereignty over the Falkland Islands, the Argentines could not receive me as Governor; indeed, they professed to have a governor of the 'Islas Malvinas' themselves, the military commander of their southernmost province, Tierra-del-Fuego. One of the few Argentines I did meet was Bishop Cutts, who not only had the diocese of Buenos Aires but was also the Anglican Bishop of the Falkland Islands. Anthony kindly invited him to lunch at the Residence and he gave me the standard Anglo-Argentine attitude to the Falklands: Anglo-Argentines were fairly treated in Argentina, it was logical that the Falkland Islands should be part of the Argentine and the Islanders had nothing to fear by joining them.[2]

The flight from Buenos Aires to Stanley took the best part of a day. There was a choice between a direct trip to Comodoro Rivadavia by Boeing 737 and several hours' wait there before catching the Fokker F27 Friendship to Stanley, or flying on the 'milk-run' from Buenos Aires by Friendship all the way, landing at various internal airstrips en route. Richard had recommended the former because, he said, the British acting consul had been alerted to meet us at Comodoro Rivadavia and he would show us the town. It meant a 4am start, but Richard nobly collected us from the Residence and eased our way through the airport formalities at the Aeroparque, which to my astonishment was situated in the heart of the city. The Argentine officials were helpful and courteous and we had a good flight to Comodoro Rivadavia in a little over two hours. The further south we flew, the more lunar became the landscape. I began to understand why no self-respecting Argentine cared to live more than sixty miles south of Buenos Aires.

The acting consul, Mr Quinn-Coles, was not at the airport to meet us, but we managed to contact him by telephone and he arrived about an hour later, grumbling about the bad communications. A colourful character from the pages of Graham Greene, he was over eighty years old and had been in Comodoro Rivadavia since the 1930s. His lean frame was as hard and ravaged as the surrounding landscape, for this was oil country, where the land was exploited, not cared for. As he drove us into town in his ancient car, almost as old as himself, I was reminded of Seria, the Brunei oil town, but with a difference; Comodoro Rivadavia had no greenery. We did not see a single garden, shrub or grass verge. Mr Quinn-Coles took us to the town's only hotel, and we hoped that we would never be marooned there overnight.[3].

Back at the airport, we were delayed for an hour and a half while the loadmaster sorted out an overbooking problem, finally departing for Stanley with twenty-six passengers. One of them was Vicecomodoro Eduardo Santozo of the Argentine Air Force, who had been stationed in Stanley two years before. He was friendly and helpful and invited me up front to catch my first glimpse of the Falkland Islands. The sky was overcast and visibility poor, so we were making a low approach from the sea. Fortunately, as we negotiated our way round a squall, the sun broke through and lit up Stanley directly in front of us. It was as if some stage-hand had acted on cue and switched on the floodlights. I stood behind the pilot and co-pilot, admiring the gaily painted roofs dotted along the hillside. But the little town seemed terribly vulnerable, as if at any moment a landslide would wipe it off its precarious perch and sweep it into the harbour. Behind was a rocky and rugged skyline. As we lowered flaps and undercarriage and made a wide sweep over the town, I

17

saw for the first time the distinctive peaks that were to become so well known in 1982: Mount William, Mount Harriet, Tumbledown, Two Sisters, Mount Kent, Mount Longdon and Wireless Ridge. Stanley was a thrilling sight, but I remember thinking – as many British soldiers thought after me – 'How small!'

We turned on finals and I moved to go back to my seat for the landing, but the pilot grabbed my arm and beckoned me to stand behind him, holding firmly on the back of his seat. I thus had a marvellous view of the approach and landing. Not only did the runway appear to be rushing towards us at an alarming speed, it seemed much too small for an aircraft of our size. It was also coming at us at an angle of some forty-five degrees. Observing that the windsock was horizontal and blowing at right angles to the runway (the pilot told me later that it was a 50-knot crosswind), I braced myself for an interesting landing. Over the threshold, he flared at precisely the right height, cut the throttles and kicked the aircraft straight at the last second, the induced skid exactly counteracting the drift. We touched down so smoothly that I doubt whether the other passengers knew that we had landed. It was a perfect demonstration of a crosswind landing in severe conditions and I was filled with admiration at the Argentine pilot's skill.

We taxied in to a small apron in front of an unfinished looking control tower, the sun shining on a group of people and a red taxi. I thanked the pilot and crew and stepped out into a typical Falkland wind. My immediate reaction was one of relief that I was not in uniform – a wooden head would certainly be needed to keep my hat on in this. At the foot of the steps was the Chief Secretary, Dick Baker, who had been Acting Governor during the inter-regnum (protocol dictated that Governors should not overlap) and his wife Connie who, despite the wind, managed to look as smart and neat as when we had first met two months ago in London. Dick introduced a gentleman dressed in the Royal Marines' old Number One uniform and another in the familiar blue of an English bobby. This was my first meeting with Falkland Islanders. The military gentleman was Phil Summers, normally Deputy Financial Secretary, but now in his territorial role of Commanding Officer of the Falkland Islands Defence Force and aide-de-camp to the Governor. The policeman was Toddy McMillan, the Chief Police Officer. Dick explained that the swearing-in ceremony had been arranged for 4pm in the Town Hall and that, despite our late arrival, there was still time for us to meet the staff at Government House and for me to change into uniform.

We walked over to the red taxi and had our first meeting with Don Bonner, who was chauffeur, valet, steward, majordomo and general factotum at Government House and was to become my fishing mentor, snooker opponent and very good friend. He was also to become my main source of information about what went on in the Falkland Islands. He knew everybody and, even more important in a small community, he knew who was related to whom, who had been married to whom and who was speaking to whom at any given moment. He had a photographic memory, a lively inquiring mind and a great sense of humour. The Bonner family had been in the Falkland Islands for four generations. Some had been more respectable than others, but they had all contributed to the local folklore. San Carlos, soon to become known around the world as the beachhead for our Task Force, had once been owned by Jack Bonner. Indeed, it was still known in the Islands as 'JB' to distinguish it from the neighbouring farm, Port San Carlos, which was known as 'KC', after its owner, Keith Cameron. Don claimed to have come from the less respectable side of the Bonner family. Brought up at Port Howard, in West Falkland, he had tried his hand at most things. Like many of his contemporaries, he had worked down in South Georgia on the whaling stations; he had volunteered for the Royal Navy as soon as he was old enough and served in minesweepers; he had returned home to become a shepherd, winning the Islands' sheepdog trials three years in succession; and he had been a renowned drinker. He had turned teetotal when his attractive and long-suffering wife, Vera, threatened to walk out, with all seven children. He had also given up smoking, and could be utterly relied upon to look after the stocks of alcohol, cigars and cigarettes in Government House.

I did not, of course, learn all this until later. On that first afternoon, Don greeted us with a welcoming smile and kept up an informative commentary as he drove us the four miles from the airport into Stanley. On the right was Canopus Hill, named after the battleship beached in the bay below after the Battle of Coronel and whose guns had fired the first shots in the Battle of the Falklands. If we looked back we could catch a glimpse of the two 6in naval guns left there since the First World War. On the left was Surf Bay, where we could often see dolphins and seals. Those handsome birds on the shoreline were kelp geese, the pure white the male and the browny black the female. We were now rounding the bend into the Canache, and the slanting masts were those of the wreck of the *Lady Elizabeth*. 'Fine iron hull,' said Don, 'You can get good mussels off her.' Nearer to town, we could see the hulk of the *Golden Chance*, which Don had helped to sail out from Wivenhoe. 'Had to be towed to the three-mile limit before we set off', said Don, 'Department of Trade wouldn't give her a seaworthiness certificate!' We were now passing the town's main peat banks. Every householder was allocated a bank and had to cut and 'rickle' his own peat (I was learning new words, too). If we looked right we could see the Narrows, the entrance into Port Stanley from Port William. Ships' captains lined up the two posts with the solid white triangles to ensure a safe run in. Now we were approaching the Cable and Wireless transmitting station, and 'them cattle' grazing around the aerial masts were Ayrshires belonging to Malcolm Ashworth, who ran the town dairy. 'Not an Islander, but does pretty well, considering', said Don.

We reached a row of unkempt white prefabs, which Don called 'the white city', and passed the 20mph sign and 'Welcome to Stanley'. We slowed down (from 15 to 10mph) and Don recounted names of people, streets and houses too numerous to absorb. I remembered 'Hodson's Villas' on the left – 'Worst slums in Stanley'. They consisted of two single-storey blocks, flimsier looking than beach huts in England. Then we were at the top of a steep hill, looking down on the town and harbour beyond. The houses were mainly of wooden construction, with corrugated iron roofs, brightly painted in reds, yellows, greens and blues. Most of them had colourful, orderly gardens and fences, caringly maintained. Lupins were everywhere and clearly thrived in this climate, despite the wind. At the foot of the hill was the Philomel Store and, off-set a little to the right, the public jetty. This was the favourite sledge-ride for the young in winter, and the not-so-young, said Don. Even Harold had been sledging down here last year. 'Harold?' I asked. 'Harold Rowlands, the Financial Secretary', said Don. I'm going to like it here, I thought – a chauffeur who sails an old tub out from England and a senior civil servant who sledges down Philomel Hill. It looked a hazardous operation to manoeuvre a speeding sledge round the S-bend and onto the jetty, and Don confirmed that occasionally some of the 'young fellers' failed to make it and finished up in the harbour.

We turned into Ross Road, which ran the length of the harbour, past an imposing terrace of brick-built houses called Jubilee Villas – 'Queen Victoria's Golden Jubilee, 1887' said Don, proudly –

then Christ Church Cathedral, a most attractive building, but the trees outside drew our attention (they were the first we had seen) as well as a huge whalebone arch, twice as big as Whitby's, in an adjoining square. Next came the West Store, which looked more like a collection of storage sheds than the town's main shop and supermarket, run by the Falkland Islands Company, then the Upland Goose Hotel and the Colony Club. I was more interested, however, in the harbourside of Ross Road, where on the pleasant greensward lay part of a huge mast. 'The mizzen from the *SS Great Britain*,' said Don. Further back lay another black hulk, the deck of which had been incongruously covered with shiny aluminium sheeting. 'The *Charles Cooper*', explained Don, 'She used to be a wool store.' Then, too quickly to take in properly even at our slow pace, we passed the telephone exchange, the police station, the Town Hall, St Mary's (the Roman Catholic Church), the Government jetty, the LADE[4] office, Public Works Department, the Secretariat, the hospital and nurses' quarters and were driving over a cattle-grid and up a narrow drive lined with thick gorse bushes to Government House.

We fell in love with what was to be our home for almost the next six years as soon as we saw it. Although badly in need of a coat of paint, and extended in an apparently haphazard manner, it had a Victorian charm and great character. There was a peace and permanence about it that reminded me of a vicarage in the Yorkshire dales. It was James Herriot country, and I felt immediately at home. Mavis was delighted with the gardens, which were clearly lovingly tended, and she could not wait to meet Gene Williams, the head gardener. I left Mavis chatting with the staff as Don took me upstairs to change into uniform. Although I had tried it on many times in Hogg and Johnstone's, this was the first time 'for real' and I must confess to feeling decidedly embarrassed when I finally appeared before the Government House staff. I had been unable to fasten the tight neck, and Don, Phil and I struggled with the wretched hooks until I was red in the face; but to no avail. Mavis came to the rescue and the woman's touch worked. I realised how sensible one of my predecessors had been in choosing a taxi as the Governor's official carriage. Even with my lack of inches, I would have had difficulty in getting in and out of a normal car in full uniform.

For the first of many times, Don took us on the two-minute drive from Government House to the Town Hall. The then Officer Commanding NP 8901, Major Sandy Lade, invited me to inspect the guard of honour, which made an interesting contrast between the Royal Marines in their modern 'Number Ones' and the Falkland Islands Defence Force in their old 'Number Ones'. We went inside for the formal swearing-in, the first of many memorable occasions that we were to attend in the Town Hall over the next six years. The senior magistrate, a dignified Falkland Islander called Harold Bennett, administered the oath of office in a simple but impressive ceremony and, in a welcoming speech, Dick said that I could expect a 'tranquil but absorbing way of life' in the Islands. I replied that I would do my utmost to discharge my responsibilities in the best interests of the Falkland Islanders, after which we took tea and sandwiches with the leading citizens. Our first impressions, which we never had cause to change, were of a friendly, open people who welcomed newcomers with genuine warmth and intuitive good manners. We returned to Government House feeling confident that we would enjoy our tranquil sojourn 'out of the main stream' (as the FCO had described it) after six hectic years in Kuala Lumpur and Saigon.

Notes

1. My predecessor, James Parker, did not have the opportunity to try on his hat in London and finished with a bleeding head on several windy occasions.

2. As some leading Anglo-Argentines were to discover when they visited the Falkland Islands during the occupation, this argument did not appeal to Falkland Islanders, who pointed out that Anglo-Argentines had made the free choice of becoming Argentine citizens and living in a foreign country, whereas Islanders had chosen to remain under British rule. Indeed, several of them had relatives who had gone to Patagonia from the Falklands and made their fortunes; but they did not envy them their wealth. Islanders preferred the British way of life, despite harsher conditions and more modest rewards.

3. Our son, Tony, had to spend a night there on one of his trips from school. He said it was an experience not to be repeated.

4. Lineas Aereas del Estado, the Argentine Air Force's civilian airline.

2

A Violent Death

For the next week, however, life was as hectic as it had ever been. We had arrived in the Falkland Islands at the end of the shearing season. Traditionally both East and West held a week-long programme of horse-racing and general festivities, when farm workers and anyone who could leave Stanley got together, relaxed and enjoyed themselves after the busiest time of the sheep-farming year. Each of the major settlements in East and West Falklands took it in turn to host the sports and, for many, it was the only time that they saw people from elsewhere. All the hosts' houses were filled to overflowing. The women caught up with the family news as they shared the cooking and the washing-up; the children enjoyed playing with others of their own age (often not possible in the smaller settlements) and the men ran the various events and swapped yarns as they quaffed gallons of beer.

On the day after our arrival, we were invited to join the sports on West Falkland, which were being hosted by Hill Cove, before proceeding to Goose Green for the East Falkland sports. As Don drove us to the Beaver hangar, half-a-mile or so to the west of Government House, I looked forward to my first flight with the Falkland Islands Government Air Service (FIGAS) and, incidentally, my first flight in a floatplane. Mavis had never liked flying in light aircraft, and was somewhat apprehensive. We watched as the ubiquitous Land Rover towed the Beaver on its wheeled cradle out of the hangar and lowered it gently down the slipway. Two groundcrew in waist-high waders stood in the icy water, holding on to the floats as they floated free from the cradle. There was a gangway on wheels for the passengers. We were introduced to the groundcrew, two of whom were technicians seconded from the RAF, a fitter to look after the engines and a rigger the airframes. They wore civilian clothes and the current incumbents, Al Watson and Bill Hughes, said that they enjoyed the change from service life. They had obviously adapted well to the Island community. The senior pilot and Director of Civil Aviation was an ex-RAF bomber pilot, Jim Kerr. He invited me to climb aboard and take the right-hand seat. Mavis climbed on to the float and hoisted herself nervously into the back.

The first thing that struck me was that one had to be a seaman as well as a pilot to handle a floatplane. As soon as Jim started the engine and waved our helpers away, the Beaver began to drift towards the shore. A sharp burst of throttle and a kick on the rudder put us on course for the deeper water and a clear run for take-off; but Jim had constantly to take both wind and current into account. It seemed a tricky business manoeuvring the craft into position while carrying out the normal take-off checks. I was intrigued by the technique of rocking the aircraft to get up on the step of the floats during take-off, thus breaking the suction of the water.[1] We were airborne after an incredibly short run and climbing slowly to the west, over the most magnificent scenery of wild, open moorland and craggy hills. Jim was an excellent guide as we flew the route (in the opposite direction) that the Royal Marines and paratroopers would 'yomp'[2] in 1982: up the Estancia track, Mount Kent on our left, Longdon on our right, to Estancia House, across two creeks separated by Sparrow Rincon, past lower Malo House to the fishing hut on the Malo (the best river in the Islands, said Jim, for sea trout – a fact I was able later to confirm); Teal Inlet settlement away on the right, looking smart and neat and tidy with its green roofs and green paddocks; the mighty Mount Usborne filling the skyline to the south, dark and solemn and higher than we were; Douglas Station further away to our right, barely discernible but with roofs glinting in the sun; over a pimple on the plain called Bombilla Hill; the upper reaches of San Carlos river, winding like a serpent and growing bigger and wider by the minute; then over a promontory and suddenly there was Port San Carlos below and San Carlos Water, Fanning Head and Falkland Sound beyond. It was a breathtaking view in the summer sunshine. The Mediterranean could not have been bluer. As we climbed to cross the Sound, we had a panoramic view of the West Falkland. Westerners, said Jim, called the West the best and, looking at the sight before us, we could not disagree.

Once across the Sound, Jim let me take over and it was good to handle an aircraft again. Mavis commented on the lack of sheep. We had not expected to see much evidence of human settlement but, with a sheep population of over half-a-million, we were surprised to fly for mile after mile without noticing a single one. Jim explained that ninety per cent of the sheep congregated on ten per cent of the land. This might have been an overstatement, but it was certainly true that the sheep tended to stick to the valleys, and there were vast tracts of land that appeared to be totally untouched. Indeed, I found this vision of nature's unspoilt domain, before man had tampered with it, the most attractive feature of the Falkland Islands.

The scenery changed dramatically as Jim took back the controls and dipped down over a neatly laid-out settlement, with green paddocks and a ribbon of trees nestling under the sunny northern slopes of Mount Adam. We had arrived at Hill Cove. Like all the old settlements in the Falkland Islands, it was situated on the coast. Before the advent of the flying machine, the only communication was by sea, so a good harbour was the first requisite. The next was fresh water and the third was peat. It was also desirable to face north to catch the sun. Hill Cove was one of the most attractive sites on the Islands and combined all of these. Founded by Robert Blake, from Crewkerne, in 1889, it had remained in the family and we were met at the jetty by the present manager, Tim Blake. I admired Jim's skill when, after alighting gently on the water, he taxied to a stop with his wing-tip overlapping the jetty and switched off as Tim held the wing. We stepped out as simply as disembarking from a landplane.

The manager's house was some distance from the main settlement and, as we drove there in the inevitable Land Rover, Tim explained that they were about to start the sheepdog trials. In the 'big house' we met Tim's vivacious wife, Sally, and most of the other farm owners and managers in West Falkland before donning anoraks and wellingtons and going to watch the trials. The setting was perfect, with magnificent hills behind and the bright blue of Byron Sound in front. The weather was cold but beautifully sunny, with a clarity and crispness in the air that reminded me of winter on the North West Frontier. We watched as shepherd and dog – border collies mainly – acted in unison to round up, by British standards, uncommonly wild sheep, guide them through seemingly impossible obstacles and finally pen them in a tiny enclosure with a triumphant slam of the gate. Not all were successful, but a surprising number were and we marvelled at the intelligence of the working dogs and the understanding between them and their masters. Tim enthused and encouraged and gave us an expert commentary. He clearly loved his life as a sheepfarmer and, in this setting, I could understand why.

Like most Islanders at that time, he and Sally gathered on

horseback, and their description of riding out with dogs and colleagues for a day's gathering sounded perfect bliss.[3] Sally explained how at the beginning of the week she had ridden up to the ridge behind the settlement to spot approaching guests and been rewarded with the unforgettable sight of thirty or more horses moving leisurely towards her from the south. People had ridden and led them for days, coming from as far afield as Port Stephens, eighty miles away, joined by others from Fox Bay West, Fox Bay East, Dunnose Head, Chartres and Port Howard until there they were in an impressive troop toiling up the last ridge before Hill Cove. Others had come overland by Land Rover (as I was soon to discover, a Falkland Islander can take a Land Rover where no ordinary mortal would dare to tread, let alone drive), some had flown in and others had come from neighbouring islands by boat.

After the sheepdog trials, we returned to the 'big house' for lunch. I must have looked somewhat anxiously at my watch, because Sally explained to me that camp[4] time was different from Stanley time. A previous Chief Secretary had tried to impose Summer Time throughout the Islands, but campers had taken no notice, so for the summer months Stanley was one hour ahead of camp. This was my first experience of the Falkland Islander's stubborn independence. Sally was descended from a leading Islander family, the Clements. She had strong views, expressed clearly and forcefully but with great good humour. Tim had served on both Executive and Legislative Councils and had represented the Falkland Islands at Commonwealth Parliamentary Association conferences in India and the Caribbean. Sally had accompanied him to India and both were regular visitors to England, where Tim had been born and educated. Well travelled as she was, however, I noticed that Sally maintained the kelper[5] tradition of rolling her own cigarettes.

All too quickly it was time to be off again to the jetty for the flight to Goose Green, on East Falkland. We flew across the Sound and over the route subsequently taken by Colonel 'H' and the 2 Paras (and, incidentally, our future son-in-law) from San Carlos to Darwin, landing at the jetty at nearby Goose Green. We were met by Brook Hardcastle, the General Manager of the Falkland Islands Company, and one of his house-guests, Adrian Monk, then manager of San Carlos. Brook ran all the company's farms from his base in Darwin. He was a fellow Yorkshireman who had married a Falkland Islander and, apart from a short spell in New Zealand, had spent most of his working life in the Islands. Adrian was a Falkland Islander in all but birth, with relations on his mother's side going back to the original settlers. One of the Islands' senior Councillors, he had represented them at talks with the Argentines, held decidedly strong views about the sovereignty dispute and expressed them well. At his father's behest but against his own inclination, he had gone to sea at an early age and become a master mariner. As soon as he could, he had abandoned the sea and, like many another ex-seafarer, had taken to farming, first in Wales and then in the Falkland Islands, starting on Pebble Island before moving to San Carlos. I did not learn all this at our first meeting but, as we left the jetty and rocked and bounced our way along the rough track from Goose Green to Darwin, I did learn that he had a lively sense of humour. He ribbed Brook about his driving, the state of the track, the flocks of upland geese (Brook was renowned for shooting them), the condition of his sheep, the paddocks, gates and fencing all the way to the 'big house'. Brook for his part was not slow with an answer and the repartee was as informative as it was amusing.

At the 'big house', a comfortable modern building with a large, warm kitchen (all Falkland Islanders have large, warm kitchens), we met Brook's wife Eileen and their eldest son, Gavin, who gave me expert advice on the best motorcycle to buy for our son when he came out. We then went off to watch the steer-riding. Like the sheepdog trials, I found it fascinating, but Mavis thought it cruel and vowed never to watch it again. It was unfortunate that the first steer we saw had its horn ripped off by a lasso, though most of them did not appear to suffer any lasting harm. I must admit, however, that the poor beasts were wide-eyed with fear as they came out of the corral, bucking and kicking in their frantic (and usually successful) efforts to dislodge their riders. The most exciting part was not the actual steer-riding but the retrieving of the steer once it had discarded its rider. Three men manoeuvred their horses at speed near enough to the fleeing animal to be able to throw a lasso around its neck and bring it to a halt. I marvelled at their dexterity in controlling the horse over rough ground while lassoing a dodging target. Once halted, the steer stood surprisingly still while one of the cowboys – for such they were, in the best Wild West tradition – removed the restricting harness and let it wander docilely away. In the early days, apparently, gauchos from the mainland had hurled bolas to bring down the wild cattle; but that skill had disappeared.

As at Hill Cove, the afternoon passed all too quickly and Brook drove us back to the 'big house' for a hot bath, change and dinner before attending the dance and prize-giving in Goose Green community hall (where many of those present that night were subsequently to be incarcerated by the Argentines). Every item of the delicious dinner was home-produced, starting with Brook's speciality, smoked mullet, caught that morning at Camilla Creek and smoked by Brook minutes before serving, followed by roast duckling (domestic, reared by Eileen) with the tastiest new potatoes and vegetables from the garden and finishing with freshly picked strawberries and feathery light meringues made from penguins' eggs. Brook even had a choice of homemade or imported wines.

We made the community hall by ten o'clock and I was grateful to my mother for having taught me old-fashioned dances like the St Bernard's Waltz, the Valeeta and the Gay Gordons, for they were all played, and danced, with great gusto. One attractive young girl came up to me and said, 'Come on, Guv, let's 'ave a dance', whisking me off into a Military Two-Step before I could draw breath. One dance with which I was unfamiliar but quickly learnt (after a fashion) was the Circassian Circle, the dance equivalent of the Falklands' signature tune. A progressive dance for young and old, it was most popular throughout the Islands and no festivity was complete without it. Mavis presented the prizes to the week's winning jockeys, runners, tug-of-war teams, shepherds and steer-riders (the star cowboy, Dennis Whitney, collecting a prize for his expert lassoing) and we left the dance with all present enjoying a most convivial and good-natured occasion.

We went down to breakfast the next morning to be greeted with the news that an Islander had been knifed in the stomach by one of the Chilean farmhands after we had left the dance and was at that moment in a critical condition in the Goose Green bunkhouse. Brook had been called out in the early hours by Eric Goss, whom we had left at the dance festooned with rosettes and celebrating victory as champion jockey over his great friend and rival, Ron Binnie. The Gosses and the Binnies were two of the longest-established families in the Falkland Islands, going back to the Chelsea pensioners of 1849. Eric and Ron both worked for the Falkland Islands Company and were managers of adjoining farms, Goose Green and Fitzroy. Ron had the right build for a jockey while Eric was more the burly farmer; but they were both fine riders and judges of horses. Once mounted, Eric's weight did not appear to be a handicap and he and Ron battled annually for the top prize of champion jockey. As host manager that year, Eric had been mainly responsible for the organisation of the week's events and he had told me during the dance how relieved he was that everything had gone off without a hitch. Now this.

I realised that the manager of a settlement did much more than run the farm. He was in effect the old-time colonial District Officer, responsible for the lives and welfare of all his charges. Brook told me that they had already contacted Dr Summers by radio and he was now on his way from Stanley by Beaver. Eric had done what he could for the victim, Tony Kirk, and put the wretched Chilean in custody. One of the nursing sisters from Stanley, who had come to Goose Green for the sports, was now looking after the patient. Brook took me to Goose Green, where we found that Peter Summers had already arrived. He said that the patient was still haemorrhaging badly, his intestines were hanging out and he was in too bad a state to move. The Beaver had gone back for Peter's assistant, Alison Bleaney, nurses and operating equipment, and Peter proposed to perform an emergency operation in the bunkhouse before flying him to Stanley.

Eric, who had had no sleep at all that night, told me how it had happened. The Chilean, Francisco Burgos, was an outside shepherd (that is, one who lived not in a settlement but on his own in one of the more distant shanties) and normally went into the settlement only at weekends for provisions. A quiet, retiring man and a good worker, Burgos had come in for the sports and, like most others at the dance, had been drinking. Leaving the men's lavatory, he had bumped into Tony Kirk's girl friend, who was going into the Ladies. It was probably an accident but Kirk and his friends had chosen to think otherwise. Eric had heard about the incident and quietly advised Burgos to head for home. Burgos had followed Eric's advice, gone to the bunkhouse and collected his riding gear (which included a knife), intending to saddle up and ride for home immediately; but his way out had been barred by Kirk and his friends, who had advanced on him along the corridor. Kirk had punched him in the face, breaking his nose, whereupon Burgos had drawn his knife and stabbed Kirk in the stomach. A simple tale no doubt enacted nightly in countless taverns around the world; but there had not been a violent killing in the Falkland Islands for over fifty years. The unforgivable crime in Falkland Islanders' eyes was that Burgos had pulled a knife. Punch-ups occurred frequently, usually after drinking and over women, the men outnumbering the women by five to one. Farm managers normally sorted out the culprits without calling in the police. To that extent, the Islands were largely self-policing. But a knife was different; it was alien to the Anglo-Saxon culture. It was what those 'dagoes' used on the mainland . . . I was learning fast.

Owing to the emergency, our flight back to Stanley was delayed, so Brook took the opportunity to show us round the wool-shed, said to be the biggest in the southern hemisphere. Empty at the end of the season, it was difficult to imagine the noise and bustle during shearing time, with sweating men shearing up to three hundred sheep a day. We flew out in the Beaver that brought in the medical team. The pilot was Ian White, one of two Falkland Islander pilots flying for FIGAS. He was following in the air his father's nautical footsteps; Captain White had been a familiar figure to all visitors to the Falkland Islands as master of the steamship *Darwin*, which had carried passengers and mail between Stanley and Montevideo and was the only means of travel to and from the Islands from 1957 until 1971. Ian had learnt his flying in Canada, where he had piled up hours on the Beaver floatplane and probably now had more experience on that type of aircraft than any other British pilot. He met us with the news that we would have to go back to Hill Cove before returning to Stanley, as he had another casualty to pick up there and take to Stanley hospital. I was delighted to fly over to the West again and savour the magnificent scenery. Our casualty turned out to be a cheerful Royal Marine, who had broken his wrist steer-riding, which was quite a common occurrence for the inexperienced. Ian let me fly most of the way and we arrived back in Stanley after an hour's flight and an eventful twenty-four hours in camp.

Don met us at the Beaver hangar with the red taxi. Dick was also there – he was always punctilious in meeting me back in Stanley, though my frequent absences placed a heavier load on his already overburdened shoulders. As we drove the Royal Marine to hospital, Dick told us the latest information on Kirk. Peter Summers had stitched him up and intended to bring him to Stanley; but the grave news was that he had been found to be suffering from DIC (Disseminated Intravascular Coagulopathy) and they had been unable to stop the bleeding. It was touch-and-go. We agreed that there was likely to be a murder charge against Burgos and sent a warning signal to London to alert Sir Peter Watkin-Williams, who as a retired judge from the Colonial Legal Service was retained to hear serious cases in the Falkland Islands and St Helena (coincidentally, he had served as a Resident Magistrate in Uganda when I was there).

My next appointment was a complete change. A banking expert from the Cayman Islands, Robin Benbow, had been investigating the possibilities for off-shore banking in the Falkland Islands. He joined us for a late lunch and we had a long discussion on the banking scene afterwards. He spoke highly of the integrity and ability of the Financial Secretary (Harold Rowlands) but was not optimistic about developing the Islands as a tax-haven or an off-shore banking centre. We were too remote and lacked the communications and expertise to attract the right sort of bankers. We were too small to have a commercial bank.[6] I was beginning to despair; no banker, no solicitor, no accountant, no estate agent, no cobbler, no greengrocer, no dry-cleaner, no hairdresser, no garage mechanic, no mason, no builder, no undertaker. How did the Islands work? Dick gave me the answer succinctly that night, at dinner: 'FIG, FIC, and DIY.'[7]

Next morning we experienced our first Falklands' hailstorm. I took to having breakfast in my dressing-room and had a magnificent view to the north, across the harbour to the Camber and, on a clear day, Mount Low beyond. This morning, the hailstones hammered down on the iron roof like grapeshot and fierce, swirling squalls obliterated the harbour. Between the squalls I could see the *Penguin* bucking and tossing on her moorings. She was a small schooner moored opposite Government House, and she became a good guide to the wind strength. If it blew over sixty knots, she would start to drag her anchor. I never ceased to enjoy my breakfast view: the water was always on the move and the wildlife a constant joy. In front of me were two resident loggers[8], jealously guarding their territory against aggressive neighbours. As I ate my breakfast, stinkers[9] would pass one-by-one up the harbour, not four feet above the sea wall, gliding swiftly on huge wings like big black bombers on a dawn raid, heading for their breakfast at the slaughterhouse. Above them was the fighter escort, flights of kelp and dolphin gulls, heading purposefully for the same target. The stronger the wind, the more they seemed to enjoy it. In winter, the turkey vultures would come into town from the hills, wheeling and soaring above the gulls and often coming down to rest with a noisy scramble on our iron roof (we once counted twenty-three on the roof at the same time). Their favourite perch was on top of the small drawing-room chimney, wings unfolded to catch the heat from

31

the peat fire or, perhaps, to fumigate their feathers. Occasionally, one would nestle down on the chimney, causing a smokescreen in the small drawing-room and a hurried evacuation until dislodged by a well-aimed stone.

Frequent companions of the loggers were the grey duck and visitors from further up the harbour, kelp and upland geese, with occasionally the beautiful night herons which lived on the wreck of the

Jhelum, the last East Indiaman, just out of sight beyond the Battle Memorial on my left. From the tree immediately below came the chatter of our resident sparrows, and on the white fence was the odd splash of brilliant red from the chest of a Falkland robin.[10] Most exciting was when the surface of the harbour broke to reveal the head of a patrolling seal. I had not expected seals to come through the Narrows, but Don said that they quite often came all the way up the harbour, particularly when the shoreline turned pink, indicating large concentrations of krill.[11]

On that first Sunday morning, however, the sea was hardly visible, let alone seals. Even the gulls were grounded during the hailstorms. I went into the office, sorted out my desk, donned an anorak and walked across to the hospital to see Tony Kirk. Alison was on duty. She explained that Kirk had survived the flight the previous afternoon, but that they had had to operate again immediately upon arrival at Stanley hospital. He was still in a critical condition and she advised against disturbing him. Even the gravest of situations have their lighter moments. Alison had a young baby, Daniel, whom she was breast-feeding at the time. Owing to the emergency, she had not fed him for far too long that day and, in her own words, her breasts were like water-melons. As they worked at the operating table (Alison was the anaesthetist), she could feel the milk running inside her blouse, down her leg and on to the floor. Peter, the professional surgeon (and, it must be said, a somewhat fastidious bachelor) had cried out 'What's that mess?' only to recoil in embarrassment when Alison told him.

I walked to the Police Station and found a worried Toddy, unhappy at the prospect of having to look after Burgos until a judge arrived from England, in a cell that was really only adequate for overnight drunks. Burgos had been flown in from Goose Green after his unfortunate victim the previous afternoon. Eyes swollen and black from his broken nose, he was not a pretty sight. His English was poor, but enough to express regret for what he had done and to apologise for causing so much trouble. He looked immensely relieved when I told him that Kirk was still alive. It was hard not to feel sorry for the man. Toddy's problem was how to mount a twenty-four-hour guard with a total complement of two police constables. In his twenty years' service, from constable to superintendent, he had never had to deal with a capital offence. He mentioned an old-age pensioner who occasionally acted as nightwatchman for other government departments. We agreed that Burgos was unlikely to be violent (in the event, he proved a model prisoner) and I authorised Toddy to engage the old-age pensioner to stand in for the police at night.

The weather cleared up remarkably quickly (as we were to discover, the Falkland Islands could experience all four seasons in one day) and that afternoon Dick and Connie took us on their favourite walk with their two young daughters, Karen and Helen. We drove to the end of the rough track to the east of the airport, which had been used by contractors to collect sand from Yorke Bay (and was to be used again in 1982 by Argentine amphibious personnel carriers), and walked across the sand dunes behind Yorke Point to Pilot Bay. Almost immediately after leaving the car, we came across a small pond brimming with speckled teal. They were rather shy and took off as soon as we appeared. Not so the gentoo penguins over the next hummock, who surveyed us curiously and seemed undecided whether to come towards us or move away. It was our first sight of penguins in the wild. There must have been upwards of sixty of them, standing in a bunch between the sand dunes. Their white was whiter than white and their black shone like gloss paint. They were handsome and comic at the same time. We tried to move round without disturbing them but made the mistake of going to the seaward side. One or two took fright and started running between us towards the beach and the open sea. The rest followed, panic spreading and the pace quickening until the last few scurried past not on their legs but on their bellies, all dignity gone but moving surprisingly quickly with the use of their flippers. We followed them down to a magnificent stretch of beach. We had basked on tropical beaches in many parts of the world, but nothing to surpass this. A thousand miles further north and it would have been as popular (and probably as crowded) as Waikiki; but then, it would not have had the wonderful spectacle of wildlife that now unfolded before us.

Apart from the gentoos, there were hundreds of loggers and upland geese all along the shoreline, and jackass penguins[12] coming and going between dunes and sea. It was a busy but peaceful natural scene, unspoilt by man. We walked slowly along the beach, feeling like trespassers as the birds and penguins near the shoreline made for the water and the penguins further up the beach headed back towards the dunes. One or two changed their minds at the last minute, scurrying back on their bellies a few yards in front of us and darting away like fish as soon as they entered the water. Looking back, we could see them resuming their old positions, like the sea settling down again in the wake of a ship.

It was a joy to watch the penguins coming ashore. They sped in to the shallows, flicked themselves upright at the last second and, legs going twenty to the dozen, ran out of the water and up beyond the shoreline, where they stood preening and congratulating themselves on a successful landing. Some, however, failed to get the timing right and finished in the shallows with an ignominious belly-flop, shaking their heads at their own clumsiness. We could have watched them all day but, although the sun was shining, there was a cold wind and we had to keep moving. Among the loggers and upland geese were two kinds of oyster-catcher, the black and the Magellanic, and a white pigeon-like bird that we later discovered was the snowy sheathbill, locally called the Cape pigeon. As we drew level with an exceptionally green patch of grass between the dunes, the pungent, fishy smell of a penguin colony hit us. This was the site of the main gentoo colony in Pilot Bay.[13] The chicks had hatched and they and the parents had moved off by now, but there were still one or two stragglers. Dick drew our attention to a cow[14] which, head down, was tossing a black and white object on its horn like a rag doll. Immediately, other cows ran up to join in, like a pack of hounds round a fox. We could not believe that the normally placid cow could be so vicious. As we ran to the rescue, another cow moved in and tried to gore the penguin with its horn. We shooed them off and found the poor creature still alive but too shocked or hurt to move. I picked it up, carefully grabbing the beak first. There was blood on its chest. We hoped that it might revive in the sea and were delighted when, on contact with the water, it was transformed from the limp, dead thing in my arms to a lively, darting torpedo. Karen's and Helen's faces were a joy to behold.

At the end of the beach, where the sand turned to rock, we came upon a pair of handsome kelp geese. We were to observe them regularly over the next two years and watch them raise (and lose) two broods of goslings. One of the sad consequences of the war in

1982 was that we were to be denied access to this bay, which had by then become for us, as it had for Dick and Connie, our favourite Sunday walk. The Argentines laid mines in the area and it was considered too risky to re-open it to the public. On that first Sunday, however, as we walked back to the shelter of the dunes, thoughts of war could not have been further from our minds. We returned to Stanley exhilarated at the prospect of observing this wonderful natural pageant throughout the coming seasons.

That evening we went to our first evensong at Christ Church Cathedral. Intended as the cathedral church for the southern part of the South American continent, as well as the parish church for the Islands, it was built on the grand scale. We were a little embarrassed to find that our seats were reserved in the front pew on the right and that I had a special hassock. Most of the small congregation sat many pews further back and we would rather have melted in with them. The choir consisted of two ladies and one man. The ladies made up in volume what they lacked in numbers. Vivienne (Viv) Perkins was slight in stature but had a remarkably strong and pure voice. She was a Gloucestershire girl, ex-WRNS, who had gone out to the Falkland Islands in 1966 and decided to make her home there. Rene Rowlands was a fourth-generation Islander, built more like an operatic singer, with a voice to match. Together they drowned the solitary male member of the choir, but encouraged the rest of us.

The service was conducted by the Reverend Harry Bagnall, Anglican chaplain of the Falkland Islands. Harry was another fellow-Yorkshireman who had arrived with his wife, Iris, just a few months before us. As he later explained, he had taken the post because he knew how to cut up sheep. The advertisement in the *Church Times* had listed butchering one's own beef and mutton as one of the qualifications needed for the job and Harry had had experience of the wholesale butchery trade before being ordained. Iris had read the advertisement and said to Harry, 'Perhaps it's you they're looking for.' He had the assistance of a lay reader, Stan Bennett, brother of the senior magistrate, Harold, and it was a joy to listen to the prayers enunciated in his rich, baritone voice. The accent was difficult to place. It was not pronounced but it was distinctly colonial, gentler than Australian, with a slight Westcountry burr. After the service we met the organist, an effervescent little round lady called Vi Robson, who was inseparable from two other elderly companions, Vi Bonner and Cissie Short, all of whom became dear friends. Vi had played the organ at Christ Church Cathedral for the last fifty-four years.[15]

We went home after evensong for a quiet evening to ourselves. This became the practice we tried to follow every Sunday. It was the only time we normally had on our own and even that was impossible when we had house-guests. Don would drive us back to Government House and join me in the snooker room after dinner for a relaxing frame or two. He was much the better player – like most Islanders, he had an excellent eye. It was no surprise to me after the war that the Falkland Islands Defence Force beat regular British army units in the march-and-shoot competitions, or that the Islands were represented at Bisley and the rifle-shooting events in the Commonwealth Games.

We turned in about eleven o'clock, and I was asleep when the telephone rang. It was Dick to say that Tony Kirk had died. Oh dear, I thought, fifty years without a murder and now one in my first week. Was this a bad omen?

Notes

1. I was told on my return to Stanley after the Argentine occupation that one of their pilots had tried to fly the Beaver but, after tearing up and down the harbour at full throttle without getting airborne, he had given up. He had failed, literally, to become unstuck.

2. 'Yomp' is a Royal Marine expression meaning to march with full pack across country. The paratrooper's equivalent is to 'tab'.

3. Sadly, motorcycles and Japanese three-wheelers have been creeping in over recent years to take the place of horses.

4. 'Camp' is the local term for countryside, ie all the land outside Stanley.

5. 'Kelper' is the name given to those born and bred in the Islands. It is derived from the kelp (seaweed) that grows in profusion around the Falklands.

6. The 1982 war changed all this. Thanks to Lord Barber's vision, the Standard Chartered Bank decided to build a branch in Stanley. Opened by Lady Young in 1984, it has since become the most profitable branch for its size in the Standard Chartered empire.

7. The Falkland Islands Government, the Falkland Islands Company and Do-It-Yourself.

8. The local name for the Falkland Islands Flightless Steamer Duck, also

called the 'steamer' because of its habit when alarmed of increasing speed by thrashing its small wings on the water like a paddle-steamer.

9. The local name for the Giant Petrel, so called because of the habit of its young of spraying the unwary egg-hunter with evil-smelling vomit.

10. The local name of the Longtailed Meadowlark. Also incorrectly but understandably called the military starling.

11. A shrimp-like crustacean on which sea birds, seals and whales feed.

12. The local name for the Magellanic penguin, a migratory bird that breeds in the Falkland Islands and goes north for the austral winter. It is the only one of the five regular species on the Islands that burrows into the ground to make its nest.

13. Happily, it survived the war. The troops kept their distance because it was in the middle of an Argentine minefield.

14. Stanley townsfolk had grazing rights on the common and, before 1982, kept cattle and horses there.

15. She went on to play until the week of her death in 1987, at the age of eighty-five.

3

The Busy Season

We had arrived in the Falkland Islands to catch the tail-end of the summer sailing season. Traditionally, the Royal Navy's ice patrol and Falklands guard ship, HMS *Endurance*, returned to Stanley after her third work period down south and took the Governor on a local trip before setting sail for home. The British Antarctic Survey ships, the RRS *Bransfield* and the RRS *John Biscoe*, usually called in and, for the last few years two cruise ships, the *Lindblad Explorer* and the *World Discoverer*, had visited before heading for warmer climes. This year, we also had four yachts tied up at the jetty, resting and recuperating after qualifying for the exclusive Cape Horners club.

We were glad to continue the Falklands tradition of offering hospitality to all visiting seafarers, who usually reciprocated by having us back on board. On one of the smallest yachts, the *Expeditus*, owned and crewed by an Australian, Mike Lewis, and his English wife, Gay, we were surprised to be offered port and mead. In return, we gave them fresh vegetables and waved them off, England-bound in their tiny but tidy craft. In contrast, the following day we went aboard the SS *World Discoverer*, which was probably the largest ship to anchor in Stanley harbour before 1982. Its captain, Herr Heinz Aye, from Hamburg, told us that Stanley was his favourite port and that he preferred the cruise round the Falklands, South Georgia and the Antarctic to any of his other cruises, which included exotic places like Bali, Tahiti and Hawaii. He introduced some of his passengers, the Chilean Mayor of Punta Arenas, the German Ambassador to Uruguay and a former Peruvian Ambassador to Chile, and I was somewhat taken aback when he grabbed a microphone and announced to the general assembly that I wanted to speak to them. I had to think quickly of some appropriate words of welcome and made a mental note to be better prepared in future. The party was abruptly terminated when an officer hurried up to Captain Aye and whispered something in his ear. 'The wind is getting up', said the Captain, 'And I know this harbour. There is not a moment to lose.' Showered with presents and seaspray, we jumped into an already bucking launch and made the jetty with nothing more than a mild drenching. This was our first encounter with the vagaries of Stanley harbour: as thousands of our troops were later to discover, it was only too easy to be trapped on board (or on shore) by a gale that blew up within minutes. We were fortunate to get back that evening, particularly as we were giving a dinner party for the yachtsmen. Some of them had to stay on board their yachts, despite being moored to the jetty.

During the next few weeks, I visited all the government departments, the Falkland Islands Company and Cable and Wireless, made my first broadcast on the local radio (the Falkland Islands Broadcasting Service or FIBS, for short) and became acquainted with the snooker-playing fraternity in the Colony Club. Mavis and I also attended the funeral of Tony Kirk and had our first chilling experience of the bleak town cemetery on the bare hillside, which I was to visit many times over the next six years. I went on board the two local coastal vessels, the *Forrest* and the *Monsunen*, and Mavis awarded prizes at the annual horticultural show, the centrepiece of which was a magnificent arrangement of vegetables by Gene. As the only professional gardener on the Islands, he was ineligible to compete for any of the cups and prizes.

One of my most pleasant tasks fell on Commonwealth Day, when I visited the primary and secondary schools in Stanley, read out the Queen's message and ended by declaring a school holiday. There was an excellent atmosphere in both schools and the standard of pupil and teacher seemed every bit as high as in England. One of the Falkland Islander teachers, Hulda Stewart, told me at dinner that evening that she had taught in Singapore and that the Stanley primary school compared favourably with anything she had seen there. She and her Scottish husband, Iain (head of Cable and Wireless) had invited us into their home to partake of a Falkland Islands speciality: upland goose and diddle-dee jelly. It was delicious. The goose was drier and less fatty than the domestic variety, more like turkey only tastier. As we discovered later, an old male could be tough, but Hulda's bird was a tender female, shot after feeding on ripe diddle-dee berries. We were saddened to learn that a popular pastime for youngsters in camp was to chase immature upland geese and run them to earth before they could fly. With no other land predator, however, the upland goose was in no danger of becoming an endangered species. Indeed, as Brook Hardcastle had told us at

Darwin, they were generally regarded as a pest whose numbers had to be kept down for the sake of the sheep. Estimates varied, but some maintained that three upland geese ate as much grass as one sheep. The diddle-dee jelly came from the berry of a heathland bush which was widespread in the Falklands and the nearest indigenous equivalent to heather. The berry was a coal-fire red, too tangy in the raw for the human palate but a favourite with the upland geese. As a jelly, it tasted like cranberry, only sharper. I tried to trace the origin of the name, but without success.

Another guest at dinner was Captain James Lord, of HMS *Endurance*. He had brought the 'Red Plum'[1] into Stanley that day and paid his formal call on me. We discussed my return call and our subsequent trip round the Islands. Next day I was duly piped aboard and inspected the Royal Marines guard of honour on the flight deck. James then took me on a tour of the ship, including the shop (with civilian NAAFI[2] manager) and laundry (with Chinese laundryman). The total complement was 139, and a better and happier band of men it would be hard to find. After a drink in the wardroom, I returned ashore for lunch followed by a formal inspection of Naval Party 8901 at Moody Brook. I was shocked at the state of the buildings, some of which dated back to the First World War. Sandy Lade said that they had been condemned years ago and that MOD had agreed in principle to build a new barracks, to the east of Stanley, but that financial constraints had meant indefinite postponement. Despite the poor living conditions, however, morale was high and most of the detachment said that they had enjoyed their year in the Falklands; indeed, many had volunteered for the posting and several had already asked to return for another tour.

Before giving dinner that evening for *Endurance* and the departing NP 8901 officers, we had the mixed pleasure of watching our first soccer match, the local 'Derby' between Stanley and HMS *Endurance*, on the sloping hillside next to Government House. Our coldest memories of the Falkland Islands are waiting on jetties and airstrips; but the Stanley football and rugby fields ran them a close second. We later experienced katabatic winds in South Georgia and the wind that almost invariably blew from Sapper Hill between the power station and Government House could fairly be described as a mini-katabatic. It whistled across the football field, combining with the slope to produce some interesting football. Local knowledge was all important: the knowing player kept the ball low and aimed off like a clay-pigeon shooter. The knowing spectator did not stand where the action was, along the downwind touchline, but on the opposite side, with his back to the wind. Better still, he parked his Land Rover above the pitch and stayed inside with the heater on.

Next day, we went aboard HMS *Endurance* for our trip round the northern coastline to San Carlos. The harbour was as calm as it had been rough on our return from the *World Discoverer* and we had a smooth run out through the Narrows and into Port William. There we saw our first Polish factory ship. It was grimy, weather-beaten and smelly. Kelp and dolphin gulls wheeled and shrieked overhead, stinkers sat heavily in the water, overfed and reluctant to move out of the way. We scattered loggers, shags and penguins as we steamed towards Cape Pembroke lighthouse in glorious sunshine. Both jackass and gentoo penguins were there, still fishing for their young. They darted away as we approached, leaping porpoise-like out of the water to gain extra speed. The inquisitive shags, both the common and the beautiful blue-eyed, winged low over us, heads twisting and turning, more interested in us than in where they were going (they occasionally hit the rigging, James said, and plopped down stunned, but otherwise unhurt, in the forecastle). James also said that whales used to be quite a common sight coming out of Port William, but, sadly, no more. As we increased speed and drew away from the shore, the wind freshened and the gulls disappeared. A few stinkers remained, but they looked dull compared with the handsome black-browed albatrosses that now joined us, soaring and gliding in our wake and coming so close to the deck that it seemed we could have caught them with a butterfly net – except that they had a wingspan of 8ft. James told us that even the black-browed albatross, or mollymawk, to give it its local name, was dwarfed by the wandering albatross, which had a 14ft wingspan and was an even more superb flyer. We should certainly see the wanderer further south, he said, but they were not uncommon around the Falklands and our chances of spotting one on this trip were quite good.

The weather deteriorated sharply during the night. I was sleeping in the Secretary's cabin (at that time the guest cabin had only one bunk, a second being fitted after the current deployment) and was awakened by the noise of books tumbling to the deck. In my landlubber's way I staggered out of the bunk, replaced them on the shelves, and went back to sleep. A few minutes later, the same thing happened. By then I was awake enough to leave them where they fell. The next morning, feeling a little queasy, I went out on deck for some fresh air. It was more than fresh; it was blowing a gale. I staggered with difficulty to the rear of the boat deck and there, above the boiling wake and heaving sea, soaring serenely in a Force Nine gale, was a beautiful white bird with black wingtips, unmistakably the wandering albatross. It was a marvellous, unforgettable sight. I felt the same thrill as when I had stumbled on an elephant (almost literally) in the Imatong mountains on the Uganda/Sudan border. I was to see many more wanderers on subsequent trips, and they never ceased to fascinate me. Standing, as now, until numb with cold, I would wait in vain for them to flap their wings. They followed a regular pattern of flight, a figure of eight, swooping down in the wake, coming very near to and sometimes level with the ship, then veering off and up, winging over in a stall-turn, picking up speed and going away down the wake to the surface and then up again, repeating the process at the other end of the figure of eight. It was all done without a single flap of the wings; the nearest thing to perpetual motion. I could not understand how they generated enough speed to glide back and catch up with the ship from well over a quarter-of-a-mile away. It was, and remains, a mystery to me.

We had planned to fly ashore that morning in one of the ship's helicopters, but the gale ruled out any possibility of getting airborne. James steamed up and down Falkland Sound (so named by Captain John Strong in 1690 after Viscount Falkland, then Treasurer of the Navy) waiting for the gale to subside. He wished to go into Brenton Loch to resupply the ship's hydrographers, who had been camping there while conducting a survey of the treacherous waters that all but cut off Lafonia from the northern half of East Falkland. We lunched on board as the weather cleared and the movement of the flight-deck dropped to within flying limits. One of the groundcrew brought our bright orange 'once only' suits and lifejackets to the cabin and we struggled into them.

'What does it mean, "Once only"?', asked Mavis, 'If you have to use it, you've had it?' 'Oh, no', said our helpful minder, 'You are only supposed to wear them once. But of course, we don't ditch them until they get too full of holes.' They were total immersion suits, made of very light, thin plastic, completely waterproof as long as there were no holes or tears in them. As I discovered later, the most vulnerable parts were the soles of the feet. Walking a few paces could puncture them and ruin the whole suit. Today, however, we had spanking new suits, without blemish. 'Make sure to tie the cords round your ankle and knee', said our minder. 'If you don't you'll float upside down.' Mavis glanced at me and I thought of the occasion in Jesselton when I took her up for her first flight in a little Piper Cherokee. I was doing no more than a Rate One turn when she leant in, grabbed my arm and yelled 'Put me down this instant!'. I wondered how she would cope in a helicopter without doors, taking off from a rolling, pitching deck over a distinctly uninviting sea. We walked like clumsy spacemen to the hangar at the rear of the ship, where our Wasp was waiting. 'What, no doors?' Mavis exclaimed, in alarm. The pilot, David Acland, explained that, without doors, the Wasp had a bigger payload and a longer range. 'Also', he added significantly, 'It is easier to get out in a hurry.' He then ran through the procedure for ditching. He showed us the flotation bags on each side of the cabin. They would automatically inflate on impact and keep the helicopter afloat; but, as they were situated above our heads, the cabin would be submerged. 'Take a deep breath as we go under', he said, 'And be careful to swim round the bag. Don't inflate your lifejacket until you are clear.'

If Mavis had not been trussed up in immersion suit and lifejacket, I think she would have made a dash for it; but the cool discipline of the Royal Navy prevailed and, before she had time to object, she had been strapped and plugged into her seat behind the pilot, while I was escorted to the other side and tied down behind the observer. The Wasp was secured to the deck by four stout red straps. The last thing the pilot did prior to take-off was to signal for the removal of these straps, whereupon four stalwarts dashed forward underneath the whirling rotor blades and removed one each, signifying that they had done so by brandishing it aloft. As the last red strap was waved, it was as if our umbilical cord had been cut. We were now on our own and it was up to the pilot to clear the heaving deck before it threw us overboard of its own volition. I found the take-off an exhilarating experience and even Mavis, who had kept her eyes tightly closed until we were well and truly airborne, admitted that she was thrilled as well as frightened.

It was bitterly cold without the doors, but the unrestricted view more than compensated for the discomfort. We climbed up over the Sound and headed east, over Cat Island and Wreck Point into San Carlos Water. Visibility after the storm was even better than usual and I was impressed again by the gin-clear air of the southern hemisphere compared with our polluted north. Every detail was in sharp focus, as through a magnifying glass. Below us lay the sad remains of the Ajax Bay freezer factory, oil drums littering the grass like elephant seals. A product of the post-war Colonial Development and Welfare Corporation (best known for the ill-fated Tanganyika groundnuts scheme), it was built in the wrong place, at the wrong time, and without proper research into the markets or sources of supply. Intended to utilise the surplus mutton on the Islands, it went bankrupt after three seasons.[3] Now, looking down on this monument to man's folly, I little thought that within two years it would be seething with activity as Rick Jolly and his team operated to save British and Argentine lives amid the meat-hooks of the abandoned abattoir.

Across San Carlos Water lay our destination, the settlement of San Carlos. We could see the roofs glinting in the sun and, behind and beyond the ridge of hills, far over to our left, we could just make out Port San Carlos. Descending rapidly over what the world now knows as Blue Beach, we landed in a field next to the manager's house. Adrian Monk was there to meet us. We had been flying for only fifteen minutes. David told us to keep the flying kit and be ready for him at 2.45pm the next day. As he ascended like a lift directly above us, I noticed the aircraft's number – 435. We were to share in its last flight the following year in South Georgia.[4]

As the high-pitched buzz of the Wasp receded (it was aptly named) peace once more descended on San Carlos. Adrian took us into his comfortable, rambling home where Nora, his English-born wife, served tea. She told us what a shock the Islands had been on first arrival; but she had been brought up in the English countryside, loved horses and dogs and cats and had adapted quickly to the Falklands way of life. She was happy in San Carlos, but wished that it was not quite so far away from the family. Her parents and daughter were in England and their son, a Cambridge graduate, was in America taking a PhD in biological mathematics at the Massachusetts Institute of Technology. Neither son nor daughter was likely to return to live in the Falklands.

After tea, Adrian took me for a walk round the settlement while Nora showed Mavis the garden. As this was our first stay in a typical Falklands settlement, it may be useful to describe it in some detail. The 'big house' was about half-a-mile away from the rest of the settlement. Like most of the other thirty-two farms in the Falkland Islands at that time, San Carlos was run by a manager and owned by a company. Adrian held a few shares but the major shareholders lived in England. As we splashed in our wellies between gorse hedges, sheltered a little from the biting wind but thankful for our anoraks and woolly hats, Adrian explained that he managed 107,000 acres, carrying about 26,000 sheep. He had a foreman, four shepherds in the settlement and two outside, a mechanic, a handy-man and four general hands. There was also a cook to look after the unattached men who lived in the bunkhouse and a cowman/gar-dener who supplied Nora with fresh milk and cream and helped her in the garden. With wives and children, the total population of the settlement was twenty-six, plus another six who lived in the out-side shepherds' houses and came into the settlement at weekends to stock up with groceries, paraffin, methylated spirits, beer and rum. Apart from the half-dozen or so houses, the settlement had a sheep-shearing shed, dog kennels, two store-sheds, workshop, community hall (used as a schoolroom when the travelling teacher came), community shop, slaughter house, generating shed and a jetty. That was it. 'We don't farm', said Adrian, 'We ranch.' Sheep, cattle and horses remained outside throughout the winter.

After lambing in the spring (October) came 'marking' time, which consisted of cutting the farm's identification mark on the lamb's ear, castrating the males and clipping the tails to reduce soiling of the fleece. Then came the busiest time of the year, shearing, which went on from November to February. This meant that all available hands (including wives and children old enough to ride) were involved in gathering and driving sheep to the home paddocks and assisting the shearers. Some farms still had enough skilled hands to do their own shearing, but more were beginning to employ travelling contract shearing gangs. The manager was usually responsible for the classification of the fleeces into their different grades, on which the reputation of the farm and hence the prices obtained in the Bradford wool auctions depended.

Each house had its own vegetable plot and cats, domestic ducks, geese and hens abounded. The cats were much larger than the average in England, due to unlimited supplies of mutton and upland goose. Dogs were not allowed to roam freely because of the risk of hydatid disease. This was a dog-borne liver parasite that was transmitted to sheep and to man and could prove fatal. Stringent regulations enforced by farm managers kept dogs in kennels when not working and ensured that all sheep's offal within a reasonable distance of the settlement was either buried or burnt. In addition, all dogs were dosed regularly with Droncit. The dog and the horse were the shepherd's workmates, the cat the domestic pet. Outside every home was a peat-stack. It was the responsibility of every householder to cut his own peat, though the farm provided the tractor and trailer to cart it from the banks to the settlement. Little did I think as we walked past the biggest peat-stack that my future son-in-law would be bivouacking in it in 1982.

That evening, we went down to the community hall to meet the settlement people. They were a little shy at first but chatted more freely after a beer or two. I was impressed by how well-informed they were, not only on Falklands' affairs but also on world topics. On the way back to the 'big house', Adrian explained the reason in two words: 'BBC Overseas'. Without television or daily newspapers or a choice of radio station, they depended almost entirely on BBC Overseas for news and entertainment. As we were to discover later when we went into Islanders' kitchens, their radios were invariably on, tuned in to the local FIBS during its broadcasting hours in the evening and BBC Overseas at other times. Many of the BBC Overseas programmes were also relayed by FIBS. In addition, most people had their own 'diddle-dee radio', the amateur band, the world of the 2-metre set, which had spread like wildfire throughout the Islands over the last few years. Many households had two sets, one in the house and one in the Land Rover. VHF and supposedly line-of-sight only, it defied the experts and bounced off and round hills to give freak reception at unheard-of distances. The experienced hams (which meant most wives as well as husbands) could transmit a message through the diddle-dee network across the length and breadth of the Islands within minutes. It was often more efficient than the Post Office's 4.5m HF network, which was installed in managers' houses and served instead of the telephone. It was also a boon to the traveller, who could call up for help if he broke down or simply warn his wife that he would be late home if he became bogged.

We were further impressed that night by the closeness of the community we had joined. One of the girls, Susan, was a sister of Tony Kirk, and another was one of Nanny's nieces.[5] Everyone knew everyone else. Susan's loss was everyone's loss. It was a truly caring community and we felt privileged to be part of it.

Nora and Adrian showed us that living in camp need not be as hard as we had been led to believe. After an excellent dinner of roast beef and all the trimmings, we had champagne with dessert and, after coffee, twelve-year-old malt whisky. We went to bed as the generator switched itself off at 11pm and slept like logs.

Next day, the tranquillity of San Carlos was broken by the noisy Wasp coming to take us to the adjoining settlement, Port San Carlos. It was only a ten minutes' flight away, but overland would have taken all morning. It brought home to me the benefit of helicopters: sea and river, hill and peat-bog were all the same to them. Traversing the lot in that short flight gave one a tremendous sense of superiority over the elements (to be humbled, I must admit, when the elements turned nasty). Alan and Carol Miller were standing in their garden to greet us. Port San Carlos was up-river from San Carlos Water, on an eastward-facing bend and more sheltered than San Carlos. We saw it at its best, on a lovely sunny day. Looking back, it is hard to picture that idyllic scene now. In 1982, it became both a Harrier strip and the base for the RAF's biggest helicopter, the Chinook. Tents were pitched between the farm buildings. Slit-trenches and fuel and ammunition dumps scarred the hillside. It looked like a Royal Flying Corps field in Flanders in the First World War. In 1980, however, the only signs of violence were the bloody fleeces draped over the fence to dry, and the only marks in the hillside were the neat lines of peat-banks. Alan and Carol took us into the 'big house', which was more modern than Adrian's but built on the same large scale to accommodate numerous guests. Like San Carlos, it was some distance away from the other buildings, except for the cowman/gardener's house. The garden was well protected by thick hedges and several recognisable trees. Alan walked me round the settlement, explaining as we went that he, like Adrian, was manager of the farm, but unlike Adrian he did not have shares in the company. The farm had been started three generations ago by William Keith Cameron, whose son had married a previous governor's daughter, Anne Henniker-Heaton. On his death, she retired to her native Ireland, but continued to maintain a keen interest in the farm, visiting it regularly and usually accompanied by one of her family. We had in fact entertained her and her son, Alastair, to lunch in Government House on their way home the previous week. Alan said that he would dearly love to own his own farm. He had made a bid for the only one on the market at the time, the adjoining Douglas Station, but the owner was asking far more than he could scrape together. He wondered why the FIG could not make more loans to aspiring Falkland Islands farmers like himself.[6]

In area, 'KC' was a little smaller than 'JB', though still over 100,000 acres. It carried more sheep – about 36,000 – because it had better breeding ground. As Alan put it, 'JB' contained a lot of 'rubbish' in No Man's Land (Mount Usborne and the Wickham Heights), which was fit only for the wild cattle. I was intrigued. Wild cattle? From where? 'Probably introduced by de Bougainville in 1764', said Alan. 'They prospered and multiplied and roamed wild after the islands were abandoned. There are still a few left.' I kept my eyes open whenever we flew over the hillier parts after that but, to my regret, never saw them.

We met the rest of the settlement for drinks in the 'big house' before lunch and again found them rather shy. When visiting settlements subsequently, we made a point of calling on them in their own homes and found them much more at ease. To begin with, they would usher us into their front rooms, but we soon realised that this was almost as inhibiting as the 'big house' (it was also usually perishingly cold) and we found that the answer was to make for the back door, which was always open, leave one's wellies in the porch and go into the kitchen, which was always full of warmth and life. The centrepiece was invariably the kitchen range, usually an Aga or Rayburn (though some still had the old Victorian 'Modern Mistress'), with a peat bucket on one side and a fat cat or two on the other. Most kitchens seemed to be full of children and children's toys, with something cooking on the stove and the 2-metre set crackling in the corner.

Carol served us a delicious lunch of teal duck, which Alan had shot, and diddle-dee jelly, followed by teaberry pie and fresh cream. The teaberry was another indigenous plant, a little like the bilberry (or blueberry) in appearance, but with a whitish pink berry more like a wild strawberry. It had a subtle taste, sweet and slightly scented, different from anything we had had elsewhere. Carol was a most attractive English girl, from Manchester, who had come out to the Falklands originally as a teacher. All too soon, we heard the high-pitched whine of the Wasp and David was back in the garden to take us to Stanley. He had the doors on this time, and gave us helmets instead of earphones to keep us warm for the longer, thirty-minute flight. I was to think about this during the great 'yomp' of our troops two years later: so easy by air and so difficult by foot, particularly with an 80-100lb pack on one's back. We landed on the edge of the football field next to Government House, where Dick was waiting to meet us. Sandy Lade was also there to supervise the refuelling of the Wasp from a 44-gallon drum. We said our grateful thanks and farewell to David, who was returning to the *Endurance* in Brenton Loch. There was no doubt about it, the helicopter was the most painless way of getting round the Falkland Islands. We were grateful to have, for once, a Saturday evening to ourselves. Dick had no urgent crisis to report, so we took our regular walk along the harbour, past the Battle Memorial (a beautiful sculpture, erected to commemorate the Battle of the Falklands, 8 December, 1914) and the wreck of the *Jhelum* as far as the Beaver hangar and back. The night herons were still on the *Jhelum*, the kelp geese on the nearby shoreline and our own two pairs of logger ducks still squabbling over their territorial boundary. It was good to be home.

The busy season was not yet over. Although the nights were beginning to draw in, the days were generally sunny and clear, like the best of autumn in England. HMS *Endurance* went off to Montevideo to collect the new Royal Marine detachment and RRS *Bransfield* departed on her last trip south to stock up the BAS bases for the winter before beginning the long journey back to England. We were due to have lunch on her in Stanley harbour, but the wind blew up suddenly and the launch could not make it across the choppy water. On a better day, shortly afterwards, we managed a farewell sail with Cas and Joan, the last of our summer yachtsmen, in their comfortable trimaran *Tortuga Too*. Our regular supply ship from Gravesend, the MV *AES*, also called at about this time. I went on board to pay my respects to the Danish captain and expressed surprise that such a small ship, with a crew of only seven, could supply virtually all the Islanders' needs and take away the total wool crop in four round trips a year. Captain Jensen made light of this, saying modestly that it was a job like any other and, indeed, a boring way to earn a living. He obviously had the sea in his blood and I ventured to suggest that it took a special sort of man to spend most of the year cooped up in a tiny cabin in a small ship on some of the most unfriendly seas in the world. 'Yes', he said, his eyes twinkling, 'A bloody fool.' We leant over the ship's rail as the jetty gang loaded the bales of wool on which the Islands' economy depended: wool straight off the sheep's back, compressed by the same hydraulic presses (Platts) that I had seen in the cotton ginneries in Uganda. Raw wool and raw cotton. Both facing fierce competition from man-made fibres; but no real substitute. Prices determined by auctions over which the producer had no control. Freight charges by weight and volume.

How much expensive dirt was being transported in those bales? I remembered as an Assistant District Commissioner swooping on the cotton stores in Uganda to check the buyer's scales. I would creep up on the unsuspecting buyer (usually an Indian) and slap my 56lb weight on his Salter's scales. If they registered under weight, I would confiscate them, charge him under the Cotton Ordinance and remove his licence. He would then usually remove himself without delay, to avoid being lynched by the African growers. It did not happen often – one or two prosecutions early in the season had the desired effect. More frequent were the grower's attempts to cheat the buyer, most commonly by putting stones in the middle of his or her cotton. Fortunately, we had no such problems in the Falklands; but, as the bales went down into the *AES*'s hold for their long journey to Bradford, I reflected on how much more we could add to their value by having a local scouring plant and woollen mill.

Apart from the shipping activity, our lives revolved round the twice-weekly LADE flights from Comodoro Rivadavia. The size of the weekly diplomatic bag dictated how long I should have to sit at my desk, and the passenger list indicated how long I should have to spend on visitors. Naturally, we had more visitors in the summer than the winter, for not only was the weather more agreeable, but the wildlife was more interesting and, of course, summer in the Falklands was winter in Europe. It was also the fishing season. On our return from Port San Carlos, I was informed that the Italian Ambassador for Uruguay had arrived with his family and was staying at the Upland Goose. I called on him there after evensong the following night and, on my way out, met a party of Irish anglers who had spent the previous two weeks fishing for sea-trout.[7] In their considered opinion, the Falklands offered the best sea-trout fishing in the world, and their enthusiasm increased my impatience to try out my new fishing tackle, brought from home on the advice of a previous governor and keen angler, Sir Edwin Arrowsmith.

The handling of visitors quickly fell into a pattern. They would make a formal call on me in my office and I would then invite them to a meal or drinks in Government House. If they were staying in the Upland Goose or on board ship, I would then return their call and, if they were extending their stay by a visit to camp, I would usually see them again on their return to Stanley before departure. With only two flights a week, it was possible to meet most visitors to the Islands and offer them some hospitality. This was one of the joys of living in a small, isolated community and, during the summer months at least, it enabled us to meet a variety of interesting people. For example, we combined lunch for the Italian Ambassador,

Emiliano Guidotti, his wife and daughter with the Master and Chief Engineer of the *Bransfield* and a senior member of the British Antarctic Survey. We usually tried to include a few Falkland Islanders, with the result, I believe, that many visitors left the Islands with a better understanding of the situation in the South Atlantic and a more sympathetic attitude towards the Islanders.

I confess, however, that we held out little hope of influencing our next party of distinguished visitors, who were the President of the Automobile Club of Argentina (appropriately named Mr Carman) and some of its members, including the ex-world racing champion, Juan Manuel Fangio. I was delighted to meet one of my heroes, but surprised to find that his English was almost non-existent and his Spanish little better; his native tongue was Italian. Vicecomodoro Hector Gilobert, the resident Argentine Air Force Commander, told me later that Italian was widely used in Buenos Aires, which in fact now had a larger Italian population than Spanish. We did not of course touch on sovereignty (I had already learnt that Argentine minds were closed on this issue), but we were able to put them right on one basic fact: Mr Carman wanted to organise a car rally round the Islands. We pointed out that we had only seven miles of road! In the light of events in 1982, I have often wondered about the real purpose of their visit. Another member of the party was Mr Allemans, the Assistant Minister of Finance, but he purported to have come as an ordinary member of the Automobile Club and not in his ministerial capacity. I could only conclude that this was another ploy in their 'hearts-and-minds' campaign to win over the Islanders, though its only effect was to strengthen Islander opinion that all Argentines were crazy.

It was at about this time that Dick alerted me to trouble brewing over the proposed LADE house. It sounds a trivial affair, and was so regarded by the FCO (and by me, at first), but it was to provide my first insight into the strength of feeling against the Argentine presence in the Islands and Islander suspicion that we, the British (or, at least, the 'Foreign Office'), were conniving with the Argentines to increase that presence so as eventually to hand over the Islands. I had not been there long enough to realise that, to the Islanders, the LADE house was seen as another nail in the coffin. We had entertained Hector Gilobert and his lovely wife, Teresa, at Government House and met their children. Hector had shown me round the LADE office, proudly demonstrating his powerful radio transmitter, which gave instant and clear communication with

Buenos Aires (a sore point, incidentally, with neighbouring Islanders, because it interfered with their reception of BBC Overseas, and
with the Postmaster General, who was forbidden under the terms of
the Argentine-British agreement to charge any licence fee). Hector
had apologised that he was unable to reciprocate my hospitality
because his house was totally inadequate. There had followed, a
few days later, an application to erect a prefabricated house on a
suitable piece of land near the racecourse. An acrimonious discussion in Executive Council had ensued, in which I had had to remind
members that, under the terms of the agreement, we were obliged
to have a number of Argentines residing in Stanley and it followed
that they had to have somewhere to live.

The upshot was that Executive Council agreed to the lease of
a government plot on condition that the house to be built thereon
would not exceed a stipulated floor area and that no flags would
be flown. The reason for these seemingly petty conditions was a
rumour that the Argentines were planning to build a huge official
residence to rival Government House.[8] Plans were duly submitted
and approved and the house was transported from Brazil by
Argentine Air Force Hercules. I was embarrassed to find that it
exceeded the stipulated floor area, although no one in his wildest
dreams would call it palatial. Feelings were running high when the
Argentines added insult to injury by proposing to hold a grand
housewarming party, with a host of VIPs and journalists from
Buenos Aires, including their Chief of Air Staff. Both the FCO
and our ambassador in Buenos Aires thought that the Islanders
were being unreasonable in opposing this, and it was only when I
warned that I should have to call out the Royal Marines to guard
the house that the Argentines were persuaded to drop the idea. As
one of the (more responsible) councillors put it afterwards, 'If you'd
let them carry on, they would have had a housewarming all right –
we'd have burnt the place down.' 'Surely, not you', I said, to which
he replied, 'I'd have been there with the first torch!'

In the event, Hector had a quiet housewarming, with only
locals present (including councillors). He and Teresa entertained us
several times after that and, although they made the best of it, they
could not overcome the fact that the house was designed more to let
in the soft Brazilian breezes than to keep out the Falkland gales.[9]

Between dealing with correspondence and visitors, my round
of Falkland Islands Government departments took up any spare
time. Despite a population smaller than most English parishes, the

Islands carried the full panoply of a colonial government. There was a Secretariat, with the Chief Secretary in charge; a Treasury, headed by the Financial Secretary, who was also Governor of the only bank on the Islands – the Government Savings Bank – and Chief Currency Officer (the Islands had their own currency); a Legal Department, with a Registrar and a Senior Magistrate; a Government Printer, who published the official gazette, all government forms and reports and many other things besides; Posts and Telecommunications (the Islands issued their own postage stamps – many of the designs by local artists); Customs; Central Stores; Air Service; Police; Fire Brigade and Agriculture, Education, Harbour, Medical, Meteorological and Public Works Departments. All where chronically understaffed and lacking in funds, but the two most glaring omissions, which I determined to rectify as soon as possible, were the posts of Attorney General and Agricultural Officer. In my previous experience, a colony always had an experienced triumvirate of Chief Secretary, Financial Secretary and Attorney General. These were the three sides of the pyramid which supported the Governor. As for the post of Agricultural Officer, it seemed inconceivable to me that a country which depended for its livelihood on agriculture should have the Customs Officer in charge of the Agricultural Department.[10]

Perhaps the most interesting visit was to the Government Printing Office. This was a working museum. Housed in an unprepossessing hut behind the Secretariat, it was presided over by a colourful Falkland Islands' character called Joe King, amongst whose many contributions to island life was a regular double act on the local radio with our head gardener, Gene (pronounced 'Gen'), 'In The Potting Shed'. Joe invariably started with one of the corniest jokes imaginable and Gene responded with an infectious 'Ho-ho-ho' that came from the bottom of his gardening boots. It was a simple, homespun programme, full of good humour and practical gardening tips. Joe's assistant in the Printing Office was Tony Pettersson, an Islander of Scandinavian descent who subsequently represented the Falklands in rifle-shooting at the Commonwealth Games. On this first visit, however, I found him grappling with printing machinery that looked as though it had been made long before the rifle was invented. Joe explained how by a series of ingenious modifications and improvisations he had managed to keep the presses turning for over forty years. He should have retired, but maintained that there was no one to take over (I suspected that Tony would have been perfectly capable, had not Joe kept some of the art to himself). He showed me how he melted down the aluminium ingots in a pan on a little stove and set up the plates. He dug out old prints from the archives to illustrate the variety of his talent: covers for the Fancy Dress Ball, 1938; scripts for the pantomimes written in verse by Governor Hodson every Christmas from 1934 to 1938 (governors must have had more spare time in those days) and even a scorecard for the Stanley Open Golf Championship, 1936, showing no fewer than thirty-two entries. Joe was a master craftsman who took a great pride in his job and loved his antiquated machinery.

The evenings were no less full than the days. When we were not entertaining in Government House, there were social events in the Town Hall, Moody Brook and the Colony Club and dinner parties in the homes of other Stanley residents. A particularly busy time began with the arrival of the new Royal Marine detachment from Montevideo on HMS *Endurance*. This was her last call before re-turning home, and a full sports and social programme was usually followed. The outgoing Royal Marines stayed in friends' houses in Stanley, the new detachment settled in at Moody Brook and as many as possible of the *Endurance* crew had a run ashore. This year, however, the traditional festivities had to be curtailed because we received news that RRS *Bransfield* had struck an uncharted, submerged rock near Rothera, a BAS base almost 1,200 miles south of Stanley. James Lord immediately prepared for sea and set off to the rescue, which put a damper on our party the following evening to say farewell to the outgoing Royal Marines and to welcome the new detachment, commanded by Major Robin Gilding.

We were relieved subsequently to hear that the *Bransfield* had managed to free herself without serious damage and did not require assistance from HMS *Endurance*, though she was reassured to have company through the notorious Drake Passage.[11] The incident brought home to me the hazards inherent in operating in the Antarctic, thousands of miles away from any search and rescue organisation.

Notes

1. So nicknamed because she was painted red, to stand out in the ice.

2. Navy, Army and Air Force Institute. A civilian non-profit-making organisation which supplies comforts and recreational facilities to HM Forces.

3. Even this fared better than the other C.D. & W. venture in the

Falklands: a sealing factory, built at Port Albermarle in West Falkland and completed only after most of the seals had disappeared. It lasted for only two seasons.

4. See page 170.

5. 'Nanny' was Mary Fullerton, housekeeper at Government House (see page 215).

6. FIG had made a start in this direction, with the purchase from the FIC of Green Patch and its subsequent division into six separate farms (see page 60). Sadly, by the time more loans and sub-divisions became available after the war, Alan had died of cancer, at the early age of forty-two.

7. Introduced by Governor Sir Miles Clifford in 1948, the brown trout quickly established itself (sadly, to the detriment of the smaller, indigenous species), went out to sea to feed like salmon and returned to the main rivers to spawn in increasing numbers and size. The largest sea-trout caught up to 1985 was 21½lbs.

8. Fanciful though this may sound, Islanders had heard the Argentine radio refer to the Vicecomodoro as the Governor of Islas Malvinas and they knew that the Argentines had done other strange things to assert sovereignty, such as sending pregnant mothers to bases in British Antarctic Territory to have their babies and stamping visitors' passports there with Argentine entry permits.

9. After the war, the house became the residence of the Commander, British Forces Falkland Islands, and was renamed 'Britannia House'. Despite the valiant efforts of the Royal Engineers, the roof continued to leak and buckets had to be placed at strategic points around the dining table. In 1989, it became the Stanley Museum.

10. To be fair, there was a Grasslands Trials Unit, headed by professional agriculturalists from the UK and including a veterinary officer who did valuable farm extension work as well as research; but in my view their presence made it more desirable to have a government Agricultural Officer, not less.

11. There was a friendly rivalry between the BAS ships and HMS *Endurance*. The *Bransfield* was overjoyed to be able to repay this favour when *Endurance* became impaled upon a submerged rock in 1984 and *Bransfield* towed her free (though *Endurance* maintained that she could have got off under her own steam, as the *Bransfield* had in 1980).

4

Exploratory Talks and Travels

Mavis was looking forward to Easter, when Tony was due to visit us from school in England. She was disappointed that our daughter, Diana, was not coming, too, but she was taking 'A'-level French in the forthcoming June and had decided to go on a school trip to Paris. We met Tony off the F27, looking remarkably fit considering that he had been up at 4am. Richard Gozney had looked after him in Buenos Aires and he had enjoyed his first taste of South America. He settled in immediately to life in Stanley and made many friends among the Islanders.

My next trip to camp was to Pebble Island, and Tony came along. John Ferguson, the head of the Grasslands Trials Unit, had invited me to see some experiments that he and his veterinary officer, Steve Whitley, were conducting there, with the help and co-operation of the Dean Brothers' manager, Griff Evans. I was amused to learn that the Dean Brothers were in truth two elderly ladies residing in Tunbridge Wells (and a younger one in Surrey). The brothers had inherited the farm from their grandfather, John Dean, who had gone out from High Wycombe to the Falklands in 1840 and obtained the freehold to Pebble Island in 1869, the first to be granted in West Falkland. The brothers' only male offspring had shown no interest in the farm, hence the daughters had inherited. Griff and his wife Gladys – 'Glad' to one and all – were both short and round and bubbling with warmth and hospitality. In addition to Tony and myself, John and Steve, they were also accommodating Mike and Alison Bleaney and their baby, Daniel. Alison had come out to the Islands from Scotland, where she had been trained as a doctor, and had met Mike in Stanley, where he had been stationed before leaving the Royal Navy and taking his present job with the Falkland Islands Company. They were spending a few days' leave with Griff and Glad, who were close friends; indeed, Griff had married them.[1] Others wandered in and out of the homely kitchen and helped themselves to Glad's seemingly never-ending supply of hot food and drinks, while Griff sat rolling a cigarette, or, with one

56

lolling unlit from his mouth, passing comments on the ceaseless chatter from the radio. The topic of the day was a praiseworthy attempt by Jim Clement, the secretary of the Sheep Owners Association, to organise the sale of surplus sheep to a Chilean entrepreneur called Maslov for transporting live to an abattoir and freezer plant in Punta Arenas. With about 23,000 carcasses a year going to waste, it was clearly desirable to find a market for them, if possible. Griff was, however, sceptical about Senor Maslov's ability to produce the ship or the money (correctly, as it turned out.)[2]

After an excellent lunch of roast mutton, as tender as any lamb and twice as tasty, Tony and I went off with John and Steve to have a look at their trial plot to the east of the island. On our way, we saw hundreds of gentoo, jackass and rockhopper penguins, and the now-familiar upland and kelp geese, logger and grey duck and dolphin and kelp gulls. A special treat was the sight of forty-eight black-necked swans on a shallow lake. Steve warned us to approach quietly, as they were exceedingly timid. The absolute opposite was the Johnny Rook, or striated caracara, which we saw the next day, when Griff took us to the western end of the island. The bird was so bold that he perched on the front of our Land Rover and followed me to the gatepost as I went to open a gate. I had never experienced such a tame bird in the wild. He was a handsome, but cruel, bird of prey, and no friend of Griff's. 'They attack the new-born lambs', he said, 'And if they find a cast sheep, they'll have its eyes and tongue.' After that, I could understand his antipathy towards the Johnny Rook; but I could not understand why he was giving the jackass penguins such a wide berth. They seemed harmless enough. 'Don't you believe it', said Griff, 'Them little beggars are full of fleas – one bite and I come up in big lumps.'

Mike took Tony shooting that evening and Tony came back with a brace of upland geese, the first birds he had ever shot. Next morning, we went with Steve to the slaughterhouse. Griff's son Raymond and John Betts were killing some of Steve's trial sheep, so that he could examine the ovaries. He was conducting an experiment in ovulation to ascertain the best time to put the rams to the ewes. Tony had no qualms about shooting a bird, but he could not stand a sheep having its throat cut. He retired as the grisly but necessary business went on. It was not a pleasant sight, but it was expertly done and the sheep did not appear to suffer any pain. The throat was cut and the neck broken at the same time. I asked Raymond and John how they felt and they said that killing a sheep or a cow did not bother them; but neither could kill a horse or a dog.

I walked round the settlement and met everyone there. That was not difficult because, apart from Griff and Glad, there was only Raymond, their son, and his wife Biffo (daughter of Tony Pole-Evans, manager of nearby Saunders Island); the foreman, Bernard Betts, and his wife Marian (she was a champion jockey, as the cups and rosettes around the house showed); John Betts and his eighty-year-old mother Cinty; Ken Berntsen, shepherd, and his wife Arena, cowhand; Nobby Clark, carpenter, and his wife Fiona; Norman Morrison, mechanic and Cyril (Bernard's father and Cinty's step-son), who was cook for Norman in the bunkhouse. Including the women, that amounted to fourteen pairs of hands to keep 13,000 sheep and themselves alive on an island of 23,000 acres. There were also nine young children. Griff was proud of his school, which Dean Brothers had bought in prefabricated form in England and he and his men had erected. It was a spacious, sunny building with lovely views over the bay, well equipped by the Falkland Islands Education Department and run by a travelling teacher. Nobby, the 'chippie', was putting the finishing touches to the teacher's sleeping quarters at one end of the classroom. The Falkland Islands Government supplied the teacher, who usually covered three settlements, spending a fortnight in each, but the farm had to provide the accommodation. When not in use as a classroom, it was used as a community hall for film shows, dances, parties and church services. Under Griff's easy-going but effective management, Pebble Island was a happy settlement, and I was to feel for them in 1982 when they were all locked up in the 'big house', and harshly treated by the Argentines after the SAS raid on their airstrip.

The Easter holidays passed all too quickly, there were the usual tearful farewells when Tony had to go back to school and the inevitable flatness about the house without him. He had made a great hit with the staff and they seemed to miss him as much as we did. Fortunately, our heavy baggage arrived from England just before he left and we busied ourselves making Government House a home by complementing the official furnishings with our own familiar objects. Receiving one's heavy baggage in the Diplomatic Service – usually after a lengthy separation – was like having an extra Christmas Day.

In the office, my main preoccupations were with the Falkland Islands Government Air Service and the forthcoming round of talks with the Argentines on the Islands' future. FIGAS had suffered two accidents to their Islander aircraft shortly before I had arrived, relatively minor in themselves (there were no casualties and the aircraft was reparable) but potentially serious. It may seem strange nowadays, but there was a body of opinion both within and outside the air service that believed that it was a mistake to introduce landplanes into the Islands and that we should stick to the tried and trusted floatplanes. The two incidents had fuelled the anti-Islander lobby and, if farmers were not to be discouraged from constructing their own airstrips, there was an urgent need to restore confidence in the Islander aircraft and FIGAS's ability to operate it.

Much as I loved the old Beaver floatplane, I had no doubt that the landplanes could offer a better service to the public, and was reassured to find that the inspector who had been sent from the British Civil Aviation Authority to investigate the accidents held the same view. He had produced an excellent report and I spent many hours discussing with FIGAS staff, councillors and farmers how best to implement its recommendations. As air communications within the Islands were of vital importance, affecting as they did all Islanders' lives, I thought it only right to tell the public through the local radio exactly what was going on. I made no attempt to conceal the differences of opinion or the clash of personalities of those involved. My broadcast produced a surprisingly grateful response. 'At last we are being treated like adults', said one. 'Thank goodness we are no longer being kept in the dark', said another. I resolved to continue to be as open as I could in all my dealings with the Islanders. In a small, isolated community like the Falklands, rumours spread like wildfire and molehills became mountains overnight. Although everybody knew what everybody else was doing, there was always an underlying suspicion that 'they' (FIG or the Foreign Office, depending upon whether the subject was domestic or external) were up to no good and that everything 'they' said or did had an ulterior, usually a sinister, motive.

Nowhere was this suspicion stronger than over Britain's relations with Argentina. The mere mention of talks between the two governments brought accusations of 'sell-out' from some and genuine anxiety about the future from all. My first Executive Council meeting demonstrated the strength of feeling on this subject. The Falkland Islands Government was based on traditional colonial lines, with a Legislative Council consisting of six elected members and two officials and an Executive Council consisting of the same two officials, two of the six elected Legislative Councillors and two members nominated by the Governor. The Governor presided over both councils and had a casting vote. I spoke to Executive Council on instructions from the FCO, stating that Lord Carrington (then Secretary-of-State for Foreign and Commonwealth Affairs) was seeking confirmation from Council that it was its wish that exploratory talks with the Argentine Government should be resumed, with new terms of reference.[3] In fact, Mr Ridley had already held exploratory meetings with the Argentine Deputy Foreign Minister, and relations had been improved by the reinstatement of Ambassadors in Buenos Aires and London. Councillors strongly opposed the inclusion of sovereignty on the agenda; indeed, some were against *any* talks with Argentina.

As the issue was of fundamental importance to the Islanders, I wanted the views of all the elected members of Legislative Council as well as those of Executive Councillors. I therefore called a meeting of Joint Councils. This was an informal body with no official status under the Constitution, but it was the fairest way of sounding Islander opinion. After a lengthy but dignified and good-tempered discussion, councillors decided by the narrowest of margins (five to four, with abstentions from me and the only other expatriate official, Dick Baker) to give Lord Carrington the confirmation that he was seeking. They remained unhappy at the inclusion of sovereignty in the terms of reference but, recognising that the pass had already been sold (without their approval) by the previous British government, they sought to contain the damage by insisting on representation at the resumed talks and directing their representative to seek the same sort of 'sovereignty umbrella' that prefaced the 1971 Communications Agreement, which stated that nothing in the Agreement affected the position of the two governments regarding the sovereignty of the Islands. Dick and I withdrew and left it to councillors to select their representative. They chose Adrian Monk.

The next day marked an important milestone in Falkland Islands' history. The FIC had agreed to sell one of its farms on favourable terms to the FIG, which in turn offered soft loans to six selected Falkland Islanders to buy their own farms. It was now my pleasurable duty to present the title deeds to the new owners. Green Patch was split up into six subdivisions, roughly 15,000 acres and 3,000 sheep apiece. We held a simple ceremony and celebration in Government House before lunch and the joy on the faces of the young farmers and their families told clearly what it meant to them.

For the first time, they had a stake in their own land. Most of the councillors were present, having stayed on after our council meeting for a meeting of the Standing Finance Committee, due to be held that afternoon. There was a slight panic when its most important member, the Financial Secretary failed to turn up. Eventually, Harold was found fast asleep in the mortuary, where he had gone for a little peace and quiet after our lunchtime celebrations.

The following day Mavis and I visited the Polish factory ship in Port William. We went out in the FIC's little tug, the *Lively*. As we went through the Narrows, our now-familiar escort of Commerson's dolphins joined us, playing in the bow wave like children in a shower, and loggers and overweight stinkers splashed out of our way. Mavis's heart sank when she saw two trawlers tied up on each side of the factory ship, the *Gryf Pomorski*. There was a considerable swell and the rope ladders between each vessel were moving several feet. 'I didn't marry a diplomat to be a circus acrobat', she said, as we climbed gingerly up and down the three lots of swinging ladders. We were met on the factory ship's deck by an all-pervading smell of fishmeal and a jaunty little man with red hair and a pointed red beard who introduced himself as Captain Szostak. He looked more like an Irish buccaneer than a Polish fishing captain. Escorting us to his spacious cabin, he said 'I have to be comfortable – I have one hundred and thirty-five days at sea.' His English was passable, though not as good as his steward's, whom we assumed to be from the Polish equivalent of the KGB. We had an excellent choice of cold meats and fish, with particularly good hors d'oeuvres, washed down with liberal quantities of Polish vodka. As the meal progressed, the steward continued to refill my glass but kept missing out Captain Szostak's. He had evidently decided that his captain had had enough. But Captain Szostak had other ideas: whenever the steward disappeared, he would wink at me and switch his empty glass with my full one. This suited us both for I was beginning to wonder how I would negotiate those rope ladders. The steward must have wondered at my prodigious capacity; he eyed me oddly, but carried on replenishing my glass.

After the meal, Captain Szostak took us on a tour of the ship. It was most impressive. He had already loaded about 4,000 tons of fish and fishmeal and had another 4,000 tons to load before he could sail for home. It would take him fifty days to get to Gdansk, calling at the Polish fishing fleet off Dakar on the way to off-load blue whiting. To quote Szostak, 'They are full of worms – can't sell them in

Europe but they sell well in Africa, where they like the big eyes!'

Blue whiting comprised the main catch, with Patagonian hake second, though the most profitable catch was squid, which was seasonal and came in two varieties. Szostak had been fishing around the world for over thirty years and had some interesting observations. The blue whiting were worm-infested because they were too old. He maintained that they should be fished more intensively, to bring the average age down. He had seen this happen off the Aleutian Islands with pollock, which was similarly worm-infested and fit only for pet-food on the North American continent until they had brought the average age down from seven to two or three years. Pollock was now the main ingredient in fish-fingers in supermarkets across America, he said. We watched as one of the men opened up a blue whiting and flicked the yellow worms out of the white flesh. Szostak explained that he could only do that with a freshly caught fish: the worms turned white after a short while and were then difficult to find. In any event, it was too labour intensive to de-worm the many thousands of whiting that the trawlers brought in to the factory ship every day. Patagonian hake, on the other hand, was a high-quality fish in great demand and short supply. Squid, too, was much sought around the world and commanded high prices. He said that both varieties were in danger of being over-fished in the waters round the Falklands and he could not understand why we did not have a licensing regime to control fishing, like other countries. He added, with a twinkle and a smile, that he would of course expect the Poles 'as old allies' and the fishermen who had been there the longest to be given priority. I asked him what he thought would happen if we did not impose controls and he answered, 'Your squid will go the same way as your whales.' From then on, I was to advocate the declaration of a fisheries zone round the Falklands and their Dependencies.[4]

We were amazed at the size of the crew – two hundred and thirty, including a few women – and the facilities on board. Captain Szostak was proud of his sick bay, complete with operating theatre, dentist's chair and X-ray equipment (though we were soon to discover that he preferred to send his injured and sick to our hospital in Stanley). The games room was equally well equipped. Captain Szostak challenged me to a game of table-tennis and I was thankful that we had played a lot at school. I managed to win, though this was probably due to his higher consumption of vodka.

We were then ushered into a huge cinema, complete with

curtains, wide screen and tip-up seats. The only thing lacking was a Mighty Wurlitzer. As the lights dimmed, a bottle of vodka and two glasses materialised from nowhere and a Polish title appeared on the screen, with the English sub-title *A Bridge Too Far*. It seemed unreal, sitting in a plush cinema on a Polish ship in a Falkland harbour, watching the efforts of British paratroopers to seize and hold a Dutch bridge against a German Panzer division. To cap it all, whenever a Pole appeared on the screen (a Polish airborne brigade took part in the action) my proud host dug me in the ribs, shouted 'Polish' and made me drink to 'The Victorious Allies'. I was glad that the Poles did not feature too often in the film. Despite the vodka (or perhaps because of it) and carrying a Polish icon and a book on Stettin, we had no problems negotiating the rope ladders on our way back. We were to entertain, and be entertained by, Captain Szostak many times over the next few years, until he retired to his beloved Stettin. He brought his wife out twice and, although she spoke not a word of English, she and Mavis struck up a warm relationship that needed no common language to communicate. I hope that he still wears the Falkland tie I gave him and thinks as fondly as I do of our times together down south.

The *Bransfield* and the *John Biscoe* arrived shortly after our visit to the *Gryf Pomorski*, making their last calls of the season, and we entertained many interesting BAS characters at Government House. One of these was Bob Headland, who was later to produce the definitive book on South Georgia.[5] He showed us his excellent slides and whetted our appetite to see the place ourselves. Rick Airey also showed us his slides, which included some of the BAS bases further south. As High Commissioner of British Antarctic Territory, it was my pleasurable duty to visit these bases and I was able to get to all except one over the next four austral summers. The exception was Halley, which the *Bransfield* visited only once a year and the round trip necessitated too long an absence from Stanley.

Two curious visitors from Argentina introduced themselves as architects from the University of Buenos Aires. One was an Anglo-Argentine called Stuart Elder and the other of Italian origin called Alberto de Paula. They said that they were studying early Stanley architecture and asked to be shown round Government House. In my innocence, I took them into every room, which they photographed avidly, and showed them all the old plans, some of which were exquisitely drawn and tinted by Victorian draughtsmen, more works of art than architect's drawings.[6] They even photographed the plans. I thought at the time that they were merely eccentric enthusiasts but, after the invasion in 1982, I realised how naive I had been. They were charming gentlemen and Mavis and I entertained them to drinks before they departed, thanking us profusely and no doubt laughing at our lack of guile.

Most parts of the Commonwealth celebrate The Queen's official birthday in June but, as this was midwinter in the Falkland Islands, we were allowed to celebrate her actual birthday on 21 April. The Queen's Birthday Parade was an annual ceremony, held on Victory Green, with the Royal Marines, the Falkland Islands Defence Force and the Girls Brigade and a twenty-one gun salute. After the parade, tradition dictated that senior officials and councillors repaired to the FIDF drill hall and stood rounds of drinks for the members. As they came from all walks of life and spanned most age groups, it was an excellent opportunity to listen to their views on current issues. Adrian Monk was one of the councillors present and they left him in no doubt what they thought of the forthcoming talks with the Argentines. We held a Queen's Birthday Party for over a hundred that night and retired to bed happy with the thought that we had got to know so many of the Islanders in three short months.

A few days later, Sir Peter Watkin-Williams arrived to try the Burgos case. He took little time in finding Burgos not guilty of murder and sentencing him to nine months for manslaughter. Islander bias showed itself unpleasantly at this verdict. The extenuating circumstances were ignored and there was widespread indignation that the death of one of their own at the hands of an outsider had not been properly avenged. I was surprised at the strength of feeling and unprepared for a notice painted in huge capital letters on a hangar on our way to the airport which read 'F. . . off Williams, we don't want your kind of justice here.' Fortunately, I was on the hangar side of the red taxi and Sir Peter was on the harbour side, next to me. I quickly leant forward and drew his attention to an imaginary penguin in the water. With any luck, he did not see the offensive graffiti. Poor Toddy was distraught at the prospect of having Burgos in his police cell for nine months; however, he turned out to be a useful handyman and Toddy eventually was sorry to see him go. In the circumstances, I had no alternative but to sign a deportation order at the end of his sentence. One of our Spanish-speaking Islanders escorted him to Comodoro Rivadavia and thence by bus south to the Chilean border, where he was left to make his reluctant way home.

Before Sir Peter left, we took him overland to Bluff Cove to give him a taste of travelling in camp. Although only fifteen miles from Stanley, the journey by Land Rover took two hours each way, driven by one of the best camp drivers in the Falkland Islands, Mickey Clarke. As we slipped and slithered in the mud, he complained about the men who had decided to site the capital at Stanley in 1843. They were seafarers, he said, who were only interested in the harbour; to get out of Stanley in any direction overland meant struggling through some of the worst peat bogs in the Islands. The art of not getting bogged involved picking out the firmer patches ahead and avoiding the tracks of those that had gone before, with the result that on the well-used approaches to Stanley one had to diverge more and more from the recognised track.

We learnt how difficult this was when we tried to drive round Stanley harbour to the Royal Navy installations on the north side, known as the Camber. The 'track', such as it was, ran along the line of the old light railway, which the Royal Navy had built in the First World War to link the jetty on the Camber with their huge radio transmitting station in Moody valley, a distance of some three-and-a-half miles. We must have covered almost twice that distance, criss-crossing the old railway line like a snakes-and-ladders board. We eventually reached the solid, stone-built house of the Royal Navy's custodian, Hector Anderson. He and Don were old shipmates and they reminisced about their voyage from England on the *Golden Chance* as Hector's wife, Millie, weighed down the table with a Yorkshire high tea of homemade bread, scones and cakes. Destined for service with the sealing factory then under construction at Port Albermarle, the *Golden Chance* and a larger (and slightly more seaworthy) vessel, the *Protector*, under the command of Adrian Monk, were purchased at Wivenhoe in Essex. The *Golden Chance* had been built in Lowestoft in 1914 as a steam drifter. She was a little under 90 tons, 84ft long with a beam of 19ft. Then forty-five years old, the Department of Trade had refused to issue her with a seaworthiness certificate and, as Don had mentioned on our first day in the Islands, she had had to be towed outside British territorial waters before being left to her own devices on the high seas – hardly an auspicious start to an 8,000-mile voyage. After a laborious beat up the English Channel, Adrian in the *Protector* realised that they could make better time by towing the *Golden*

Chance the whole way. They ploughed through the Bay of Biscay in this fashion, averaging a good six knots, until they were abeam of Lisbon, whereupon the *Protector* caught fire. They managed to contain the damage but had to put in to Lisbon for repairs. Such were the temptations of that city that Adrian had to set sail again before the repairs were properly completed, otherwise he would have had no crew left to man either vessel. Even with the fire damage on the *Protector*, they could still make better speed with the *Golden Chance* under tow than on her own. After an eventful crossing of the Atlantic, Don was on night watch about a day out of Rio de Janeiro when he heard plopping noises coming from the main deck. Thinking they were flying fish landing on board, he went to investigate. To his horror, he found that the pitch between the deck-planks was bubbling up, the bursting bubbles causing the plopping noises. Further investigation showed that the *Golden Chance* had broken her back. Expecting her to split in two at any moment, they nursed her into Rio, where she was splinted up while the crews had another great run ashore. Finally, sixty-three days after leaving Wivenhoe, they sailed triumphantly into Stanley harbour.

Although the sealing venture lasted for only two seasons (killing a little over 3,000 sea lions) the *Protector* and *Golden Chance* continued to give useful service round the Islands until finally *Protector* was beached in New Island and the *Golden Chance* in the Canache. Hector was also beached on the Camber, where he took the job of looking after the Royal Navy diesel tanks, warehouses, pumping station and reserve stores. He showed me round and I was saddened to see the rusting remains of two shunting engines, one piled up with other scrap metal at the edge of the jetty and the other partly submerged.[7] Back in England, enthusiasts would have had them restored to pristine condition and probably running along the original track.

As a sideline, Hector and Millie, who both loved animals, ran the Islands' quarantine station, which was situated near their house towards Navy Point. Although only ten minutes from Stanley by boat, to drive round as we had done took over an hour, and there were occasions when even a Land Rover could not get through. Hector said that, in the old days, if the wind was in the right direction, Islanders would hoist a sail on a railway carriage and be blown along the line – a more elegant and faster way to travel than a bumpy Land Rover.

Our next trip to camp was by the traditional method – by

sea. We boarded the MV *Forrest* at the Government jetty and sailed off to visit some of the settlements to the north of Stanley. Although owned by the FIG and crewed by Falkland Islanders, the *Forrest* was on annual charter to the Ministry of Defence for the use of the Royal Marines. Major Robin Gilding and six of his men accompanied us and one of our doctors, Hilary King, came along to carry out hydatid tests on the people in the settlements. Although no one had died from the disease for some years, the Medical Department continued precautionary screening throughout the Islands. If caught early enough, it could be cured by surgery.

The *Forrest*'s skipper, Jack Sollis, was a popular Islander who had been sailing around the Falkland Islands since the Second World War and probably knew the local waters better than any man alive. He appeared to navigate without looking at the charts and with only an occasional glance at the compass. In good visibility, he lined up one known landmark with another and steamed serenely between the kelp beds into the narrowest and shallowest of harbours. He knew the tides and currents like the back of his hand and was deservedly proud of the fact that he had never run aground or even scraped the side of any vessel in his command. With a kind, craggy face, and a soft, gentle voice, he was every child's idea of the salty sea captain. I found him a mine of information and learnt more about the Islands (and the Islanders) on my trips with him than from anyone else except Don. This morning, as we headed out of Port Stanley towards Kidney Island, he told me how he had helped to carry the wounded off HMS *Exeter*, moored on the spot which we were now passing, after the Battle of the River Plate in 1939.[8]

Kidney Island was our first port of call. It was an uninhabited nature reserve, with a tremendous variety of wildlife. A naturalist wished to carry out research there later in the year, and Robin had agreed to renovate an old hut, which had been used for the same purposes some years ago. Mavis stayed on board and Robin and I went ashore in a Gemini rubber inflatable. The island was thickly covered with tussock grass, which grew in huge mounds well above our heads. We were making our way uphill through these mounds towards the hut when we suddenly came face-to-face with a huge bull sea lion. He reared up between the tussock, towering above us and snorting angrily. His mane was fully grown and he looked every bit as handsome as his four-legged namesake. But we had no time to stand and stare, as the magnificent beast started to come downhill, moving surprisingly quickly for such an ungainly animal.

We broke ranks, Robin to the right and me to the left, and the sea lion rushed between us towards the sea. We found the hut intact, but in a delapidated state. Robin left three of his Royal Marines to sort it out, with instructions to keep a wary eye open for sea lions, and we reboarded the *Forrest* to sail round to Berkeley Sound.

The first settlement on the north side of the Sound was Johnson's Harbour. As the tide was low, we went ashore by Gemini, to be met by the owner/manager, Osmund Smith. One of the few farms to be owned entirely by a Falkland Islander at that time, it was registered in the name of the Smith Brothers and had been in the Smith family since 1870. Osmund was the only son in a family of four. In his mid-sixties and still a bachelor, he had never been out of the Islands. He visited Stanley infrequently and lived quietly with his mother, to whom we were introduced over smoko, the Falkland Islands equivalent of 'elevenses' but in content more like a high tea than the normal coffee-break. Mrs Smith was a formidable lady. Well over eighty, she was in full command of her faculties and the farm. Osmund treated her with both affection and deference and, in her presence, spoke only when spoken to. Mrs Smith lamented the fact that not one of her daughters, though married, had produced a grandchild for her and that, when Osmund died, that would be the end of the line. I ventured to suggest that there was yet time, whereupon she shook her head vigorously. 'My daughters are all over fifty', she said, then, with a toss of her head in Osmund's direction, 'and he'll never get married.' This sounded more like a command than a statement.

Osmund was modest about his farm and his generosity. Jack had told me that he produced some of the finest wool in the Islands and that, by good management, hard work and prudence, he had become one of the Islands' wealthiest farmers and was always willing to help others who were struggling to make ends meet. He also held enlightened views on conservation: his farm had the largest King penguin colony in the Islands, near Volunteer Point. In 1947, Osmund had espied four King penguins in a gentoo colony. He left the area undisturbed and had been delighted to see their numbers increase over the years until there were now over sixty.[9] He had a shepherd's shanty near Volunteer Point, well stocked with food, fuel and bedding and he kindly invited us to stay there whenever we wished. We found it a marvellous escape from Stanley and were only sorry that we could not take up his generous offer more often.

After lunch with Osmund and his mother, we went back on

board the *Forrest* and sailed across Berkeley Sound to Green Patch, where we met the new owners busily preparing for their first season. Jock and June McPhee and their attractive daughter, Trudy, were planning to drag the house that had been allocated to them in the settlement out to their farm at Brookfield, a distance of over three miles across peat-bog, diddle-dee and white grass. We had heard that moving house in the Falklands was different from back home, but had not imagined that they meant it literally. Their plan was to jack up the house, slide wooden sledges underneath and drag it with a team of tractors to the new site. We were unable to witness the actual move, but we visited the house at Brookfield shortly afterwards and Trudy said that everything had gone well. They had left some glasses in a kitchen cupboard by mistake, and even they had survived the journey. She showed us a door which at Green Patch would not shut properly: it was now a perfect fit. Only the chimney had to be rebuilt.

We left Green Patch a little before dusk and sailed the short distance across the sound to Port Louis. We were looking forward to seeing the Islands' first settlement. Even in the twilight, it was obvious why de Bougainville had chosen the spot: the inner harbour was completely land-locked except for an extremely narrow entrance. Indeed, the entrance was so small that Jack had to anchor the *Forrest* outside and we went in by Gemini. As we approached the lights of the settlement, I reflected upon how tiny the old ships must have been – the *Forrest* was only 144 tons gross and 86ft long.

We were met by Len and Millie Grant and taken to their house, which was built upon the solid stone walls constructed by Louis Vernet in 1826. Vernet was an interesting character. Born in France, his Protestant parents had taken him to Hamburg at an early age. At fourteen, his father had sent him to the USA to train in business and, after eight years, he had gone to Lisbon for a spell before establishing himself in Buenos Aires in 1817 as a successful, cultured and highly intelligent businessman. He went to Port Louis in 1826 and, after many vicissitudes, set up a promising enterprise, rounding up wild cattle, supplying beef, fresh vegetables and dairy produce to the increasing number of ships calling at the Falkland Islands and even exporting dried beef and salted fish to Brazil and wool to London. To control the North American sealers, who were exploiting the Islands' seal population in ever-increasing numbers (and helping themselves to Vernet's cattle), he applied to the Buenos Aires government for a man-of-war but, owing to the civil war then waging on the mainland, it could not provide. Instead, it appointed him Governor. The sealers refused to recognise his authority and the British Government protested against the appointment, claiming prior British rights of ownership. When Vernet attempted to exert his authority over a North American sealer, the US Consul in Buenos Aires despatched a corvette, the USS *Lexington*, to the Islands 'to protect the rights of US citizens there'. The captain of the USS *Lexington* carried out his instructions by flattening Port Louis with his cannon. As a result, only two sides of the original house remained.

While we chatted with Len and Millie, Hilary set up his clinic in their house and we met the other ten inhabitants of Port Louis as they filed through for hydatid screening. Jack joined us later for dinner and explained that he took a particular interest in Port Louis because both he and his wife, Maud, had a substantial share in the company that owned it. The other shareholders were also Islanders. Though comparatively small, with 10,000 sheep and a hundred cattle, it paid a modest dividend. A pressing problem was to find a replacement for Len, who was due to retire as manager shortly. Experienced managers were becoming more and more difficult to find. Like most Islanders who spent their working lives in camp, Len and Millie had scrimped and saved to buy a house in Stanley in preparation for the day that they had to retire. Once they ceased to be employed on the farm, they had no option but to move into town.

We were up early the next morning to see what we could find of Port Louis' past history. Apart from the manager's house, little remained: fragments of stone wall here and there, the foundations of de Bougainville's fort and a reasonably well-preserved stone corral. The most poignant reminder of the settlement's turbulent past came at the cemetery where, prominent among smaller headstones, stood one engraved with the name 'Matthew Brisbane'. He it was whom Vernet had left in charge in 1831, after seizing the North American sealer the *Harriet* and taking her to Buenos Aires to prosecute the master.

Brisbane was another interesting character. He had sailed from England with the Antarctic explorer Weddell and had helped him to chart the South Shetlands. He had been further south than Captain Cook before being shipwrecked on the coast of Tierra del Fuego and making his way in an improvised boat to the Falkland Islands, where he had joined Vernet in 1830. After the destruction of the

70

settlement by the USS *Lexington*, he had suffered the ignominy of being clapped in irons and taken by her master, Captain Silas P. Duncan, to Montevideo for trial as a common pirate. Thanks to the intervention of the British Consul, Woodbine Parish, he had eventually been released and, at Vernet's request, he returned to Port Louis in 1833, where he had impressed Captain Fitzroy of the *Beagle*, who described him as 'an honest, industrious and most faithful man, who feared no danger and despised hardship'. As Vernet's agent, he was responsible for Vernet's property but, in trying to restore order, he antagonised the gauchos whom Vernet had originally recruited from the mainland and who had been roaming at will since the *Lexington* raid, using Vernet's horses to kill cattle as they pleased and selling the beef to sealing vessels. On 26 August, 1833, the ringleader, Rivero, took Brisbane by surprise and killed him.[10] Four other murders followed, including that of a fellow-Englishman, William Dickson, who had been Vernet's storekeeper. We could not identify his or any of the other graves.

After breakfast with Len and Millie, we went on board the *Forrest* again and set sail for Salvador. It was another calm day and we had a fascinating run round the coast, thrilled with our first sight of fur seals. Watching them basking on Volunteer rocks, it was difficult to imagine how anyone could club the harmless animals to death: yet in the last century they had been hunted almost to extinction, with over three million skins taken from the Islands over a seven-year period. Fortunately, the few that survived had multiplied and several rookeries like this one off Volunteer Point now appeared to be well established. Turning into the narrow channel that led to Port Salvador, we passed Little Shag and Big Shag Islands, Goat Point, Fish Creek, Rat Island and Rabbit Island until eventually we anchored off the attractive settlement of Gibraltar Station, Salvador. This was the home of Robin and Jene Pitaluga. Robin's antecedents originated from Italy, but his great-grandfather had come here from Gibraltar where, as Robin put it, the respectable part of the family had remained, achieving high office in that colony's administration. At one time his great-grandfather had owned most of the East Falkland north of Stanley but, living up to his role of black sheep, he had lost over 100,000 acres one night on a £6 wager; but Robin still had enough land to carry over 16,000 sheep and a hundred cattle, and his cousin, Diana, had about half that number on the other side of the channel.

Robin took us to his extremely comfortable home, which was

unique in having a Royal Navy helicopter at the bottom of the garden. It was an old Whirlwind from HMS *Endurance*, before she was re-equipped with Wasps. The pilot had ditched after a fuel supply problem. Fortunately, he had managed to come down in shallow water not far from the settlement and the Navy had salvaged what they could and bequeathed the remains to Robin, whose two sons had used it as a supertoy. Mavis was delighted to find that Jene hailed from London, where she had met Robin during one of his leaves. Life as a farmer's wife in the Falklands could not have been more different, but Jene had adapted well and met the challenge. I was delighted to find that Robin was interested in flying. He owned his own Cessna Skyhawk and had taken his private pilot's licence at Biggin Hill. He showed me the hangar that he had built for it himself; it was tailor-made for the Skyhawk, with not a foot to spare. Instead of returning to Stanley on the *Forrest*, he offered to fly us back – sixteen minutes by air, compared with six-and-a-half hours by sea. I jumped at the chance, though Mavis took some persuading.

First, however, we were due to visit the other settlements in Salvador Water: Teal Inlet, Douglas Station and Rincon Grande. After a most pleasant night ashore with Robin and Jene, we climbed aboard the *Forrest* and steamed the seven miles to Teal Inlet. Looking back on this trip in 1982, I prayed that our Task Force would not decide to land there: the ships would have been sitting ducks in those restricted waters. Teal Inlet was as attractive on the ground as from the air. Its owner/manager, David Barton, and his wife Col (Robin's sister) were away and we were entertained to smoko by the settlement's oldest inhabitant, Mrs Newman. In her eighties, Mrs Newman was the daughter of Fred Cheek, who had lost an arm at the tender age of ten. He had fallen from a horse and sustained a compound fracture. This had happened in West Falkland and it had taken three weeks to get him to hospital in Stanley, by which time gangrene had set in and amputation was the only course. Undeterred, Fred had grown up to perform all the duties of a normal shepherd, learning to shear with one arm, saddle up (using his teeth to tie knots) and ride with the best of them. The only thing he could not do, said Mrs Newman, was to fasten the buttons on his shirt-sleeve. He worked for many years as a postman in the West Falklands, on horseback and leading any number of packhorses carrying the mail. Mrs Newman had obviously inherited her father's grit: she loved fishing and during the season drove off alone in her

Land Rover up the Malo River, where she camped for days on end.

We lunched on board the *Forrest* on the way to Rincon Grande, Diana's farm opposite Salvador. Diana and her husband, Ron Turner, ran the farm with only one other couple, the Whitneys. Their young son and daughter also helped, though still in their early teens. Diana did not believe in sending them away to boarding school, nor did she hold with travelling teachers. She employed a full-time tutor, who also helped out on the farm. Diana invited us upstairs to their living room, which she had had built on the first floor with large picture windows on three sides to make the most of the spectacular view. To the west lay the channel into Salvador Water, with Robin's farm beyond; to the east, Bacon and Ham paddock, Standing Man Hill, Twelve O'clock Hill and Shanty Ridge; and to the south, the Rincon, Horseshoe Bay and, away in the distance, Smoko Mountain. To welcome us, Diana opened a couple of bottles of champagne and hoisted the Union Jack (almost all the farms we visited raised the flag, but Diana was the only one who capped it with champagne). Her first love was horses. She had over seventy on the farm, including some handsome thoroughbreds imported from the mainland. She professed to keep sheep only to provide the wherewithal to indulge her love of horses, but she was also an expert sheepfarmer and regularly obtained the highest prices for her wool.

As dusk fell, Jack took us back to Gibraltar Station and we were able to visit all the houses there before returning to Robin and Jene's for dinner and bed. Hilary had carried out hydatid tests in the settlements we had visited and, happily, none was positive. Next morning, we set sail for Douglas Station, which was about as far to the west of Salvador as Teal Inlet was to the south. Unusually, the jetty was four miles from the settlement, at Moro Point. We were met there by Michael Clarke, son of Mickey, who had driven us with Sir Peter Watkin-Williams (and was to be my regular camp driver) and he drove us in glorious sunshine to Douglas Station. Hilary accompanied us and we met all the residents as they gathered for their hydatid screening. We had smoko with Bill and Clara McKay. They had been the longest residents on the farm and when the owner, Harland Greenshields, retired in ill health to his native Wales, he had left Bill in charge. But Bill was not happy as manager; he much preferred the life of an outside shepherd. He and Clara had not moved in to the 'big house', which was beginning to look rather shabby and forlorn. Indeed, the whole farm had a feel of decay and neglect about it, and the residents lacked a sense of purpose. It was barely ticking over, awaiting a new owner. Michael said that it was carrying 14,000 sheep when it should have had 22,000. He estimated that a good third of the farm was not being used. He would have liked to buy it, but not at the price being asked.

We returned on the *Forrest* to Salvador, where we said farewell to Jack, Hilary and Robin Gilding and his Royal Marines and had a leisurely lunch with Robin and Jene while the *Forrest* steamed back to Kidney Island to pick up the Royal Marines that we had left there. They eventually arrived in Stanley at 8.30pm. We took off from Robin's airfield (the only one on the Islands to boast three strips) at 3.15pm and were in Government House before 4.00pm. I think that it was this trip that made me determined to buy my own Cessna. Much as I had enjoyed the *Forrest*, the advantages of having one's own aircraft to get round these scattered settlements were overwhelming. There were, however, two snags: my pilot's licence was out-of-date and I did not have the money. I could overcome the first by renewing the licence during my home leave in 1981 and, fortuitously, I reached the notional age of sixty in the same year and so became eligible for a gratuity.[11]

Notes
1. Farm managers could be authorised by the Governor to perform marriage ceremonies. Griff was a popular choice and conducted several during my term of office, including Steve's.

2. See page 154

3. The previous Labour government had agreed to hold negotiations with the Government of the Argentine Republic concerning 'future political relations, *including sovereignty*, with regard to the Falkland Islands, South Georgia and South Sandwich Islands'. A number of inconclusive meetings had been held, at which the Falkland Islanders had not been represented.

4. One was eventually declared round the Falklands in 1986 (but not 200 miles). There is still no fisheries zone round South Georgia or South Sandwich Islands.

5. *The Island of South Georgia*, by Robert Headland (Cambridge University Press).

6. All these plans had disappeared when I returned to Government House after the Argentine occupation in 1982.

7. These were 'Wren' class locomotives, built in 1915 by Kerr Stuart

& Co Ltd of Stoke-on-Trent, 6 x 9in cylinders, 0–4–0 ST 20in diameter wheels of 24in gauge.

8. See page 325.

9. At my last visit, in 1985, there were over four hundred.

10. For this dastardly act, modern Argentina acclaims Rivero as a national hero and, for a while during the occupation in 1982, renamed Stanley 'Puerto Rivero' in his honour.

11. The Diplomatic Service used to classify certain countries as 'hardship posts' and these counted time-and-a-half towards retirement. As most of the posts in which we had served were thus classified (though we never found them so in practice) I was due to become a notional sixty at the age of fifty-five.

5

A Wet and Gloomy Winter

First on the agenda on my return to Stanley was another meeting of Joint Councils to hear Adrian's report of the talks with the Argentines in New York. Although the Argentines had begun by restating their position on sovereignty, Mr Ridley had managed to get agreement that the fundamental difference of opinion on this matter should not inhibit further discussions of the possibility of co-operation in the development and conservation of the resources of the South-West Atlantic. Adrian gave it as his opinion that the Argentines would not co-operate on anything unless Britain first conceded sovereignty. He went on the local radio that evening and gave a summary of the talks, which was meant to reassure the Islanders that nothing was being negotiated behind their backs; but over the next few weeks I found a pervading feeling of gloom, pessimism and suspicion. The mere fact that we were having talks with the Argentines could mean only one thing: the present British Government, like the last, was considering the transfer of sovereignty. My constantly reiterated reminder that any solution negotiated with Argentina would have to be acceptable to Islanders cut no ice. Those 'clever people' in the Foreign Office would trick them into it and they would be presented with a *fait accompli,* as they had been in 1971 with the Communications Agreement.[1] They were afraid that their councillors would be either hoodwinked or browbeaten into submission. I had more confidence in their chosen representatives: I could not see Adrian Monk or his fellow-councillors being hoodwinked or browbeaten by my diplomatic colleagues.

I reported Islander reactions faithfully to the FCO and could have wished for similar frankness in return. Indeed, FCO reluctance to keep me fully informed – let alone to invite me to comment on drafts before they were submitted to ministers – was to become the main bone of contention between us for the rest of my time in the Falklands. Until the Franks report was published in 1983, for example, I did not know that the Cabinet Defence Committee had agreed in July, 1980, to attempt to reach a solution of the dispute on

76

the basis of a leaseback arrangement.[2] This decision had been based upon a memorandum by Lord Carrington which must have been drafted initially by South American Department, then my parent department in the FCO; yet I was neither informed nor consulted at the time. It has always been, of course, the complaint of the man on the spot that Whitehall knows best; but it was particularly frustrating in the context of the Falkland Islands, where the point at issue was the future of the Islanders themselves.

The FCO was not the only Whitehall department that knew what was best for the Islanders. Second on the agenda with Joint Councils was the crisis over the school hostel. Long before my arrival in the Islands, a decision had been taken to close the Darwin boarding school and build a new hostel in Stanley. This was a sound decision on educational grounds, since the number of secondary schoolchildren could not justify two secondary schools and, with over half the population in Stanley, the obvious choice was to expand the secondary school there and build a boarding hostel nearby to accommodate the children from camp. By thus concentrating secondary education in one school, the children would enjoy better facilities and a greater variety of subjects to take at 'O' level. The British Government had generously agreed to finance the project, which had been entrusted to the ODA.[3] Although scheduled for completion by the beginning of 1979, it had run into all sorts of problems and was far from finished by the time of my arrival in February, 1980. I had paid regular visits to the site and was appalled to see, slowly growing from the mud and chaos, a forbidding concrete structure that looked more like a blockhouse on the Maginot Line than a children's hostel. The root cause of all the problems and delays was that ODA had chosen the wrong design, the wrong contractor and the wrong method of construction. The hostel was a single-storey, flat-roofed building made out of a novel method of spraying ready-mixed concrete under pressure onto a frame of thin metal bars. The contractors were a firm established for the purpose by Charringtons, which had then owned the FIC but were subsequently taken over by Coalite. As Ted Needham, the head of Coalite, said to me later, we had both inherited 'a can of worms'. One small example will suffice: wet concrete from a pressure-gun in the Falkland wind was, to say the least, wasteful. So much intended for the roof and the walls finished up on the ground that Willie Bowles, the local carpenter (and at that time a Legislative and Executive Councillor) had to cut two inches off all the fitted wardrobes.

A crisis had occurred because maintenance on the Darwin school had been kept to a minimum for the last few years in anticipation of moving into the Stanley hostel, and its generator had finally gone up in flames. The children had been sent home and emergency measures were needed to restart their education and fill the gap until the new hostel was ready. The only vacant building in Stanley suitable for use as a hostel was Stanley House. This was a fine Victorian building owned by the FIC and once the residence of the company's 'Colony Manager'. The post had long ceased to exist and the last occupants of the house had been the contractors who had built Stanley Airport in 1977. They had left it in a bad state of repair and standing empty for three years had led to further deterioration; but it was basically sound and councillors gave me authority to negotiate with Coalite for its use as a temporary hostel. I soon discovered that the FIC's Stanley manager, Harry Milne (who was naturally sympathetic to our needs) had no delegated authority and that I was dealing with Mr Needham, who had the reputation of being an extremely tough negotiator. After several diplomatic approaches had failed, I decided on a different tactic. Harry had told me that Mr Needham was a hard-headed Yorkshireman, so I began my next telex: 'As one hard-headed Yorkshireman to another. . .' to which he replied 'I am not a Yorkshireman, I come from Derbyshire, but I am equally hard-headed. . .' I could not resist the rejoinder: 'Sorry you are from the wrong side of the border, but I do not hold that against you.' I think it was from this point that the ice began to crack and we later became good friends. Ted sent out a strong team to negotiate on the spot and the upshot was that we were able to use Stanley House as a temporary hostel for a peppercorn rent. We for our part undertook to restore the building to the condition in which we had found it once the children moved into the permanent hostel. A welcome sequel to this visit was that one of the team, Harry Camm (not a Coalite man but a personal friend of Ted Needham) became interested in farming in the Falklands and subsequently bought Douglas Station from Harland Greenshields.

Not so welcome was a continuing wrangle over the new hostel. Ted naturally wanted to conclude the wretched contract as quickly as possible. Given the chance, he would never have entered into it in the first place. I shared his views but, before I could sign the completion certificate on behalf of the FIG, I had to be sure that the building had been constructed according to specification. My new Director of Public Works, John Brodrick, was an experienced engineer on secondment from the British firm of Roughton and Partners, and he had grave doubts about the structural safety of the main hall. Also, one did not need to be an engineer to see that the finish was well below the normal British standards that had been stipulated in the contract. On John's advice, I refused to take over the building until certain tests and remedial works had been carried out. We went through a farcical period, with a hapless Harry Milne bringing the hostel keys to my office (on Ted's instructions) and my returning them to him. The matter had not been resolved before the Argentine invasion in 1982.

June 1980 saw my first budget session of Legislative Council. The FIG followed the US financial year, 1 July to 30 June. Harold Rowlands prepared the budget, we discussed it in Executive Council, I gave a round-up of the past year in my opening address to Legislative Council and Harold then presented his estimates for the coming year. After general comments from the councillors, I withdrew and the whole house went into select committee to examine the estimates item by item, calling in heads of department where necessary to explain and justify their provisions. That first year, FIG's revenue was £2½ million. When I left in 1985, it had risen to £6 million. The main sources of revenue were corporation tax (primarily from profits from the export of wool), income tax (similar levels to Britain) and philately. If world wool prices were low, it meant a bad year for the FIG, which suffered all the disadvantages of a one-crop economy. For 1980-1 there was scarcely enough to keep the government departments ticking over, let alone to provide the basic infrastructure on which development depended. The only development projects in hand were the ill-fated school hostel already mentioned and the almost equally ill-fated Stanley-Darwin road, both financed and supervised by the ODA. Instead of buying new, specialised roadmaking equipment, the ODA had foisted upon Public Works Department worn-out vehicles and machinery left behind by the airport contractors. As a result of this false economy, not even the modest target of six to seven miles of road a year (gravel, not tarred) could be achieved. At the 1980 rate of construction, it would have taken over twenty-two years to complete the sixty-five miles of road. And this was to be the main highway in East Falkland!

The need for more rapid progress was well illustrated during

79

Farmers' Week, which was held annually in Stanley in July – arguably the worst month of the year. Adrian and Nora Monk took nine hours to drive from Darwin in their Land Rover, at an average speed of 7mph. Others were more fortunate, but half-a-dozen boggings a trip at that time of the year were quite commonplace. All travellers carried heavy jacks, wooden planks and towropes and it was not unusual to have to jack up each wheel separately, the wooden plank disappearing into the peaty mud as the wheel rose enough to insert sprigs of diddle-dee, stones or any other objects on which the tyres might grip.

As if to cock a snook at the long nights and wintry weather, Stanley's busiest social life was held at this time. Starting with the May Ball, at which the May Queen and Prince Charming were selected for the year, the programme ran through the Johnny Walker darts competition (won in 1980 by a Royal Marine); three church bazaars (Christ Church, St Mary's and the Tabernacle); the Badminton Club's Fancy Dress Ball (held on or near midwinter's night, in which almost everybody entered, young and old, singly and in groups); the Governor's Cup darts competition (I was knocked out in the second round by a charming young girl, Marilyn Bonner, one of Don's many nieces); the Sports Club's annual dance; the Grassland Trials Unit's party; the final of the Sheepdog Trials; the School Concert and the Falkland Islands Home Handicrafts exhibition.

Farmer's Week gave us the opportunity to meet most of the farm managers and owner-occupiers and to entertain them at Government House. I learnt a lot by sitting in on some of their discussions in the Sheep Owners Association. By coincidence, Argentine National Day (9 July) also fell during this week. Hector and Teresa Gilobert gave a drinks party, which was well attended by the farmers and held in a cordial atmosphere. We agreed beforehand that there would be no speeches or national anthems. After the trouble over their new house, I did not want a similar embarrassment to the one I had witnessed on Japanese National Day in Jesselton (now Kota Kinabalu), Sabah. There, as the national anthem began, Donald Stephens, the Chief Minister, and most of the locals had pointedly turned their backs on the Japanese Consul and carried on talking. It was a calculated insult, understandable perhaps in Donald's case, since the Japanese had killed his father.

Our next trip to camp was in August and we took Diana and Tony, who had joined us for their long vacation. Flying with them to Fox Bay East in the Beaver, we all agreed that we had never seen such a desolate landscape. Through the snow squalls, we could make out a grey, lifeless, watery land. There had not been enough snow to hide everything under a white blanket – just enough to blur the features and deaden the colours. I was glad that we were flying over that inhospitable land and not plodding through it. To add to the monotony, our route took us across Lafonia, the flattest and least interesting part of the Falklands. Despite the bad weather, we felt perfectly safe in the experienced hands of our pilot, Ian White. Our travelling companion was Shirley Knight, wife of the Fox Bay West manager. Her accent left no doubt where she came from – Northern Ireland.[4] Our hosts at Fox Bay East were Richard and Grizelda Cockwell, both from England. They had two young sons, Adam and Ben, and already had two house-guests from the yacht *Sea Leg*, John Dalby and Ros Hall, who had decided to winter in the Islands; but Grizelda cheerfully accommodated the four of us and made us most welcome.

Fox Bay East was owned by Packe Brothers and Company Limited, the main shareholders of which were Islanders. Richard was the manager and explained the difficulties of running a farm that was split between Packe's Port Howard (north of Port Howard settlement) and the central part of West Falkland. Even without the northern section, Fox Bay East was badly situated to run a farm that stretched as far west as Dunnose Head. Overland communication was so bad that he had to keep a separate settlement there, not merely an outside shepherd's house. To complicate matters, Packe's Port Howard had the best breeding ground, which meant a four-day drive of large flocks of sheep over forty-six miles every season. The whole farm carried about 31,000 sheep and was clearly an early candidate for sub-division.[5]

That first afternoon, Richard took us for a walk along the coast to the nearest penguin colony. The sun shone between the snow squalls and all the usual shore and seabirds were there in profusion. Riding majestically at anchor in one of the bays was Richard's pride and joy, *The Compass Rose*, a superb ocean-going yacht which he had bought for a song from its American owner who, after being dismasted and disillusioned, had abandoned it in Port Stanley. In the evening, Mavis and I walked round the settlement and met the residents in their own homes. There were nine families, plus three men in the bunkhouse – about thirty people altogether, including children. Historically, Fox Bay East had housed the Post Office and the doctor for West Falkland. The doctor had gone but the

Assistant Postmaster remained. Ken Halliday, ably assisted by his wife Joyce, dealt with a continual stream of letters from dealers and collectors seeking the Fox Bay East cachet. They took their responsibilities seriously and stamped each envelope carefully by hand to ensure that the cachet was legible and in exactly the right place. They knew that it was much valued in philatelic circles. They also operated and maintained the radio and teleprinter link with Stanley and serviced the generator. In addition, like most kelpers, Joyce kept chickens and a cow or two. We returned to look at their Post Office the next morning and were interested to see the old births and deaths register, which Ken kept in the safe. Going back to the mid-nineteenth century, it contained a striking number of young deaths. We also noticed that a frequent cause of death among older people was alcoholism.

Fox Bay West looked very close, not ten minutes across the water; but there was no boat available. Richard kindly offered to drive us there, which meant going up the creek for a considerable distance before being able to cross. It took forty minutes of hard driving. Fox Bay West was one of two farms on West Falkland owned by the FIC (the other being the adjoining Port Stephens). Slightly smaller than Packe Brothers, with 29,000 sheep, the population was also less and Nigel Knight was able to take us round all the houses and outbuildings before lunch. They were generally in better shape than those of Fox Bay East and confirmed our previous impression that FIC looked after its employees well and maintained a higher standard than most. Shirley and Nigel entertained us to an excellent lunch and we returned to Fox Bay East for the night. In our absence, the *Forrest* had arrived to take us to Speedwell Island.

Standing on the jetty early next morning, we decided that it must be the coldest spot in the Falklands. There was nothing between us and the Antarctic and the wind was howling up from that direction. We were thankful to join Jack in the cosy warmth of the *Forrest's* bridge. The wind was whipping up the water and we had a choppy passage across the Sound. I was surprised to see so many stinkers until Jack explained that a nearby island was the main breeding colony for the whole archipelago. He said that the stinkers passing Government House every morning on the way to the Stanley slaughterhouse probably came from here. It seemed a long way to fly for breakfast. Diana and Tony began to feel a little seasick after two hours of rolling across the swell, but they soon recovered when we reached the lee of Speedwell Island. We went ashore by Gemini and had smoko with the island's only residents, the Larsens. Ronnie had moved there quite recently from North Arm, where he had been for thirty-one years. He and his wife Yvonne had a grown-up daughter and a young baby and looked after 9,000 sheep, forty-nine cattle and fourteen horses on Speedwell and adjoining islands. They and the islands belonged to the FIC. Despite the isolation, the Larsens were very happy, though Ron said that he would prefer to own Speedwell if he could.[6] Yvonne was a Jaffray, one of the main families in Lafonia and aunt of our two maids in Government House.

On our return trip to the *Forrest*, we shared the Gemini with gory mutton carcasses destined for friends in Stanley. Jack was heading homeward, through Eagle Passage and round Bull Point (another renowned spot for wildlife); but before he did so he was dropping us off at Flores Harbour, where Tony Blake, the manager of North Arm, was due to meet us. We loaded ourselves and our suitcases into the Gemini and the snow swirled around as we pulled away from the *Forrest*, obscuring both ship and shore from view. It was an odd sensation, sitting in a snowstorm in a little rubber boat in the middle of nowhere, looking at our cases still bearing stickers and labels marked 'Buenos Aires', 'Kuala Lumpur', 'Singapore' and 'Saigon'. We grounded on a shallow, stony beach and splashed ashore in our wellies before discerning three figures huddled in front of a small sandbank. They looked cold and wet, but Tony greeted me with a cheerful, 'Dr Livingstone, I presume,' and introduced his foreman, Alec Jaffray (Yvonne's brother). The third member of our welcoming committee was John Ferguson from the Grasslands Trials Unit. Their three Land Rovers were parked behind the sandbank and they loaded our cases as we said farewell to our Gemini driver, Nut Goodwin.[7] Rather him than me, I thought, trying to find his way back to the *Forrest* in that snowstorm. I realised how easily accidents could happen in such conditions.

Tony led the way with Mavis and Diana, our Tony went with John and Alec brought up the rear with me. We had an exciting two-hour drive to North Arm; smoother than normal, said Alec, because the ground was frozen. We skidded on ice rather than slithered in mud. And, when bogged, it was reasonably easy to be pulled out without using the big jack.

Shedding our sodden anoraks and muddy wellies, Tony led us into a lovely warm kitchen. His wife, Lyn, was cooking and the most appetising smells emanated from the Aga. Both Tony and Lyn were New Zealanders. Tony and Brook Hardcastle had worked together at Telford farm training institute, in New Zealand, where Tony was a lecturer and Brook farm manager. Lyn was a trained children's nanny. Brook's enthusiasm for the Falklands had rubbed off on Tony and when Brook returned and offered him a job with the FIC, he had gladly accepted. They had now been in the Falklands for nine years and loved it. Lyn said that she could not imagine a better place for bringing up their children, Heidi and Tom. John Ferguson was already staying with them, but there was room to spare for the four of us. The dining table easily seated ten and, after an excellent dinner, Tony took us to the club for the Saturday dance. North Arm was the second largest settlement after Goose Green and everybody – children included – seemed to be at the dance. Tony was responsible for over 70,000 sheep, 850 cattle, 300 horses and almost a hundred humans. There was a great community spirit in the clubhouse, with music provided by an accordion, a guitar and – Tony's speciality – a 'lagerphone'. This was an old broomstick from which sprouted various arms festooned with metal bottle-tops. The noise resulting from banging it rhythmically on the wooden floor was a cross between a double bass and a tambourine. In Tony's capable hands, it was most effective; but I was not so successful. It took me back to the skiffle group we used to have in the Gulu Club in Uganda in the fifties. There we had, not a 'lagerphone', but an old tea-chest, a piece of cord and a broomstick. The Islanders' favourite music was 'Country and Western'. It had something to do, I suppose, with those wide, open spaces and all that time spent in the saddle. Inevitably, we also had the Circassian Circle and the old-fashioned waltzes. The party was still going strong when we retired at 2am.

We were up early the next morning and off with John Ferguson to see some trials that Tony was carrying out on pasture management. He believed that heavy stocking could rid the pasture of the poor, white grass and give the more nutritious grasses a chance to establish themselves, thereby improving the pasture without expensive imported fertiliser. It was noticeable how much greener the grass was in his more heavily stocked paddocks. John agreed that, if the sheep had no alternative, they would eat the poorer grasses and that smaller, more succulent shoots would emerge; but one had to be careful not to push the sheep too hard or they would quickly lose condition and the wool yield would fall. The object of Tony's experiment was to see just how far he could go before this happened. I remembered remarking to Brook Hardcastle how green and lush all the home paddocks looked compared with the general camp and he had explained that that was because they were so well manured by the sheep coming in from the outlying paddocks. He was a firm believer in the old Yorkshire maxim, 'Tha' can only get out of't land what tha' puts in'. Nevertheless, Tony was convinced that the pasture in the Falklands could be dramatically improved by judicious pasture management.[8]

We returned to Lyn's delicious cooking of upland goose, whereupon Tony (our son) went off shooting with Gavin Hardcastle (Brook's son) and his girl-friend, Debbie, who was visiting from England, and came back with another eight. Tony (Blake) took me to the club, and on the outskirts of the settlement pointed out a sign that I had missed the night before: 'Welcome to the People's Republic of North Arm', followed by 'Watch Out For Children, Dogs and Crawling Drunks'. We chatted to a few of the settlement characters, including a smartly dressed gentleman called Ben Minell, who looked and behaved like a perfect Jeeves. I was not surprised to learn that he had once been valet to the Colonial Secretary (predecessor of the Chief Secretary). He explained that he had left because his 'greedy' master would not allow him to share his drinks. Previous Colonial Secretaries, he said, had been more understanding. Also present was Peter Morrison, whom I had knocked out of the Governor's Cup darts competition. To demonstrate what an amazing fluke that had been, he massacred me on his home ground.

The Beaver was due to fly us back to Stanley the following afternoon, but the weather in the morning was foul and all flying was cancelled. We decided to wait for a weather check at noon and then, if the forecast gave no prospect of the cloud lifting, to go overland. If the weather remained bad, we should be able to make Stanley by the following night, only twenty-four hours behind schedule. Tony and John Ferguson nobly volunteered to drive us as far as Goose Green. This was where the diddle-dee radio came into its own. It took only minutes to arrange overnight accommodation there. Eric and Shirley Goss said that they would be happy to have the four Hunts, despite the short notice (indeed, they laid on a dinner party for us) and there was no shortage of volunteers to look after Tony and John.

We spent part of the morning before departure looking at North

Arm school. Because of its size, the FIC employed its own school-master, a quiet Scot called Philip Hutton. He and his wife, Isobel, had been in the Islands since the fifties, most of the time at North Arm. The school was a model of its kind and compared favourably with a village school in England (it reminded Mavis of the school in *Anne of Green Gables*). Philip was a dedicated teacher who loved children, horses and gardening and appeared to combine all three very successfully in North Arm. On our way back to the 'big house', we called at Alec Jaffray's for smoko. He and his wife Elliot were the parents of our two maids, Valerie and Joan, and were pleased to hear how they were getting on.

The noon forecast showing no signs of improvement, we had an early lunch and were on our way by 1.30pm, Tony taking Mavis and me in front and Diana and our Tony with John in the rear. About half-an-hour out of North Arm, with the settlement barely out of sight, we lost John's Land Rover. Retracing our tracks, we found a bedraggled John under the front of his vehicle. A track rod had worked loose and his steering had gone. Finding the missing bits in the muddy and icy pools seemed an impossible task. Once again, the 2-metre set proved invaluable. Tony called up Alec, who took details of the wanted parts and promised to be out with them as quickly as possible. Meanwhile, the six of us groped up to our elbows in the mud along the tracks made by John's Land Rover. I carelessly let the water come over one of my wellies and had a frozen foot for the rest of the journey. Suddenly John let out a triumphant cry and brandished a metal bolt, quickly followed by a nut and bracket. Undaunted by the cold or the wet or the mud, he lay on his back under the Land Rover and proceeded to re-assemble the track rod. As Mavis said, one had to be resourceful to travel in winter in the Falkland Islands. He had almost completed the repair when Alec turned up with the spare parts. Alec escorted us through the third gate from the settlement (distances were measured more by gates and fences than miles and kilometres) to make sure that the track rod would hold before he left us and returned to North Arm.

We took four-and-a-half hours to cover the thirty miles to Goose Green. Tony said that the camp was the wettest he had ever known. John got bogged once and it took us half-an-hour to pull him out. We drove over Bodie Creek bridge in the dark. Built in 1935 by the FIC, using its own farm labour and steel from Dorman Long (my father's employers for most of his working life), it was over 400ft long and had been erected to link Goose Green with Walker Creek, another FIC settlement on the southern shore of Choiseul Sound; but it also cut several miles off the journey to North Arm.

A hot bath brought feeling back to my foot and we all revived quickly in Shirley's warm and cheerful house. After such a journey, there was a pleasant sense of achievement; it was almost worth the discomfort to defeat the elements. During the party I was soon in animated conversation with Veronica Fowler, the attractive wife of the headmaster of Darwin School. Both she and her husband John came from Yorkshire and had been in the Islands (like the Blakes) for nine years. Although we found that we had a lot in common, Veronica's political views were well to the left of centre and somehow our conversation turned to Margaret Thatcher, about whom Veronica had strong and decidedly critical opinions. I vigorously defended the Prime Minister, and our voices were clearly heard in the next room, where Mavis happened to be talking to John. 'Who is that female giving Rex such an ear-bashing?' asked Mavis, to which John replied, 'That, I'm afraid, is my wife.'

After a most entertaining dinner, we walked over to the community hall, where Veronica and I buried the hatchet over a game of darts (she won) and John agreed to show me round Darwin School the next morning. I was to think of this first meeting with Veronica when I was standing with Margaret Thatcher in the community hall in 1983. Sadly, Veronica was no longer there so I did not have the pleasure of introducing her.[9]

We ended the evening with a quiet nightcap in Nick and Sheila Hadden's house. Nick was a Scot who had come out to work as book-keeper for the FIC and decided to stay. Sheila was a true kelper but of Scottish origins – her father was Murdo McLeod, one of the characters of Stanley. Sheila ran the company store but Nick was approaching retirement and they were looking for a house to buy in Stanley.

Next morning, John Fowler took me to look at Darwin School. The damage caused by the generator fire was not as bad as I had expected and, with a little help from PWD, we agreed that two rooms could be made reasonably habitable. I promised John to take it up with the DPW on my return.[10] We then visited the temporary class in the bunkhouse, which had the great advantage of being warm, though it could only be used until the shearing season began in October. What a contrast between the present cheerful atmosphere and my previous visit, when Kirk was lying there. After a walk round the settlement with Eric Goss and a call on Sheila in the store, which was stocked as well as any mini-supermarket in England, we heard the familiar drone of the Pratt and Whitney Wasp of the Beaver. Eddie Anderson had braved the low cloud and come to save us a six-hour drive (at least) to Stanley. The jetty was just a stone's throw from Eric and Shirley's house and we got there as Eddie taxied in. Mount Usborne and the Wickham Heights were totally obscured, but the cloud-cover was broken over the coast, and Eddie wisely headed for Fitzroy, keeping well clear of the high ground. We crept between Tumbledown and Mount William into Port Stanley and Eddie switched off at the Beaver slipway after a thirty-five minute flight. 'What would have happened', I asked, 'If Stanley had closed in?' 'I'd have gone back to Goose Green,' said Eddie, 'It's often clear when Stanley is out.' 'But if Goose Green had closed in?' I persisted. 'No problem – I could have put down in any of those bays along the coast and waited for it to clear.' That was one advantage of a seaplane over a landplane.

The in-tray on my office desk was, as always after a few days' absence, piled high and my engagement book crowded. I was working late a few nights later when a worried Robin rang from Moody Brook to say that one of his Royal Marines was missing. The *Forrest* had taken a few of them to North Arm and Marine Addis had failed to return to the ship before sailing time. Jack Sollis made it a rule to sail at the appointed hour and had departed without him. He reported Addis's absence over the radio and at first it was thought that he had simply missed the boat. However, a check of the houses in the settlement drew a blank and Tony reported that Addis had last been seen leaving the club and heading for the jetty. He had instituted an immediate search of all the ground between the club and the jetty (which was some distance from the settlement) but with no result.

At first light the next morning, despite the appalling weather, we organised an intensive search by sea, land and air. The Beaver flew for most of the daylight hours, the *Forrest* went back to North Arm with divers, who kept diving in the icy water until Robin, fearful of their safety, ordered them to stop, and Tony used all the able-bodied people in the settlement, plus Royal Marines, to comb the surrounding countryside. Addis's body was never found. The ensuing inquest had no alternative but to return a death by unknown causes. There were many theories – some exceedingly wild – but Jack Sollis's was the most likely. It had been a dark and bitterly cold night, with a severe frost and gusty winds. The jetty was long and narrow and the wooden planking, along which ran a narrow-gauge railway for loading the bales of wool, was treacherous underfoot. Addis could easily have slipped off into the sea and, in that wind, the duty Marine on watch would have heard nothing. A few minutes in the icy water would have been enough to induce hypothermia. The currents could have taken the body into the kelp beds, which would have prevented it from floating to the surface. After this tragic incident, which again emphasised the need to respect the natural elements, Robin instituted the 'buddy' system, whereby Royal Marines always went in pairs when travelling in camp.

An interesting visitor about this time was the Argentine naval transport, the *Bahia Buen Suceso,* bringing drums of petrol, oil, kerosene and aviation fuel, gas cylinders and animal feed from the mainland. She was later to hit the headlines by landing the scrap-metal merchants illegally at Leith, in South Georgia, in March, 1982; but this was an authorised routine visit under the communications agreements. Nevertheless, it always rankled with Islanders that she came into Port Stanley without flying the courtesy flag. The explanation I was instructed to give was that warships (and, by extension, naval transports) did not have to fly the courtesy flag when entering a foreign port; but it sounded unconvincing, particularly as there were experienced seafarers on the Islands who knew that our Royal Fleet Auxiliaries flew the courtesy flag whenever they entered another country's port. I could only answer, somewhat lamely, that the Argentine fleet auxiliaries were manned by serving members of the Argentine Navy, whereas ours were crewed by civilians.

Hector Gilobert had already introduced me to Captain Gaffoglio, of the Argentine Navy, who used to fly over to Stanley in advance of one of his ships to make the necessary arrangements with the FIC, whose jetty they used. Gaffoglio now introduced me to the master of the *Bahia Buen Suceso*, Captain Pizzagali, who invited Mavis and me on board for dinner. Hector and Teresa came, too, and we had a pleasant evening, with platitudinous speeches of mutual friendship and co-operation. If I had known then of Gaffoglio's 'hobby' of photographing the beaches around Stanley every time he came over, I would not have been so diplomatic. The ship was comfortable and the Captain's cabin well appointed, and I was sad when she was sunk by the Royal Navy on Trafalgar Day, 1982.[11]

Another interesting Argentine visitor was Mr Crosby (I did not get his first name), who introduced himself as a veterinary surgeon and a politician opposed to the current military regime.

He was travelling with his wife, three daughters and a secretary. According to him, he led the world in artificial insemination techniques for sheep. He saw a great future in the Falkland Islands as a UN-declared disease-free zone, producing semen from pedigree rams for export to both South and North America. Mr Crosby believed that, being of low bulk and high value, it could profitably be transported by air and would more than cover the cost of establishing a pedigree flock. I pointed out that we first had to get rid of our last two diseases, hydatid and brucellosis; pedigree flocks would also need imported feed. It was, however, an interesting thought for the future.

The inevitable day arrived when Diana and Tony had to leave, at the end of their summer vacation. Mavis was too upset to come to the airport. Don drove the three of us in the red taxi along the now all-too-familiar 4½ miles of metalled road. Diana knew every inch of it because I had been teaching her to drive in Mavis's Ford Fiesta (better known as Fifi) and this was the only stretch of road outside Stanley suitable for a saloon car.[12] Tony had ventured further on his 'scrambler' motor cycle. Learning the hard way, it had taken him 5½ hours to ride to Fitzroy – a distance of about 20 miles – and 6½ hours to get back. He had turned up so covered in mud that he was unrecognisable. The occasion had been Fitzroy's 'two nighter'. Most settlements threw a big party once during the winter and held it over two nights. 'I can understand why now,' said Tony, 'It takes a day to get over the journey!' At the airport, it was reassuring to see Robin Gilding, whose turn it was to carry the diplomatic bag. He would see Diana and Tony safely to and through Buenos Aires. I promised Tony to look after his motor cycle and give it the occasional run (thought not to Fitzroy) and then they were off and away into a lovely blue sky. Don looked as miserable as I felt as we drove back to Government House.

A harassed Toddy McMillan brought me some much-needed light relief. He regretted to have to report an embarrassing incident concerning his latest prisoner. For reasons that will become clear, I refrain from giving details of the prisoner, except that he was an Englishman, married to a kelper. He had had an argument with his employers, the FIC, and had either walked out or been given the sack. Whatever the cause, he had felt aggrieved and, after drinking more than was good for him, had hurled a stone through the window of the West Store, filled up an old metal dustbin with loot and attracted the attention of a sleepy policeman by rolling it past the police station in the early hours. Hardly a professional job, but the magistrate had decided that he could not let him off with just a fine and had sentenced him to three months' imprisonment. The previous evening, Toddy had let him out of the cell for his regular exercise in the courtyard, which was walled in, but the barbed wire on top of the wall had long since fallen down. It was not a particularly athletic feat to take a running jump and climb over it. This the prisoner had done while Toddy was busy at the front of the police station. Confronted with an angry customer demanding to lodge a complaint, Toddy had picked up his pen and was about to enter the details in the station log when he glanced up and realised that the complainant was his prisoner. 'What are you doing out there?' he asked. 'Never mind what *I'm* doing' said the prisoner, 'There's a Marine in bed with my wife – what are *you* doing about that?' Poor Toddy had no sooner locked him up again when in stormed the irate wife, wanting to know what Toddy was doing letting her husband out of jail. 'I thought I was safe!' she said, not unreasonably.

Knowing how Mavis would miss the children, I was determined to get her out to camp as soon as possible. Pending and in-trays gradually diminished over the weekend and by 1am Monday they were empty. We were on our way to Roy Cove by 8.30am. Eddie Anderson was our pilot again, with fellow-passenger Councillor Bill Goss (Eric's father), whom we dropped off at Green Patch. He had undertaken the difficult task of supervising the splitting-up of the settlement. With the best will in the world, it was not easy to dismember a farm and distribute the assets fairly amongst six individual (and independent) farmers. Green Patch was the first of its kind, there was no precedent to follow and the rules had to be made as we went along. It was Bill's scrupulous fairness and practical common sense, combined with the new farmers' co-operative spirit, that ensured success. Regrettably we were not so fortunate with our next sub-division, which was to be Roy Cove; hence the reason for my present visit.

Roy Cove was one of the more picturesque settlements. After an hour's flight, Eddie dipped down towards a deep gully and, as we crested the last hill before the sea, the settlement swung suddenly and dramatically into view. Nestling at the head of the creek, on sheltered hillsides, with a clump of trees near the manager's house, it could have been a small hamlet in Lorna Doone country. We counted six houses, plus the bunkhouse, shearing shed and outbuildings. The jetty was well down the creek, towards the sea and, almost before Mavis had time to close her eyes, Eddie had chopped the throttle, put the Beaver down gently on the water and was gliding towards it. Without another touch of throttle, we came to a standstill with the port wing over the jetty, and it required only the slightest touch by a man in a blue woolly hat to steady us until Eddie had thrown out a line. It was an impressive display of precision landing.

The man in the woolly hat was Joe Newell, the manager, and as soon as he spoke we knew that he was one of the more recent settlers from Northern Ireland. His three daughters, Donna, Paula and Cara gave us a hand with the luggage and Joe drove us in his Land Rover to the 'big house' where his wife, Trudy, was waiting with smoko. Trudy was a true kelper from an old Islander family, the Johnsons. Her sister was married to George Betts, master of the *Monsunen*, whom we were to see later on this trip. Roy Cove was owned by a local company, with 70,000 acres but currently carrying only 18,000 sheep. In its heyday, under the dynamic management of Syd Miller, now a retired senior citizen in Stanley, it had carried 22,000 but the extensive reseeding he had done with Yorkshire Fog had been neglected and carrying capacity had been decreased.[13] Joe showed us the vast area that Syd had seeded as we drove to the new reseed trials being conducted by the Grasslands Trials Unit at Herbert Stream house. There they were using an assortment of seeds and having great trouble keeping away the upland geese. Despite scarecrows, noise scarers and our own presence, there were hundreds gobbling up the fresh green shoots. We drove mile after mile through overgrown Yorkshire Fog. Seeing its long white fronds waving in the wind, we could understand why Falkland children said that the colour of grass was white.

That evening and the next, we climbed up and down the steep hills on which the settlement was built, meeting all the residents in their homes. The main complaint was that their favourite BBC programme, *The Archers*, had ceased to be relayed over the local radio (we had been arguing with the BBC over costs); their own uncertain future came second. Syd Miller, one of the farm's directors, had authorised me to tell Joe that he would be given first choice of sub-division but, to my surprise, he said that he was not interested; he was thinking of going back to Northern Ireland. The head shepherd was a Scotsman, Tom McGhie. He and his wife, Moira, loved the Islands and wanted to stay, but he was getting on in years and neither of them fancied the prospect of retiring to Stanley. Back in the highlands of Scotland, he would have no trouble continuing to work as a part-time shepherd well into his seventies. I did my best to persuade both Joe and Tom to stay – they were key figures for the splitting up of the farm – but to no avail.[14]

This was only the first of our troubles with Roy Cove. The next was finance. The FIG did not have the money to offer soft loans to all six sub-division owners, as it had done with Green Patch. To overcome the shortfall, it was proposed at first that three of the sub-divisions should be offered to overseas buyers at the going market rate and that the money thus realised would be used to make soft loans to three deserving Islanders. This was later amended by councillors to two overseas buyers and four Islanders. There were unavoidable administrative delays but, eventually, the two overseas buyers turned up, one from Scotland and one from New Zealand. The local owners were already on their sub-divisions and relations were difficult from the start. To compound matters, the official handing-over ceremony was due to be held on 2 April, 1982 – the day of the Argentine invasion. In the circumstances, it was perhaps not surprising that the experiment failed. It was not tried again.

On this, our first, visit to Roy Cove, however, the farm was running smoothly and there were no storm clouds on the horizon. Joe took us to an outside shepherd's house at Dunbar, a delightful spot along the peninsula towards Byron Heights. The outside shepherd was a young man called Willie Ross, whose new bride, Odette, was a Goss. It seemed the ideal honeymoon hideaway. Roy Cove, the nearest settlement, was 1½ hours' tough ride by Land Rover. At the head of a small creek, looking north towards Carcass and Saunders Islands, the house was perfectly sited, with lovely views in all directions. The vegetable garden was well established, the chicken run neat and tidy, the dog kennels clean and the peat plentiful. I envied Willie and Odette their peace and self-sufficiency.[15] On our way back, we drove close to a large gentoo penguin colony. That afternoon, young Donna Newell raced me up Cooke Hill, behind the settlement, from the summit of which we had the most spectacular views south over King George Bay: Rabbit and Hummock Islands, The Crouching Lions and, behind them, the Passage Islands, stood out in sharp relief in the cold, clear sunshine. In the UK, it would have been a celebrated beauty spot. In the evening, we helped Trudy feed the ducks and Joe the pigs before completing our round of the houses in the settlement. We were thankful for the warmth of Trudy's kitchen on our return, but found the bathroom the coldest we had yet experienced. Syd and Betty Miller must have been tough to have lived there for thirty-six years.

Next day, it was Ian White's turn to pick us up in the Beaver and fly us to Dunnose Head. Jimmy Forster was waiting for us there, in a rowing boat. He did not seem to notice the cold, but we were feeling it by the time we reached the shore. Jimmy was a Manchester man who had given up the city for the wide, open spaces and had adapted to his new life so well that in the previous year he had won the Islands' sheepdog trials, beating the Islanders, as it were, at their own game. His young wife Ginny (with a hard 'g') was a Pole-Evans and a true kelper. We had smoko with all the residents, nine in all, plus our jolly accordionist from North Arm, Jimmy Miller, who was there on a short holiday. Jimmy then took us round the settlement. His latest and proudest acquisition was the shearing shed. Designed on New Zealand lines, it was the best and most modern we had seen. He also showed us the airfield that he was laying out. Unlike most farms, which had or were making a single grass strip, he was being more ambitious and making two. This would cut down the cross-wind component, but it was to have serious consequences during the conflict in 1982.[16]

Jimmy and Ginny served up a huge lunch and then it was time to be rowed out again to the buoy to await the Beaver. Eddie was the pilot for the afternoon, and he flew us to Weddell Island, thirteen minutes across Queen Charlotte Bay. It was a glorious day and we could see New Island and Beaver clearly beyond Weddell. Below us, like a toy green boat in a paddling pool, was the *Monsunen*, her wake giving the only indication that she was moving. The wind was in the wrong direction for a landing close to the jetty, so we alighted in Gull Harbour and taxied to the buoy, where Bob Ferguson was waiting in a rowing boat to tether the Beaver and take us ashore. Bob's father had emigrated from Scotland. He was manager for Hamilton Estates Limited and responsible for all the islands in the south-west except New Island, amounting to 78,000 acres altogether. Weddell was the largest, at 54,000 acres, followed by Beaver (12,000) and the Passage Islands (6,000). Hamilton had been an illiterate Scottish shepherd, but he was both enterprising and industrious and, having established himself in the Falklands, had gone across to Patagonia and helped to open up that vast region of Argentina, making a fortune in the process. He had died leaving several daughters, one of whom was still alive in Argentina and the main beneficiary of the estate. The company itself was registered in Jersey, with Hamilton's old Scottish lawyer as chairman. One of the trustees was Argentine. In addition to the Weddell group, Hamilton's also owned Saunders Island. These were the only farms in the Falklands with Argentine connections (it was ironic that Saunders was where the British first settled in 1765).

There was a warm reception committee to meet us at the jetty: Bob's Welsh wife, Thelma, his sister, Tina, and husband Joe Short, Colin and Irene McDonald, two old characters, Peter Kiddle and 'Chum' Binnie, and what seemed like dozens of young children. The Shorts were descended from the thirty Chelsea Pensioners who had come out to the Islands in 1849.[17]

Off-season or no, the farm was a hive of activity in preparation for the *Monsunen*'s visit. Bob was selling four hundred sheep to the FIC and *Monsunen* was about to arrive to transport them to Port Stephens. We watched as Bob and Joe expertly worked their dogs and sorted out the sheep into the various pens. All was ready by the time the *Monsunen* tied up. The tide was low and the gangway sloped steeply down into the hold – too steeply for some of the frightened sheep, who lost their footing and ended up in a bleating heap at the bottom. It seemed cruel, but George Betts, the master, assured us that no harm would befall them and that he would not lose any on the short passage to Port Stephens. Loading took the rest of the day and George decided to stay overnight. He had his young son, Owen, with him and they both came to dinner with us at Bob and Thelma's. Owen was having the time of his life on board the *Monsunen*. He was only ten and preferred this to school any day. There was no doubt about the attraction of the sea to most young Islander boys; Bob and Thelma were proud of their son, who had joined the Royal Navy. They were looking forward to seeing him next summer, when he was due down on HMS *Endurance*.[18] Most young boys I spoke to wanted either to go to sea or to fly. It was understandable but did not bode well for the future of farming in the Islands.

Next morning, Bob took us in his ramshackle old Renault jeep to Swan Point, the northernmost tip of Weddell. We went inland on the way out and back along the coast. It was a spectacular trip for wildlife. We identified most of the eighty-seven species of birds commonly seen in the Falklands, saw fur seals and sea lions at Loop Head and came face-to-face with Bob's biggest problem – foxes. Apparently Hamilton had been fond of introducing non-indigenous animals into the Islands. He had brought foxes to Weddell in the hope that they would reduce the upland goose population; but they had found lambs an easier prey, with the result that the upland geese had increased and Bob had had to stop lambing altogether. He now sent his breeding flock by boat across to Beaver, where Tony Felton was able to keep the foxes under control. Bob shot a particularly cheeky fox, which stopped on the path behind our jeep, eyeing us curiously as if it had never seen a human being. It made no attempt to run as Bob raised his rifle. Bob said he usually bagged one or two whenever he drove out of the settlement, but he could not hope to eradicate them. 'They've multiplied like rabbits,' he said and, pointing to a nearby stone run, 'They're safe as houses in there.'

Stone runs, or stone rivers, are an interesting geological phenomenon, claimed to be unique to the Falkland Islands. Thought by Darwin to be of volcanic origin, the modern theory is that the present mountains were once much higher and that, after a period of freeze-thaw weathering, the softer layers of quartzite broke down into mud, causing the harder layers to crumble and ooze down the mountain-side. A remarkable feature is the distance that some of these have travelled; boulders several feet across and weighing up to fifty tons or more can be found miles from the original mountain peaks. We clambered over some of the huge, angular rocks and could hear the trickle of water through the stones many feet below. We agreed with Bob that it would take a veritable army of huntsmen and terriers to flush out foxes from a stone run such as this. We later called in at a shanty which Bob made freely available to Royal Marines for a rest and recreation. The only obligation was that they should shoot as many foxes as possible; but Bob said that they made a bigger impression on the upland geese.

Every time we stopped, Bob had to coax the tired old jeep back to life. Hamilton Estates Limited had refused to buy him a Land Rover. All the farm possessed in the way of vehicles was one ancient tractor (the jeep was Bob's own). The saddest loss, however, had been the farm boat. The old schooner, aptly called 'Weddell', had come to the end of its working life.[19] A new vessel had been ordered from France; but the final purchase price was astronomical and wool prices were low, so the trustees had decided to sell it upon completion. Without a boat, Bob could not work the Passage Islands, from which all sheep had been removed, or his other outlying islands. He had to use Tony Felton's small boat to transport sheep to and from Beaver. On Weddell itself, Bob said that he had been denied funds for fencing and, as a result, was carrying only 8,000 sheep when, with proper management, he could have been carrying almost twice that number.

On our return to the settlement, we walked round the houses and found them in a poorer state than anywhere else we had visited. No money had been invested in the farm for years. It was the worst example of absentee landlordism that we had seen (and this was confirmed after we had visited all the other settlements). When Bob told me that, as manager, he was getting less in basic pay than an ordinary farm-hand on other farms, I determined that, despite the political implications, we would take over Weddell, Beaver and Saunders from Hamilton Estates.[20]

After dinner, Bob and I left Thelma and Mavis to do the washing-up and went to the community hall to watch a James Stewart western, *Two Rode Together*. All the settlements had a 16mm projector (this was before the days of video) and films from the central library in Stanley were transported by the *Forrest* and the *Monsunen*. Westerns were the most popular. Next morning we called at the bunkhouse to see old Peter Kiddle, the cook. He was at least eighty and his only inmate, Chum Binnie, was himself over seventy. Peter was sitting in front of the stove, bathing a foot in hot water. His ankle had swollen overnight and he could not get his boot on. Chum was already at work in the wool shed. Despite the ankle, Peter had cooked breakfast for Chum and greeted us cheerfully. When I proposed suggesting to the doctor that he should include Weddell in his next camp tour, Peter snorted and said that he was perfectly capable of looking after himself and 'didn't want no doctor fussin' around'.

Ian White brought in the Beaver and we covered the short hop to Beaver Island in ten minutes. Tony and Vi Felton were there to meet us, with their daughter Faith (later to be a maid at Government House) and Tony's daughter from a previous marriage, Sonia, with her second husband and two children from her previous marriage. These complicated marital relationships were not uncommon in the Falklands and it behove the newcomer to tread warily lest he find himself maligning an ex-wife or ex-husband or, worse, someone's mother or father. Both Tony and Vi could trace their ancestry back to the original Chelsea Pensioners (Vi's maiden name was Short). Tony's first wife had been Winnie Miranda, née Jones, and he was Vi's third husband. Tony and Winnie's daughter, Sonia, had first married Royal Marine Geordie Gill (who figures later in this story) and was currently married to another English-man, Brian Paul. Sonia was a gifted artist who drew exquisite miniatures of Falkland wild flowers, but sadly, arthritic fingers were to curtail a promising talent. Tony and Vi's eldest daughter, Rhoda, was training to be a nurse and their son, Gavin, was work-ing at Port Stephens.[21]

Beaver Island was a single-family farm, carrying 2,000 sheep, though Tony said, like Bob, that with proper management the island could support twice that number. We had smoko on a magnificent table, which Vi explained had been washed ashore from the *Yarra Yarra*, a ship that had disappeared with all hands off Beaver in 1885. Apparently she had been spotted from the settlement between squalls with all sails set, making for Smylie Channel, then the snow and sleet had blotted out the view and she was never seen again. Only the table had been washed ashore at Beaver, though hundreds of candles and the ship's medicine chest had been found later on George Island. While we were having smoko, Ian flew to New Island and now returned to take us to our next destination, Port Stephens, which took us over some of the most rugged scenery in the Falklands. He flew low over Staats Island to give us a good view of the guanaco, which Hamilton had introduced in the early 1930s, presumably for its fine-quality wool. A small brother of the llama, it had flourished on Staats (nearly four hundred had been culled in the 1950s) but had been unable to swim to the surrounding islands. From a distance, the Horse Block stack to the south-west of Weddell looked like an aircraft carrier. Closer, one could see why it was so named, rearing up out of the water like a gigantic Trojan horse. Cape Orford loomed up and we were once more over land and dipping down into the sheltered harbour of Port Stephens. Named as early as 1766, after Sir Philip Stephens, First Secretary of the Admiralty, it had been the last acquisition of the FIC. The farm extended to the boundary with Fox Bay West and included the whole of the southern part of West Falkland, a total of 250,000 acres. Its manager, Peter Robertson, was on the jetty to meet us. A true kelper, he had gained some of his early farming experience in Argentina, where he had met his charming wife, Ann, whose grandparents had emigrated from England. She was, however, intensely loyal to the Falkland Islanders and strongly supported their right to remain British.

As Peter took us into their comfortable home, we were again struck by the high living standards maintained by FIC – in marked contrast to our last two ports of call. We were also struck by Peter's likeness to his father, Charlie, who had been manager of Port Stephens before him and was now in Stanley, where I often saw him in the Colony Club. One day he had related to me how he almost got into the First World War. Born in 1900 in the Falkland Islands, he was being educated in England at the outbreak of war in 1914. He was desperately keen to join up, but was under age and his father had given his guardian strict instructions that he should finish his education. Having ridden since a tiny tot, he was entirely at home with horses and, seeing a troop of the Household Cavalry parading through the streets of London, he had followed it back to barracks and helped in the stables. He had so impressed the troop sergeant with his handling of horses that he had been wheeled in front of the recruiting officer. Lying about his age, and tall enough to carry it off, he had been duly sworn in and given the King's shilling. His troop was about to go to France when his guardian tracked him down and revealed his true age to the commanding officer, who reluctantly had to discharge him. The guardian was taking no more chances: he sent Charlie under escort by train to Liverpool, where he was kept under guard until his ship sailed for Montevideo.

Charlie said he had always regretted missing the war.

Peter explained to us that, although the farm covered such a vast area, much of it was poor grazing, currently carrying only 30,500 sheep with a possible maximum of 40,000. The settlement was small for the size of the farm, with under twenty residents. They were an interesting mixture; an American Bahai couple, Debbie and Don Youngquist (she was keen to get a private pilot's licence; he was a hovercraft enthusiast, with exciting ideas as to their use in the Falklands); an English couple, Clive and Rosemary Wilkinson (he had an agricultural degree, she was a qualified teacher, both strongly Church of England);[22] an old Scottish handyman, Jock Fairlie, who had emigrated from Scotland in 1955; a Chilean farm-hand, José Maldonal, and the rest true kelpers (one of whom, Keva Smith, was later to become our cook at Government House).

Our first excursion from the settlement was with Peter and Ann past the attractive little cemetery and through a large gentoo penguin colony to Wood Cove (named for the driftwood that was washed ashore – there were no trees!) and Stephens Peak, from which we had magnificent views, to the north over the settlement and harbour and, to the south, a spectacular coastline of towering cliffs and weird rock formations. Peter collected his dogs from the kennels and let them run behind the Land Rover. This was the off-season and it was good to give them some exercise, he said. During the season, they would happily run anything up to a hundred miles a day, wearing out their pads if the shepherd was not careful. Peter exercised his dogs regularly in the winter to keep their pads hard. We were interested to see that the older ones totally ignored the penguins. One or two of the younger ones approached them playfully but returned to the Land Rover on Peter's command.

Next day, Peter took me to see his best breeding ground and the old sealing station at Port Albermarle. It was a rough, two-and-a-half hour drive and Peter wisely had his head shepherd, Leon Berntsen, and his cowman/gardener, Gerard Smith, to accompany us for most of the way. It was sunny but cold with superb visibility, and we had marvellous views of the sea to the south and the hills to the north. We drove between Mounts Alice and Young, both over 1,000 feet, and down into Albermarle Harbour, with Dismal Swamp to our left and The Big Mollymawk towering above the harbour to our front. It would have been a delightful beauty spot without the ugly remains of the old sealing station. Lying derelict since 1952, most of the buildings had been taken or blown down; but the foundations remained and rusty pieces of metal were scattered everywhere. The worst eyesore – and potential threat to wildlife – was a stack of 44-gallon drums of heavy fuel oil, about a hundred tons altogether, some of it seeping out of the drums and into the water like thick black treacle. We had our picnic in these dreary surroundings, wondering how we could stop the pollution. Some older ship's engines still used thick oil rather than the modern diesel fuel and I undertook to invite any such vessels calling at Stanley to come to Port Albermarle and take what they needed.

On our way back to Port Stephens, we called at a picturesque spot called Kit's Creek. According to Peter, Kit was a large American negress who somehow came south on a whaler or sealer in the last century and was dumped ashore here. Undaunted, she constructed a stone house partly in the cave at the head of the creek, from which she dispensed her favours to passing seafarers in return for furs and seal-skins. Kit's Creek became well-known among sealers and whalers and she finally returned to North America, so the story goes, a wealthy woman.

Every trip that we made into camp taught me a little more about sheep. This time, I noticed that they always ran away from us in the same direction. 'Yes', said Peter, 'Sheep always run into wind.'

He brought his breeding ewes down to the south-east paddocks to give them better grazing during gestation, which normally lasted 150 days. The lambs were weaned here before facing the rougher pastures to the north and west.

The Robertson's children, two girls and a boy, were at school in Argentina. Under the communications agreements, the Argentine government had offered scholarships to Islander children and, since 1972, about thirty had gone over to schools in Buenos Aires and Cordoba. The scheme had not proved popular, however, and by 1980 the Robertsons were about the only Islander children remaining in school over there. Paul, the son, had actually been born in Argentina and would be liable to military service if he stayed. He was interested in a military career, but in the British Armed Forces, not the Argentine.[23]

Eddie Anderson collected us from Port Stephens and we flew back to Stanley via Darwin, where we picked up three schoolgirls returning to the hostel. We hit some bad squalls on the way, but the girls were as unconcerned as if they had been on a school bus.

Notes

1. This was an agreement between Britain and Argentina which covered a wide range of communications matters under a 'sovereignty umbrella' (ie without prejudice to either side's position on sovereignty), the most important of which was the establishment of an air service by Argentina to replace the monthly passenger service by sea to Montevideo, hitherto provided by the Falkland Islands Company ship, the RMS *Darwin*.

2. *Falkland Islands Review:* Report of a Committee of Privy Counsellors, January, 1983 (Cmnd 8787, page 22).

3. Although under a Conservative Government the ODA was technically a part of the FCO, in practice it operated as a separate department, with its own Minister of Overseas Development.

4. The FIC and J. C. Waldron Ltd (Port Howard) had recruited employees from Northern Ireland, several of whom subsequently settled in the Falklands.

5. In 1982 it became the third farm to be split up, after Green Patch and Roy Cove.

6. His ambition was partly realised after 1982, when the FIC introduced a share-ownership scheme for their outlying islands.

7. Nut was First Mate on the *Forrest* and took over as Master when Jack Sollis retired in 1983.

8. This became more practical after 1982 with the greater use of electric fencing, which was more mobile, easier to erect and dismantle than traditional fencing and enabled the farmer to manage his pastures to greater effect.

9. When Darwin School had to close, John came into Stanley and later became Superintendent of Education. He and Veronica stayed on loyally during the conflict but decided to return to England afterwards. They were a sad loss to the Islands.

10. The building functioned as a day school for the children from Darwin and Goose Green from October, 1980, until the invasion, when it was totally destroyed by 2 Para in the battle on 28 May, 1982.

11. See page 352.

12. Mavis had Fifi in the Falklands for almost six years. The mileage on the clock when she brought it home was 1,100, though it had travelled 16,000 miles by sea.

13. Yorkshire Fog is a hardy type of grass that grows well in the Falkland Islands.

14. Joe took his family to Northern Ireland, but they could not settle and I was delighted to welcome them back in the Falkland Islands before we left in 1985. Tom and Moira returned in 1989.

15. After the sub-division, Dunbar became a farm in its own right and flourished in the capable hands of Marshall Barnes, who had been Bill Luxton's navvy boss at Chartres.

16. Seen as a possible enemy base, it was strafed by Harriers. Jimmy and Ginny luckily escaped injury but Councillor Tim Miller, who was with them at the time, received a piece of shrapnel in the skull and lost the sight of one eye.

17. They were not the octogenarians we think of as Chelsea Pensioners today. The youngest pensioner was twenty-six, the oldest fifty-three and the average age for the thirty was forty-two.

18. He was with *Endurance* throughout the 1982 conflict and was highly commended by Captain Barker.

19. Don, my driver, is now the proud owner and it rides at anchor in Port Stanley.

20. It was a long struggle but, in 1986, Bob finally became the owner of

Weddell, Tony Felton of Beaver and Tony Pole-Evans of Saunders Island.

21. After the conflict in 1982, Gavin was tragically to take his own life with a captured Argentine automatic rifle.

22. Clive and Rosemary later purchased a sub-division of Fox Bay East and now live at Dunnose Head.

23. After 1982, Paul was selected for training as a FIGAS pilot. He passed his flying course at Kidlington, Oxford and is now flying Islanders in the Falklands. His sister, Janet, was selected for sixth-form education at Atlantic College, the first Falkland Islander to attend that prestigious school. She subsequently obtained a university degree, and is also now back in the Falklands.

6

A Test of Loyalty

We were delighted on our return to Government House to see that the daffodils and crocuses were in bloom; but I was dismayed to find in my mail a letter from the FCO advising against the FIG making a financial contribution to the Falkland Islands Committee in London. This was an unofficial body established in 1968 by an English barrister (and one-time member of the Foreign Office) Bill Hunter Christie, to rally support for the Falkland Islanders. Its membership included Members of Parliament from all the main political parties and it had been instrumental in persuading the government of the day not to attempt to reach a settlement with Argentina on the basis of a Memorandum of Understanding that made no reference to the Islanders' wishes. Drawn up by officials, the relevant part of this Memorandum read:

> The Government of the United Kingdom . . . will recognise Argentina's sovereignty over the Islands from a date to be agreed. This date will be agreed as soon as possible after (i) the two governments have resolved the present divergence between them as to the criteria according to which the United Kingdom Government shall consider whether the interests of the Islanders would be secured by the safeguards and guarantees to be offered by the Argentine Government, and (ii) the Government of the United Kingdom are then satisfied that those interests are so secured.[1]

The then Secretary of State for Foreign and Commonwealth Affairs, Mr Michael Stewart, had assured Parliament that the British Government would continue to insist on the paramountcy of the Islanders' wishes and the Memorandum of Understanding had never been put to the Argentines. Falkland councillors were naturally grateful to the Falkland Islands Committee and, at a recent meeting, they had decided to respond to an appeal for financial help. At the time, the FIG could not afford to establish its own office in London and the arguments for helping the Falkland Islands Committee seemed compelling. The FCO took a different view. They argued that a financial contribution from the FIG would give the Falkland Islands Committee an official status and that the Committee would then be seen as the FIG's spokesman in London. It would be dangerous to have a mouthpiece over which the FIG had no control.

Here was my first test of loyalty. The FCO expected me to put their arguments convincingly to the councillors; at the same time I sympathised with councillors' desire to help their well-wishers in Britain. Governors are different from Ambassadors and High Commissioners, in that they wear two hats. Not only is it their duty to represent their home government and put across its policies, but they are also head of the colonial government to which they are appointed and have a duty to carry out that government's decisions and policies. This difference was not always perceived in the FCO. Conflicts of interest were bound to arise and I had previously determined that, if it should ever reach the stage that the FCO instructed me to pursue a policy that I believed to be against the best interests of the Falkland Islanders, I should have no alternative but to resign. This particular issue did not warrant such drastic action; but it was enough to trouble my conscience. I resolved to do my best to put over the FCO arguments and then, when the councillors stuck to their guns (as I thought they would) I would support their decision to the FCO. To my surprise, councillors accepted the force of the FCO arguments and all but one (Stuart Wallace) agreed to reverse their previous decision. In the event, the Falkland Islands Committee managed to struggle on with voluntary donations and its office performed sterling work during the conflict in 1982. The FIG subsequently established its own office in London, maintaining close relations with the Falkland Islands Committee and its larger offspring, the Falkland Islands Association, and contributing to its running costs.

Welcome house guests at this time were 'Survival' photographers, Cindy Buxton and Annie Price. They had spent three months the previous summer filming for Anglia Television on New Island and the Jasons and planned to spend the coming season on Carcass Island. Full of life, attractive, resourceful, unaffected and genuinely fond of the Islands and Islanders, they were extremely popular and were to prove excellent ambassadors for the Falklands in the years ahead. Their films *Penguin Christmas* and *Penguin Summer* were deservedly successful and did much to counter the rather grim and depressing pictures taken by the war photographers in 1982. Cindy was also highly competitive and took me on at snooker, squash, carpet bowls, croquet and any game that was going. She and Annie even turned out for a ladies' rugby team against the Royal Marines.

Saturday, 20 September was Chilean National Day and we were invited to attend the celebrations at the ESRO (European Space Research Organisation) building between Stanley and Moody Brook. According to the latest census, there were twenty-two Chilean men and five Chilean women in the Islands. Most of the men worked for the PWD in Stanley and lived in the ESRO building, which had been converted into a hostel. It looked as though all the Chileans in the Islands had come into town for their National Day. They had excelled themselves in decorating the hall, dressing up in national costume and preparing Chilean dishes. I was glad to see that they were far outnumbered by their Islander guests, who were entering fully into the carnival atmosphere. The Burgos affair seemed happily behind them.

Earlier that day, we had attended our first Falkland wedding. Don's niece, Marilyn (who had knocked me out of the Governor's Cup) was getting married to David Ford. The Fords, like the Bonners, were a long-established Falkland family. She was given away by Don's eldest brother, Harry, who we knew was not Marilyn's father. On the way home in the taxi, I asked Don what had happened to the father. 'Oh, he died a long time ago', replied Don, 'Of fire extinguisher fluid and anti-freeze.' He said this as casually as if it had been a heart attack.

The reception was held in the Town Hall, with tables groaning with food, children tearing around uncontrollably, Marilyn leading the dancing in her wedding gown and everyone, young and old, joining in. The two Vis (Vi Robson and Vi Bonner) never missed a dance. Although both in their eighties, they were remarkably light and nimble on their feet. I was chatting to Charlie Robertson and mentioned Don's remark to me about his brother's death, which he confirmed, adding that stranger deaths had occurred in the Islands. In the old days, he said, all the shepherds dressed up in suit and tie on Sundays, without fail. Their observance of the sabbath did not, however, extend to abstention from drink, and one poor soul after a heavy session had strangled himself trying to take off his tie.

Our aim was to visit all the settlements in the first year. After Cindy's and Annie's praise of Carcass and its owners, Rob and Lorraine McGill, we arranged to make that our next destination;

but strong winds at Carcass caused the flight to be cancelled. Unfortunately, we could not delay the rest of the programme, which included Golding, Keppel and Saunders Islands, because it had to fit in with the *Forrest's* schedule. We flew first to Pebble Island, to drop off Griff and Glad Evans, who had been in Stanley for a few days, and we then made the short hop to Golding and were rowed ashore by Fenton Hirtle's son, Tony. Fenton owned Golding and two smaller islands, Middle and East, amounting to 18,000 acres in all. He had 1,100 sheep on Golding and 800 on each of the other islands, but reckoned that these numbers could reasonably be increased. He believed in fencing, rotovating and reseeding and was sinking all his money and exerting all his efforts to that end. Generally regarded as the hardest working man in the Falkland Islands, Fenton had spent twenty-three years at Hill Cove, saving every penny until he could buy his own farm. He had borrowed from no one. Everything he had achieved was through his own efforts, though the Grasslands Trials Unit had advised him on seed and fertiliser and the FIG had contributed £1,000 towards his fencing programme (Fenton himself having paid £4,000). When he had to move sheep from island to island, he did so at night. Fenton said that he had started doing this to save the daylight hours for rotovating, but had discovered that the sheep were more docile at night and easier to move. Every penny went back into the farm. He wanted a Land Rover; his wife, Linda, wanted an indoor lavatory (theirs was the only farm in the Falklands without one); they both wanted to move the house to a more central spot on the island; but these would have to wait: fencing, seed and fertiliser came first.

While Mavis stayed with Linda and their two younger children, Odette and Gerald, I rode on the back of Fenton's Polish tractor to see his rotovated plots. They were most impressive, but Fenton was the first to admit that he was taking a gamble: a strong gale could blow all of his topsoil into the sea before the new grass had time to establish itself. (In the event, it was not the wind that subsequently caused disaster, but fire. He was progressing well until fire struck in 1983, ravaging hundreds of acres. As we surveyed the blackened land after the fire, Fenton was down, but not out. 'It will put me back a few years', he said, 'but I intend to carry on.' On my last visit, in 1985, fresh shoots were sprouting through the ashes and the new grass looked as green as any English meadow.)

Fenton showed me the four miles of fencing that he and Tony had laid and his plans for extension. We picked up a number of dead lambs. 'Under-nourished mothers', he said, sadly. On the way back, he pointed out a reef that was covered at high tide. 'Seven sheep were marooned there', he said, 'they had to swim for it and them dam stinkers went for their bellies. Come ashore with their tripes hanging out they did and I had to kill 'em.'

After lunch with the Hirtles, we boarded the Gemini and splashed our way out to the *Forrest*, which had arrived to take us to Keppel. Both Keppel and Saunders Islands were named after officers who had sailed in Admiral Anson's squadron in 1740. Anson was perhaps the first man to appreciate the importance of the Falklands. Writing to the Admiralty after his expedition he said, 'It is scarcely to be conceived of what prodigious import a convenient station in the Falklands might prove, situated so far to the southward and so near to Cape Horn.' He was obviously thinking of the Islands' naval and strategic significance; but the first settlers on Keppel saw the Falklands as the key to missionary work with the aboriginal tribes of South America. The imagination of Christians in England had been fired by Captain Fitzroy's attempt to spread Christianity and civilisation in Tierra del Fuego by taking three natives (whimsically named York Minster, Jeremy Button and Fuegia Basket), educating them in England and returning them with a young English missionary, Richard Matthews, to the Beagle Channel (named after his ship) three years later. After only ten days, the natives had turned against Matthews, and York Minster and Fuegia Basket had sided with them. Fitzroy had taken Matthews back on board and sailed for the Falkland Islands. When he returned a year later, he could hardly recognise Jeremy Button. In the words of his illustrious passenger, Charles Darwin, 'Instead of the clean, well-dressed stout lad we left him, we found him a naked thin squalid savage.' The full story was not told in England until after the completion of the *Beagle's* epic voyage round the world in 1836 and it was not until 1855 that the Patagonian Missionary Society succeeded in obtaining the grant of Keppel Island. For a peppercorn rent, the Society founded a settlement 'that might be a durable centre of operations, a place of rendezvous for the Missionaries, a safe depot for stores, a model community for the natives from South America and finally a farm to produce a considerable revenue'.

After many trips to Tierra del Fuego, the Society's secretary, the Reverend Despard, succeeded in getting some of the Yahgans to return with him to Keppel. One of his adopted sons, Thomas

Bridges (later to establish the mission station at Ushuaia) was a gifted linguist and, at the age of eighteen, quickly became proficient in the Yahgan language. He elected to stay at Keppel when Despard returned to England and accompanied Despard's successor, the Reverend Stirling, on many trips to the mainland. Between 1860 and 1864, over fifty Yahgans were taught at Keppel. The Patagonian Missionary Society became the South American Missionary Society and Stirling became Bishop of the Falkland Islands, with the largest diocese in the world, embracing the whole of South America. Thomas Bridges was recalled to England to take Holy Orders and duly returned to Keppel as a reverend (and with a wife from South Devon). Keppel continued as a training mission until 1898 and as a farm for the Missionary Society until 1911, when the island was sold to Dean Brothers of Pebble Island.

The present owners, Sam and Hay Miller, greeted us at the jetty as the sun set in a blaze of red behind Mount Keppel. The site for the settlement had been well chosen. It nestled in a horseshoe-shaped valley with the Bishop's residence, 'Sulivan House', standing proudly on the elevated ground in the centre, and the other buildings spread along the sloping hills between it and the cove. We walked round them the next morning and found the solid stone walls in good condition, despite the clay mortar. They were so dry on the inside that we could read clearly the pages of a 1907 *Tatler* which had been pasted on as wallpaper to serve, no doubt, both as entertainment and insulation.

Sam had about 3,000 sheep on the island, two hundred more than Bishop Stirling had estimated in 1877, but only 47 cattle, compared with Stirling's 500. With more fencing, Sam reckoned that he could increase the carrying capacity to 5,000. He had constructed four miles of fencing but, at £1,000 a mile, he could not sub-divide his 9,000 acres as he would have wished, even with a 25 per cent government subsidy. Unlike Fenton Hirtle, Sam had had to take a commercial loan (from FIC) to buy Keppel, and the interest payments were proving a heavy burden. Sam was a true kelper, son of Syd and Betty Miller and brother of one of the Councillors, Tim. Hay was a daughter of Jim and Bunny Clement and sister of Margaret (better known as Tooie) Evans, wife of another councillor, Derek. The Clements were a long-established Falkland family, but Bunny was English, having met Jim during the Second World War. He had paid his own way to England and enlisted in the RAF, where his seafaring skills were put to good use on a

Sunderland flying boat squadron. Their son Peter was at that time one of the *Forrest* crew and joined us for dinner that night.

Our trip to Saunders on the *Forrest* was surprisingly rough. We encountered a short, sharp sea as we sailed through Island Channel and into Port Egmont, which Commodore John Byron had described to the Earl of Egmont in 1765 as one of the finest harbours in the world and where, he declared, 'The whole navy of England might ride in perfect security from the winds.' Surveying Port Egmont from the bridge of the *Forrest* in 1980 I had to agree that, despite our rough passage from Keppel, it was certainly an excellent harbour, land-locked on every side and easy to approach. Jack Sollis confirmed that, for the most part, the holding ground was good, the tidal streams minimal and there was rarely a swell. 'It could still take the whole of the Royal Navy,' said Jack.

We tied up at the jetty and were greeted by Tony Pole-Evans and his grown-up sons, Bill and David. Bill was married to Shirley née Alazia) and they had two young children, Lisa and Ian. This was the sum total of the population on an island of 31,000 acres. Tony had lost his wife some years before and lived with David in the 'big house', while Bill and his family had a separate house in the settlement. Tony managed the farm for Hamilton Estates Limited. If anything, it was even more run down than Weddell. Existing fencing was in a bad state, most of the buildings were in need of repair and all the farm machinery – what there was of it – was old and worn out. With his sons' help, Tony looked after 8,000 sheep but reckoned that with another six miles of fencing he could increase the carrying capacity by 2,000 or more. He had asked for a new Land Rover and a rotovator as well as fencing, but to no avail. Like Bob Ferguson on Weddell, he received less basic pay as a manager than a normal farmhand elsewhere. He amazed us by saying that he had not taken leave since 1948, although, to be fair to his employers, he said that he had no real desire to leave Saunders. His great hobby was amateur radio, through which he kept in touch with the outside world. He was also an avid listener to BBC Overseas. He hoped one day that he or his sons would own Saunders Island, but until then they lived happily enough, keeping the farm going as best they could.

They certainly lived well: for lunch we had the most excellent roast beef. Saunders beef was always in great demand in Stanley, and now we could understand why. There must have been something special in the grazing. Indeed, Commodore Byron had remarked upon the abundance of geese – 'it was seldom that we took less than one hundred wild geese in a day for each ship' – and it was known that they always concentrated on the best grazing. Byron also recorded that the soil was extremely good and that 'the land is all covered with wood sorrell and wild Sellery, which are the best antiscorbuticks in the world'.[2] His successor, Captain John McBride, had been less enthusiastic, but then he had had to spend a winter at Port Egmont. The Lords of the Admiralty, having heard rumours of a French presence on the Falklands, had instructed him, after erecting a blockhouse at Port Egmont, to survey those parts of the Islands that Byron had been unable to explore and acquaint the subjects of any foreign power who might be found that, the Islands having been first discovered by the English and being the rightful property of the Crown of England, they had no right to establish a settlement and were directed to transport themselves off the Islands within six months. If they failed to do so, His Majesty's ships were authorised to take them off, treating them 'with all tenderness and care, and protected in every respect from injury, either to their property or persons in their return to the Dominions of that Power to which they belong'.[3] Unfortunately, McBride's storeship, the *Experiment*, and the sloop *Carcass* took a month longer to reach Port Egmont, consequently he could not get round to Port Louis before the winter set in.

We thought of McBride and his brave band as we strolled round the remains of the blockhouse that afternoon. Well fed on fresh beef, we felt for them existing for the winter on oatmeal, 'portable soupe' and 'sourkrout', with only the upland goose (and presumably 'sorrel and wild Sellery') to supplement their ship's provisions. As McBride said in a letter to the Earl of Egmont, 'Every person who comes this way should be well provided with guns and dogs, as his dinner in a great measure depends on it'. He also made a wise prophecy: 'This country, I believe, must have abler farmers than sailors to make anything of it'. His ubiquitous Royal Marines set about being farmers and, by 1767, had established a vegetable garden, acquired livestock, erected various wooden and stone buildings (in addition to the blockhouse) and organised a plentiful supply of peat. It was difficult to believe, looking at the few remains, that at one time this had been a thriving settlement of well over a hundred men. Tony had told us that there were four Royal Marine graves on the slope of the hill to the north of the blockhouse. We found three mounds in the diddle-dee, but could

111

only surmise a fourth. Little remained visible above the ground because the Spanish had destroyed the settlement in 1779.

We tried to unravel the story as we walked back through the diddle-dee to the present settlement, a distance of about one-and-a-half miles. Captain McBride had duly carried out his instructions. In December 1766, he had sailed up Berkeley Sound to Port Louis and given the French notice to quit. They had rejected the British claim to the Islands, but the meeting had been amicable. Following an agreement between France and Spain, the French had then handed over Port Louis to the Spanish in 1767, by which time McBride had returned to England, leaving Captain Rayner, shortly to be succeeded by Captain Hunt of the *Tamar*, in charge of Port Egmont. Hunt had not ventured into Port Louis and did not come across a Spanish ship until 1769, when he gave its commander the same formal notice as McBride had given the French. The Spanish commandant at Port Louis, now renamed Port Soledad, had returned the compliment by giving the British notice to leave.

This farcical exchange had continued until June, 1770, when five Spanish frigates had appeared off Port Egmont with a force of soldiers and sailors amounting to some 1,600 men. Hunt had by then sailed for England, leaving Captain Farmer in charge, with only his sloop *Favourite* and four 12lb cannon on shore to defend the settlement. Farmer had sent a message to the Spanish Commander, Madariaga, requesting him to depart and, in reply, Madariaga had landed troops and artillery half-a-mile from the settlement (where we were now walking), moored his frigates close inshore opposite the blockhouse, and opened fire. Farmer had returned the fire, but the result was a foregone conclusion and, in the presence of such an overwhelmingly superior force, Farmer had had no alternative but to raise the flag of truce.[4] Under the terms of capitulation, he had surrendered the blockhouse and agreed not to sail for home for twenty days after the departure of the Spanish frigates (to make sure, the Spaniards had removed the *Favourite*'s rudder). When Farmer eventually reached England, in September, 1770, there was an outcry and the British Government had demanded restitution of the settlement at Port Egmont to the *status quo ante*. Both sides prepared for war and it was the Spanish monarch who finally climbed down, disavowed the action taken by his Governor in La Plata and, in a written agreement, undertook to restore 'the port and fort called Egmont, with all the artillery and stores, according to the inventory'. Restitution had been formally made on 15 September,

1771 but, thanks to a weak and vacillating Prime Minister (Lord North), the British Government had not insisted upon the removal of the Spanish garrison from Port Soledad.

The settlement had continued at Port Egmont for a further three years until, owing to a general reduction of naval forces overseas, the garrison had been withdrawn. They left behind thirty-eight gardens, which had produced every kind of vegetable except peas, 'which the mice ate', and a lead plaque affixed to the blockhouse door which read:

> Be it known to all nations that Falkland Islands , with this fort, the storehouse, wharfs, harbours, bays and creeks thereunto belonging, are the sole right and property of His Most Sacred Majesty, George the Third, King of Great Britain, France and Ireland, Defender of the Faith etc. In witness thereof this plate is set up and His Britannic Majesty's colours left flying as a mark of possession.
>
> By S.W. Clayton
> Commanding Officer at Falkland Islands, AD1774

Five years later, on orders from Madrid, the Spaniards had demolished the settlement and removed the plaque to Buenos Aires, whence it disappeared during the British invasion in 1806. The Spanish garrison and penal colony had remained at Port Soledad until 1811, when they finally abandoned the Falklands.

Having tied up at the jetty for the night, Jack Sollis was able to join us for dinner. Looking at him and Tony Pole-Evans, I could imagine them living in Port Egmont two hundred years ago, taking both Spaniards and weather in their stride. They were worthy successors of Byron, Farmer and McBride.

Next morning, David took us in his old (1956) Land Rover, which he had towed from Hill Cove on a raft, over the central saddle to the northern cliffs. There we had our first, unforgettable sight of a black-browed albatross colony. We had seen them in flight and at sea; but not at close range, sitting on their nests. The first thing that struck me was the orderliness of the colony; the nests looked like rows of grey chimney-stacks and the mollymawks sat upon them sedately, not squawling and pecking at each other like the penguins and gulls, but minding their own business and at peace with the world. A mark of distinction was the thick black line that ran over and through the eye. Despite its huge size – it had an 8ft wingspan – and a vicious looking beak, it looked a gentle, dignified bird. David wanted to show us an egg, so he sidled up to a nest and leant softly on the sitting bird, keeping a stick between him and its mighty beak. The bird did not attempt to snap at him; she merely clucked a few times as he picked the egg out of the nest and settled down again contentedly after he had put it back. He said that they laid only one egg, early in October, and the fledgling would not leave the nest until March or April. Nesting pairs returned to the same nest each year, building it up a little each time (hence the chimney-stack effect) and might well have circumnavigated the globe during the year. The young ones would return to start breeding in their fourth or fifth year, having spent all the intervening period at sea.

David gave us a fascinating trip back to the settlement along the shoreline, which was teeming with jackass and gentoo penguins, sanderlings and the usual dense flocks of ducks, geese and gulls. Spring was in the air and one could feel the sense of urgency and excitement among the birds. Sadly, we had no time to linger and, after smoko with the Pole-Evans, Ian White arrived to take us back to Stanley in the Beaver. On the way he told me of a problem that had arisen over the aviation fuel, which the Argentines supplied under the fuel agreement of 1974. Because of the lack of a fuel jetty in Stanley, all Argentine fuels were imported in 44-gallon drums. The last batch, said Ian, had been contaminated. Gerald Cheek had rejected the whole consignment, but Hector Gilobert, acting on instructions from Buenos Aires, had refused to take it back or replace it. The matter was urgent because the reserve stocks would only allow for a few more days' flying.

I saw Gerald and Hector and our two RAF technicians, Bill Hughes and Al Watson, on my return. Al was quite adamant that the whole consignment was contaminated. He and Bill had spent the weekend sampling every drum and he strongly advised against the use of any of it in aircraft. Hector was most embarrassed but stuck to the Buenos Aires line that nothing could be wrong with the fuel. Eventually he was persuaded to accompany Gerald and Al to the drums to see for himself. He admitted that some of the drums were contaminated, but not all. It looked as though we were in for a prolonged argument before the Argentines would replace the fuel and, if FIGAS was to continue to fly, we had to get uncontaminated fuel quickly. Eddie Anderson came up with the answer: why not send the *Forrest* to Punta Arenas? We loaded her with empty drums and Jack Sollis sailed while we negotiated with the Chileans. He returned exactly one week later with a load of uncontaminated aviation fuel. Harold Rowlands did his arithmetic and came up with a surprising result. Taking account of a week's loss of charter from the MOD, the *Forrest's* steaming and crew costs, harbour and loading dues in Punta Arenas and the cost of the fuel itself, the price worked out at a mere ten pence a drum more than that charged by the Argentines. And the main selling point of the Fuel Agreement had been that the fuel prices in Stanley would be those in force on the Argentine mainland. Much had been made of the fact that the Argentines were transporting the fuel free of charge. Harold's figures were an eye-opener. We never got a satisfactory explanation. Our embassy in Buenos Aires suggested that YPF might be charging more for other fuels to compensate for their losses on diesel, which the Argentine Government pegged at an artificially low price for political reasons. If this were true, since YPF did not supply diesel to the Falklands, the Islanders were in effect subsidising the Argentine peasant by paying over the odds for petrol, kerosene and aviation fuel.

I could not refrain from pointing this out to Colonel Balcarce, of the Argentine Foreign Ministry, when he was lecturing me on all the good things that the Argentines were doing for the Falkland Islanders. I also mentioned the number of times that postbags had been taken off the aircraft at Comodoro Rivadavia because of weight restrictions, and yet sacks of fresh fruit for Argentine personnel stationed in Stanley still came through. Such things were unlikely to win over the hearts and minds of the Islanders. Balcarce had been for many years, if not the architect, then certainly the main proponent of this policy of wooing the Islanders. A great survivor, he had seen several regimes, and Foreign Ministers, come and go, but had stayed secure on his 'Islas Malvinas' desk. He visited the Falklands regularly, but this was the first time I had met him. I had been warned that he was fond of telling everyone that he had been educated at Downside and, sure enough, it came out in the first few minutes of our meeting. All I can say is that his English did not do credit to his old school. He was pleasant enough, but Mavis summed up my feelings after we had entertained him in Government House: 'I wouldn't trust him an inch.'

The main purpose of Balcarce's visit was to discuss the construction of a fuel jetty for the YPF. Under the Fuel Agreement, the Argentines had been permitted to build a tank farm on the eastern outskirts of Stanley for the bulk storage of fuel. It had been envisaged in the Agreement that the YPF tankers would be able to use the FIC jetty (without payment of fee or tariff) for the off-loading of fuel both in bulk and in drums; but a safety expert had subsequently decreed that the jetty was not safe for bulk off-loading, consequently most of the tanks in the tank farm were standing idle. Provision had been made in the Agreement for the Argentine Government to construct a jetty, 'should it deem it appropriate', but the Argentines had asked for a financial contribution from the British Government, and long delays had ensued. Agreement on this tricky issue seemed now to be within reach, and Balcarce wished to discuss the operating procedures. He had with him Captain Gaffoglio (no doubt taking more photographs of beaches) and Comodoros Gutierrez (recently Air Attaché in London), Remorino and Benvenutto. I could not understand what these gentlemen had to do with YPF or a fuel jetty, but there they were. We held a reception for them, at which they met a good cross-section of Falkland Islanders and, of course, behaved impeccably.

Two further irritating incidents occurred at this time which indicated that, beneath the smooth diplomatic talk, Argentine attitudes remained both arrogant and insensitive. Dick came into my office one day with the commander of the Polish fishing fleet, Captain Edmund Sieminski. He wished to make a formal complaint against the Argentines. Two of his trawlers had been stopped on the high seas, boarded by Argentine Navy personnel, accused of fishing in Argentine waters and ordered to haul in their nets and depart. They were about forty-five miles south east of the Falkland Islands at the time. His skippers had complied and reported the incident to him. He believed that they had been fishing in Falkland, not Argentine, waters and he had come to Stanley to request an official certificate from me to that effect. I said that I could certainly give him a certificate to state that they were not Argentine waters, but I could not state that they were Falkland waters because we had neither a fisheries nor an exclusive economic zone round the Islands; all we had was a 3-mile territorial limit. He was astonished at what he clearly regarded as a grave omission on our part and expressed his indignation at the 'cheek' of the Argentines in claiming that their 200-mile exclusive economic zone included the Falklands. He was grateful for my offer of a certificate, which I duly prepared on a piece of parchment, signed and sealed with the Governor's seal and ceremoniously handed over, though of course we both knew that it was utterly worthless. He nodded when I suggested that his best course of action would be to report the incident to his government with a demand for an official protest to the Argentines at the highest level. He said that he had already alerted his employers in Gdansk; but I got the impression that he did not expect them to push his government very hard.

We had an interesting conversation on fishing in the South Atlantic. His English was excellent and he spoke directly and honestly (in marked contrast to Colonel Balcarce). He had a crew of ninety-five on his fillet freezer trawler, they were paid on results and his normal production was 25 – 30 tons of fillets a day. At present he was catching mainly blue whiting, which (as Szostak had told me) were heavily infested with parasites. Normally they would be processed for fishmeal but, as he had an order for fillets to fulfil for West Germany, he was having to scrape off the parasites before filleting, and this reduced production to 9 tons a day. His crew were, he said, very unhappy. We arranged a football match between them and a Stanley XI and he left in great good humour with my certificate under his arm, like a telescope.

The other incident concerned the Transglobe Expedition's Twin Otter. Giles Kershaw and Jerry Nicholson had landed at Stanley to refuel before the long hop to Rothera on their way to the South Pole. In this case, there was no question of lack of fuel or contamination. The Twin Otter used the same fuel as the Fokker F27 and there was plenty of it at the airport; but Hector Gilobert had felt obliged to report to Buenos Aires before giving authority. His masters had replied, insisting that Giles must report for clearance on the mainland before heading for the Antarctic. To make sure that he followed this instruction, Hector was to give him only enough fuel to get to Rio Gallegos. We argued with Hector that this was illogical; if his masters wanted to make the point that Argentina was the gateway to the Antarctic, since they claimed that the Falklands were Argentine, Giles would be leaving from Argentine soil anyway. Eventually, Hector helpfully turned a blind eye when the fuel went into the extra tanks (which took up the whole of the fuselage), Giles filed a flight plan to the mainland (which he had no intention of following), and we waved him off early one Sunday morning, clutching his cricket bat and determined, as the mad Englishman he was, to use it at the South Pole. He and Jerry landed at Rothera eight hours later.

We were into November, spring was coming along apace and shearing had begun. Our weekend walks along Yorke Bay produced new surprises: one Sunday we spotted a King penguin, standing in solitary splendour on a sand-dune. Perhaps it had wandered from Osmund's colony at Volunteer Point. We saw it the following weekend and, by the next, it had gone. I was giving Tony's motor cycle a run along the beach one Saturday afternoon and came across a leopard seal. He was hauled up at high-water mark, exhausted and suffering from a gaping wound on the back of his neck. A great chunk had been taken out of him, the result perhaps of a fight with another leopard or, more probably, an attack by a killer whale. I was able to walk up very close and admire his beautiful spotted skin in detail. He eyed me suspiciously and showed his serrated teeth, but was too weak to move more than his head. I went back the next day. He was still there, but closer to the sea. The following weekend, he was nowhere to be found. He must have recovered and gone back to sea, otherwise some evidence of his body would surely have remained. On a gentler note, Karen, Helen and I spent another Saturday morning watching jackass penguins cavorting in Gypsy Cove. The water was so clear that we could see them from our vantage point on the top of the ridge, darting about playfully beneath the surface. On our way back, we picked Pale Maidens from the old naval gun-site.

As spring blossomed, the FCO gave me somewhat short notice of a forthcoming visit by Mr Nicholas Ridley. For reasons unknown, news of the visit was not to be announced until further notice. I was naturally pleased that a minister of the Crown was taking the trouble to come so far to see us; but I was also apprehensive about the purpose of the visit.Although it meant preparing programmes, briefs and personality notes, I was determined to get out to camp to see some shearing before he arrived, also to sound out more Islanders on their political views. In my visits to date, I had canvassed their thoughts on the future and one clear message had emerged: they wanted to stay British. Argentine performance since the 1971 Communications Agreement had been such a combination of arrogance and incompetence that, if anything, it had strengthened their resolve to stay British. Any talk of handing over sovereignty to the Argentines, or sharing it with them in any way, was anathema to the kelper.

Before Mr Ridley arrived, I also wanted to see for myself the difficulties that lay ahead of the PWD in constructing the road to Darwin. If we were to improve the rate of progress, we should need support from the FCO to argue the case for more resources from the ODA. We therefore decided to drive to Darwin, calling at Bluff

Cove and Fitzroy on the way. Since our last visit to Bluff Cove, it had changed hands. The old owners, George and Rose Stewart, had retired to Stanley and the farm had been bought by an unlikely partnership of barrister, bosun and baker. Kevin Kilmartin, the barrister, had opted out of the rat-race in England and emigrated to the Falklands in 1975. A bachelor, he had worked on several farms as a farmhand, learning to shear and handle sheep the hard way before taking the plunge and going into partnership with Mike Bleaney and Tim Dobbyns. Mike was a sleeping partner and continued to live in Stanley and work for the FIC (he had previously been a bosun in the Royal Navy). Tim was a big, bluff Irishman who had been running the Stanley bakery for ten years but had always hankered after a farm of his own. With only 5,000 sheep (albeit 40,000 acres), Bluff Cove was barely enough to support three owners; but it had been the only farm available at the price that they could afford. Tim and his wife, Jean, were an enterprising pair but were as independent as Kevin and it came as no surprise when their partnership split up and Tim went off on his own to negotiate for a piece of adjoining land from the FIC (later to be called Riverside Farm). The partnership of barrister and bosun lasted a while longer but that, too, eventually broke up, leaving Kevin in sole charge.

With Mickey Clarke as our camp driver, we reached Bluff Cove without mishap in 2½ hours, had lunch with Kevin and Tim and Jean, and took a further hour to reach Fitzroy, where we spent the night with the manager, Ron Binnie, and his wife Linda, whom we had last met at the Darwin sports. We had time to walk round the settlement before dark and found it as neat and well laid out as it appeared from the air. The credit for that, said Ron, went to Jim Clement, who had managed the farm for twenty-four years. An early night suited us all – with over 25,000 sheep to shear, Ron had to be up before dawn. The shearing shed was already bustling with activity when we got there after breakfast. The first formality was to have my shoes chalked as I crossed the threshold. Ron explained that this was the custom when visitors entered a shearing shed for the first time. He went on to say that, in return, visitors were expected to donate a bottle of rum to the thirsty shearers. It was the first of many bottles that this quaint, but expensive, custom was to cost me. I never discovered whether it had a genuine origin or was specially devised for greenhorns like myself. We watched in admiration as the shearers turned the compliant sheep this way and that between their legs, removing the complete fleece in under two minutes. Ron, himself a champion shearer, said that the sheep was compliant only if you held it in the right way. We saw what he meant a few moments later when an obvious beginner had trouble holding what appeared to be a hyperactive sheep. Ron took over and within seconds the animal was as docile as a lap-dog. The wrestling match resumed as soon as the novice took over again. Unfortunately, he snipped a piece off the sheep's ear. The blood made the wound seem a lot worse than it was; but it put Mavis off watching shearing for the rest of our time in the Falklands.

We had to be on our way because John Brodrick, the DPW, who had also spent the night at Fitzroy, wanted to show me the line of the new road and the difficulties to be encountered in crossing the various rivers and creeks. The first obstacle was the Frying Pan, an awkward crossing at the confluence of two streams, then the going was relatively easy alongside Long Pond and up onto March Ridge, the firmest stretch of camp between Fitzroy and Darwin. From here we had a magnificent view across the plain to the north, with Mount Pleasant an unmistakable landmark, sticking up like a pimple at the end of the Wickham Heights, and Mount Usborne towering menacingly behind. Little did we realise that less than five years later we would be looking down from this same spot on an international airport. From March Ridge we had a tricky crossing of the valley to L'Antioja Ridge, leaving Mount Pleasant shanty to our right, along the ridge and down into L'Antioja Stream – a difficult crossing this, as we were to find to our cost later – and a wet slither and slide to Swan Inlet. Here we had a puncture, and the spanner with which we had been supplied refused to budge the wheel nuts. Thanks to the diddle-dee radio, we were able to contact John and Basil Morrison, the PWD roads supervisor, whom we had left at L'Antioja Stream, and they had a man-size spanner that did the trick. Meanwhile, however, we could not have been marooned in a more delightful spot. We were looking down on Swan Inlet and there we counted seventeen handsome black-necked swans. There were also countless upland geese and loggers taking their goslings and ducklings for an outing on the water. Yet again, we were privileged spectators in a world of unspoilt nature, with no sign or sight of man.

We should have been in Darwin for lunch, but the puncture delayed us and we met Brook Hardcastle on the track, coming out to look for us. As he escorted us in, we met a huge flock of sheep being driven back to Swan Inlet and Laguna Isla paddocks, having been shorn at Goose Green. There must have been a few thousand, moving at a steady but unhurried pace, dogs darting here and there to check the strayers and the stragglers, responding to the calls and whistles emanating from somewhere behind in the dust-clouds kicked up by thousands of hooves. Horses and riders materialised one by one out of the dust, spread in a line until we could make out five altogether. They had kerchiefs over their faces to protect themselves from the dust, but the effect was of a rustling scene from some Wild West film. The nearest rider had a sheep straddled over the saddle in front of him – Brook said that there were usually one or two weaker ones who failed to keep up with the main flock and had to be carried in this fashion. They normally recovered after a rest.

At Darwin, Brook took us to see how the school was progressing and then proudly showed us his latest experiment. We walked along the jetty to the wreck of the *Vicar of Bray*,[5] which formed the jetty-head, and there he pulled up two pots absolutely teeming with small red crabs. He said that, when they were originally hauled out of the water, not only were the pots full but there were dozens of crabs crawling round the outside, trying to get in. They had been caught in Choiseul Sound in 17 fathoms in 2½ hours. There must have been over fifty crabs altogether, of the *Centolla* (spider) variety. The *Centolla* was a profitable export from Chile and he saw no reason why a similar industry could not be built up in the Falklands.[6]

At the jetty was the small FIC coaster, the *Ilen*, loading up with men and supplies to shear the sheep on the smaller islands belonging to the FIC. We could not see how fourteen men were going to spend three weeks on that small vessel; but they appeared cheerful enough. The skipper of the *Ilen* was a highland Scot, Jim Burgess, whom Brook had recruited from the Isle of Mull. After seeing them off, we went to the shearing shed to observe the largest shearing operation in the Falklands. Brook said that they had sheared 22,000 sheep in the last ten days. He had a mixture of contract shearers and FIC employees, seven of the former and nine of his own experienced men from Goose Green and Walker Creek. The shed had enough bays to accommodate twenty-four shearers in all, but sixteen were enough to cope with the number of sheep at present.[7] The peak of the season would come later. We watched the busy scene, with women and children scurrying with the fleeces from the floor to the table, where Eric Goss was classing them into different bins, and the poor sheep were bundled unceremoniously between the shearer's legs through a trapdoor to the counting-out pens. Brook said that they would survive the cold, but were at risk if unlucky enough to have a heavy rainstorm immediately after being shorn.

As usual, Eileen looked after us extremely well. John Brodrick and Basil Morrison were also house guests, and we had useful discussions with Brook on the best route for the Stanley-Darwin road. Before leaving the next morning we visited the school again, this time with John Fowler, and agreed further work to be done by PWD. As this was the weekend before Mr Ridley's visit, I wanted to have a chat with Adrian Monk. The FCO had not briefed me about the visit, but it did not require prior knowledge to guess that leaseback would feature in any discussion on sovereignty, and Adrian would be an implacable opponent. Ian White picked us up in the Beaver from Goose Green jetty and in fifteen minutes we were alighting on the placid waters of San Carlos. Adrian had just got in from gathering. We fed the dogs and dined ourselves on delicious, freshly caught smelt. Adrian said that the mullet were running and suggested an early fishing expedition the next morning to Head of the Bay.

Despite the occasional snow squall, it was a glorious morning and Head of the Bay was teeming with mullet. To my surprise, Adrian said that he did not like fishing and stretched out in the sun while I landed some satisfying 2½ pounders. After lunch, Adrian's foreman, Pat Short, invited us to his house to see the first videotape that he had received. Pat was one of the pioneers of video in the Falklands. His namesake Peter in Stanley was an enthusiast and was thinking of setting up a video library. He had asked my advice on the best system. Two or three people in Stanley had already bought the Betamax but, after consulting my expert in this field (Mike Peake, who had made his own television and video), I had recommended VHS. This was what Pat had bought and we were delighted to see the excellent quality of the picture. The power from the ordinary farm generator was adequate and Pat's demonstration convinced me that this was the next great innovation in the Falkland Islands, following the 2-metre radio.[8] It was uncanny to sit in Pat's house in San Carlos watching Alan and Joan Roote's magnificent 'Survival' film *Two In The Bush*, depicting scenes of Africa all too familiar to Mavis and me about twenty years before. Impressed though Pat and Isabel and their daughter, Michelle, were with the cheetah, hornbill, spitting cobra, wildebeeste and hippo in their sitting room, they were nothing compared with the horse-racing and show-jumping that featured in the next tape.

That evening, Adrian and I tossed the sovereignty issue back and forth until the lights went off at 11pm. Adrian's attitude was simple: we had a good freehold title to the Islands, why give that up for a leasehold? He did not accept my argument that there was no harm in talking about a possible leaseback solution with the Argentines and that, as long as we kept on talking, the Argentines were unlikely to take any other form of action. I suggested that we could go on discussing the terms of a leaseback for ever; we could argue for years, for example, over the length of the lease. Adrian maintained that, if we once allowed the Argentines to think that we were prepared to give up sovereignty under certain conditions and guarantees, then whatever conditions and guarantees we might negotiate would not be worth the paper they were written on. He accepted that, if the talks broke down, the outlook would be bleak. The Argentines could make life very difficult for the Islanders; but Islanders would put up with hardship rather than make any concession on sovereignty. One thing on which we were agreed: the Argentines would not be so stupid as to attempt to take the Islands by force – not, at least, until they had tried all the other options. Having failed to win the 'hearts-and-minds' campaign, we thought that they might try Islanders' pockets. They could wave the big stick and dangle the carrot at the same time. It would not be difficult to offer more generous aid than Britain had given, though Adrian doubted whether this would have the slightest effect on any but a very few of the younger generation. I turned in that night convinced that Adrian was right, and that Mr Ridley was in for a difficult time.

The next day being Sunday and a day of rest, even during the shearing season, Adrian and Pat drove us round the head of the creek to the old freezer plant at Ajax Bay. It was a beautiful, sunny day and, as we wandered through the derelict buildings, we lamented the waste of British taxpayers' money and considered how some of it might yet be salvaged. We thought of many possible uses, but certainly not a military field hospital. Entering the old skin-drying shed, we startled a white owl, which flew to the far end and perched on one of the steel beams. Tiptoeing out, we beckoned to Mavis and Nora to come quietly; but we upset the owl again and it flew past us to the other end of the shed, disappearing with a sickening bang and a cloud of feathers through the ventilator fan, which looked far too small to accommodate an owl and in any event was spinning in the strong wind at a seemingly lethal rate. We dashed out and round the corner expecting to pick up the minced pieces, but there was no sign of the bird. Somehow it had squeezed through the fan-blades and carried on flying. I was excited at the thought that perhaps we had made the first sighting of a snowy owl in the Falklands; but the experts told me later that it was probably a barn owl.

While Mavis and Nora prepared the picnic, we walked across to the fuel dump to inspect the oil drums. There a tragic sight met our eyes. A thick tar-like substance had seeped out of many of the drums, leaving sticky black pools into which unsuspecting lambs had wandered, stuck and starved to death. We counted five in all, ranging from a day or two old to several weeks. Adrian was understandably angry and told us to grab armfuls of diddle-dee; he would set fire to the wretched oil. It was surprising – and a lesson – to me to see how quickly the diddle-dee caught fire. Without the help of paper, and using only one match, it smouldered, crackled and then burst into flames. We soon had several bonfires going on the pools of oil and round the drums. But it was the same heavy fuel oil that Peter Robertson had shown me at Port Albermarle and the flames appeared to be having no effect. Dishevelled and disconsolate, we rejoined the ladies and were finishing our picnic when there was a loud bang and a dense cloud of thick black smoke billowed into the sky. One of the drums had exploded. There followed a spontaneous firework display: drum after drum went up as we watched with the guilty pleasure of the arsonist.

That night, we joined the rest of the settlement in the community hall. They knew me well enough by then to subject me to an ear-bashing on everything from FIGAS to the Argentines. We were due to fly back to Stanley the next morning, but it was too windy for the Beaver and the San Carlos airstrip was not yet ready for the Islander (which at long last had resumed flying). We therefore arranged over the radio that Brook would drive out from Darwin to meet us at the boundary and take us to Goose Green, where the Islander should be able to land. We thus travelled the route that Colonel 'H' and his 2 Paras, guided by our future son-in-law, were to make famous in 1982; but we did not 'tab' for two days, we went by Land Rover, in 2½ hours. Adrian had trouble getting up Sussex Mountain, but it was plain sailing after that as far as the boundary, where Brook was waiting.

On the way to Camilla Creek, Brook pointed out a night heron sitting on her nest on a little island. He said that the same pair was there every year. We stopped for coffee at Camilla Creek House, where Mrs Christel Mercer, from Grangemouth, Scotland, was living with her American husband, Giles, and young baby. Christel said that she loved the Falklands and wished to stay. So did her husband, who was away lamb-marking at the time of our visit.[9] We did not stop at Burntside House but carried on to Darwin, where Eileen kindly gave us lunch, and then to Goose Green airfield to await the Islander. Ian White and a new pilot, Mike Selwood, landed with one of the teachers from the Stanley senior school, Richard Cain, who had brought with him a party of schoolchildren to climb Mount Usborne. We wished them well and climbed aboard for our first flight in the FIGAS Islander. Ian was enthusiastic but surprised that Britten-Norman, the designers, had given the aircraft such tiny wheels. 'For operating in rough, wet conditions, like the Falklands', said Ian, 'it should have big wheels, with low-pressure tyres.' He was to be proven right time and time again. Apart from this, the aircraft was ideal for the job.[10]

Notes

1. *Falkland Islands Review:* Report of a Committee of Privy Counsellors, January, 1983 (Cmnd 8787, page 6).

2. From a letter from Commodore Byron to the Earl of Egmont, 24 February 1765.

3. From a letter from Mr Secretary Conway to the Lords of the Admiralty, 20 July 1765.

4. On our last visit to Saunders, in 1985, Tony Pole-Evans kindly presented us with one of two cannon-balls that he had found lying at Port Egmont. It is now a doorstep in our home: but we do not know whether it is English or Spanish.

5. The *Vicar of Bray* was built in 1841 by Robert Hardy of Whitehaven, England. Of wooden construction, she was rigged first as a brig, later a barque. She is the only surviving vessel to have participated in the California gold rush of 1849. Thanks to an intuitive captain, she was made ready for sea and was thus able to escape from San Francisco as the earthquake struck – the last ship to get out of the harbour.

6. After two years of trials, the Falkland Seafood Company was established in 1987 in Stanley to harvest and process these crabs.

7. After the capture of Goose Green by 2 Para in 1982, over 3,000 Argentines were held in this shed.

8. By 1985, almost every house in camp had a VHS video cassette player.

9. The Mercers moved into Stanley before the war and no one was occupying Camilla Creek House when Colonel 'H' set up his headquarters there in May, 1982.

10. We took up the question of improving the undercarriage with the manufacturers, but were given technical reasons why it could not be done.

7

Mr Ridley's Visit: No to Leaseback

Back in Stanley, anxiety was mounting over Mr Ridley's visit. A stream of Islanders came to my office to express their concern, with the result that briefs were completed just hours before his aircraft landed. As he arrived on a Saturday, Mr Ridley was able to enjoy the weekend fishing and sketching. We were unlucky with sea trout, but caught a few mullet. Sunday happened to be the ninetieth birthday of Mrs Liz Perry, the Islands' oldest female resident, and she was delighted to receive congratulations and birthday greetings in person from a Minister of State.

During the ensuing week, Mr Ridley was exposed to as wide a cross-section of Islanders as possible, starting and finishing with Joint Councils and including the Sheep Owners Association, the General Employees Union, the Falkland Islands Committee, the Social Club, the business community, individuals who had asked to see him, a public meeting and interviews on the radio and with the local press. In camp, he visited Goose Green, Fox Bay East and West, Chartres, Hill Cove, Roy Cove, Carcass and Green Patch, and at these settlements he met also representatives from North Arm, Port Howard, Port Stephens, Port Louis and Johnson's Harbour. He was treated courteously and listened to intently wherever he went. The only disagreeable note was struck by a demonstration at the airport upon his departure, which was out of character with the good manners normally shown by Islanders. Indeed, their natural reluctance to express disagreement with distinguished guests probably caused Mr Ridley and his officials to leave with an over-optimistic impression of Islander reaction to their leaseback proposal. This could be the only explanation of the Franks Committee's summing-up of the visit: 'On leaseback, Islander opinion appeared to be divided, with a substantial minority opposed to it and the majority undecided.'[1] By my reckoning, the vast majority were opposed to it, with a minority prepared to talk about it with the Argentines, not with any real intention of reaching a leaseback agreement but simply as a means of keeping talks going. No Islander seriously believed, for example, that the Argentines would agree to a leaseback spanning 'two or three or more generations', which was what Mr Ridley was suggesting. Other conditions that Islanders considered crucial to a leaseback agreement but impossible to achieve were the right of self-determination at the end of any lease and a reversion to the *status quo ante* if the Argentines broke the agreement.

Mr Ridley's message to the Islanders was simple: the 'dead hand' of the sovereignty dispute was stagnating the Islands' economy. It was therefore in the Islanders' interest to resolve the dispute; his advisers had suggested three possible solutions: condominium, sovereignty freeze or leaseback. He would welcome further suggestions from Islanders, but he favoured leaseback and wanted to know what Islanders thought before he put such a proposal to the Argentines. Her Majesty's Government would, as always, be guided by Islanders' wishes.

In Joint Councils, some councillors wanted no negotiations with the Argentines whatsoever, but the majority favoured talks and wanted to be represented at such talks. They took Mr Ridley's point that, if there were to be talks, he must have something to talk about; but they were not happy with any of his suggestions and, as they had received no prior notice, they asked for more time to consider them and to consult their constituencies. Mr Ridley readily agreed and asked for their considered views early in the new year.

The two main dates in the Falkland Islands' calendar were the Queen's birthday, 21 April, and Battle Day, 8 December.[2] The battle commemorated was the Battle of the Falklands, 1914, when, thanks to the perspicacity of Winston Churchill, two of the Royal Navy's latest battle cruisers, HMS *Invincible* and HMS *Inflexible*, had arrived in the nick of time to save the Falklands from a raid and possible occupation by the German navy. The day was a public holiday, with a service in Christ Church Cathedral and laying of wreaths at the Battle Monument. Coming shortly after Mr Ridley's visit, and in the middle of the public debate on sovereignty, Islanders took the opportunity to demonstrate their Britishness and loyalty to the Crown. They sang the National Anthem lustily and shamed me by knowing the second verse off by heart (I had forgotten it since leaving the Boy Scouts). After the parade, one of the younger councillors, born after the Second World War, told me that he had been deeply moved by the ceremony and that he had changed his mind about leaseback 'for the umpteenth time' since Mr Ridley's visit.

The public debate continued throughout December, over FIBS

and the diddle-dee radio, in the local press, during the Stanley races (held between Christmas and New Year), in the pubs and on the farms. A rousing, Churchillian address by Adrian Monk over FIBS on 2 January made a big impact. Four days later, Joint Councils met and, after a last-ditch stand by the 'no-talks-at-all' lobby, agreed to talks on the basis of a sovereignty freeze. The next day, Legislative Council passed the following resolution (except for Adrian, who voted against) and asked me to forward it to the FCO:

> While this House does not like any of the ideas put forward by Mr Ridley for a possible settlement of the sovereignty dispute with Argentina, it agrees that Her Majesty's Government should hold further talks with the Argentines at which this House should be represented and at which the British delegation should seek an agreement to freeze the dispute over sovereignty for a specified period of time.

In other words, the elected representatives of the Islanders rejected the leaseback proposal.

Meanwhile, the busy season was upon us again. The first of the tourist ships to arrive was the *World Discoverer*, with our old friend, Captain Aye. He gave another sumptuous party on board, and again asked me to speak (I was better prepared this time). We had our first visit from the *Lindblad Explorer* and were delighted to meet again Sonja Lindblad, whom we had last met in the Seychelles. HMS *Endurance* came into the harbour in the traditional way with her new commander, Captain Nick Barker, firing a 17-gun salute and the FIDF returning the compliment.

The RRS *Bransfield* and RRS *John Biscoe* arrived with the summer migration of scientists from BAS headquarters in Cambridge. *John Biscoe* limped in with a faulty propeller and had to be towed to Montevideo by HMS *Endurance* before she could resume her Antarctic programme. Their misfortune was our gain, because it meant that David Attenborough and his film crew had to spend Christmas in Stanley. They were filming for the TV series *The Living Planet* and David's team consisted of Ned Kelly, the producer, Hugh Maynard, the cameraman and Dicky Bird, the sound recordist. We enjoyed having them in Stanley over the festivities. They came to our Christmas night party at Government House, during the course of which I introduced them to billiard-table hockey, a vicious game that the Tochi Scouts had taught me on the North-West Frontier. David reckoned that it was the most dangerous thing he had ever done. Ned was a keen and knowledgeable jazz enthusiast and listened to my collection of old seventy-eights, played on an even older wind-up grafanola, until the sun came up.[3]

Other visitors during this period were Ted Needham, the head of Coalite, who was as formidable an opponent at golf and snooker as he was at the negotiating table; Harry Camm, who was proceeding with the purchase of Douglas Station; Len Hill, who had bought Grand Jason and Steeple Jason in 1970 for £5,500; Cindy and Annie, who were in town for more film, which was overdue and lost somewhere in Argentina; and a number of colleagues from our Embassy in Buenos Aires, including the Ambassador, Anthony Williams. The weather was so good during Anthony's visit that we were able to play croquet on Government House lawn (albeit in anoraks!). He spent one night in camp, at North Arm, and in Stanley met a fair cross-section of kelpers from camp who were in for the annual sports. These were traditionally held on Boxing Day and the two following days. The main events were horse racing, but there was also a gymkhana, steer-riding, running, potato and sack racing and tug of war. Tony and Diana had joined us again for the Christmas holidays and, despite his mother's strong opposition, Tony tried his hand at steer-riding. He was dismounted after a few seconds but did not come to any harm. One of the Royal Marines finished up in hospital, again with a broken wrist. He joined his Commanding Officer, Robin Gilding, who had earlier broken his collar bone in a rugby match between NP 8901 and *Endurance*.

We had another tragic death during this same period. A Scotsman, Len Minto, killed his Islander wife, Gladys. He had lived in the Falklands for many years and was known to be of a violent disposition, particularly after a few drinks. He had beaten his wife several times, she had finally left him and the magistrate had warned him not to attempt to molest her. For her own safety, we had allowed her to sleep in the hospital and, to give her some money of her own, we had engaged her as a maid at Government House. She was a good worker and it was encouraging to see how well she responded to kindness instead of cruelty. On the morning of the murder, Len Minto had been summoned to appear in the magistrate's court to be given formal notice that any further molestation of his wife would mean imprisonment. Unknown to us, and against advice from the hospital, Gladys had nipped home to press her husband's suit, so that he might appear respectably dressed before the magistrate. He had already gone off to his job at PWD, but returned earlier than she had expected in order to change for the court hearing. He had found her at the ironing table, picked up a kitchen knife and stabbed her to death.[4] Not a murder for fifty years, and now two in my first year.

The last event of note in 1980 was the census. Taken normally every ten years, the last census had been in 1972; but councillors desired up-to-date figures in view of fears expressed of an accelerating exodus. Making allowances for visitors and Royal Marines, the population over the eight years had dropped by 108. In the same period, births had exceeded deaths by 136, which indicted that 244 people had left the Islands over the past eight years – an average of a little over thirty a year. With a total population of only 1,813, this was a worrying figure. To add to the problem, the census showed a significant drift from camp to Stanley. Other interesting results of the census confirmed that the vast majority (1,723 or 95.04 per cent) were British,[5] with 30 Argentines (all except 2 of whom were members of the armed forces, YPF or Gas del Estado serving short tours of duty in the Islands); 27 Chileans (mainly farm and road workers) 24 Americans (mainly of the Bahai faith); 2 Uruguayans, 1 Colombian, 3 French, 1 German, 1 Yugoslav and 1 Dane. The census also provided information on the standard of living and the amenities enjoyed. Of the 589 residential buildings occupied in the Islands (363 of them in Stanley), 582 had piped water, 580 had baths, 513 had water closets and 418 had freezers. All had electricity (mains in Stanley, private generators elsewhere) and peat was used for cooking in 447 households. There were 371 Land Rovers or other four-wheel drive vehicles and 78 tractors.

Early in the new year, the FCO asked for the names of two councillors to represent the Islanders in the next round of talks with the Argentines. Councillors chose their senior elected representative, Adrian Monk, and their youngest, Stuart Wallace. They went to New York in February with Mr Ridley and his team of officials from the FCO. Mr Ridley proposed a sovereignty freeze which, as expected, the Argentines rejected, asserting that a freeze was in effect what they had endured since 1971. The two councillors arrived back in Stanley on 28 February in sombre mood. The options had narrowed down to leaseback or deadlock. The Argentines were pressing for 'substantive' talks and Anthony Williams in Buenos Aires urged the FCO to have at least one further round of talks during the year. Councillors were loath to commit themselves before the Legislative Council elections, which were due to be held in October. Mr Ridley's visit had focussed people's minds on the sovereignty issue and had aroused all the old doubts and suspicions that the FCO was trying to get rid of them. Even being present at the talks was enough to damn councillors in some kelpers' eyes (as we shall see, it cost Stuart Wallace his seat). As the months went by, attitudes crystallised until the winning slogan for the October elections became 'Sovereignty is not for sale at any price'; but I am anticipating events.

1981 started on a gloomy note with a down-turn in wool prices, warnings of redundancies on some settlements and the FIC talking of 'severe cuts and money-saving measures'. We continued our round of settlements as opportunity offered, starting with two of the finest islands for wildlife: Westpoint and Carcass. Roddy and Lily Napier, the owners of Westpoint, successfully combined sheep-farming with wildlife conservation. Their beautiful island was the most mountainous we had visited, with Cliff Mountain, 1,211ft, and Mount Ararat 794ft. In between was the largest mixed colony of black-browed albatross and rockhopper penguins that we had seen to date. The rockhopper chicks were almost the size of their parents and looked ridiculous trying to hide under them. The albatross chicks were like soft cuddly toys, balls of whitish-grey cotton wool with shiny black buttons for eyes. But Roddy advised against trying to cuddle one. Like the stinker, he said, they could emit a foul-smelling liquid from that lovely beak of theirs. We noticed a mature bird that had caught its wing in one of Roddy's fences (erected, incidentally, to keep the sheep away from the breeding birds). Roddy laboriously climbed down to it and, with the utmost patience, gently disentangled the wing from the wire. The huge bird flapped it a few times, clucked its beak as if to say thank you and took off into the gale.

Roddy was a true kelper, a cousin of Adrian Monk and with interests in various parts of the Falklands, including at that time half of New Island; but he preferred to live on Westpoint. The Napier family had been improving the pasture there over a period of thirty-five years by replanting tussock-grass (30,000 plants) and limiting the number of sheep to around 2,000. Roddy had shown that, with proper management, sheep and wildlife could live happily side-by-side. As we took off from Westpoint, we sighted the impressive Jason Islands in the distance. Len Hill had bought them from Dean Brothers without sheep and had been criticised in the

Falklands for his stated policy of keeping sheep off the Islands in order to preserve the wildlife.

Our next stop, Carcass, provided another example of how the two could be compatible. Here the owners were Rob and Lorraine McGill, the most recent of a line of enlightened conservationists who had endeavoured to keep Carcass Island as nature intended it to be. Named after HMS *Carcass*, which surveyed the island in 1766, it was bought by Charles Hansen in 1870 and remained in the Hansen family until 1952. After a short spell under Bertrand and Monk, Cecil and Kitty Bertrand became the owners and lived there for twenty years, until 1974, when Rob and Lorraine took over. Jason Hansen (Charles's son) had early realised the importance of tussock-grass as a winter feed and had fenced and planted extensively, using pack-horse or horse and cart to transport the tussock roots from one part of the island to another and dibbing them in by hand. He and two assistants had planted many thousands over the years. As a result, by the late 1940s, all sheep except the old wethers were wintered in tussock paddocks and the island, with only 4,200 acres, carried over 2,000 sheep. But Hansen did more than improve the land; he was also a keen conservationist and interested in growing trees. He made the island a virtual wildlife sanctuary by forbidding the import of cats and ensuring that no rats or mice came ashore. The Bertrands and the McGills continued this policy and, as a result, the island now teemed with birds of many species, all incredibly tame.

As Rob led us towards the compound, our first surprise was a thick copse of fir trees (macrocarpa) groaning under the weight of scores of night herons and their nests. We stopped and stared as a cheeky tussock bird alighted on the toe of my wellington. Rob warned us not to stand under the trees, unless we wanted to be covered in night heron droppings. It must have been strong stuff, because the foliage had died off in places. Almost all the trunks and main branches were splattered in white. To our astonishment, as we entered the sheltered garden there, in front of us, was a palm tree. A palm tree, in the Falkland Islands? We thought we must be seeing things; but no, there were several more around the house. Rob said that, as long as they were facing north and sheltered from the wind, they thrived. He took us into the kitchen, which was large even by Falkland standards. It needed to be, for every available surface was loaded with food. Lorraine had been baking for days in preparation for an impending invasion by over a hundred tourists from the *World Discoverer*. She explained that she had an arrangement with the tour operators of both the *World Discoverer* and the *Lindblad Explorer* to provide a traditional smoko or afternoon tea for all who ventured ashore. There were buns, scones and cakes of every description, giving off a most appetising aroma and all baked by Lorraine in one peat oven.

The McGills' delightful seven-year-old daughter, Janie, took us up the slope behind their house to the first of two cottages, which Rob had loaned to Cindy and Annie for the season and which they had kindly invited us to share for the next two nights. John Cheek was staying in the other cottage with his family. He was the brother of Gerald, the Director of Civil Aviation and a senior member of Cable and Wireless in Stanley. His wife Jan was a daughter of Basil Biggs, now the senior lighthouse keeper at Cape Pembroke but for many years the police officer in South Georgia, where Jan was born.

Cindy and Annie took us in the 'Blue lady', a 1954 Land Rover which Rob had loaned them, to see the ingenious hide that they had constructed to film the inside of a jackass burrow. Barely enough room to take Cindy and her equipment, it was cold and cramped and smelly and we wondered how she could sit there for hour after hour, waiting for the two chicks and their minder to do something of interest. Stamina and patience were clearly essential requirements for a professional wildlife photographer.

Satisfied that her jackass film stars were in good shape, Cindy drove us to a tern colony, where we were overwhelmed by sheer numbers. On our arrival, thousands of terns suddenly took to the air screaming harshly and filling the sky with their white wings. Then, panic over, they settled down as quickly as they had scrambled. On the way back, we stopped at the copse that Jason Hansen had planted and, crawling on our hands and knees, followed Cindy in to a turkey vulture's nest – if a scrape in the ground could be so grandly described. There was one solitary chick, looking much more attractive than the full-grown bird. It made a strange hissing noise as we approached. Not wishing to frighten it or invite attack from a mother with sharp talons and a 5ft wingspan, we quietly withdrew. Back in the cottage, we were warming ourselves in front of the Aga cooker when we heard a scampering on the tin roof. It sounded like an outsize rat, but we knew that there were no rats on Carcass. 'Ah', said Annie, 'That's Senior, come for his supper.' Senior turned out to be a night heron, so tame that he would perch over the front door and take titbits from the hand.

Next day, Cindy and Annie took us to the crowded gull colonies on the north-west point. There were thousands of kelp gulls and the smaller but prettier dolphin gulls resplendent in dove grey, with deep red bills and legs. We were dive-bombed by angry skuas, known locally as sea-hens, as we walked over their breeding ground. We could now understand why Cindy and Annie carried sticks. It seemed that all the birds on the island were busily guarding or feeding their young: upland, kelp and ruddy-headed geese, Johnny Rooks, Caranchos, black and Magellanic oyster-catchers, logger and grey ducks, as well as the smaller dotterels and plovers – we even saw a little wren's nest – all combined to convey a remarkable variety and fecundity. A notable first for us was a pair of magnificent red-backed hawks and, for a change, the female was the larger and more beautiful. To add to the congestion along the shoreline, dozens of elephant seals were laid up, smelling foul and looking like down-and-out tramps as they shed their tatty skins. Watching some of them in a wallow, which looked and smelt like the hippo wallows in East Africa, we saw how cruel nature could be. A tussock bird hopped a little too close to a night heron and was immediately gobbled up. Had the four of us not witnessed it, we would not have believed that a night heron could take a whole tussock bird. At about 8in, it was the size of a thrush. To round off a perfect day, we went to the other side of the island to see a large king cormorant colony. The largest and most beautiful of the cormorant family, the king shag, to give it its local name, was black above with a metallic bluish green sheen and white underparts. The most striking features, however, were its intensely blue eyes and orange-yellow caruncle above the base of the bill. Neither as dignified as the albatross nor as belligerent as the rockhopper, they nested in similar cliff-top positions on columns of mud, tussock-grass and seaweed.

Back at the settlement, Cindy suggested a walk to the beach to see if any mullet had been trapped in the specially constructed rock-pools as the tide went out. To our delight, there were three four-pounders, more than enough for an excellent supper for us and for Senior. Cindy expertly broke their necks, but not expertly enough for Annie and Mavis, who screamed when they seemingly came to life again in the kitchen sink. We had drinks with the McGills that evening and were most impressed with young Roy who, though only eleven years old, talked and thought like someone twice his age. He was a fund of knowledge of the island's wildlife and its habits, with a natural scientist's powers of observation and analysis. After he and Janie had gone to bed, we discussed their future with Rob and Lorraine, who were naturally reluctant to send them off the island (which they clearly loved), but also wanted them to have a good education and meet other children of their age. It was the dilemma that most families in camp had to face at one time or another. Lorraine was resolved to go into Stanley with the children when Roy reached secondary school age, even though this would mean leaving Rob on his own on Carcass for long spells. They were more fortunate in this regard than most, as they had a house in Stanley and Rob was able to shut up shop on the island and join the family for the winter months.[6]

We were sad to leave Carcass and vowed to return as often as we could. We went back several times and were never disappointed. There was always something of interest to see. On one occasion, we watched in horror as a sea lion caught a penguin a few yards off the beach and tossed it around like a rag doll. Within seconds the stinkers had finished it off and all that was left was a lengthening oil slick and a piece of black skin washed ashore, over which two skuas were having a tug of war. On another, Rob took me to the very tip of North-West Point and there was the biggest and most handsome bull sea lion I had seen, keeping a watchful eye on a solitary female and preventing her from going into the sea. It was early days for breeding and she clearly did not relish being the first in his harem.

On our return to Stanley, life was even more hectic than usual because we were due to embark on our first major voyage on HMS Endurance in four days' time and I had an important Executive Council meeting, a visiting television team, an ODA visitor and the usual backlog of mail and local people wishing to see me. The main issue before Executive Council was the draft YPF Jetty Agreement, which caused me another crisis of conscience. I had to do my best to get it through but was uneasy about many of its provisions, which to my mind gave too much control to the Argentines. Councillors did not like it but accepted my arguments with good grace and decided not to oppose any of the draft provisions.[7] The television team came from BBC's Pebble Mill studios in Birmingham and was due to accompany us on HMS Endurance, making a series of films named after the presenter, Bob Langley. Neither he nor the producer, John Smith, was slow to pick up the loaded political atmosphere in the Islands following Mr Ridley's visit and they decided to devote one whole episode to the Falklands. The obvious settlement to visit was Pebble Island. Griff was co-operative and the necessary arrangements were quickly made.

As usual, I was working until the last minute in the office, left myself less than a quarter of an hour to pack and then we were ceremoniously piped aboard HMS *Endurance* to begin our great adventure – South. Mavis was fortunate in that, as the wife of the High Commissioner of the British Antarctic Territory, she was one of the few women entitled to travel on a Royal Navy ship. She was also fortunate in having a cast-iron stomach and never feeling sea-sick. We had a rough ride through Drake Passage, with green water over the bows on several occasions. The film in the wardroom that evening was 'Great Expectations', which summed up our hopes for the next two weeks. We were not disappointed.

We headed due south for the first two days, during which I read William Jameson's book *Wandering Albatross* and was able to confirm for myself the accuracy of his observations. We were rarely without at least one of these graceful birds, gliding and soaring in our wake. Late on the second day, we glimpsed our first iceberg, a slab-sided flat-top about the size of St James's Park. 'They come much bigger than that', said Bill Hurst, the navigation officer, who was spending his second summer in the Antarctic; 'The biggest ever reported was over 12,000 square miles – bigger than Belgium.' Known as tabular bergs, these huge chunks of ice break off the vast ice sheet that covers most of the Antarctic continent and float wherever the winds and currents take them. Some run aground on the Antarctic Peninsula or the islands of the Southern Ocean, others drift further north until melted by the warmer waters. Thanks to radar, they are no longer a serious hazard to shipping, but it is wise to give them a wide berth, as they are larger underwater than they appear above, and the older ones tend to be unstable and easily rolled over by the disturbance caused by a passing ship. More dangerous are the growlers, small bergs barely discernible above the water but big enough to damage a ship's hull.

We were now south of the 60th parallel and, to conform with the Antarctic Treaty, the *Endurance's* two 20mm cannon were put under wraps. This treaty, ratified by twelve nations[8] in 1961, put all territorial claims south of the 60th parallel 'on ice' for thirty years, during which Antarctica was to be used for peaceful purposes only. Military bases were prohibited, though the treaty did not prevent the use of military personnel or equipment for scientific research 'or any other peaceful purpose'. At the end of thirty years (1991), any member could request a conference of all contracting parties to review the operation of the treaty, and changes could be made on a majority vote. In other words, if no member requested a review, the treaty carried on beyond 1991 as before. Although it expressly stated that no act while the treaty was in force would create any right of sovereignty in Antarctica, the Argentines had invested a lot of money establishing 'scientific' bases in British Antarctic Territory (which the treaty allowed them to do – freedom of scientific investigation was guaranteed) and operating them as if they were exercising sovereignty over British territory. The scientific importance of these bases seemed to be considerably less significant for them than the long-term political and military aspects. The FCO had warned me not to visit any Argentine base, lest my official presence should imply recognition of Argentine sovereignty or be used at some future date to support their territorial claim. This was disappointing, but the prohibition did not extend to the bases of other nations, of which there were many on our route.

First, however, we were due to pay a nostalgic visit to unoccupied Elephant Island, the most northerly of the group called South Shetland Islands, which before the Antarctic Treaty had been part of the Falkland Islands Dependencies and was now British Antarctic Territory. It was to Elephant Island that Sir Ernest Shackleton had led his marooned band of men from the Weddell Sea after his ship, the *Endurance*, had broken up in the ice in 1915, and from Elephant Island that he had sailed on Easter Monday, 1916, in the *James Caird*, the largest of the three boats salvaged from the *Endurance*, on his epic voyage to South Georgia and eventual rescue. The BBC television team wished to re-enact Shackleton's arrival and the crew of the present-day *Endurance* entered into the make-believe world with gusto. Buffer donned a wig and old sailor's rig and drilled his oarsmen to simulate rowing in the smallest of the *Endurance*'s boats, the *Dudley Docker* (the three boats carried by the *Endurance* were named after Shackleton's famous three: *James Caird*, *Stancombe Wills* and *Dudley Docker*, which were themselves named by Shackleton after three generous benefactors to his expedition). Surveying the barren, inhospitable rocks of Elephant Island, we wondered how Frank Wild and his twenty-one stalwarts had managed to survive under two upturned boats for 105 days, and imagined the relief

138

and joy they must have felt when they saw Shackleton coming to rescue them.

Once the *Dudley Docker* had deposited the camera crew safely on the beach, we were able to look at the wildlife, which abounded on Elephant Island's steep slopes. There were thousands of the attractive chinstrap penguins, skuas, stinkers, terns, pintados and Wilson's petrels. They were not the only ones fishing in those rich waters: we counted eight Russian trawlers round Elephant and Clarence Islands. Judging from the smell and the hundreds of screaming seabirds, they had made a good catch.

That night, the camera crew safely back on board and the *Dudley Docker* once more restored to its 1981 role, we sailed cautiously down the east coast of the Antarctic Peninsula, past Vega Island to the northern tip of James Ross Island. As the rise-and-shine pipe was played over the ship's Tannoy, we hurried up onto the bridge and were thrilled to see that we were surrounded by pack ice. I climbed up into the crow's nest and had a magnificent view of the *Endurance*'s strengthened bows riding up on the ice and then crashing down, sending cracks running in all directions like a splintering windscreen. Occasionally the ice was too thick for this battering technique and Nick had to reverse and try again. It was a slow business but, by the judicious selection of likely leads, we managed to inch our way south. Nick wanted to see how far he could get between James Ross Island and the mainland. The scenery was breathtaking in its magnificence, with ice cliffs and awesome snow-capped peaks as far as the eye could see to our right and craggy, windswept rocks to our left. It was difficult to imagine that before us stretched an icy desert of some five and a quarter million square miles, about twice the size of Australia. It slowly became apparent that ahead lay a dead end, the accumulation of years of floes, brash and pack ice blown by the wind into an indescribable tangle on the edge of the fast ice, which we could now see joined James Ross Island to Graham Land. There was no way through here. It was Sunday and I had to tear myself away from this wondrous sight to attend the church service down below. The surroundings gave special meaning to our singing of the seamen's hymn 'For those in peril on the sea'. And, of course, above it, too. As soon as the service was over, the Wasps were airborne, landing supplies on James Ross Island for a BAS geological expedition due to camp there the following summer. The little helicopters looked so vulnerable against that gigantic backdrop. If their single engine decided to pack up, there was little chance of survival.

Having satisfied himself that there was no way through to the south, Nick determined to try skirting James Ross Island to the north and east. By late afternoon, we were beset. Stuck hard for the night, we had drinks with the television team, dinner with Nick and Bill Hurst and watched an American film about teenagers in the fifties. It was still light when we turned in fifteen minutes past midnight. Sleeping in a stationary bunk seemed strange after so many nights at sea.

Feeling some movement the next morning, we went on deck to find Nick was wiggling the stern. With the propeller driving forward, and turning the rudder from side to side, he was breaking up the ice behind us and slowly widening the gap. When he reversed the engine, we began to move backwards, imperceptibly at first until, after two hours, the bows were free. During the night a solitary penguin had waddled up to the ship to investigate. There were fresh footprints across the virgin snow to within two paces of the ship's side. Curiosity satisfied, he had obviously returned whence he had come, for there was a parallel set of prints receding as far as the eye could see.

North of Vega Island, Nick tried another lead to the east. We were more fortunate this time and, after crashing through some heavy pack in spectacular fashion (and leaving some of our red paint on the broken ice), we reached clear water north of James Ross Island. The excitement was not over, however, for we were in uncharted waters and suddenly, after cruising for some time at a consistent depth of forty metres, the seabed started to shoal at an alarming rate. The seaman calling out the depth remained impassive as the distance between us and the seabed lessened from thirty to twenty-five to twenty metres in as many seconds. Nick quietly rang the engine speed from a half to a quarter ahead (he had told me that, before going into reverse, he had to stop the engine, which did nothing to ease my mind) and the unemotional voice continued, 'Nineteen . . . eighteen . . . sixteen . . . fourteen . . . fourteen . . . fifteen . . . twenty . . .' The *Endurance*'s draught was five metres. We had passed over a submerged pinnacle with nine metres to spare – ample, as it turned out, but we had no idea when the shoaling would stop. I was expecting a sickening crunch at any moment, and the expressions on the faces of my fellow land-lubbers from Pebble Mill showed that they were thinking the same; but Nick and his men on the bridge remained as cool as the ice around us. There was no sign of panic, only the same good-humoured banter between them as there always was, as if shoaling in uncharted seas was an everyday occurrence.[9]

Here is as good a place as any to pay tribute to Nick Barker and his captaincy of HMS *Endurance*. She was obviously a happy ship, as one could sense as soon as one stepped aboard. Mavis and I visited all the other rates' messes, from the Chief Petty Officers to the Able Seamen, and got to know them well. We heard nothing but praise for 'the Boss'. ('The Boss' had been the name given to Shackleton by his men on the original *Endurance*.)

We negotiated our way through bergy bits and broken pack ice to the east of Seymour Island, where we parked for the night. This was a rocky windswept island, sheer-sided and flat-topped like a tabular iceberg, just to the north of Snow Hill Island. On its flat top, the Argentines had constructed their biggest air base in British Antarctic Territory, called Marambio. Nick contacted the base commander, who invited him to call the next day. I could not accompany him, but flew over the base in the other helicopter on the way to Cockburn Island, an extinct volcano sticking out of the sea to the west of Seymour Island. On the ground at Marambio were two Chinook helicopters and two Twin Otters. The strip looked rough and scarcely long enough for a Hercules, but Nick said on his return that one came in on average about once a week. The Argentine Air Force kept about fifty personnel on the base, relieved every two months. It looked a desolate place from the air but Nick said that the accommodation was extensive, warm and comfortable. It was Marambio into which Argentina had flown pregnant women to have their babies, with the notion that this would in some way strengthen their claim to sovereignty.

It was also Marambio from which other Argentine bases were supplied, including their illegal base at Southern Thule, in the South Sandwich Islands. All the islands in the South Sandwich group are north of the 60th parallel and therefore outside the Antarctic Treaty region. Nevertheless, in 1976 the Argentines established a base on the southernmost island of the group, without prior reference to the British authorities and in violation of British sovereignty. In December, 1976, a helicopter from HMS *Endurance* spotted the base and reported its presence to London. The British Government protested to the Argentine Government in 1977 but did not make the news public in the United Kingdom until May, 1978. By then it was clear to the Argentine Government that the British Government was not going to react strongly, and it proceeded to build up the base. Despite earlier assurances that the station would not be permanent and was purely for meteorological observation and research, the Argentines constructed accommodation for over a hundred men, fuel tanks, a large hangar and a heavy-lift helicopter pad. Apart from a formal complaint once a year, Britain did nothing. It is difficult to escape the conclusion that this was one of the factors that led Galtieri and his advisers to believe that, if they invaded the Falklands, Britain would not respond.

On Cockburn Island, I was left to wander on my own while Tony Ellerbeck, the flight commander, went off on another mission. The steep slopes were free from snow but were covered in grey, volcanic ash. Near the shoreline was a splash of green, which turned out to be moss fed by the droppings of countless Adelie penguins. Neither the Adelie nor the chinstrap penguin ventured as far north as the Falklands, but they were the main species in Antarctica, and we saw thousands of them on this trip. Unfortunately, we did not get far enough south to see the pride of Antarctica, the Emperor penguin, which was even larger than the King and confined to the coldest latitudes on earth.

I had a wonderful feeling, standing alone on Cockburn Island, with only the Adelies for company. It was a beautiful morning, sunny and cloudless and not a breath of wind. Once the noise of the Wasp had gone, a marvellous quiet descended, as if time itself had stopped. I was not only looking at a still-life picture, I was part of it. Here, in a hostile environment, miles from a fellow human being, was perfect peace, tranquillity and harmony. I savoured the moment. To add to my good fortune, this was the very island on which Sir James Clark Ross had first set foot to take formal possession of the region for Britain in 1843. All too soon, the angry drone of the Wasp assailed my ears and the moment had gone. Tony flew me back over the blown-out top of the volcano and we were irritated to see a hut there flying an Argentine flag with 'Air Force' painted boldly on the roof. There was no sign of life and we assumed that it was not permanently occupied.

That evening, we left James Ross Island and the Weddell Sea and during the night steamed through Hope Bay towards our next destination, Deception Island. We crossed Bransfield Strait and entered the narrow entrance, called Neptune's Bellows, into a fine natural harbour created by a sunken volcano. We anchored in Whaler's Bay, near a derelict whaling station, where we found the German research ship, the *Meteor*. It was flying the Argentine courtesy flag, which annoyed me as Deception was British territory and we had had a permanent presence there from 1944 until 1969. Britain's claim was based on early exploration – South Georgia, the South Sandwich, South Shetland and South Orkney Islands and Graham Land were all discovered by British expeditions. The formal acquisition of these lands was promulgated by Letters Patent published in 1908 (amended in 1917) declaring the Antarctic sector between longitudes 20′W and 80′W to be Dependencies of the Colony of the Falkland Islands. At that time, no other nation challenged our sovereignty. Argentina first claimed the South Orkney Islands in 1925, extended the claim to South Georgia in 1927 and by 1937 was claiming the right to all the Dependencies. During the Second World War, when things were going badly for Britain, Argentina, believing that the Axis powers would win, sent an expedition to Deception Island and purported to take possession of the whole Antarctic sector between longitudes 25′W and 68′ 34″W. When the British Government received formal notification of this, it despatched HMS *Carnarvon Castle* to Deception Island, where she anchored in January, 1943 and sent a party ashore to obliterate Argentine marks of sovereignty, hoist the Union Jack and record Britain's prior right to the island. It was galling for me, therefore, to go ashore and walk through the sad remains of the old BAS base, abandoned after volcanic eruptions in 1967 and 1969, and yet not be allowed to go across the harbour to the Argentine base. Nick paid a visit there but found only the cook present; the other five residents were being entertained by the Germans on board the *Meteor*.

The volcano was still active, as we discovered when we walked to a steaming pond and found the water piping hot. One or two seals were 'taking the waters', basking flat on their backs like Colonel Blimps in a Turkish bath. We did not recognise them at first because they were silvery white; but on closer examination they turned out to be the ordinary crabeater, the most common of Antarctic seals (incidentally, the name is misleading; they feed entirely on krill). The unusual colouring must have been caused by the sulphur or perhaps the hot water.

It was uncanny: steaming hot water on the shoreline and snow on the slopes behind. *Terra firma* felt anything but firm. Undeterred, the Royal Marines were eager to test their ski legs. Despite jagged rocks that awaited them below the snowline they hurtled down in gay abandon. I was persuaded against my better judgement to join in, but soon decided that snow conditions were too hazardous for me.

Back on board, Nick got in touch with the *Meteor* and invited the captain to drop in with his Argentine guests when returning them to their base. Two German scientists accompanied the Argentines, who appeared to be military men. They were affable and pleasant but did not appear to be very active in scientific research. Life was not easy for them on Deception, under the ever-present threat of another eruption, though they had the comforting thought of a Chinook on Marambio to lift them off at short notice should anything happen.

We left Deception the next morning, creeping through Neptune's Bellows in fog, and set course for the BAS base at Faraday. Britain has had a base there since 1947 and the hut used by the British Graham Land expedition, 1934–7, still stood. It took us a little over twenty-four hours to make the passage from Deception, keeping well clear of the coast and most of the ice until we had to head east to the base. There was a way through, but it was a slow business, so Nick and I went ahead by helicopter. The base commander, Chris Jeffes, met us and proudly took us round his excellent new building, the showpiece of which was a superbly crafted bar. There were twenty-five men on the base, reducing to fifteen for the winter. How young they all looked – including the base commander and the doctor – and yet many of them had spent years qualifying in their particular sciences and most were experienced Antarctic hands. The main work of the station was in the atmospheric sciences: meteorology, magnetism, ozone, radiation and ionospherics, with some seismological measurements. Chris's enthusiasm was infectious as he attempted to explain the complex instruments to an ignorant non-scientist like myself. My field was more in human relations and, talking to those who were to winter together (some for the second year running), I could understand why Dick Laws, the Director of BAS, set such store on selection. There was no room for a square peg here.

We were having a farewell drink at the bar when a commotion occurred outside and we dashed to the window to see a bedraggled sailor being fished out of the icy water. A few minutes later, huddled in blankets but still chattering with cold, he was escorted into the bar and given a stiff rum. It transpired that one of the BAS men had allowed him to try his hand with a skidoo – something like a motor tricycle on skis – and he had opened the throttle and roared straight into the 'oggin'. Nick groaned when he discovered that it was 'Scotty'. 'Every ship has one', he said, 'I wouldn't trust Scotty with a tin-opener.' Retrieving the skidoo was a major operation, requiring divers and lifting tackle, followed by stripping all the working parts to get rid of the salt water; but Chris was unperturbed. 'It will give us something to do over the winter', he said cheerfully, though he demurred when the television crew asked if Scotty could do it again for the cameras. After interviews with Bob Langley for his 'Langley South' series, we returned by boat to the *Endurance*, which had by then been able to anchor within half-a-mile of the base.

Next day was awaited with great anticipation by newcomers to the Antarctic; we were to sail up the spectacular Lemaire Channel, known by the old hands as Kodak Gap because it was so photogenic. The morning brought low cloud and snow, not ideal for photography; but no camera could catch the awesome beauty of the channel, no matter how good the conditions. We sailed between towering cliffs and rugged peaks, dodging icebergs in subtle shades of translucent blue. Suddenly a snowball came whistling up from the foredeck and cameras were forgotten as a furious snowball fight ensued. It was irreverent, like choirboys flicking pellets in church, but great fun.

Above the Lemaire Channel lay the American base, Palmer Station, on Anvers Island. FIDS (the Falkland Islands Dependencies Survey), which was the original name for BAS, had built a base there in 1955 to investigate the possibility of copper on the western side of the Lemaire Channel (one of the peaks was called Copper Peak because of its green-stained rocks) but no copper was found and the base was closed at the end of 1957. When later the Americans were looking for a site on Anvers Island, FIDS had loaned them their abandoned hut while they built a much more prepossessing base on the nearby Bonaparte Point. Now, as we approached it by boat, we were impressed by its size and aspect. Despite a continual stream of visitors during the austral summer – it was a popular stop for tour ships and yachtsmen – Don Wiggins, the base commander, greeted us warmly and showed us round. The senior scientist, Dr Dave Morrisa, a physiologist, also gave generously of his time and both spoke highly of the help and co-operation that they had received from BAS. We were surprised to meet two women in Dr Morrisa's scientific team, one of whom was intending to winter over. Dick Laws held strong views about women serving on Antarctic stations and would not allow them on BAS bases. Despite the size of Palmer Station, there were only twenty-five personnel – the same number as Faraday – and in winter they were due to reduce to seven or eight. Faraday's accommodation was basic compared with Palmer's, which also had a much greater choice of amenities and leisure facilities. The Americans were, however, more restricted in their movements off base. As their main scientific purpose was summer biological and glaciological work, in the interests of safety the winter maintenance staff were not equipped with skis or camping equipment and were thus unable to explore the rest of the island, whereas the men on Faraday could get out and, as the Penola Strait normally froze over during the winter months, they could reach and explore the mainland. Even within the confines of Palmer Station, danger lurked in the form of a leopard seal, which had twice attacked the rubber inflatables, fortunately without harm to the occupants.

We entertained our hospitable hosts on board HMS *Endurance* that evening, together with the French crew of a yacht which was sojourning at Palmer Station for the summer. They amazed me by declaring their intention of going *south* in a few days' time, to winter at Faraday. It is curious that the French have made yachting in the Southern Ocean their particular speciality; we were to see several yachts in subsequent seasons and almost all were French.

Next morning we continued to sail north, through the Neumayer Channel, which was almost as spectacular as Lemaire. It was a beautiful, sunny day, without a cloud in the sky, and the television crew took full advantage by going ahead of the *Endurance* in a Gemini and taking what they hoped would be striking shots of the 'Red Plum' bearing down upon them. At times we appeared to be about to cleave the Gemini in two, but the cameraman stuck to his task as the Royal Marine at the helm swerved out of the way at the last moment. Between going up on deck to photograph the best selection of icebergs that we had seen to date, we carried on with our round of the ship's messes and finished a most interesting and enjoyable day with a few rubbers of bridge in our cabin. My lasting impression of the day was of lazy seals on icebergs and, in particular, one small floe on which at one end lay a leopard seal, snake-like and sinister, and at the other a lonely chinstrap, standing nervously on the edge, looking over his shoulder and wondering, 'To jump, or not to jump'.

The following day saw us off Brabant Island, with the helicopters dumping supplies for the forthcoming Joint Services Expedition. It turned foggy as we approached the Antarctic Convergence, the natural dividing line between the cold Southern Ocean and the warmer waters of the South Atlantic, and then we were rolling and pitching our way once more through Drake Passage. An increase in seabirds showed that we had reached Birdwood Bank, a rich fisheries area. We still had four or five of the glorious wanderers behind us; but the small pintados and Wilson's petrels had gone, and the familiar stinker had taken their place. Another night, and we were off Fitzroy for breakfast. We thanked Nick for a truly memorable trip, and Tony Ellerbeck flew us off the flight-deck in Wasp 435 to Government House.

A warm welcome awaited us. Apart from Government House staff and Major Robin Gilding, Annie Price was there (Cindy was busy filming on Carcass) to introduce us to Cindy's father, Lord Buxton, and her younger sister, Vicky. They had arrived to spend a week or two on Carcass and we were delighted to look after them while in Stanley. We had first heard about Aubrey Buxton's 'Survival' team in Uganda, when he was filming an attempt to save the white rhino; but we had not had the pleasure of meeting him before. 'Survival' had gone from strength to strength under his guidance. He was a dedicated naturalist and expert ornithologist and, as a member of the House of Lords, had always taken a keen interest in the political situation in the South Atlantic and Antarctica, staunchly supporting the Falkland Islanders. We were to be grateful also for his personal friendship in 1982.

There was the usual mountain of mail to be dealt with before donning my uniform and going out to meet the *Endurance* as she sailed into harbour. This was for the benefit not only of the Pebble Mill television team, but also for an Anglia TV team which Aubrey had brought in. After three inspections of the Royal Marines on the flight deck, both producers pronounced themselves satisfied. Over the next few days, they interviewed me about the political situation. Bob Langley was more aggressive than Anglia's Malcolm Allsop, but both were perfectly fair. Bob boxed me into a corner about Britain's likely reaction to a possible Argentine invasion. I suppose my reply should have been, in time-honoured fashion, that I did not answer hypothetical questions; but with Argentine ears in mind

I said, 'If the Argentines landed here, we should have to dislodge them.' Thank goodness Bob did not follow up by asking me how. I could not have answered. The perceived wisdom in Whitehall at that time was that the Islands were 'indefensible'.

Looking back, it was perceptive of BBC and Anglia to send film crews down to the Falklands a year before the Argentine invasion. Until then, there had been very little coverage by the British media; indeed, before 1982 few people in Britain either knew or cared where the Falkland Islands were. Both films, Pebble Mill's *Langley South* and Anglia's *More British Than The British*, reflected Islander opinion at the time and accurately predicted the result of the October election.

February saw the most elegant visitor to Stanley harbour, a tall ship of classic lines but built only a year before: the magnificent Polish barquentine, the *Pogoria*. Her master, Captain Baronowski, a well-known Polish TV personality, was on his way home after replenishing the Polish Antarctic bases for the winter. He explained that a modern sailing ship made economic sense; the *Pogoria* could sail down to Antarctica from Poland and back in almost the same time as a modern motor vessel and at a fraction of the cost. She had, of course, an auxiliary engine, and also up-to-date navigational aids and first-class accommodation. He showed us round and it was lovely to see the wooden timbers and panelling. The contrast with his fellow-Pole's ship in Port William could not have been more striking. Captain Skelnick invited us aboard his factory ship, the *Zulawe*, which took it in turn with the *Gryf Pomorski* to mother the Polish fishing fleet. No polished mahogany on her, only the all-pervading smell of fishmeal. To round off our nautical visitors in February – and end our first year in the Falklands – we welcomed the Royal Fleet Auxiliary *Plumleaf* to replenish our diesel tanks. The next time her captain, Phil Roberts, was to be in Falkland waters was in command of the ill-fated RFA *Sir Galahad*, in 1982.

Notes

1. *Falkland Islands Review:* Report of a Committee of Privy Counsellors, January, 1983 (Comnd 8786, page 23).

2. Since 1982 a third has been added: Liberation Day, 14 June.

3. After the invasion in 1982, we were delighted to receive a telegram of support from Ned and his team, high up in the mountains of Nepal.

4. He was later convicted of murder and sent to the United Kingdom to

serve his sentence. His conviction was reduced on appeal to manslaughter but he remained in detention 'at Her Majesty's pleasure'.

5. This included 7 British Nationals born in Australia, 5 in Canada and 5 in New Zealand.

6. Lorraine took Roy and Janie into Stanley after the war and was invaluable as a house parent in the school hostel, and, later, its supervisor. Both children did well in their 'O' levels and went to England for further education. Roy was subsequently selected for training as a FIGAS pilot.

7. Fortunately, the agreement was not implemented before the Argentine invasion.

8. Argentina, Australia, Belgium, Chile, France, Japan, New Zealand, Norway, South Africa, United Kingdom, USA and USSR. Another nineteen nations have since acceded to the Treaty.

9. HMS *Endurance* was not so fortunate in 1984, when she struck an uncharted submerged pinnacle in the Orleans Strait.

8

The Wrong Signals

Looking back on our first year, we had certainly found it full and absorbing, as Dick had predicted: but scarcely tranquil. We had failed in our ambition to visit all the settlements and meet all the people, though we were well on the way. During February, we had managed to stay with Ian and Maria Strange, on New Island, but I could not do that wonderful island justice as I had to get back to Stanley to field an inspection team from the FCO. Mavis was able to spend longer there (and make another trip to Carcass), with our house guest, Mary O'Hare, an old friend from Uganda days, and the judge and prosecuting counsel from the Minto case, Peter Watkin-Williams and Aden O'Brien Quinn. The psychologist in the case had had to return to England immediately after the trial. By an unfortunate coincidence, his name was also Minto. Another welcome visitor over this period was Harold Briley, who was then the BBC's Latin American correspondent, based in Buenos Aires. He was knowledgeable on Argentina and his sympathetic approach to the Islanders won him many friends.

Not so welcome was an Argentine trespasser into Falkland waters in the shape of a seismic survey vessel, which Eddie Anderson espied skulking in a bay on the unfrequented side of Weddell Island.[1] He was flying the Beaver from New Island to Port Stephens at the time. Fortunately, HMS *Endurance* was within reach and Nick readily agreed to investigate. The Argentine skipper apologised and said that he had had to run before a violent storm, which had driven him from Argentine waters as far as the Falklands. He had sought temporary shelter at Weddell and had been unable to raise Stanley on the radio. He intended to depart immediately. The only part of the story that rang true was the foul weather. We had had quite a blow for a couple of days; but it was more than likely that he had been carrying out seismic surveys much closer to the Falklands than he was prepared to admit. His presence also lent credence to Bob Ferguson's oft-told tales of sheep disappearing and dogs being heard and seen on the west of Weddell. Bob was convinced that

Argentine vessels carried sheepdogs aboard and raided his sheep from time to time.

We were reminded of this incident later in the year when Argentina invited bids for concessionary blocks for oil exploration which straddled the putative median line. Lord Carrington took the unprecedented step of issuing a formal notice in oil magazines, warning international oil companies against bidding for blocks over which the Argentines had no right. Regrettably, we did not take the next logical step, which would have been to declare our own exclusive economic zone and invite bids for blocks on our side of the median line. Indeed, some of the major internationals (not British) applied for the Argentine blocks, regardless of Lord Carrington's warning. The war came before exploration in the disputed blocks had begun, though of course commercial drilling had been going on nearer the Patagonian coast for some time.

Now into our second year, life fell into a familiar pattern. The end-of-season sports in East Falkland were held at Fitzroy. They were postponed from the end of February until the second week in March owing to the untimely death of Linda Binnie's father. We drove overland in convoy from Stanley. It was bitterly cold on Fitzroy racecourse and spectators stayed in their Land Rovers, engines running and heaters on. Eric Goss was again the champion jockey and Melvyn Summers won the shearing competition with the fastest time for one sheep of one minute and eight seconds.[2] On the way home, Mickey Clarke, our driver, never forgave himself for getting bogged between Fitzroy and Bluff Cove. As he painfully jacked up each wheel, less experienced camp drivers sailed past, regaling him with choice invective. In truth, our bogging had more to do with Mickey's alcohol consumption the night before than the state of the track, wet though it was. Tim and Jean Dobbyns kept up a continuous smoko at Bluff Cove for the passing hang-overs. The Darwin road had now reached seven miles out of Stanley, and never was a firm surface more welcome.

Apart from a brief visit with Mr Ridley, I had not been to Chartres, in West Falkland, and Mavis had not seen it at all. We flew there a week after the sports and spent two most enjoyable days with Bill and Pat Luxton. Bill was a true kelper, whose great-grandfather had been one of the Royal Marines sent out to the Falklands in the 1840s. He had taken his discharge in Stanley in 1863 and worked for many years as Mr Dean's gardener. Bill's grandfather had worked at Port Stephens before moving to

Chartres in the early 1900s. Pat was from Storrington, near Worthing, in England and had come out to the Falklands in 1966 as a book-keeper and teacher. Bill had his own Cessna and generously let me fly it round his farm. He gave me valuable advice on buying an aircraft and the cost of maintaining it and confirmed the opinion I had formed at Salvador that a Cessna of my own would be well worth while. He kept his almost literally at the bottom of his garden, in a tailor-made hangar like Robin's. A little distance away was an excellent trout-stream, with the massive bulk of Mount Philomel to the south and a most attractive harbour to the west, abounding with upland geese and teal duck. We could understand why Bill's grandfather had decided to settle here and why Pat had fallen in love with it. The settlement itself was of medium size, with twenty-four residents in all. They had not quite finished shearing, with 21,000 shorn and 4,000 to go. The work force was more permanent than most: Jimmy Duncan had been at Chartres since the 1930s and Jack Harvey since 1940. The new Islander pilot, Mike Selwood, from the Channel Islands, came to collect us and made an impressive crosswind landing. He then demonstrated what an all-rounder a FIGAS pilot had to be by pulling out a spanner and releasing the pressure from the starboard brake, which had locked the wheel as he turned.

Back in Stanley, we prepared to receive the children again, for Easter, said farewell to Robin Gilding and his Royal Marines and welcomed Gary Noott and the new detachment, which HMS *Endurance* had brought from Montevideo. During the Easter holidays, Diana met Gary's second-in-command, Lieutenant John Thurman, at a party in Government House. I managed to get away for a weekend with Tony to the Malo where, under the expert guidance of Terry Spruce, chairman of the Stanley Angling Club, I was fortunate to land an 8½lb sea trout, my largest to date. Thanks to Nick Barker, Tony and I were also able to have a short trip on the *Endurance* before she sailed for home, visiting Carcass, Westpoint and Hill Cove. We had arranged for the *Endurance* to take Minto back to the UK to serve his sentence but, at the last minute, the MOD instructed Nick not to embark him without prior guarantees from Montevideo and Buenos Aires that they would allow *Endurance* to call at their ports with Minto aboard, and such guarantees were not forthcoming in the time available. Fortunately, the *Bransfield* arrived in Stanley shortly after the *Endurance* had sailed and her captain, John Cole, and BAS's senior officer on board, Eric Salmon, took it upon themselves to deliver Minto safely to the prison authorities in England. This was no light responsibility; the psychologist, Dr Minto, had warned that Minto could be violent and suicidal. Unlike HMS *Endurance*, the *Bransfield* did not have a proper lock-up on board and Minto had to be put in an ordinary cabin. I went to see him before he left and told him in no uncertain terms to behave himself on the voyage. Happily, he caused no trouble and, to Toddy's intense relief, duly became the responsibility of HM Prisons.

My next trip to camp was to Roy Cove, where morale was low after the announcement that the farm was to be split up. I did my best to reassure the residents that they would not be left jobless or without a roof over their heads, but failed again to persuade Joe Newell to take a section. He had made up his mind to return to Northern Ireland. While there I took the opportunity to inspect the airstrip, which Joe was constructing a few miles from the settlement. The need for it was reinforced by our having to wait for the Beaver, sitting in a small boat, chilled to the marrow, for over an hour in an icy wind. Ian White was apologetic when he eventually turned up, but it was not his fault – he had been inspecting the Westpoint airstrip with Roddy Napier and somehow the radio message postponing his estimated time of arrival had failed to get through.

All too soon, the Easter holidays were over and we were seeing off Diana and Tony again on the LADE flight. This time they were accompanied by Cindy and Annie, who had livened up Government House for the last two weeks, having completed their filming on Carcass. We were sorry to see them go and made a date to meet them next season in South Georgia. It was still just an idea in Cindy's head – but Cindy had a way of turning ideas into reality.

The regular fixtures, like the Queen's Birthday Parade, came and went without incident and life was placid on the surface, though from all sides it was impressed upon me how strongly opposed the Islanders were to any ceding of sovereignty. Opinion was hardening against talks on leaseback, even as a device for keeping the talks going. The announcement by MOD of the withdrawal of HMS *Endurance* after the 1981-2 season was received with dismay. Islanders perceived immediately how this would be seen from Buenos Aires (a factor that appeared to have been totally ignored in the decision-making process in Whitehall). The British Press were beginning to take an interest and the *Daily Express,* which had championed the Islanders' cause in 1968, sent down their Chief Correspondent,

153

Michael Brown, and photographer, Harry Dempster. In 1968, at the time of Lord Chalfont's visit, the *Express* had published a picture of a group protest meeting outside the cathedral, complete with banners and placards, and Michael explained that his editor wanted an update of the same picture. I thought that such a picture at the present time might well exacerbate relations with Argentina and suggested that an equally effective one for UK readers but less damaging for Anglo-Argentine relations would be a group photograph on Government House lawn with flags but no banners, instead of which he could have me and the Royal Marines in uniform. Michael readily agreed and one cold, Saturday morning half of Stanley turned out to be photographed. Michael and Harry became good friends of ours and staunch supporters of the Falklands. Indeed, to show their appreciation, the Islanders invited them back for the 150th Anniversary celebrations in 1983. Several other journalists followed them down to Stanley, including a Frenchman from Associated Press and two Americans, James Evans and Jack Epstein of the *Pacific News*. John Ferguson brought in an Argentine soil scientist, Carlos Puricelli, and escorted him round the Islands, taking soil samples for analysis in his laboratory in Argentina, which had better facilities than our own in the Grasslands Trials Unit. John said that he found the resulting data helpful – as, doubtless, did the Argentines.

By far the most entertaining visitor in 1981, however, was Mr Maslov, or rather Mr Maslov's ship. He was the gentleman who had offered to buy the Islands' surplus sheep and about whom Griff Evans had spoken so scathingly. He had conducted two trial runs in 1980 from Punta Arenas, in Chile. The first had been successful, with few casualties and reasonably prompt payment. The second had not, with many deaths on the way across and several farmers still waiting for their money. Maslov had blamed the vessel, which everyone agreed was unsuitable for transporting live sheep in bulk, and he had promised to renew the trade once he had acquired a more suitable and larger ship. News had filtered through of a tank landing craft from Italy, which Maslov was converting into a sheep-carrier. After various false alarms, and farmers gathering their surplus sheep in the home paddocks and then having to release them when Maslov's ship failed to materialise, it turned up one glorious Sunday in May. Maslov's son was on board and he invited most of Stanley to a reception in its spacious hold that evening.

Despite its size (1,144 tons and 83 metres long), the *Maritza*

Arlette was able to come into the public jetty and, to demonstrate how ideal it was for the job, the captain brought it in bows on, with doors open and ramp down. Two anchors trailed out behind and two ropes and a gangplank secured the ship to the jetty. As Don was quick to point out, this meant that its huge slab side was facing the prevailing westerly wind. 'If the wind gets up', said Don, 'She'll take the jetty with her.' We went on to the reception from evensong at the cathedral, which meant that I was dressed in my Sunday-best and Mavis in a fur coat instead of our more practical anoraks. The captain's opening remarks were puzzling. 'How do you do', he said, 'I am not the captain who killed the cook. I am the fourth captain since then.' Feeling that this had something to do with the false alarms, we waited until we had a quiet moment with Maslov Junior and asked him what the captain had meant. 'Oh, did you not know?' he exclaimed, as if all the world had heard the story, 'The captain who brought the ship from Italy killed the cook and is now in prison in Miami. We had terrible trouble finding another, but after three duds, we got this one.' He then went on to assure us that he had every confidence in 'this one', that his seamanship was of the highest order and his temperament such that he was unlikely to kill the cook, no matter how bad the cooking. Judging from the fine spread before us, there was no risk of that. After the buffet, I was invited to say a few words of welcome, and the captain had launched into a fulsome reply when one of the ship's officers sidled up and whispered something in his ear. 'Excusa me', he announced, 'I am wanted onna the bridge. Uno momento,' and dashed out. I looked round for Don, but he had sniffed the wind and had also disappeared. The captain returned first, looking a little flustered, but determined to carry on with his speech. He was getting into his stride again when Don returned with the dramatic news that the gangplank had gone. Suddenly everybody was shouting and dashing hither and thither; the poor captain never did finish his speech. The wind had sprung up and, fortunately for Stanley, the ropes had either broken or come adrift, otherwise we would have lost half the public jetty. Eventually, the FIC's *Lively* came to our rescue and managed to take us back to shore, though not without a soaking in seaspray. Many of the guests spent the night aboard.

Maslov was due in Goose Green the next morning, but was still in Port Stanley when an irate Brook Hardcastle rang me to ask where he was. 'I'm afraid he's got his anchors in a twist', I said, 'And he tells me it will take all day to clear

155

them.' Brook was naturally concerned because he had gathered a large flock for Maslov on the home paddock and could ill afford to waste the grazing on scrag sheep that otherwise would have been slaughtered. In the event, it took the captain two days to disentangle his anchor chains and, to add insult to injury, when he finally arrived at Goose Green, he smashed into Brook's jetty, causing substantial damage. That was the last we saw of Maslov, his fourth captain or the *Maritza Arlette*. He never paid for the sheep and we later heard that the Chilean Banks were after him.

Mid-tour leave was almost upon us and we had not yet visited Port Howard, an omission that we were determined to rectify before we left. It was the last of the major settlements on our itinerary, and one of the most attractive. More than any other, it resembled a typical English farm, with stables, barns and all the outbuildings normally associated with farming in England. Don had warned us that it was a Bonner stronghold and he was right: every other person we met seemed to be a Bonner. Don's daughter, Carol, was married to the assistant manager, Rodney Lee, whose brother, Robin, was the manager. The Lees had been associated with Port Howard for even longer than the Bonners. The first Lee had arrived in the Islands almost a hundred years ago. He had taken a contract to deliver a flock of sheep from Britain to another company and then return home, but on the outward voyage he had fallen in love with a girl who was bound for Patagonia and had persuaded her to get married and stay in the Falklands. It had to be a whirlwind romance because the girl was allowed to remain in the Islands unmarried for only three days. He had then taken a job as shepherd on Port Howard in 1890 and the Lees had worked and lived there ever since. Robin's wife, Susan, was another Pole-Evans, whose father had managed Port Howard for many years before Robin. The farm was owned by a British firm, J.L. Waldron Ltd, who though absentee landlords were both caring and imaginative.[3] The Matthew brothers, who were connected with the Waldron family, took it in turn to come out each year during the shearing season, and the company had paid for Robin to study agriculture in New Zealand before assuming the managership. It was a large farm, even by Falkland standards: 177,000 acres, 38,000 sheep, 1,100 cattle and 300 horses. Robin made enough oaten hay to be able to feed the working horses and milking cows during winter, a practice not followed anywhere else in the Islands at that time.

There were forty-eight people altogether in the settlement, including eight children, with a smart little schoolroom and teacher. Two of Don's sons, Timothy and Simon, were shepherds there (as Don had been himself) and one of his nephews, Paul, was tractor driver and mechanic.[4] We met them all in the community hall that evening, a happy and harmonious band. Next morning, Robin drove us round the creek to Packe's Port Howard, which came under Richard Cockwell's management from Fox Bay East. Robin and Heather Smith had recently moved there from Port Howard. Robin Lee said how sorry he was to lose him; but they preferred the peace and quiet of an outside house to being in the settlement. I was to think of this when I stood amid the wreckage of a Harrier on that same spot a little over a year later.

Our last visitor before we went on leave was John Ure, a senior FCO official. The purpose of his visit was to encourage Islanders to make an early decision in favour of leaseback. He was also spending some time in Argentina, where he hoped to reassure the Argentine Government of the British Government's wish to make progress towards a solution and to seek to persuade them not to force the pace. Councillors were in Stanley for the budget session of Legislative Council when John arrived. The first evening, I introduced them to him at Government House and showed the Pebble Mill film on the Falklands, which stimulated a lively discussion. John had many opportunities in the days that followed to discuss the sovereignty issue with them, both collectively and individually. We also met the Sheep Owners Association and we managed to fit in a trip to the young farmers at Green Patch, where we spent two nights as guests of Neil and Glenda Watson, at Long Island. Neil had won the Governor's Cup that year on a handsome mare called Sally and John enjoyed an early morning ride on her along the magnificent stretch of beach that was the Watsons' front garden. In this, their first year, Neil had taken thirty-three bales of wool from his sheep, worth about £9,000. Not a lot with which to bring up a family and keep the farm running for a year, but Neil had no regrets – it was a lovely way of life and he had no wish to change it. Like all the young farmers, he was uncompromisingly against leaseback.

We drove back to Stanley in two Land Rovers. It was very wet and we were bogged down five times on the way. Perhaps with prophetic anticipation, John elected to walk in from the Two Sisters. The date was 13 June. Exactly a year later, the Paras and Royal Marines were 'yomping' over the same route, the day before the Argentine surrender. We also found time to take John on board the *Gryf Pomorski*, which was back in Port William with Captain Szostak. He had his wife with him on this trip and we helped to celebrate their twenty-seventh wedding anniversary. Another celebration on the same day was the award of the Queen's Police Medal to Toddy McMillan, who was about to retire after more than twenty years in the police force. We were also losing the longest serving kelper in the senior school, the woodwork master, Jim Lellman, who at the age of seventy-six decided that it was time to retire and join his English wife in Bristol.

John Ure left the Islands with the impression that opinion had not hardened irrevocably against leaseback. I was not so sanguine. My expectations were that the elections in October would bring more hardliners in to Legislative Council and that it would be difficult to get them to agree to keep *any* talks going. It was not as if we were dealing with a mature, stable country like, say, Norway. Argentina's track record was there for all to see and it was not surprising that Islanders wanted nothing to do with the Argentines.

Mavis departed on the same flight as John, to visit her mother and sisters in Zimbabwe on the way home. I followed a week later, leaving the Islands in the capable hands of Dick Baker and relieved to know that the Sheep Owners Association and the General Employees Union had reached agreement on pay and conditions for the coming year. In view of the depressed wool prices, the Union had acted responsibly and accepted a fifty per cent cut in the automatic cost-of-living increase.

The LADE flight from Stanley to Buenos Aires took seven hours, including a 1½hr stop at Comodoro Rivadavia, and there was no direct connection with London for the next two days. As Anthony Williams had already gone on leave, I stayed with John and Margaritha Chick, who had visited us recently in Stanley. He was Chargé d'Affaires in Anthony's absence and, although they looked after me very well and introduced me to some charming Argentine friends, I did not feel comfortable in Buenos Aires. After the Falklands, it was all too garish and strident, and I could understand why many Islanders disliked having to spend two days there on their way 'home' to Britain. I savoured, too, the treatment that some of them received from Argentine officials. LADE had treated me with the utmost courtesy, ushering me through Comodoro Rivadavia and Aeroparque without even asking for my passport, but an irritable official at Ezeiza, the international airport, did not see how he could stamp my passport to show that I was going out of the country when there was no stamp to show that I had come in; yet he could not allow me to leave without a stamp. The problem was only resolved after a telephone call to John and the intervention of the Ministry of Foreign Affairs.

Almost immediately after my arrival in London, Mr Ridley called a meeting to consider the situation in the South Atlantic. He took the chair and FCO officials included Sir Michael Palliser and John Ure, together with Anthony Williams and myself. John said that he had found Argentine Foreign Affairs Ministers and officials reasonably relaxed about progress, or lack of progress, on the Falklands negotiations and well disposed towards the leaseback idea. They had warned, however, that the military leaders were less patient and might require a more 'forward' policy at any time. In the Islands, he judged that, in order to secure agreement to leaseback, much more would need to be done to educate opinion about the danger of inaction and the safeguards on which the Government would insist in any leaseback arrangements. He suggested a number of measures to assist a campaign of public education, including assurances to the Islanders on access to the United Kingdom, a resettlement scheme for those dissatisfied with any arrangements reached, further land distribution schemes, and the initiation of more productive economic schemes for the Islands. Anthony said that ground had been lost since February (the New York talks) both because it was less possible to depend on continued Argentine patience and understanding and because Islander opinion of the realities of the situation had been allowed to slide back. He advocated a 'sales campaign', perhaps mainly by bringing home to British opinion the potential cost of any alternative.

As the day wore on, I listened to the debate with mounting incredulity. The Islanders they were talking about were not the Islanders I had come to know over the last sixteen months. My colleagues talked as if Falkland Islanders could be manipulated or persuaded or 'educated' into doing something that they had made perfectly plain they had no wish to do. There was an air of unreality in the meeting, far removed from the 'realities of the situation' in the Falklands. My only contribution was to reiterate that the Islanders wished to have nothing whatsoever to do with the Argentines and did not believe that any terms that might be agreed for a leaseback settlement could ever provide them with the guarantees that they would require. The conclusions at the end of the day were that the immediate aim should be to play for time with Argentina; that the new Legislative Council, when elected, should be persuaded to allow talks to continue; that a paper for the Defence Committee should be prepared recommending a major public education campaign, and that up-to-date contingency plans should be prepared.

I went to the House of Lords that evening with a heavy heart, sure in my own mind that putting pressure on the Islanders would only be counter-productive. The best we could hope for was that the new councillors would agree to another round of talks before the end of the year. The debate in the Lords was on the Falkland Islands and the first thing that struck me was the empty chamber: there were only five opposition and six Government members. Perhaps a public education campaign *was* necessary, starting with Parliament! Aubrey Buxton made a strong speech on the folly of withdrawing HMS *Endurance* and the strategic significance of the Falklands and their Dependencies. Lord Trefgarne spoke for the Government, confirming HMS *Endurance*'s withdrawal after the forthcoming season. Other concerned spectators in the gallery with me were Cindy, Michael Brown and Nick Barker. We had a sombre drink afterwards and I caught the midnight train to my father's home in Burnham.

After rounding up the family - Diana from Woldingham, Tony from Radley, and Mavis from Heathrow – I enrolled in the Three Counties Club at Blackbushe to renew my Private Pilot's Licence. The other 'must' during leave was a visit to the Orkney and Shetland Islands, where I hoped to learn lessons that could usefully be applied in the Falklands. First, however, it was flying from Blackbushe whenever the weather and FCO permitted. One of the urgent matters to be resolved with the FCO was the appointment of an Attorney General. Another was the future of the BAS base at Grytviken. Dick Laws had dropped a bombshell by announcing that the only way the BAS could absorb a ten per cent cut across the board, as decreed by its parent department, was by closing one of its bases and, as he considered that Grytviken was the least important scientifically, it would be the one to go – unless of course money could be found from elsewhere. The FCO had no funds for this sort of thing and the only possible source was the Falkland Islands Government. In fact, the Falkland Islands Dependencies' budget had always been kept separate from that of the Falkland Islands and, thanks to Harold Rowlands' prudent management, a considerable surplus had accrued over the years from stamp revenues and harbour and water dues (obtained mainly from Russian trawlers). The running costs of the base, however, would be more than the anticipated annual revenue from these sources and it would be only a matter of time before the Dependencies were bankrupt. Nevertheless, it was politically imperative that a British presence be maintained at Grytviken and BAS scientists were the obvious people to be there. Faced with this ultimatum, I undertook to try to persuade councillors upon my return to the Islands to agree to fund the BAS base with effect from the following financial year. I made the point, however, that this would be seen by Islanders (and Argentines) as yet another sign of Britain's diminishing interest in the South Atlantic.

A subject of more immediate concern was the British Nationality Bill, which threatened to exclude third, fourth and fifth generation Falkland Islanders from British citizenship. Islanders had not been impressed by the argument that granting them British citizenship would open the door to three-and-a-half million Chinese from Hong Kong. They saw themselves as British in everything except their place of birth and better qualified to reside in their mother country than the Gibraltarians, who by some quirk in European Community rules found themselves entitled to British citizenship. I attended the debate in the House of Lords, which incidentally took place on the eve of the Royal Wedding of the Prince and Princess of Wales, and watched a spirited attempt by Lady Vickers to force an amendment which would have given all Islanders the right to British citizenship. She was ably supported by Lords Buxton and Shackleton and other friends of the Falklands, but the amendment was defeated by one vote. Standing in Hyde Park that night, watching the firework display with 300,000 fellow British subjects, I felt for the 800 or more loyal descendants of British stock in the Falkland Islands who would no longer have the right of access to, or abode in, their home country.[5] More to the point, I could imagine how the wires would be buzzing between the Argentine Embassy and Buenos Aires on this latest indication of Britain's lack of commitment to the Islanders.

On our way north to Inverness, we stopped at Whitby to perform a twinning ceremony between Stanley and that attractive Yorkshire seaport. Not only were there historical ties dating back to Captain Cook, but the current Mayor, Richard Wastell, had been billeted on the Bonner family in Stanley during the Second World War. In Inverness, we were met by Bob Storey, who had been on Lord Shackleton's team in the Falklands in 1976. He worked for the Highlands and Islands Development Board and had kindly arranged our programme on Orkney and Shetlands. The similarity between these islands and the Falklands was striking: the fresh air, the wild grandeur of the moors and the crags, the lack of trees, the spectacular coastline and the all pervading presence of the sea. The Scottish islands were greener (they had a heavier rainfall), but the greatest difference was man-made: Orkney and Shetland had good, metalled roads, built mainly by the military in two World Wars. If I had needed convincing that the key to the development of the Falklands was roads, this trip would have done it.

We paid interesting and useful visits to a variety of small enterprises: a fish factory, a cottage knitwear industry, stone cutters, sheepskin curing, a peat-cutting machine and a domestic woollen mill. All were relevant to the Falklands and have since been developed there. The woollen mill, run by the enterprising Jamieson Brothers, was perhaps the best example of what could be done with a bit of imagination and flair in the Falkland Islands. They took the wool off the sheep's back – as their advertisement proclaimed, 'naturally Shetland Wool' – washed, scoured, spun and knitted it into the well-known 'Fairisle' sweater and sold it in up-market department stores. Smart packaging ensured an extremely good profit. If we could get a Falkland Islands pattern as distinctive as the 'Fairisle', I was sure that our finer quality wool would be able to compete in the top market range, despite the extra transport costs.

The Jamiesons operated modestly from their back yard. At the other end of the scale was the £1.25 billion oil terminal at Sullum Voe. If we were to strike oil and gas in commercial quantities in Falklands waters (and be allowed to exploit it), this was likely to be the scale of the enterprise. My main interest was in the social consequences of such a huge influx of men and money on the island community, and the Convenor and Chief Executive of the Shetland Council were reassuring. Their canny islanders had adapted well, reaping the benefits of the oil bonanza but using them wisely and with an eye on the long-term future after the oil ran out. I was confident that the kelpers would be every bit as canny. The Chief Executive also gave me useful advice on how to negotiate with the major oil companies.

We ended a fascinating stay with a visit to the Lerwick Harbour Trust and one of the local food suppliers to the drilling rigs. There

162

were useful lessons here for the Falkland Islands, whether for servicing oil companies or fishing fleets. On our way through Orkney, we met Andy Alsop, who had introduced the Islander aircraft to the Falklands and expressed a wish to return to fly for FIGAS, but was having problems with ODA over his contract and conditions of service. He had gained a high reputation in the Islands for piloting skill and selfless service, and we wanted him badly. Despite our best endeavours, however, bureaucracy prevailed and he did not arrive for another year.

Going south, we stopped off to see Al Watson, now returned to the RAF from FIGAS and servicing Nimrods at Kinross – a far cry from Beavers in Stanley. We inspected the salmon hatcheries at Almondbank and I flew over to Campbeltown to see a salmon ranching scheme, which was another possible prospect for the Falklands.[6] Back in England, we were the guests for two nights of Ted and Kath Needham, at Chesterfield, where as well as a return golf match with Ted and Harry Camm (on a much better course than Stanley's) we had a helpful discussion on the Stanley school hostel.

Home again in Sunningdale, I resumed flying and just managed to complete the obligatory solo cross-country (Blackbushe–Thruxton – Shoreham) and pass the general flying test before the end of my leave. Creeping down to Shoreham and back to Blackbushe in dirty industrial haze, I consoled myself with the thought that the Falklands enjoyed clear, unpolluted air and, apart from the occasional squall, I should have no problems over visibility. Between flights, I made a dash to Slimbridge for a meeting with Sir Peter Scott and fellow trustees of the Falkland Islands Foundation, a trip to Bourton-on-the-Water to see Len Hill and 'Birdland' and another meeting with Dick Laws in Cambridge about the BAS base at Grytviken. As I had feared, running costs had already escalated from £180,000 a year to £237,000, with additional capital costs for repair and renovation of £98,000. At this rate, the money would run out in seven years. A more helpful meeting was with Mr Elliott, of Salvesen's, the firm that had the lease of the old whaling stations in South Georgia. I wished to persuade him not to renew Davidoff's option to the scrap there after it ran out in April the following year. He was sympathetic and said that, in view of Davidoff's non-performance to date, he thought that Salvesen's would agree to let it lapse.[7]

In the FCO, my last meeting was with the Secretary of State,

Lord Carrington. The usual officials were there, but Anthony Williams had already returned to Buenos Aires. Mr Ridley was present and the Lord Privy Seal, Sir Ian Gilmour. To my relief, Lord Carrington did not accept the recommendation for a 'public education' campaign. He considered that the political realities were such that it would be counter-productive.

I recounted this to Anthony Williams when I stayed with him on my way through Buenos Aires a week later and expressed my conviction that we should never be able to persuade the Falkland Islanders to accept a transfer of sovereignty. If we were to go all the way down the leaseback road, and not use it merely to keep the dialogue with Argentina going, we should have to overrule the Islanders' wishes and impose a settlement upon them – a course of action to which I was totally opposed. Early the next morning Anthony came into my room in his dressing gown to say goodbye. I was flying on the 'milk run'; Aeroparque 7.30am, Stanley 3.30pm, with four stops on the way. We both expected difficult times ahead; but neither of us contemplated invasion within six months.

It was good to be back in Stanley again, even though the weather was foul and we had to creep in past Cape Pembroke lighthouse. Once again, I was filled with admiration for the Argentine pilots. Dick and the other Councillors were at the airport and I introduced them to Michael Shersby and Eric Ogden, two MPs who had accompanied me on the flight. Every few years the Commonwealth Parliamentary Association organised a visit by two Members of Parliament and, fortuitously, the Falklands' turn had come up again in time for the run-up to the Legislative Council elections. Dick and Connie gave me dinner that night, Mavis having stayed at home to see Diana into London University. She was due to follow me in a month or so. Dick said that listeners to Argentine radio had reported a stepping-up in the propaganda against the British, blaming us for the lack of progress in the talks on 'returning' the Malvinas. The local newspaper, the *Penguin News*, had reported a 'deepening crisis' with Argentina and commented indignantly on an Argentine note which had stated that Islanders' wishes could not be considered as there was a great lack of knowledge in the Islands as to what happened on the mainland. 'In other words,' said the *Penguin News*, 'Falkland Islanders are not wise enough to determine their own future.'

Dick had arranged a full programme for the MPs, in Stanley and in camp, meeting a wide cross-section of Islanders. Eric

Ogden amused me by saying that he did not wish to stick to the programme, he wanted to get out and meet the 'real' people. I said that the people who were expecting him would be disappointed; but that was up to him. In the event, Michael Shersby met more 'real' people by sticking to the programme than Eric did by going off on his own. None the less, both returned to the United Kingdom firm friends and supporters of the Falkland Islanders, and have remained so ever since.

During their visit, the election campaign was in full swing. Without television and daily newspapers, this amounted to candidates broadcasting over the local radio, with those in camp travelling round the settlements as best they could and those in Stanley going round the houses or holding public meetings in the Town Hall. Although the electoral roll was a mere 1,034, the electoral procedure was cumbersome in the extreme. First, there were elections for Stanley East, Stanley West, East Falkland and West Falkland; then there were elections for Stanley and Camp Divisions. As unsuccessful candidates in the first round could stand for election in the second, and nomination day had to be a fortnight before election day, this meant that the elections took a whole month. Only one candidate, Tim Blake (West Falkland), was unopposed. Only one out of six expatriates standing was successful – Tony Blake – and he had lived in the Islands for over ten years. The others were fourth and fifth generation kelpers. Their names read like a roll-call of the original settlers: Blake, Binnie, Goss, Cheek and Peck. There was a seventy-eight per cent turn-out of voters and almost all of them voted for the sovereignty hardliners. Stuart Wallace lost his seat because voters thought that he had 'gone soft' on leaseback. He lost to Bill Goss, who was opposed to talks of any kind with the Argentines. Stuart's companion to the February talks, Adrian Monk, was ineligible for re-election because he had joined government service as Agricultural Officer.

Having experienced every type of electoral malpractice in Uganda and Borneo, from burning ballot boxes to physical intimidation, it was refreshing for me to observe an election as devoid of any hint of rigging as a general election in Britain. There was not a single complaint, petition or protest and the police reported no incident before, during or after the elections. Without the slightest shadow of a doubt, the six new Legislative Councillors faithfully represented the views of the vast majority of Falkland Islanders. During the campaign, however, I had one dissenting voice. A young kelper came to my office with the proposition that, if the British Government were to offer all Islanders £100,000 a head to become Argentine, with guaranteed entry to the UK if they did not like it, the majority of under twenty-fives would accept the money and 'give it a go' (the over twenty-fives could retire to the UK). This shocked me so much that for a time I made a point of asking every young Islander I met if they would be interested in such a deal. There were no takers.

My first aim with the new councillors was to secure their agreement to a further round of talks with the Argentines before the end of the year. After lengthy discussion, they agreed, provided that sovereignty was not on the agenda. Subsequently, they relented to the extent that their chosen representatives (Tim Blake and John Cheek) were authorised to join in any discussion on sovereignty, but with the sole aim of convincing Argentina that Britain had the stronger claim to the Islands and that the Islanders were determined to stay British. They were to emphasise that there could be no negotiations on the *transfer* of sovereignty. If, despite their protests, either side entered into such negotiations, they were to walk out of the meeting. Talks were arranged to be held in Geneva in December but, because of the change of government in Argentina in that month, the Argentines asked for a postponement until January, 1982. In the event, the talks were further postponed until the end of February and the venue changed to New York because Mr Luce, who had taken Mr Ridley's place in the FCO, had other commitments in January.

Meanwhile, life continued as usual in Government House, with colonial administration taking up much more of my time than conventional diplomacy, although the one impinged upon the other in the vexed area of YPF payments for the use of the FIC jetty, which the FIC claimed were outstanding and Hector Gilobert maintained were covered by the Fuel Agreement. After poring over the small print (oh, for an Attorney General!) it seemed to me that the FIC was right and Hector wrong; but Hector could be stubborn, and he wheeled in Colonel Balcarce in support. We made little progress before the invasion rendered the argument irrelevant in 1982.

Harold Rowlands was dismayed when I told him about the deal I had been forced to make with BAS over Grytviken. He had not husbanded the Dependencies' resources for many years only to see them exhausted over the next few. The hostel saga rumbled on, with John Brodrick refusing to accept the building from the FIC.

He took me round one morning after a rainstorm and we counted eighteen leaks and eighty-four ceiling tiles down. Our old friend Captain Szostak returned to Port William. He was worried about the situation in Poland and concerned for some of his crew, who were leading Solidarity members. He intimated that one or two might jump ship and expressed the hope that, if they did, we would treat them well. Over the next few months, six of his men presented themselves at the police station and requested political asylum. In each case, their belongings mysteriously appeared a few days later off the *Gryf Pomorski*. Unfortunately for these hapless Poles, it was out of the frying pan into the fire: before we could get them away to their preferred destinations, the Argentines had invaded.

Other old friends who reappeared were Captain Aye and the *World Discoverer*, the *Bransfield* and the *John Biscoe* and, in time for our Battle Day celebrations, Nick Barker and HMS *Endurance*. It was a poignant moment as we stood together on the saluting base and Master-at-Arms Barry Brennan led the *Endurance*'s flag-bearing party past us for (as we then thought) the last time. The ship's two Wasps flew past in close formation, the White Ensign and the Falkland Flag suspended beneath them, and Nick and I laid wreaths at the foot of the Battle Memorial. Nick had carefully chosen the wreath-bearers, burly stokers Tab Hunter and Nick Carter, as the two most unlikely lads in his crew to be seen carrying flowers; but they were extremely smart and performed as to the manner born. There were the usual sporting engagements: NP 8901 beat *Endurance* at rugby; we squared the golf match between Stanley and *Endurance*, and *Endurance* beat NP 8901 at soccer.

Notes

1. This was the *Yehuin*, which was to be captured by the British in 1982 and renamed the *Falkland Sound*, but better known locally as the *Black Pig*.

2. Melvyn died a little later in a tragic accident while fence-laying: a post under tension whipped back and fractured his skull.

3. In 1987, they sold the farm to Robin and Rodney Lee, who continued to run it as before, but with Rodney as manager and Robin his assistant (Robin had a serious operation which made it inadvisable for him to perform the heavy manual tasks required of a farm manager. He now runs the old 'big house' as a tourist lodge).

4. Simon was later to get his own farm at Roy Cove. The head shepherd, Danny Donnelly, was also to take a subdivision there.

5. After the war in 1982, Lady Vickers' amendment was passed in the House of Lords and Michael Shersby piloted it successfully through the House of Commons.

6. Brook Hardcastle's son, Simon, started a salmon farm in Fox Bay East in 1987. Salmon ranching has yet to be tried.

7. Senor Davidoff was an Argentine citizen who had entered into a contract with Salvesen's (a British registered firm) to purchase the scrap from the old whaling stations on South Georgia. My predecessor had tried to prevent this, pointing out the political implications, but Salvesen's said that they had received no other offers and the FCO had taken the view that it could not interfere in a purely commercial transaction.

9

South Georgia Interlude: An Unforeseeable Outcome

We embarked on HMS *Endurance* on 9 December, 1981, to sail to South Georgia and Signy (in the South Orkney Islands) before returning to Stanley for Christmas. As things turned out, we never made Signy. The three-day crossing to South Georgia was uneventful, except of course for the fascinating bird-life. The wanderers joined us on the second day out and stayed with us long after the stinkers and mollymawks had gone. It was misty as we crossed the Antarctic Convergence and the sea temperature dropped to 2°C. In the old days, this would be a likely spot for seeing whales, but we searched in vain. Another day and night and we awoke to find the ship surrounded by thousands of pretty black-and-white pintados, swooping and soaring against the grand back-drop of Royal Bay.

To readers unfortunate enough not to have visited South Georgia, it is difficult to convey the thrill of one's first sighting of this magnificent island. After days of nothing but sea, the rugged skyline of snow-covered peaks and majestic sweep of enormous glaciers takes the breath away. Although a sub-Antarctic island, the central spine of mountains rises to over 9,000ft and is perpetually mantled in snow. On board with us were the members of a Joint Services Expedition, who were to spend the summer season climbing a few hitherto unconquered peaks. We stood on the bridge with Bob Veale, the leader, as he told the helicopters by radio where to drop the expedition's supplies. With their loads swinging beneath them, the Wasps looked as frail as daddy-longlegs flying over the water. The helicopter pilots were already having difficulties with the katabatic winds that blew up suddenly over the mountains and whistled down the glaciers with great force.[1] Tim Finding, the ship's second pilot, reported a 30-40knot wind over the Ross Glacier, which was to be the expedition's advance camp. Despite the exacting conditions, the *Endurance*'s two Wasps managed to off-load eight tons of equipment and ferry the whole JSE team of sixteen ashore. They also landed a BBC television crew, with three of the *Endurance* seamen, on the Ross and Hindle Glaciers to take location shots for a film of Sir Ernest Shackleton's epic journey across South Georgia in 1916.

Having accomplished these arduous tasks, Tim's next detail was the relatively simple one of ferrying Mavis and me to St Andrews Bay, where BAS had a field hut which Cindy had persuaded Dick Laws to allow her and Annie to use for the season. Apart from its great natural beauty, the main attraction of St Andrews Bay was a colony of over 30,000 King penguins. As we flew over the spur separating St Andrews from Royal Bay, I was busily filming the spectacular scenery with my cine-camera. Tim started descending over Cook Glacier and we made out the little hut on the scree below the snowline as we banked in towards the Heaney Glacier. As we got closer, we saw a large Union Jack flying from a small flagpole – the flag, no doubt, that Cindy's local had given her in Langham, which we had visited during our leave. It was stiff as a board, pointing inland, indicating a strong on-shore wind. I caught a glimpse of Cindy and Annie standing outside the hut, waving, and wondered when Tim was going to turn into wind for the landing; but we kept going downwind and descending rapidly – too rapidly. We hit the ground going forward at speed, like a fixed-wing aircraft, and tipped up on our nose. For a fraction of a second, I thought we were going right over, but the rotor blades saved us by hitting the ground and throwing us back and then over onto our side. We were all well strapped in and came to no harm, except that Mavis was slightly bruised. I was still holding my camera, and kicked myself for not having the presence of mind to have kept on filming. There was smoke coming from the engine behind us, so we did not loiter.

The Royal Navy lived up to its gentlemanly tradition: the crewman, Bob Nadin, helped Mavis out first before climbing out himself. I picked up a camera from the floor (I think it was Tim's) and followed him out, still clutching my cine-camera. Poor Tim was mystified. He thought at first that the engine had failed to respond – he kept opening the throttle and we still kept going down. The answer was, of course, the unpredictable wind, which in Royal Bay twenty minutes before had been blowing hard off-shore, but had veered 180° by the time we landed in St Andrews. We literally ran out of lift and were blown to the ground.

Cindy and Annie were considerably more at risk than ourselves. Huge pieces of rotor blade and pylon were flung over a hundred yards from the crash. The gearbox assembly whistled past Cindy's ear. Unfortunately for the pictorial record, but reassuringly for us, she and Annie had put our safety before photography and rushed back to the hut to grab fire extinguishers. As we emerged from the wreckage, there they stood, extinguishers poised and ready to douse us in foam. Luckily, the aircraft did not catch fire (thank goodness for kerosene and not high-octane petrol) and the extinguishers were quickly replaced by mugs, not of tea, but of stiff gin-and-tonics. Tim used Cindy's radio to report the accident and Tony Ellerbeck was soon overhead in the other Wasp. He landed cautiously and surveyed the wreckage. 'I'm afraid it's a write-off,' he said, 'which means we cannot go south. We're not allowed to operate in the ice with only one aircraft.' But he was relieved to find us all unscathed and in good heart and returned to the *Endurance* with Tim and Bob, while Cindy and Annie took us down to the beach, which was littered with hundreds of elephant seals. Dotted here and there amongst them were small groups of King penguins (the main colony was at the other end of the bay). Cindy playfully tickled one of the young elephant pups and it bent its flipper over her hand, like a child grabbing hold of its mother.

The temperature was so mild out of the wind that we were able to sit in a sheltered spot on the beach and watch 'life's rich pageant', South Georgia style. A few feet in front of us was a young elephant seal, lazily flicking sand over its back with its flippers. Beyond, near the shore-line, lay serried ranks of elephants, so close together that a party of King penguins, darting in from the sea and catapulting themselves upright, had to paddle along the water's edge before they could find a gap. Above, in the brilliant blue sky, soared the beautiful light-mantled sooty albatross, cousin of the mollymawk and, if anything, even more graceful. I climbed up the tussock hill behind us and watched them only three feet away, unconcernedly sitting on their eggs and clucking contentedly. So handsome with their grey head and wings and delicate pale grey breast, their most striking feature was a pure white crescent around the eye, which gave them a look of perpetual surprise. Although occasionally spotted in the Falklands, this was my first sighting.

Towards evening, after a most enjoyable day, the *Endurance* appeared in St Andrews Bay and we went back on board by boat. Cindy and Annie accompanied us and we all gathered in the wardroom for an excellent buffet dinner. Later that night, I stupidly trapped my finger in the cabin door and lost my nail.

In less time than it took to grow a new one, the Argentines had occupied South Georgia and the Falklands and the British had assembled a task force, transported it 8,000 miles across the ocean, retaken South Georgia, landed at San Carlos, 'yomped' across East Falkland, recaptured Stanley and despatched over 10,000 Argentines back to the mainland.

The next day, we went ashore again by boat, and Cindy and Annie took us across the foot of the glaciers and through the melt streams to the King penguin colony, which was about a mile from the hut. We were amazed to see thousands of fat fledglings, covered in thick, woolly down and huddled together in large groups, like rows of brown bearskins, in the middle of adult birds incubating eggs on their feet. Cindy explained that the breeding cycle of the King was different from the smaller varieties of penguin. It took more than a year to rear a chick, so that a breeding pair would lay early one summer, late the next and miss out on the third. Looking at this crowded rookery, teeming with life as far as the eye could see, it was difficult to imagine that it had been a mere thirty birds in 1914. Sealers and whalers had slaughtered the King almost to extinction by then. Now, without man, it could more than hold its own against its natural predators.

We returned to the *Endurance* by helicopter. Mavis approached it with some apprehension but managed to contain herself until alighting on the flight deck, when to her annoyance she burst into tears. We went ashore the next morning in the *Stancombe Wills*, together with Nick, Mike Green (the First Officer) and Neil Munro (the ship's doctor). The flight crew had almost finished picking the pieces off our wrecked Wasp. Its skeleton looked forlorn on the grey scree. We all had a last drink with Cindy and Annie in gorgeous sunshine, sitting on their 'verandah'. Getting ice for the gin and tonic was simple – a few paces to the glacier on the left of the hut and there was a never-ending supply. We watched as the Christmas parcels and mail were unloaded. The ship's surprise birthday present for the girls was a hand-made thunder-box, superbly crafted by the 'chippies', Stan Bugg and Adge Cutler. It was a wooden throne with canvas sides, complete with padded back-rest and dangling lavatory chain and handle. Cindy carried it up the beach in the most practical manner, box on shoulders and blond head through the polished seat. There was only one snag: it had been designed for burly six-foot sailors.

We left Cindy and Annie in peace once more, alone with

their elephants and Kings, after an invasion almost as traumatic as the one that we would all shortly share. Our next stop was Grytviken, where Nick's first task was to lay a wreath on Sir Ernest Shackleton's grave. The sun was so warm that I was able to go ashore in an ordinary suit, without overcoat or anorak. Nick conducted a simple but moving service in memory of 'The Boss', and we all paid our respects. It was interesting to read the various metal plaques on the grave, mainly from visiting Russian and Polish ships.[2] The carved granite headstone stood prominently among the graves of sealers, whalers and others who had died on South Georgia since 1846. Although only forty-eight when he died, Shackleton must surely rank as one of the greatest explorers of all time. On the reverse of his headstone was the quotation from Robert Browning 'I hold that a man should strive to the uttermost for his life's set prize'. No one could have striven harder than Shackleton, not only to achieve *his* life's set prize, but to have done it without losing the life of a single fellow man.

We walked from the cemetery to the old whaling station. Where once was all bustle and carnage and slaughter, all was now still and quiet, except for the occasional grunt of the elephant seal, whose reign was once more supreme. Gone, one hopes, forever are the days when whalers were licensed to take 6,000 bulls a year. As whales became scarce, the shore-based industry became less profitable and, by 1967, all whaling and sealing from South Georgia had ceased. Man's greed had destroyed his livelihood; but at least the demise of the whale had meant the reprieve of the seal.

Standing on the 'plan', the vast wooden apron onto which the huge whales were winched for flensing, the scene was more like an abandoned film set than an old whaling factory. Surely the snow-capped mountains were a painted backdrop, the white church a cardboard cut-out and the half-sunken whalers plywood models? To me, Grytviken was not a ghost town, as many had described it: there were no ghosts because it seemed too artificial ever to have been alive. We climbed the wooden steps from the 'plan' to the meat cookery, then through the guano factory to the bone cookery and meat extract plant, out onto the path and up to the church past the laundry, bath house, barracks and cinema (wherein we found reels of 35mm film scattered all over the projection room). The attractive white church had been built and used in Stromwen, Norway, before being dismantled and taken to Grytviken in 1913.

It was re-erected and re-opened on Christmas Day. We wondered whether the last Norwegians to leave had re-created their opening day, because the church was decorated for Christmas, with a crib and a Christmas tree near the pulpit. The organ still worked and the two bells (cast in Tonsberg) still chimed. We walked back to the harbour past the hospital, the whale oil tanks, the power house, the centrifuges, the blubber cookery and boiler house. Whaling had ceased in Grytviken in 1964, though caretakers remained until 1971, after which it was totally abandoned. BAS personnel had volunteered to look after the dam and watering facilities (which earned some revenue), one of the piers, the football pitch and the church; but the rest of the station was at the mercy of the elements and the mindless vandalism of visiting ships' crews.

We spent the afternoon at King Edward Point, with the BAS base commander, Peter Witty, and his deputy, Steve Martin. They had excellent accommodation in Shackleton House, which the FIG had built as a three-storey administrative building for its staff to serve the whaling industry. Unfortunately, as so often seemed to happen in the South Atlantic, it had just been completed when shore-based whaling ceased. FIDS (as BAS was then called) was thinking of extending its biological programmes at Signy at the time and a deal was struck by which FIDS was allowed to use all the FIG property and equipment at King Edward Point in return for taking over the Dependency's administrative functions. As well as base commander, Peter was therefore magistrate, harbour master, customs officer, immigration officer and assistant postmaster. These were not sinecures; as the years went by, more tour ships, yachtsmen and fishing vessels dropped anchor in Cumberland Bay and came ashore, wanting stamps, water or simply an unusual 'chop' in their passports. As we shall see, the most testing time was about to descend upon Steve Martin, who was due to take over from Peter Witty at the end of the summer.

That evening, we sailed for Bird Island to visit the BAS field station there. Bird Island was off the western tip of South Georgia, which meant that we traversed the island from end to end, a distance of about a hundred miles. Next morning, it was blowing a Force Nine gale, which ruled out flying. During a lull, Tony was able to drop mail at the hut, but conditions were too bad to transport passengers. We therefore sailed back to Leith, where we were able to go ashore by boat. Leith was the largest of the old whaling stations, and the last to close, in 1966. Here was no romantic setting, like Grytviken: this was Teesside compared with Speyside. Ghosts were everywhere. We even found a half-finished meal of rice on a plate, dried solid, as if the Japanese (the last to use the base) had been interrupted during lunch. Elephant seals had moved in. We opened one door and a startled bull came roaring out, lolloping across the railway lines that ran down to the jetty as if they were fronds of seaweed. Every building was an Aladdin's cave: there were lathes, generators, steel plates, iron girders, well-seasoned timber, hammers, picks, shovels, axes, nails, screws, nuts and bolts, coils of wire, cooking utensils, ladders, trolleys, tools, flensing knives and harpoons. Most remarkable was the hospital. Nick was upset that it had been ransacked since his visit the previous year, but it was still packed with equipment and medical supplies. There were rolls of cotton wool, lint and bandages. The dentist's chair still stood in the middle of the room, surrounded by dentist's tools, though vandals had smashed the windows and the snow was creeping inexorably towards it. There were thousands of medicines on the shelves. The operating theatre was largely intact, with oxygen bottles still standing at the head of the table and scalpels in the sink. The ward still contained beds, though mattresses, pillows and blankets had disappeared. In one room, we found a *Daily Herald* and a *Daily Mirror*, dated 15 August, 1960, in excellent condition.

More valuable to Senor Davidoff was the floating (now semi-submerged) dock at Stromness. We landed there by helicopter and it was immediately apparent that this had been the main ship-repair yard for the whaling industry. The ship's propellers lying near the jetty were of considerable value and there was more heavy equipment inside the warehouse. If Davidoff refloated the dock (and it looked as though only one corner needed pumping out), he could load it with scrap and tow it to South America. A costly exercise, but we calculated that he could reasonably expect to make over £1 million from the sale of the dock and the scrap.

The third whaling station in Stromness Bay was Husvik, and it was there that we saw our first reindeer. They were much whiter than we had expected, and quite timid. The original importation of three stags and seven hinds from Norway, probably in 1911, had been made at Ocean Harbour, south of Grytviken, and their descendants formed the southern herd, which had spread as far as St Andrews and Royal Bay. They had been unable, however, to cross the glaciers to the north and the reindeer that we now saw had come from a later importation of three stags and four hinds at

Husvik in 1925. They had developed into the present northern herd, which had access to more areas than the southern. It is possible that, if glacial recession were to continue at its present rate, the two herds might join up at some time in the future. At the time of our visit, the total population was estimated at about 2,000. Shooting for sport and fresh meat was permitted, but only under licence issued by the base commander at Grytviken. (Incidentally, one of the conditions in Davidoff's contract was that he was not allowed to hunt or shoot reindeer.)

We left Husvik with one piece of loot that we thought Davidoff would not miss: an outsize rolling pin. The weather having abated somewhat, Nick decided to try again to get into Bird Island. Although flying conditions were marginal (Mavis decided against), we managed to find a landing spot some distance from the BAS hut and, despite being surrounded by soaring wanderers, touched down safely. A baby skua scuttled away as we unstrapped and a wandering albatross sat sedately on its nest not ten feet away, totally ignoring the noisy Wasp and its down-draught. The base commander, Peter Prince, came up to meet us. He had a stick and advised us to stay close to him as we walked through the fur seal rookery to the hut. The bulls, he said, were apt to be aggressive and could give one a nasty bite. The approach to the hut was amazing: fur seals lined the valley down to the beach, which was as crowded as Blackpool on a summer's day, and little black pups scampered from under our feet; indeed, we had to walk round one mother and baby who refused to budge. There were seals everywhere, even under the BAS huts. At one time, all the shores of South Georgia had been like this, but by 1830 the demands of fashion for ladies' fur coats had resulted in the population being all but exterminated. Peter said that 40,000 pups had been born in the rookery in the past fortnight, so the species was in no danger now. All would not survive, but he estimated that the population was increasing by about ten per cent a year. The handsome bulls were much bigger than the females and fought each other fiercely to win or defend their breeding territory. They normally had a harem of anything up to fifteen cows and guarded them jealously.

On our way down to the hut, we had noticed several bull carcasses. Peter explained that the old bulls, exhausted by too much fighting and mating, would crawl up the valley to die. He and his colleagues had been tagging pups (and wandering albatross) since 1957 and the station had been manned every summer for the last ten years. Now, to my surprise, they were building a new hut with improved facilities and accommodation for eight men, their current strength, and intended to operate it as a permanent base. It was clearly a useful ornithological and seal research station, and a naturalist's paradise, but I wondered how BAS could afford to do this at a time when there were insufficient funds to keep Grytviken open. On our way back to the helicopter, Peter demonstrated that the wanderer was just as gentle as her smaller black-browed cousin. He lifted out an egg from under a sitting bird, which did no more than make a few clapping noises with its beak.

Back on board, Nick received the welcome news that a RAF Hercules was flying another Wasp out to Montevideo to replace Number 435, so it was time to say farewell to what old BAS hands derisively termed 'the banana belt' and head back to Stanley. Signy would have to wait until next season. The weather was extremely bad for the first two days. At the Sunday church service, it was difficult to stand and, playing bridge after dinner, the table toppled over. We were glad to see Diana and Tony waiting for us at Stanley jetty, home for the Christmas holidays. We did not know it at the time but, as the *Endurance* battled through the South Atlantic gales away from South Georgia, the Argentine naval ice-breaker, *Almirante Irizar*, was on the way there from Buenos Aires. On board was Senor Davidoff, the scrap-metal merchant, who had notified our Embassy in Buenos Aires of the visit in a letter which arrived after he had departed. Normally, radio courtesies would have been exchanged between the two ships but, on this occasion, the Argentine navy maintained radio silence.

We celebrated Christmas, 1981, in traditional style. On Christmas Day, Mavis and I went round the hospital in the morning and held our Christmas party in the evening, with guests from the *Endurance* and the *Bransfield*. The Stanley Sports started on Boxing Day in glorious sunshine and most of us got badly sunburnt. The steer-riding was completed without accident and the whole meeting declared a resounding success. The only sour note to the festive atmosphere was a signal from Peter Witty that the Argentines had made a clandestine landing at Leith on 20 December (two days after we were there). The *Almirante Irizar* had been seen by the crew of a visiting French yacht. Peter had gone to Leith to investigate on 23 December to find that the birds had flown but had left ample evidence that they had been ashore. Chalked on the BAS emergency depot was a notice claiming possession of South Georgia in the name of Argentina – and the date.

The other pieces of the jigsaw came from our Embassy in Buenos Aires and from Salvesen's in Edinburgh, whom Davidoff had also notified on the day of his departure from the mainland. In landing at Leith without reporting to Peter Witty at Grytviken, Davidoff had not only broken the terms of his contract with Salvesen's, he had also broken the law of the Dependencies, with which he had pledged to comply. More significantly, Captain Trombetta had violated all the norms of international law by taking his vessel – a naval ship – into British territorial waters without prior diplomatic clearance, ignoring the recognised port of entry and sending a landing party ashore without permission. In my view, he would not have done this without the approval of Admiral Anaya, the Commander-in-Chief of the Argentine Navy, and my immediate reaction was that here was the beginning of another Southern Thule. Anaya was once again testing the water and, if we allowed him to get away with it, the Falkland Islanders would have another nail in their coffin. I recommended to the FCO that we should institute proceedings against Davidoff and make the strongest protest to the Argentine Government. The FCO sent instructions to Anthony Williams to deliver a formal protest in the strongest terms, but instructed me not to institute proceedings against Davidoff under Falkland Islands Dependencies law because, as the telegram put it, this 'would risk provoking a most serious incident which could escalate and have an unforeseeable outcome'.[3]

The last day of 1981 was overcast, with strong chill winds, violent hail squalls and the menace of worse to come. It was an appropriate harbinger of 1982.

Notes

1. 'Katabatic' is a meteorological term for a body of air that flows downwards with great force, gathering momentum as it goes. In South Georgia, it tends to build up over the mountain tops and sweep down the glaciers to the sea. It is a great menace to all who travel by land, sea or air.

2. Sadly, on our last visit to the grave, in 1985, most of the plaques had disappeared – taken, presumably, by souvenir hunters.

3. *Falkland Islands Review:* Report of a Committee of Privy Counsellors, January, 1983 (Comnd 8787, page 48)

10

The Gathering Storm

In my address to the Legislative Council on 5 January, I tried to strike a more cheerful note by pointing out that, although 1981 had been a depressing year in many ways, there was a brighter side with the start of our policy of giving the Islanders a stake in their own land. It was an inescapable fact, however, that the Islanders' relations with both Britain and Argentina had deteriorated during the year. The leaseback initiative was effectively dead, but Islanders' suspicions of the British Government's intentions had been increased by a number of other unconnected matters, including the announcement of the withdrawal of HMS *Endurance*, the denial of British citizenship to Falkland Islanders and financial cuts to BAS, especially the threatened closure of the Grytviken base.

Argentina had further antagonised the Islanders by a series of actions which had demonstrated a combination of arrogance, insensitivity and inefficiency, notably the recent reduction of the air service from two flights a week to one without warning or explanation; unauthorised overflights by Argentine Air Force Hercules (there had been six recently); the LADE house affair; the *Yehuin* incident; the contaminated fuel argument; the YPF bills squabble and, now, the *Almirante Irizar*'s unauthorised call at South Georgia. Islanders had also noted with unease the change of government in Argentina in December. General Galtieri was the first president to retain his position as Commander-in-Chief of the Army and was therefore in a stronger position than any of his predecessors. He was also a close friend of Admiral Anaya, who was known to be the most hawkish of the senior commanders on the Falklands issue. The new Foreign Minister, Dr Costa Mendez, was remembered by Islanders as the minister who had conducted negotiations with Britain during the last sovereignty crisis in 1968.

On the domestic scene, the year started badly with a strike by the Stanley jetty gang, who refused to follow their camp colleagues and accept a fifty per cent cut in the cost-of-living bonus. Determined action by David Britton, whom Ted Needham had appointed as the

London-based Managing Director of the FIC, resulted in a speedy collapse of the strike; but industrial relations were not as harmonious as they had been. On a personal note, my Cessna aircraft, which had been expected from the factory in the USA before the end of 1981, failed to appear. The ferry company reported difficulty in finding a pilot willing to bring it as far as the Falklands.

There was the usual flat feeling after Diana and Tony left at the end of the Christmas holidays. Tony was due to rejoin us for Easter, but Diana would not be coming out again until the (northern) summer. Her relationship with John Thurman had developed apace and he would be on leave in England for Easter. To his everlasting regret, he was to miss the night of the invasion because, as second-in-command, he had arrived a month ahead of his detachment and would thus be leaving correspondingly earlier. We gave him a farewell party in February little realising that, when we were next to meet, it would be at their wedding in Sunningdale.

There were still some smaller settlements that we had not yet visited, but urgent problems and visitors kept me in Stanley for the early part of the year. Hector Gilobert brought in his successor, Roberto Gamin, a Hercules pilot, who seemed pleasant enough but whose English was poor. I hoped that it would improve as much as Hector's had during his two years with us in Stanley. We gave a farewell party for Hector and Teresa and were genuinely sorry to see them go in early February. Interesting visitors at this time included a lone yachtsman, Paul Rogers, who was attempting a *twice*-round-the-world trip in his yacht *Spirit of Pentax*, and a team from the Scott Polar Research Institute which included the lovely Norwegian scientist, Monica Kristensen, who was later to achieve fame by leading a valiant but unsuccessful expedition to retrace Amundsen's route to the South Pole, using dogs (but not killing them). Leader of the team was Dr Vernon Squire and they were joining HMS *Endurance* for a trip south to study the behaviour and break-up of Antarctic tabular icebergs. We saw them both before and after their trip and, like us, they developed a great affection for the *Endurance* and her crew. It so happened that we were entertaining them in Government House when Don announced that *Endurance* was leaving. We dashed into the garden and watched her steam slowly out of sight. Monica could not hold back the tears.

A new Polish mother ship came into Port William to replace the *Gryf Pomorski*. She was the *Kuszaby II* and we had an excellent outing to her, with over a dozen Commerson's dolphins playing at the *Lively*'s bows as we went through the Narrows. Her master, Captain Krolikowski, was much younger than Captain Szostak, but an equally charming and generous host. He took us along to the ship's cinema to see 'Hair', which brought back memories of our turbulent time in Saigon; but there was no toast to the Allies during this film.

Mavis managed to get away to Darwin for the East Falkland Sports, but I had to stay in Stanley to see Dick Laws and Sir Donald Logan, who came in on the *Bransfield*. Sir Donald was a diplomatic colleague who had been Britain's representative at the Law of the Sea Conference, and at Dick's request was conducting an inquiry into fire precautions on BAS bases. Fire was an ever-present hazard in the hostile environment of the Antarctic and there had been some serious incidents in the past. My discussions with Dick naturally centred on Grytviken and how we could increase revenue and reduce costs.

Eventually, on 19 February, my aircraft arrived. It had been abandoned by the ferry pilot at Rio Gallegos. He had made one stab at getting to the Falklands, but the prospect of all that water had apparently frightened him off. He had returned to Rio Gallegos and caught the next flight back to the USA. Eddie Anderson came to my rescue: he and 'Robbie' Robson, one of the two RAF technicians, volunteered to go to Rio Gallegos and fly it over for me. After many difficulties, Eddie talked his way into the airfield and persuaded the Argentine authorities to release the aircraft. The ferry tank took up all the passenger space (enough fuel for a twelve-hour flight) so Robbie had to return the way they had gone, via Comodoro Rivadavia and LADE. Eddie flew solo from Rio Gallegos to Stanley in three hours. As soon as I had some free time, Robin Pitaluga took me in my aircraft to his airfield at Salvador. His three strips enabled me to become familiar with take-offs and landings more-or-less into wind before tackling cross-wind landings at the single runway in Stanley.

On 24 February I saw off Councillors Tim Blake and John Cheek, bound for New York and the next round of talks with the Argentines. The day before, they had called on me at Government House and had met Lord and Lady Buxton, who had flown in that day to sail south in the *Endurance* on her last work period before going home to the scrapyard. Lord Buxton told me that he had had a private conversation with Dr Costa Mendez (the Argentine Foreign Minister) before leaving Buenos Aires, and had received the impression that, though the Junta were increasing pressure on him to produce a solution to the sovereignty issue, an invasion of the Falklands was unlikely. He could not, however, rule out unopposed landings elsewhere, probably in South Georgia.

That same day, Senor Davidoff had called at the British Embassy in Buenos Aires to apologise for the problems caused by his visit to Leith on the *Almirante Irizar* in December and to give notice that he intended soon to return to South Georgia with a party to start collecting the scrap. In order not to cause further difficulties, he asked for full instructions on how to proceed. Mike Hickson (who had taken over from Richard Gozney as the Embassy's 'Mr Falklands') had told him that he must report to Grytviken on arrival and follow the procedures laid down by the base commander. Mike gave me this account when he arrived in the Falklands for a week's visit on 9 March. He agreed that Davidoff had been deceptively naive, knew full well that he had to report to Grytviken and had known in December. I expressed the view that he had been let off too lightly; he should have been told that he had already broken the law, that he was extremely fortunate in being given another chance and that next time he must give adequate notice and stick rigidly to the terms of his contract, otherwise he would be declared a prohibited immigrant.

Fortuitously, Peter Witty was in Stanley during Mike's visit, on his way home after handing over to Steve Martin. We both briefed Mike on exactly what he should tell Davidoff when he next made contact. Meanwhile, however, Davidoff had followed his December tactic by notifying the Embassy on the day that Mike flew to Stanley that he was sending forty-one workmen to South Georgia only two days later. He had prudently decided not to accompany them, but was sending his son. They would stay at Leith for an initial period of four months and would be transported on the *Bahia Buen Suceso*. On 11 March, Davidoff's lawyer had telephoned the Embassy to confirm the imminent sailing of the *Bahia Buen Suceso* and, in Mike's absence, David Joy had taken the call and stressed that the ship should first report to King Edward Point, Grytviken, for entry purposes. In any event, the ship's master, Captain Briatore, was an experienced Argentine naval officer and must have known that Grytviken was the official port of entry and that he had to report there before proceeding to Leith.

Hard on the heels of the *Bahia Buen Suceso*'s sailing came the disappointing news from Salvesen's that they were prepared after all to extend Davidoff's contract for another two years, until 31 March, 1984, upon receipt of an additional payment.[1] The FCO stuck to the view that this was a purely commercial transaction with which it could not interfere, while our Embassy in Buenos Aires sought to play down the role of the Argentine navy and portray the whole affair as 'just a piece of low-level bravura combined with Davidoff's well-known fecklessness'. Seen from Stanley, Davidoff was being used by the Argentine navy (if not the Junta) in a carefully planned operation to exert the Argentine claim to South Georgia by establishing a physical presence at Leith. British reactions were being tested and worse would follow if the response was timid and the illegalities condoned. I sent a warning signal to Steve Martin, outlining the procedure to be followed if the *Bahia Buen Suceso* turned up at King Edward Point.

As events moved inexorably towards a crisis in South Georgia, councillors considered the situation in the aftermath of the New York talks. Tim Blake and John Cheek had arrived back in Stanley on 2 March. Unknown to us at the time, on that same day General Galtieri was breaking the news to General Menendez that a decision had been taken to recover 'Las Islas Malvinas' by force and that he was to be the Governor. Tim and John explained to Joint Councils (less Bill Luxton, who was still shearing) the background to the joint *communiqué* issued after the talks, which stated:

> The meeting took place in a cordial and positive spirit. The two sides reaffirmed their resolve to find a solution to the sovereignty dispute and considered in detail an Argentine proposal for procedures to make better progress in this sense. They agreed to inform their Governments accordingly.

According to Tim and John, the Argentine delegation had started the talks by proposing a system of monthly meetings of top-level officials with a pre-established agenda and at a pre-arranged meeting place, with the aim of achieving recognition of Argentine sovereignty over the Falklands, South Georgia and South Sandwich Islands by the 150th anniversary of Britain's 'illegal usurpation of Las Malvinas', ie 3 January, 1983. The British delegation had of course rejected these proposals but had agreed, *ad referendum*, to establish a permanent negotiating commission. Most of the subsequent discussion had been about the detailed arrangements for this commission: for instance, it would be presided over by ministers, who would direct its work and decide on the agenda of, and participation in, meetings. Islanders could be represented and 'all elements' in the dispute would be considered. The period of operation of the commission would be for one year, at the end of which ministers would review progress and reach conclusions on whether the commission should continue its work. Tim and John stressed that no fixed agenda or timetable was agreed. Either party could terminate the commission at any time, meetings would be held alternately in the capitals of the two countries and would be chaired by the host minister or a senior official nominated by him.

This was bad enough; but councillors had been led to expect worse by a misleading *communiqué* which the Argentine Ministry of Foreign affairs had issued on the same day as the joint *communiqué* (and before the Argentine delegation had returned to Buenos Aires) setting out the Argentine delegation's opening position as if it were the conclusion reached by both parties at the end of the talks. The general public in the Islands had picked this up on the radio and were naturally alarmed: they wanted to hear the truth from the two councillors who had been there. Unfortunately for Tim and John, the FCO would not allow them to go on the air and put the record straight because both parties at the talks had agreed that the proposals for the commission would remain confidential until their respective governments had been consulted. It made no difference that the Argentine Ministry of Foreign Affairs had already broken the agreement. Tim and John were therefore confined to denying the Argentine statement without being able to say exactly what *had* been agreed. No wonder, then, that the *Penguin News* was extremely critical, unfairly blaming the FIG for keeping the Islanders in the dark on a fundamental issue affecting their future. Nor were the Islanders placated by Mr Luce's reassuring statement in the House of Commons that there would be no contemplation of transfer of sovereignty without consulting the wishes of the Islanders. Councillors were angry but, to their credit, there was no breach of confidentiality; they all realised what a sensitive position we were in and had no wish to make life more difficult for Mr Luce or Lord Carrington. After the unilateral *communiqué* of the Argentine Ministry of Foreign Affairs and the bellicose attitude of the Argentine press, however, councillors were opposed to *any* further talks.

On 9 March, the FCO asked for councillors' views on a draft

message which Lord Carrington proposed to send to Dr Mendez. It expressed Lord Carrington's pleasure at the progress that had been made in New York towards setting up new procedures for carrying forward and giving fresh impetus to negotiations about the future of the Islands, which reflected his Government's determination to achieve a peaceful solution to a difficult issue that would be acceptable to both governments and to the people of the Falkland Islands, while expressing disappointment at the statements which had been made in the press reports in Buenos Aires following the talks. It sought agreement on two essential points: first, that the negotiating commission would encompass all aspects of possible approaches to a solution of the dispute, without prejudice to either side's position on sovereignty – 'these talks must be genuine negotiations and cannot be based on any predetermined assumptions on what the outcome might be' – and, secondly, that the negotiations could not be pursued against a background of threats from either side of retaliatory action if they broke down.[2]

As councillors had dispersed only the weekend before (and it was still the busy season in camp), we were unable to re-assemble before 16 March. To my relief, councillors agreed unanimously that Lord Carrington's message should go to Dr Mendez, without amendment, and the FCO was so informed. Events in South Georgia were now, however, to overtake this initiative, and the message was never sent.

On the evening of 17 March, while HMS *Endurance* was on her way from Grytviken to Stanley and we were giving a farewell party in Stanley for the *John Biscoe*, the *Bahia Buen Suceso*, observing radio silence, was approaching South Georgia. The next morning, she did not sail in to Cumberland Bay to report to King Edward Point, but crept in to Leith harbour. That same morning, a field party set out by launch from King Edward Point to Carlita Bay with the intention of trekking overland to Husvik and thence to Leith to finish moving emergency stores from the manager's house to the smaller customs house, which they would then batten down for the winter. Following the *Almirante Irizar*'s illegal landing in December (and some subsequent looting by French yachts), the base commander had had a substantial wooden noticeboard constructed in bold red and white lettering stating: 'British Antarctic Survey – Leith Field Station – Unauthorised Entry Prohibited', the last line being repeated in Spanish, Russian, Polish and

French. One of the *Endurance*'s helicopters had deposited the noticeboard at the manager's house and it was the field party's final task to erect it outside the customs house before returning to King Edward Point.

After spending the night at Husvik, the four BAS men trekked to Leith, arriving in the early afternoon. At almost the same time, HMS *Endurance* was dropping anchor in Port Stanley and the Argentine navy's latest support ship, the *Bahia Paraiso*, was one day out from Ushuaia, flying the pennant of the navy's senior officer, Antarctic Squadron, Captain Trombetta, and carrying a party of *buzo tactico* – marine commandos – under the command of the notorious Lieutenant Alfredo Astiz, with instructions to land at Leith and secure the scrap-merchants' base.

Approaching Leith harbour, the BAS men heard several rifle shots and saw the *Bahia Buen Suceso* berthed at the deep-water jetty. Cargo was being unloaded and there were almost fifty men ashore, some in civilian clothes and others in white military-style uniforms. An Argentine flag flew from the top of the generator station. They entered the manager's house and found twelve men sitting at the table eating reindeer steaks. The word 'British' on the noticeboard had been scrawled over and 'Argentina' substituted.

Finding no English speaker, two of the field party, Trefor Edwards and Neil Shaw, went aboard the *Bahia Buen Suceso* and met Captain Briatore, who to their relief spoke English. In an amicable atmosphere, they advised him that he should have reported first to Grytviken for clearance formalities and he replied that the British Embassy in Buenos Aires had given him permission to land at Leith and that the base commander at Grytviken should have been so notified. Trefor Edwards had a VHF set with him and relayed this information to Steve Martin at King Edward Point. Bob Headland laboured over the antiquated and unfamiliar cyphers that were our only secure link between South Georgia and Stanley and eventually, having failed to raise Cable and Wireless, managed to pass the message to me via the *Endurance*. It arrived while we were having dinner at Government House with Lord and Lady Buxton, who were spending a few nights ashore with us.

Early the next morning, I went on board the *Endurance*, spoke to Steve Martin over the ship's radio and sent him the following message to be delivered to the leader of the Argentine shore party at Leith:

1 You have landed illegally at Leith without obtaining proper clearance.

2 You and your party must go back on board the *Bahia Buen Suceso* immediately and report to Base Commander, Grytviken, for further instructions.

3 You must remove the Argentine flag from Leith.

4 You must not interfere with the BAS depot at Leith.

5 You must not alter or deface any of the notices at Leith.

6 No military personnel are allowed to land in South Georgia.

7 No firearms are to be taken ashore.

I then reported the facts and my action to the FCO, giving my view that the Argentine navy was using Davidoff as a front to establish an Argentine presence on South Georgia and suggesting that, since this was the second violation by Davidoff, the party should be ordered to leave South Georgia even if it did report to Grytviken. Having consulted Nick Barker, I also suggested that, if the Argentines did not comply with my instructions, HMS *Endurance* should sail to South Georgia the next day with Royal Marines embarked to ensure that the Argentines left.

The FCO demonstrated the speed with which Whitehall could move in a crisis by responding within hours in a most helpful and positive manner. It agreed with my instructions to the base commander and instructed the Ambassador in Buenos Aires to tell the Argentine Ministry of Foreign Affairs that the incident was regarded as serious and that, if the *Bahia Buen Suceso* did not leave forthwith, the British Government would have to take whatever action seemed necessary. The Argentine Charge d'Affaires in London was also summoned and given the same message.

While we waited to hear whether Nick would be going to Montevideo to collect the new detachment of Royal Marines or to South Georgia to evict the scrap-metal merchants, *Endurance*'s football team secured their first-ever win of the Stanley Shield. I presented it to their captain, Sergeant Peter Leach, who was shortly to do even better at Grytviken and receive the DSM for bravery.

The expected telegram arrived that evening as Iain and Hulda Stewart were giving their traditional farewell supper party for *Endurance*. Nick and I withdrew to Hulda's kitchen and, while she and Iain passed to and fro dispensing trays of food and drink, we read the following signal from the FCO: 'CINCFleet is sending instructions to Captain HMS *Endurance* to leave for South Georgia at 0930Z on 21 March.'[3] We brought Aubrey out of the party because he and Maria had been expecting to go to Montevideo in the *Endurance* to catch their homeward flight, and consequently had left most of their luggage on board. Nick arranged a boat for them at first light the next morning. He had planned to leave the flight and the ship's section of Royal Marines in the Falklands while *Endurance* collected the new detachment of NP 8901. Now all was changed and he gave instructions for the Wasps to be recovered immediately from Green Patch. We agreed that his thirteen Royal Marines should be augmented by nine men from NP 8901, bringing them up to platoon strength, and Gary Noott went off to organise them and their kit, with additional arms and ammunition. It did not occur to any of us at the time that they might be needed to defend Stanley. Nick decided that there was no time to recover the *James Caird* from Berkeley Sound. The hydrographers would remain in Stanley, to work on their charts and, incidentally, to leave more space on board for the extra Royal Marines. Finally, Nick despatched all the members of the *Endurance* present to round up the rest of the crew from various parts of Stanley.

The FCO required us to conceal the *Endurance*'s change of destination, but I am afraid that it was a forlorn hope. Too many Islanders were aware of – indeed, were involved in – the arrangements that had been made in anticipation of her run to Montevideo, and the ham radios were already buzzing with news of the Argentine landing at Leith. Confirmation came with the announcement that the *John Biscoe* was returning to Stanley with the new Royal Marine detachment from Montevideo. Nevertheless, we maintained the pretence by adhering to the FCO's form of words: 'HMS *Endurance* is still in Falkland waters and available to assist if necessary.'

We were up at six on a cold and bleak Sunday morning, 21 March. I accompanied Aubrey and Maria across a choppy harbour to say farewell to Nick. On the jetty, my nine Royal Marines were assembled, looking extremely warlike with their weaponry and combat gear. They were brimming with confidence and asked me to make sure that they would be allowed to land at Leith and evict the 'Argies'. On board, Sgt Leach promised to look after the Stanley Shield and bring it safely back, and I took the opportunity to have what was to become my daily early morning schedule with Steve

Martin at Grytviken. The field party had withdrawn the previous day from Leith, having delivered my instructions. They noticed that the Argentine flag had been hauled down, but had heard more shots fired as they left, presumably aimed at the reindeer. At my request, Steve established an observation post at a high pass west of Jason Harbour, overlooking Stromness Bay. With powerful binoculars, it was possible from there to observe the activities at Leith and, with a VHF radio, to monitor the Argentines' ship-to-shore communications. Bob Headland understood Spanish and was able to maintain a running commentary back to Steve at King Edward Point. Despite the freezing cold, the small BAS contingent – ten in all – bravely manned this observation post until relieved by the Royal Marines from HMS *Endurance* four days later. Their observations on 21 March indicated that more drums of fuel were being unloaded and that Captain Briatore hoped to finish unloading and sail at 4pm. The shore party invited him to lunch on barbecued reindeer meat and he asked for another reindeer to be shot before he sailed.

Back in Stanley, shortly after lunch, the new chief police officer, Ronnie Lamb, reported an incident at the LADE office the night before. Apparently someone had entered, using a key, draped a Union Jack over the Argentine flag next to the Vicecomodoro's desk, carefully removed the trays from the desk, stacked them neatly in a corner and inscribed on the desk-top in toothpaste: 'Tit for tat you buggers'. When asked why it had taken him so long to report the incident, Gamin had explained that he had been trying to work out from his English-Spanish dictionary what the words meant! Two nights later, someone sprayed on the LADE office window the letters 'UK OK' in aerosol paint.

These two incidents were magnified out of all proportion by the Argentine press: 'Barbarous Piratical Reaction – LADE Offices Attacked' was one of the more sober headlines. Our Embassy in Buenos Aires quoted Ministry of Foreign Affairs spokesmen as alleging that this was a 'parallel insult' to Davidoff's party hoisting the Argentine flag in Leith. More realistically, a senior official pointed out to Anthony Williams that the captain of an Argentine naval support vessel should not have been expected to request permission to enter what Argentine law did not recognise as foreign territory, and that these problems should have been faced before the salvage contract was authorised. This was one point on which we could agree.

On Monday, 22 March, on our early morning schedule (which

by now all the radio hams on the Islands were listening to), Steve reported that the *Bahia Buen Suceso* had sailed from Leith the previous evening and that his two observers, Neil Shaw and Peter Stark, had since seen no sign of the shore party. We arranged a twice-daily schedule thereafter and, in the hope that Captain Briatore was intending to follow my instructions and report to Grytviken for clearance, Steve and Bob Headland began to prepare the necessary paper work for fifty temporary immigrants. During the day, Aubrey made use of my communications facilities to send a personal message to Lord Carrington, stating that it was naive to regard Davidoff as a casual scrap-dealer and that his contract should be rescinded immediately in view of the deliberate breaches of its terms. He judged that, if the British reaction was placatory, more illegal landings would follow, the next time probably in the Falkland Islands. We both thought, however, that a full-scale military action against the Islands was unlikely until all other forms of pressure had been exhausted. The logical scenario was deadlock in the talks; international action at the United Nations; diplomatic and commercial reprisals and then, and only then, military invasion. As to the time-scale, I envisaged deteriorating relations until the failure of a final attempt by Lord Carrington and Dr Mendez to reach a diplomatic solution at the October UN meeting, followed by a withdrawal of the air service and other economic action against the Islanders, with a possible invasion to coincide with the 150th anniversary in January, 1983 (ironically, I had held a meeting that day of our own 150th Anniversary Celebrations committee).

On our evening schedule, Steve reported (as we had feared) that some Argentines, later estimated to be about thirty, were still at Leith and that a French yacht, the *Cinq Gars Pour*, which had been in King Edward Cove, had ignored his instructions and sailed into Leith harbour. Peter Stark had observed it helping the Argentines to recover a barge which had been blown from Leith jetty overnight to a position directly below the observation post. He had also spotted six men on Leith jetty operating a crane. Nick Barker reported that he had intercepted a message from Argentine naval headquarters congratulating the *Bahia Buen Suceso* on a successful operation and directing her to return to Buenos Aires as soon as possible.

In Stanley, Dick and Connie Baker entertained us, the Buxtons and two American businessmen to dinner, during which the main topic of conversation was kelp. The Americans were interested in our massive kelp beds, which they said were the largest reserves in the world. They were extremely knowledgeable about the international alginate industry and saw a bright future for Falklands kelp, using a new, wet-processing method on board a factory ship and cropping the top four feet of the kelp *ad infinitum*. We naturally welcomed this as much-needed diversification for our one-crop economy. Back home, Aubrey and I relaxed before retiring (as we did each evening) with a game of snooker, which he invariably won.

There was no change in the scene at Leith on 23 March, and we spent much of the day in discussion with our American visitors on a future kelp industry. The LADE flight arrived as usual and we went to the airport to meet Tony, who was due to spend his Easter holidays with us. He struggled with a suitcase laden with books that he should have studied during the last two terms. He had a lot of catching up to do before taking 'A' levels in June.

In London, Mr Luce told the House of Commons about the landing at Leith and said that arrangements were being made to ensure the Argentines' early departure. In Buenos Aires, Anthony Williams was instructed to tell the Ministry of Foreign Affairs that the British Government had decided that HMS *Endurance* should continue to South Georgia in order to remove the remaining Argentines. He was summoned to see Dr Mendez, who expressed surprise that the British Government was proceeding so rapidly to such very grave action, without exhausting the diplomatic options; if action to remove the Argentines was not postponed, moderates like himself would lose control of events. Anthony warned the FCO that, seen from Buenos Aires, the British Government's reaction to Davidoff's 'trivial and low-level misbehaviour' could do lasting damage to the whole structure of bilateral relations. FCO Ministers decided to make a further attempt to resolve the problem without provocation. HMS *Endurance* was advised to change course for Grytviken and await further instructions, while Anthony was instructed to deliver a personal message from Lord Carrington to Dr Mendez, agreeing to the removal of the men by the *Bahia Buen Suceso* but making it clear that, if this was not done without delay, we had no choice but to remove them ourselves. The overriding need was to secure the right political climate for mutual efforts to resolve the Falkland Islands dispute peacefully through negotiations.[4]

Anthony finished a busy day by carrying out these instructions and telegraphing the FCO to say that Dr Mendez had welcomed

Lord Carrington's message and assumed that it would be possible for another Argentine ship (not necessarily the *Bahia Buen Suceso*) to remove the men. He was about to discuss this with the military. Anthony commented that he thought Dr Mendez was trying to be helpful and sensible.

Early the next day, 24 March, Anthony reported that Dr Mendez was hopeful of arranging the evacuation of the Argentine workmen, not by the *Bahia Buen Suceso*, but by an alternative Argentine vessel. In Stanley, we were also up and about early, to run Aubrey and Maria to the airport for the LADE flight at 7.30am. Fellow travellers with the Buxtons were Fred and Cecilia Gooch, long-time Stanley residents (he had been manager of the first ill-fated alginates enterprise) but not kelpers. Cecilia was in a wheelchair and Fred was taking her over to Comodoro Rivadavia for treatment. I wished her a speedy recovery and exchanged a few words with him. How I wish he had told me then what he told me upon his return after the war; namely, that Captain Gaffoglio had been in Stanley for the last two weeks, asking him details about Mullet Creek and walking along the beaches between the airport and Cape Pembroke. Dashing back to Cable and Wireless for my morning schedule with Steve Martin, I was relieved to hear that the *Endurance* had arrived off King Edward Point at 6am and that the Royal Marines were taking over the observation post from the hard-pressed BAS men.

At lunchtime, we entertained a couple who had arrived on the LADE flight the day before with Tony: John and Pamela Dixon. He was a freelance photographer working on an assignment for the *Daily Mirror* and she was gathering material for an article for *Woman's Own*. More to the point, they had kindly brought with them the blocks for our 150th Anniversary celebrations. Designed by Father Monaghan, they were required so that Joe King could make a start with the advance printing of the programmes, posters, etc. Joe was delighted when I handed them over to him that afternoon. Despite the impending crisis in South Georgia, normal work had to proceed and the rest of the afternoon was occupied with a meeting to work out the arrangements for the sub-division of Roy Cove. We agreed that I should fly there on 2 April to present the title documents to the new owners. Later that evening, as Tony and I were watching England beating Wales in the rugby international on video, I received a copy of another signal from Anthony to the FCO, saying that he had seen Dr

Mendez again, who was looking exhausted and had told him that he was having great difficulty, particularly with Admiral Anaya, and asked for more time to devise some alternative to action by *Endurance*.

The next morning, 25 March, my spirits rose when Steve reported that the *Bahia Paraiso* had arrived at Leith Harbour at dawn, but they were quickly dashed when he said that the ship appeared to be *un*loading, not loading. Nick confirmed this from the *Endurance* later in the morning, adding that three landing craft and a military helicopter were plying between the *Bahia Paraiso* and Leith jetty, off-loading stores and equipment.

During the day, there were more diplomatic exchanges between London and Buenos Aires, culminating in instructions to Anthony to tell Dr Mendez that, as an ultimate effort of goodwill, if the Argentine party went to Grytviken, documentation would be issued to enable it to return to Leith. On the BBC Overseas news that evening, it was reported that the Argentines had despatched several warships to support the *Bahia Paraiso*.

On my morning schedule, 26 March, I asked Steve to prepare certificates of identity and immigration forms in case the Argentines decided to comply with the British Government's final request. Dr Mendez had suggested merely stamping the Argentines' 'white cards', with which they had been issued by the Ministry of Foreign Affairs before departure from Buenos Aires (thus indicating, incidentally, the MFA's collusion in the navy's plans); but I had argued that the 1971 Communications Agreement, under which the 'white cards' were issued, did not apply to South Georgia but only to the Falkland Islands, and that proper documentation meant stamping the Argentines' passports with a normal entry permit. If, as seemed likely, the scrap workers did not possess passports, the base commander would issue them with temporary certificates of identity, bearing an entry permit for sixteen weeks, which was the time estimated by Davidoff to complete the work. This was imposing a heavy burden upon Steve and Bob Headland (in the event, about twelve hours' typing) but it was important to uphold the principle that the 1971 Communications Agreement did not apply to the Dependencies. Nick Barker made contact later to say that the *Bahia Paraiso* had sailed from Leith but that, because of the foggy conditions, it was not possible to tell whether it had taken off all the Argentines. We had to wait until early afternoon for the fog to clear. Nick then reported a continuing Argentine presence: although only two men had been sighted, there was smoke coming from several buildings, two boats were moored alongside the jetty, sixty-five drums of fuel and large quantities of stores and equipment stood on the jetty and the shore party had worked late into the evening the previous day, unloading and stacking supplies. It was clear that they were now established for a long stay in Leith. It was also clear, said Nick, that the operation had been pre-planned for some time, as the *Bahia Paraiso* had come from Antarctica and not direct from Argentina.

From Buenos Aires, Anthony reported that Galtieri wished to discuss the position in South Georgia with his Commanders-in-Chief and that a response to Lord Carrington's message would probably not be made until the evening.

In London, ministers agreed to the retention on station of HMS *Endurance* 'for the time being' and to postpone the departure of the outgoing NP 8901 from Stanley.

In Stanley, I was beginning to be bombarded with calls from the world news media. There was little I could tell them. To my surprise, an Argentine journalist presented himself at my office, announced that he had arrived on Tuesday's flight and requested an interview for a French magazine, *Gamma France*. He was a pleasant character called Rafael David Wollmann, but seemed to be more interested in taking photographs of me and Government House than in asking questions. That evening, Steve Martin had nothing to report, though Nick confirmed that the *Bahia Paraiso* remained in the vicinity, but had made no attempt to go into King Edward Point. I called on Monsignor Spraggon and Father Monaghan for what had become a regular chat. They had their ears close to the ground and accurately reflected the mood of Stanley folk. There was genuine anxiety and concern, together with the understandable complaint about lack of information from Government; but also there was an iron resolve against appeasement. The Monsignor was absolutely certain that Islanders were prepared to face the consequences rather than give in to Argentine pressure in South Georgia. He shared my view that concessions today in the Dependencies would lead to concessions tomorrow in the Falklands, and he was sure that the vast majority of Islanders thought the same way. Later that evening, at a drinks party given by Tony and Annie Chater for the camp teachers, who were in Stanley for a teaching seminar, there was unanimous endorsement of this point of view.

Saturday morning, 27 March, was one of my North West Frontier days, when the sun shone brightly through a clear blue sky, with a crisp nip in the air and incredible visibility. Perfect flying weather. As soon as my morning schedule with Steve was over (still nothing to report), I dragged Tony out of bed and took the Land Rover to the airport. We pushed my Cessna out of the hangar, she started first time and we were airborne and looking down on a sleepy Stanley within minutes. No southern English haze here. No radio or maps needed to navigate. There was the road (the one and only) snaking away past Sapper Hill and Mounts William and Harriet towards Bluff Cove. We flew lazily in that direction, all the sky in the world to ourselves (FIGAS did not fly on a Saturday), doing gentle stall turns and wing-overs. I let Tony try a few steep turns until we were regularly hitting our own slipstream; then we meandered down as far as Fitzroy, from above which we could see the whole of Lafonia and even, far out on the horizon, Beauchene Island. All too soon, it was time to turn back for my mid-morning schedule with Nick, sitting off Grytviken. To my great satisfaction, I managed under Tony's critical gaze to do a 'greaser' of a landing. It was the last landing I did in Cessna VP-FBA. I had flown it for a total of six hours.

Nick had nothing further to report: the *Bahia Paraiso* was still in the vicinity, but Captain Trombetta had declined to meet him, despite the fact that they were old acquaintances and that, in normal circumstances, they would have exchanged courtesy calls. We deduced that, like Nick, he was awaiting instructions.

Anthony sent disturbing news from Buenos Aires. He feared that events over the night had reinforced the growing impression that Dr Mendez had been less than honest with him and that the Argentines had been 'playing us along'. After the Commanders-in-Chief had met the previous evening, Dr Mendez did not summon him, as they had agreed, but instead held a press conference at which he announced that a firm decision had been taken to give the men on South Georgia all necessary protection, adding 'Nor is this diplomatic protection only, since there is also a navy ship, called the *Bahia Paraiso*, in the area to provide any necessary protection'. Anthony was seeking an urgent interview with Dr Mendez to clarify this statement. Later in the day, he reported that he had seen, not Costa Mendez, but a senior official, Sr

Ros, who declined to answer his questions and said that revised instructions had been given to the Ministry of Foreign Affairs and that these would be conveyed in a message from Dr Mendez to the British Government.

The RRS *Bransfield* paid its last call of the season to Stanley and her captain, Stuart Lawrence, came in for an update on the political situation. It appeared that London had not been keeping BAS headquarters in Cambridge fully informed of events. The two hydrographic officers from HMS *Endurance*, Richard Ball and Chris Todhunter, also called in and I gave them the latest news from Nick. That evening, we entertained the *Bransfield* crew and BAS members to drinks at Government House.

On Sunday, 28 March, the expected message came from Dr Mendez. It was uncompromising. It did not suggest any constructive way of proceeding and withdrew Dr Mendez's previous proposal for the completion of formalities at Grytviken. It attempted to maintain that the activities of the Argentine workers at Leith were known in advance by the British Government and in any case that they were being carried out on territory 'subject to the special regime agreed in 1971 between the Argentine and Great Britain'. Anthony concluded that the Argentines intended no move to resolve the dispute, but to let matters ride while they built up their naval strength in the area.

Nick reported from the *Endurance* that the *Bahia Paraiso* had taken up station fifteen miles off the north coast of South Georgia and that there were more than a dozen, possibly eighteen, men at Leith.

Press reports from Buenos Aires indicated that five Argentine warships had been despatched towards South Georgia and that all naval leave had been cancelled. On my evening schedule with Steve Martin, he reported that the Russian deep sea tug *Storki* had arrived at Grytviken from the South Shetland Islands (almost 1,000 miles away), ostensibly for water.[5]

Later that evening, as we prepared to go on board the *Bransfield* to say farewell, I received a copy of a message from Lord Carrington to the US Foreign Secretary, General Haig, seeking his good offices as a mediator and suggesting that the matter could be resolved either by the Argentines seeking permission at Grytviken to regularise their position or by their evacuation by a third ship. Talking to the BAS dentist on the

Bransfield, Derek Bielby, we discovered that we were both ex-RAF, but he had served throughout the Second World War, flying Wellingtons, Warwicks, Mosquitoes, Lancasters and Sunderlands. The *Bransfield* was heading for Punta Arenas and then Faraday. I went home hoping that Derek was not about to be embroiled in another war; he had done more than his share in the last.

On Monday, 29 March, Steve and Nick had nothing to report from South Georgia. Gary Noott came in to report that Moody Brook was clear of the outgoing NP8901 and ready to receive his successor's detachment, due later that day on the *John Biscoe*. His remaining strength was twenty-six and these were scattered round Stanley, billeted on friends and acquaintances. They could, however, be mustered at short notice. We agreed that one section would be on duty at the airport overnight on Tuesday, while the LADE aircraft was on the apron. After the LADE office incident, this was more to reassure Vicecomodoro Gamin than to serve any useful purpose: as I had explained to him, it was highly unlikely that Islanders would deliberately sabotage their only link with the outside world. Gary said that he would be handing over command to his successor, Mike Norman, on Thursday 1 April.

During the day, I received several overseas calls from the media, including one from Radio Australia. I was surprised at the amount of interest shown and astonished at the ignorance displayed; most enquirers thought that South Georgia was but a stone's throw from the Falklands – some even asked for flight details. The *John Biscoe* dropped anchor in Port Stanley at 6.30pm, but I was unable to go aboard until later as we were entertaining the camp teachers at Government House. It was good to see the two BAS ships together in the harbour; their calls rarely coincided. Stuart Lawrence joined me in Malcolm Phelps' cabin and we exchanged the latest news. Malcolm said that he had been 'buzzed' by an Argentine Hercules on the way from Montevideo, but had not seen any Argentine ships. He was anxious to sail for home as soon as the Royal Marines were disembarked, as he was already overdue. Stuart intended to stick to his programme if humanly possible. We waved goodbye to the *John Biscoe* later that evening.

Next morning, 30 March, Gary brought Mike Norman in to meet me. The official photographer took us shaking hands outside Government House. John and Pamela Dixon were also there. It was a happy, carefree occasion, with Gary in distinctly end-of-tour mood and Mike looking forward to a pleasant year of outdoor activity and isolated command. Built like a second-row forward, he exuded confidence and solid dependability.

I was busy all day preparing letters for the diplomatic bag, which my assistant, Michael Growcott, was due to take to Buenos Aires on the LADE flight. There were the inevitable overseas calls from the media and Patrick Watts came in to tape one of my regular broadcasts on the local radio. I could tell listeners little more than they had already picked up from the BBC and the Argentine radio: Lord Carrington and Mr Luce had both made statements in Parliament summarising developments. It was reassuring that HMS *Endurance* would remain on station for as long as was necessary, that the Falklands would be defended if necessary (but with what?) and that their wishes were paramount; but, as one said to me afterwards, 'Our paramount wish is for the British Government to act immediately to remove the Argentines from South Georgia.' The Argentine radio reported major demonstrations in Buenos Aires by labour unions against the government's austerity measures. I could neither confirm nor deny British press reports about the sailing of a nuclear-powered submarine in support of HMS *Endurance*. I had heard nothing officially.

The LADE flight arrived on time, bringing with it Hector Gilobert, whom Gamin brought in to see me about the LADE office incident. Hector said that Air Force headquarters were extremely concerned about the safety of LADE personnel in Stanley and about their F28 overnighting at Stanley airport. They had sent him over to seek assurances from me that no harm would befall either. He admitted that his masters had over-reacted to the incident ten days ago and expressed his satisfaction with the precautions that we had already taken. He would recommend upon his return that the weekly flight should continue.

The LADE aircraft also brought in four British journalists. They called on me for a general briefing and advice on how to get to South Georgia. I explained that there was no way of getting to South Georgia from the Falklands and that their best bet was to catch the next flight back to the mainland; there was no story here. I then excused myself for my evening schedule with Steve Martin and invited them to drinks later.

On Wednesday, 31 March, the Fokker F28 took off as normal and I called Gary Noott and Mike Norman to discuss (of all things) LADE security in the light of my meeting with Gilobert and Gamin. We did not wish to give the Argentines the slightest pretext for cancelling the weekly flight. My next visitors were Count and Countess Bardeau. He was Austrian, naturalised Spanish; she was Spanish. They expressed interest in buying San Carlos farm and had arrived on the LADE flight to have a look at it. I advised them how to contact FIGAS and, after coffee, wished them a pleasant stay. I never saw or heard of them again.

There were the usual interruptions during the day from overseas calls and more than the usual number of telegrams, including one from Buenos Aires reporting that Argentine press comment on the South Georgia dispute had been overshadowed by violent demonstrations in Buenos Aires against the government's economic policies. The popular press had given prominence to reports of the despatch of a nuclear-powered submarine from Britain and Dr Mendez was widely quoted as telling reporters that Argentina would not give way to threats of force and that the group on South Georgia was on Argentine soil. Too late that evening for me to receive copies, the FCO sent instructions to Anthony to deliver Lord Carrington's reply to Dr Mendez, which proposed sending John Ure as a personal emissary to Buenos Aires with constructive proposals for a solution allowing the salvage contract on South Georgia to be carried out. It went on to say that the defusing of the South Georgia incident would prepare the way for a resumption of the dialogue on the broader issues discussed in the New York talks in February. The MOD also sent instructions to HMS *Endurance* to return to Stanley with all despatch, having first put ashore the Royal Marines at King Edward Point. Not mentioned in the telegrams was the crucial information that, in the early evening, Mr Nott (then Secretary of State for Defence) had been briefed by MOD officials on the latest intelligence report, which indicated that the early morning of 2 April had been set by the Argentines as the time and day for 'action'. Taken with earlier intelligence reports, analysts had assumed that the action intended was an invasion of the Falkland Islands. The FCO had also seen these reports.[6]

In blissful ignorance of what was about to befall us, Mavis and

I hosted a party that evening for fourteen islanders in honour of Harold Bennett, who was retiring after fifty years of government service. Finishing as Senior Magistrate, Harold had held a number of posts in the Falkland Islands Government and was universally liked and respected. His father before him had also enjoyed a distinguished career in the public service, pioneering conservation of the Islands' wildlife and building up links with the British Museum and the London Zoo. He had taught himself taxidermy as a hobby and assembled a unique collection of Falkland birds, which had tragically been lost when the first town hall (an elegant, wooden building) was destroyed by fire. Harold had inherited his father's love of nature and was also an avid gardener, with the best roses in Stanley. He and his hospitable wife, Grace, always gave me a warm welcome whenever I dropped in during an evening stroll, and invariably sent me back to Mavis with a lovely bunch of roses or daffodils or whatever happened to be in bloom at the time. We had asked Harold and Grace to choose the guests, so it was a relaxed, friendly party with lots of kelper anecdotes and reminiscences. Aubrey Buxton had left us a video cassette of the Anglia film 'More British Than the British' and we showed it after dinner to an appreciative audience. Harold Rowlands voiced the opinion of the rest when he urged me once again to press for the eviction of the Argentines from South Georgia. None of us realised at the time that this was about to be overtaken by more immediate events. Harold Bennett afterwards referred to our dinner party as 'The Last Supper'.

Thursday, 1 April, began the same as any other day. My early morning schedule with Steve Martin was uneventful (he could not tell me over the radio that HMS *Endurance* had sailed) and there was nothing from Nick because he was maintaining radio silence. Telegrams arrived from London during the morning about movements of the Argentine navy and activity in Washington and New York; but nothing about invasion on 2 April. Bill Luxton flew in from Chartres and called to see me. I explained the gravity of the situation but could not forecast what might happen. The usual overseas calls from the media interrupted my normal paper work until luncheon, which passed quietly with the family. We were pleased that Tony appeared at long last to be getting down to serious study for his 'A' levels. I returned to the office for more overseas calls and dictating until 3.30pm, when the fateful telegram arrived.

Notes

1. Davidoff never made the additional payment, so legally the contract lapsed on 31 March, 1982.

2. *Falkland Islands Review:* Report of a Committee of Privy Counsellors January, 1983 (Cmnd 8787, page 46)

3. Z signifies Greenwich Mean Time.

4. *Falkland Islands Review:* Report of a Committee of Privy Counsellors, january, 1983 (Cmnd 8787, page 53).

5. This could have been a genuine coincidence: Russian ships had called at Grytviken for water in the past.

6. *Falkland Islands Review:* Report of a Committee of Privy Counsellors, January, 1983 (Cmnd 8787, page 67).

11

'Make Your Dispositions Accordingly'

Couched in cautious, diplomatic language, the FCO telegram read:

We have apparently reliable evidence that an Argentine task force will gather off Cape Pembroke[1] early tomorrow morning, 2 April. *You will wish to make your dispositions accordingly.*

My communicator, Brian Wells, placed it on my desk with the cheery comment: 'They might have added goodbye and the best of British. . .' I made a quick calculation. Fifteen, sixteen hours at most to 'make my dispositions accordingly'. I asked my secretary, Christine, to get me Moody Brook. Christine was married to Brian. It was not often in the Diplomatic Service that a husband-and-wife team could work together in the same post. They were a dependable pair, comforting to have with me at a time like this. With Michael Growcott on the bag run, I knew that his wife, Avril, would be worried. She lived with three young children in a house in the centre of Stanley. Brian and Christine were more vulnerable in Government House grounds (their house had been at one time the head gardener's cottage), so I suggested to Christine that she should go to Avril's and stay with her overnight, and that Brian should join them as soon as we closed down communications. First priority, however, was to put all available hands on shredding and burning classified papers. I had learnt during our evacuation from Saigon in 1975 just how long it took to dispose of paper. Although we had carried out regular and rigorous weeding, it would still take many hours to destroy all our sensitive material.

As Brian headed for the shredding machine, Christine put me through to Mike Norman at Moody Brook. I asked him to get Gary and come immediately to Government House (our telephone link was anything but secure). Reading the telegram again as I waited, it brought to mind the Admiralty signal to

202

Governor Allardyce in 1914. I took *The Battle Of The Falklands* from the bookshelf behind me and looked up the exact wording:

> German cruiser raid may take place. All admiralty colliers should be concealed in unfrequented harbours. Be ready to destroy supplies useful to the enemy and hide codes effectively on enemy ships being sighted.

It had decidedly more style (and guidance) than my bald telegram; but then, according to legend, it had been drafted by Winston Churchill. Mike and Gary arrived within fifteen minutes. I showed Mike the signal. 'It looks as if the buggers really mean it this time,' I said. We ran through the contingency plans that Gary had updated during the year and agreed that they were the best we could do with the resources available and the minimal intelligence we had on the composition and intentions of the Argentine task force. We discussed the possible lines of attack and decided that the most likely landing beach was near the airport in Pilot Bay, to the east of Yorke Point. We assumed that they would use infantry landing craft (we were not to know until later that they had embarked amphibious personnel carriers) and the beach we chose offered the best approach for such craft, free from kelp and steeply shelving, thus reducing the wading distance for disembarking troops. As if to underline our choice, it was also the site of our resident gentoo penguin colony. They had chosen it presumably for the same reason: it gave them the best chance against their enemy, the leopard seal. I agreed that it was the obvious place for a machine-gun section, but could not help feeling sorry for the poor penguins and the rude awakening that we were planning for them.

We were fortunate in having more men available than Gary had envisaged when he updated the contingency plans. There were sixty-nine Royal Marines, forty-three of the new detachment and twenty-six of the old, plus ten hydrographers from HMS *Endurance*. Although primarily trained to use a mapping pen, they all knew how to fire a gun. In addition, there was the Falkland Islands Defence Force. Lacking radio communications, its main task was to guard key positions in Stanley such as the power station, the telephone exchange and Cable and Wireless installations. Its active membership in Stanley amounted to about forty; but many of those were filling essential civilian posts, which they would be expected to man in an emergency.

Immediately behind our chosen landing beach lay Stanley airport. This was an obvious target and somehow we had to render it inoperative.[2] Unfortunately, the Royal Marines had no suitable explosives with which to crater the runway and, though the Director of Public Works had dynamite for quarrying purposes, he advised that to do an effective job would take days to lay the charges. We knew that the 4,100ft runway would take Hercules because they had brought in the LADE house, making three or four flights and using (I now recalled) different and double crews each time. The most recent landing had been an emergency diversion of a flight from Marambio to Buenos Aires with an alleged fuel leak. Many of us had been suspicious at first; but it had seemed genuine when the Director of Civil Aviation reported the Hercules taxying in with fuel streaming from one of its tanks. In any event, there was no need for the Argentine Air Force to manufacture excuses to fly into Stanley airport; as we have seen, the British Government had given Argentina the right under the Communications Agreement to operate an air service between the Islands and the mainland and, by now, the Argentine Air Force had plenty of pilots who were familiar with it.

To locate the airport in bad weather, the Argentines had installed a radio beacon (a constant source of annoyance, incidentally, to the many radio hams in the Islands because it transmitted the letters MV for Malvinas and not FL for Falklands). We would have to put that out of action. I told Mike that I would arrange for FIGAS and PWD to put obstacles on the runway and Mike detailed a section to defend it under the command of one of the more experienced corporals from Gary's detachment, a colourful character called Figgy Duff. He and fellow-Royal Marine Corporal Nick Williams were well known to the Islanders because they presented a popular weekly request programme on FIBS called 'The Nick and Fig Show'. The remaining sections were to be deployed at tactical points covering the four-mile stretch of road between the airport and Stanley, with instructions to hold out for as long as they could before leapfrogging back, covering each other as they retreated until they reached the eastern outskirts of Stanley ('the white city'), there to disengage and move as rapidly as possible through the town to Government House, to the west of the main residential area. With the harbour to the north and the rising ground of Sapper Hill to the south,

204

Government House was almost impossible to defend. Nevertheless, it was the seat of government and had to be the last redoubt.

We also intended that one section, under Gary Noott and comprising his most experienced men, would take off to the south and go into hiding in camp. Gary had prepared plans for this purpose, but there had been no time to deploy food and ammunition to the chosen sites. We agreed that the MV *Forrest* should proceed to the outer harbour in the hours of darkness and use her radar to warn us of any incoming ships. Assuming that the actual landings would not take place until after dawn, I arranged for the FIGAS Islander to be refuelled and flown to the racecourse at dusk, ready for a dawn reconnaissance flight. Mike and Gary went off to organise their men, and I asked Christine to invite all FIG departmental heads to come to a meeting in the main drawing room of Government House at 4.30pm.

A pressing problem was the number of Argentines in our midst. Apart from the half-dozen or so LADE staff, we had two Spanish teachers and about a score of YPF and Gas del Estado employees. Normally these amounted to only two or three; but a party of sixteen had flown in on the previous week's flight, ostensibly to build loading ramps for their gas cylinders. They were in civilian clothes, but it had not escaped our notice that they were all fit, young men of military age. We had not suspected them as precursors of an invasion at the time; but they had caused concern because Islanders were always sensitive about the number of Argentines allowed in under the fuel and communications agreements. They were convinced that the Argentines deliberately overloaded their presence in Stanley in the belief that it would somehow boost their sovereignty claim to the Islands.

I had been trying for some time to reach agreement on the maximum number of Argentine officials permitted to reside in Stanley and also to establish a procedure for regulating the number of temporary workers allowed in for specific jobs such as this. The agreements contained a general clause that both LADE and YPF should be allowed to station in the Falkland Islands the personnel necessary to look after their installations and operations; but they also stated that the composition of such teams of personnel should be as agreed in the Special Consultative Committee, a body established by the 1971 agreement consisting of representatives of the Argentine Ministry of Foreign Affairs and the British Embassy in Buenos Aires, with local representatives in Stanley (the Chief Secretary and the Vicecomodoro). There was the added complication in this particular case that, strictly speaking, Gas del Estado was not covered by the 1974 Fuel Agreement, which referred only to YPF 'or their representative'. It appeared that they had been allowed to creep in, as it were, on the back of YPF.

It was obvious with hindsight that the sixteen Gas del Estado gentlemen were not what they purported to be. Whatever they were up to, I wanted them out of harm's way, and the sooner the better. It would also be prudent to lock up all the LADE personnel, not only to prevent them from warning the task force that we knew they were coming (using their powerful radio link with Buenos Aires), but also for their own safety. I also wanted to warn the Islanders of the impending invasion as soon as possible, without of course saying anything over the local radio that might compromise our intelligence sources. While waiting for the departmental heads to assemble, I therefore despatched a signal to the FCO stating that I intended to round up all the Argentines in Stanley before dawn tomorrow and seeking advice on when the Islanders should be informed. The FCO replied that, while the evidence of Argentine intentions to attack the Islands the next day was highly suggestive, it was not yet entirely conclusive and diplomatic action was being taken to prevent an attack. When I informed the Islanders was left to my discretion. Oh dear, I thought, no wonder we are called 'the better-notters' by the rest of Whitehall.[3]

Leaving my office, I noticed that three of the 'droggies'[4] from HMS *Endurance*, Lieutenants Richard Ball and Chris Todhunter and Petty Officer Vind, were helping Brian and Christine with the shredding and burning of confidential files. They had been working in my conference room, mapping surveys carried out earlier in the season of Berkeley Sound and Rothera (in the Antarctic) and had responded willingly to Brian's request for help. Walking along the corridor and through the dividing door that separated the office from the domestic side of Government House, I never ceased to contrast these few paces with my daily commuting by train and tube when working in the Foreign Office. Even now, I had no desire to change places.

The main drawing room of Government House had an old-fashioned elegance. A picture of the young Queen Victoria hung over the fireplace, with portraits of the Queen and the Duke of Edinburgh on the opposite wall. On the other walls were Pollard prints of horses, inns and stagecoaches generously donated by Jack Abbott, who though not Islander-born had married a Falkland Islander and, since her death, had chosen to live in Stanley. Through the French windows on the northern side lay the conservatory, a magnificent Victorian edifice with ornate metal brackets, antiquated heating and clumsy ratchets and levers to operate the ventilation system. As usual, the conservatory was a blaze of colour; pelargoniums, sweet peas, climbing geraniums, African Marigolds and begonias. How Gene managed to keep a good show there throughout the year I shall never know, though after twenty-seven years in the job he had an unrivalled knowledge of the plants and the seasons. Looking past the departmental heads who were present, I noticed through the French windows that the vine was heavy with ripening grapes and wondered idly who would be eating them.

When all were assembled, I read out the telegram and explained that we were seeking an immediate meeting of the Security Council in New York; but we had to prepare for the worst. I was sorry for the short notice. We could not now get the boarding children out to camp or evacuate the old people and children from Stanley. I would go on the radio after the meeting to explain the situation as fully as possible and would probably have to declare a state of emergency before dawn. I asked the Postmaster General if he could get his engineers to rig up broadcasting facilities for me in Government House and keep the broadcasting studio and telephone exchange open all night. Bill Etheridge, a quiet Falkland Islander with whom I normally discussed nothing more exciting than designs for our next stamp issue, nodded slowly and said it would be done. I then turned to the Superintendent of Education. 'No school tomorrow, John,' I declared, thinking as I said it that I normally gave a holiday only on Commonwealth Day. 'Would you make sure that somebody stays with the hostel children from now on, and arrange for camp parents to be kept informed?' Some settlements were linked with Stanley by telephone, others by radio only; but I knew that John and Veronica would get through to the parents somehow. To the Chief Medical Officer I said, 'Daniel, I think you should alert all your staff for early duty tomorrow.' The disturbing thought struck me that, if we did have heavy fighting and lots of casualties, our tiny hospital and staff would never be able to cope. Daniel Haynes was the senior of three expatriate doctors, one of whom was his wife, Hilary, who also had three small children to look after. Supporting staff consisted of matron and three State Registered Nurses. The King Edward Memorial Hospital was smaller than most cottage hospitals in England, with about twenty beds, most of which were already occupied by geriatric and other patients.

The Director of Public Works employed the largest number of workers in the public sector in the Falkland Islands and was responsible for water and electricity supplies as well as roads, refuse disposal, stormwater drainage and the construction and maintenance of all public and many private buildings. He was also responsible for the fire brigade. I asked John to put his heaviest equipment on the runway as soon as the Islander had taken off and ensure that the power station and water filtration plants were fully manned, with maintenance staff standing by to effect emergency repairs. I also asked him to alert the Fire Brigade Superintendent, Patrick McPhee. I asked the Director of Civil Aviation, Gerald Cheek, to put his fire tender and fuel bowser on the runway and to warn the FIGAS pilots[5] and groundcrew to be ready for a dawn scramble. Gerald was in a quandary because, as well as being Director of Civil Aviation, he was also a senior NCO in the FIDF. Recalling the 'Condor' incident in 1966, when an Argentine Douglas DC4 had landed on the racecourse, we thought that helicopters from the task force might follow its example. We therefore solved his dilemma by making him responsible for the section guarding the Islander and the racecourse.

We were discussing plans for the *Forrest* with the Customs Officer and Harbourmaster, Les Halliday, when the door opened and Mavis appeared. Hearing voices on her return from shopping at the West Store, she wondered who was occupying the drawing room at that unusual hour. 'Sorry, Mavis', I said, 'I forgot to tell you about this meeting.' Looking puzzled and a little suspicious, she tactfully withdrew. I asked Les to make sure that Basil Biggs did not light the lighthouse that night. The Cape Pembroke light-house was a museum piece, but still performed a useful function. Apparently there was only one other like it still in use, and that was on Perim Island in the Red Sea. Built around the turn of the century, its light came from a gigantic mantle, fuelled by paraffin and lit with an elephant-sized tray of methylated spirits. Despite its size, it was just like an overgrown Tilley lamp and reminded me of our happy safaris in Uganda. Thanks to skilfully crafted prisms, its beacon could be seen for fourteen miles and I saw no point in helping the Argentines by lighting their way in.

I asked the Chief Police Officer, Ronnie Lamb, to keep an eye on Argentines and Argentine property in Stanley and told him that I would need his help in rounding them up as soon as I decided the time was right. He confirmed that Anton Livermore, his only male police constable, knew where they were staying.

I ended the meeting by wishing them the best of luck and advising them to keep tuned in to FIBS. As they filed out, there was none of the usual chit-chat. Harold Rowlands had not said a word throughout the meeting. Descended from a Scandinavian sailor said to have jumped ship in the Falklands, he normally looked like a benign Edward G. Robinson. As the meeting went on, how-ever, the lines on his face deepened and the frown became more pronounced. As he left, his blue eyes looked at me in disbelief. All I could do was to give a helpless shrug: there were no words to answer that anguished gaze.

I motioned to Dick to stay behind and, as soon as the others had gone, asked if Mavis and Tony could stay with Connie for the night. 'Of course', he replied. Echoing my fears about the Argentines in our midst, he urged that we should grab them without delay. I showed him the FCO telegram. He snorted. 'I'm afraid we'll have to wait', I said, adding, 'I'd feel a lot happier if you would round them up – you and the droggies.' 'Fine' said Dick, 'I'll be ready when you give the word.'

I then asked him to brief the Stanley councillors ahead of my broadcast. Except for Bill Luxton, we could not get word to Camp councillors in advance as we had no secure means of communicating with them. 'What about the journalists?' asked Dick. 'I was due to see Simon Winchester at 4.30 and had to cancel when you called your meeting. He's bound to suspect that something is up.' I under-took to brief them immediately after my broadcast and to ask Cable and Wireless (which normally closed down at 6pm) to stay open so that they could file their stories.

I had a final question for Dick before he left: 'How do I declare a State of Emergency?' It was not something I had done before. We discussed various ordinances and other pieces of legislation and decided that I would have to go back to 1939 to find a suitable precedent.

I returned to the office to look up my Laws and found Patrick Watts waiting with his apparatus. Neither of us knew it at the time, but he was about to start a marathon session at the microphone that was to end over sixteen hours later with an Argentine gun in his back and bring him a well deserved MBE. Patrick had a natural flair for journalism and broadcasting and excelled at sporting commentaries. He was a keen footballer himself and knew everyone in the local football league; his darts commentaries made the matches more exciting to listen to than to watch and his racing commentaries were every bit as good as Peter Bromley's, with the added advantage that he could rattle off the past histories of all the horses and riders. He was a 'natural' for giving a live commentary on an invasion.

'I'm not staying in here, Patrick,' I said, 'It's too exposed. I'll be in Michael's office, at the back.' Patrick went off with the Posts and Telecommunications engineer, Bill Roberts, to turn the First Secretary's office into a temporary broadcasting studio.

I telephoned Iain Stewart and asked him to come and see me. His offices were next door to Government House and he arrived within minutes. I asked him if Cable and Wireless could stay open all night. Anticipating my request, he said he had already alerted his staff. They would keep transmitting and receiving until the 'Argies' stopped them; but he was worried about possible sabotage to his transmitters. I said I shared his concern, explained the situation with regard to the Argentines in Stanley and said that both the transmitting and receiving stations would be guarded by the FIDF all night.

No sooner had Iain left than Bill Luxton appeared. I was glad to see him because dusk was fast approaching and I wanted to give him the opportunity of flying his Cessna from the airport to the racecourse. 'Are you going to move yours?' he asked. 'I haven't time, I'm afraid', I said, 'but I've told FIGAS to bring the Islander over. With luck you might be able to get back to Chartres first light tomorrow.' 'No', said Bill in his calm, matter-of-fact way. 'If the bastards are coming, it's too late now.' As the senior member of Executive Council, I had come to value his balanced judgement and advice. An outspoken and consistent critic of our policy towards Argentina, he was too kind to say 'I told you so'; but it was there in his eyes. He had never disguised his dislike of the Argentines and we both knew that he must be at or near the top of their 'hit list'. But his face betrayed no emotion as he left to work out how he was going to get himself and his family back to the farm. Thinking about the shock in store for Pat, I realised that I had still not explained what was happening to Mavis. She was in the kitchen, chatting with Nanny and Keva as they prepared lasagna for Brian and Christine and the 'droggies', who were still busily shredding and burning. I took her into the small drawing room and explained the situation. I said that the Royal Marines would shortly be arriving to set up operational headquarters at Government House, and that I did not want her or Tony or any of the staff to stay overnight. I knew that she would object but guessed that, after the inevitable outburst, common sense would prevail and she would go peacefully. Her opening gambit was, 'You made me leave you in Saigon and I'm not going to leave you now.'

'Darling, it's not like Saigon', I said. 'You'll only be down the road at Dick and Connie's, not in Hong Kong.' She had no answer to that.

'Tony is out, at the Smiths, I believe', she said.

'Well, would you call and tell him to come home immediately? And tell the staff to spend the night with friends – tell them to take their most treasured possessions with them, but say I don't expect their rooms to come to any harm'.

I returned to Michael's office for the broadcast, which was now scheduled for 8.15pm. I had hung on in the hope that London would have confirmed by then that an emergency meeting of the UN Security Council had been arranged; but there was still no news. Deciding that my broadcast could be delayed no longer, I told Brian, who was dashing between the telex and the shredding machine like a champion sprinter, to bring any telegram in to me, even if I was on the air, and telephoned Patrick at the FIBS studio to say that I was ready. One of his part-time announcers, Mike Smallwood, a quiet American who had settled in the Falkland Islands because he enjoyed the peace and tranquillity, introduced me, and I began:

Good Evening. I have an important announcement to make about the state of affairs between the British and Argentine Governments over the Falkland Islands dispute. We have now sought an immediate emergency meeting of the Security Council on the grounds that there could be a situation which threatens international peace and security.

I don't know whether it has been possible to arrange a

meeting to-day, but our spokesman has been asked to make the following specific points:

'The Secretary General has today summoned the British and the Argentinian Permanent Representatives to express his deep concern over the situation in the South Atlantic and has urged restraint on both sides. It is right that the Security Council should endorse and back up his approach. We for our part have continued to make every possible effort to re-solve the current problems by diplomatic means. The British Ambassador in Buenos Aires yesterday delivered a further message to the Argentinian Government urging a negotiated settlement to current problems and offering to send a senior emissary to Buenos Aires. The Argentinian Foreign Minister had today responded to this approach in negative terms. He had declined to discuss further the problems occasioned by the illegal presence of Argentine nationals on South Georgia and he had specifically stated that he no longer wished to use diplomatic channels to discuss the situation in South Georgia. In addition to the Foreign Minister's unwillingness to pursue diplomatic exchanges there is mounting evidence that the Argentine armed forces are preparing to invade the Falkland Islands.

In these circumstances it is essential that the Security Council urge that there should be no resort to armed force and that diplomatic negotiations should be resumed.'

Now these are the points that our spokesman in the Security Council has been asked to make – if he can get a meeting today.

In these circumstances, I think it is necessary to take certain precautionary measures here in Stanley. I don't think that the camp is at risk and I don't think that any measures need to be taken out there. But here in Stanley, I have alerted the Royal Marines and I ask now for all serving – all active – members of the FIDF to report to the Drill Hall as soon as possible.

They will be on guard tonight at the key points in the town. Schools will be closed tomorrow. The radio station will stay open until further notice. If the Security Council's urging to keep the peace is not heeded by the Argentine Government, I expect to have to declare a state of emergency, perhaps before dawn tomorrow. I shall come on the air again as soon as I have anything to report, but in the meantime I would urge you all to

212

remain calm and keep off the streets. In particular, do not go along the airport road, stay indoors and please do not add to the troubles of the security services by making demonstrations or damaging Argentine property. This would play into their hands and simply provide them with the excuse they need to invade us. So, please, do not take the law into your own hands. Let us show our visitors that we are responsible, law-abiding and resolute citizens.

I shall let you know as soon as I have anything further to report.

Patrick followed me on the air, stating that FIBS would stick to the ordinary evening programme until closing time (10.30pm), and that music and other entertainment would then be provided throughout the night, interspersed with news from London and from me in Government House as and when it became available. He then handed the microphone back to Mike, who helped to set the tone by saying in his soft American accent, 'Well, as it says in those large frenzied letters on the cover of *A Hitch-Hiker's Guide To The Galaxy* – DON'T PANIC!' He then played as his next choice of record 'Strangers in the Night'. I smiled as I listened to the familiar lyrics, so smoothly delivered by Frank Sinatra. We would certainly be sharing something before the night was through, I thought, but it wasn't love that was 'just a glance away, a warm embracing dance away' – it was the wretched 'Argies'.

To the background of Sinatra, I looked up the 1939 Emergency Regulations. They seemed to fit the bill so I set about drafting my statement, hoping against hope that some miracle would happen and I would not have to make it. As I wrote, Neville Chamberlain's declaration of war on 3 September, 1939, came back to me and I remembered the sound of the air-raid warning as his voice faded from our old Philco wireless set. I hoped that we would have a little more time than that.

I was thus engaged when Simon Winchester and his colleagues appeared. They had heard my broadcast and were anxious to file their stories in time for the morning papers at home. I did my best to answer their questions and off they dashed to Cable and Wireless next door.

In my outer office, Chris Todhunter and his men were still cheerfully shredding and burning. 'We've almost finished', said Chris, looking and smelling like Guy Fawkes. 'Hardly a Navy job',

I said. 'But I hope to offer you something more appropriate in a little while. Would you like to join the *Forrest* when she goes out to Port William?' Chris responded enthusiastically, 'Fine', he said, 'Richard and I will be happy to go.' It suddenly struck me, with a great surge of relief, that HMS *Endurance* could not possibly arrive in Stanley before the Argentine task force. If she had been within striking distance, I knew that Nick would have followed his illustrious predecessor, Sir Christopher Cradock, at Coronel and steamed in with all guns blazing (two 20mm cannons and a few small missiles from his Wasps). He would have been as outgunned as Cradock and would assuredly have been sunk in the same way, with similar heavy loss of life.

I went through to Mavis and Tony in the small drawing room. The atmosphere between mother and son was a little strained. Mavis explained that this was because, after hearing my broadcast, Tony had wanted to report to the Drill Hall for duty with the FIDF and she had refused to let him go. Though not a member, he had been in the Combined Cadet Force at Radley and was familiar with the FIDF's weapons. I knew that he would never forgive us if we did not let him go. Islander friends of his age (seventeen) were members and would be reporting for duty. After a little prompting, Mavis agreed and Tony dashed off eagerly on his motorcycle. When he had gone, I explained that Phil would certainly not entrust a rifle to his care. Sure enough, a disappointed Tony returned shortly afterwards to say that the FIDF had no use for his services. 'Not even as a despatch rider', he said dejectedly. 'They said they had no despatches to deliver.' 'Not to worry,' I replied, 'Your place tonight is with your mother. Help her pack Fifi and take her to Dick and Connie's after dinner.'

As we sat down and attempted to eat, Dick arrived to remind me of something I had overlooked – the Argentine VOR beacon. He had received an ingenious suggestion from Bill Curtis, a Canadian who, like Mike Smallwood, had come to settle in the Falkland Islands to get away from the strife-torn world. Bill reckoned that he could falsify the position of the beacon so that aircraft homing in on it would land in the sea. I did not understand how this could be done; but at least it seemed worth a try, so I gave my agreement and Dick went off to tell Bill that, if he could not bend the beacon, he was to break it.

I suddenly realised that Mavis was serving dinner herself. 'Where's Donna?' I asked, knowing that she was the maid on duty that evening. 'They have all gone – all except Don', Mavis replied. I was upset at not being able to say goodbye and thank them for looking after us. They were more than our staff, they were part of the family: the two maids Donna Gleadell and Doreen McLaren and cook Keva Smith (who had joined us from Port Stephens) and the housekeeper, Nanny. Nanny's real name was Mrs Mary Fullerton but she was known to everyone as Nanny because she had started in that position at Government House in 1965, looking after Sir Cosmo and Lady Haskard's small son, and the name had stuck. She had left her husband years before and her only son had been tragically lost at sea in his twenties. Her only home since 1965 had been Government House and I was worried that she would not take kindly to my instruction to leave; but Tony said that she had accepted it with good grace and in the right spirit – she had gone off with a picture of the Queen under one arm and a bottle of gin under the other.

It was an awkward farewell to Mavis in the hall. Neither of us knew what to say; but Tony rose to the occasion and bustled his mother out with a cheerful 'See you in the morning'.

After they had gone, I decided to grab a weapon to defend myself. The only firearm in Government House at the time was my .12 bore shotgun, which was in the rodroom with the fishing tackle. I opened the door to find that Don had already beaten me to it. He was tipping out cartridges on to the top of the spare freezer, which stood below a window overlooking the front drive and flagpole. Propped beside the freezer was my shotgun. Don nodded towards the flagpole and said grimly 'I've left the flag up tonight, Sir, and I'll shoot any Argie bastard who tries to take it down.' I felt tears of pride well up and had to turn on my heel. 'How dare the Argentines try to walk over people like this?', I thought, anger rising in me for the first time. I suppose I had been too busy until that moment to feel any emotion. Don's words now brought it flooding out. Shock, indignation and anger. As the shock subsided, the anger mounted. I had intended to ask Don why he had not left with the rest of the staff; but I knew now that it was pointless. Moreover, I was glad to have him there with me. He followed me into the small drawing room and asked if I would like a drink. 'No thank you, Don,' I said. 'We've a long night ahead of us.' I looked at my watch; 11.45pm. We should know shortly the result of our approach to the Security Council. I switched on the radio and waited for the news on the hour from BBC Overseas. The Falkland Islands were the main topic, and the bulletin contained excellent reports from our Ambassador to the UN, Sir Anthony Parsons, and from Harold Briley in Buenos Aires. It was reassuring to have Tony Parsons batting for us in New York. If anybody could save us at this stage, he could. I had worked for him in the Foreign Office in the Middle East Department and formed the highest regard for his ability and intellect. And there was no one in Buenos Aires who had a more helpful attitude to the Islanders than Harold Briley. Somehow it was comforting to hear their familiar voices on BBC Overseas. It was clear from the bulletin, however, that there had been no response from Argentina to the call by the President of the Security Council to refrain from the use of force. I therefore decided to broadcast again.

As I made my way through the dividing door to the office end of Government House, I was amazed at the transformation that had taken place. There were Royal Marines, automatic weapons and boxes of ammunition everywhere. Sergeant Short had installed his radio in one corner of the First Secretary's office – now the 'Ops room' – and it was already humming and crackling as he spoke to the various sections in the field. I went along to the cypher room to see if any fresh news had come in from the Foreign Office. Brian was sitting at the telex but had nothing new to report. I retraced my steps to the Ops room and went on the air for the second time that night:

Good morning,
    You probably heard the outcome of the Security Council meeting on the BBC – both Britain and Argentina were called upon not to use force to settle their dispute over the Falkland Islands. We must now wait and see what effect this has upon the Argentine Government.
    As I speak, there is no indication that the Argentine Navy task force heading this way has changed course. Unless it does, we can expect it off Cape Pembroke by dawn. Now please don't be inquisitive and go and see for yourselves. You'll just get in the way. Stay indoors and we shall keep you informed by radio.
    That's all for now.

As I switched back to the main studio, I heard another part-time announcer, Dave Emsley, fade in with 'How Deep is the Ocean'. Dave had also come to the Falkland Islands for a peaceful life. He was a gentle, quietly spoken Englishman and an ex-Boeing 707 pilot. I negotiated the rifles and the boxes of ammunition in the corridor and went back to Brian in the cypher room.

'All the classified files destroyed?' I asked.

'Yes', said Brian, 'In fact, *all* the files have been destroyed.'

'And Christine?'

'Gone to Avril's.'

'Good. Now, what about the cypher equipment? Do you know how to destroy it?'

'Yes – to make sure I asked FCO for destruction procedures and I'm all set to destruct as soon as you give the word.'

'Well done', I said. 'As soon as we know for certain that the invasion is on. We may not have much time, so let's have the last signal ready to go.' I scribbled down the simple message: 'Invasion has started. Closing down.' We agreed that, after destroying the cypher equipment, Brian would lock the security doors and combination blisters, throw the keys into the harbour and join Christine at Avril's.

At that moment, the telex started chattering and we watched as the decoded signal confirmed what we had already heard over the BBC: Argentina had not responded to the President of the Security Council. The FCO went on to state, however, that President Reagan was making a final attempt to talk personally to President Galtieri to urge him to refrain from military action. The outcome of this approach was not expected before 3.30am local time. My immediate reaction was an upsurge of hope; but second thoughts persuaded me that nothing would deter Galtieri now. He was committed to invasion and was invading because he was convinced that we would not respond, no matter what President Reagan or anyone else might say. Laudable though the President's intervention was, its effect was that yet again I had to postpone tidying up my own little world; I could neither declare a state of emergency nor round up the Argentines.

Dick took the news stoically. 'Nothing much we can do now before 3.30, Dick,' I said. 'So I suggest you do what I'm going to do.' 'What's that?' he asked. 'Get some sleep.' And, with that, I went to bed.

Notes

1. The entrance to Stanley's outer harbour, Port William.

2. Someone in Whitehall had also thought about this. The last telegram

217

from the FCO to me, despatched but never received, gave me discretion to blow up the runway 'to prevent it being used after invasion to resupply an invasion force'.

3. This rather unkind but not entirely unjustified tag had been given to the Foreign Office by military members of the Ministry of Defence who, familiar with regimental nicknames like 'the cherry-pickers', had coined the phrase because of the FCO's propensity to say 'better not' to any proposed course of action.

4. A nickname for Royal Navy hydrographers.

5. FIGAS had three pilots at the time, two kelpers and one expatriate.

12

Undefeated in Defeat

Refreshed after a couple of hours' sleep, I sat in the soft glow of the peat fire, turning and cocking the ugly little 9mm pistol that the Royal Marines had given me. I was in my favourite room in Government House, the one that usually conjured up images of gracious living. Tonight, however, my mind went back thirty-five years, to the North-West Frontier and Colonel Grant-Taylor's staccato instructions: 'Turn – Cock – Turn – Squeeze.' The trick was to turn the gun outwards, flick the hammer back with the thumb, turn it inwards again and squeeze the trigger, keeping the same grip on the butt throughout. It sounds straightforward but it was not easy, even with the little pistol I now held. With a heavy .45 revolver it was decidedly difficult. Grant-Taylor maintained that you fired a pistol with the base joint of the thumb. How ridiculous, I remembered thinking, surely you fire a gun with the trigger finger. 'Squeeze the butt as if it were an orange', he used to say and, after two days of dry gun-play, turning, cocking and squeezing until our wrists and fingers ached, it began to work. Grant-Taylor was the British Army's leading small-arms expert and had become a legend in his own lifetime. Before we went on his course, none of us could hit the proverbial barn door from fifteen yards, using RAF issue .38 Smith and Wessons. At the end of the course, we fired a .45 Colt from each hand and put the contents of both chambers into a solitary sandbag.

Grant-Taylor was a great believer in the stopping power of a .45. To prove his point, he related an incident during his secondment to Hoover's G-men in the United States, when his best friend was gunned down by 'Babyface' Nelson after Nelson himself had been hit with a .38 bullet. 'A .45 would have bowled him over', he said. He called the .38 Smith and Wesson a mere toy: 'OK for Hollywood but no good in a real fight.'

Sitting in our cosy drawing room in Government House, waiting for the Argentines, I wondered what Grant-Taylor would have called the little 9mm in my hand. A peashooter, perhaps, or a popgun. Nevertheless, I was determined to use it on the first 'Argie' who came through the door. My main concern was whether I would be able to identify friend from foe before squeezing the trigger. How terrible, I thought, to shoot one of our own men by mistake.

I was mulling over this problem when the familiar green beret of the Royal Marines appeared in the firelight. The face under it was blackened and streaked with brown and green. The effect was both sinister and eerie. Underneath the face was the nondescript camouflage clothing that all combat troops seem to wear these days. The green beret was the only distinguishing feature. But perhaps some of our Royal Marines would not be wearing berets? Identifying friend from foe was indeed going to be difficult. When the camouflaged figure spoke, I recognised Mike Norman's reassuring voice. 'All Royal Marines deployed by 0200 hours and ready to repel boarders, Sir', he reported cheerfully. Obviously here was a good man to have in a tight corner.

'Thank you, Mike,' I said, 'Anyone left at Moody Brook?'

'No, sir. All HQ staff are here, Marine Berry on Sapper Hill and the rest deployed east of Stanley.'

'Good'. I looked at my watch: 3.15am. 'Well, unless Reagan can make Galtieri see sense, all we can do now is pray for a Force Nine gale.'

'Not much chance of that,' said Mike ruefully. 'Jack Sollis came back a little while ago. He said the sea's as flat as a pancake, little wind and no moon – ideal conditions for an invasion.'

'Why did Jack come back?'

'Oh, he thought he had a radar contact. But it was a false alarm. I've sent him out again.'

'With the droggies?'

'Not this time – Dick needs them to round up the Argies when you give the word.'

'It won't be long now,' I said.

We walked to the cypher room and, shortly after 3.30am, Brian received the expected signal from the FCO. It confirmed our fears: Galtieri had rebuffed President Reagan's personal appeal on the telephone. Nothing could stop the invasion now. I gave Dick the order to round up the Argentines. I wanted them safely locked up before I broadcast a state of emergency. Dick estimated that he could complete the operation in forty-five minutes so we agreed that I would go on the air at 4.15am. I told Dick to go home as soon as he had rounded them up, and off he went with Chris Todhunter and a handful of droggies and Royal Marines to rendezvous with PC Livermore at the Upland Goose, where most of the Gas del Estado men were staying. Richard Ball with five other ratings went to the Town Hall to be ready to receive and guard the prisoners.

I sat down to prepare my broadcast. There was not much to say. The civilian population had behaved impeccably well up till now, they had heeded my warning to stay indoors and there had been no attempt to retaliate against Argentine property or persons in Stanley. I could not rule out the possibility, however, that a few hotheads might take to the streets and attempt to resist the invaders or, while there was yet time, wreak vengeance upon the Argentines in our midst. I therefore decided to be tough in my address; in retrospect, unnecessarily so, for the Islanders continued to show the utmost dignity and restraint. I went on the air at 4.15am:

Good Morning,

It is with the deepest regret that I have to report a complete lack of response from the Argentine Government to the Security Council's call to refrain from the use of force against the Falkland Islands.[1]

As a last resort, and at our request, President Reagan spoke direct to President Galtieri a little while ago to urge restraint and to offer to send Vice-President Bush to Argentina. Galtieri replied that he appreciated President Reagan's concern, but if the UK did not agree tonight to recognise Argentine sovereignty over the whole of the Falklands, with provision for transfer within the next few months, they would take whatever action was necessary. Argentina considered that it had full freedom to use force. The idea of a mission by Bush was rejected.

Now it is difficult to see what further steps we could take to deter the Argentines. I therefore have no alternative but to declare a State of Emergency with immediate effect, under the Emergency Powers Ordinance of 1939.

Under these emergency powers, I can detain any person, authorise the entering of any premises, acquire any property and issue such orders as I see fit.

I must again warn people in Stanley to stay indoors. Anyone seen wandering on the streets from now until further notice will be arrested by the Security Forces, so please don't make things worse for them and add to their difficulties by going out.

I have no further news about the Argentine Navy task force, but may I just say that the morale of the Royal Marines and the FIDF is terrific, and it makes me proud to be their Commander-in-Chief.

That's all for now – I'll report when anything has been observed.

As Patrick faded me out with more music – Mantovani this time – I returned to the small drawing room and the peat fire. I heard my 'minder' settle down again outside the door. Mike had thoughtfully provided his armourer, Marine Harry Dorey, to be my personal bodyguard. He was to be my loyal shadow throughout the night, never more than a yard or two away.

Like many another that night, in the final lull before the storm, I found myself reflecting upon the past. I reached the conclusion that I had had a hugely enjoyable, interesting and satisfying life, blessed with devoted parents, a wonderful wife and two marvellous children. It was a relief to find that I could face the prospect of death with equanimity. I recalled that the closest I had been before was at the age of nineteen, when my Spitfire had had an argument with a tree while low flying near Wimborne Minster. In a 'Mayday' call, I had reported glycol in the cockpit, engine temperatures off the clock, oil pressure gone and ailerons stuck. I had finished my message with a panic-stricken 'What shall I do?' and it had taken a laconic 'Bale out, chum' from an anonymous pilot to bring me to my senses and nurse the stricken aircraft back to base. Sitting in front of the peat fire, I remembered the Australian Wing Commander's comment after I had landed. 'Son', he said, shaking his head in disbelief, 'You're living on borrowed time.' 'Borrowed for this?' I wondered. Too late to see action in the Second World War, I had felt restless and unfulfilled ever since attaining my wings. No matter how good the training, one could never be sure how one would react when it came to the real thing. Now, it seemed, after all this time, I was to have my baptism of fire.

I considered Mavis's future without me and concluded that she would probably be happier on her own. I had always been difficult to live with, for the past thirty years I had dragged her uncomplainingly around the world, and all she had really wanted for several years now was to settle down in our house in England, tend her beloved garden and watch the seasons come and go. The children had all but flown the nest, so I had no worries on their score. I was, however, desperately concerned about the Royal Marines and the members of the FIDF. Many of them were not much older than my own son, on the threshold of life and with everything to look forward to. The thought that a decision of mine could cut off their young lives was to be my main worry until the final outcome.

I remembered reading in some General's memoirs that, once the battle had started, he could do nothing but wait. The action was out of his hands and he had to leave it to his subordinates. I was happy and relieved to leave the direction of our troops (all seventy-nine of them!) to Mike – as a civilian it would have been presumptuous of me to interfere anyway – but I knew that there could be only one outcome to this particular battle and that I would have to decide when to call it a day. I had had enough experience of the Royal Marines to know that they would fight to the last man unless I ordered them to stop. We clearly had to make a fight of it; but equally clearly there was no point in throwing lives away. The Royal Marines were there to provide a trip-wire. They could not possibly repulse the invader. There was no nuclear submarine within thousands of miles, no relieving cavalry about to charge over the horizon. We were on our own and I would have to give in at some stage. The crucial question was, 'When?'

Mike Norman reported at about 4.45am that he had been out at Lookout Rocks, a good vantage point to the east of Stanley, at 4.30am and thought he had heard the sound of helicopters from the south. This was worrying, if true; but Mike said that his ears might have deceived him. We decided to await corroboration. We went along to the Ops room and it was not long in coming. Marine Michael Berry, alone on Sapper Hill, reported by radio that he, too, thought that he had heard helicopters at about the same time, from the direction of Mullet Creek. But, like Mike, he could not say for sure. If they were landing there, our plans had gone seriously awry. But it seemed unlikely that their main force would land two-and-a-half miles south of Stanley when they had much easier access from the east. In any event, we had no reserves to deploy to the south, so we could only sit tight and await developments. The evidence was insufficient to warrant 'The-invasion-has-started' signal to London – we had already had one false alarm, from the *Forrest*, and I did not want another. The most worrying aspect was that, if the Argentines *had* landed at Mullet Creek, and were now moving towards Stanley, they would cut off the planned escape route for Gary and his section.

A little before 5am, Brian came along from the cypher room to report that Cable and Wireless had asked if they could shut down their link with Rugby and switch to Portishead. I said they could switch anywhere as long as they kept some link open with the UK.

At 5.15am we received the first positive news of the Argentine task force. Jack Sollis on the *Forrest* reported three large blips on his radar screen off Mengeary Point and heading west into Port William. No false alarm this time. He retreated into Stanley Harbour as fast as the *Forrest*'s old engine would allow – all of eight knots. As he entered the Narrows, he did not realise how close he was to being blown out of the water by Corporal York and his section of Royal Marines, who were covering the entrance to the harbour with anti-tank missiles. They recognised the *Forrest* in the nick of time.

Immediately after Jack Sollis's report, Basil Biggs at Cape Pembroke lighthouse reported one large and two smaller vessels, which looked like landing craft, heading towards Yorke Point. I went along to the cypher room and told Brian to send off 'The-invasion-has-started' signal and returned to the Ops room where the military radio was crackling with reports coming in thick and fast. There was understandable confusion and one report of a landing craft approaching the Narrows, which in retrospect must have been the earlier sighting of the *Forrest*: but it caused us concern at the time. We waited eagerly for news from Marines Wilcox and Milne, who were sitting behind their machine-gun in the sand dunes overlooking our chosen beach in Pilot Bay. As they told us later, they had the frustration of seeing a large ship sail past them and on into Yorke Bay. This was a shallow-shelving beach, ideal for amphibious landing craft, which the mother ship presently began to disgorge. The craft trundled unhindered up the beach towards the airport and the road to Stanley. Before we heard about this, however, Marine Berry on Sapper Hill reported that he could see flashing lights approaching from the direction of Mullet Creek. A little later, he estimated upwards of a hundred hostiles coming each side of him and (using the very words that I had used in panic all those years ago) yelled 'What shall I do?' Mike grabbed the microphone and gave him sound practical advice, 'Keep your ruddy head down!'

We were lamenting the fact that this had put paid to Gary's plans to go into hiding when a worried Brian appeared to report that Cable and Wireless had been unable to raise Portishead. They had tried to regain contact with Rugby but to no avail. We were completely out of touch with the UK and he had been unable to send off the invasion signal. My immediate reaction was that the Argentines had sabotaged the Cable and Wireless transmitters, but Brian assured me that they were still working normally: there appeared to be something wrong at the receiving end. I accompanied him to the cypher room and asked for Brian Summers, the duty officer at Cable and Wireless (Phil, his father, had pleaded for him to turn out for the FIDF, since he held the pivotal post of Sergeant Major; but he was also essential at Cable and Wireless). He came along within minutes and confirmed with a cheerful smile that everything was all right at his end and that it was probably the ionosphere playing up.[2] He would keep on trying to raise Portishead or anywhere else in England. I told Brian Wells to despatch the invasion signal *en clair* as soon as contact was re-established and to destroy the remainder of our cypher equipment. 'Then', I said, 'Beat it to Avril's.'

On my return to the Ops room, Mike told me that, in the light of Marine Berry's report, he had ordered two sections back from the east to reinforce our defences at Government House. In the event, only one of them made it.

A few minutes before six o'clock we heard the sound of gunfire coming from the west, followed by what sounded like mortar-bomb explosions. 'Moody Brook', said Mike. I felt immense relief that we had not left any Royal Marines there. 'I'd better go on the air again,' I said and called Patrick at the studio, who switched me through immediately:

This is the Governor speaking. This is just to let you know that the first Argentine ships have been sighted in Port William and one landing craft is approaching the Narrows. Everything is under control. We are keeping them under surveillance. There have been one or two bangs at Moody Brook, but we consider that this is a diversion. That's all for now.

After Patrick had faded me out with 'Fingal's Cave', we heard some very loud bangs and automatic fire so close that they seemed to come from the courtyard between us and the staff quarters. I dived for the floor and the shelter of the office desk and was surprised to find Brian on the floor with me. 'I thought I told you to go to Avril's', I said. 'No chance', said Brian, 'The shooting started as I

225

was coming back from the harbour. They're all round us.' I glanced at my watch – five minutes past six. About half-an-hour to go until dawn. The attack on Government House had started.

The noise for a while was deafening. It numbed the senses, like an anaesthetic, and made thinking a conscious effort. We surmised later that the Argentines were throwing stun grenades but, at the time, we thought we were being mortared. Outbursts of automatic and rifle fire interspersed the bangs. My first rational thought was surprise that the windows had not shattered. My second was to wonder why we had no pieces of metal flying round. Our Royal Marines were obviously firing back at the enemy, but I could not differentiate between incoming and outgoing fire; it all sounded exceedingly close. After what seemed an eternity, I raised my head gingerly and peered out. It was still dark but there was the faintest glimmer of dawn. More bangs close by sent me under the desk again and then, in a lull in the firing, a weird, unearthly voice, distorted by a loudhailer, called out in a thick, Spanish accent: 'Meestair Hurnt – You are a reasonable man. Come out and surrendair.' To which a Royal Marine responded, with commendable initiative and choice lower-deck language, 'F. . . off you bloody spic!' followed by a burst of automatic fire. The shooting then intensified on both sides and Gary urged me to leave the Ops room as the enemy was now just outside.

Brian and I dutifully followed him on our hands and knees down the corridor and into the outer office, but another burst of fire from even closer convinced me that I had been safer under my solid desk in the Ops room. In any event, I did not wish to be separated from my radio link with the Islanders. As I groped my way back down the corridor, I stumbled on a hunched-up figure in the corner and was surprised to find that it was Dick Baker. 'What are you doing here?' I asked. 'I thought I told you to go home.' 'Sorry', said Dick, 'I wasn't able to round up all the Argies before this started. Gilobert and Gamin are still in the LADE house.' Apparently the Gas el Estado boys had taken longer to winkle out than Dick had anticipated. He had rightly concentrated on them and, having made sure that they were safely under guard in the Town Hall, was about to go to the LADE house when he heard firing at Moody Brook. I suspected that he had seized on this as an excuse to return to me rather than do as I had instructed because, loyal second-in-command that he was, he considered his proper place to be at my side. I had not wanted any of my civilian staff to be put at risk by remaining in Government House. Now I had three: Don, Brian and Dick. I must admit, however, that I was glad to have them. Dick was to be particularly useful later on, and it was fortuitous that he had not had the time to pick up Gilobert and Gamin.

Having resumed my position under the desk, I stretched up and grabbed the microphone from the desk-top. I tried speaking into it. It was dead. I grabbed the telephone. With growing apprehension, I propped myself against the side of the desk and cranked the handle to get the operator. To my great relief, the friendly voice of Hilda Perry came through from the exchange, 'What number do you want, Sir?' she asked, as calmly as if it were a normal working day. 'I'm sorry, Hilda', I replied, 'I can't remember the number but can you get me Patrick at the FIBS studio?' 'Certainly, Sir', she replied and after a little delay, there was Patrick's voice on the line, anxiously asking if we were all right. He had heard the firing at Government House and, failing to raise me on the radio link, had feared the worst. I told him that my microphone was not working and he advised me how to check it. As I crawled across the floor, checking the wire into its socket, I realised that the firing had subsided and that it was beginning to get light. As dawn broke, we looked at each other across the floor of the Ops room and grinned as the truth dawned upon us that we had repulsed the enemy's first attack. It was a great feeling; but of course it did not last. We knew in our hearts that the respite was only temporary and that, when they came again, we were done for. But we savoured our brief moment of victory.

I could not get the wretched radio to work. As I fiddled with the wires, Sergeant Short, who had sat calmly operating his radio in the corner throughout the firefight, reported that six APCs (armoured personnel carriers) had been observed heading out of Yorke Bay towards Stanley along the airport road. I asked Mike what armament they carried.

'30mm cannon', he replied.[3]

'What does that mean?'

'It means that they can knock the shit out of us and we can't do a thing about it,' he said calmly.

While Mike began his rounds of Government House to check on casualties, I telephoned Patrick and told him that I had failed to coax any life out of the microphone. Patrick said that he would try putting the earpiece of his telephone to the studio microphone and decided that it was good enough to transmit. So I went on the air again. I gave a summary of what had happened at Government House and reported the sighting of the armoured personnel carriers. I said that it was only a matter of time before we were over-run but that we would hold out for as long as we could. Patrick asked me about casualties and I replied honestly that I knew of none, though inwardly I was sure that there must have been some on both sides. He asked if I was going to surrender and, conscious – indeed hopeful – that the Argentines would be listening, I said 'No – I'm not surrendering to any bloody Argie,' but added that I was prepared to talk if they would send someone to talk to me. I vaguely had in mind some sort of truce or cease-fire to get the wounded to hospital; but I knew in reality that I was simply postponing the inevitable because the prospect of surrender was so distasteful.

Meanwhile, I was anxious that there should be no reprisals against members of the FIDF. Phil obviously shared my concern because he rang immediately after my broadcast and requested further orders. 'Tell them all thank you from me, to go home and get out of uniform', I said, 'And do the same yourself.' Unfortunately, some were unable to get home and were rounded up subsequently with the Royal Marines.

Sporadic firing from the Argentines surrounding Government House continued, but they made no attempt to launch another attack. Fortunately for us, and sensibly of them, they were waiting for the extra fire power of their APCs and were content to keep our heads down. Mike returned with the (to me) incredible but joyous news that no Royal Marine guarding Government House had been killed or wounded. He had, however, heard groaning from the vegetable garden, where there were at least three badly wounded Argentines.

My immediate reaction was 'Good grief, were they that close?' (not fifteen yards from where we were sitting). 'Can we do anything for them?'I asked. 'Two of the lads have already tried', said Mike, 'They were being sniped at but they got near to the first chap, who's in a really bad way – guts spilling out – when he started to pull a grenade. So they left him.' He died where he lay a little later, not actually in the vegetable garden but in the chicken run between the vegetable garden and the staff quarters.[4]

About this time, we received the heartening news that the section led by Mike's second-in-command, Bill Trollope, had knocked out the first APC. They put an 84mm rocket into the tracks and a 66mm rocket into the passenger compartment. They stood ready to shoot anybody who got out, but nobody did (the normal passenger complement was ten). The following APCs stopped, deployed their troops and opened fire on Bill's section which, having exhausted its anti-tank rockets, was forced to withdraw. Unfortunately, the incident occurred on a stretch of the airport road not far from the 'white city', whose civilian occupants took some of the return fire. It was a miracle that no one was killed or injured in this exchange. The first news of it came not from the military radio but from a telephone call to Patrick from Alistair Grieves, a laboratory technician with the Grasslands Trials Unit. He and his wife and child occupied one of the 'white city' bungalows and Patrick broadcast the telephone conversation. Alistair reported heavy bangs, some machine-gun and small-arms fire close by and smoke. Patrick asked him if he could see the APCs but Alistair said that he was lying on the floor and was not prepared to stick his head up to have a look.

Some time later a neighbour, Tom Davies, telephoned to say that his bungalow had received a direct hit. He and Gwen were sheltering on the floor when a mortar bomb struck the galvanised iron water tank above their heads and exploded into thousands of fragments. Had it missed the water tank, it would have exploded on impact with the floor and almost certainly killed them. As it was, the fragments flew harmlessly over their heads into the bedroom and all they got was a good drenching. When Tom rang Patrick, he and Gwen were ankle deep in water, frantically baling out. Tom had visited the Falkland Islands regularly over the past eight years, advising the Grasslands Trials Unit from his base at Newcastle. On reaching the age of sixty and completing a distinguished career in England, he could have settled down to a well-earned retirement, but such was his attachment to the Islands that he had accepted a contract to serve as full-time agronomist in the Grasslands Trials Unit (after the war, he was to take over from John Ferguson as Director of its expanded off-spring, the Agricultural Research Centre). Gwen had never served overseas before but had willingly joined him in Stanley.

Other people began to pick up their telephones and speak to Patrick, who relayed their voices over the radio. The dairyman, Malcolm Ashworth, whose dairy was to the east of Stanley, near the YPF fuel depot (and most of whose cattle were subsequently to be killed and eaten by the occupying forces), reported two Argentine flags flying at the airport. Alistair Grieves called again to report a white helicopter landing at the airport. I was delighted to hear

Peter Felton telling all the anxious parents in camp that their boys were safe and in good heart at Stanley House. They were having breakfast and at the first sign of shooting nearby they would take refuge in the solid stone cellar, where they would be safer than anywhere else in Stanley. John Peatfield called from the girls' hostel to say that they, too, were in good heart and that there had been no shooting near them. No panic, he said, and no tears. They were also having breakfast.

Doctor Daniel called from the hospital to say that everything was fine there, all the staff were on duty, breakfast was being served, they had received no casualties but were ready to look after any that might be brought in. Perhaps the most bizarre call came from the Chief Police Officer, Ronnie Lamb, who said that he had just apprehended Henry Halliday, on his way to work at PWD because, he said, he was shortly to retire and did not want to jeopardise his pension. Rhoda Felton reported from the high ground near the Grasslands Trials Unit that she could see 'armoured cars' entering Stanley and Royal Marines falling back – 'all very colourful' she observed cheerily.

Colourful, it may have been but, if the APCs carried on at this rate, they would be outside Government House within ten minutes. I decided that it was time to talk, picked up the telephone and asked the ever-faithful Hilda to get me the Vicecomodoro. When Gamin answered, I asked to speak to Hector, as his English was better and anyway I had known him for much longer; but, when he came on the line, he sounded very agitated and had difficulty expressing himself in English. I had naturally assumed that he was privy to the invasion plan and indeed that he had a part to play in it. In reply to my request to be put in touch with the commander of the invasion force, however, he said that he did not know who the commander was.

'Come off it, Hector', I said, 'You must know - surely that's why they sent you back.'

'Your Excellency', he replied (he was always very formal with me), 'I beg you to believe me. I know nothing about this, absolutely nothing. It is the most terrible thing that has happened.' There followed an emotional outburst, in a mixture of English and Spanish, explaining that the invasion was the work of the navy and the army and that the air force had nothing to do with it. He and his family had spent some of their happiest days in Stanley, his sons had played football with the Islanders, we were his friends and this was the last thing in the world that he had wanted to happen. He had been sent over to look into the LADE office incident and that was all. He was as surprised and shocked as I was. . . It was a most convincing performance. If he was acting, it was acting worthy of Laurence Olivier.

'All right, Hector', I said, when I could get a word in, 'I believe you. But would you get an Argentine flag and go and find out who *is* in charge? We need a truce to get your wounded to hospital.'

'I haven't got an Argentine flag', he replied lamely.

'Well, go to the office and get one', I said. The conversation was becoming farcical.

'Oh no, I can't go to the office' he replied, with feeling. I had to admit that he had a point, because Government House lay between his house and the LADE office.

'All right', I said impatiently, 'Get a white flag and come here. We won't shoot you, but I can't speak for your people.' There was a pause; then, to his everlasting credit, he replied, 'Give me ten minutes.'

When I told Mike and the others in the Ops room, they fell about laughing. Partly relief, no doubt; but the situation had its funny side. There were we, surrounded by an overwhelmingly superior Argentine force, and there was Hector, coming to *us* with a white flag. He was as good as his word and I like to think that he did it as much for the Islanders as for his fellow-Argentines. Mike warned our Royal Marines not to shoot and yelled to the Argentines to hold their fire; but there was a burst as he opened the door to let Hector in and it was a very shaken Vicecomodoro who appeared in the Ops room. I thanked him for coming and he repeated that he did not know who was in charge of the invading force. Knowing his trigger-happy countrymen, he was reluctant to venture forth again; but it occurred to me that he and Dick Baker, as the local representatives of the Special Consultative Committee, were the right pair to initiate consultations with our uninvited guests. When I put this to Hector, he saw the force of the argument and agreed to go and meet the advancing APCs if Dick would go, too. Dick readily volunteered to accompany him. As we crawled in single file down my 'commuting' corridor (the Argentines were still sniping at us) I picked up one of the white net curtains that had been shot from the window. I also suffered my only 'injury' in the course of the invasion. I bruised my knee on a hard object on the floor. Looking down, I saw our red, smiling Buddha gazing up at me. A memento

231

from Penang, he normally resided on the window-sill; but, like us, he had obviously decided that the floor was the safer place to be. I was glad to see that he was undamaged, and put him back in his proper place (where, incidentally, I found him, still smiling, on my return after the war). I tied the net curtain to my umbrella, which I collected from the stand next to the front door, and gave it to Dick. My last words were, 'Don't lose my umbrella, Dick – I paid the earth for it from Briggs in Piccadilly.'

Corporal Geordie Gill was guarding the front door. As we watched Hector and Dick walk bravely down the drive towards the town, white flags fluttering, Geordie turned to me in dismay. 'Does this mean I can't shoot at the bastards any more?' he asked, his face a picture of disappointment.

'Not at all, Geordie', I said (though unsure myself of the Geneva Convention), 'If they shoot at you, you shoot back. And if they try to move, you shoot.'

'Ah, thank you, Sir', he said beaming as if I had just given him a week's run ashore. 'You see, there's one of them just up there, behind that rock, and he'll have to move some time.' Geordie was a crack shot, one of NP8901's best and most experienced marksmen, with two previous tours in the Falklands. He loved the Islands and, though no longer married to Sonia, was deeply concerned about her and their children's safety. I did not rate highly the chances of survival of that Argentine behind the rock.

As Dick and Hector disappeared from our view along Ross Road, there was a burst of fire from the football field. I dashed back to the Ops room, praying that they had not been the target. Happily, a few minutes later, Ronnie Lamb came on the telephone to report that he could see them approaching the Town Hall. At the same time, Patrick reported that an Argentine had been trying to contact him on our local radio frequency. The voice was indistinct and the message unclear, but it seemed that he was an official spokesman of the task force. I asked Patrick to tell him to meet my Chief Secretary and the LADE Vicecomodoro outside the Town Hall. Meanwhile, Dick had gone into the Town Hall and now contacted me by telephone. I told him that we were in touch with the enemy by radio and would he and Hector wait outside the Town Hall for the task force commander or his representative to come along from Ross Road East, where the APCs appeared to have stopped.

While we were waiting for them to make contact, we heard a couple of bursts of automatic fire from the staff quarters, followed a few minutes later by an ebullient Gary Noott, grinning from ear to ear and announcing proudly that he had caught three prisoners. Corporal Mick Sellen, who with Marine Paterson had shot the three Argentines in the chicken run, had reported to Gary that he had seen three others make for the staff quarters, and he suspected that they were still there. Gary had gone to the foot of the stairs with Geordie Gill and Marine Harry Dorey and fired a burst into the roof, whereupon a babble of excited Spanish voices had emanated from the store-room on the first floor. Another burst had produced a clatter of arms and three frightened 'Argies' with their hands up. As Gary said later, if these were their crack troops, he was not overly impressed: he had expected them to come out with guns blazing. It was perhaps fortunate for Gary and his men that they had not. I remember thinking at the time, 'What on earth are we going to do with three prisoners when we are surrounded by hundreds of the blighters?' I was relieved, however, that I had insisted upon the staff leaving the night before.

Shortly after this incident, Dick saw three men, whom he later described to me as looking like characters from an American war film, walking towards him along Ross Road from the Upland Goose, followed closely behind by an APC. All wore combat gear and had pistols strapped to their waists. The tall man in the centre of the group introduced himself to Dick as Admiral Carlos Busser, commander of the task force. Dick invited him to come to Government House without the APC. Busser gave an order to one of his aides: the APC stopped and the party of five, with Dick and Hector still carrying their white flags, started to walk in line abreast along Ross Road towards Government House. As they walked, Dick saw steel-helmeted Argentine troops appearing on the ridge behind the football field and heard them chanting 'Argentina'. Suddenly, there was a burst of gunfire. Dick was about to dive for cover in the gorse hedge when Admiral Busser barked a command in Spanish that would have done credit to a Guards' sergeant-major and the firing stopped as abruptly as it had started. Busser smiled at Dick and said, in English: 'And they call this the age of electronics!'

I was sitting behind my desk in the Ops room, working out in my mind how to conduct the interview, when the door opened and Busser strode in. His appearance took me by surprise. He was tall, lean, pleasant-looking and, despite his warlike trappings, almost gentle of aspect. My anger mounted, however, as he shook hands with my colleagues, for all the world as if he were paying a diplomatic courtesy call and his troops had not been shooting at us moments before. I stood up as he approached my desk. He proffered his hand and I almost took it from habit; but then the anger welled up and instead I had a momentary desire to pull my pistol out of the drawer and empty the magazine into his chest. He must have seen the anger in my eyes, for he dropped his hand with a hurt look and I immediately felt ashamed of my behaviour. What programmed creatures we are, I thought – not a moment ago I had wanted to kill him. His eyes showed not anger but weariness: the tell-tale rings indicated that he, too, had been a long time without sleep. I told him that I could not shake hands with someone who was invading British territory, that he had landed unlawfully and was to leave forthwith. He replied in good English that he was in charge of the landing force and had come to reclaim for Argentina what was rightfully theirs. I pointed out that our two governments had agreed in the UN to settle the dispute by peaceful means and he said, almost apologetically, that he was a soldier merely obeying instructions. Before I could make the obvious point that those instructions had come from a military junta, he went on to say that he had brought an 'overwhelmingly superior force' with which to take the Islands so as to avoid casualties. He complimented me on the 'bravery and professionalism' of my troops but appealed to me now to order them to lay down their arms in order to save needless bloodshed and damage to property. I said that I would certainly agree to a truce so that we could get his badly wounded to hospital. He thanked me for my concern for his wounded but again urged me to order my men to lay down their arms. 'Otherwise', he said, 'you will be held responsible for the further casualties that will inevitably occur.' I retorted that it was the people who started the shooting that were responsible for the casualties, not the people who resisted. But I had to admit to myself that I would be putting both Royal Marines and civilians at unnecessary risk by carrying on an obviously futile resistance. With a heavy heart, I turned to Mike and told him to give the order to lay down arms. I could not bring myself to use the word 'Surrender'. Mike's face was a mixture of relief and anguish: it was not part of his training to surrender, but his good sense told him that there was no real alternative. As Gary accompanied Busser to tend the wounded round Government House, Mike told his radio operator to instruct all sections to down arms and wait to be collected. I started preparing my final broadcast to tell the Falkland Islanders that it was all over. Glancing up from my desk, I noticed that somehow Simon Winchester had managed to slip in to the Ops room and was standing scribbling away in the background. I had to admire his journalistic enterprise.

For the last half-hour or so I had been unable to listen to the local radio: but most Islanders had had their ears glued to their sets and heard the dramatic announcement that the FIBS studio had been taken over. Patrick had carried on playing music (setting the scene with 'Spanish Eyes' and 'Granada') and relaying telephone messages until the Argentines burst open the door and stormed into the studio. Listeners heard an excited Spanish voice, followed by an indignant Patrick saying:

Just a minute. Take that gun out of my back. I'm going to transmit. You take that gun away. I'm not speaking with a gun in my back. . . Well, we have been taken over as expected by the Argentines. . . They have just given me some tapes they want to broadcast. . . Huh, they are arguing amongst themselves now – the three Argentines. . . They've disappeared and left me alone in this room. Good. I still hope that we can get His Excellency the Governor's message to you. . .

It was at this moment that I rang through. Patrick said, over the radio and on the telephone to me,

Sir, I've just been taken over by the Argentines; but they've gone into an argument now. Right. Well, HE the Governor is on the line now and he's going to speak to you before we have to play the Argentine tapes. Yes, Sir, go ahead please.

Trying to hide the emotion I felt, I began:

Hello, Kelpers and Islanders. I hope that you can hear me on the 'phone. The machine here doesn't work. I'm sorry it happened like this. The Admiral came along – I must pay tribute to Vicecomodoro Gilobert, who was very brave in coming in here, and also to Dick Baker, for the two of them going down and waiting for the Admiral when shots were whipping about all over the place – the Admiral came along to me and I told him that he had landed unlawfully on British sovereign territory and I ordered him to leave forthwith. He refused, claiming that he was taking back territory that belonged to Argentina and that it was Britain that was unlawfully in possession. I said that it was reprehensible that

Argentina should have seized the islands by force after Britain and Argentina had agreed in the UN to settle the dispute by peaceful means. He said he was a soldier merely obeying instructions, but he appealed to me to cease needless bloodshed as he had an overwhelmingly superior force. I said I couldn't argue with that but I would not have agreed to a ceasefire had we anything like comparable forces. He paid tribute to our troops and called them very brave. I told him that he had got three seriously wounded at the back of my staff quarters and offered him medical help. He gladly accepted. He gave assurance that no Islander would be harmed in any way. I said I had heard that some of his troops had already broken in to some of the Islanders' homes and he immediately told his second-in-command to investigate and to discipline them afterwards. I sincerely hope that that happens. I asked if he was taking over from me as military governor. He said no, an army general would be coming to take over from me in about an hour.

That's all I've got to say. I'm sorry it's happened this way. It's probably the last message I'll be able to give you. But I wish you all the best of luck and, rest assured, the British will be back.

I had no grounds for making that last remark except the deep conviction that the British public would recognise right from wrong and would not let wrong prevail. I hoped that it would both reassure the Islanders and put fear into the Argentines.

No music from Patrick to fade me out this time. Instead, an anxious voice as my telephone went dead: 'Sir? Hello?. . . I'm sorry, I've lost the Governor. . .' In more senses than one, I thought, sadly. Then the line crackled back into life and Patrick asked: 'Can you tell me what the next step is that the people should take now please?' I advised them to continue to stay indoors for the time being, as there were still plenty of troops around who were fidgety with their triggers: but that, when things settled down, kelpers should carry on as much as possible as normal. Government departments would doubtless be taken over, as Patrick's had been, but officials should continue to run their departments in the usual way for the sake of the Islanders. Patrick asked if he personally should carry on. I said that he was performing a valuable service for the Islanders, he had done a tremendous job throughout the night and that he should keep it up for as long as they let him – even with

236

a gun in his back. He asked me what I thought the British reaction would be. I said that we would have to declare war on Argentina: Argentines had taken by force a piece of British sovereign territory and we had no alternative. I added that no respectable nation in the world could do other than condemn the Argentine act and I was sure that it would have won the Islanders many friends that they did not have before. I ended by saying that I would continue to broadcast until somebody stopped me.

The time had come to take stock of the damage to Government House. As I had instructed everyone else to lay down arms, I thought that I had better do something about my own pistol, which was still lying fully loaded in the desk drawer. I handed it over to a surprised Argentine guard and headed for the kitchen, which Don told me had been wrecked by hand grenades. Passing the front door, I saw some Argentine soldiers carrying two bodybags over Mavis's rockery, which was on the right of the main drive. They were stumbling on the uneven surface under their heavy loads and I had no doubt that the bags contained dead Argentines. I must say that I was not prepared for the sight that greeted me when I reached the kitchen; it was as if a hurricane had struck it – I could not believe that one or two splinter grenades could wreak such havoc. The freezer had been blown apart: there were loose and frayed wires, broken glass and debris everywhere. To make matters worse, water was cascading down through the ceiling, hissing and spluttering as it hit the bare wires. Don and I switched off all the switches and unplugged all the plugs that we could find and went up to the attic to try to locate the stopcock. On the way, I glanced into Diana's room. Apart from the water pouring down from above and the broken windows, there were two bullet-holes in the wall and another perfectly placed in the posterior of Picasso's blue nude, a print of which John had bought Diana as a Christmas present. It was marksmanship worthy of Geordie Gill.

In the attic, we had trouble finding the stopcock; but we found several bullet-holes in the water-pipes and were attempting to plug these when we heard the sound of helicopters arriving at the football field. We had an excellent view from our vantage point in the attic. Two Lynx helicopters landed, and out poured a horde of red-hatted, gold-braided gentlemen who proceeded to hug, kiss and embrace each other in typical Latin fashion. 'Just look at the silly buggers', said Don, 'You'd think they'd won the World Cup.' I looked at my watch: 10.30. The Military Governor was starting punctually. I dashed along to my bedroom to spruce up a little to receive the General. It was the first time I had been there since my nap in the early hours. The room faced the harbour and had thus escaped most of the shooting; but the roof on the southern side and the bathroom had been peppered and the sunshine through the holes gave a pleasant, dappled effect.

I went down to my main office to await the Argentine general. Dick was already there. We watched sadly as Argentine soldiers assembled our Royal Marines on the lawn in front of us. We were alarmed to see some members of the FIDF. They were Gerald Cheek's and Pat Peck's sections, who had been caught between the Argentines attacking Moody Brook and those surrounding Government House. As I learned from Pat later, their worst moment was when they had been lined up against the wall outside the Chief Secretary's house and told to straighten their berets. Pat had expected a 'Mexican execution' but, instead, they had been offered cigarettes. Now, they were apart from the main body of Royal Marines and we wondered anxiously what the Argentines might have in store for them. We were particularly concerned over the fate of two ex-Royal Marines, Jim Fairfield and Taff Davies. They had married Islanders and were living in Stanley. They had not joined the FIDF but 'once a Royal Marine, always a Royal Marine' and, after hearing my broadcast the night before, they had reported for duty at Moody Brook. We saw them now, sitting on the lawn with the rest of the Royal Marines, and hoped that they would not find themselves locked up and sent away. Yet we did not want to draw the Argentines' attention to them because, as civilians, their status was, to say the least, questionable. In the event, we need not have worried, because Pat Peck managed to extricate them from the Royal Marines and infiltrate them into his section. After handing in their firearms, all the FIDF members were allowed to go home and there was no subsequent evidence of victimisation (though Gerald Cheek was banished to Fox Bay East).

Dick and I assumed that the ten hydrographers would be treated as combatants, in the same way as the Royal Marines. We considered the position of our two RAF technicians and decided that, as they were for all practical purposes civilian, it was probably better to say nothing about their military status.

After about a quarter of an hour, an Argentine officer appeared to take me, he said, to General Garcia in the Town Hall. I told him to go back and tell his General that I would see him here, at Government House. He dutifully departed to return about half-an-hour later with an escort to say that General Garcia 'commanded' me to appear before him at the Town Hall. I said that I did not take instructions from his General, Government House was the seat of government and that, if his General wanted to see me he should come here. The poor man looked most unhappy, but withdrew once more. Finally, a little after midday, Hector Gilobert turned up in his car and implored me to go with him peacefully to the Town Hall, otherwise the soldiers would 'escort' me there. My first reaction was 'Let them'; but the thought of being frog-marched to the Town Hall was too undignified, so I finally agreed to go. Dick came with me. As we drove the short distance from Government House to the Town Hall, past the now-stationary APCs and hordes of laughing, chattering Argentine soldiers, I thought of the many times I had travelled that route in the red taxi to the formal opening of Legislative Council, when the Royal Marines and FIDF had looked so smart and proud in their Number Ones. Now they were sprawling dejectedly on the grass outside Government House, untidy in combat gear, faces blackened and bodies limp with fatigue.

Hector led us up the stairs and into the refreshment room to the right of the main hall, where we normally went for a drink and a chat between dances on a Saturday night. The room was full of Argentine soldiers, pressmen and cameras. They had even rigged up special lighting to capture their moment of glory. A sallow little man with general's epaulettes came towards me, arm outstretched and a fixed, sickly smile on his face. Cameras whirred. It was all beautifully stage-managed, doubtless for the rejoicing Argentine public back home; but I failed to respond to cue. I put my hands pointedly behind my back. The cameras stopped. The smile disappeared. The sallow cheeks twitched with annoyance and Garcia said sharply, through a naval interpreter: 'It is very ungentlemanly of you to refuse to shake my hand', to which I replied, 'It is very uncivilised of you to invade my country.' As the interpreter struggled in some embarrassment to translate this, I looked directly at the General and said the words that I had rehearsed to myself while waiting in the office: 'You have landed unlawfully on British territory and I order you to remove yourself and your troops forthwith', whereupon Garcia retorted angrily, raising his voice, 'We have taken back what is rightfully ours and we shall stay FOREVER.' 'We could go on arguing over sovereignty forever', I said, 'But what you cannot

239

deny is that your government and mine pledged to settle the dispute by peaceful means. Do you call this peaceful?'

I spread my arms to indicate the assembled soldiery. Garcia turned away impatiently and conferred with his aides, while Dick and I stood there, feeling ill at ease (though not, I hope, showing it). Garcia turned to us again and, once more in control of himself, said that we must leave by four o'clock that afternoon. The tension eased when I replied that we could not possibly leave by then: 'You didn't tell us you were coming', I said, 'So we haven't packed.' This drew a genuine smile from Garcia. He nevertheless insisted that I and 'all my colonial officers' must leave by four, but gave his personal assurance that our belongings would be looked after, properly packed and forwarded to us. We could take now only what we could pack in the next few hours. I said that the administration of the Islands would break down completely if all the expatriate officers left with me. My diplomatic staff should accompany me but, apart from them, all the expatriate officers should stay until the Argentine Government had made proper arrangements to replace them. Garcia conferred again with his aides and then gave his agreement. I said I could not leave without 'my troops' (ie hydrographers as well as Royal Marines). There was another conference and Garcia confirmed that they would be flown by Hercules to join me in Comodoro Rivadavia. I would go with my staff in a Fokker F28. I then pointed out that three of the Royal Marines were married to local girls and had children: those families should also come with me in the F28. After further consultation, Garcia agreed. That was the end of the interview and I did not see him again.

As Hector drove us back to Dick's residence, he volunteered to look after my aircraft and see that it was safely delivered to France, if I could pick it up from there. I wondered why he had chosen France but told him not to worry, we would be back before he could do anything about it. We bade each other farewell, Hector still mumbling apologies for the whole sorry business, and Dick and I went inside to rejoin our families.

Notes

1. I was wrong here. The call came from the President of the Security Council, with the support of the majority of members.

2. At the time of the invasion, we had only short-wave radio communications with the outside world and these were sometimes disrupted by movements of the Heavyside Layer in the ionosphere, from which the

April 1982   Stanley — Commodore Riv.

2 Friday

8 am A long night. Sat in front of peat fire, cocking pistol. Came to terms

9 with not being here this time tomorrow. 0230. Mike reported all Marines deployed.

10 0330 Reagan's appeal to Galtieri rebuffed. No chance now. Told Dick to round up

11 Argies.

4.15 — went on air & declared state of

12 emergency.

4.30 — reports of helicopters from South.

1 pm 5.15 — tried to signal FCO, landings started, from Marines in lighthouse + York Bay.

2 Brian Summers miss circuit gone. Rugby out — tried Portishead. No joy.

3 5.50 Bangs from Moody Brook. 6am. Shots at us in GH. ½ hr of bedlam.

4 Lights out, on floor. They withdrew. As dawn came, groans from wall. 3 there.

5 Gary caught 3 in Maids' quarters. 15 APCs landed & approaching town. 30mm cannon.

6 Rang Hector Gilobert. He came with white flag. Dick went with him to Town Hall. Admiral

7 Busser (?) came. 9.25 ordered ceasefire. General Garcia arr. 10.30. To Town Hall. Hector

April took over when... 12.15 Notes Back to Connie's
Sunday   4 11 18 25 for lunch. Then packed. Pay.
Monday   5 12 19 26
Tuesday 6 13 20 27 Dowling (Int. Officer) To Radio
Wednesday 7 14 21 28
Thursday 1 8 15 22 29 Station. Patrick Watts was terrific.
Friday   2 9 16 23 30 But put it by now. Recorded
Saturday 3 10 17 24 message. And to Goytwicke. Left
6 pm. With Avril, Wells & Marine wives.

Extract from my diary, 2 April 1982 (*Express Newspapers*)

Previous page Government House in the foreground, looking east over Stanley. The Argentines attacked through the vegetable garden (lower right). Three were shot in the chicken run behind the staff quarters (centre right) and three caught in the staff quarters. My operations room was immediately to the left of the large garage. This picture was taken in 1983, after the war but before the hospital fire (*Crown Copyright – BFFI Photographic Section*)

With Mavis and Cindy Buxton in front of our crashed Wasp, St Andrews Bay, South Georgia, 1981. (*Cindy Buxton & Annie Price: Survival Anglia*)

Stanley under the Argentines. Drive on the right! (*R. S. Whitley*)

Stanley town plan (*FIG*)

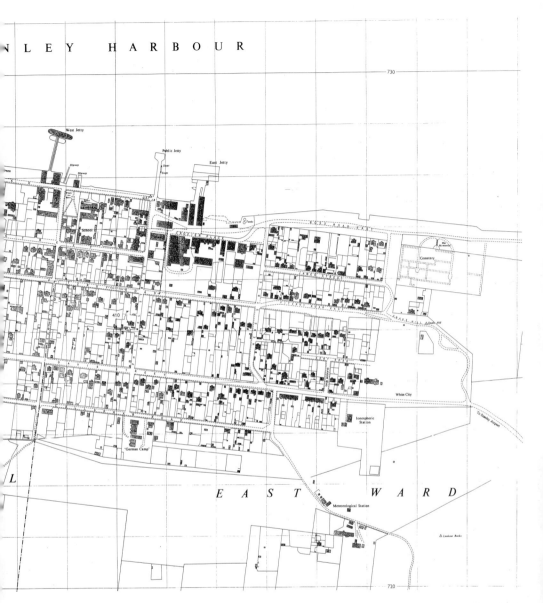

Taken from D.O.S. 153 © Crown Copyright 1966, with additional labels

Below Farewell dinner on board HMS *Invincible*, Port William, 24 August 1982. From left to right: Councillors Terry Peck, Tim Blake, Maj Gen David Thorne, Captain Jeremy Black, myself, Rear-Admiral Derek Reffell, Harold Rowlands (Financial Secretary), Dick Baker (Chief Secretary), Councillor Bill Luxton and Commander Tony Provest (*Crown Copyright – HMS* Invincible *Photographic Section*)

Left Meeting the Prime Minister at No 10 Downing Street with Gary Noott and Mike Norman, 5 April 1982 (*Express Newspapers*)

Right Opening Brabant Island Post Office, 17 February 1984. Postmaster Chris Furse in the tent, Captain Colin MacGregor on my left (*Ted Corbett*)

Below Welcoming the Secretary of State for Defence to the opening of Mt Pleasant Airport, 12 May 1985. From left to right: Bridget and Maj Gen Peter de la Billiere, Mavis, myself, Mr Michael Heseltine. On the steps, in ascending order: Mrs Anne Heseltine, Lord Strathcona, Lord Shackleton and Lord Buxton, Air Marshal Sir Peter Harding, Mr Ian Gow and Sir Humphrey Atkins (*Crown Copyright – BFFI Photographic Section*)

radio waves normally bounced back to earth. As we discovered later, ionospheric conditions were notoriously bad at Falklands latitudes at that time of the year and that hour of the day.

3. It transpired that they were armed with .5in machine guns, not 30mm cannon, but they still outgunned us.

4. He was Captain Giacchino, commanding the *Buzo Tactico* detachment which attacked Government House. He was the only fatal casualty admitted by the Argentines and was deservedly given a hero's funeral in Argentina.

Above left Prince Andrew at Blue Beach Cemetery, 11 May 1985. Monsignor Spraggon and Padre Carruthers behind. (*Crown Copyright – BFFI Photographic Section*)

Below left Farewell to Stanley, 13 October 1985. On board RFA *Sir Geraint* watching MV *Forrest* returning to harbour. (*Crown Copyright – BFFI Photographic Section*)

13

A Strange Homecoming

Mavis and Connie were naturally relieved to see us. They had followed events on the radio and had received one or two stray bullets in Sulivan House as the Argentine troops had passed by on their way from Moody Brook to Government House. We were recounting our experiences when a distraught Patrick appeared with his nine-year-old daughter, Amara. Though drooping from fatigue, he was too distressed to sleep. Dick gave him a whisky and he told us what had happened at the studio. Apparently, the three Argentines had settled their argument, returned and ordered Patrick to play their first tape. It began with a painful rendering of the Argentine national anthem, played at the wrong speed, followed by a recorded voice in Spanish reading four communiqués, which were then translated into English by a voice that sounded suspiciously like that of Colonel Balcarce. The communiqués started by greeting the people of 'Malvinas' and exhorting them to co-operate with the new authorities and to comply with all future instructions. The 'colonial and military authorities' of the British Government would be sent back to Britain immediately, with their families and personal effects. For the time being, all people were to remain in their homes and anyone found outside would be arrested (shades of my emergency declaration). However, the Argentine Government guaranteed the continuity of the Islanders' way of life in an atmosphere of peace, order and harmony. As we were to learn later, subsequent edicts showed how hollow was this guarantee: for example, one decreed that all traffic should travel henceforth on the right-hand side of the road and another that Spanish would be the official language and the teaching medium in schools. Needless to say, Islanders took not the slightest notice, driving as they had always driven, on the *best* side of the road, and continuing to speak English. Schools remained closed, though some of the teachers held lessons (in English of course) in private homes. Patrick went on to say that the Argentines had then put on the second tape, which began with the Argentine national anthem, followed by Argentine military music. Eventually, we managed to persuade Patrick that his best place now was bed and Amara, showing a maternal instinct well beyond her years, took him home.

Connie served mutton for lunch. Despite having had nothing to eat since dinner the night before, I could not work up much of an appetite. Now that it was all over, a great lethargy descended and it took my more practical wife to remind me that we had no time to waste if we were to be packed by 4pm. As we drove back to Government House in Fifi, we met the dentist, Robert Watson, and his American wife, Cathy, walking along Ross Road. We stopped to say goodbye and I was saddened to see tears streaming down Cathy's face. She was too upset to speak. I wished them all the best and turned into Government House drive with indignation and anger mounting again. How could Galtieri cause such unhappiness to decent people like Robert and Cathy? They were of the Bahai faith: unselfish, upstanding citizens who had lived in the Falkland Islands for over ten years, dedicated to improving the dental health and general welfare of the Islanders.

I was in no mood to be greeted at the door of my own home by a tall, smartly dressed, heel-clicking Gestapo-type Argentine who introduced himself as Major Dowling, military intelligence. He spoke excellent English and described himself as Irish-Argentine, though his demeanour suggested classical Prussian. He flourished a list of names and demanded to know what I had done with my missing marines. I was shocked to see that he had a complete roll-call of both outgoing and incoming detachments, all correctly typed with ranks and initials. He must have brought it with him from Buenos Aires and obtained it, I presumed, from an airline agent in Montevideo (the Royal Marines flew from the UK to Montevideo by civilian airline, so the passenger manifest would have been readily available). I glanced down the list and my heart beat faster when I saw that the unticked names included those from Gary's detachment whom we had sent to South Georgia on the *Endurance*. Good, I thought, they are in for a nasty shock when they try to land there. Corporal York and his section from the new detachment were also unaccounted for. I feared for them because they had taken off to the north camp, whereas Gary's plan had been to go south. They knew nothing of the countryside or the Islanders. To Dowling, I naturally feigned ignorance. 'I only know the officers', I said, thinking of the Argentine attitudes to their own men, 'I don't bother about the other ranks.' This seemed to satisfy him.

He folded the list primly and put it in his pocket with a confident 'We shall find them.'

I declined his invitation to accompany him to my office, saying that I was in a hurry to pack. He explained that his primary objective was my cypher room. He knew what was in there; he knew that it was protected by three combination locks; all he required from me were the three combinations, otherwise he would have to blow the door. I said that in that case he would have to blow the door; would he now kindly let me get on with my packing. He followed me upstairs and kept pestering me until eventually, to get him out of my hair, I told him that I would go down and open the first combination blister for him, but that I did not know the others; he would have to get them from my assistant. He strode down the stairs ahead of me and along the corridor like an eager schoolboy. I was pleased when he banged his head on the lintel of the green baize door (I usually warned tall people that it was rather low). The first combination blister normally contained the keys to the filing cabinets and the strongroom door (which had a second combination blister over one of its locks). I knew that those keys were now at the bottom of the harbour. As I twirled the knob and swung open the door, Dowling's smile turned to a scowl. Stabbing a finger at the list on the inside of the door, he barked 'Where are these?' 'I don't know', I replied, in all innocence. 'They were there the last time I opened it.' In a rage, he stalked off to find Brian. I returned to my packing, happy in the knowledge that, even if Brian did open the second combination, Dowling would not open the strongroom door without the key, and that greater disappointment lay in store for him when he finally broke into the strongroom, for we had destroyed all the security material therein.

I was about to pack my ceremonial uniform and wondering how best to stow the awkwardly shaped hat and feathers when Tony came in from his bedroom. 'Why don't you wear it, Dad?' 'Don't be silly', called Mavis, from our bedroom, 'He can't travel in that.' Perhaps not, I thought, but it might hearten the Islanders to see me leave in style. I could think about getting out of it afterwards. So I put it on. Taking the tunic from the wardrobe, I noticed that my medals had gone. I was puzzled. Why should anyone steal my medals? Dowling was the obvious suspect. He must have been skulking about inside Government House in our absence. I resolved to accuse him directly, but more pressing problems arose when he reappeared and the medals slipped my mind. His temper had not been improved by his wild-goose chase. Nor did the sight of me in my uniform do anything to sweeten it. 'You can't go in that', he said. I shrugged and carried on closing the suitcases. He hesitated. Good, I thought, he is obviously under orders not to lay hands upon me. Changing tack, he said that we were already late and his instructions were to take me to the airport: where were the keys to the Land Rover? I replied that Tony had them and that he would drive the Land Rover after loading our baggage. Tony winked as he went off with Dowling, taking him deliberately the long way round, by the office entrance. As soon as they had gone, our faithful Don, previously alerted, brought the red taxi to the front door and hoisted my pennant as Mavis and I jumped in. We were well away before Dowling realised what had happened.

'Stop at the studio, Don', I said, 'I want to broadcast a farewell message.' We drove past groups of Argentine troops who gaped in surprise at the Union Jack fluttering proudly from the red taxi. We went past the Secretariat, from which hung an enormous Argentine flag, out of all proportion to the modest flagpole,[1] up St Mary's Walk and stopped outside the studio in John Street. Mavis and Don sat in the taxi and I went inside. I was surprised but pleased to see Patrick there, with two Argentines. I explained my intentions and the Argentines said that they would have to get General Garcia's permission. I said that I was prepared to wait and, emerging from the studio, found Dowling glowering at me from beside the taxi. Emboldened by our last encounter, I said I refused to go to the airport until I had broadcast a farewell message to 'my people' and that I should be obliged if he would report that to his general. To my surprise, he acquiesced and headed off in the direction of the Town Hall. Fortunately, it was a dry, sunny afternoon and an increasing number of Islanders ventured out of doors and gathered round our little convoy as the news spread that we were there. Don took the opportunity to check that Avril and the children and Brian and Chris had been collected from the Growcott's house, which was nearby, and Dowling returned with the news that General Garcia would not allow me to broadcast live, but that I could record a message on tape, to be broadcast after I had gone, provided that at the same time I would broadcast instructions to any of 'my troops' who might be in South Georgia to lay down their arms. I said I would do no such thing but that I would give them a factual account of what had happened here (they would almost certainly have picked up the earlier broadcasts on shortwave anyway).

While Dowling relayed this to Garcia, I set about writing my farewell message, leaning on the bonnet of the taxi, with frequent interruptions from Islanders who wanted to bid me farewell. John Dixon appeared from nowhere to photograph me at this time. Monsignor Spraggon came up from St Mary's, accompanied by Father Monaghan. Seeing me in uniform, he determined there and then to wear his full regalia each day until the Argentines departed. 'The Islanders will need you more than ever now, Monsignor', I said. 'I know you'll do your best for them.' 'And I know you'll be back', said Monsignor, with absolute conviction. Daniel Spraggon was a remarkable man. The son of a Newcastle butcher, he had been called to the priesthood with the Mill Hill Fathers and served for many years in West Africa, for much of the time as chaplain to the forces. Mavis and I had known several of his colleagues in Uganda, where they ran schools and clinics in remote areas. Now in his seventies, Daniel had been in the Falkland Islands for over ten years and was universally liked and respected. He was to prove a tower of strength during the occupation. Hector Gilobert came along, to bid farewell to Mavis; but I noticed that he slipped away as soon as Dowling reappeared. Harry Bagnall also came to express his sadness at our departure and to assure me that he and Iris would stay on for as long as the people needed them. He, too, was to perform sterling service during the occupation.

Dowling came back with orders to present my message to General Garcia before I recorded it. Off he went with my rather scruffy hand-written text and the crowd swelled until he returned with Garcia's agreement for me to put it on tape. Dowling insisted, however, that I recorded it in the studio in his presence and waited until he played it back to make sure that I had not strayed from the approved text. By now it was well after 4.30pm and we were slipping further behind our estimated time of departure.

I cannot remember the contents of my farewell message. I have neither a copy of the text nor a recording of it; but Garcia was true to his word and allowed it to be broadcast. I know that I ended by reiterating that we would be back. We drove away from a silent, tearful crowd in John Street. Don paused as we drew alongside Lois Cottage, the home of Syd and Betty Miller, who were both at the gate to say goodbye. They were heartbroken. Tears streamed down their cheeks and they were too distressed to speak. They grabbed my hands in theirs and clung on. I shall not forget the anguish on their faces as I pulled away, as gently as I could. They remained frozen at the gate as we drove down John Street and rounded the bend into Philomel Hill.

Approaching the airport, Mavis said that she would jump out as soon as Don stopped and grab the pennant. Her female intuition must have warned her what was to happen for, as soon as we stopped and before she could move, Dowling had appeared from nowhere and seized the pennant. I asked him to hand it over but he merely smiled and put it in his pocket. He told Don that he must not hang around the airport. I had dreaded saying goodbye, but Don made it easier. 'Don't you worry, sir', he said, 'I'll make sure them fellers don't use the taxi – or Fifi. And I'll pop in every day to see that your kit is OK until you're back.' I watched as the taxi trundled off towards Stanley, praying that I would see him – and it – again.

We were relieved to find the other civilian passengers already mustered in the airport lounge. I felt sorry for Avril, with three small children and no husband. She was beside herself with anxiety for Michael's safety in Buenos Aires. While Tony played with the children, I did my best to reassure her that no harm would come to him. We had a long wait in the airport lounge because Dowling insisted upon going through every item of my baggage. With two assistants, the inspection took over two hours – almost as long as we had been given to pack. Whether Dowling actually believed that I would be stupid enough to have the combinations written down somewhere, I do not know; but he searched through every pocket and read every piece of paper. He tore the suitcase linings, took the backs off framed photographs and confiscated every file and document. One file he seized upon eagerly contained the minutes of our 150th Anniversary Celebrations Committee. He seemed to think it particularly significant. Naturally I protested, claiming diplomatic immunity, but he said nothing, smiled coldly and carried on in his clinical way. I managed to win an argument over my personal diary. I had made the mistake of using an official HMSO publication, from which he inferred that it contained official records. He spent a good ten minutes flitting through its pages and reading several innocuous entries before throwing it across the table back to me.

The inspection was carried out behind a curtain in one corner of the airport lounge. It occurred to me that here was a good opportunity to get out of my uniform, which, as Mavis had said, was not the ideal apparel for long hours of airline travel. As Dowling was taking out my suits and running through the pockets, I took off my gloves and hat and handed them over to him. He took them automatically, then paused and gave me a flash of his cruel blue eyes. I thought for a second that he was going to throw them back at me; instead, he slowly turned the hat over, looked inside, ran his fingers round the lining and handed it, gloves, feathers and all to one of his assistants. I took off my sword and belt and handed them over. He showed great interest in the sword, pulling it out of its scabbard. 'Ah, Wilkinson', he remarked. I next unbuttoned my tunic and handed that over. He felt in all the pockets and passed it to his assistant. The same with my trousers and, finally, boots, which he did not bother to inspect – evidently they were unworthy of his scrutiny (which showed, incidentally, that he was not as professional as he made himself out to be). I stood in my socks, underpants and vest and pointed to a shirt. His assistant passed it to Dowling, who handed it over to me. I pointed to trousers; the same sequence, followed by jacket, tie and shoes. Not a word passed between us. When they started repacking, I derived inordinate pleasure from watching Dowling and his henchmen folding and packing the ceremonial uniform of Her Majesty's Colonial Service.

Tony followed me in and they went through his luggage. 'Thank goodness they didn't make me strip like you, Dad', he said afterwards, thinking that I had been made to take off my uniform. 'I have Simon Winchester's report in my shoe.' Apparently Simon had managed to intercept Tony and slip the report to him while Dowling was otherwise engaged. Tony had put it inside his shoe and was using it as a sole.

After an interminable wait at the airport, we were eventually escorted to a Fokker F28 and told to board. Mavis confirmed that the Royal Marines had already boarded a Hercules alongside the F28 and the escorting officer assured me that it would follow as soon as we were airborne. I had no option but to rely on General Garcia's good faith. As we walked across the tarmac, I kept my eyes open for any useful details. Stanley airport had never been so busy; there were jeeps and trucks, boxes of ammunition and supplies piled high and men scurrying around everywhere. I tried to pick out cap badges and shoulder flashes but most of them seemed to be wearing unmarked anoraks over their uniforms and nondescript woolly hats. Apart from our F28 and the neighbouring Hercules, there were two Sea King helicopters and one other Hercules taxying in. There was also a caravan with a radar scanner on its roof.

As we accelerated down the runway, our last glimpse of Stanley airport was of the blue and white flag of Argentina, usurping the

Union Jack on the airport flagpole. The time was 9.15pm, exactly twelve hours since I had told the Royal Marines to lay down their arms. The last time I had taken off from Stanley in an F28 was for my mid-tour leave. We had been a happy, carefree bunch of passengers then; Hector and Teresa Gilobert going back to see their families in Cordoba; David Britton returning to London after one of his routine visits for the FIC; PWD works supervisor Derek Turner at the end of his contract and our future son-in-law, John Thurman, whose turn it was to carry the diplomatic bag. As we took off on that occasion, Hector had invited me up front to catch a view of Stanley in the early morning and I had stood between the pilot and co-pilot looking down on a peaceful, sleepy town just beginning to stir, the peat smoke curling up towards us (the smell of peat will always remind me of the Falklands). Tired then, I remembered, after a late night and early morning, it was nothing to the weariness I felt now. Trying to work out how much sleep I had had, I came to the conclusion that my arithmetic must be faulty. Surely it was more than two hours in the last forty? Giving up, I fell asleep on Mavis's shoulder – thank goodness I had never had any trouble dozing in an aircraft.

The flight to Comodoro Rivadavia took one hour forty minutes. On arrival, we were all escorted into the VIP room, doubtless because the Argentines wanted to keep us segregated from other passengers. We had assumed that we would be flying onwards to Buenos Aires but, to our surprise and relief (except for Avril), we were now told that we would be flown direct to Montevideo. Poor Avril almost had hysterics. I tried to reassure her that in all probability Michael would be waiting for us at Montevideo; but she would not be comforted. Tony once more came to the rescue and looked after the children.

We had a long wait for the Royal Marines. Their Hercules eventually landed and taxied to the far end of the runway, where they were immediately transferred to a waiting Boeing 707. We were driven there by coach. It was a great relief to see them all again, and in good heart despite the events of the past twenty-four hours. Sadly, the guards would not allow any communication between wives and husbands; they patrolled up and down the aisle, brandishing their weapons. I wondered whether they would be stupid enough to use them at 35,000ft. One or two were surlier than the rest and showed their disapproval of my moving round chatting to the Marines; but they did not physically restrain me. Mike had already collected a tally of ammunition expended and casualties inflicted: 6,450 rounds of 7.62 calibre; five 84mm and seven 66mm rockets and two white phosphorous grenades; five kills, seventeen hits, three prisoners and one armoured personnel carrier knocked out. On our side; not a single man wounded, although six (Corporal York and his section) were unaccounted for.

Mike explained that, after they had been gathered together and searched on the front lawn in front of Government House, the Royal Marines had been separated from the FIDF and taken ten at a time to Moody Brook, where they had been given ten minutes to collect their personal belongings. Some were lucky and retrieved most of their kit; others had found little. Items of value like cameras and radio cassettes had disappeared. Gary Noott told me with great relief that he had rescued my golf clubs and bag, which he had borrowed and had hoped to use in the last few days after handing over to Mike. I was not bothered about the clubs, but had felt a pang about losing the bag, which the British businessmen in Malaysia had kindly presented to me on my departure in 1979.

I slept fitfully on the way to Montevideo, where we touched down at 2.15am on the Saturday morning. Our Ambassador, Patricia Hutchinson, was there to meet us, together with a large reception party of Uruguayan officials, led by their Minister of the Interior. They had been waiting for us since well before midnight. 'Blame Major Dowling', I thought. Despite their long wait, they could not have been kinder or more solicitous. They were obviously under great pressure from the media but, as Patricia subsequently explained, they had agreed to accept us and help us on our way only provided that there was no publicity. They were in a delicate position with regard to their big neighbour and I could understand their anxieties. Mavis, Tony and I were whisked away from the rest of the group as soon as we stepped off the aircraft and I had no opportunity to pass on to Avril the Ambassador's news that Michael was indeed in Montevideo, waiting at the Residence. Patricia said that the Uruguayan authorities had arranged to accommodate everyone in the same hotel; Mavis, Tony and I would stay with her.

After thanking the Minister of Interior for his kindness and concern for our welfare, we fought our way through a crowd of reporters outside the airport and sank into the comfort of the Ambassador's Jaguar (quite a change from my old taxi). Michael's face as we arrived at the Residence was a mixture of joy and incredulity. He could hardly believe that we were there, in the flesh, or that

Avril and the children were with us in Montevideo. Patricia packed him off to the hotel and we went into the lounge for a much needed drink and sandwiches. I was almost too tired to eat, but Patricia said that I could not go to bed because the Prime Minister would be telephoning at 4.15am. It was then 3.15 and I suggested that an hour's nap would do me the world of good; but she would not hear of it. Mavis and Tony went off thankfully to their beds and Patricia set about the task of keeping me awake until the Prime Minsister called, maintaining a continuous stream of questions and information, including the welcome news that the RAF was sending a VC10 to collect us the next day. The telephone rang at a quarter to five. Mrs Thatcher came on the line immediately. Her first question was about the safety of the Falkland Islanders and our Royal Marines. She said with feeling, 'Thank God', when I told her that we had suffered no casualties that I knew of. She then said that they had been puzzled by the fact that I had not signalled the start of the invasion. I apologised and said we had tried but had been unable to get through – why, I did not know. She replied that she was not blaming me but that the lack of news had caused her considerable difficulties (I learned later that this was something of an understatement). I recounted briefly the events in Stanley over the previous twenty-four hours and she finished by asking me to convey her thanks and best wishes to the Royal Marines. As I put the telephone down, Patricia appeared from behind the door, which I noticed she had carefully left ajar, saying with an apologetic smile, 'I'm afraid I eavesdropped shamelessly; but it's not every day that we get a call from the Prime Minister.' I said I would forgive her if she would now let me go to bed. I hit the pillow and went out like a light.

I was awakened after about four hours with a cup of tea and (wondrous to behold) fresh pawpaw and a slice of lime. While Mavis and Tony explored the lovely Residence garden in glorious sunshine, I closeted myself away in Patricia's study and began the tedious business of composing my report to the FCO. How many times had I sat like this, with a blank blue form XY42 *Outward Telegram* in front of me, in various parts of the world, wondering how to begin? *File No* – I could not fill that in, for a start. My files no longer existed – Brian and the 'droggies' had seen to that. With some satisfaction, I wrote 'Destroyed'. *Department* – 'Lately Government House, Stanley'; *Drafted by* – that was easy. *Tel Extn* – not applicable. *Security Classification* – I supposed I had better make it 'Confidential', though all the world would know what I was reporting about by now. *Precedence* – too often we were accused of giving telegrams a greater priority grading than they warranted, particularly from a sleepy hollow like Stanley; but this time there could be no doubt: 'FLASH – DESKBY . . .'. But what to put in there? I had lost track of Greenwich Mean Time. I was not even sure of the day. My watch said 1000 hours, but that was Stanley time. Four hours behind London, which I remembered was now on British Summer Time, so three hours behind GMT. Right – 'DESKBY 031600Z'. That would give me two hours to compose it and the communicators an hour to transmit (the 'deskby' tag meant the time by which the telegram should be on the recipient's desk). *Time of Origin* – assuming Montevideo was the same as Stanley time, 031300Z. *To* – FCO; *Repeated to* – UKMIS New York, certainly, and Buenos Aires, if we were still operating there. I put it in, just in case.

The preamble was the easy part. Now for *Text*. I began with difficulty but, as usual, once the memory was jogged and the flow started, composition became easier. I recounted the events as factually as I could remember them and finished the telegram before lunch. Although communications were normally closed at weekends, Patricia had her communicator standing by and kindly offered to take it to the Embassy herself. I asked if she would bring back a copy for me and, to my surprise, she refused, reminding me gently but firmly of our rules on document security. She was right, of course, but I could not help smiling at the absurdity of the situation. Here I was, going home directly in a Royal Air Force aircraft, escorted by over sixty Royal Marines, and yet I could not carry a classified document!

Before she left for the Embassy, Patricia warned me that a number of journalists had telephoned wanting to interview me, and that I must not speak to any of them while she was out, because she had given a firm assurance to the Uruguayans that I would not make any statement to the Press while on Uruguayan soil. Shortly after she had gone, her other house-guest (an English lady) invited me to the telephone to speak to someone who claimed to be a personal friend. Knowing the ways of journalists, I asked if she would first identify the caller. It turned out to be our old friend, Harry Dempster. True, he worked for the *Daily Express*, but as a photographer, not a reporter. This was sufficient to ease my conscience. I picked up the telephone. Harry was genuinely concerned about our welfare and was delighted that we were all well. It was good to hear his cheerful voice again; he was in Montevideo and trying to get down to Argentina. Could I oblige him with an interview? I explained the position and Harry, to his credit, did not try to persuade or press me in any way. But he had not been in Fleet Street for most of his working life to give up that easily. He asked whether we would be strolling in the Residence garden at any time: if so, he would endeavour to find a vantage point overlooking the grounds and the rest would be up to him. The warm sun and Patricia's lovely garden were too tempting for us to resist after our Falklands autumn, and we spent much of our remaining time there. Harry told me later that he got his photograph.

After lunch, I asked to pay a visit to the Royal Marines and my staff at the hotel; but Patricia thought it wiser for me to stay inside the Residence. A prisoner in the Falkland Islands, I thought, and now a prisoner in Uruguay. But I could see the point in keeping me out of reach of the media – almost anything I said in Montevideo would be likely to cause embarrassment to the Uruguayans; and they had gone out of their way to be helpful. Instead of my visiting the hotel, therefore, Mike Norman, Gary Noott and Brian Wells came to the Residence to see me. They reported everyone in good heart after a refreshing sleep. The hotel was comfortable and they were being well looked after. They were all delighted at the prospect of flying home next day. We ran through my report and had another inquest on the sequence of events. As a result, I sent a follow-up telegram to the FCO. We were hopeful that the Royal Marines left in South Georgia would give the Argentines a rude shock; but we were concerned about the fate of the section we had left behind in the Falklands.

We had a quiet evening with Patricia and her other house-guest and retired early to bed. I did not sleep well and was up before seven. Patricia confirmed that the RAF VC10 would be taking off at 1.30pm and warned us to be ready to leave for the airport after midday. I was glad to be on the move again. We had been looked after very well, but it was like being in limbo. My thoughts were divided between the good people we had left behind and the action being taken in Britain. I had told the Islanders that we would be back. But how? And when? I was eager to get home to find out. There was at least one crumb of comfort: everybody in Britain would now know where the Falkland Islands were!

Before leaving the Residence, we received a signal from the FCO asking for our accommodation requirements. Our tenants in

Sunningdale could not be expected to vacate without reasonable notice and I knew that I would be required to be within easy reach of the FCO. After consulting Mavis, I replied asking for one double and one single room in an hotel close to Whitehall for the first few days, until we could make more permanent arrangements.

The Royal Marines were in fine form as we boarded the VC10, but their spirits quickly turned to anger as they read the headlines in the English newspapers. They were the previous day's edition and it was clear (as I tried to explain) that the reports of the invasion were based upon scant and inaccurate information. The worst was the *Daily Mail*, with a one-word headline four inches tall: 'SHAME'. The article claimed that the Royal Marines had surrendered with scarcely a shot having been fired. Other reports were less sensational but in similar vein; it was sickening to see the primeval clamour for a blood sacrifice. Evidently, Fleet Street would have felt better had we sustained casualties, the more the merrier. I promised the Royal Marines that I would put the record straight at my first Press conference.

The RAF crew were, as usual, most helpful and attentive but, as with all RAF aircraft, the VC10 was 'dry'. Anticipating this, Mavis had packed a bottle of brandy and a bottle of whisky in her cabin luggage and I was able to do the rounds, topping up plastic cups for those who felt in need of a strong drink. After six-and-a-half hours, we landed at Wideawake airfield, Ascension Island. Our reception committee lived up to the name, despite the fact that it was late at night their time. The first person to greet me at the foot of the steps was the British Administrator, Bernard Pauncefort.[2] He was an old FCO colleague and had been one of the first to greet me after I was evacuated from Saigon. 'You mustn't make a habit of this', he said, with a friendly grin and a warm handshake. His wife, Patricia, was also there and, next to her the United States Air Force Officer-in-Charge at Wideawake, Lieutenant-Colonel Bill Bryden and his wife, Mary Lou, and the Pan American Airways representative, Dan Coffey. They could not do enough for us. Bill had told the cafeteria to stay open and to lay on their full menu – breakfast, lunch and dinner – all on the house. The Royal Marines surveyed the groaning counters with amazement and proceeded to demolish fried eggs, burgers, bacon, T-bone steaks, chicken, peas, beans, chips, roast potatoes and a bewildering variety of sweets and ice creams.

We boarded the VC10 again after fifty minutes of wonderful hospitality. The Captain announced that we had a good tail wind and would be flying non-stop to Brize Norton, landing in eight-and-a-half hours. Anticipating a Press conference on arrival, I ran through the timing and sequence of events again with Mike, Gary and Brian and returned to my seat to marshal my thoughts. I had no idea what awaited me in England, but there was little doubt that the leading questions would be: 'How did it happen?' and 'Why were we caught napping?' There were no simple answers.

Undoubtedly, diplomacy had been at fault on both sides. It was clear that we had misread the Argentines and that they had misread us. We never thought that Galtieri would invade – not at least until he had exhausted all the other options – and he never thought that we would respond. How had such a misunderstanding arisen? Sitting facing, and thinking, backwards in the VC10,[3] high over the Atlantic, I wondered whether his Malvinas watchers had read too much into a long chain of events, from Southern Thule to the withdrawal of HMS *Endurance*. I could hardly blame them if they had; but, at the same time, his diplomats in London must have displayed a lamentable ignorance of the British character.

We could have had no illusions over Argentine intentions. Since first raising the issue in the United Nations, they had consistently maintained their demand for the transfer of sovereignty within a reasonable time. On the other hand, successive British governments, while indicating to the Argentines that the door was open to a transfer of sovereignty, had said that they were not prepared to push the Islanders through it. The resulting uncertainty had increased the anxiety of the Islanders and the expectations of the Argentine leaders, who held the rights of the individual in such scant regard that they thought nothing of liquidating thousands of their fellow-countrymen; why should Britain pay heed to the wishes of a mere 1800? In the United Nations, the Argentines had always made much play of the difference between wishes and interests, pointing out that the original UN resolution had referred to Islander interests and that these were not necessarily the same as their wishes. They had then proceeded to make the arrogant assertion that they would act in the Islanders' best interests irrespective of their wishes. Here, perhaps, was the key to our misunderstanding: to them, the Islanders' wishes did not matter; to us, they did.

As the first of the sun's rays turned the tops of the clouds below us into salmon pink, I pondered the other question; why had we received such little notice? Either our intelligence was seriously at fault or our analysts had misinterpreted the signals. A task force of that size could not possibly assemble overnight, and the Argentine planners must have been busy for weeks, if not months. My own guess was that Galtieri had given the green light to Anaya in December, as a *quid pro quo* for Anaya's support for his presidency. Anaya had then used Davidoff as a convenient sounding board to test our reaction. Had we submitted meekly (as with Southern Thule), he would have argued this as a further indication of our lack of commitment and pressed for a landing on the Falklands, probably to coincide with the 150th anniversary in 1983. By reacting strongly, we gave Anaya the excuse to press for the military option immediately. The timing coincidentally suited Galtieri because it diverted public attention from his worsening economic problems.

We were now passing over the Canaries, discernible through the broken cloud eight miles below. The captain had said earlier that he would invite me up to the cabin for a first glimpse of England. As we approached the coast there was cloud over Cornwall and Devon, but the Bristol Channel was clear and Bristol stood out attractively in the morning sun. I could see the River Avon snaking up through the gorge to the city docks and thought of the SS *Great Britain* down there, where she belonged. Thank goodness she had been brought home from the Falklands before the balloon went up. As we started the descent to Brize Norton, I spoke to the Royal Marines over the public address system for the last time. I thanked them for looking after me, praised them for their bravery, professionalism and selfless devotion to duty and said how proud I would always be to have been associated with them on the night of 1–2 April, 1982.

Taxiing in to the apron in front of the terminal building at Brize Norton, we were amazed to see a huge crowd assembled there to meet us. 'Good grief', I muttered to Mavis, 'This is worse than the night of the invasion.' The first person up the steps was the Chief Clerk from the FCO, Derek Day, who said that I would not be giving a Press conference immediately, but that one had been arranged for the afternoon in the FCO. He was followed by Mr Richard Luce, the FCO minister responsible for South American affairs, and Mr Jerry Wiggin, a junior minister in the MOD, whom we had entertained in Kuala Lumpur some years before, as a backbencher. They greeted us warmly and were most solicitous about our welfare. At the foot of the steps stood Sir Stuart Pringle who, despite serious injuries from an IRA bomb, had resumed his full duties as Commandant-General of the Royal Marines. I was

glad to have the opportunity to tell him how well his men had performed in Stanley. Mavis was about to meet him when she heard a
cry from the crowd and espied Diana. All others were forgotten as
mother and daughter were re-united. We had not expected Diana
to be there, and it was wonderful to have the family together again
– even for a few brief moments on the tarmac. Diana explained later
that she and John had been holidaying in Venice when the news of
the invasion had broken. They had flown back to London on the
first available flight and John had telephoned a colleague in the
MOD to offer his services with the Task Force. His colleague had
told him to report to Plymouth and given him the FCO Emergency
Unit telephone number, which Diana had called to ask if she could
be given a lift to Brize Norton to meet us. The Emergency Unit had
replied that they were much too busy to make any arrangements for
her, whereupon John had seized the telephone and threatened to
ring the *Daily Express*, saying that they would certainly be happy
to take her to Brize Norton. This had done the trick.

Mike Norman, Gary Noott and I were whisked away to the
VIP lounge, where various senior officers of the Task Force were
waiting to debrief us, while Mavis, Diana and Tony were escorted
to another room. There was a great sense of urgency, as the Task
Force was sailing from Portsmouth that night. After an all-too-brief
debriefing, I rejoined the family to be informed that Diana would
be coming to London with me to collect her case, but that Mavis
would be going with Tony to her brother's home, near Bury St
Edmunds. There was no time to argue, the Andover that was to
fly me to Northolt was already waiting, with engines running, and
Diana and I were bundled off after the hastiest of farewells. Once
on the aircraft, Mr Luce gave me the startling news that he, Lord
Carrington and Mr Humphrey Atkins would be announcing their
resignations that afternoon. He said that I was due to see Lord
Carrington at 12.00pm and the Prime Minister at 12.30pm. Mike
Norman and Gary Noott (also on the aircraft) were to see the
Secretary of State for Defence and then join me at Number Ten.
We would meet up again for a Press conference at 3pm.

Sitting in the VIP Andover, I recalled the last time I had been
in a similar aircraft, at Jesselton, Sabah, in 1967, when the then
Commander-in-Chief, Far East, Sir John Grandy and Lady Grandy
visited us from Singapore. For the previous three years Britain had
been conducting a war against the Indonesians in Borneo, and had
prosecuted it to a successful conclusion. I hoped that we would do

the same in the Falklands, but that it would not take so long or cost so many lives.

Memories came flooding back, too, as we landed at Northolt. The last time I had landed there was from Germany, in 1948, shortly before leaving the RAF. Little had changed – there was even an old Dakota standing on the apron. No customs or immigration formalities this time, however, but straight from the aircraft to a waiting car and out to join the London-bound traffic on the Western Avenue. 'Join' is scarcely the right word: we had a police escort of two motor cyclists, who cleaved our way through the traffic with consummate skill. They were in a different league from the noisier and larger escorts I had experienced elsewhere. In Jakarta, for example, when accompanying our new ambassador to present his credentials to President Suharto, we had eight 'snowballs' on huge machines, sirens going incessantly, and still slowed to a crawl. Here with our two unobtrusive helpers, we tore through traffic lights and junctions and made Downing Street from Northolt in twenty minutes. After a quick farewell to Diana, I was ushered in to the Secretary of State's room in the FCO at 12.05pm. Lord Carrington expressed his relief that we had suffered no casualties and showed deep concern at the plight of the Falkland Islanders. He wanted every detail of the night of the invasion. He slapped his thigh when I told him of my conversation with General Garcia and told me to repeat it at the Press Conference. At no time did he intimate that he was about to resign or show any sign of the strain that he must have been under. His thoughts appeared to be totally with 'our people' down in the South Atlantic. At 12.25pm, he said that I was required at Number Ten, and that he also had something to do. As I walked across the road with John Ure, Lord Carrington announced his resignation.

Mike and Gary were waiting for me and we were led in to the Prime Minister. It was my first meeting with Mrs Thatcher. She was smaller and more feminine than I had expected. We gave our account of the night of the invasion and conjectured upon the breakdown of communications.

Mike dashed off to make arrangements for his detachment to go south again with the Task Force (all volunteered to go) and I returned to the FCO for a beer and sandwiches with Sir Michael Palliser and his Deputy Under Secretaries. It was a strange working lunch. There was general gloom at Lord Carrington's resignation and the loss of Richard Luce and Humphrey Atkins. The crisis could not have broken at a worse time for Sir Michael, who was in his last week as PUS, or for his successor, Sir Antony Acland. The change meant ramifications down the chain of command, perhaps the most important being the chairmanship of the Joint Intelligence Committee.

The afternoon Press conference was not as bad as I had feared. The head of News Separtment, Nick Fenn, handled it well, sheltering me from awkward political questions, and Mike Norman and Gary Noott gave solid support. I took the opportunity to put the record straight when a *Daily Mail* reporter asked a question. 'Is David English still your editor?' I asked, and, when he nodded, I said, 'Will you please tell him that I was most grateful for the kind acknowledgement he published when I helped his orphans out of Vietnam in 1975, but I should value much more now an apology for the slanderous report he published of our Royal Marines' surrendering with scarcely a shot fired.' I then read out the details of the ammunition expended and casualties inflicted.[4] Before the end of the conference, I was also able to pay tribute to Lord Carrington and express my sadness at his resignation. Back in Nick's office, he said that I could expect many direct approaches from the media, but that I must refer them all in the first instance to News Department and not give an interview without prior approval of the FCO. This suited me, but it turned out to be impossible to follow in practice.

Sir Michael asked to see me again that evening and spoke kindly about the Press conference. As I was about to leave, he asked if transport had been provided to take me to my hotel. I said not and that I was hoping to find a taxi in Whitehall. He generously offered his car after his driver had dropped him at the Houses of Parliament. I collected my cases and went with him back to Parliament Square. His driver then took me to the aptly named Diplomat Hotel, in a part of London unfamiliar to me, at about 7pm. My room was tiny but at least it had a telephone and television set. I had neither my brother-in-law's telephone number nor his address, but I knew that he lived near Bury St Edmunds. It took an age to raise Directory Enquiries. With one ear glued to the telephone, I caught up with the latest Falklands news on the television. When Directory Enquiries finally answered, the operator was most helpful and eventually tracked down the right number. Mavis vented her anger about being separated from me yet again. Fortunately, Aubrey Buxton had thoughtfully sent a letter to await our arrival at Brize Norton, offering us the use of Cindy's cottage in Langham.

As he put it, Cindy was unlikely to be using it for some time, and he was sure that she would not mind. I promised Mavis that I would collect my car as soon as I could get away from the FCO, pick her up and avail ourselves of Aubrey's kind offer.

After watching *Panorama* on television, I decided that it was time to eat. The proprietor of the hotel, a pleasant Polish gentleman, explained that his establishment was non-catering but suggested one or two reasonable restaurants nearby. In fact, he said, he was about to go for dinner himself, would I care to join him? It thus transpired that my only companion for my first dinner in England after the Argentine invasion was a Pole whom I had not met before. Some homecoming!

Notes

1. It later brought the flagpole toppling down in a typical Falkland wind. The Argentines took this as a bad omen.

2. Later to become my Chief Secretary in the Falkland Islands.

3. All the seats in RAF VC10s faced backwards for greater passenger safety.

4. I understand that David English subsequently published a retraction of the offending article, unusually placing it on the front page.

14

Frustration

I had been promised a car for my first appointment the next morning, but it was an hour late in turning up. The frustration that I was to feel for the next three months was beginning to show by the time I arrived at the FCO, to be told that I could not get past reception without a pass. I asked to speak to Robin Fearn, the head of South American Department and the person with whom I had had most dealings over the previous two years. He had vacated his office, I was told, and was now ensconced in the Emergency Unit, at the top of the building. I tried to ring, but all numbers were constantly engaged. Eventually I got hold of Alex Smith, one of the juniors in South American Department whom I had known and found most helpful on previous visits. He came down to reception, arranged for me to be issued with a temporary pass and escorted me to the Emergency Unit. The sight that confronted us reminded me of those Hollywood films of the Thirties, with newspaper editors wielding telephones in each hand, reporters scurrying to and fro and typewriters clattering. The only props missing were the black eye-shades and the cigars. Spotting Robin across the 'open plan' layout, I negotiated my way to his desk, sat down and waited for him to finish on the telephone. No sooner had he put one down than another rang. It was impossible to carry on a serious conversation. I retreated to the quieter haven of Alex Smith's office in South American Department, leaving poor Robin to his telephones.

Alex handed me a message from the Labour Party Secretary: would I call on the Party Leader, Mr Michael Foot, in the House of Commons today? I asked the private office for advice and was told that the request would have to go to the new Secretary of State (Mr Francis Pym) for approval. Other telephone calls were pouring in and Alex virtually gave up his own work to help me. One call was from a Senior Superintendent of the Metropolitan Police, who introduced himself as Bill Richards, born in the Falkland Islands. He offered his services 'in any capacity' when I went back. He was to remain true to his word, returning to the Falklands on one of

269

the first Hercules to carry civilian passengers. In Stanley, he was to be a tonic to the Islanders, walking the beat in his Senior Superintendent's uniform.

The private office conveyed the message that Mr Pym agreed to my seeing Mr Foot, but I was to watch what I said. Arriving at the Houses of Parliament, I was ushered into a pleasant office overlooking the Thames, where Mr Foot was waiting with Mr Denis Healey, the shadow Foreign Secretary and one of the Silkin brothers (I was not sure which). I had met Mr Healey many years ago when, as Secretary of State for Defence, he had visited Sabah and I had taken him to meet the Yang di Pertuan Negara and the Chief Minister; but I did not expect him to remember me. I had seen him on the *Panorama* programme the night before, at one point in which he had drawn a similarity between the present situation in the Falklands and the Indonesian invasion of Sarawak and Sabah in the Sixties. I made the mistake of disagreeing with him, pointing out that the Argentines had invaded British sovereign territory whereas in Borneo we had gone to the aid of a fellow Commonwealth country, Sarawak and Sabah being by then part of Malaysia and no longer British Colonies. I do not know whether it was this that riled him or (more probably) that he was deliberately provoking me into providing ammunition with which he could belabour the government; but he was certainly aggressive. What orders had I received? Why had I not cratered the runway? Why had I allowed an Argentine Hercules to land at the airport last month? Why had I surrendered so soon? He seemed to be suggesting that I should have suffered casualties before giving in. Thankfully, Mr Foot intervened at this point and expressed his gratitude to me for giving him and his colleagues a first-hand account of the invasion.

Aubrey Buxton rang on my return to the FCO and kindly invited me to stay in his London flat. He arranged for his car to collect me from the hotel that evening. Another caller was Councillor John Cheek, who was on a course in the Westcountry with Cable and Wireless. He had come up to London and would like to see me. We arranged to meet at St Stephen's Tavern and, when I eventually managed to get away from the incessant telephone calls, I found him there, chatting to Ted Rowlands. Mr Rowlands had been Minister of State at the FCO in the Labour Government and had conducted talks with the Argentines in 1976. He had visited the Falklands and was popular with the Islanders. To my astonishment, he revealed that we knew how to crack the Argentine codes: why then had we received such little notice of the invasion? I could only tell him what little notice I had received. John was fortunate in having his wife and children with him in England, but he was naturally worried about the relatives and friends that they had left behind. I gave him all the information I could and promised to keep him informed of any further news. He volunteered his services in any capacity and, though shy and retiring by nature, he subsequently never flinched from appearing on television and became an excellent ambassador for the Falkland Islands, both in Britain and the USA.

Life was considerably more comfortable in Aubrey's flat, though the pace was hectic. He was at that time Chairman of the Independent Broadcasting Authority as well as Director of Anglia Television, and I arrived in the middle of a drinks party that he and Maria were giving for a host of television administrators. It was good to see them both again, in surroundings very different from our last meeting on a windy Stanley airport. As soon as their guests had departed, they took me to Independent Television News for a quick dinner before watching the live transmission of *News at Ten*. It was a pleasure to meet the presenters, Alastair Burnett and Trevor McDonald, afterwards, though Maria and I naturally disagreed with the former's views on the Falklands. He maintained that they were not worth fighting for. I was also sorry that it was not Sandy Gall's turn to present the news. One of my last acts in Saigon in 1975 had been to bequeath to Sandy our house, together with our excellent steward, Jacques, and a well-stocked bar, so that he could await the arrival of the Communists in some degree of comfort.

Next day, the telephones were already ringing when I arrived in Alex Smith's office at 9am. Clearly, I could not go on monopolising his desk and time. Alex's normal work was piling up and anyway I needed an office and a secretary of my own. I went across to Curtis Green to see Derek Day, the Chief Clerk. He was engaged, but I left my request with his secretary and took a train to Sunningdale to collect my car. To my relief, it started first time. The licence had expired and it needed an MOT test, but I hoped the police would be sympathetic. The local garage put some air in the tyres and I returned to London.

I managed to get away from the FCO for the Easter weekend. Collecting Mavis and family from her brother's in Suffolk, we arrived at Cindy's cottage to find that Maria had been across from Stiffkey and thoughtfully stocked the larder with food and wine and brightened the rooms with freshly cut flowers. It was good to be on our own again as a family. There was, however, no peace from the wretched telephone. It did not take the media long to find out where we were and a large part of the holiday was spent in fending off would-be interviewers. We compromised by allowing some photographs to be taken and I gave a few interviews in Norwich. An urgent call came from a Brigadier Peter de la Billière, asking if there was a suitable landing pad near Cindy's house for a helicopter. I said there was a tennis court in the garden and he said he hoped to send one of his men to ask me a few questions. I described where we were in the village, but no helicopter turned up. Peter was later to become a good friend and colleague as Commander British Forces Falkland Islands.

Another call was from Protocol Department, to say that the Queen would be pleased to receive Mavis and me at Windsor Castle on 14 April. Aubrey and Maria, who had entertained us royally at Stiffkey over Easter, again offered us the use of their Mayfair flat. Leaving Diana and Tony at Langham, we drove up to London on the 13th, where I went to Bush House to record a message to the Islanders on 'Calling The Falklands'. Reacting quickly to the invasion, BBC Overseas had increased the frequency of broadcasts to the Falklands from weekly to daily and, in the capable hands of presenter Peter King, it was to prove an invaluable link between Britain and the Islanders in the months ahead. In this, my first broadcast since leaving the Islands, I told the Islanders that I was in no doubt about the British Government's determination to come to their rescue, that I would be back soon and that, out of the present tragedy, the Falkland Islands would emerge stronger and with more support than ever before.

My first visit to Windsor Castle had been during the Second World War. I had been directed then to the highest tower, where my brother had been on duty as a spotter in the Royal Observer Corps. On this occasion, we were directed to the private apartments, where we were greeted by the familiar figure of Philip Moore. He had been the Deputy High Commissioner in Singapore when we were in Kuching and Jesselton. He soon put us at our ease and, on the dot of midday, ushered us into the Queen's private room. It was less formal than Buckingham Palace but still very grand. The Queen was sitting looking out on a lovely part of the grounds, secluded from the public. She expressed her concern for the Islanders and we discussed the situation in the South Atlantic at length, returning to Langham late that night.

At 8.30am the next morning, the telephone rang to say that Dick Baker and family and a host of others from the Falklands were coming into Gatwick at lunchtime. I dashed down from Norfolk and arrived in the nick of time. It was wonderful to see Dick, Connie, Karen and Helen emerge from the aircraft, followed by Bill and Pat Luxton and their son, Stephen. Pat flung her arms round my neck and wept with relief. Bill told me later that they had managed to get back to the farm but that it had taken them a week, being passed from one settlement to another. On the day after their return to Chartres, Dowling had arrived by helicopter and told them to pack while he flew on to Port Stephens. He gave Bill no indication of their ultimate destination but remarked ominously, 'Do not cause trouble. We have dossiers on 500 of you Islanders.' Returning from Port Stephens, he collected Bill, Pat and Stephen and took them into Stanley. There, Bill had insisted upon seeing Vicecomodoro Bloomer-Reeve, who had once been in charge of the LADE office in Stanley and was now back as Menendez's civil administrator. (He had been recalled from his post as Air Attaché in Bonn, presumably because he knew the Islanders and had made a good impression on them while he was there.) Bloomer-Reeve was clearly distressed over Bill's plight but had explained that he was powerless to intervene. Fearing that he was about join the *desparecidos*, Bill had stayed close to Dick during their transportation through Argentina. Pat said that she had expected him to be dragged away from her at any moment. Also on the flight was Ronnie Lamb, the Chief Police Officer, and a number of expatriate teachers and other government officials. Apparently the weekly LADE flight to Comodoro Rivadavia was still running and the Argentines had announced that anyone who wished to leave the Islands was free to do so. There, were, however, three snags: there were no extra flights, priority was given to Argentines, and fares had to be paid in advance. We managed to help over fares – the Prime Minister gave an assurance that no one who wished to leave the Islands would be prevented from doing so by lack of funds – but we could do nothing about priorities.

As soon as we could get through the hordes of Press at Gatwick, I took Dick to the FCO, where we met Mr Luce's successor, Mr Cranley Onslow, and Dick described the latest situation in Stanley. Next day, we managed to have a meeting with Robin

Fearn, at which we were joined by Bill Luxton and Ray Checkley, the senior registrar, who had arrived on the same flight. My main concern was to nail a report in the Press that heads of government departments in Stanley had signed a petition calling for a truce and the evacuation of all civilians until the fighting was over. If true, this was worrying on two counts: first, if the Islanders were evacuated, they would be unlikely to get back; secondly, there would be little support in Britain for risking British lives to take back islands devoid of Islanders. To my relief, Dick and his colleagues confirmed that this was an initiative by some of the remaining expatriates and did not reflect the attitude of the majority of kelpers.

On the administrative side, Robin offered Dick and me the use of his office for as long as he was required full-time in the Emergency Unit. It was not possible to have a private secretary, but we could use the typing pool. Requests for speeches and appearances were pouring in, as well as numerous inquiries about the whereabouts of individuals. We simply did not have the facilities or supporting staff to cope. This was where the Falkland Islands Office, staffed and run by volunteers, proved invaluable. Under the dynamic leadership of Bill Hunter Christie, who virtually abandoned his law practice for the duration of the conflict, his wife, Merle, Air Commodore Brian Frow and a team of dedicated helpers and supporters handled a bewildering variety of queries, from long-lost relatives to would-be immigrants. Indeed, their office became the welfare centre and focal point for Islanders in the UK.

Tony Parsons had done a brilliant job in the United Nations in winning support for the British case, but the Argentines were conducting the diplomatic battle with great energy. Effective countermeasures were urgently needed. The FCO launched a major campaign through Embassies and High Commissions to convince the rest of the world of the justness of our cause. Fact sheets and booklets on the historical background and the origins of the dispute were hurriedly compiled and distributed. At the same time, the hard-pressed Emergency Unit and South American Department were engaged in producing papers for parliamentary debates and questions and for the peace talks being conducted by the US Secretary of State, General Alexander Haig. My role and that of my exiled councillors was never defined, but clearly the most effective way of putting the Islanders' case was for their own representatives to speak out. Neither Bill Luxton nor John Cheek relished the limelight, but both entered wholeheartedly into the fray, speaking frequently on television, to the Press and at public meetings. Dick went with Bill to address the European Parliament in Strasbourg and John went to the USA to support our Ambassador, Sir Nicholas Henderson, who was doing so much himself to win over American opinion. I found myself invited to address bodies like the Royal College of Defence Studies, Camberley Staff College, the Royal Military Academy and the Royal Marines Training Centre at Lympstone. On one occasion, we joined forces to answer questions from about 300 MPs in one of the committee rooms in the Houses of Parliament. Afterwards, we were buttonholed by the parliamentary correspondents. I had not expected to be interviewed by them and had not sought prior approval from News Department; but it would have looked odd had I left Bill and John to face them alone – I was after all still the official head of the Falkland Islands Government.

One of the questions I answered was about leaseback. I had not heard any recent statement by Ministers on this, and had made what seemed to me the rather obvious comment that the Islanders would be even less likely to accept a leaseback solution after the Argentine invasion than they were before. They had emphatically rejected it in 1981, surely no one seriously believed that, given a free choice, they would accept it now?

I found myself wondering whether leaseback might be an element in General Haig's peace negotiations. I was not privy to these, nor had I had been consulted in the preparation of ministerial papers for them. My only involvement had occurred by accident. I happened to be in Alex Smith's office when his telephone rang and the caller wanted to know the composition of Executive and Legislative Councils. Alex looked inquiringly at me and I told him. The next question was: 'How many in the Islands' police force?' 'That's easy', I said, 'One Chief Police Officer, one Police Constable and one Woman Police Constable.' The next question was: 'How many Argentines on the Islands?' 'What, now?', I asked, 'Who's putting these questions?' Alex passed me the telephone and, to my surprise, I heard Anthony Williams's voice on the other end. When I asked whether he wanted the number of permanent Argentine residents before the invasion or temporary residents like LADE, YPF and Gas del Estado personnel, he said, 'You'd better come down here – I'm in the Senior Legal Adviser's office.' Puzzled, I went down and found Anthony sitting at a table with Sir Ian Sinclair. He explained that they were working on a draft reply to Haig's latest proposals and it had to be submitted by the evening; hence the rush. What was the Argentine population in the Falklands before the invasion? I said there were thirty shown in the 1980 census but these included temporary birds of passage. To my knowledge there were only two Argentines permanently resident in the Islands on 1 April, and I had heard that one of them had since returned to Argentina. The sole permanent Argentine resident now was Stuart Wallace's mother-in-law.

It was not until Mrs Thatcher's statement in the House of Commons on 20 May that I discovered the reason behind these questions. Under the proposed interim agreement (which the British Government was prepared to accept), a UN administrator was to appoint one representative from the Argentine population 'normally resident on the Islands' to each of the two councils. Listening to the Prime Minister from the public gallery, I heaved a sigh of relief that the Argentines had rejected our proposals. No Falkland Islands Councillor would have agreed to sit on Executive or Legislative Council with an Argentine member (even Stuart's mother-in-law!). The question relating to the police had arisen from a similarly ludicrous proposal for a joint police force during the interim administration.

Before all this had been revealed by the Prime Minister, I was decidedly uneasy that, in the admirable desire for peace, concessions might be made that would be unacceptable to the Islanders. It seemed to me that, despite the oft-repeated statement that their wishes would be taken fully into account, a solution could be imposed upon them without their representatives having had the slightest say. Three of their ten Councillors were in England, but they had not been consulted. Nor had I. If the negotiations appeared to be progressing on the basis of leaseback or a condominium or UN trusteeship, I considered that it would be my duty, as head of the Falkland Islands Government, to speak out on the Islanders' behalf. I wrote in this vein to the FCO. Implicit in my letter was that I would submit my resignation if I decided that HMG was acting against the Islanders' interests.

Fortunately for the Islanders (and myself), Galtieri turned down the peace proposals. Thereafter, Mrs Thatcher did not waver in her resolve to re-establish British administration on the Islands. Early in May, she invited me to call on her again, together with Bill Luxton and John Cheek. She made clear to us that, by British administration, she meant my return and the restoration of Executive and Legislative Councils. Despite her incredibly busy schedule, she found time to give us a fascinating tour of Number Ten. Later that same day, I went to Bush House to transmit a message from the Queen to the Falkland Islanders. Some days earlier, loyal greetings on the Queen's birthday (21 April) had been smuggled out of the Islands and delivered to Buckingham Palace. I expressed my pleasure at being instructed to convey the Queen's warmest appreciation of these greetings and her message in reply: to each and every one of her loyal subjects in the Islands, she sent her prayers, and those of her family, for their safety and well-being. I said that I regretted being unable to deliver this message from Government House, Stanley, but looked forward to being back for Her Majesty's birthday next year, as usual.

During the two-and-a-half months of occupation, the BBC allowed me to send many messages of support to the beleaguered Islanders. I cleared them whenever possible with News Department and stepped down when a minister found time to speak on behalf of HMG. Mr Onslow was the government's main spokesman and Islanders told me upon my return how heartening they found these regular broadcasts. I also continued to give speeches to selected audiences and to meet evacuees and repatriated British from the war zone. After the Easter holidays, we left Cindy's delightful cottage in Norfolk and moved to the house of an old friend in Loughton, but even this proved too far out of London for my long and irregular hours and, after about a month, we moved again, to a small flat in Fulham. This was the result of a visit to Stanley by Judge Peter Mason and his then fiancée, Sara. We had come across them one evening walking along Ross Road and, as was the custom and courtesy in those days, seeing that they were strangers, we stopped and chatted. They enjoyed taking their holidays in out-of-the-way places, and thus began a lasting friendship. Hearing that we were looking for accommodation, Sara (now Mrs Mason) offered us her old flat. We were most grateful and stayed there until I flew back to the Falklands.

We were still in Loughton, however, when we heard that the BAS personnel and the Royal Marines from Grytviken were due to land at Brize Norton one morning at 4am. I arrived there to find Sir Steuart Pringle, Mr Wiggin from MOD, Dick Laws, head of BAS, and a crowd of Pressmen. Lieutenant Keith Mills led his valiant Royal Marines down the steps from the VC10, followed by Steve Martin, Bob Headland and the other members of BAS who had been captured with them. I complimented Keith on giving the

Argentines such a warm welcome and, when I next saw him (as best man at Diana's wedding) was delighted to find him wearing the ribbon of the Distinguished Service Cross.[1] To my great relief, the six Royal Marines whom we had left behind in the Falklands were also on the aircraft, together with Leading Seaman Brook, whom the hydrographers had left at Green Patch to maintain tidal records during the austral summer. The total complements of NP 8901 and HMS *Endurance* were thus accounted for. The only casualty was Corporal Peters, who had been shot in the arm during the action in South Georgia. Not all the BAS men, however, were safely home. Some thirteen remained in the field huts on South Georgia; and, of course, Cindy and Annie were still in St Andrews Bay, filming the King penguins, while HMS *Endurance* lurked among the icebergs.

Like most of the British public, my ears were glued to the radio for the latest news from down south. The most up-to-date information, however, came from a party of about thirty Islanders and expatriates who arrived at Gatwick on 22 April. Mavis and I met them and heard about the silly edicts that the Argentine authorities had issued.[2] The build-up of troops was continuing, but there was no evidence of ill-treatment of civilians. Dick met the next and, as it happened, the last batch of civilians to fly out of Stanley a week later, while I was passing out the King's squad of Royal Marines at Lympstone. Further commercial flights were brought to an abrupt halt by the bombing of Stanley airport on 1 May. Between these last two civilian flights, we heard the great news that our forces had repossessed South Georgia. Despite appalling weather conditions, which caused two of our Wessex helicopters to crash (fortunately without the loss of a single life), we managed to insert SAS and SBS reconnaissance parties, land assault troops and retake Grytviken, with 170 prisoners and without casualties. Perhaps the greatest prize was the Argentine submarine *Santa Fe*, which was caught on the surface and disabled by our helicopters, the two Wasps from HMS *Endurance* both scoring direct hits with their missiles. Following the fall of Grytviken, the Argentine force at Leith hoisted the white flag on 26 April. It consisted of forty-eight of Davidoff's scrap workers and sixteen Argentine marines, commanded by Lieutenant Commander Alfredo Astiz.

On 28 April, I was recalled from Camberley Staff College to record a message to the Islanders explaining the imposition of a Total Exclusion Zone round the Falklands, which HMG declared on 30 April – the day, incidentally, on which HMS *Endurance* sailed into

St Andrews Bay to rescue Cindy and Annie and three of the BAS personnel who had been keeping them company. On that same day, I let slip in my address to the Royal Marines at Lympstone that our daughter had become engaged to one of them. John had written to me from HMS *Fearless*, on his way to Ascension, asking for Diana's hand in marriage. Mavis and I were naturally delighted, even though it meant that Diana would not finish her degree course at London University. Apparently, on the night before he sailed, John had telephoned with a final request: if he came back in one piece, would Diana marry him? Until then, she had been determined not to get married before attaining her degree; but Galtieri's invasion changed all that.

Further cause for celebration came the next day, with the announcement of the Vulcan attack on Stanley airport. It was an inspired, imaginative strike, the first of five Vulcan missions directed against the airfield and adjacent radar installations. The refuelling logistics were stupendous, requiring at least fifteen Victor tanker sorties and eighteen air-to-air refuellings to get one Vulcan to Stanley from Ascension and back. Despite a direct hit on the runway, Hercules transport aircraft continued to use it until almost the day of the surrender. Of greater strategic significance, however, was the fear that it instilled in the Argentine Air Command of possible raids on the mainland; if we could bomb Stanley, we could bomb Buenos Aires.

Next day came the announcement of the sinking of the Argentine cruiser, the *General Belgrano*. The strategic importance of this was overshadowed by the ensuing political controversy, but the fact remains that, after the loss of the *Belgrano*, Argentine naval surface forces never again ventured outside their twelve-mile territorial limit. Political opponents accused Mrs Thatcher of deliberately starting the shooting war in order to sabotage the Peruvian peace initiative. They ignored the fact that the Argentines had started the shooting war on 2 April and that it was only by the greatest good fortune that we had not suffered any casualties then. It was in any event wishful thinking to suppose that the Peruvian peace proposals stood any more chance of success than those initiated by General Haig: the gulf between the two sides remained too wide. As for the claim that it was somehow hitting below the belt to launch a salvo of torpedoes at the *Belgrano* when she was outside the Total Exclusion Zone and heading westwards, it was not generally realised that the Argentine Navy's plan had been to attack the British Task Force with aircraft from the carrier *Veintecinco de Mayo* (from outside the Total Exclusion Zone), knock out one or both of the British aircraft carriers and then send in the *Belgrano* to destroy the remainder of the Task Force. The plan was aborted because there was not enough wind across the deck of the Argentine carrier to launch her heavily laden Skyhawks. As dawn was fast approaching, the naval commander ordered his ships to turn back to safer waters until the wind increased. Evidence from Argentine official sources after the war made no mention of any warship being recalled to port. The deduction must be, therefore, that the withdrawal was temporary and that the ships were to head eastwards again when the wind blew up sufficiently for the carrier to launch the air strike.

Later in the day, and before the sinking of the *Belgrano*, two Super Etendards of the Argentine Navy took off from Rio Grande, armed with Exocet missiles and intending to attack the British warships, but their strike had to be aborted because they failed to accomplish a successful air-to-air refuelling off the coast. The fact that the *Belgrano* was outside the Total Exclusion Zone when she was sunk was irrelevant. By warning *all* ships and aircraft (not only Argentine) to keep out of a 200-mile zone round the Falklands, the British Government was imposing a blockade, not restricting its own area of operations. It would be absurd if the aggressor could dictate the limits within which the war that he started should be fought; yet this was the implication of those who cried 'Foul' or, as one Argentine proclaimed in the UN, 'Britain may not rule the waves, but she certainly waives the rules.'

Shortly after the sinking of the *Belgrano* came the news of a successful Exocet attack on HMS *Sheffield*. Some weeks later, Dick and I were having lunch with Sir John and Lady Fieldhouse at Northwood and the *Sheffield's* captain, Sam Salt. He gave us a graphic account of his ship's last moments. For over four hours he and his men had tried to bring the fierce fires under control, until the deck became too hot to walk on and he had to give the order to abandon ship. Twenty of his crew were lost but 236 were saved, demonstrating the value of helicopters in rescue work at sea.

The sinking of the *Belgrano* and the *Sheffield* had a profound effect on the British public. Until then, I had been impressed with their feelings of outrage and indignation at the injustice committed on innocent Islanders, of a clear wrong that must be put right; but the general view seemed to be that this would be achieved without serious loss. We had retaken South Georgia without a casualty on either side.³ The Falklands would be retrieved in the same way. Now, everyone realised that we were in for a bloody war and that more ships and more men would be lost before final victory. If anything, however, this served merely to harden people's determination. There may have been some faint hearts in Westminster and Whitehall, but I did not meet any in the country. Ordinary people from all walks of life, young and old, came up or wrote to me to express their support and sympathy for the Islanders. As in 1939, the war brought out the best in people, and Mavis and I were showered with kindness. When we went to Southampton, for example, to talk to the Falkland Islanders there, we had so many questions that we were too late to get back to the hotel for dinner. Even the late-night restaurants were closing; but one, run by a Cypriot family, stayed open to serve us and refused to let us pay, saying that, as islanders themselves, they could understand the plight of our Falkland friends. On another occasion, in London, I happened to hail a red taxi in Victoria Street. The driver, who was not the chatty type, took me to Waterloo without a word. As I pulled out the fare, he turned down the flag and said 'Can't charge you for riding in your own taxi, Guv!' Perhaps the most surprising incident, however, occurred under the arches of Charing Cross Bridge. We had been to the Players' Theatre and the tramps were tucked in to their cardboard and newspapers for the night when one of them got up, shook me by the hand and said, 'Well done, Guv!' He had obviously read the papers before sleeping in them.

I paid one more visit to Brize Norton to greet incoming passengers. On 13 May, we received the good news that Cindy and Annie and the thirteen BAS men from South Georgia were due in at 2.30 the next morning. I arrived to find a large contingent of the Buxton family, led by Aubrey and Maria, and Annie's mother and sister, with an even larger contingent of the media. Dick Laws and Eric Salmon were also there from BAS. It was a joyous reunion: now all the civilians from the Falklands Dependencies were safely back home. I prayed that this one-hundred-per cent record would continue on the Falkland Islands themselves. Cindy brought greetings from Nick and his men on HMS *Endurance*. She and Annie had hoped to travel on her at least as far as Ascension, but she was still needed down south and they had been transferred to HMS *Antrim* and, subsequently, HMS *Antelope*. Later, on 21 May, in Falkland Sound, HMS *Antrim* was struck by a bomb that failed to explode. HMS *Antelope* was less fortunate. On 23 May, she was also hit by a bomb that failed to explode, but it went off while a bomb disposal team was attempting to defuse it, killing one of the team and seriously injuring the other. The resulting fires caused the ship to be abandoned and she later sank.

Meanwhile, the focus of attention on the diplomatic front had shifted to the United Nations, where the Secretary-General, Senor Perez de Cuellar, had launched a peace initiative. That same weekend, the Prime Minister recalled Tony Parsons (and Sir Nicholas Henderson) for consultation before presenting Britain's final proposals for a draft interim agreement to the Secretary General. I had earlier submitted, through the usual channels, a paper giving my thoughts on the future of the Falkland Islands, in the hope that it might help to counter the arguments of those who advocated concessions that I knew would be unacceptable to Islanders. In it, I had expressed my optimism about the future, provided that we upheld the principle of self-determination for the Islanders. I stated my belief that any referendum or plebiscite held after the war would result in an overwhelming vote by Islanders to remain British and that they would reject any solution – leaseback or otherwise – that would involve a transfer of sovereignty to Argentina, no matter how generous the terms that we were able to negotiate.

I then went into detail on how and why I thought that the Islands could prosper without Argentina, based upon the assumption that the British Government would not impose a settlement upon the Islanders against their wishes. If Britain would only make clear to the world after the cessation of hostilities that it was prepared to continue to defend the Islanders' right to stay British, we could reverse the population drift and attract private investment for development. British Government aid would be needed to rehabilitate and improve the basic infrastructure, starting with an imaginative housing development scheme, but private investment would surely follow. I finished by expressing the hope that the Islands' security would be assured not only by Britain but also by the USA and the United Nations, and that in time the Argentines might come to recognise the Islanders' right to have the government of their own choosing. In the event, my paper lost the battle of the pending tray and did not reach the Prime Minister's desk until long after the peace initiatives had run into the sand. But I need not have worried: Galtieri's intransigence saved the Islanders.

As the war progressed, we prepared for the aftermath. The need for more Diplomatic Service staff than before the invasion was recognised, in order to cope with rehabilitation and liaison with the military, who would clearly have to remain on the Islands in greater strength than the old NP8901. To my regret, I could not take back with me Brian and Christine Wells, who had already been posted to India; but Personnel Department did their best and gathered together a first-rate team.

Anticipating that the Royal Engineers and the Public Works Department would have to work closely together, we arranged a meeting on 21 May with ODA and MOD at which John Brodrick raised a few eyebrows by forecasting (accurately as it turned out) how much it would cost to rehabilitate the road, electricity and water services. He pointed out that the Stanley roads had never been constructed to withstand the weight and volume of the heavy military vehicles that the Royal Engineers would be using and that the electricity and water supplies would be totally inadequate (even assuming that they were undamaged) to support a military garrison of any size. What we could not foretell, of course, was how much damage would be suffered during the final assault. We did not know it at the time, but the land fighting had started in earnest early that morning, with our troops going ashore at San Carlos. We heard the news on the car radio that evening, as we drove to the Westcountry with Diana to spend half-term with her godmother. I tried to re-assure her over John's safety, saying that he would not have gone ashore with the first wave because he was on the headquarters staff and much too valuable to be put at risk. My credibility suffered when we heard later that John had been in the leading landing craft and was indeed the first to knock on the manager's door and say, 'Hello, Pat, I'm back again.' Pat Short did not recognise him at first, in his camouflage paint, but had then calmly invited him in for a cup of tea as if it had been four o'clock in the afternoon and not four in the morning. Next day, when the grim news was coming in of the loss of HMS *Ardent*, with twenty-two lives, and damage to HMS *Argonaut* (two lives lost) and HMS *Antrim*, I changed my tune and sought to persuade Diana that John was far safer ashore than afloat. He would remain at headquarters, I said, behind the front line and well protected from air attack. My credibility in Diana's eyes was finally destroyed when we heard that John had accompanied 2 Para in their advance on Goose Green and had been with Colonel 'H' when he was killed.

Before that heroic action, the Task Force suffered its heaviest loss to date with the hitting by Exocet of the SS *Atlantic Conveyor* on 25 May – Argentina's National Day. The Argentines claimed to have sunk one of the aircraft carriers – both were in the vicinity at the time – and there was evidence to suggest that chaff or Lynx helicopters successfully decoyed two Exocets away from them, one going harmlessly into the sea and the other relocking on the container ship. The loss of a carrier would have been disastrous, but the loss of the *Atlantic Conveyor*, with its precious cargo, was a severe blow. Three Chinooks, six Wessex and one Lynx were destroyed, together with large quantities of spare parts, Harrier cluster bombs, numerous vehicles, thousands of tents and aluminium matting for a forward airstrip. Fortunately, all the Harriers brought south by the *Atlantic Conveyor* had been flown off, as had one Chinook, which later broke all records (and the maker's specifications) in the loads that it carried. For the majority of the troops, however, the loss of the other three Chinooks meant that the only way to Stanley was by Shanks's pony. Sadly, twelve men, including the master, Captain North, were also lost in this action.

The SS *Atlantic Conveyor* was not the only casualty on Argentine National Day: HMS *Coventry* was hit by several bombs and subsequently capsized with the loss of nineteen crew. The Argentine Naval and air forces had demonstrated that, despite heavy aircraft losses and intense air activity since 21 May, they were still capable of launching raids and inflicting heavy damage.

Although the obvious aim of landing at San Carlos was to move directly to Stanley, the military staff at Northwood decided that the Argentine troops at Goose Green posed a threat to our right flank and to the beachhead and had to be neutralised before the advance on Stanley could be fully developed. The 2nd Battalion, The Parachute Regiment was given the job and what started as a 'major raid' turned into one of the decisive actions of the war. I knew nothing of this at the time, of course, and went to Bush House on 28 May to make my normal broadcast, following the Prime Minister's announcement in Parliament the previous day that our troops had broken out of the San Carlos bridgehead. I had no inside knowledge of the military plans. I had never been invited to the daily briefings in the FCO but had not protested because I could hardly claim the need to know. The only information I had was the Prime Minister's statement and the morning's headlines, a typical one of which was the *Daily Mail*'s 'Troops Attack On All Fronts'. After sending best wishes to the people at 'JB' and 'KC' (from which some newspapers deduced I was speaking in code!) I said, 'Those of you listening in

Darwin, Goose Green, Douglas Station and Teal Inlet may already know more than I do at this end'. I mentioned all four settlements because they were the only possible routes that the troops could take overland from the bridgehead.

I did not know that, at the time of my broadcast, Darwin had already fallen and Goose Green was under attack by 2 Para, or that 3 Para and 45 Commando, Royal Marines, were marching on Douglas Station and Teal Inlet. Early next morning an agitated duty officer rang me from the FCO to say that the Permanent Under Secretary, MOD, had telephoned to protest at my divulging military secrets. I was flabbergasted at the time, but understood MOD sensitivity later when John told me that he had been with Colonel 'H' at Camilla Creek at about midday on 27 May (the day before my broadcast) when someone tuned in to BBC Overseas and heard the announcement that 2 Para were advancing on Darwin. Some say that, as a result of this, the original garrison of some 650 at Goose Green was reinforced on 28 May by an additional regiment.

The facts of the battle for Goose Green speak for themselves: a force of 450 men overcame an Argentine force more than treble its size, dug in to well-prepared positions and supported by radar-controlled 35mm anti-aircraft guns, Pucara ground attack aircraft, artillery, mortars and machine guns. Sixteen Paras and one Royal Marine were killed. The exact number of Argentines killed was never ascertained, but estimates varied from 40 to 250. Over 1,000 prisoners were taken and large quantities of artillery, air defence weapons and ammunition captured. Most heartening from my point of view was that all 112 Islanders, who had been confined in the community hall for the past three weeks, were released unharmed. This would gladden the hearts of the besieged Stanley folk. The victory would also demoralise the Argentine troops waiting in the hills round the town.

As our troops prepared for the final assault, I wrote a letter of congratulations on behalf of the Falkland Islanders to John Fieldhouse for the relief of Goose Green and drafted a letter of condolence to the next-of-kin of those who had lost their lives in the battle. I had discussed this with Dick Baker, John Cheek and Bill Luxton and we agreed that it would be appropriate for me, as head of the Falkland Islands Government, to write to the next-of-kin of all who had died in the conflict to express the everlasting gratitude and deepest sympathy of the Falkland Islanders. Incomprehensibly, the FCO did not agree and, as I was dependent upon FCO staff and facilities to produce the letter, it was never sent. Meanwhile, the Task Force was reinforced by the arrival of the 5th Infantry Brigade, which had been transported in great secrecy by the RMS *Queen Elizabeth II* to South Georgia, where they were transferred to the SS *Canberra* and MV *Norland* and disembarked at San Carlos on 31 May. The build-up for the final battle continued during the early days of June, in the course of which we sustained the heaviest casualties of the campaign, when the Royal Fleet Auxiliary landing ships *Sir Galahad* and *Sir Tristram* were bombed while disembarking troops and supplies at Fitzroy (incorrectly called Bluff Cove by the media). The 1st Battalion, Welsh Guards, was the worst hit, with forty-two killed. Eight others brought the total to fifty. The tragedy was vividly portrayed on television screens throughout Britain, calling into question again the wisdom of allowing cameramen to accompany the Task Force. Such mishaps were bound to occur in war and, as Vietnam had shown to the Americans, bringing them into Everyman's living room did not necessarily help the war effort – or the service chiefs responsible for its conduct. In the event, the bombing, grievous though it was, did not delay the final assault on Stanley.

On the day of the *Sir Galahad* bombing, I had closeted myself in the flat at Fulham to prepare a speech for the 30 Club[4] at Claridge's that evening. The telephone rang and it was John Ure, whom I had not seen at the FCO for some weeks. To my surprise, he said that he had been on leave. He said that he was concerned about Bill Luxton's remarks to the Press about my being left out of the decision-making process in the FCO and suggested lunch with me, the councillors, himself, Robin and the Deputy Under-Secretary, Sidney Giffard (whom the Councillors had never met). Finding a date to suit all of us was difficult, but we eventually met on 14 June, the day of the Argentine surrender, and, incidentally, the day that I finally acquired a personal secretary (to be shared with Dick).

Before that, however, Dick and I had had a busy week concerned, of all things, with our Falklands murderer, Mr Minto. He had appealed against his conviction and sentence and the Court of Appeal, sitting in London, had reduced the conviction to manslaughter on the grounds of diminished responsibility. He was confined at Her Majesty's pleasure and the Home Office now demanded from the Falkland Islands Government not only the appeal costs but also the daily cost of keeping him in a criminal mental institution in England. I pointed out that the appeal fees alone exceeded the annual budgets of the Falklands' Police, Prison and Justice departments put together. We managed to reach a practical compromise, but only after protracted meetings at Lincoln's Inn, the Home Office and the FCO.

Another topic that had exercised us that week was the launching of the South Atlantic Fund. This was a MOD initiative and we were disappointed to learn that it was restricted to members of Her Majesty's Armed Forces and their relatives. While we fully supported the aims of the fund, we saw the need also to help Falkland Islanders who might suffer loss or injury as a result of the war. As legal obstacles prevented us from including them in the South Atlantic Fund, the Falkland Islands Association, with my full support, decided to launch a Falkland Islands Appeal, which we announced at the Royal Commonwealth Society on 10 June. It was inevitably overshadowed by the South Atlantic Fund, to which many donors contributed under the mistaken impression that they were helping the Islanders as well as our own servicemen, and we failed by a considerable margin to meet the modest target of £1 million. Nevertheless, the money raised, which included a generous donation of £250,000 from the sympathetic States of Jersey, was put to good use and much appreciated by the Islanders.

On 11 June, as General Moore was preparing to launch the first phase of his attack on Stanley – the capture of Mount Longdon, Two Sisters and Mount Harriet – Mr Onslow presided over the inaugural meeting of an inter-departmental rehabilitation group, consisting of ministers and officials from FCO, ODA and MOD, to which Falklands' councillors were invited. The group laid down a useful framework for future co-ordination and co-operation. the big question was, of course, how much of Stanley would need rehabilitating after the fighting. The next day, 12 June, was the Queen's official birthday. While the 3rd Battalion, The Parachute Regiment, was digging in on Mount Longdon under heavy artillery fire, we gathered in Horse Guards Parade for the Trooping The Colour. The Prime Minister had kindly invited Mavis and me to join her guests and, despite the showers and umbrellas, we had an excellent view, surrounded by Commonwealth representatives whom the Prime Minister entertained to drinks afterwards. We were invited to stay on for an informal lunch – so informal in fact that Mrs Thatcher was helping to serve – and naturally all thoughts were with our fighting men and the Stanley folk waiting to be liberated. I mentioned to a fellow guest, Lady Tilney, Diana's anxiety for John's safety and she was most sympathetic. She had lost her husband at the end of the last war and had been through it all herself. She offered to talk to Diana if anything happened to John.

Happily, we did not have to avail ourselves of Lady Tilney's kind offer. Had General Moore's plan gone through to the third phase, we might well have done, because John had been detailed to guide 3 Commando Brigade from Moody Brook past the ESRO building and slaughterhouse, up Felton Stream and across the golf course (on which he had played with me) to take Sapper Hill. After the second phase – Wireless Ridge, Tumbledown and Mount William – Argentine resistance crumbled and the white flags began to appear over Stanley. Phase 3 was never launched. On the night of 14 June, General Moore took the formal surrender of the Argentine forces on the Falkland Islands from General Menendez, and sent his famous message: 'The Falkland Islands are once more under the government desired by their inhabitants - God Save The Queen.'

My telephone never stopped ringing: journalists asking for comments; well-wishers offering congratulations; Islanders and expatriates wanting to return; associations wanting me to speak; would-be immigrants wanting to know how to get out to the Falklands. I had arranged to go to Exeter on 15 June, to open a maritime exhibition, but had to postpone that for a day because Mrs Thatcher was making a statement in the House of Commons. The atmosphere inside the chamber was electric. Surprise at the suddenness of victory combined with feelings of joy, relief, pride and thankfulness to produce a spirit that I had not experienced in London since VJ-Day, 1945. There was sadness and compassion, too, at the loss of so many young lives on both sides. I was particularly grieved over a report from Argentine sources that three civilians had been killed by British shelling on the day before the surrender. Confirmation came as I was about to leave for Parliament. Apparently, naval gunfire had been directed on to the western part of Stanley under the mistaken impression that civilians had been evacuated from that area, and three women had been killed.[5] Grievous though this loss of life was, one could only thank God that Menendez had been sensible enough to surrender before the final assault on Stanley.

The Prime Minister's statement in the House of Commons was both firm and unequivocal: 'What we have won we hold.' She pledged that the Falklands would never again be the victim of unprovoked aggression and that the sovereignty of the Islands was not negotiable. In answer to a question from Mr Michael Foot, she said, 'Our forces did not risk their lives for UN trusteeship. They risked their lives to defend British territory, the British way of life and the right of British people to determine their own future.' It was an emotional moment and I confess that, like many others, my eyes were moist. If only we had given that message loud and clear over the last decade, I thought, the invasion would never have happened.

In her speech, the Prime Minister mentioned that I would be going back to Stanley as Civil Commissioner, not as Governor, and that I would work alongside a Military Commissioner. I had not been involved in any of the discussions leading up to the change, and on returning to the FCO from the House of Commons, I was taken aback to be told that I would be giving a Press conference within the next hour to explain the change and to express my sentiments about returning to the Islands. The latter was easy – I was naturally delighted – but I could hardly explain the change in title when I did not know the reason myself.

From a quick reading of the Order-in-Council, it appeared that all the functions of the office of Governor and Commander-in-Chief would be exercised by the Civil Commissioner except those relating to defence and internal security (excluding the police), on which it was mandatory for the Civil Commissioner to consult the Military Commissioner and act in accordance with his advice. To me, it seemed that the simplest way would have been to remove 'Commander-in-Chief' from the old title and retain 'Governor'; but I understand that there were legal objections to this. Realising that a legal explanation would not satisfy the Press, I decided to make light of the change and, when asked the inevitable question, how did I feel on being 'demoted' from Governor to Civil Commissioner, I replied that I couldn't care less whether I was called Governor, Civil Commissioner or Senior Sixer as long as I could get on with the job. Frankly, however, the more I thought about the titles, the less I liked them. We had just heard the Prime Minister talking about the right of the Islanders to live under a government of their own choosing, yet here we were imposing a constitutional change upon them without even consulting their representatives in Britain. To the outside world, the mere fact of having a Military as well as a Civil Commissioner would imply a degree of military control, at a time when Argentina itself was moving from a military dictatorship to a civilian democracy. At the practical level also, I could foresee difficulties unless both commissioners had a sound understanding of the constitutional position, exercised their powers with tact and goodwill and established a close and harmonious working relationship.[6]

The main point, however, was that the war was over, we had won and I was going back. After my Press conference, I went to Bush House to send a joyous message to the Falkland Islands on BBC Overseas. The next week was a mad scramble to tie up the loose ends before leaving. First priority was to give evidence to the reconstituted Shackleton Committee. At the beginning of June, the Prime Minister had invited Lord Shackleton to update his 1976 economic report and he had lost no time in re-assembling his original team in the Old Admiralty building. I spent over two hours giving my views and suggestions on how the Islands could be made not only economically viable but also prosperous. Essential ingredients were a longer runway to take big jets and the declaration of a 200-mile exclusive economic zone (EEZ). Further subdivision of the larger farms would also be desirable.

I had a meeting with Mr Francis Pym, my first since he had taken over as Secretary of State for Foreign Affairs. He explained that he had not troubled me earlier because he knew that I had been seeing the Prime Minister and assured me that my return to the Islands had never been in question (there had been Press reports that the FCO was against my return). I said that I had never had any doubts myself and had dismissed the reports as idle speculation. I raised the question of the Total Exclusion Zone and recommended the declaration of an EEZ before it was lifted, but he said that this would present serious difficulties. The PUS called me in for a last meeting before I left. He was justifiably indignant over an allegation by Mr Eric Ogden that the FCO had been destroying secret papers in anticipation of an official inquiry into the affairs leading up to the Argentine invasion; but I was astonished when he appeared to suspect me as a possible source. I explained that the only time I had seen or spoken to Mr Ogden since his trip to the Falklands in 1981 was at the meeting with about 300 other MPs on 27 April. I knew him only slightly and had no idea why he should have made such a scurrilous charge.

Over the weekend, my newly acquired personal secretary, Joyce Jamieson, nobly volunteered to come into the office and I was able to catch up with the backlog of mail. The Crown Agents called in to show me the artwork for a special postage stamp issue, a £1 + £1 rebuilding surcharge, which turned out to be a great success. The Chartered Bank expressed interest in opening a branch in Stanley, which was most encouraging, and various firms rang to offer to supply prefabricated buildings. How different, I thought, from pre-invasion, when there was scarcely any interest in the Falkland Islands. Mr Onslow held another meeting of the inter-departmental rehabilitation group, which, unlike the first, I found depressing. There were plenty of constructive proposals, but no department would accept financial responsibility. Expense had been no object in our regaining the Islands, but I could see that, unless the Prime Minister intervened, rehabilitating them would become bogged down in Whitehall red tape. Fortunately, the Prime Minister did intervene and, as a result, £16 million were allocated to ODA for rehabilitation. (Subsequently, Parliament voted £31 million for a five-year development programme based upon the Shackleton Committee's recommendations.)

Dick Baker and I had drawn up a list of thirty-four civilians who we considered should return with us on the first aircraft. These included councillors' wives and their children and my personal secretary, but not our own wives. I called on the Chief of Defence Staff, Admiral Sir Terence Lewin, and he confirmed that both he and the Prime Minister had agreed that the civilians on my list should have top priority. On the day before we were due to fly, however, the RAF decreed that no women or children could travel on the Hercules. It was a sad blow and the only reason I was given was that the toilet arrangements on board were inadequate. Apparently, female members of the Armed Forces, including nurses, could use the somewhat primitive Elsan, which was hidden from other passengers by a curtain, but civilians could not.[7] John Cheek elected to come without his family, but Bill Luxton decided to wait and accompany Pat and their son by sea from Ascension. My new secretary, Elspeth Disney, was most disappointed and did not arrive in Stanley until after our other two girls who, because of their lower priority, had been booked on the first ship to leave Ascension.

Somehow in that last hectic week we managed to find the time to take my father out for lunch to celebrate his eighty-ninth birthday. It was to be his last. The morning of departure dawned with a posse of Pressmen outside our little flat in Fulham. Fortunately, it was fine and sunny, for there was no room to have them inside. One of the reporters produced a bottle of champagne and early morning commuters raised eyebrows as we celebrated on the pavement of the Fulham Road. Mavis accompanied me to Brize Norton, where the Station Commander, Group Captain Phil Walker, presented me with another three bottles of champagne, a gift from all the RAF personnel on the base. Dick Baker, John Cheek and John Brodrick were already there, together with two new members of my FCO team, Simon Fuller and Bill Greenham. They were to prove a great help to me in the first few weeks back in Stanley. Our pilot was No. 10 Squadron's Commanding Officer, Wing Commander Bunn, who presented me with the squadron crest and a magnificent picture of a VC10. He invited me up front for the take-off and, as the pleasant green fields of the Cotswolds receded and the Bristol Channel loomed into view, I thought of the Royal Marines who had been with me on our homeward flight ten long weeks ago and wondered if they had all survived the fighting. How satisfying it must have been for them to walk back into Government House – captors this time, not captives – and how I wished I could have been with them.

Back in my seat, reflecting on the past ten weeks, I realised that I was a sadder, but wiser, man. Harold Nicolson once said that the qualities required of a diplomatist (he eschewed the modern word 'diplomat') were truth, accuracy, calm, patience, good temper, modesty and loyalty. Well, I had been as truthful and accurate as my memory would allow, but had fallen down badly on calm, patience and good temper. I hoped I had been modest and I had certainly been loyal – loyal that is, to the people for whom I had been made responsible, the Falkland Islanders. And therein lay the rub. Some of my friends may have concluded that I had 'gone native.' If sticking up for one's own kith and kin was 'going native', then I was happy to plead guilty. The result, however, was that I had lost the trust of some of my colleagues. Looking ahead, we still had to face the re-emergence of the argument that we were right to seek 'some accommodation' with the Argentines and that the war had vindicated this policy, not exposed it as the cause. The argument ran that the only alternative was 'Fortress Falklands', which we could not afford, and so, once the dust had settled, the old 'leaseback' idea would reappear. Fortunately for the Islanders, the Prime Minister was firmly in the driving seat and unlikely to listen to this line of appeasement. Nodding off to sleep as we headed for West Africa,

I thought, not for the first or last time, 'Thank God for Maggie Thatcher.'

Notes

1. For a full account of this action in South Georgia, I commend *Operation Paraquat* by Roger Perkins.

2. See page 250.

3. One Argentine was killed after the surrender on the stricken *Santa Fe*, the result of a tragic misunderstanding.

4. The 30 Club was a group of leading personalities in the newspaper, printing and advertising industries.

5. For the full details see page 302.

6. Happily, the arrangement worked well with all the Military Commissioners except one. See page 405.

7. The rule was subsequently relaxed and many female civilians, including my wife, travelled by Hercules and coped perfectly well.

15

A Happy Return

We changed crews and refuelled at Dakar, in Senegal, after a six-hour flight. It was my first stop there and I found it pleasantly warm in the early evening as we stood next to the monsoon drain, watching the lizards gobbling up the mosquitoes. We were kept away from the main terminal building because the Senegalese authorities did not wish to draw attention to British military aircraft and personnel. We had a small RAF detachment there, but they kept a low profile, working inconspicuously to speed the flow of men and materials between the UK and Ascension. Theirs was an unsung but valuable effort in the Falklands war. We owe a debt of gratitude, too, to the Senegalese Government for allowing us to use Dakar as a staging post.

The flight to Ascension from Dakar was only 3½ hours and we touched down a little before midnight, to be met again by Bernard Pauncefort, Bill Bryden and Don Coffey. It was a happy reunion and an augury of things to come in the Falklands. We had, however, jumped the gun a little in arriving at Ascension before the RAF had tested the damaged runway at Stanley. They wished to make a proving flight before carrying civilians. For the first of many times, Bernard took me to the Administrator's official residence halfway up the mountain. It was originally the Royal Marines' hospital and had been built in a square, with a central courtyard and a large verandah which afforded a magnificent view of Georgetown and the sea.

After breakfast, Bernard drove me down the countless hairpin bends, the temperature increasing by leaps and bounds as we descended to Wideawake Field, where we were informed that the first RAF Hercules was on its way to Stanley and that, if it landed and took off successfully, we could get airborne while it was on its way back to Ascension. The flight took between thirteen and fourteen hours and we could expect to take off at about 4am next morning, 25 June. I took the opportunity to see as much of Ascension as I could. Armed with my 16mm cine-camera, I jumped aboard a

Chinook which was about to take some St Helenian children on a flight round the island. It was a fascinating trip. Unlike all the other mountains I had seen, Ascension had more foliage at the top than at the bottom. On the peaks were lush bamboo forests, but the greenery became less and less lower down the slopes until all was bare and brown at the bottom. Older than Krakatau, which I had flown over in the Air Attaché's aircraft in Indonesia, it was still comparatively recent in geological terms, and plants had not had time to establish themselves on the lower slopes of volcanic ash. But they were spreading slowly, said Bernard, and ultimately Ascension would become a tropical paradise like Mauritius or the Seychelles. Indeed, over the next three years I was to pay several visits to Ascension and each time the advance of foliage down the slopes was noticeable.

During our joy-ride round the island, the pilot received instructions to inspect a Russian trawler, which had been reported skulking on the three-mile territorial limit. We returned to Wideawake, disembarked the children and flew quickly to the spot, where we hovered beside the trawler's bridge, taking photographs. I was intrigued by the veritable Christmas tree of aerials that sprouted from its superstructure. The men (and one woman) on the bridge photographed us in return and we parted with friendly waves. That afternoon, wanting to take some film in Georgetown from the ground, I espied a superb vantage point on top of a flagpole near the main square. I climbed up its ladder and was happily filming when a horrified Bernard appeared and called for me to come down. Apparently, the pole had been unsafe for years and was liable to topple over under the slightest extra weight. Bernard said he did not want a dead Governor (or Civil Commissioner) on his hands.

Tricia gave an excellent dinner party that evening, with fresh crayfish tails and, after what seemed like a ten-minute nap, Bernard was waking me at 3am for a 4.30 take-off. The first Hercules had signalled the green light and we were on our way. Fortified by a full English breakfast, fried in a field kitchen on the airfield and eaten off a trestle table in a marquee, we sat in canvas bucket seats ranged down the side of the aircraft and wondered how we would be feeling after twelve hours. The last time I had travelled in a Hercules was when we were evacuated from Saigon, in 1975. We were the last fixed-wing aircraft to leave Tan Son Nhut airport before the communists started shelling and rocketing it. But that had been a comparatively short flight, to Singapore, and in a warm climate. We waited on the ground while two Victor tankers took off, and then it was our turn. I sat in the jump seat between and behind the first and second pilots. The heavily laden aircraft took an age to build up flying speed. We trundled past the hills on each side of the runway (which were too close, I was told, to comply with normal civilian regulations) and eventually became airborne. As the vibrations from the wheels ceased, I experienced the same thrill I always had at the moment of take-off, whether in a Tiger Moth or Concorde.

To get our Hercules to Stanley took three Victor tankers. In case the runway became unserviceable or the weather made it impossible to land, the Hercules had to have enough fuel on arrival at Stanley to be able to fly all the way back to Ascension. The first in-flight refuelling was scheduled for four hours out of Ascension, the second, ten hours. The captain, Flight Lieutenant Harry Burgoyne, had been flying Hercules for eleven years. He was full of praise for Marshall's of Cambridge, who had fitted refuelling probes on the Hercules in twenty-one days. In normal times, he said, it would have taken months. Pilots had quickly got the hang of formating close under the tail of the tanker aircraft and connecting their probe first time. I was to see him demonstrate this to perfection later but, as the sun came up, I went back to my seat to write a few letters.

The biggest snag in travelling by RAF Hercules was the poor lighting. At night, it was almost impossible to read or write. Another drawback was the heating system. It was too hot near the blowers, too cold elsewhere. Some passengers found the high noise level irritating. It made conversation difficult, but I did not mind that – there was always plenty to think about. As I became a seasoned Hercules passenger (thirteen in all), I learned to grab a stretcher beside the bulkhead. This was out of everybody's way, near to a light and not far from a hot-air blower. Unfortunately, the stretchers were removed from the normal Hercules and fitted into specialised 'casevac' aircraft, so latterly this option was not available. There was a bunk on the flightdeck and most crews were generous in inviting me to use it; but as it was really intended to let them stretch out I always felt that I was depriving one of them of a much-needed rest. The truly expert Hercules passenger, however, carried his own hammock and slung it at the back, above the sloping ramp, as soon as we were airborne, there to remain warm and snug until a few minutes before touchdown. Food was provided in picnic boxes, cold but plentiful, which the loadmasters distributed by swinging like trapeze artists from the central rigging. Again I was privileged in usually being invited up to the flightdeck for hot meals, which were normally reserved for the crew.

On this first flight, my next invitation to the flightdeck was to witness the in-flight refuelling. They gave me earphones so that I could listen to the conversation between ourselves and the tanker, which was already in view on our starboard side. I could sense the increased tension as we eased our way behind the Victor and slowly lessened the gap between us and the basket at the end of the trailing hose. With a solid clunk, the probe was locked in first time and the fuel began to flow. We took on 3,200 gallons on that first refuelling, losing height during the operation from 21,000 to 8,000 ft. A gentle descent was necessary because the Hercules could not fly fast enough straight and level to keep up with the Victor. It was twenty minutes of total concentration by both pilots, and I was full of admiration. Harry Burgoyne said he actually looked forward to the refuelling – it broke the monotony of an otherwise boring flight.

After the second refuelling, we waved goodbye to the last Victor and settled down for the final leg of the flight. Stanley lay about three hours ahead. I felt sorry for the Victor crew, who had to go all the way back to Ascension without even seeing the Falkland Islands, and prayed that we should not have to follow them. Somewhere along the way, we had crossed the first Hercules, whose captain had reported that the Stanley runway was 'no sweat', provided that the crosswind did not exceed 25 knots. There was a thrill of expectancy as the engine note changed at 800ft, over a grey and uninviting sea. I was in the jump seat again, straining for a sight of land. Suddenly some rugged rocks appeared, then a jagged coastline followed by Cape Pembroke lighthouse. We were bang on course. Harry made a low-level run over Stanley airport and I was appalled at the devastation. There were craters and wrecked aircraft and vehicles everywhere. The one direct hit on the runway had sliced off half the width, about halfway along its length. It was the first of a stick which had cut a swathe across the airfield between the Islander hangar and the terminal building. The Islander looked very sad, with its back broken, and our three Cessnas were in varying stages of disrepair. I was pleased to see that mine looked more-or-less intact. My greatest pleasure, however, was to see the Union Jack flying again from the airport flagpole. Harry was more concerned with the windsock. It was blowing at right angles across the runway (shades of my first landing there) at an estimated 25 knots. I glanced inquiringly at Harry. 'No sweat', he said, and started the downwind checks for landing. I do not know how the approach speeds of the Hercules and the Friendship compare, but we seemed to be coming in faster and steeper than ever before. It looked impossible to land on that half-strip of runway but, despite the crosswind, we touched down sweetly, the propellers whined as Harry reversed the pitch and we stopped with plenty of runway to spare. As we taxied back, I noticed that the port wing went over the Vulcan crater. There was precious little room for error.

Harold Rowlands and Don were on the apron to meet me. I could not have chosen a better reception committee. Jeremy Moore's *aide-de-camp* was also there to escort us by helicopter to the football field next to Government House where, despite the heavy rain, the whole of Stanley seemed to be assembled to greet me. There was also a guard-of-honour, which I was delighted to see included detachments of the Royal Marines and the FIDF, and a military band. The two victorious commanders, Sandy Woodward and Jeremy Moore, welcomed me back but, before I could take the General Salute, I was engulfed by the crowd. Normally not renowned for displaying emotions, even the miserable weather could not dampen their spirits. In that sea of faces I saw Syd and Betty Miller, crying this time from joy, not sorrow, and Monsignor Spraggon, in all his finery still and beaming goodwill and happiness. Eventually, Sandy prised me away to take the Salute and inspect the troops. The poor bandsmen had to pour the water out of their instruments before they could play and everyone was soaked. It was, nevertheless, a joyous occasion and, having seen the Pope on television kneeling down and kissing the good earth after a flight, I felt like doing the same. But the Falklands good earth was dirty wet mud, not a clean red carpet, so I settled for kissing it in spirit instead.

Jeremy took me into Government House, which he was still using as his headquarters, and apologised for the shambles. There were about a dozen soldiers in the small drawing room, working at trestle tables; telephone wires were scattered all over the place, through broken windows in the conservatory and out to Gene's precious lawn, on which were parked Royal Signals lorries and Land Rovers. There was mud everywhere and I was glad that Mavis was not there to share the scene with me. It was comforting, however, to see familiar objects like the smiling red Buddha, the old Chinese fisherman, Mavis's pieces of

Ming and our pictures still hanging on the walls, albeit at crazy angles.

I asked Jeremy if John Thurman, Mike Norman and the other NP8901 Royal Marines were still in Stanley and he said that they were aboard the *Canberra*. We had seen the 'Great White Whale' at anchor in Port William as we flew in and I asked if I could visit them before she sailed. To my dismay, he said that she had left while we were on the football field. Most of the Royal Marines and the Paras had gone with her. Bill Luxton had asked me before I left England if I could keep hold of our friend Major Dowling. I asked Jeremy about the Argentine prisoners, but he said that most of them had already been transported back to Argentina. He had no knowledge of Dowling.[1]

Nanny appeared from the kitchen, as bright and cheerful as ever. She said that she had been staying at Don and Vera's since the liberation (John had also stayed there before boarding the *Canberra*). Before that, she had been with friends in the police cottages and had received a nasty shock when one of our helicopters had launched a rocket into the police station close by. General Menendez had been meeting with other top brass in the Town Hall at the time and she guessed that this had been the target (a few yards to the right and the rocket would have scored a bull's eye). Nanny had visited Government House regularly during the occupation to make sure that Jenny, her cat, was safe. She said it was like an army barracks and, though neither she nor Jenny was ill-treated, she never wanted to experience 'that lot' again. She had been tidying up the kitchen and noticed that various pieces of GH silver and china had disappeared. Discerning souvenir hunters had concentrated upon those with the 'VR' markings rather than the 'GR' and 'ER'. The freezers had been cleaned out and cases of wine and spirits had gone. Nanny and Don had packed our clothes, except for the anoraks, which the Argentines had snapped up in the first few days.

To my relief, all my books had been left intact. Indeed, the only one that had been removed from the shelf was a bound volume of *The Illustrated London News* from the First World War, which Menendez had taken through to the office. It was bizarre to think of him leafing through those pictures of death and destruction on the Western Front while similar scenes were being enacted in the hills around him. He must have been something of a hypochondriac because an office drawer was full of pills of every description. There was also a scented pink lip salve, marked 'Avon Dew Kiss – Lapiz humectante para labios'. There were more pills in the bedroom, drawers full of them. In the bedside cabinet was a pair of pyjamas, which I assumed to be Jeremy's. When I asked him, however, he reacted strongly: fighting soldiers did not wear pyjamas. They must have belonged to Menendez and, as they were thicker and warmer than mine, I had no compunction about wearing them.

Keeping warm became one of my main preoccupations. The Argentines had tried to use thick oil fuel in the central heating system, consequently the boiler was completely blocked. Electricity was erratic and we were urged to use it as economically as possible; this meant using the fan-heater first thing in the morning only. Fortunately, the Argentines had not made use of the peat that Don had stacked in the shed, so we were able to have a peat fire in the small drawing-room; but there was no fireplace in the office and the shelling seemed to have loosened all the doors and windows. Everything rattled whenever a helicopter flew past, which was almost non-stop during daylight hours. Indeed, the 'triangle' in front of Government House became for a while the busiest helipad in the world. Doors refused to close and windows stuck. My office must have been one of the draughtiest places in Stanley. Despite a Korean anorak, newly purchased from the West Store, and my fur-lined boots, I would slowly freeze at my desk. The only answer was exercise and this took the form of a small trampoline, which we had left in the drawing room. I would work at my desk until my toes went numb, then adjourn into the drawing room for twenty or thirty jumps on the trampoline.

Water was another problem. The water filtration plant near Moody Brook had received a direct hit from one of our 105mm shells, which fortunately had struck a corner of the main tank and exploded with most of the blast going outside. The tank itself, though displaced several inches on its foundations, had survived. However, many of the distribution pipes had been fractured and, as a result, the reservoir was almost empty. Water was rationed and we were asked to use as little as possible. Miraculously the 'Teasmade', which we kept beside the bed, had survived, and still worked. Nanny and I quickly fell into a routine: she would fill my hot-water bottle at night and the water would remain warm enough for me to use for washing the next morning. The water left in the 'Teasmade' after making my morning tea was enough for me to shave in; and I cleaned my teeth in an egg-cupful of cold water. Baths were out, despite my smelling of rubber from the hot-water bottle.

All our chickens had gone, but somehow Nanny produced me scrambled egg for breakfast. One duck had survived (she was still there when we left in 1985). Gene and the two assistant gardeners turned up for work on the first morning that I was back. Gene was utterly disconsolate when he saw the conservatory; only the grapevine appeared to have survived. He sat on the steps, elbows on knees, glum face in cupped hands, and said that he could never get it back to what it was. 'Nonsense, Gene,' I said, 'Six months and I bet you'll have it as good as ever.' I do not know how he did it (it took several months to get the glass from England) but after six months it was a blaze of colour again and, within a year, sweet peas, pelargoniums, geraniums, African marigolds and roses were back in profusion.

The vegetable garden and greenhouses behind Government House were, if anything, a sorrier sight. Our shelling had cratered Gene's potato and swede patches, broken most of the greenhouse glass and wreaked havoc with the strawberry, raspberry and currant bushes. Don said that two dead Argentines had been found in the potato shed, which had somehow survived a near miss. Government House itself had a few more holes in it than when I left and pieces of shell had ripped gashes in the corrugated iron walls of the garage, incredibly without causing damage to the red taxi or Mavis's Fifi. Don had removed the distributor from Fifi and immobilised the diesel engine of the taxi so that the Argentines could use neither. He had gone into GH regularly to pack our things and also to keep an eye on the place. Menendez had not slept there latterly, he said, but had moved round various points in Stanley, apparently fearful of a Special Forces' attempt to kill or capture him.

The roof leaked badly. We quickly identified the spots and put buckets, basins and any other containers we could find to catch the drips. The result was a cacophony of sound, which at first kept me awake but soon became a familiar background noise. The Argentines had stacked sandbags at all the windows but stupidly had put them inside. As a result, the lovely Persian carpet in the drawing room had been completely covered in mud and sand (we were picking up sand in the vacuum cleaner over a year later). They had also criss-crossed the windows with sellotape to reduce the risk of flying glass. It took an age to pull off and we never did get rid of the marks completely.

My most pleasurable task on the first day was to remove the pictures of Galtieri and San Martin from the main drawing room and to replace them with those of the Queen and the Duke of Edinburgh, which Menendez had thoughtfully placed behind the door, anticipating that his stay was only temporary. He had not touched the young Queen Victoria over the fireplace or any of the other portraits of British royalty along the hallway. In the office was an odd piece of headgear in a handsome glass case, a present to Menendez from some admirers in Buenos Aires. It was the ceremonial hat of the President's praetorian guard and I thought that it would go well in the great Falklands auction, a fund-raising event which I had discussed with the organisers before leaving England. I assumed, perhaps wrongly, that it could not have meant much to Menendez, otherwise he would have taken it with him. After all, he had had more time to pack than Garcia had given me. In due course, the hat was taken back to London and fetched an excellent price for the South Atlantic Fund. The successful bidder was Ted Needham, who bought it for the Coalite boardroom in Bolsover. Subsequently I received an official reprimand for giving away something that was not mine to give. The FCO considered that it would make more difficult the retrieval of the things that I had lost. I could only reply that it had not struck me for a moment that I had the slightest chance of getting any of my things back from Argentina.

After recording a message for the local radio with Patrick Watts and holding a Press conference for the few British journalists who remained in Stanley, my first and sad duty was to see the next-of-kin of the three civilians who had been killed. Don's elder brother, Harry, had lost his wife, Doreen, and it had hit him badly. Tragically, their only child, Cheryl, was spastic and, though now twenty-eight years old, required the care and attention of a young baby. Doreen had devoted her life to looking after her and Harry could not possibly cope on his own. There were no proper facilities in the Falklands, but he was understandably reluctant to send her away to strange and unfamiliar surroundings in England. He was still in a state of shock, reluctant to face up to the inevitable, and it took a deal of persuasion to convince him that it was in Cheryl's best interests, as well as his own, for her to go for specialised care and treatment in England. Eventually, he gave his consent and the Falklands Appeal came to the rescue. She was placed in a home in Camberley, where I found her when I went on leave in 1983 under the excellent care of the Ockenden Venture, with whom I had worked in Saigon. Sadly, Harry never recovered from Doreen's death. He lost the will to live, sought solace from the bottle, and died on New Year's Eve, 1982. He was, in truth, the fourth civilian casualty of the war.

Don took me from Harry to Laurie Goodwin, whose mother, Mary, had been killed with Doreen. She was quite elderly and had been living on her own for some time. Laurie himself was disabled and the Falklands Appeal was able to help him by supplying a new car with special controls, for which he was most grateful.

We found Steve Whitley at Mike and Alison Bleaney's. His young wife Sue had been the third fatality. Steve himself had received a nasty gash in the back and one of the nursing sisters, Karen Timberlake, was dressing it when we arrived. Sue had come out to the Falklands as a teacher at the Stanley secondary school and she and Steve had been married by Griff Evans at Pebble Island the previous year. During the occupation, they all gathered in John and Veronica Fowler's house because it was more substantial than their own and afforded greater protection. Anticipating that the British forces might think that there were no civilians in the western part of Stanley, they had pointedly put washing out in the garden and stoked the fire, hoping to show any gunnery observers looking down from the outlying hills that the house was still inhabited. Sue and the other ladies had just gone into the kitchen to make a pot of tea when a shell landed in the front garden. Before the men could get the ladies back into the front room, a second shell landed in the back garden, showering metal fragments into the kitchen and killing Sue and Doreen instantly. Mary died later, from shock.

According to the head of the Naval Historical Branch of the MOD, this incident was the only 'accidental infringement' of the general policy of the Task Force, which was to refrain from deliberately firing upon the built-up area of Stanley.[2] Steve was understandably bitter. He and Sue could have left the Islands with other expatriates recruited by the ODA in the first few weeks of the Argentine occupation, but they had chosen to stay to do what they could to help (Steve was the only veterinary surgeon in the Islands). I was told later that he had waged his own war against the Argentines, going round Stanley with castrating shears, cutting Argentine telephone cables. To add to Steve's chagrin, his house had been occupied and several of his possessions taken, the most valuable and irreplaceable of which was a rare collection of Falkland Islands coins.

Sitting in the familiar surroundings of Alison's kitchen, which had always been one of the most popular meeting-places in Stanley, I found it difficult to imagine the trauma that they had been through in the past two-and-a-half months. They looked tired and drawn and were clearly in need of a rest – I determined to get them on leave as soon as possible – yet they chatted and joked as if nothing out of the ordinary had happened: Alison breast-fed Emma as she prepared a meal; Mike bounced Daniel on his knee and the radio crackled away in the corner. There was a reluctance to talk about their recent experience, as if too painful to recall. Indeed, I found this to be general throughout Stanley, which incidentally made my task in preparing citations for decorations extremely difficult. For a good year after the war, the Stanley folk did not want to talk about it. For the second year, they talked of little else. By the third year, they were beginning to look ahead. I did not hear Alison's story from her own lips until she visited me from her new home in Australia five years later.

After the Argentines had banished Daniel Haynes, the Senior Medical Officer, and his family to Fox Bay East, Alison had carried on running the hospital with the help of Mary Elphinstone, another qualified doctor who had come out to the Falkland Islands for a holiday a few days before the invasion. They soon established the practice of seeing Captain Hussey and Vicecomodoro Bloomer-Reeve every morning. These were the two most approachable members of the occupying force. Captain Hussey was an Argentine Navy officer who had visited the Islands several times before the invasion. Alison and Mary then took it in turn to go to the R/T hut, which Eileen Vidal stoically manned throughout the occupation, to receive medical calls. Menendez had at first ordered the R/T station to be closed; but with Bloomer-Reeve's help Alison had persuaded him that it was necessary for the health and welfare of the Islanders in camp.

Each settlement had a medicine chest issued by the Medical Department and, upon hearing a patient's ailments over the radio, the doctor would prescribe the relevant medicine. This daily surgery by radio had become a regular feature of Islander life and to stop it would have caused great hardship. Keeping the link open, however, was a constant battle. After the power cable to the R/T station had been cut for the fifth time, Alison and Mary had gone yet again to protest to General Menendez, whom they had found in a nasty mood. He was decidedly unco-operative until Alison pulled out her breast and started to feed Emma: this completely disarmed him and they got what they wanted. Alison took Emma everywhere and found her a tremendous help. Tense and trigger-happy troops relaxed when they saw the baby and let them pass with a pat and a smile.

The few days before the surrender had been difficult. Alison had made her medical calls as normal on the Thursday morning. A patient in Fox Bay West badly needed medicine that was not in the medicine chest and Alison had offered to take it herself by Argentine helicopter; but Captain Hussey had refused to let her go. The helicopter had duly left, with the medicine but without Alison and, though painted white and red with crosses prominently displayed, was shot down by its own troops. On the Friday, Eileen Vidal had been ordered to close the R/T station and dismantle the equipment.

As our troops tightened the ring round Stanley, Alison and Mike had taken the children into the hospital, sleeping in a cupboard in the operating theatre. There were about a hundred civilians in the hospital over that last weekend, crammed into part of a building normally catering for thirty-four patients. The Argentines had occupied the other part. They had their own doctors and excellent equipment, but Alison said she was disgusted when one of them, called Mario, simply abandoned his patients and went off in the hospital ship, the *Bahia Paraiso*, which had arrived in Stanley on the Thursday (and which, incidentally, had been observed by Islanders living near the jetty off-loading ammunition and troops during the night).[3] Alison was also disgusted with the team from the International Commission of the Red Cross, which arrived on board the *Bahia Paraiso*. Consisting of one Swiss, one French and one Spanish (whom Alison mistook for an Argentine), they made only the most cursory inspection of the hospital, saying that they could not stay long as they were due to have lunch with General Menendez. (Harold Rowlands told me that he and other senior members of the Falkland Islands Government had asked to see the ICRC team but that their request had been ignored.)

On Monday morning, 14 June, the day of the surrender, Alison had been working in the hospital as usual and listening to her portable radio, which she left tuned in to the R/T station frequency in case of emergency calls from camp, when she heard a voice speaking in English and Spanish calling for the Argentine forces to surrender.[4] Failure to respond, said the voice, would lead to unnecessary bloodshed in Stanley. Carrying Emma in her arms, Alison had gone in search of Captain Hussey. In the rapidly deteriorating situation, Hussey and his staff were moving from house to house and it had taken about two hours to find him. She reported the broadcast and warned that, if the Argentines did not surrender, they would all be destroyed, civilians and soldiers alike. Hussey passed this on to Menendez but returned to Alison with the grim response: 'No surrender'. 'Well, that's it', said Alison, shaking Hussey by the hand and wishing him goodbye. He turned ashen grey and shook visibly. 'Wait a minute', he said, 'I'll try again.'

On the second attempt, Menendez agreed to talk. Hussey went with Alison to the R/T station in Davis Street, where Alison dug out the equipment from the cupboard and set about re-assembling it. A critical moment occurred when she had to connect the wires to two identical sockets: the wrong way round would have blown the set. By good fortune, she got it right first time and made contact with Captain Bell. Hussey told her not to mention that he was present but simply to ask for the terms of surrender. Armed with these, Hussey went back to Menendez. He asked Alison to accompany him because, he said, she was his 'lucky penny'. After receiving further orders from Menendez, he returned with Alison to the R/T station, authorised this time to speak to Bell and to arrange the surrender. By then it was about 3pm.

Alison walked back to the hospital feeling very relieved. Sanity had prevailed and, despite orders to the contrary from Galtieri, Menendez had made the humane decision.[5] The people of Stanley were saved. At about 4pm, Alison saw a helicopter trailing a white flag land at the football field. Out of it stepped Captain Bell, a signaller, and Lieutenant Colonel Mike Rose, whom Alison at the time mistook for General Moore. As they walked past the hospital, Rose called, 'You Alison?' She nodded. 'You did a great job'.

But Alison's job was not over. Within twenty-four hours of the surrender, she was back in the operating theatre, handing instruments to dishevelled Para doctors who, still in their combat gear and camouflage paint, were operating by Tilley lamp on a trooper whose friend had been skylarking about with a captured Argentine revolver. A bullet had gone through his cheek and lodged in the shoulder. The incongruous touch was that Alison still had Emma clasped in one arm, swathed in radiant pink.

After visiting Mike and Alison Bleaney, Don took me to see John and Veronica Fowler. They had moved into the hospital after their house had been shelled but were now in another government quarter. They had both been badly shaken and were obvious candidates for home leave. I was delighted to find Tony Blake with them, from North Arm. He was as cheerful and ebullient as ever as he recounted how he had hunted, captured and looked after an unfortunate Argentine pilot who had been shot down in Lafonia. North Arm settlement had emerged from the conflict unscathed and they had not been short of food or fuel.[6] BBC Overseas had been their lifeline during the occupation. They had quickly converted their outdoor aerials to be portable, so that they could haul them down as soon as an Argentine aircraft was heard and put them up again immediately it had gone.

My next port of call was Harold Rowlands, who lived by himself in a pleasant house overlooking the harbour on Ross Road East. Already the slipway opposite, hastily constructed by the Royal Engineers, was a hive of activity, off-loading supplies and equipment from flat-topped lighters, known as Mexeflotes, which plied between the shore and the ships too large to tie up at the jetty. The scene looked more like Hong Kong than Stanley harbour. Harold looked tired and wan, but his sense of humour had not deserted him. Apparently the Argentines had tried to get him to switch the Islands' currency from pounds sterling to pesos, but he had refused. 'I told them I was far too old', he said, 'to learn about all those noughts.'

Another man who had not lost his sense of humour was Monsignor Spraggon. I called on him after attending evensong in the cathedral (at which I dried up reading the lesson – it was all a bit too much) and he showed me the damage that a trigger-happy Argentine had caused to his new house. Imagining our Special Forces in the shadows, a nervous conscript had loosed off twenty-seven rounds into the house, one of which had ripped through Monsignor's theological books. 'He got through them a lot quicker than I did', commented Daniel. The morning after the shooting, he had stormed into Bloomer-Reeve's office, dressed in his finery and protesting in his finest Geordie accent, and dragged poor Bloomer-Reeve back to his house to view the damage. Two bullets had gone through the lavatory at lethal height. 'Look at that', said Monsignor, 'If I'd been answering the call of nature, you'd now be answering to God.'

The Monsignor must have sorely taxed the Argentines. In the early days of the occupation, they had offered television sets to Islanders on generous hire-purchase terms, £10 deposit and £10 a month. Monsignor had exhorted the townsfolk to buy, explaining that it was an excellent bargain – only £20 or £30 at most, since the British would be back within a couple of months. He never doubted that we would win. 'God was on our side,' he said simply and made this abundantly clear to the Argentines. He preached to mixed congregations every Sunday and many Argentine soldiers sought him out privately and expressed their misgivings. He said that Bloomer-Reeve knew they were done for as soon as we had announced the sailing of the Task Force. He also thought that Menendez felt the same way but dared not admit it. He sought and received an assurance from Menendez that there would be no fighting in the streets of Stanley. On the Queen's birthday, he and Harry Bagnall had insisted on holding the traditional joint service, finishing with the National Anthem, which had been sung lustily by a bigger-than-average congregation. In the months ahead, I was to hear many tales of bravery and selflessness shown by both Monsignor Spraggon and Harry Bagnall. They tended their flocks in the highest Christian tradition.

That first Sunday of my return, before evensong, I had given Fifi a run. She started first time and I drove out to the airport and back and along to the Beaver hangar. The road had deteriorated somewhat since before the invasion but was still passable for a saloon car. At the airport, I examined the wreckage of the Islander and the three Cessnas. Although my aircraft appeared to be the least damaged, close inspection revealed various holes in the wings, tail-fin and fuselage, the result of accurate cluster-bombing by our Harriers. The aircraft were fair game because the Argentines had been using them to get around the Islands, but it was sad to think that they might never fly again (subsequent inspection by qualified engineers declared them total write-offs). Outside the Beaver hangar, the two Beavers, VP-FAT and VP-FAV were also a sorry sight. Both had been parked on the slipway by the Argentines, who had painted huge red crosses on the hangar and used it in the latter stages of the war as a first-aid post (some Islanders who lived nearby said that it was more a mortuary than a first-aid post, with bodies taken out by boat and dumped at sea). FAT had been virtually demolished by the British bombardments on 11 and 12 June, but FAV appeared to be reparable. The immediate requirement was to put it out of bounds to the souvenir hunters who were descending upon the Argentine aircraft like locusts. The Army Air Corps was using the hangar for its 'teeny-weenies' so all we could do for the time being was to cover the engine and cabin with tarpaulins and tether the aircraft securely to the ground. Unfortunately, we did not make it secure enough. On 28 July it was blown over onto its back in a gale and completely wrecked.

On my way home, I called on Ron and Nidge Buckett. Ron was an expatriate, ex-British Army, with the impossible task of looking after FIG transport. Nidge had been born in Yorkshire of Polish stock. They had both elected to stay in Stanley during the occupation and Alison had told me what a fine job they had done, looking after the old people, carrying them to and from 'safe houses' at night and generally administering to their needs. Nidge gave me the names of the elderly who had been hardest hit and agreed to take me to see them. She said that seven houses had been destroyed and about twenty more too badly damaged to live in. John Brodrick later confirmed these figures and identified forty-five more damaged but inhabitable and 122 slightly damaged. As the total number of houses in Stanley was only 366, and there had been a shortage of housing even before the war, this exacerbated an already serious problem. Anticipating the need, John had wisely ordered supplies of the two most important commodities, timber and glass (which arrived in August), but the general shortage of accommodation – housing, storage and office space – was to remain the biggest problem in Stanley for the rest of my time there.

Returning to Government House, I noticed several of our troops swarming over the Puma, which had either crash-landed or been hit on the ground at the side of Ross Road near the bottom of my garden. The craze for 'razzing'[7] as our troops called it, had caught on rapidly, and everyone seemed to want a bit of Argentine memorabilia. The Puma was not airworthy but was reparable – or rather it would have been before it was 'razzed'. General Moore tried to put a stop to it, but there was so much war booty around and so many ships with space aboard going home that it was an impossible task. The story goes that the Military Police put a notice on the Puma ordering trespassers to keep off and warning that it had been booby-trapped by the Argentines, but some bright spark 'razzed' the notice. Of greater value was the Chinook which the Argentines had abandoned behind Government House. It was believed to have been grounded with engine trouble, but externally it looked in perfect condition – perfect, that is, until the 'razzers' got to work. Eventually all that was left of the hulk was lifted away by an RAF Chinook and taken to the *Tor Caledonia* for carriage to the UK. I understand that it never flew again.[8]

Notes

1. Monsignor Spraggon told me later that Dowling had disappeared from the scene long before the British troops closed on Stanley.

2. *The Royal Navy and the Falklands War* by David Brown; page 321.

3. Reliable witnesses saw two oblong containers being off-loaded and driven away on the back of a lorry. Their observations fitted the description of Exocet missiles. On 12 June, HMS *Glamorgan* was hit by a land launched Exocet, killing thirteen of her Ship's Company.

4. This was Captain Rod Bell, a Spanish speaker on General Moore's staff.

5. In reply to a request to surrender earlier in the day, Galtieri had ordered that the fight should go on 'as the British were probably as exhausted as the Argentines were'. (*The Royal Navy and the Falklands War* by David Brown, page 333).

6. Over ninety per cent of the Falkland Islands was untouched by the war. This is not to say, however, that the inhabitants were unaffected.

7. From RAS – replenishment at sea.

8. *Falklands: The Air War* by Messrs Burden, Draper, Rough, Smith and Wilton, page 75.

16

So Much Owed by So Few to So Many

Despite the freezing office, we started work at 7am on the Monday morning and carried on thereafter until at least 7pm most days, with a short break for lunch. Simon Fuller and Bill Greenham lodged with me in Government House and our cook, Keva Smith, returned to help Nanny and Don, so we were quickly back in business. We were joined on 29 June by another FCO colleague, Julian Chandler, who came in on the second Hercules to carry civilians. Julian had served with me in Kuala Lumpur and volunteered to do a full tour in the Falklands. I was delighted to have him. Indeed, I could not have wished for a better team. They all set to work with a will and made light of the immense task of clearing up the mess left by the Argentines. There were no demarcation rules: everyone tackled the job in hand, from sweeping up to carrying peat to blocking up broken windows. Bill soon had the telex and cypher machines working and it was good to see him sitting there pounding the keys in his anorak. A minor irritation was that the only working telephones were in my study and the kitchen. They were of the hand-cranked variety and much time was wasted dashing to and fro making and answering calls (though it helped the circulation, and there was usually tea or coffee in the kitchen). We were lucky to have telephones at all, since many lines were down in town and heavy military vehicles being off-loaded at slipway 'B' were knocking them down almost as quickly as the hard-pressed telecommunications engineers were putting them up. Without a secretary, everything had to be written laboriously in manuscript, though this was eased somewhat when Myriam Booth, a Falkland Islander who was employed by BAS but had worked for my predecessor as social secretary, kindly offered to come in and type in the afternoon.

The Welsh Guards undertook the mammoth task of removing the sandbagged dug-outs from round Government House, while Gene and his two assistants began to bring back some semblance of order in the garden. We were all told to clear out quickly one morning when a guardsman found a suspicious-looking canister in one of the dugouts. It could have been a booby-trap but, in the event, it turned out to be a tin of bully beef.

There was so much to be done; the only way to proceed was to select the priorities and allocate the areas of concentration. First priority was clearly to ensure the security of the Islands by providing a credible deterrent to the continuing military threat from Argentina – the Argentines had not formally declared a cessation of hostilities, nor had they renounced the use of force.[1] Our aircraft carriers had already spent too long at sea and an adequate land-based air defence system was essential. Top priority must therefore be given to strengthening and lengthening the 4,100ft runway at Stanley airport to take Phantoms, and to constructing the radar stations needed to direct them. The Prime Minister and her Chiefs of Staff had already initiated action on this by ordering aluminium matting from the USA and authorising the despatch of the radar and other ground equipment necessary to sustain a Phantom unit. As the fighting troops went home, the Royal Engineer units built up until, at the peak, there were over a thousand sappers on the Islands. Before the aluminium matting could be laid, the runway base had to be extended to 6,000ft, the apron more than doubled in size and new roads and taxiways made. All the hard core needed for this, plus the foundations for the radar stations and the buildings to house the troops, had to be quarried locally, which put quarry equipment and, above all, dumper trucks, at a premium. John Brodrick needed aggregate and hard core for road repairs and houses and his perennial cry was to become not, like Richard III, 'A horse! A horse! My kingdom for a horse!' but a dumper truck.

Given that everything had to be subordinated to the runway, PWD handed over its Rose Hill quarry, which was close to the airport, to the Royal Engineers. The only other quarry was further away from Stanley at Pony's Pass, and the chronic shortage of dumper trucks meant that civilian rehabilitation had perforce to proceed more slowly. I explained the situation to councillors at our first meeting of Joint Councils on 29 June and they pledged their fullest support to the armed forces. They were so grateful for being liberated, nothing was too much for our troops. They readily agreed that we should share the hospital, the post office, the Secretariat, the police station, the drill hall, the harbourmaster's office and the Town Hall and that any public or private building with room to spare should be made available to them. With over 3,000 troops in and around Stanley, and a civilian population of little over 1,000, every nook and cranny was needed if all were to have a roof over their heads for the rest of the winter.

Councillors were puzzled (as I had been) by the change in my title, but I stressed the practical side and said how gratified I was to have a major-general to relieve me of my military responsibilities. They said that they would welcome his presence at their council meetings and endorsed my proposal to establish a joint civil and military rehabilitation committee, consisting of senior FIG officers and members of the general's staff. At the end of a memorable meeting, we repaired to the Upland Goose for lunch, which I considered an appropriate occasion to open the bottles of champagne so kindly presented by RAF Brize Norton. Not only was it our first council reunion since the invasion, it was also my birthday.

I went on the local radio that evening to explain what we had discussed at the meeting and to tell Islanders about the Joint Rehabilitation Committee. I also took the opportunity to scotch a rumour which had been growing during the occupation that HMG had prior warning of the invasion and to exonerate the two councillors who had represented them at the February talks from any hint of collusion or duplicity. I urged Islanders to look forward, not back, into the better and brighter future that Galtieri's folly had created for them. I also explained that anyone who had suffered loss or injury or damage as a direct result of the Argentine invasion and the subsequent armed conflict should submit his or her claim to the military Claims Officer, who had been given an office in the Secretariat.

Before my broadcast, I called on Harry Milne and Terry Spruce of the Falkland Islands Company, who had stayed at their posts in Stanley throughout the occupation. We discussed the future use of their jetty, which was the only one in the harbour capable of off-loading freight in any quantity. They readily agreed to allow the military to use it, except when the *AES* called, and to share their warehouses and offices with the Royal Corps of Transport. Harry said that the Argentines had ruined many of the bales of wool waiting to be shipped: they had dragged them out of the warehouse for use as super sandbags, ripped several open and even fouled some. As a nasty farewell present, they had left grenades with their pins out wedged between bales, to be activated when the bales were moved.

On my way back to Government House, I called on Gem Baylis, who had arrived on the same Hercules as Julian. Gem was a teacher at the senior school and had left the Islands with his family in the first few weeks of the occupation. To him fell the main task of cleaning out the school and getting it going again. The classrooms were in an indescribable mess. I do not know how many Argentine troops had been billeted there, but judging from the excreta left everywhere – including in desks and drawers – there must have been hundreds. Gem was ex-army himself and was used to hardship; he had been on a tough Joint Services expedition to Elephant Island, in the South Shetlands. He knuckled down to his novel job of nightsoil porter and, aided by a noble band of volunteers from the RAF, had the school ready for pupils in an incredibly short time. The Army Education Corps moved into part of the junior school and helped not only with the cleaning but also with the teaching until we were able to bring the civilian establishment back to full strength.

Other welcome passengers who flew in with Julian and Gem were Bob Handley and Bob Headland. The former was a doctor with BAS, who had helped us out before as a locum, and he had contrived to secure a priority flight, knowing that our Medical Department could use him. I was delighted to see him at Gem's house, because it meant that Alison could go on leave (though I had a hard job persuading her). Bob Headland was waiting for me when I returned to the office. He had done a great job in South Georgia, acting as intermediary between the attacking Argentine force and the Royal Marines and preventing cypher and postal equipment from falling into enemy hands. With characteristic initiative, he had talked his way onto the Hercules and I had no doubt that he would soon talk his way onto a naval ship going to South Georgia, where Dick Laws wanted him to prepare an inventory of damage to BAS property and equipment. He hoped also to salvage the bags of cyphers and seals that he had thrown into the water off King Edward Point jetty.

At the end of a hectic but satisfying day, it was good to relax after dinner with a few frames of snooker with Simon, Bill and Don.

Next day, 30 June, we held our first meeting of the Joint Rehabilitation Committee (JRC) and Jeremy Moore introduced me into the world of military acronyms, or rather reintroduced me, because I had first come across this jargon in Borneo. DOBOPS had rolled nicely off the tongue and seemed appropriate for General George Lea, who was a big man in every sense. It stood for Director of Borneo Operations, based with his staff in Labuan. Down in Kuching we had a FAC or Forward Air Commander. To my regret,

I never ascertained whether there was a BAC. BFFI (pronounced Biffy) sounded right for the British Forces, Falkland Islands, but CBFFI (pronounced Seabiffy) was a little clumsy for their Commander. SRAFOFI, or Senior RAF Officer, Falkland Islands, took a bit of getting used to, but the best was SNOFI, or Senior Naval Officer, Falkland Islands. It was pronounced with a long 'o' if the incumbent was liked, a short 'o' if not. Jeremy had a strong team: Brigadier Tony Wilson, Commander 5 Infantry Brigade; Commodore Michael Clapp, SNOFI (definitely with a long 'o'); Group Captain Bill Wratten, SRAFOFI, and Colonels Kennedy, Brownson and Baxter. I had Dick Baker, Harold Rowlands, John Brodrick and Simon Fuller. Goodwill abounded and there was a refreshing unity of purpose in tackling the immediate problems, which we agreed were: clearing up the debris of war, most importantly, the mines so recklessly laid by the Argentines and the vast amounts of unexploded ordnance, arms and ammunition; increasing the water and electricity supplies; repairing the roads, telephone wires and houses; controlling shipping in Port Stanley and Port William and re-establishing air and sea links with the settlements. Between meetings, I saw Jeremy almost every day, and John Brodrick and Colonel Kennedy met even more frequently.

The atmosphere at my meeting with heads of FIG departments that afternoon was in stark contrast to the optimism and energy of the JRC. It was not as gloomy as my last, on the day before the invasion, but there was a listlessness and apathy that I found most depressing. It was not until later that I realised that they were still in a state of shock. If they were not to be overwhelmed by the sheer size and dynamism of our armed forces, they were going to need a lot of propping up. Discussing the situation over dinner with Simon, Bill and Julian (who had also moved into Government House), we agreed that goodwill was not self-generating but the product of a two-way traffic and that it would not last unless we worked hard at it. As the day of liberation receded, conflicts of interest were bound to arise. The next priority after the security of the Islands must therefore be civil/military relations. I decided to concentrate on this myself and told Simon to make it his main job also. He liaised with the Commander's staff major and quickly struck up a useful rapport, which enabled us to iron out snags long before they built up into major problems. I gave Julian the task of looking after the expatriate officers in FIG and dealing with complaints from the public. He had a sympathetic ear and a friendly, genuine disposition, which soon made him popular with Islanders, expatriates and the military alike. Bill had a full-time job restoring and running the office, but he also had close contacts with the military in the communications field and established excellent relations there.

My next priority was to visit all those in Stanley and in camp who had suffered as a result of the war. With Nidge Buckett's help, I was slowly making my way round the damaged houses and the elderly inhabitants of Stanley. With Jeremy's help, by way of a Gazelle helicopter, I was able on 1 July to get to my first settlement, Darwin/Goose Green. Sergeant Keates of the Army Air Corps flew me and we landed in Brook's garden at Darwin, carefully avoiding the shell-holes in his lawn. Brook and Eileen were in great form and quite happy to tell me about their ordeal on the night of 2 Para's attack. They showed me where they had lain in the corridor, as far away from the outside walls as possible, while they were shelled from both sides. Miraculously, the house was not hit. Brook and I walked the few hundred yards to the gorse gully where 2 Para had been forced to halt, then round the spur of a hill to the next gully, where Colonel 'H' had lost his life in getting the attack moving again. It was uncanny to think that John, my future son-in-law, had been there at the time, reconnoitring the top of the gorse gully on the left while Colonel 'H' was probing to the right. John had found it clear at the top and was on his way down to report when Colonel 'H' was shot.

I retraced their steps, from breaking cover at the end of the bay, where they first came under fire, to the gorse bushes where they had joined 2 Platoon of 'A' Company. Much of the gorse was flattened and burnt. Spent cartridge cases littered the ground and pieces of clothing fluttered in the wind, snared on the prickly gorse. I struggled to the top of the gully, wondering how anyone could get through with rifle, ammunition and webbing. 'A' Company Commander, Major Dair Farrar-Hockley (whose father I had known on DOBOP's staff in Labuan), had led some sixteen men up there. I walked back down the side of the gully, where Captains Dent and Wood and Corporal Hardman were killed by withering fire from a trench not twenty yards up the slope. It was presumably this position that Colonel 'H' was attempting to outflank from the right when he was hit from another foxhole on the further slopes. I retraced his steps, round the bottom of the hill and up a shallower, gorseless gully to the spot where he had fallen. Brook and Eileen and others from the settlement had put flowers there (artificial at this time of the year), but the wind had scattered them. I collected and embedded them as firmly as scratching hands could in that stony soil. (On a subsequent visit, I found that someone had planted a sprig of heather there. The label was still legible: 'Gardener's Best Guaranteed. *Calluna vulgaris*. Darkness. Flower crimson purple, Aug-Sept.' I hoped that it was able to adapt to the austral seasons).

The Argentine foxholes were littered with the detritus of war. They had the stale, sour smell of faeces and death. It was the sort of smell you could taste; a taste that lingered in the mouth long afterwards. There seemed to be more tubes of toothpaste – 'Odol Crema Dental' – than spent cartridge cases; either the Argentine troops were mad keen on dental hygiene or they did not bother to clean their teeth at all. Among the cast-off clothing, webbing and blankets, I noticed an odd gym shoe, marked 'Industria Argentina'. It was scarcely bigger than a child's.

John told me later that the Argentines had started to come out of their bunkers, hands up and waving white flags, shortly after Colonel 'H' had been killed. Many of them had lost control of their bowels and smelt awful. They had had to squat in their own excrement all day. He helped one who, despite having had what seemed like half of his head shot away, was still conscious and walking. Another was screaming from the bunker and, when John went to help, died in front of him. Both his legs had been blown off, probably by a 66mm rocket. In the confusion, a Land Rover drove up while they were standing beside the captured positions and out stepped two Argentines. They were told to drop their weapons, but one put his up to the shoulder and was instantly cut down. The other somehow escaped.

Brook and Eileen had listened to the noise of the battle from the floor of their house, but had not known the outcome until a paratrooper knocked on the door and told them that the British had taken Darwin Hill. This was by no means the end of the fighting, which had carried on doggedly all day in the capable hands of the battalion's second-in-command, Major Chris Keeble; but the commanding heights had been secured and total victory was almost within 2 Para's grasp. Perhaps the greatest danger came from the Oerlikon 35mm radar-controlled anti-aircraft guns, which had been deployed to defend Goose Green airfield against air attack but were now ranged against the paratroopers who had to advance over open ground from Darwin ridge. At least three of the guns were situated on the eastern tip of Goose Green, immediately behind the settlement and the community hall in which the civilians were incarcerated. Brook had been most impressed with the Harrier strike on these guns. It was a clinical raid, he said, missing the settlement but hitting the congested tip of land behind and creating havoc amongst the enemy. John told me later that he had looked down on this raid from the gorse ridge and had heard the screams even from that distance.[2] In his estimation it had finally broken the Argentine will to carry on fighting.

Brook drove me to the top of the ridge, which gave us a grand, sweeping view of Goose Green and Choiseul Sound. There, visible from both Darwin and Goose Green, the grateful people of the two settlements had erected a monument to 2 Para. It was a rough stone cairn and a fitting tribute to Colonel 'H' and his brave men, who had triumphed against all the odds.[3] From there we drove down into Goose Green and had smoko with Eric and Shirley Goss. Eric described how, after the first Harrier raid on the airfield on 1 May, the Argentines had bundled all the civilians into the community hall. They suspected (wrongly) that one of the hams had been in radio contact with the Task Force and guided the aircraft in. The raid had caught them by surprise, the three Harriers releasing their bombs on the airfield and getting clear before the Argentines could bring their anti-aircraft guns to bear. The only reaction from the ground had been some ineffective small-arms fire. Subsequent raids were not so fortunate. We walked along a trail of Harrier bits, strung out over 300yd near the airfield. This was Lieutenant Nick Taylor's aircraft, shot down by the Oerlikon guns as he commenced his bombing run on 4 May. We walked further, past a similar trail of wreckage from an Argentine Skyhawk (also shot down by the Oerlikons), until we came to Nick Taylor's grave, behind a hedge near the racecourse. On the other side of the hedge were seven other graves, those of a Pucara pilot and six groundcrew killed during the raid on 1 May. (These bodies were later moved to the Argentine cemetery on the other side of Choiseul Sound.) At the request of his widow, Nick Taylor was left where he fell, tended by the grateful residents of Darwin and Goose Green.

We walked back across the airfield, which was strewn with damaged Pucaras. My abiding memory is of three of these sinister-looking aircraft, tilted crazily on their noses and silhouetted against the skyline. They brought to mind Wellington's remark, 'There is nothing worse than a battle won except a battle lost.' We passed a party of Gurkhas piling up captured Argentine equipment: a stack of steel helmets; a mountain of rifles and automatic weapons; boxes of every calibre of ammunition, from 9mm to 105mm, and rockets, missiles and bombs of all sizes. Brook pointed to what looked like wing tanks for the Pucaras. 'Napalm,' he said. John told me later that he had seen napalm dropped during the battle for Goose Green, but fortunately it had fallen harmlessly off target. We walked round the settlement and I was surprised to see how quickly it had returned to normal. Children were playing on a slide that just over a month ago had been used by the Argentines as a rocket launcher. The community hall was clean and showed no sign of its use for twenty-eight days as a prison. Eric said that, after patient negotiations, they were able to establish a roster for cooking and washing clothes in the bunkhouse and, towards the end, he and Brook had been allowed to move back to their own houses with their wives. Eric had played a vital role in the negotiations leading to the Argentine surrender on 29 May. The houses occupied by the Argentine troops had been vandalised and left in a filthy mess. Excreta in the drawers and baths seemed to be their favourite calling card.

The Gurkhas were most popular with the local residents. Disciplined, cheerful and willing to help in every possible way, the loss of one of them, blown up by a grenade while tidying up a trench, was felt as a family bereavement. Eric took me to the Mess of the 1st/7th Duke of Edinburgh Own Gurkha Rifles where, in the absence of their Commanding Officer, I thanked the second-in-command. It was obvious that civil/military relations here were excellent and the residents' only regret was that the Gurkhas would not be staying longer.

Sergeant Keates picked me up from the Gurkha Mess in his Gazelle and we were soon in Fitzroy, landing in Ron Binnie's garden. Ron and Linda were the same as ever, unaffected by the war and completely unflappable. Their daughter Michele told me how the telephone had rung one day and she heard an English voice at the other end asking if there were any Argentines there. She yelled 'Dad, it's the British!' and Ron had confirmed that the Argentines had left. 'Fine', said the voice, 'We'll be with you shortly.' The voice belonged to Colour Sergeant Morris of 2 Para, whose commander at Brook's suggestion had sent him with a scouting party to Swan Inlet, an outside shepherd's shanty about halfway between Goose Green and Fitzroy, which Brook knew had a land-line connection with Fitzroy. Bert Ford now took up the story. He had spent most of the war driving food and people between Stanley, Bluff Cove, Fitzroy and Goose Green. Monsignor Spraggon had helped him to get permission to travel, but one day he had advised him to go out to Fitzroy and stay there. The best moment of his life, he said, was when he answered a knock on the door one morning and found seven Paras standing outside. 'Any Argies around?' they asked. 'No', he said. 'Good', was the reply, 'We'll bring our lads in.' Within a few hours, Bert said that he was astounded to see more 'fellers' gathered in one place than he had ever seen in his life before.

Although Bert did not tell me, I discovered later that he had used his Land Rover to help our troops to move forward from Fitzroy towards Stanley and had virtually driven it into the ground. When the subject of claiming compensation came up, I urged him to submit a claim for his Land Rover, but he demurred. 'After what them fellers did for me,' he said, 'I'm not submitting a claim.'

As we took off from Fitzroy, we circled over the scene of the *Sir Galahad* tragedy. The *Sir Tristram* was still there, stricken where she lay but still afloat, her superstructure a tangled mass of twisted iron and burnt metal. Yellow life-jackets drifted up and down the shoreline and a lifeboat lay beached in the bay. Ron told me that the smell of burnt flesh had pervaded the settlement for days. We flew over Fitzroy bridge and landed at Bluff Cove, which was surrounded by dug-outs, fox-holes and trenches. The 105mm battery was still deployed there. Tim and Jean Dobbyns were in good heart. Like Bert Ford, Tim had driven his Land Rover in support of our troops, until they had hit a minefield. The Land Rover in front of him, driven by Mike McKay, had been badly damaged, but fortunately no one was hurt. After this incident, the civilians were kept to the rear. Kevin Kilmartin had acquired a wife since my last visit. Diana had come out to Stanley originally as a nurse, and this had stood her in good stead when the Scots Guards struggled ashore, frozen and exhausted after seven hours in landing craft in a 70 knot gale. Unlike Tim, Kevin was dejected and depressed. His farm had taken a pasting as 2 Para, the Scots Guards and then the Welsh Guards had passed through; now the gunners. He had my sympathy. He had not opted out of the rat-race in England for this and it was understandable that he had taken it harder than the kelpers themselves. Indeed, I was to find generally that it was the recent immigrant who had difficulty adjusting to the new way of life, not the fourth- or fifth-generation kelper.

Sergeant Keates dropped me back at the triangle next to Government House at 4.30pm. Thanks to the helicopter, I had been able to visit three settlements in daylight and still had time for paperwork in the office both morning and evening. Before dinner, I called on Iain and Hulda Stewart to get up-to-date with Cable and Wireless. They were staying with Mollie Morrison because their house, which was west of the Battle Memorial, had been damaged and subsequently occupied by our troops. They were the first to alert me to the bitterness that was felt by some of those who had stayed in Stanley against those who had gone – particularly those who had left the Islands altogether. This was to be my next priority: to try to heal the wounds within the community.

Thank goodness there were no quislings or collaborators. One Argentine family with dual nationality had gone to Argentina in the first week or two of the occupation and the only true kelper who had thrown in his lot with the Argentines, Alec Betts, had left later. His motives were personal, not political. He had deserted his second wife, Rosita (a Chilean), leaving their children and those of his first marriage for her to look after without any financial assistance, and had gone off with the Giloberts' nanny. He spoke good Spanish and had been employed by LADE in its Stanley office. He was one of two kelpers whom the Argentines were thereafter to parade on the UN stage every year in New York to speak 'on behalf of' Falkland Islanders. The other was a youngster called Rozee who had fled from the Islands before the war to escape a charge of carnal knowledge of a girl under sixteen.

I was anxious to bring back to Stanley all the expatriates who had left. We needed every pair of hands we could get and those familiar with the Islands were likely to be more useful than those that were not. I sought to lessen feelings of resentment against them by rewarding those who had stayed. I was already compiling material for citations, but the honours system was never one to assuage feelings of resentment; indeed, it often had the opposite effect, for far more people deserved medals than ever got them. With councillors' approval, I announced that all FIG staff who had remained at their posts in Stanley during the occupation would receive a month's holiday or an extra month's salary in lieu (as we were so short-staffed, most of those eligible had to take the latter). It seemed fair at the time but, with hindsight, it was a mistake. It took no account, for example, of those who had remained at their posts but done nothing, compared with others, such as the water, telephone and electricity workers who had toiled night and day, often in dangerous circumstances, to keep the essential services running. And there was the reasonable argument that staff who could not carry on with their work in Stanley, such as FIGAS and teachers, were acting in everyone's best interests in getting out of the town when they could. My announcement also embarrassed the other main employers in Stanley, FIC and Cable and Wireless. Sadly, it did nothing to heal the rifts in our small community; we had to leave it to time to do that.

On 2 July, Sandy Woodward brought in his successor, Rear Admiral Derek Reffell, to meet me and I gave Sandy a farewell lunch, with Jeremy Moore and Michael Clapp. I believe that this was the last time that the Task Force, Land Force and Amphibious Warfare commanders sat down together in the Falklands. After lunch, John Brodrick came in to arrange priorities for the technical personnel needed from Britain and no sooner had he gone than in came the eight Poles who had jumped ship before the war. With commendable initiative, they had found a Polish speaker in the British army, Sergeant Kot, who had taken them under his wing and now proved most helpful in ascertaining their intentions and explaining the difficulties in getting them to their desired destinations. Not surprisingly after what they had been through, they did not wish to stay in the Falklands. They were, however, usefully employed until we could authorise them to travel.[4]

Next morning Captain Middleton of HMS *Hermes* called to say goodbye, bringing with him a magnificent iced cake as a present to the children of Stanley. With HMS *Hermes'* departure, Derek Reffell flew his flag from HMS *Bristol*, although the other carrier, HMS *Invincible*, was to remain on station until relieved by HMS *Illustrious*.

My next engagement turned out to be one of the most harrowing experiences of my life. Steve Whitley had previously explained that Sue had expressed a wish to be buried on Sea Lion Island. He hated the thought of her remaining on the bleak hillside that constituted Stanley cemetery and had arranged for the Welsh Guards to help him to transport her to Sea Lion. On a miserable, rainy morning with low clouds scudding overhead, a small group gathered at the graveside: Steve, Mike and Alison Bleaney, nurse Karen Timberlake, Dr Bob Handley, Father Monaghan and myself. The grave had been ripped open by a military JCB, which was now perched on the top corner of the cemetery, looking down on us like a brooding vulture. A major supervised seven guardsmen as they eased the coffin out of the ground and carried it to a waiting Sea King. We climbed aboard and sat facing each other, knees up against the coffin, which lay between us. It was muddy and the JCB had damaged one corner. Mercifully, the noise of the helicopter prevented conversation. We sat with heads bowed until we landed at Sea Lion.

Terence Clifton met us outside his house and led the way into the kitchen, where Doreen had hot coffee waiting. Terence and Doreen were then the sole occupants of the island, on which they ran 1500 sheep, 15 cattle and 4 horses. It was a hard, isolated life but neither of them would have changed it. They had two young daughters, who received irregular visits from a camp teacher and otherwise depended upon lessons on the radio and from Doreen. Visiting house-guests were Margaret Minell, who had worked for a time as one of our maids in Government House, and Gary Hewitt from Stanley. Terry and Gary had started digging Sue's grave at nine that morning, but had made slow progress in the heavy soil. Steve went with Terry to the spot and decided that it was still too shallow. With the help of the guardsmen, they dug it deeper. It was slow work, because only one person could dig at a time.

Meanwhile, Doreen prepared lunch for us all in true kelper fashion: roast mutton, potato, swede, cabbage, carrots, cake and coffee. In the afternoon, Steve and Terry declared themselves satisfied with the depth of the grave, the guardsmen loaded the coffin onto Terry's Land Rover and we walked behind, an odd-looking cortège in anoraks and wellingtons. Terry had chosen a lovely spot for Sue's last resting-place and had built a small fence round it to keep out the sheep (and, in season, the elephant seals). Father Monaghan conducted a simple service beside the grave and afterwards we all helped to fill it in. The Sea King collected us and I was back in my office by 4pm.

Harry Milne brought David Britton along to see me at 6pm. David had managed to get down for a long stay to assess the damage to FIC property, prepare a claim for compensation and generally help to rehabilitate the company. Julian came in at the same time to announce that he was the proud father of a baby son. David was a highly competitive snooker player so, to celebrate, Julian and I took on the combined might of the FIC – and lost. During the evening I mentioned that I was unable to pick up BBC Overseas on my little transistor radio (my large shortwave had disappeared with the Argentines) and next morning Harry called in and kindly presented me with a spare until a fresh consignment arrived. Evensong that night was well attended by the military (who had improved the choir out of all recognition) but the resident congregation had dropped markedly. Life was reverting to normal only too rapidly for Harry Bagnall. He had hoped that kelpers would have perceived God's hand in the war, seen the light and changed their ways. He had preached to large congregations during the occupation and was disillusioned now that they had dropped away. I tried to explain the inevitability of this: people would always turn to God in their hour of need and ignore him in normal times. But Harry took it to heart.

As things settled down, the social life hotted up. Journalists started to pour in and I had to add them to Julian's many other duties. One of the first to return was Simon Winchester, who had languished in an Argentine prison in Ushuaia for most of the war. He presented me with a bottle of champagne, one of a pair that he had salvaged from Moody Brook on the day of the invasion. They had remained in his baggage in Buenos Aires throughout the war; he had opened one to celebrate his release from prison and now he wanted me to have the other to celebrate his return to the Falklands. It was a kind thought and I accepted with gratitude. I was only sorry to read his article later in the *Sunday Times*, which started the canard that Islanders were ungrateful and sullen. The three people quoted by him were well known for their individual and untypical views (one of them was not even an Islander) and to attribute their attitude to Islanders in general was totally false. I could only assume that he had deliberately struck a discordant note to hit the headlines and make up for his wasted time in prison.

There were incessant parties for departing units and ships and for their replacements. My first shipborne dinner was on a Type 21 frigate, HMS *Avenger*, with Captain Hugo White. He had had a lively war, bombarding Argentine positions, landing special forces and narrowly missing bombs from a pair of Skyhawks. His gunners claimed the distinction of having shot down an Exocet missile with their 4.5in gun. If true, it was a remarkable piece of shooting. Unfortunately, it could not be confirmed because the same Exocet was also claimed by HMS *Exeter*, who had fired a Sea Dart at it. As neither ship had seen the Exocet, another possible explanation was that it had been decoyed by the *Avenger*'s chaff rockets. I did not go aboard HMS *Exeter* but Captain Balfour was able to bring most of his crew ashore for a special service in Christ Church Cathedral in memory of the men who had been killed on her predecessor during the Battle of the River Plate, 1939. The German pocket-battleship, the *Admiral Graf Spee*, had inflicted heavy damage, scoring over a hundred hits, killing sixty officers and men and wounding twenty. The stricken ship had limped into Port William and the whole ship's complement of over 600 men had been accommodated ashore in private homes in Stanley. Some of the badly wounded had died in the hospital and were buried in the town's cemetery. There was thus a special bond between HMS *Exeter* and the townsfolk, many of whom could remember looking after the crew. After the service, we repaired to the Rose Hotel, where the redoubtable Velma Malcolm opened her private rooms and laid on drinks and a buffet, as her mother had done for the other *Exeter* crew forty-three years ago.

The Welsh Guards entertained me proudly at Stanley House, which they had taken over as the battalion mess. The battalion band gave an excellent concert in conjunction with the primary schoolchildren and brought a new dimension to entertainment in Stanley. Their Commander, Lieutenant-Colonel Johnny Rickett, bore his battalion's misfortunes with great fortitude and morale was high, despite another alarming catastrophe, when eight guardsmen were seriously injured by Sidewinder missiles accidentally fired from a Harrier about to take off. The men had been helping to clean up the airfield and, by one of those cruel strokes of ill-luck, happened to be in line with the Harrier when the Sidewinders were launched.

Headquarters BFFI were established in the ill-fated school hostel, which began to grow rapidly, with Portakabins and signals huts sprouting all round the grim concrete structure. 5 Brigade gave a farewell dinner to Jeremy Moore in the main hall, which John Brodrick had condemned before the war. I glanced somewhat apprehensively at the ceiling when the Royal Marines band from ss *Uganda* was playing, and even more so when the Gurkha pipes marched round the dining tables; but the roof did not come tumbling down.[5]

The most remarkable farewell party on land was that of the 1st/7th Gurkhas at Goose Green. The Commanding Officer, David Morgan, invited Jeremy and me to Beating Retreat on their last Saturday evening. We flew together in a Gazelle from Stanley and arrived in a snowstorm. After tea in the mess, we donned our warmest clothes and went out to watch the Beating Retreat in driving snow. It was blowing horizontally from the South. David had thoughtfully provided seats and braziers (Coalite by courtesy of the FIC) and we sat with our backs to the wind, feet and hands as close to the braziers as we dared. Opposite us, across an area the size of a football field, was a mock-up of a North-West Frontier fort. A searchlight picked out a solitary bugler on the battlements and, as his bugle call ended, the main gates of the fort swung open and into the glare of a dozen searchlights – and the driving snow – marched the Gurkha pipes and drums. They marched and countermarched for twenty minutes, hands bare and snow gathering on their eyelashes. It was a spine-tingling performance. I remembered the last time I had watched a Gurkha band beating retreat, in Razmak on the North-West Frontier in 1947. Then, I had been dressed in tropical kit, an iced John Collins in my hand. Now, as soon as the ceremony was over, we repaired to the transit shed, where we were thawed out by fiery curry and hot toddy. The Gurkhas then entertained us to their traditional dancing, some of them acting most convincingly as flirtatious girls. After a while, we were invited to join in and I had to keep telling myself that the attractive girl who was attempting to seduce me on the dance floor was in reality a professional soldier – and one of the toughest in the world at that. Goose Green had seen nothing like it; as one of the Islanders remarked to me, 'Beats the Circassion Circle, don't it Guv?'

The Gurkhas had been ready to go through the Scots Guards after Tumbledown and take Mount William; but the white flags had appeared and they had been saved the trouble. They naturally regretted not getting into action but, as David Morgan said, 'If you can win a battle by reputation, it's better than fighting.' They certainly left a high reputation behind them in the Falklands, not only as fighters but also as kind and courteous guests.

The most memorable farewell party at sea was that given by Captain Jeremy Black on HMS *Invincible*. He anchored his carrier in Port William as near as her draught would allow to the spot on which Admiral Sturdee had anchored his flagship of the same name on 7 December, 1914. Jeremy had kindly invited all the councillors on board for the night. We followed the same menu as Admiral Sturdee on the night before his famous action. Anticipating having to make an after-dinner speech, I had done my homework on the battle, but Jeremy spoke first and gave a much more interesting and amusing account of it than I had prepared. The only addition I could make was that the then-Governor, Sir William Allardyce, had jumped for joy when he saw the tripod masts of the Royal Navy's latest battle cruisers sticking up over Yorke Bay and I could vouch for the accuracy of this because the woman who had been standing beside him at the time had mentioned it to me only the day before. She was Liz Perry, who had been Allardyce's cook, and was still alive and well in Stanley. I added that she was short of gin and oranges and that I could get her the former but not the latter. I left HMS *Invincible* loaded with oranges.

The worst moment in all the speeches I have made came towards the end of this particular one, when I realised that the ship's name had slipped my mind. It was one of those silly mental blocks that sometimes occurs when introducing a close friend or relative. Concealing (I hoped) my rising panic, I glanced round the wardroom as I spoke, searching for a clue. All the menus had been removed, there was no lifebuoy bearing the ship's name – nothing. I thought of *Indomitable, Indefatigable, Illustrious, Intrepid, Inflexible* – even *Endurance*. I knew they were not right. Thankfully, as I was about to duck the issue and propose the toast to 'this glorious ship and all who sail in her', the name came. Afterwards, I was privileged to meet many of the pilots and crews who had played such an important part in the war, including Prince Andrew. They were naturally proud of their ship and would never have forgiven me had I forgotten her name. Prince Andrew had been ashore in Stanley but had not called at Government House because he was there as a serving naval officer and not as visiting royalty. Subsequently, Claud Molkenbuhr, who had the Murrell farm near Stanley, told me how he had met a bearded officer walking alongside the Murrell River and invited him in for coffee. He asked him where he came from in England. Prince Andrew (for it was he) replied that his parents had a house in London, and one or two in the country, to which Claud's comment was, 'They must be bloody wealthy!'

Liz Perry was one of the first of the senior citizens on whom I called after my return to the Islands. Her daughter Kathy and son Tom had tried to persuade her to move out of her house and into the hospital, but she had refused until the Argentines had burst into her house for the fourth time. They had poked her with guns and pulled out drawers, scattering the contents all over the floor. She said they suspected that she was harbouring British special forces in her home, and it was this that finally persuaded her that she would be better off in hospital. She had moved in expecting to remain until, as she put it, they took her out feet first. However, on Daniel's return from internment in Fox Bay East, she had had a flaming row with him and walked out. After his rudeness, she said, she wouldn't be seen dead in the hospital! I took her the oranges from HMS *Invincible* and she was most grateful.

Before leaving the carrier, I had been shown a captured Bell Huey helicopter which one of the pilots had flown aboard from Stanley. The groundcrew had repainted it in bright red with FIGAS emblazoned on its side. About a dozen Hueys had been left by the Argentines, several of them in good flying condition, and we hoped to reconstitute FIGAS by using them to replace our wrecked Beavers and Islander. (I had flown in Hueys in South Vietnam and knew what a reliable workhorse they were.) They could carry more passengers and freight than the Islander and, though more expensive to operate, would give years of service for the cost of new fixed-wing aircraft. We were fortunate in having helicopter pilots in the Royal Navy and the Army Air Corps who were not only qualified on type but also held instructor's ratings. Eddie Anderson started to receive lessons and Bristows agreed to let us have a Falkland Islander, Ian McLeod, who was a qualified engineer on Hueys. He was due for leave from West Africa and coming over to see his family in any event, but Bristows generously allowed him to extend his stay. Sadly, his inspection of the 'Red Herring' revealed evidence of a heavy landing at some time in its short life, necessitating an alignment check of the main rotor-head and pedestal, which could only be done in the UK. Bristows offered to do this free of charge if we could get it to Redhill. Arrangements were well advanced (indeed, a Chinook had put it aboard a merchant vessel about to sail) when we received information from the Civil Aviation Authority that, even if Bristows passed it, they would not authorise a civil airworthiness certificate. The type was not registered for civilian use in the UK (though it was in the USA) and exhaustive and expensive trials would be required, without any guarantee that a certificate to allow it to carry fare-paying passengers would be issued at the end of the day. It was a disappointing end to an imaginative idea.[6]

We now concentrated on replacements for our fixed-wing aircraft. The tide had turned in favour of landplanes, but some of the smaller settlements did not have airstrips and could not easily construct them, so we ordered two Islanders and one Beaver floatplane.Beavers were becoming increasingly difficult to find, but eventually we located a suitable one in Canada. This had to be dismantled, shipped across the Atlantic to the UK and re-shipped down to the Falklands. It was a lengthy process but, even so, it arrived in Stanley before the Islanders, which had to be built from scratch. We had hoped to save time (and money) by ferrying them out – with extra fuel tanks, they could easily have flown to Stanley from Montevideo, or down through Chile and across from Punta Arenas – but the FCO could not agree to such a course of action.

Thanks to the unofficial efforts of the RAF, with its Chinooks and Sea Kings, the Royal Navy with its Lynx, Wessex and Sea Kings and the Army Air Corps with its 'teeny-weenies', Islanders did not suffer at first from the lack of a FIGAS. Indeed, in the immediate aftermath of the war, there was so much helicopter activity that people in camp (or, at least, in some of the luckier settlements) were more mobile than they had ever been. As things settled down and peacetime regulations began to be applied, rides in military helicopters became more difficult, although it was comforting to know that they were always available for emergencies and civilian mail continued to be carried to and from settlements that happened to be along the military routes. The Beaver did not enter service with FIGAS until the end of January, 1983, with the Islanders following at the end of March. A most useful supplement to FIGAS came a little later with the introduction of Sikorski S-61s, operated by Bristow helicopters under contract to the military. It was agreed that civilians could take up any spare seats not required by the military for the same price as FIGAS fares and this proved to be a very popular mode of travel. Bristow crews were mainly ex-servicemen and were every bit as friendly and helpful to Islanders as their serving colleagues.

In the early days after the conflict, the 'teeny-weenies' were a great boon to me. There was so much work in Stanley that I could not afford to spend lengthy periods travelling between settlements, yet it was most important for me to show an interest in the farms on which the Islands' economy depended and in the isolated outposts of the servicemen who were defending them. With my own aircraft a write-off and FIGAS out of action, I was utterly dependent upon the military. Jeremy Moore and subsequently his successor, David Thorne, could not have been more helpful. If they were visiting military units, they invited me to join them and we combined the visit with a call on a neighbouring settlement. If I wished to go anywhere else, there was usually a Scout or a Gazelle at my disposal. The pilot would collect me from the triangle and deposit me in the garden of 'the big house' at a settlement. In that way, I was able to visit three or four in a day and still clear the in-tray in my office.

I have already described my first trip, to Darwin/Goose Green. Next on my priority list was San Carlos. Sergeants Sutherland and Beverley flew me there in a Gazelle. The ravages of war were hidden under a blanket of fresh snow. The sky was clear and the sun shone. It was difficult to imagine the battle that had waged in that peaceful bay only a few weeks before. Pat and Isabel Short were in good heart, despite sharing their house with thirty-five men of the Royal Navy (and Eddie Anderson, who was learning to fly the Huey). A Sea King squadron was based there and every building was bursting at the seams. Pat showed me the peat-stack in which John (my future son-in-law) and a colleague had slept for the first week or so after the landings. There was ample evidence of the settlement's use as the Task Force's main bridgehead but, even allowing for the benevolent effect of the snow, there was nothing like the mess that the Argentines had left in Stanley.

We flew across San Carlos Water to Ajax Bay, where I paid homage to those killed in the war now buried in a temporary cemetery on the bleak hillside, to the south of the old freezer plant. These included Colonel 'H' and his colleagues from Darwin/Goose Green, the Scots Guards from Tumbledown, the Welsh Guards from Fitzroy, 3 Para from Mount Longdon and Royal Marines and others, including a Chinese cook. It was a desolate spot, totally unsuitable as a permanent resting place for our glorious dead. After this visit, I advocated the creation of a war cemetery at Blue Beach, San Carlos.[7]

The Scots Guards were living in appalling conditions in the abandoned freezer plant. One talented member had brightened up the abattoir with murals and composed a poem called 'Tumbledown' which he had painted in classic script on the wall. It was a harrowing place: no lovely white owl this time, only two jagged holes in the roof where bombs had penetrated (and, mercifully, failed to explode). I was glad to leave and fly across San Carlos Water to Port San Carlos, where Alan Miller was waiting to greet me. Everything there had changed; even Alan looked years older. He said he had been 'roughed up' by my old friend Dowling. He showed me the beam on the side of the woolshed where he had hit the back of his head after Dowling had struck him on the forehead with a rifle butt. 'I saw two lots of stars', said Alan.

We walked round the settlement, which was a hive of activity, the base of No. 18 RAF Squadron. There were Chinooks on every available piece of level ground; indeed, some tilted alarmingly on not-so-level ground. Tents had mushroomed between the houses. Packing cases, drums and containers lay alongside the muddy track running down to the jetty. Mechanics perched high on the pedestal of one Chinook, changing a rotor blade in bitingly cold wind. Servicing these monsters in the open air in the Falklands in midwinter was no picnic, yet the morale of the groundcrew could not have been better. We drove up to the Harrier strip above the settlement, which was also used as a refuelling spot by helicopters. Enormous rubber pillows lay on the diddle-dee and pipes snaked down to the water's edge, whence they ran unseen to a marker buoy in water deep enough to take ocean-going tankers. Alan showed me where a Harrier had ploughed in at the end of the metal strip after a partial engine failure on 8 June. Fortunately, the pilot had escaped unhurt. The crews of two Gazelles shot down on the first day of the landings, 21 May, had not been so lucky. Alan said that an Argentine patrol had moved into the woolshed the night before from the direction of Fanning Head. They were in a nasty mood and he was glad to see the back of them as they departed the next morning heading up-river towards Douglas Station. He had been horrified when two of our helicopters, a Sea King and a Gazelle, had appeared over the hills on the opposite side of the river, flying lazily in their direction. The Sea King escaped, but the Gazelle was hit by small-arms fire. It crashed in the sea not too far from the jetty and, as Alan and one or two of his men ran down to a boat to go to the rescue, they were fired at from across the bay. They watched helplessly as one of the crew helped the other towards the shore under fire from the retreating Argentines. They made it, but one of them died later and the other was badly wounded. As Alan and his men were helping this crew out of the water, another Gazelle flew over in the direction of the enemy; it, too, was shot down, crashing on a hillside at the other side of the bay. Both occupants were killed. After that, Alan mustered all the tractors and trailers and Land Rovers on the farm and helped 3 Para to off-load supplies before beginning their 'tab' across East Falkland to Stanley.

Thanks to my 'teeny-weeny', I was back in Stanley within half-an-hour, just in time to resolve an argument between Harry Milne and the naval harbourmaster over the *AES* and the military use of the FIC jetty. The old New Zealand ferry, the *Rangatira*, arrived that weekend with hundreds of Royal Engineers and RAF personnel to work on the runway extension. She became a familiar feature in Stanley harbour, acting as a dormitory for almost a thousand troops until more permanent accommodation was provided by coastels.[8] Nicknamed '*Rangatraz*' by her temporary residents, she acquired over the months a distinctive odour, which one learnt to avoid by crossing the harbour upwind of her. As a local wag put it, 'She must be the only ship that farts.' Nevertheless, she was regarded with affection by the townsfolk, particularly the children, for whom the crew organised some magnificent parties. They must have had an Aladdin's Cave somewhere on board, for they produced a seemingly never-ending supply of streamers, funny hats, crackers and toys. The chefs excelled themselves with iced cakes, sticky buns and ice cream. Stanley children had never seen anything like it. One of them summed up their feelings: 'It's like birthday and Christmas rolled into one!'

My next visit was to Port Howard. The day dawned with thick fog rolling in from the north-east and I assumed that all flying was cancelled; but I had under-estimated the 'teeny-weenies'. The only concession made to the weather (which would have kept FIGAS grounded) was to hug the coastline at about fifty feet all the way, instead of flying the more direct route overland. Robin Lee was surprised to see us loom out of the fog and touch down in his garden. As ever, he and Susan made us most welcome. The settlement had not been badly treated by the Argentines, though several of their houses had been taken over and left in a filthy condition. The Argentines had been jubilant when they shot down Jeff Glover's Harrier. The Islanders had naturally been dismayed, but were relieved to see Jeff rescued from the water, injured but alive. They were not allowed to visit him, but Sharon Middleton had managed to persuade one of his captors to take him some cakes and sweets. He was flown to Stanley the next day and subsequently taken to the mainland. (After the war, he was to return to Port Howard and thank Sharon personally for her kindness.)

Robin said that he had no knowledge of another prisoner, who had been kept under the floorboards in the 'big house', which the Argentines used as their headquarters. They allowed Robin to make use of the telephone installed there and he had been curious about a pile of knapsacks which had suddenly appeared in the middle of the room, on which two or three Argentines lounged as he entered. After the surrender, he was astonished to see a huge black man emerge from the house with the others. He turned out to be one of our Fijian SAS sergeants. He and three colleagues had been observing Port Howard from a distance when they were surprised by an Argentine patrol. The leader, Captain John Hamilton, deliberately drew the enemy fire onto himself to enable his men to get away. He was killed in the process, but two escaped and his Fijian sergeant was captured. Robin took me to the little cemetery, on a hillside a short walk from the farm, where they had buried Hamilton. (His widow, like Lieutenant Taylor's, decided to leave him there and not to have him transferred to Blue Beach Cemetery.)

I had hoped to continue to Pebble Island, but even my indomitable pilot, Captain Bourne, had to admit defeat after hover-taxying for about half-an-hour, creeping even closer to the shore and lower to the sea. The fog had thickened behind us, so there was no getting back to Stanley. We spent a pleasant night with Robin and Susan and their other guests, the Scots Guards, who were much better off than their colleagues in Ajax Bay. I had an interesting talk with their padre, who had met General Menendez on the prison ship. It was obvious, he said, that there was no love lost between him and General Joffre, whom the other officers treated with more respect, despite the fact that as Commander of 10 Brigade (which was deployed round Stanley) he came under the overall command of Menendez as Military Governor.

Next morning, the fog was still thick but, thanks to Captain Bourne's skilful flying, we managed to creep back to Stanley along the coast. I was particularly anxious to get back because I was giving a farewell party for Jeremy Moore that evening. I also wanted to make sure that the thirty civilians whom we had selected as the first to go on leave got away on the ship due to sail the following day. Steve Whitley and Cheryl Bonner were given top priority and flew off the same day. Later that morning, Jeremy brought in his successor, David Thorne, to meet me. He was bubbling with energy and enthusiasm and provided the tonic I needed after the depressing hour I had just spent with our Stanley dairyman, Malcolm Ashworth. Poor Malcolm had suffered more than most from the occupation. Of his dairy herd of sixty-five, only eleven survived. His livelihood had gone and could not be resuscitated overnight. Indeed, it was difficult to see how he could ever get started again, with his herd decimated and a large part of his pasture mined by the Argentines. He was seriously considering packing up and going back to his native Yorkshire; but the Islands could ill afford to lose a man of his calibre, and I urged him to stay. I could see no light at the end of the tunnel, all I could countenance was patience and faith in the future but, to his everlasting credit (and that of his resilient wife, Glynis) he stuck it out and triumphed in the end.[9] I heard from others that he and Glynis had continued to deliver what little milk they had to the hospital and the elderly throughout the conflict, regardless of the dangers. His bravery was duly recognised with the award of the British Empire Medal.

Rear-Admiral Derek Reffell invited me on board his flagship HMS *Bristol*, for a farewell dinner for Jeremy and to welcome David Thorne, and on Sunday, 18 July, after a joint Press conference in the morning, we gave Jeremy a rousing send-off from Stanley airport. Lots of Stanley folk turned up to see him off and wish him well. It was an emotional moment, and normally stoical Islanders were visibly moved.

The next day, Nick Barker brought HMS *Endurance* into Port Stanley for the first time since her hurried departure on 21 March to evict (we hoped) the Argentine scrap-metal merchants from South Georgia. The return was somewhat of an anti-climax: instead of the triumphant entry that she deserved, with flags flying and a gun salute from Victory Green, she had to creep in, almost unobserved, between twenty-two other ships anchored in Ports William and Stanley. Her normal berth was occupied by the *Rangatira* and she was allocated space further down the harbour. The rules for an operational zone were still in force and runs ashore were severely curtailed. The crew was naturally disappointed and there was little that Islanders could do to show their gratitude and appreciation. I tried to express some of their feelings to the ship's company on their closed-circuit television, but they had to wait until they returned to Chatham for a reception worthy of them.

Nick kindly invited me aboard for two nights and we sailed to Fox Bay, via Fitzroy. We went ashore at each of the settlements and the ship entertained the kelpers to lunch on board. The gunners had moved from Bluff Cove to Fitzroy, where Ron Binnie was happy to have them, and the Queen's Own Highlanders had a detachment at Fox Bay West. The army had established a helicopter refuelling base on the airfield at Fox Bay East. Richard Cockwell showed us how close the Harrier strike on the *Bahia Buen Suceso* had been to his house. There was a neat line of bomb craters, running from the jetty across the paddock in front of his garden towards the other houses. A degree or two to the north and his house would have been demolished. The strike was an outstanding success, immobilising the *Bahia Buen Suceso* for the rest of the conflict and causing little damage to the settlement.

Fox Bay West had not been so fortunate. Nigel Knight said that the Argentines had taken over the bunk-house, galley, hay barn, cow shed, garage, community hall and several houses. He and Shirley had accommodated between a dozen and three dozen civilians in the 'big house' for two-and-a-half months. His 4.5m radio transmitter and all 2m sets had been confiscated, aerials demolished and civilian houses searched from top to bottom. All cameras, films, binoculars and maps had been removed, a 5pm to 8am curfew imposed, a black-out enforced and lights out at 10pm (earlier towards the end). Many sheep and hens had been killed, stores and vegetables stolen and wooden fences, sheds and sheep pens torn down for firewood or to build defensive positions. Worst of all, six minefields had been laid in and around the settlement.

Not knowing the fate of his ship's boat, the *James Caird*, Nick had brought up from Leith a captured Argentine lifeboat, which the scrap-metal merchants had abandoned. The engine was faulty, but his resouceful engineers had 'razzed' another in South Georgia and got the boat to work. With typical humour, they had christened it the *James Turd*. On recovering the *James Caird* in one piece, Nick presented the *James Turd* to me, for use by the FIG as a harbour-boat. Don was delighted to have bo'sun added to his many other duties. As I was piped ashore, after an emotional farewell, I could not help reflecting that it was thanks to Galtieri that we would be seeing the *Endurance* back again next season.

On 28 July, we held our first Legislative Council since before the conflict. David Thorne was sworn in and warmly welcomed by councillors. As I inspected the guard of honour outside the Town Hall, splendidly mounted by men of the Queen's Own Highlanders and our own Falkland Islands Defence Force, I thought of General Garcia's bombastic words, 'We have taken back what is rightfully ours, and we shall stay FOREVER.' That was less than four months ago. In thanking the Task Force in my opening address I shamelessly paraphrased Churchill: 'Never in the field of human conflict was so much owed by so few to so many' and each councillor in turn expressed his thanks and offered his condolences to the bereaved.

David and I quickly struck up a happy working and personal relationship. He set his sights on finishing the Stanley runway before the summer and getting all his troops properly housed

335

before the following winter. Based on past experience, many of us were sceptical:laying 6,100ft of aluminium matting, hard-stands and taxiways in the worst months of the Falklands winter could not be done, while constructing Portakabins and the like on inaccessible radar sites and at camps round the Islands would take years, not months. David confounded us all. The first Phantom landed at Stanley airport on 17 October, 1982 and most of the tents had gone by the onset of the austral winter.

Notes

1. They had not done so at the time of writing (1989).

2. These guns and accompanying radar were eventually salvaged by an enterprising RAF officer and formed the basis of a Royal Auxiliary Air Force Regiment squadron, of which I now have the honour to be Honorary Air Commodore.

3. Now replaced by a more permanent structure.

4. The difficulties over immigration, travel documents, etc were speedily resolved and they were all accepted by the country of their choice.

5. Indeed, during the war, the Argentines had put sandbags and anti-aircraft guns on the roof.

6. All was not in vain. The 'Red Herring's' rotor-head (which was found to be perfectly sound) now drives Sqd Ldr Rob Tierney's Huey at displays in the UK in aid of the Royal Air Force Benevolent fund and the airframe was traded for two other Argentine aircraft which now belong to Stanley Museum.

7. See page 347.

8. Built originally for the off-shore oil industry, coastels were basically large barges with hundreds of containers welded on top of them. They were self-sufficient, floating hotels.

9. It took even longer than we had both feared. He had to seed and fence new pasture before he could import his favoured Ayrshires, and build a new dairy. He did not restart milk production until 1987 but, when Mavis and I visited him in 1989, both farm and business were flourishing.

17

A Remarkable Year

For the first few months after the occupation, Stanley was indescribably filthy: how anyone could have made such a mess of a town in seventy-four days was beyond comprehension. The British troops worked tirelessly to clear up the detritus of war, while Malcolm Binnie and his handful of PWD workers tried manfully to clean up the streets. Malcolm had the typical kelper's versatility in tackling everything from laying paving stones to flushing out blocked drains. Throughout the occupation, he and his small gang had virtually kept the town going, emptying dustbins, cleaning drains and doing any odd job that was required. Now, they faced an insurmountable task. Councillor Terry Peck, who had distinguished himself during the occupation as a scout and guide to 3 Para, and was now helping me to organise the few odd-job men in Stanley to carry out repairs to private houses, tried to galvanise the public into a 'Clean up Stanley' campaign; but the result was disappointing. The troops joined in with enthusiasm, but the sad fact was that most civilians were more than fully engaged in rehabilitating themselves and their families. Few had time to spare for community work.

The swollen population in Stanley added to the mess left behind by the Argentines. Every building was filled to overflowing: Dick Baker had twenty-four sailors with him in Sulivan House; Waverley House had sixty-five soldiers, which was more than it had accommodated in its heyday as a brothel, before the opening of the Panama Canal. The amount of waste generated by the military came as a shock to the townsfolk. Like other islanders, the kelper was by nature a hoarder; nothing that might come in useful was ever thrown away. The average soldier, on the other hand, had been brought up in a waste-making society and was accustomed to discarding things that he had no immediate use for. For example, in the absence of trees, wood was a valuable, imported commodity, to be kept for fencing or making chicken runs and peat sheds, not burnt as firewood (Ian Strange had built his whole house with driftwood picked up from the beaches). The Gurkhas

337

pitched into tidying up Stanley with typical energy and efficiency, piling everything onto huge bonfires. They were understandably surprised when I had to ask them to desist until the townsfolk had taken what they wanted.

Before the war, the town's rubbish was collected once a week and dumped in a tip not far from Malcolm Ashworth's dairy. One small refuse lorry was more than adequate for the purpose. Within a few weeks of liberation, Malcolm took me to see the tip and I found it not only full but brimming over towards his house. I had no alternative but to order its closure and re-open an old pit towards Moody Brook, on the other side of town. Even that soon proved inadequate to cope with a dozen or so military lorries a day; but the only other possible site was behind a minefield, so we had to make do. We were still searching for an alternative site when I left in 1985. By then, the tip had become popularly known as the Stanley Supermarket, where all sorts of bargains, from crates of oranges to diesel generators, could be had for the taking.

One unfortunate consequence was severe damage to the roads leading to the tip. Most of the military activity was to the east of Stanley and the tip was to the west, so virtually all traffic had to go through the town. To exacerbate the problem, the REME servicing workshop was established at the old Royal Marine barracks at Moody Brook and this resulted in a steady stream of military vehicles, from captured Mercedes jeeps to mobile cranes and heavy lift trucks, trundling through Stanley on roads which had never been designed to take such traffic. The airport road took an even greater pounding from the tipper trucks plying to and from the quarry and the heavy loads brought ashore at 'B' slip. I drove Fifi along the airport road for the last time on 7 August; thereafter, it was a brave man who risked a saloon car over those ruts and potholes. Visiting journalists and Members of Parliament were subsequently to criticise us for the terrible state of our roads; but the task was beyond the limited resources of PWD, and the Royal Engineers had greater priorities, so nothing could be done until the ODA was persuaded to engage private contractors from the UK. A bureaucratic wrangle between ODA and MOD on apportionment of blame produced the inevitable result of 'too little, too late' and, sadly, the Stanley roads remained in a deplorable state until long after my departure in 1985.

The other long-term legacy of the war was the mines. They were of the plastic type and could not be located by normal metal detectors. Many of them had been sown haphazardly and without proper records, contrary to the Geneva Convention. Others on beaches had been washed from their original positions. The MOD decided as early as August, 1982, that no attempt would be made to raise the mines until a safe method of location could be devised. Even so, two brave officers lost limbs in attempting to delineate the minefield boundaries. Islanders fully supported the MOD decision and declared themselves willing to live with the mines rather than risk further loss of life or limb to British soldiers. The first priority was to identify the limits of the minefields and wire them off. The most extensive were round Stanley itself, but smaller fields had been sown at Goose Green, Fox Bay and Port Howard. The saddest task was to shoot the cattle and horses that had been maimed but were still alive and suffering inside the minefields. The sheep were not such a problem: their smaller hooves usually missed the mines and the odd one or two that had been unlucky enough to detonate them had been killed outright. The only safe way of shooting the animals was from a helicopter. The army veterinary officer, Brian Thompson, undertook this gruesome task, assisted by a couple of marksmen from the Queen's Own Highlanders. Brian told me that his worst moment was having to shoot a skinny calf which was trying to suck from its dead and bloated mother.

The worst affected farm was Claud Molkenbuhr's, on the Murrell River. I called there shortly after Claud had accompanied Brian on his mercy killing flight. He had only twelve cattle left out of seventy-one, ten horses out of sixteen, two pigs out of eleven and thirteen hens out of a hundred. The Argentines had smashed his house (leaving their usual calling cards in drawers, washbasins and bath), taken down two-and-a-half miles of fencing to use as firewood and props for their foxholes and slaughtered his animals for food. But Claud was not downhearted: he was about to get his tractor back from Long Island, his rotovator from Stanley and some timber from PWD to repair the house and fences. He still had 2,000 sheep (out of 3,054) and he and his wife Judy would soon have the place shipshape again. I sipped coffee in the shambles that had been their home and marvelled at his spirit.

The Chief Resident Engineer, Colonel Derek Brownson, took me to see the minefield at Rookery Bay. The Argentines had evidently expected our troops to land on this coastline and had prepared strong defences. The mines had been laid methodically in concert with the barbed wire and gun positions to give the most effective fields of fire. An attempted landing there would undoubtedly have resulted in heavy casualties. Derek pointed out some sinister circles in the sand, about the size of a wheel-hub. They were anti-tank mines. He then directed my gaze to a smaller circle nearby, about the size of a shoe-polish tin. I would have missed it without his help. That, he explained, was an anti-personnel mine; it was probably wired to go off if anyone attempted to lift the anti-tank mine. John (my future son-in-law) told me later that mines were uppermost in his mind as he waited to guide Julian Thompson's brigade into Stanley on the night of the surrender. 'I didn't mind the prospect of being shot at', he said, 'But I hated the thought of stepping on a mine.' Thank goodness the white flags appeared before the final assault.

My main anxiety with the mines was over the children. Adults would heed the skull-and-cross bones notices, but would children be deterred, particularly if they could no longer play on their favourite beach or go 'egging' in the penguin colony? I need not have worried. The bomb disposal men of the Royal Engineers (or Explosive Ordnance Disposal, to give them their proper name) did a magnificent job in the schools and on the local radio. They encouraged children to look out for and report suspicious-looking objects, rewarding them with a special bomb-disposal badge, and inculcated in them the discipline of not touching. Apart from the mines, there lay scattered around Stanley and its environs thousands of potentially dangerous explosives, which took years to clear up. It is to the everlasting credit of the officers and men of the EOD that not a single child was killed or injured during this process. It reflects well, too, on the children themselves. I heard of only one instance of foolhardiness, when two teenagers dared each other to ride through a minefield on motorcycles. Mercifully, they got away with it. Some airmen, who should have known better, were injured when they tampered with a detonator and one unlucky civilian sustained burns when he was sharpening his shears and a spark ignited some gunpowder, which had been carelessly spilt in the shearing shed by the Argentines.

Over the next three years, strenuous efforts were made to find a safe and sure way of locating the plastic mines. All the known methods were tried, but none could ensure a one-hundred-per-cent clearance. Sniffer dogs were considered but, in the event, were not sent out from the UK. A more scientific approach, using radar and computers, seemed promising; but the MOD eventually ruled out further trials on grounds of cost. I was left with the uneasy suspicion that, had there been a military need to lift the mines (which MOD maintained there was not), these trials would have continued. I spoke to one of the scientists involved, who was optimistic that they were on the right lines and that, given time, they would come up with a practical solution. By feeding into the computer the known ingredients of the soil, it could identify from the radar pattern any unknown objects, including plastic mines. The theory had proved workable; the problem was one of miniaturisation; that is, how to reduce the huge generator, computer and radar equipment to manageable proportions in the field. The scientist said that we were ahead of the rest of the world in this type of research and he was confident that, with plastic pipes replacing metal ones underground for all sorts of purposes, there would be a commercial as well as a military market for the final product. Like many other British inventions, however, he feared that some other country would step in and reap the commercial benefits.

The 1st Battalion, the Queen's Own Highlanders, was an excellent choice for the first infantry unit to be posted to the Falklands after the war. The troops settled down well and quickly became at home in the sheep-farming environment. Indeed, some of them were so attracted by the Islands that they resolved to return as immigrants at the end of their army service. Like a number of ex-Royal Marines who had already settled in Stanley, they were the best type of immigrant; people who had experienced life in the Islands before deciding to make them their permanent home. They knew what they were going to, unlike a few carpet-baggers who turned up after the war hoping to make a quick killing. One well-publicised figure arrived with a fish-and-chip van and was surprised to learn that he could buy neither fish nor potatoes. By contrast, a Yorkshireman called Dave Hawkesworth did his home-work properly, made a preliminary visit to the Islands, identified a suitable store, returned to England to arrange supplies, buy appropriate equipment and collect his wife and soon established a thriving business selling (among other things) fish and chips. He and his wife were welcomed by the Islanders because they were prepared to work and to fit in with the community. They both joined the FIDF and did so well in their business that, within a few years, they were able to buy Sedge Island, off West Falkland.

In the afterglow of victory, many people in Britain showed interest in emigrating to the Falklands, though the chronic housing shortage and transport difficulties put off all but the most

341

determined. The unofficial Falkland Islands Office in London was inundated with requests and accumulated over 600 names of prospective immigrants. It was clear that an official government office was needed, not only to process immigration applications but also to represent the Falkland Islands Government officially in London and to counteract some of the more lurid and inaccurate stories that were beginning to appear in the popular press. Adrian Monk was the obvious choice for the post and councillors voted unanimously that he should be their first representative in London. Despite the high costs involved, they decided to fund the office entirely from FIG revenues and not to seek British Government aid. Adrian had a difficult time finding suitable premises at a price that the FIG could afford, but eventually he managed to establish the Falkland Islands Government Office in London (FIGO), staffed entirely by Falkland Islanders, and it soon proved invaluable.[1]

My life became easier with the arrival of our FCO girls. Ruth Goodwin and Maggie Neville were the first to grace our bachelor and still somewhat primitive establishment, to be followed in mid-August by my personal secretary, Elspeth Disney. It was interesting to see how the number of military visitors to Government House shot up after their arrival (the ratio of men to eligible women in Stanley at that time must have been over a hundred to one). The girls never complained about being bored. To their credit, they also never let play interfere with work, turning out cheerfully at all hours, weekends included, when needed. They were a tonic to us all. Ruth and Maggie built up quite a fan club by running a weekly record request programme on the local radio which, thanks to the British Forces Broadcasting Service (BFBS), had been much expanded since before the war. Transmitting hours were gradually increased until eventually we achieved almost a round-the-clock service. The resources of FIBS were, of course, totally inadequate to sustain more than a fraction of this amount of output and we were happy to let BFBS have the lion's share of broadcasting hours (the military were, after all, the larger audience); but I insisted upon keeping the traditional hours for FIBS. Most of the personable young men that BFBS sent out – mainly from their stations in Germany and Cyprus – were sensitive to the situation and worked well with Patrick Watts and his team. One or two, however, tried to dominate the local staff and to treat FIBS as if it were just another BFBS station. When they could not get their own way on peak broadcasting times, there was a move to have two separate stations, transmitting simultaneously to the troops and the civilians. I strongly opposed this: local radio had become an integral part of Islander life; it was a unifying influence throughout the Islands; everyone listened to the same programme; troops spending a mere four months down there got the flavour of Islander life from FIBS and conversely the BFBS content of FIBS gave Islanders an insight into military life. If there had been two stations broadcasting at the same time, most of the troops would have automatically tuned in to BFBS and it would probably have had a disuniting effect on Islanders themselves, the youngsters listening to BFBS and the older folk to FIBS.

The occasional skirmish between FIBS and BFBS typified the sensitive relationship that existed in all the shared services. The military were present in such strength and had such greater resources that it was difficult for the civilians to avoid being swamped altogether. This was particularly true in the hospital, the Post Office, aviation and harbourmaster's departments. At the highest level, David Thorne and most of his staff were always conscious of Islander feelings and responded sympathetically when I had to point out that some civilian's toes had been trodden upon; but there were those who tended to behave as if they were occupying forces in a conquered territory and not British troops in a British colony. With most of the armed forces rotating every four months, no sooner had we got the message across than we had to start the process all over again. Never the most assertive of people, Islanders in senior FIG posts wilted when introduced to yet another dominating personality as their opposite number. Whenever I told them to stand up for their rights, I received the stock answer, 'But we can't argue with them – they liberated us!'

It must be said that in Whitehall and Westminster, too, there were those who behaved as if the Falkland Islands Government did not exist. A whole generation of politicians and civil servants had reached positions of responsibility with no experience of the colonial system. Considering the small population of the Falklands, it was perhaps understandable that they tended to regard the FIG (if they thought about it at all) as a local parish council, and I had constantly to remind them that they were dealing with a government which enjoyed a large measure of autonomy conferred upon it by Act of Parliament. If the Islanders were too reticent (and grateful) to stand up for themselves, someone had to. As I discovered when unexpectedly summoned to London to talks in September, this only served to increase my reputation as 'a difficult cuss'.

My recall to London happily coincided with Diana's wedding. I had previously written to Mavis to say that I could not possibly leave the Falklands at that busy time; but the FCO showed unaccustomed humanity and kindness in arranging the talks to suit. The main purpose was to give evidence to the Franks Committee, which was a committee of Privy Counsellors from all political parties under the chairmanship of Lord Franks, appointed by the British Government to review the way in which the Government had discharged its responsibilities in relation to the Falkland Islands and their Dependencies in the period leading up to the Argentine invasion. They questioned me, politely but penetratingly, for one-and-a-half hours. In reply, I had no difficulty in following Sir Harold Nicolson's first principles of truth and accuracy. The committee was both thorough and fair and, after taking oral and written evidence from over 150 persons, concluded that it would not be justified in attaching any criticism or blame to the British Government for the Argentine Junta's decision to commit its act of unprovoked aggression.[2]

During my short stay in London, I was invited to speak to the Royal Commonwealth Society, whose Chairman at the time, Sir Eric Norris, had been my High Commissioner in Kuala Lumpur. The FCO asked to see my speech, which was of course about the Falklands dispute, and I duly submitted it the day before. I was amused that it was authorised – as the British version. I walked across to Northumberland Avenue asking myself: what was expected from a British diplomat – the Argentine version?

Diana's wedding was a glorious occasion. The sun shone, the bride was radiant and the groom resplendent in his Royal Marine uniform. Keith Mills and other officers formed a guard of honour as the couple emerged from the church. One of them was Nick Barker, who had arrived home about a month before, *Endurance* having steamed 41,466 miles and spent 311 days away from base – longer than any other naval ship in the Task Force.

I attended another memorable ceremony before returning to Stanley. Mrs Rosemary Ritchie, a great-granddaughter of Lord Stanley (later 14th Earl of Derby), the Secretary of State for the Colonies and War in 1833 and after whom the town was named, wished to present to the Falkland Islanders a battle ensign which had been presented to her father, Captain Victor Stanley, by the ship's company of his battleship, HMS *Erin*, in 1917. I was taken to her flat in Onslow Square where, together with her first cousin, Major Harry Stanley, and two close friends, we toasted the Islanders in champagne out of glasses from HMS *Erin*. These were unique because the *Erin* had been built for the Turkish navy and commandeered by the Royal Navy when Turkey threw in its lot with Germany in 1914, and all the glasses bore the name of the ship in Turkish script. The battle ensign was the largest I had ever seen but, being pure silk, packed neatly into its original handsome wooden case, which I duly transported to Stanley.[3]

The return flight took ten-and-a-half hours to Ascension and twelve-and-a-half to Stanley. The first in-flight refuelling was by Hercules, the second by Victor. Apparently, this halved the fuel costs from my first flight, which used Victor tankers only. The aluminium matting made a loud rumbling sound as we landed in Stanley. My first task was to distribute pieces of Diana's and John's wedding cake to their many friends in Stanley. My next was to arrange a programme for Mr Cranley Onslow, who was following me down in two days' time.

Mr Onslow was the first government minister to visit the Islands since the war, and he was warmly welcomed. He spent a hectic five days with us, during which he had a session with Joint Councils, addressed a public meeting and travelled extensively. Thanks to helicopter mobility, we even managed to drop off at the Malo river for a spot of trout fishing, at which he demonstrated his skill by landing a three-pounder within the hour (as I was later to discover, he was also no slouch at snooker). Councillors pressed hard for a 200-mile fisheries zone, but were met with what was to become the stock answer: the cost of policing such a zone would far outweigh the income from licence fees, and there was no point in declaring a zone that could not be enforced.

Air Marshal Sir John Curtiss was visiting at the same time and we held some useful joint sessions with the military. Both our distinguished guests were reassured to find that civil/military relations were excellent, despite the overcrowding in Stanley, and they were most impressed with the rate of progress on the airfield. Sadly, I could not show Mr Onslow the same progress on the civilian side: PWD had its hands more than full in attempting to maintain the creaking fabric of the town, let alone make any improvements. Building houses was beyond its capacity. Mr Onslow was quickly convinced that the only way to increase accommodation in Stanley was to import prefabricated houses and he acted energetically upon his return to the UK. I had shown him some of the damaged houses, which the military were occupying, and mentioned the figure of twenty-seven requiring replacement or major repairs. He sent me a telegram to say that, as costs decreased with numbers, he had decided to double my figure: we should shortly receive fifty-four top-quality wooden houses, fully furnished down to sheets and blankets, freezers and washing machines. In the absence of a suitable British design, he chose an excellent Swedish model, supplied through its British agents, Brewster. As the Swedish name – Mynesjohn – was unpronounceable, they became known as the Brewster houses. Subsequently criticised by Press and politicians as too expensive and extravagant, they nevertheless brought a new standard of insulation and comfort to Stanley and have since proved very popular. Their triple-glazed windows (British made, incidentally) may not have been needed in the Falklands' climate, but such were the peculiar economies of scale that to have replaced them with double-glazing for the fifty-four ordered for Stanley would actually have cost more.

Owing to a combination of Murphy's Law and the Falklands' factor, the building programme fell disappointingly behind schedule. PWD also lacked the machinery to lay down the proper infrastructure. Slowly, however, a new road began to take shape alongside the racecourse (to be named, appropriately enough, Sir Jeremy Moore Avenue), followed by a brand-new estate on Callaghan Road. The hostel block built to accommodate Brewster's workmen was to prove invaluable as a temporary hospital after the tragic fire at the King Edward Memorial Hospital and continued to serve in that capacity until the new hospital was completed in 1987.[4]

One of the media men accompanying Mr Onslow was the BBC's Harold Briley. To show their appreciation of his support during the occupation, some Islanders met us at the entrance to Government House waving a placard, 'God Bless You, Harold'. He decided to stay on for a few days after Mr Onslow had left and was recording a couple of pieces with me for the BBC when I realised that I was late for the start of the half-marathon. In a rash moment, I had said that I would enter for this if David Thorne did. Unknown to me, he had said the same thing and our respective staffs so arranged it that we were each told that the other had entered first. Well down the field, I teamed up with a young kelper called Simon Goodwin, aged 10½ years. We made a firm pact that he, the youngest, and I, the oldest in the race would run in together but, as the winning post came into sight, he left me standing. The others were waiting patiently for me to award the prizes. Simon took his with a great big smile and thanked me for pacing him. Incidentally, we raised a considerable sum for the South Atlantic Fund.

That evening, Stewart Campbell of the Commonwealth War Graves Commission called on me and confirmed that the site for our war cemetery would be Blue Beach, San Carlos. He had discussed it with Pat Short, who was more than willing to have it on his land, and was confident that it would be properly cared for. Upon his return to England, Stewart said that he would arrange for two expert masons to come out to build the wall (with the help of the Royal Engineers) while we would organise the stone from Fox Bay, which he had seen and agreed would be suitable for the purpose. The headstones would be cut and engraved in England.

After evensong, my last task of the day was the pleasurable one of going to the FIBS studio and announcing the Falklands honours. Civilians in the Islands received three OBEs, eight MBEs and thirteen BEMs – not as many as I had submitted, but a fair proportion. On the military side, I was pleased to see that NP 8901 had been recognised by a Mention-in-Despatches to Mike Norman, but disappointed that it was not a higher honour, or that no other member of NP8901 had been decorated. In my view, their bravery on the night of the invasion before I ordered them to lay down their arms deserved more recognition than a Mention-in-Despatches to their commanding officer.

I was amazed at the mailbag in subsequent weeks. People from all walks of life, old friends and complete strangers, wrote to congratulate me on my knighthood. Letters came in from old and new Commonwealth countries, Europe, the USA, South America and several of the Eastern bloc countries. I had not realised what a worldwide impact the Falklands war had made. I was invited (with Don) to join the Vintage Taxi Club and to ride in a Beardmore taxi if ever I was in California. Offers came in for the red taxi and innumerable requests for photographs and war mementoes. Perhaps the strangest was from a Roman Catholic priest in the USA, who asked for a pair of British soldier's boots and a pair of Argentine soldier's boots. He said that he collected old boots and prayed for their previous occupants. With David's help, I was able to oblige and received a grateful acknowledgement from the eccentric priest saying how delighted he was to receive both pairs.

On 17 October, David's Chief of Staff, Roger Wheeler, took

me to the airport to welcome the first Phantom. The latest arrester gear from the USA had been firmly anchored by sinking a couple of containers filled with concrete into the ground on each side of the runway. The aircraft was brought to a halt within 800ft. The deceleration from 170 knots to zero put considerable strain on the human body, as I was later to discover,[5] but Wing Commander McFadyean showed no ill effects as he jumped down from the cockpit, looking remarkably fresh and cheerful after his long flight from Ascension. With Phantoms on station, the Sea Harrier force was no longer required. The Islanders wanted to show their gratitude by holding a formal farewell party, for they realised more than most the vital role that this aircraft and its pilots had played in their liberation, and the pilots themselves were keen to reciprocate by giving a farewell fly-past round the settlements: but MOD ordered that, for security reasons, no publicity was to surround their departure. HMS *Illustrious*, which had taken over from HMS *Invincible*, departed without ceremony on Trafalgar Day, thus ending another distinguished chapter in the history of the Royal Navy's air arm and leaving the air defence of the Islands entirely dependent upon the single runway at Stanley airport. The aluminium matting had a guaranteed life of only two years and HMG accepted that a more permanent solution had to be found if the Islands' security was to be ensured. The choice was between the construction of a brand-new airport on a virgin site or the upgrading of Stanley airport. After several feasibility studies and on-site inspections, tenders were invited from British companies giving them the choice of either Stanley or Mount Pleasant. Despite the need to construct a new port and a five-mile access road, Mount Pleasant emerged as the quicker and cheaper alternative, mainly because Stanley airport had to remain operational throughout the construction. In an incredibly short space of time, specifications and tender documents were prepared and the contract awarded, with the objective of having the main runway operational before the aluminium matting needed replacing. The contractors overcame all obstacles and succeeded in beating the deadline; but I am once again anticipating events.

Apart from my daily dealing with the military, the biggest change that the war had made in my working life was the number of visitors. Despite the long, uncomfortable ride in the Hercules, there was a never-ending stream of politicians, military officers, civil servants and journalists. In the two years prior to the war, we had seen only one government minister and two backbenchers. In the two years after the war, we were to receive visits from no less than eight ministers of the Crown and some forty or more Members of Parliament, while visitors from the media were too numerous to mention and most of the senior officers of the three armed services came down at least once.

In addition to extra visitors, I had to chair extra committees. There was a general desire amongst Islanders to commemorate Liberation Day in some permanent fashion. The obvious way was to erect a monument, although there was a body of opinion that favoured something more functional, such as a gymnasium or community hall. I held out for a monument not only because I considered it a more fitting way to honour the dead, but also because it would serve as a permanent reminder of Argentine aggression and the sacrifice that Britain had made to restore the Islanders' freedom. We formed a Monument Committee and aimed at unveiling the monument on 14 June, 1983. A Falkland Islands' architect, Gerald Dixon, offered his services without charge and we chose a prime site in front of the Secretariat. Islanders wanted the monument to be a tribute from them to the Task Force and would not hear of a fund-raising appeal in Britain. They raised all the money themselves, though they received generous help in kind from suppliers and shippers. Tarmac, for example, supplied the main granite stones from their Merrivale quarry on Dartmoor free of charge and replaced three of the huge blocks when a fire in the ship's hold damaged the originals. It was this fire that delayed the completion of the monument and the unveiling eventually took place two years after the liberation, on 14 June, 1984. Even then, it was not complete. I soon began to receive complaints about missing units, incorrect initials and ranks, and names mis-spelt. And this was after the MOD had had an extra year to check and re-check every detail, having prepared the list for us in the first place. An engraver volunteered to come out to make corrections and additions. Erecting a makeshift shelter from the biting wind, he worked long hours in the Falklands mid-winter until all was completed.

Even more urgent than the monument was the 150th anniversary of continuous British settlement of the Falkland Islands. I re-established the planning committee that we had set up before the war. Time was running out if we were to hold the celebrations on 3 January, 1983. It was on that day 150 years ago that Captain Onslow had sailed into Berkeley Sound in HMS *Clio* and re-taken the Falkland Islands in the name of King George III.

The focal point of the celebrations was the racecourse, which had been severely damaged by the Argentines, who had dug fox-holes and ammunition dumps along it, and also by our own artillery, which had bombarded the Argentine positions. Most of the fencing had been pulled down and almost all the buildings damaged. To add to our problems, Stanley Common could not be used for grazing and exercising the horses as the Argentines had scattered mines and other unexploded ordnance over it. At one stage, it looked as if we would have to postpone the celebrations for a whole year but, thanks to generous help from the UK and the herculean efforts of a few enthusiasts, both civilian and military, we were able to hold them in the last week of February, 1983. The help from the UK was largely inspired by Sir Harry Llewellyn, who publicised our needs in his regular column in the *Sporting Life* and generated a tremendous response. The Racecourse Association, United Racecourses Limited and The Jockey Club donated all manner of equipment, from the latest plastic fencing to jockey's scales. The tote house, which had been totally demolished, was replaced by Chester Racecourse, and a Mrs R. Turnell donated a colourful assortment of racing silks, which were cleaned free of charge by Sketchley Cleaners. Never had our jockeys looked so smart. Some of them had reservations about the state of the course, but the most experienced, Ron Binnie and Eric Goss, decided that, though the going was rough, it was possible to race. Despite heavy rain during the meeting, all the races were run without casualty. There were three falls – 'Tootie' Morrison, Tim Bonner (Don's son) and myself (in the veterans' foot-race) – but no injury to man or mount. Somehow all the horses brought in from camp were accommodated in paddocks round the town and we were able to confound the Jeremiahs who said that it could not be done until the following summer.

Another active committee at the time was the Falkland Islands Appeal Committee. I established this shortly after my return to advise the UK trustees on the most deserving cases for financial assistance. We quickly dealt with the obvious cases of individual hardship (like Cheryl Bonner) and a few others that could not wait for the official compensation scheme; but others were more marginal and required time-consuming investigation. We worked closely with the MOD claims officers, who were assigned the task of receiving, assessing and negotiating claims under the British Government scheme announced in Parliament by the Prime Minister, who told the House of Commons that she had instructed that claims made under the scheme would be met generously and promptly. Claims officers were authorised to settle and pay compensation in the great majority of cases without reference to London. The trouble was that many Islanders had no idea what they should claim for or, if they had, they did not know the cost of repair or replacement. Also, most of the claims officers were used to dealing with grasping German farmers, not honest Falkland Islanders. Some were excellent and carried out the Prime Minister's instructions, but others were overly suspicious and tried to bully the claimant. This was where Bill Richards was invaluable. Since his arrival on one of the early Hercules, he had spent up to sixteen hours a day on the beat, calling on most of the families in Stanley. Known and trusted by the townsfolk, he acted as honest broker between claimant and claims officer, and both accepted his view on what was reasonable. He knew the odd few who would be likely to submit false claims, and advised the claims officer accordingly. As a result, there were few appeals and only one or two disgruntled claimants.

We were concerned that most of the money from the appeal fund was going to Stanley residents. With people in camp in mind, we devised the idea of replacing some of the slaughtered livestock with animals shipped out from the UK. The result became known as the *Noah's Ark* project. There was a certain amount of opposition to the idea and perhaps the strongest opponent was John Ferguson, the head of the Grasslands Trials Unit, whose professional advice I respected; but Steve Whitley, who had returned on the Hercules with me, was strongly in favour and, indeed, became the main motivating force in the Islands and deserved most of the credit for its success. Major General Alan Mills laboured assiduously at the London end, finding a suitable ship, negotiating the freight rates and assembling the animals. The project caught the British public's imagination and their response was most generous: donations came from rare breed societies, clubs and individuals and everything imaginable was offered, from a budgerigar to a hamster. The animals most in demand were cattle, sheep, horses and ponies but, as there was room on the ship, goats, pigs, dogs, cats, ducks, chickens – and, yes, budgerigars – were accepted. *Noah's Ark* eventually sailed, with two veterinary surgeons aboard, and so successful were they at looking after their assorted menagerie that *Noah's Ark* had a bigger population when it arrived than when it started. Tim Miller and Peter Goss had asked for some Jacob's sheep and these caused a great stir, not only amongst the Islanders but also amongst the ordinary sheep, who took one look at them and ran. Tim said they thought that these strange looking animals were a new brand of sheepdog. Some of the animals failed to adapt to the Falklands' climate, but most survived and brought welcome new strains into the Islands.

On the same Trafalgar Day as HMS *Illustrious* left Falklands' waters, the Royal Navy sank the *Bahia Buen Suceso*. The submarine *Onyx* delivered the *coup de grace*. Coincidentally, I was sitting at dinner that evening in Britannia House next to the Deputy SNOFI, Mike Sizeland, who had given me my first trip in a submarine, HMS *Andrew*, in Jesselton Bay, North Borneo in 1966. The dinner was, naturally, an all-Navy affair, save for David Thorne and me, and we were given Navy issue woolly-pullies to wear. As we drank to the immortal memory, I felt that Nelson would have been proud of the men around me. Although he never served in the South Atlantic, it was because of the crisis with Spain over the Falkland Islands in 1770 that he had reported to his first ship, the *Raisonnable* (a captured Frenchman) as a midshipman at the tender age of twelve years three months. He subsequently took part in an expedition to the Arctic on HMS *Carcass*, the sloop which had helped to found the settlement at Port Egmont in 1766 and surveyed the island in West Falkland that now bears its name. I thought it appropriate that we should be celebrating Trafalgar Night in the Argentine commander's house, though I doubt whether Hector would have appreciated the mess games that took place later in the evening, or some of the lower-deck ditties that were sung.

The next government minister to visit was Mr John Nott, the Secretary of State for Defence. His programme was largely in David's hands, but he asked to see as many civilians as possible and particularly to meet councillors. As his visit was from Friday to Monday, the only time that we could arrange a Joint Councils' meeting was on the Sunday afternoon; but councillors gladly came in to express their gratitude in person to the Minister responsible for the Armed Forces. The camp councillors could not, of course, have made it without the help of the military and, to make the most of their expensive helicopter trips, we took the opportunity to discuss the Shackleton Report, which had recently been published and circulated in the Islands.[6]

Lord Shackleton and his team had prepared their new report in less than two months – a remarkable achievement. They first summarised the key changes that had taken place since their last report in 1976: wool prices had fallen and local energy costs had risen by twenty per cent in real terms; with the successful outcome of the war, the climate for investment had improved, but external communications could no longer be through Argentina, or perhaps any other country in South America; the FIC had changed hands and, in international maritime law, 200-mile limits had been widely adopted. In the light of these changes, and taking account of other factors that had remained unchanged since 1976, Lord Shackleton's main recommendations were: the creation of a Falkland Islands Development Agency; the purchase of all farms owned by absentee landlords; the expansion of the Grasslands Trials Unit; the introduction of farm grants and subsidies; the establishment of 200-mile fisheries limits; shell-fish and salmon ranching pilot schemes; the development of tourism; a local knitwear industry; a new runway not less than 8,500ft; a civil external air service, a road network throughout the Islands and a deep-water jetty in Port Stanley. Councillors voted to accept the Shackleton Report 'lock, stock and barrel'. HMG went along with most of the recommendations, but not the two most radical – the purchase of farms and the 200-mile fisheries limit. Mr Onslow had already explained to councillors that HMG favoured a gradualist approach to the process of farm ownership and a multinational approach to the South Atlantic fisheries. Subsequent experience showed that HMG was probably right on the first and wrong on the second.

On civil/military relations, Lord Shackleton urged that consideration be given to accompanied tours and maximising the number of women in the garrison; also to the use of the Royal Engineers to assist with infrastructural development, particularly roads. Mr Nott could give no assurances on these points; but he did confirm that there were no longer any plans to withdraw HMS *Endurance*. Like Mr Onslow before him, he asked councillors to consider exempting imported contract labour on the new airport from local taxes. Tender documents were under preparation and contract prices would be higher if local taxes were levied. Councillors explained to Mr Nott that Islanders were grateful, not grasping, people and that they did not want the British Government to spend more on the new airport than was absolutely necessary. They agreed to exempt imported labour from local taxes. In doing so, they doubtless reflected the mood of the majority of Islanders; but the decision was to cause difficulties later. It accentuated the difference betwen the overseas contract worker and the local labourer, whose basic pay varied from an eighth to a sixth of his imported counterpart's.

Also, duty-free alcohol and cigarettes inevitably found their way into private homes, losing much-needed revenue for the FIG.

After the Joint Councils' meeting, we gave a drinks party for over a hundred at Government House, followed by dinner at Stanley House in the mess of the Queen's Own Highlanders, with whose Commanding Officer, Colonel Nicholas Ridley (no relation to our former minister), we enjoyed excellent relations.

The next day, we all flew to San Carlos. Looking around at my fellow-passengers in the Chinook, I thought what a harvest for the grim reaper. All the councillors and senior FIG officers and their wives were present, together with all the senior officers on David's staff (David himself had gone ahead with Mr Nott). We were bound for Blue Beach cemetery to attend a service of committal and remembrance for those who had fallen during the conflict. The wall had not yet been built, but a neat white fence had been erected on the spot where it would be, and the coffins of those whose next-of-kin had chosen for them to remain in the Falklands were to be lowered into their final resting place. For the first time in British military history, I believe, the next-of-kin had been given the choice of having their loved ones shipped home or leaving them with their comrades-in-arms in the country where they had fallen. The majority had chosen to bring them home, but I think that, had they seen the perfect setting at Blue Beach and known the care with which all war graves are tended, they might well have chosen otherwise. As it was, we stood in the little cemetery as fourteen coffins were lowered in unison; sixty-four were on board the RFA *Sir Bedivere*, which stood a little way off in San Carlos water. Father Monaghan blessed and hallowed the cemetery and a moving service was conducted by Harry Bagnall and Padres Dailley and Mortimer. After the Last Post, a two-minute silence and Reveille, we turned to face seaward as the *Sir Bedivere* steamed slowly away from Blue Beach, on the long journey home, accompanied by a fly-past and saluted by the warships in the bay. As the sound of the aircraft disappeared, a piper stood alone on the beach and played a lament, while a naval launch dropped a wreath over her stern in memory of those who had perished at sea. There were few dry eyes in San Carlos at that moment. The wreath floated for a long time, drifting in the wake of the *Sir Bedivere*.

Pat and Isabel Short hosted a huge curry lunch provided by the military. Mr Nott was flying to Ascension that evening, but he managed to spend an hour or so fishing in the afternoon, during which he landed ten sea trout, the largest weighing six-and-a-half pounds. He was a happy man as David and I escorted him to his Hercules.

Not so happy was Ted Needham (the head of Coalite), whom I entertained to dinner that evening. He was still upset at FIG's decision not to accept the hostel and most reluctant to part with Stanley House for good. He naturally opposed Lord Shackleton's recommendation on farm take-overs and I invited him to meet councillors for a general discussion the next morning. Having taken three frames off me at snooker, he departed in a better mood. The Joint Councils' meeting was good-humoured, but neither side gave ground. I went to the airport to see Ted off that night, together with Councillors Tony Blake and John Cheek, who were going to New York to support the British delegation in a UN debate on the Falklands.

A most welcome addition to my hard-pressed team was Michael Gaiger, the Attorney General. It had taken a long time, first to convince the ODA that we needed an Attorney General and then to find one; but it was worth the wait, for Michael quickly settled in and soon proved indispensable. It was difficult to imagine how we had managed without him. Another excellent choice from the FCO was Reg Williams who, like Julian, had volunteered to join me for a full tour. Both he and Michael were married, but there was no housing available for their wives. Jack Abbott (who had departed on the *Canberra*) had generously offered me the use of his house, so Michael and Reg moved in there, later to be joined by our first Development Officer, John Reid. This post was the result of another of Lord Shackleton's recommendations.

Next day, I was at the airport again to meet a party of ten Members of Parliament. I remembered an old ambassador telling me that, the more senior one became in the diplomatic service, the more time one spent at airports. This visit was also to bring back a piece of advice that had been given to me and my fellow 'colonial retreads' when we first joined the service in 1963. Members of Parliament came in four kinds, we were told, and we should learn quickly to recognise which was which. It had nothing to do with political parties. The first kind was the decent and bright; he was a pleasure to deal with and could be extremely helpful. The second was the decent and not-so-bright; he was also no problem and could be quite helpful. The third was the not-so-decent and not-so-bright; he could be a problem but was usually pretty harmless. Then there was the fourth, the downright nasty and very bright; he was decidedly dangerous and needed careful watching. But they all had one thing in common, and that was an inordinate vanity, so it behove us to treat them all as VIPs. In my experience, there had been exceptions, even to this; but it was sound advice to follow. I was fortunate with these ten: there was not one of the fourth kind amongst them and plenty of the first, of whom Mr Roy Mason was perhaps the most outstanding.

We gave a drinks party for the MPs that night, with about sixty guests, and next day they split up into small groups and visited military units and ships, re-assembling for dinner at Government House that evening. Before dinner, the Queen's Own Highlanders treated us to Beating Retreat on, of all places, a roll-on/roll-off ferry. The ship was the *Baltic Ferry*, which normally carried juggernauts between Felixstowe and Rotterdam, so there was plenty of room on her cavernous deck.

On their last morning, we took the MPs on a tour of Stanley, which included the filtration plant, power station, Brewster houses, PWD and the vehicle workshop, followed by a round-up meeting with Joint Councils. My impression was that they left with a better understanding of our difficulties and a more sympathetic attitude towards the Islanders than when they arrived. Indeed, with a few notable exceptions, this seemed to be the general effect on visitors. We suggested to the FCO that an invitation should be issued to the UN Committee of Twenty-Four, whom we knew took the Argentine side in the sovereignty issue, but this was ruled out on the grounds that it would be counter-productive. We were aware that the members of the committee did not have open minds, but we thought that at least if they visited the Islands they would not be able to go back to New York and continue to claim that the Falklands were populated by poor Spanish-speaking natives oppressed by nasty British imperialists. We received glowing reports of John Cheek's and Tony Blake's performance in the UN: as the Islanders' democratically elected representatives, they spoke convincingly and well; but nothing would sway UN members' prejudice against a 'colony', except perhaps by coming to the Islands and seeing with their own eyes.

One of the MPs, Sir Hector Monro, stayed on after the rest of the party to see his son, Hugh, who was in the Queen's Own Highlanders, and to visit more of the settlements. He managed to get to Green Patch, Roy Cove and Chartres in a busy day, in which

356

I was also able to show him the Stanley rugby ground. Sir Hector typified the best kind of MP. Surveying the depressing field of churned-up mud before us, with makeshift posts leaning drunkenly in the wind (the Argentines had demolished our elegant old ones, made from ship's masts), he mentioned that, as President of the Scottish Rugby Football Union, he might be able to help; what did we need? I said everything, from balls to flags, to jerseys, shorts and stockings. He asked what colour the Stanley Rugby Club wore. I thought quickly – we had never been able to turn out fifteen men in the same colours. 'Black and white,' I said (my old school strip). Some weeks later, I was delighted to receive from the Secretary of the English Rugby Football Union a complete set of jerseys, stockings and shorts, flags, whistles and balls, and a useful set of RFU publications. The only snag was that the jerseys were not black and white, but Argentine blue and white. My fears that kelpers would refuse to wear them proved groundless: practical above all else, they donned them with glee.

Like many other things, the advent of so many servicemen led to a great improvement in the quality of our rugby. Before the war, we had been pushed to find two XVs. Unless we had a visiting ship, the pattern during the season would be Stanley v the Royal Marines one week, and the Royal Marines v Stanley the next, both played on the same ground on a Sunday morning. Kick-off depended upon how long the parties had lasted the night before. As referee, I started by going to the ground assiduously at 10.30am, but most of the players did not roll up until 11am or later. Regardless of what time we started, all the players walked off the pitch at 11.55 precisely, whether I blew the final whistle or not. 'Glory hour' in the Globe started at midday – we observed one-hour opening on Sundays – and the players did not wish to miss a minute of drinking time. Now, we had so many teams wanting to play that our only rugby pitch was suffering from over-use. The football ground was even worse but, with so few sporting facilities available, we were reluctant to close them. On one occasion, I was plodding off the field, having refereed the final of a most enjoyable seven-a-side competition, when a Chinook landed just behind the dead-ball line. A bunch of sailors from, I believe, HMS *Liverpool*, lined up facing the Chinook and, on the command of a Chief Petty Officer, proceeded with guard-like precision to take down their trousers, about turn and bare their bums. It was a most effective insult, performed in perfect unison. They had not bargained, however, on the quick reaction of the pilot. Before they could get their trousers back up, the Chinook was airborne and hovering not twenty feet above them, its down-draught bowling bare bums over like ninepins.

The golf course was another facility that we were eager to bring back into use. It had been constructed in 1939 by the Tabaris Territorials. These were British and Anglo-Argentine volunteers who, suspecting German designs on the Falklands, had come over from Buenos Aires on their own initiative at the outbreak of war to help the Islanders to defend themselves. They quickly became bored and, having nothing to do, constructed a new nine-hole golf course (the old one, around Government House, having fallen into disuse). They took the name 'Tabaris' from a not very respectable bar in Buenos Aires which they used to frequent. The course had been used by the Argentines as an ammunition dump and badly damaged by the digging of bunkers (not the golfing kind), foxholes and trenches, and by shell-holes from our own 105mm guns. Unexploded ordnance lay scattered around – we were picking up small-arms ammunition for months afterwards – but the first task was to remove hundreds of feet of barbed and concertina wire. On our first inspection, we lost the eighth hole completely. I had lost balls before, and even a club once, but never a hole. The eighth green had simply disappeared. Three others had been dug up to make bunkers, and two were pock-marked with 105mm craters. Near the edge of the ninth green, half-buried, we found a circular metal object, which looked suspiciously like an anti-tank mine. Approaching it gingerly, we scraped away the soil slowly and were relieved to discover that it was a harmless old wheel-hub from a Land Rover.

Even before the conflict, the course could never have been called first-rate. To define it in the kindest light, it was golf as the Scots had invented it, with no proper tees, fairways or greens. It was grazed by sheep awaiting slaughter in the nearby abattoir. My favourite hole was the seventh, where the green was over a rise and hidden from the tee. It was also sheltered from the wind and a popular spot for the sheep. Driving off the tee, you knew that your ball had hit the green if sheep came running over the brow of the hill towards you. The clubhouse was an old packing crate, a gift from the Royal Marines, which the Argentines had used for firewood. I wrote to *Golf Monthly* explaining our plight and, as with the racecourse, the response was tremendous. Malcolm Campbell, the editor, rounded up all the golf clubs, bags, balls, tees and flags so generously offered from various parts of Britain, and the RAF flew them down. Until we acquired a new clubhouse, Government House became the nineteenth hole and all the equipment (including our own clubs) was made available on loan from there for anyone from the three services or merchant marines who wanted to play. Sadly, the golfing fraternity did not live up to its gentlemanly reputation: bags and clubs began to disappear until we had to stop lending them out. By then, however, the news had spread that there was a golf course in Stanley, and keen golfers brought out their own clubs. The enterprising secretary of the English and International Greenkeepers Association also heard about us and wrote to me asking to be put in touch with 'my head greenkeeper and assistant greenkeepers' so that she could invite them to join her association. I could not resist replying that, as well as President of the Stanley Golf Club, I was also the head greenkeeper and that, for my assistant greenkeepers, I had a flock of sheep; but yes, please, we should like to join.

After too few ships' visits before the war, we now found it difficult to keep pace with the comings and goings. I tried to accept every invitation to go on board, but it was not always possible. In addition to RN and RFA ships, there was an assorted variety of STUFT (ships taken up from trade). One of them was the RMS *St Helena*, which normally plied between Avonmouth, St Helena and Capetown and had been commandeered by the Royal Navy for use as a minesweeper support ship. When we were considering contingency plans before the outbreak of hostilities, I had suggested to the FCO that, in the event of a withdrawal of the air service by Argentina, the *St Helena* might include Stanley in her itinerary, only to be told that the ship was considered unsuitable for South Atlantic waters. It was with some surprise, therefore, that I saw her sail into Port Stanley. Her captain, Mike Smith, laughed when I told him and said that she would have suited us very well. Carrying seventy-five passengers, she had the capacity in her hold to take all the Falklands wool clip to the UK in two trips and, as Capetown was only thirteen days' steaming from Stanley, a practical itinerary could have been worked out – though admittedly at some disadvantage to St Helena.

The largest ships I visited in the Royal Fleet Auxiliary were the *Fort Grange* and the *Fort Austin*. Both were fleet replenishment ships, capable of carrying four Sea Kings and thousands of tons of supplies. The Master of the *Fort Grange*, Captain Barry Rutterford, invited me on board for the first of many visits in August. He became a regular visitor to Government House and a good friend. We appreciated his thoughtfulness in sending us hampers of fruit from Harrods after he had returned home. He knew how scarce fruit was in the Islands. Our staff were amazed at some of the more exotic varieties, which they had never seen before.

The *Fort Austin* had Sea Kings from 814 and 824 Naval Air Squadrons embarked and they flew Mavis and me to join them for Taranto Night. This was a traditional Fleet Air Arm celebration to commemorate their heroic action in 1940, when twenty-one old Swordfishes ('Stringbags') disabled half the Italian fleet at a single stroke. The Master, Captain Dick Thorn, provided us with an excellent suite of cabins and we flew back the next morning after a most entertaining evening and comfortable night.

The largest ship taken up from trade and still in Falklands waters was the *Astronomer*, a roll-on/roll-off container ship of almost 30,000 tons. I landed on her spacious deck by Gazelle and had lunch to compare in quality and surroundings with any five-star hotel. The smallest was not a STUFT, but the captured Argentine vessel, the *Yehuin*, which Eddie Anderson had spotted skulking off west Weddell in 1981. She was renamed *The Black Pig* and used as the 'gash' ship. I accompanied the crew on one of their nightly trips, unromantic but essential (particularly with the pressure on the Stanley rubbish tip). We sailed out of Port William and into deep water to the east of the Islands before dumping the collected rubbish of the day.

The most intriguing ship I visited looked not like a ship at all, but more like an oil platform. She was the *Stena Seaspread*, an offshore support ship of revolutionary design. Built in Sweden for the oil industry and adapted in a matter of days to carry a Fleet Maintenance Group, she and her sister-ship, *Stena Inspector*,[7] proved invaluable as repair ships to the Task Force and subsequently to all the ships that served down south. Captain Mike Williams showed me the wizardry that he had at his fingertips. No dragging anchors for him: with the judicious use of propellers and thrusters from all angles, and the latest computers and navigational system, he could keep his exact position over one spot in virtually any weather. The equipment on board enabled the Royal Navy to carry out major repairs which hitherto had been possible only in a dockyard and, as the nearest naval dockyard was Gibraltar, the advantages were obvious.

Another interesting STUFT was the Russian built *Lycaon*, which carried ammunition for the Task Force. She still had thousands of rounds of 4.5in ammunition, missiles and other ordnance when Ruth, Maggie and I went aboard for lunch in November. Afterwards I invited some of the wardroom members back to Government House. They had been kept well to the east of the Falklands during the war and had had no chance to come ashore. I gave them what had become popularly known as the GH battlefield tour: my operations room and the desk under which we had sheltered; the Argentine bullet-holes in the hall, registry, snooker room, dining room, bedrooms and kitchen; the bullet-holes made by Gary in the staff quarters; the store room from which he had flushed out three prisoners and the places in the garden where the attackers had fallen. They were intrigued with the penetrative power of one bullet, which had ricochetted off the dining-room wall, scored the carpet underneath the dining table, gone up through the thickest part of the solid wooden sideboard, sliced through two tablemats and finished up in the wall.

That evening, David invited us to our first CSE show, in the Town Hall. Combined Services Entertainments were what we knew in the Second World War as ENSA: professional entertainers who volunteered to travel to operational theatres to entertain the troops. We attended all the CSE shows to which we were invited thereafter and, when time allowed, entertained the performers in Government House. They worked extremely hard during their whirlwind tours, giving shows morning, afternoon and evening, and were greatly appreciated not only by the troops but also by those civilians who were lucky enough to be invited to see them. Unfortunately, difficulties over insurance stopped shows in the Town Hall and many troupes came and went without being seen by Stanley citizens (though this did not apply to those in settlements with a military presence). Perhaps the best-known entertainers who came down were Sir Harry Secombe and Jim Davidson. I gave both of them the GH battlefield tour and Sir Harry summed up his reaction with, 'And who says Maggie started the shooting war with the *Belgrano*?'

The saddest ship I visited was the RFA *Sir Tristram*. After being refloated at Fitzroy, she was towed into Port Stanley, where she performed useful service as an extension to the FIC jetty and then as a dormitory ship across at the Camber, the men sleeping in the undamaged tank deck. Most of the superstructure was a tangled mass of burnt metal and the cabins abaft the bridge were uninhabitable. It was noteworthy that all the aluminium had gone and only the steel remained. She was a constant reminder of the Fitzroy tragedy and we were all relieved when she was eventually lifted onto a salvage ship and taken to Britain for reconstruction.[8]

Undoubtedly my happiest visit to a ship was to collect Mavis from the MV *Norland*, a North Sea ferry usually operating between Hull and Rotterdam. For military reasons, the first port of call on arrival in the Falklands was San Carlos Water, to off-load troops there before sailing round to Port William with the civilians. David kindly offered me a 'teeny-weeny' to fly over to San Carlos and thus save a day or two. Sunday, 7 November, dawned with a cloudless sky as Captain Wright landed at the triangle and picked me up. It was a Scout, not a Gazelle, and I hoped that Mavis would not be put off (the Scout being the Navy's Wasp in army clothing). Personally, I preferred the Scout: the bulbous passenger windows afforded better views and gave back-seat passengers more room than the Gazelle. We had a magnificent view of San Carlos Water and arrived over the *Norland* as she was dropping anchor. What a sensible idea it had been to fit all these ships taken up from trade with helicopter pads. We were aboard and in the Captain's cabin within minutes. Mavis was in good form, having been looked after right royally all the way from Ascension by the Master, Bob Lough, and his excellent crew, and having as travelling companion, Monsignor Spraggon, who was returning from a short trip to Ascension. The MV *Norland* was the unsung hero of the war. With 2 Para aboard, she was the first STUFT to go into San Carlos Water and the longest to remain there. Unfortunately, she did not sail home until long after most of the other participants and so, except in her home port, Hull, did not get the rapturous welcome that was accorded better-known ships like the *QE II* and the *Canberra*. Nevertheless, she and her crew will always be remembered with gratitude and affection by Falkland Islanders as their South Sea ferry to and from Ascension.

My most exciting ship's visit was to HMS *Courageous*, a nuclear-powered hunter killer submarine. I went on board by boat from San Carlos and we sailed north on the surface, clearing the Sound before diving. It was a far cry from HMS *Andrew* in 1966. When we submerged then, all the foul smells from the bilges had wafted into the living quarters and mingled with the basic, all-pervading smell of diesel. Now, there was no difference in the pure air we breathed, no matter how deep we went or how long we stayed submerged, because the submarine manufactured its own. The captain,

Commander Rupert Best, let me drive for a while. The controls and instruments were similar to an aircraft's and keeping the submarine on an even plane and at a steady depth was very much like flying by instruments. I was impressed with the speed we travelled underwater and the ease with which we could lose or gain depth. For a vessel weighing about 4,000 tons, it was incredibly manoeuvrable. After lunch in the spacious wardroom, Rupert took me on a tour of the ship and I had to keep reminding myself that I was on a submarine. The only link with tradition was a couple of hammocks slung over the torpedo tubes. It was somehow comforting to see them amid all that modern gadgetry. We broke surface well to the north of the Falklands and I was winched off by a Chinook.

With the departure of Admiral Reffell and the 3rd Flotilla, Captain Hutton became the senior naval officer at sea, on HMS *Newcastle*. Captain David Dobson (another SNOFI with a decidedly long 'o') brought him to Government House to meet me, as he did with all the ships' captains, but I was unable to return his call. I did manage, however, to get on board HMS *Liverpool*, whose captain, Frank Grenier, sent his Lynx helicopter to collect Mavis and me from the triangle. More sophisticated than the Scout or Gazelle, and considerably larger, the Lynx was able to home on the *Liverpool* in spite of dense fog. The ship's superstructure suddenly materialised out of the murk in front of us, and we were on the flightdeck and shutting down before we realised that we had arrived. As the fog cleared, we watched our first replenishment at sea, or RAS (pronounced Razz), with the RFA *Tidespring*. Routine for the crews, we found it exciting; the standard of seamanship required to keep station so close to the tanker seemed to me to be as high as the airmanship required for in-flight refuelling, particularly in rough weather. We went ashore on Lively Island and had lunch with Albert and Yona Davis, who ran the island for the FIC. After lunch, Albert took us to see a simple monument which the Royal Marines had erected in memory of their comrades who had been on a landing craft bound for Bluff Cove from Darwin on the same day that the *Sir Galahad* and *Sir Tristram* were attacked. Six Royal Marines and one naval rating were killed when a Skyhawk scored a direct hit.

Albert said that the Argentines had installed a radar station on the south of the island and killed a few of his sheep, but had not bothered him in the settlement. Yona had kept the radio going and was most grateful to BBC Overseas; it was the only way they knew what was happening in the rest of the Falklands. Isolated as they were, neither wanted to leave Lively Island. If they could buy it from FIC, their two sons, one of whom was driving for PWD and the other worked in a shearing gang, would return to help. They would also refurbish their home and the rest of the settlement, which showed signs of neglect.[9]

Other warships in Falklands' waters in this twilight period after the war (apart from the carriers and their escorts) were HMSs *Glasgow, Brazen, Antrim, Ariadne, Minerva, Charybdis, Phoebe* and *Sirices*, and I cannot praise them too highly for the dedicated way in which they performed their duties. For a long time, until the radar stations on shore became fully operational, they patrolled our western approaches, the eyes and ears of our early warning system. This meant long hours on watch, uncomfortable in anti-flash clothing under battle conditions, often in heavy seas, maintaining the highest state of readiness despite the knowledge that an enemy attack was most unlikely. Without action, or the serious threat of it, the main enemy was boredom, yet on all my visits I found morale from lower deck to captain to be of the highest.

More fortunate than the frigates, destroyers and submarines, which rarely got into port, were the survey vessels HMS *Hydra* and HMS *Hecate*. They worked closer inshore and were able to call at many of the settlements. Their captains, Richard Campbell and Chris Gobey, invited me to travel with them whenever I could and, using helicopters to get me to and from Stanley, I made full use of their kind hospitality. My first trip in *Hydra* had been in early August, from Port Stephens to North Arm where, in Tony and Lyn Blake's comfortable house, I enjoyed the luxury of a bath for the first time since returning to the Islands. The 'People's Republic' greeted me warmly in the community hall that night. Their sixty-odd population had been swollen by the influx of seventy Queen's Own Highlanders, most of them sleeping in the bunkhouse. Despite the overcrowding, relations were excellent.

My next trip was to the far west, in the *Hecate*, in October. Elspeth had been working non-stop since her arrival in August and needed a break, so I was delighted when Chris invited her to come too. We flew in the *Hecate*'s Wasp to each of the Jason Islands, something I had always wanted to do. On Jason West Cay was an old ship-wreck, perched on the central ridge of the little island like a stranded whale, surrounded by gentoo penguins, which were being pestered by scores of Johnny Rooks, skuas and sheathbills.

It must have taken a freak wave to deposit that unfortunate ship so high above the shoreline. Watching us from the seashore was a handsome bull fur seal. On Steeple Jason were thousands of black-browed albatrosses, intermingled with equal numbers of rockhopper penguins. We checked Len Hill's hut and found it intact but in need of minor repair. I could understand why he had bought the islands, and why Cindy and Annie had chosen Steeple Jason to make their film *Penguin Summer*. On Grand Jason were more gentoos and jackass and two odd King penguins. On South Jason was a crashed Argentine Skyhawk. It was halfway up the rock-face, which climbed precipitously from sea-level to over 900ft. Chris later sent in a shore-party and they found the pilot dead in the cockpit, his bomb-load still on board. How unlucky, I thought, to have hit this solitary hunk of rock on his approach to the Islands: the odds must have been thousands to one against. On the other hand, had not fate dealt him such a cruel blow, his bombs might well have caused the loss of more British lives.

From the Jasons we went to Westpoint, where Roddy and Lily Napier came aboard, none the worse for their isolated existence during the occupation. It would have taken more than an Argentine to ruffle Roddy. Chris was excellent in entertaining the kelpers from these remote settlements. Most of them had been deprived of contact with their fellow human beings, save for the radio and perhaps the odd visit from the SAS. They had not been short of food, but they had lacked variety. It was a pleasure to share with them the traditional hospitality and conviviality of one of Her Majesty's ships. From Westpoint we went to Roy Cove, where Chris had a survey party ashore. They were living in a woolshed near the jetty and their boat sat high and dry in a paddock between the jetty and the settlement. Apparently, a Chinook had dropped it there to await the boat party, not realising that they had no means of getting it to the water. In the settlement was a company of the Queen's Own Highlanders, living in the 'big house' and shared round the other houses (one was accommodating twenty-six); but here again relations were excellent, with a healthy attitude of give-and-take and no complaints. I returned to Roy Cove early in December with Mavis, where we embarked on the *Hecate* and sailed for Weddell Island, via Split and the Passage Islands, both magnificent wildlife sactuaries, unspoilt by man. Bob and Thelma Ferguson and all at Weddell had survived the war unscathed and were more determined than ever to stay put, preferably of course running the farm as their own and not as employees of Hamilton Estates. Tony and Vi Felton expressed the same view on Beaver, which Tony said he would be happy to run on his own.

With this trip to the far southwest, I managed in six months to visit all the settlements except New Island. Thanks to David's co-operation, I had also visited all the land units, from signalling stations to Rapier batteries, and most of the ships. Everywhere I found morale to be of the highest and relations between military and civilians warm and mutually beneficial. I had expected a decline in goodwill and growing friction, but found none. The only complaints I had were from farmers about the gates left open and fences knocked down by military vehicles. This was primarily an educational problem. Many soldiers simply did not know how to open or close the peculiar Falkland gates, which were no more than an extension of the fence, secured by a cross-pole between the fence posts and a stake in the ground. Some of the lazier troops tended to take short cuts by going through fences that were miles away from anywhere and seemingly served no useful purpose. Once it was explained to them that letting the rams get at the ewes at the wrong time might be good for the rams but bad for the farmer, the number of incidents decreased. But this had to be done every four months. In December, the Queen's Own Highlanders were replaced by the Hampshires. They were another country battalion who also settled down well in the Falklands environment, but few had seen a Falkland gate.

Before the Queen's Own Highlanders left, we held a simple ceremony behind Government House. The Editor of the Scottish *Sunday Post* had sent us 253 plants of white heather, one for each of the men who had died in the fighting to recover the Islands. He had arranged a similar ceremony in Princes Street Gardens, Edinburgh, to take place at the same moment on Sunday, 28 November, with the aim of dedicating identical memorial gardens in Scotland and the Falklands. He had hoped that we could plant the heather at San Carlos, but Gene advised that the white heather was difficult to grow in the Falklands and that he would need to nurse the plants for at least the first two seasons, until they were established. We therefore dedicated a temporary bed behind Government House and Gene transferred the plants into the cold frames for the next two winters.

With the coming of summer, our regular visitors began to return. Malcolm Phelps brought in the *John Biscoe* on his way to the Antarctic and Captain Aye returned with the *World Discoverer*. He held a celebratory luncheon on board and scribbled on my menu, 'HAPPY, HAPPY to be back in our Antarctic home port, Port Stanley'. Our old friend Captain Skelnik turned up with the Polish factory ship *Zulawy*, and was disappointed to find that he could no longer anchor in Port William. Instead, we offered him Berkeley Sound which, though further from Stanley, was in many ways a more suitable anchorage for the transhipment of fish and supplies. It was too far, however, to visit in the little tug *Lively*, and we were fortunate in having one of the Royal Navy's salvage tugs, the *Yorkshireman*, available in Port Stanley. Her skipper was happy to oblige and we travelled to the *Zulawy* in style. Captain Skelnik was delighted to see us back. The *Yorkshireman* was one of a trio of salvage tugs requisitioned from United Towing, Hull, which performed outstandingly well both during and after the conflict. The largest of the three, the *Salvageman*, was assigned to Nick Barker's task unit to retake Southern Thule. She was the only merchant vessel to go that far south. She had been the first to reach the Falklands operational area and was the last to leave, not returning to the UK until mid-1984. Both the *Salvageman* and the *Yorkshireman* helped with the salvage of the Argentine submarine *Sante Fe* in Grytviken. The third member of this celebrated trio was the *Irishman*. Though one of the smallest vessels sent south (686 tons), she had attempted the salvage of one of the largest, the *Atlantic Conveyor*. She managed to get the burning and listing hulk under tow but, at night and in fog, the line parted and the stricken container ship went down. After the war, masters of ships parking in Ports William and Stanley were able to sleep sounder in their bunks knowing that one of these tugs was on hand should a Falklands' wind blow up and cause them to drag their anchors.

The port of Hull had served the task Force proudly. In addition to these three tugs and the *Norland*, five Hull trawlers were requisitioned and commissioned as minesweepers: *Cordella, Farnella, Junella, Northella* and *Pict*. They were all used in Cumberland Bay, South Georgia, to transfer troops and supplies from the *QEII* to the *Canberra* and the *Norland* and Jimmy James, who was the Royal Navy Officer on the *QEII* at the time, told me that he had difficulty in recognising which was which from his elevated position on the bridge. On one occasion, he called down 'Which one are you?' and received the reply 'Cordella. Which one are you?'. Jimmy was the first SNOFI after Michael Clapp and, by a happy coincidence, he was also a cousin of Harold Bennett, our retired Senior Magistrate.

8 December saw the traditional Battle Day ceremony at the monument. It was a brilliant day and the Royal Navy and FIDF turned out in force. In the absence of the Falklands guard ship, HMS *Endurance*, David Dobson (SNOFI) joined me in taking the salute. There were bigger crowds than usual, and not just because of the excellent weather. Islanders took the opportunity to show their gratitude to the Royal Navy not only for saving them in the Battle of the Falklands, 1914, but also for winning the Battle for the Falklands, 1982. In future, there would be two great days to celebrate: 8 December, Battle Day and 14 June, Liberation Day. That evening, the FIDF held a successful dance in the Town Hall.

A few days before Christmas, Tony, our son, arrived on the *Cunard Countess*. This ship had taken over from the *Norland* on the shuttle service from Ascension. As every pair of hands was needed to prepare Stanley for the 150th anniversary, Tony was soon employed as a 'chippie's mate' on the racecourse. The Christmas festivities were much enlivened by the military presence. The band of the 1st Battalion, the Royal Hampshires, played carols round the town on Christmas Eve, the RAF provided a traditional jazz group ('Q' Oswald, clarinet, John Stirling, piano) for our Christmas party at Government House and on Boxing Day the Royal Navy organised a raft race from the Battle Monument to Victory Green. This was an hilarious occasion, blessed with perfect weather, in which most units and ships and many civilians took part. The only rule was that each raft had to have at least one female in the crew. The rafts came in all shapes and sizes, some of ingenious design and at least one with a suspected outboard motor concealed between its planks. David Dobson had instructed his experts at Navy Point to design a race-winner and had invited DSNOFI (Mike Sizeland) and Mavis to be part of his winning crew. There must have been something radically wrong with the raft (or the crew) because to SNOFI's dismay they had barely crossed the starting line by the time the leading rafts had reached the winning post. The genuine winner (the powered raft having been disqualified) was a racy raft constructed on Argentine Skyhawk drop-tanks. So successful was the race that it was decided to make it an annual event.

At the end of the year the *Lindblad Explorer* dropped anchor in Stanley harbour and we gave a New Year's Eve party for the crew and passengers in Government House. With military and civilian guests, the numbers exceeded 250. Coincidentally, at midnight we were lighting a bonfire on the hill behind Government House to mark the beginning of the centenary year of the Boys Brigade, which had long had an active branch in Stanley. A few minutes before midnight, we led a procession of our guests up the hill and, as the flames leapt skywards on the stroke of midnight, I reflected on what a remarkable year it had been and said my fervent thanks to the Task Force. Returning cold but happy to Government House, Don was waiting for me at the door. He took me aside into the rodroom and told me that his brother, Harry, had died just before midnight.

Notes

1. With the fishing boom, the FIGO assumed greater responsibilities and in 1989 was moved into larger premises.

2. *Falkland Islands Review:* Report of a Committee of Privy Counsellors, Cmnd 8787, HMSO.

3. The ensign now adorns Christ Church Cathedral.

4. See page 425.

5. See page 447.

6. *Falkland Islands Economic Study 1982*, Cmnd 8653, HMSO.

7. Later bought by the Admiralty and renamed HMS *Diligence*.

8. This was not until 1984, when adequate accommodation became available on the coastels.

9. FIC subsequently entered into a profit-sharing agreement with Albert, which gave him a bigger stake in the island.

18

Freedom and Justice in Peace and Security

The last of the Service chiefs to visit us in 1982 had been the Chief of Air Staff, Air Chief Marshal Sir Keith Williamson. He stayed in Government House and, on the first morning, asked to see me alone in my office. There he disclosed that the Prime Minister intended to visit the Islands from 8 to 12 January and handed me a letter from Sir Robert Armstrong, then Secretary of the Cabinet and Head of the Civil Service. Written in his own hand, with paragraphs and lines thoughtfully lettered and numbered to ease reply, he stressed that security must be maintained and that the only person with whom I should discuss the programme was the Military Commissioner. If news of the visit leaked out, it would be cancelled. He sketched a possible outline for a four-day visit, finishing with a postscript: 'The PM does not like much spare time on visits like this.' David and I mapped out a provisional programme and I sent it back in a handwritten letter to Sir Robert. He wrote again with a few further comments and told me to reply only if we disagreed. That was that. It was the easiest VIP programme I had ever arranged. Normally, and particularly where the military were concerned, such visits entailed weeks of preparation and discussion, with voluminous programmes and numerous printed revisions. For the Prime Minister, three handwritten letters sufficed.

It was not, of course, quite as simple as that for David, who was responsible for the Prime Minister's protection. On a strict need-to-know basis, he and his staff prepared a contingency plan 'for the visit of a VIP to the Falkland Islands'. No names or dates were mentioned, but it was planned for a Saturday arrival and Wednesday departure. The give-away was that one of the party was shown as 'VIP's wife/husband'.

As no announcement about the visit could be made beforehand, the journalists who would normally have accompanied the Prime Minister were to follow twenty-four hours later. There was a BBC television team in the Islands, led by Nicholas Wichell, but it had been there since before Christmas and was due to leave on 5 January, three days before the Prime Minister's arrival. That morning, I received a call from Bernard Ingham, the Prime Minister's press secretary, telling me to keep the team on the Islands but not to disclose the reason. I rang Nicholas at the Upland Goose, where he and his colleagues were happily packing, and asked him to come to my office. There I explained that something was likely to happen over the next week that he might wish he had stayed for and my advice was for him to postpone his departure. He said that must mean that we were expecting someone we wanted to see or someone we did not want to see; either way, he would stay (at the time, there were rumours that an Argentine intended to bring some next-of-kin to the Islands to pay homage to their dead). I think he guessed that the Prime Minister was coming but, to his credit, he kept it to himself.

I told Mavis, of course, about our forthcoming guests, but we had to pretend to the staff that they were preparing for a party of journalists who could not be accommodated at the Upland Goose. In the village atmosphere of the Falklands, the slightest hint of an impending visit by the Prime Minister would have been flashed round the Islands by 'diddle-dee radio' within minutes and Don, for all his excellent virtues, would have been one of the first on the air. I hoped that he would forgive me for denting his reputation as a reliable newsmonger. I warned Patrick Watts and other local journalists to be at the airport by 4.30pm on Saturday, 8 January, but did not tell them who was coming.

As soon as Mrs Thatcher stepped off the Hercules, Patrick telephoned the FIBS studio, which interrupted its normal programme to announce her arrival. In the twenty minutes that it took Don to drive along the four miles of pot-holed airport road, the Stanley townsfolk flocked out of their houses and gathered along the route to welcome the Prime Minister. At her request, Don stopped at various points and she and Mr Thatcher got out and shook hands with scores of people. She said to one group, 'You were all marvellous', to which Mike Bleaney, who was standing with young Daniel on his shoulders, replied 'You didn't do too badly yourself, Ma'am!' As we passed near Harold Bennett's house, he came to the taxi window and handed Mrs Thatcher a single rose. His eyes were moist and he was too choked to speak. He turned away but the Prime Minister told Don to stop, jumped out of the taxi and hurried after him. I followed and introduced him. He still could not speak and I could see that Mrs Thatcher, too, was deeply moved as she thanked him for the rose. All along the route, the crowds had gathered. It seemed that the whole of Stanley had come out to greet her. For a normally undemonstrative community, it was a remarkable display of affection – spontaneous, sincere and from the heart.

The Prime Minister's party consisted of the Chief of Naval Staff, Admiral Sir John Fieldhouse, who had been the commander of the Task Force operations from April to June, 1982, based at Northwood; her Principal Private Secretary, Robin Butler, who was later to take Sir Robert Armstrong's place as Secretary of the Cabinet and Head of the Home Civil Service; a Private Secretary, John Coles, who was seconded from the Diplomatic Service; her Press Secretary, Bernard Ingham and a duty clerk, Alan Logan. There was no security officer or personal detective. I showed Mr and Mrs Thatcher to their room and pointed out the Argentine bullet-holes in the ceiling. The Prime Minister elected to sleep in the bed beneath them. As she tidied up, Mr Thatcher came down to the small drawing room and stood warming himself in front of the peat fire. Our first engagement was a briefing at HQ BFFI and I was surprised to see that he made no move to get ready. 'Oh, I can't come', he said, 'I've not been security cleared.'

I ran through the programme with him and the secretaries who had now joined us, and pointed to one or two items that might be omitted if they thought that we had given the Prime Minister too much to do. I got a few rueful smiles in response and an assurance that she would fulfil every bit of the programme, and probably more. At the briefing, it was interesting to see the close rapport between the Prime Minister and Sir John Fieldhouse and the detailed grasp that she had of military matters. Afterwards, we had a small dinner party at Government House with a few of the leading Islanders. There were only seventeen in all, but even this was a bit of a crowd for the small drawing-room. Nevertheless, that was where we stayed because the Prime Minister decided that she preferred it (as we did) to the main drawing-room. After the other guests had gone, she naturally gravitated to Mavis's chair beside the peat fire, kicked off her shoes and relaxed with a whisky and soda – a practice she was to follow each evening.

Sunday started with a visit to Stanley airport to see the RAF units and to visit the engineering works at the nearby quarry. The Royal Engineers were producing thousands of tons of crushed stone to build roads from the airport to the coastel sites along the Canache. The first coastel had arrived from Sweden in December on the *Ferncarrier*, a semi-submersible heavy-lift vessel, and we had hoped to have it in position in time for the Prime Minister to open, but the wind and tides had to be exactly right and the correct combination did not occur until the evening of her departure.

In the latter part of the morning, the Prime Minister attended a joint meeting of Executive and Legislative Councils, followed by lunch at Government House with councillors. They each expressed their thanks and undying gratitude to Mrs Thatcher for sending the Task Force and reiterated their loyalty to the Queen. Looking to the future, they emphasised that Islanders had no wish to resume negotiations with the Argentines for as long as the Argentines equated negotiations with the transfer of sovereignty. They were grateful to Britain for providing the necessary security and for responding generously to Lord Shackleton's recommendations: they recognised that it was now up to Islanders to make the most of the opportunities thus created. Councillor Tony Blake urged the break-up of more of the larger farms and Councillor Tim Blake pressed for the development of the Islands' deep sea fisheries by using the 150-mile protection zone in which to license fishing. Tim also explained the work of the Select Committee, of which he was chairman, on revising the constitution and the electoral procedure for the Islands and expressed the hope that proposals would be forwarded to HMG by July.

After lunch, the Prime Minister visited the Rookery Bay minefield and the Camber, where the Gurkha engineers, RAF Search and Rescue and several Royal Navy units were based, and then flew back across the harbour to see the Port Squadron of the Royal Corps of Transport, finishing a busy afternoon with a visit to the Field Post Office and the bakery. The latter was, literally, a museum piece. Used in the First World War, it had been taken out of an army museum and transported to the Falklands, where it performed magnificently until the troops moved to the Canache, after which it was returned to the museum. Parked under canvas between two FIC warehouses, it was a popular place to visit not only because of the appetising smell of freshly baked bread but also because it was the warmest place in town.

Before evensong in the cathedral, the Prime Minister laid a wreath at the cross of sacrifice for those Falkland Islanders who had lost their lives in the two World Wars. She had brought a number of wreaths from England, all beautifully made with flowers rarely seen in the Falklands. David was host for dinner that night in Britannia House.

Monday was, if anything, busier than Sunday. We visited four settlements in East Falkland and two in the West. At each place, the Prime Minister gave speeches to the Islanders and to the troops and spoke to a large number of them individually. In order that she might meet as many Islanders as possible, David had kindly arranged for helicopters to bring them in from outlying settlements, so there was a large crowd (by Falklands' standards) wherever we went. Local journalists and the BBC team were joined by others from Britain who had flown in on the Sunday. Microphones and cameras were thrust in front of the Prime Minister at every opportunity and she sustained the barrage with unfailing good humour and patience. We travelled in a Sea King, with a Chinook for the Press and the infantry escort. Mrs Thatcher was welcomed with tremendous warmth wherever we landed, but none more so than Goose Green, where the men, women and children who had been incarcerated in the community hall gave her three resounding cheers and gathered round to shake her hand and offer their personal thanks.

Brook Hardcastle and Eric Goss took us to the grave of Lieutenant Nick Taylor, RN, where Mrs Thatcher laid one of her wreaths and Eric assured her that the people of the settlement would tend the grave with loving care for evermore. We then visited 'Y' Company of the 1st Battalion, the Royal Hampshire Regiment, accompanied by the battalion commander, Lieutenant-Colonel Hastings Neville. Sited near the remains of the old schoolhouse, between Goose Green and Darwin, theirs was the first camp to be provided with Portakabins and was well on the way to completion. The Prime Minister was concerned about the welfare of the garrison and hoped that David's objective of having most of them out of tented accommodation by the onset of winter would be achieved.

From Goose Green we flew to Port San Carlos, where Alan Miller and his small band were sharing the settlement with the RAF Chinook detachment, the Harrier forward operating base and a platoon of the Royal Hampshires, and thence to San Carlos to lay a wreath at Blue Beach cemetery. Pat and Isabel Short provided lunch for the Prime Minister's party: after so many VIP visits they were becoming expert hosts. Indeed, I never ceased to admire Isabel for the seeming ease with which she adapted to the changed circumstances. Before the war, she had been extremely

374

shy and retiring, but now she chatted easily to all and sundry, from the Prime Minister down. This I noted was a heartening characteristic of Islanders in general: they rose to the occasion, whether at home, like Isabel, or the UN, like John Cheek, or in London, like Lewis Clifton.

San Carlos Water was still protected by Rapiers, the crews of which lived in dug-outs reminiscent of the trenches in the First World War, but their morale could not have been higher, as the Prime Minister discovered. At Kelly's Garden, across the bay from San Carlos, the Royal Engineers were busily constructing a camp, which was intended to house the Chinook detachment and the headquarters of the ground air defence battery. Like most of the camps under construction, the biggest enemy was mud. We wore wellingtons as we splashed from hut to helicopter.

The Prime Minister refused to wear wellingtons for our next port of call, which was Port Howard cemetery. In fact, she was quite indignant when I suggested on the aircraft that she should put them on. 'I am not wearing wellingtons to Captain Hamilton's grave', she said firmly, and promptly donned her best shoes. A Gurkha guard of honour presented arms as she walked through the mud to lay a wreath on Captain Hamilton's grave. I followed in my wellies, wondering whether a male Prime Minister would have been so sensitive.

After chatting to the people in the settlement, we flew from Port Howard to Fox Bay East, where Islanders from Fox Bay West, Port Stephens and Chartres had assembled. It was also the base for 'A' Company, the Royal Hampshires, whose camp was taking shape a little way up-river, at Doctor's Creek. Returning to the triangle after so many take-offs and landings, and so long in a noisy helicopter, I think that we were all feeling tired; within half-an-hour, however, we were changed and heading for a public reception at the Town Hall. On the short journey from Government House, I warned the Prime Minister that we had a surprise in store. Councillors had decided to confer upon her the freedom of the Falkland Islands, a unique honour in that only the freedom of Stanley had been awarded before (and that only to the Royal Marines and the West Yorkshire Regiment, which had been based there in the Second World War). Harold Rowlands, as the most senior kelper in the FIG, had been chosen to present the scroll; I would introduce him and we would both speak for no more than two minutes. She would be expected to say a few words in reply, but not to make a long speech.

The Town Hall was packed. There must have been 600 or more there, in a room normally considered crowded with 200 (indeed, the Director of Public Works was concerned that the floor might not take the weight). The atmosphere was electric and the Prime Minister perked up as soon as she entered: she was engulfed in a sea of grateful well-wishers and it took the best part of an hour to guide her through the crowd to the stage at the other end of the hall. I introduced Harold and stuck to my allotted two minutes. Harold was equally brief: describing the occasion as the greatest moment in his life, he said that he was echoing the sentiments of all Falkland Islanders in expressing his pleasure at being able to thank Mrs Thatcher in person for their liberation and pledged Islanders to build a better future to ensure that the war had been worth-while and that British lives had not been lost in vain. He read out the formal proclamation, presented the scroll and then brought the house down by kissing the Prime Minister. Clearly elated, Mrs Thatcher made what many of the audience told me afterwards was the best speech they had ever heard. It lasted for twenty minutes, without notes or briefing (none of us had prepared any material for her), and touched exactly the right chord. She received the most enthusiastic reception ever witnessed in the Falkland Islands. The biggest cheer came when she said 'Today again the Union Jack flies over Port Stanley, and may it ever fly there.' This had of course particular significance for me, for it was here in the Town Hall that General Garcia had told me that the Argentines would stay 'forever'. It was an intensely moving experience for us all, including the Prime Minister's party. Bernard Ingham came up afterwards and smothered me in a huge bear-hug. Dinner that evening was a lively affair, with all the day's fatigue banished. Indeed, though well past midnight, Mr Thatcher had difficulty in persuading the Prime Minister to go to bed.

Tuesday was largely a nautical day but, before flying to HMS *Antrim*, the Prime Minister visited the junior and senior schools, the hospital, the post office, the power station, PWD, the Brewster houses and the FIGAS hangar, where the Beaver was being reassembled. At sea, she went from HMS *Antrim* to the RFA *Fort Grange*, the *Stena Inspector* and HMS *Charybdis*, returning in the evening to give interviews to the *Penguin News* and the local radio. David was host at a tri-service dinner that night, which lasted until after midnight. Relaxing in front of the peat fire before going to bed, the Prime Minister suddenly said, 'I haven't seen a penguin, I must see a penguin before we leave.' As she was due to depart at 8am that morning, there was not much time to arrange a visit to a penguin colony. Then she added, 'And I should like to walk over Tumbledown.' I groaned inwardly. 'It will mean getting up at five Prime Minister', I said. 'That's fine,' she replied. After she and Mr Thatcher had retired, David organised a helicopter and I got hold of Ian Strange. We agreed that we should be able to fit in both Tumbledown and Seal Point before breakfast.

It was a miserable morning, blowing and raining. Undeterred, the Prime Minister jumped into the Sea King and we landed in the wet on Tumbledown. Mr Thatcher urged her to put a scarf over her head, but she would have none of it. Although the dangerous ordnance had been removed, there was still plenty of evidence of the battle, sangars and foxholes festooned with bits of webbing, tattered clothes and the inevitable tubes of toothpaste. Surveying the difficult terrain in the wind and the rain, the Prime Minister marvelled that the Scots Guards had been able to storm the Argentine positions. From Tumbledown, we flew down to Seal Point, on the tip of Port Harriet, and the jackass penguins obliged the Prime Minister by coming out of their burrows and eyeing her curiously. Thanks to the helicopter, we were back at Government House and having breakfast by 7.15am.

Everything had gone without a hitch up till now; we had even managed to keep the Prime Minister's departure a secret. To convince the Press that she would not be leaving until the following day, one of the crew of her Hercules had been told to stay up late drinking with the journalists (who were sharing the Upland Goose with them). He played his part so well that, when the rest of the crew climbed out of their bedroom windows at 4.30am, he failed to surface and had to be quietly spirited away by his colleagues. Most of the Press had accepted an invitation to be flown on a wildlife tour for the day and were on their way to a penguin colony when we escorted the Prime Minister to the airport. We bade our farewells and the Hercules door closed at precisely 8am. As it was raining hard, David and I sought shelter in the helicopter and sat waiting for the Hercules to take off. We were congratulating ourselves that everything had gone well when the intercom crackled and our pilot reported that the Hercules was taxiing back. Apparently all four engines had lost power as the pilot opened the throttles. There was no danger because he had scarcely started his take-off run; but it was worrying. David and I dashed out of the helicopter and across the apron to be at the foot of the steps again as the Prime Minister and her party disembarked. We waited in the Station Commander's Portakabin while the RAF decided what to do. The Prime Minister was naturally perturbed about losing precious time; her programme was as full as ever, with a big reception at Ascension on her way home (she had passed through unknown on the way down) and she wanted to be back in London for question time in the House of Commons the following afternoon. The choice lay between checking the faulty engines, which might have taken several hours, transferring the special caravan, which had been fitted into the Prime Minister's aircraft, into the Press Hercules, or taking the Press Hercules as it stood. As switching the caravan would also have taken several hours, the Prime Minister elected to go in the Press Hercules, without trimmings. After almost an hour's delay, we said farewell a second time and breathed sighs of relief as the heavily laden Hercules lumbered off the runway and disappeared into the overcast. We had thoroughly enjoyed the visit, but another day at that pace would have been hard to bear. 'Early night, tonight, David,' I said, as we flew back to the triangle, with which he heartily concurred.

Before she left, Mrs Thatcher said that she had been deeply touched by the warmth and kindness of the welcome she had received everywhere she went and from everyone she had met. She knew that what was being expressed to her was the loyalty of the Falkland Islanders to Britain and their gratitude for the professionalism and gallantry of the Task Force in freeing them from the domination of a military invader. But that was only part of the story. What in truth the Islanders were expressing was their gratitude to Mrs Thatcher for sending the Task Force and never wavering in her determination to liberate the Islands. They believed that, had she not been the Prime Minister at the time, the Task Force would never have sailed and they would have been under Argentine domination 'forever'.

In coming 8,000 miles to meet the Islanders, the Prime Minister boosted morale as nothing else could. The citizens of shabby, shell-shocked Stanley needed a tonic and the Prime Minister's visit was the perfect medicine. It was fitting that she should come in the month that marked the 150th anniversary of continuous British settlement, the date by which the Argentines had determined that they would achieve sovereignty over the Islands. Her clear, unequivocal commitment to the Islanders both reassured them and instilled confidence in the future. Whatever other politicians or the Foreign Office might do or say, Islanders knew that they had a staunch champion at the helm in London.

At about the time that the Prime Minister's aircraft was approaching Ascension, David, Mavis and I were celebrating the successful mooring of the coastel in the Canache. We were the first to walk across the ramp and go aboard, to be welcomed by the Swedish owner, SNOFI and the naval liaison officer who had conducted the delicate operation. There was no drinking water on board – the reverse osmosis plant that was to produce fresh water from the sea was not yet functioning – so we drank a toast to the *Safe Dominica* (as the coastel was then called) in neat Schnappes, the only drink that our Swedish host possessed. The installation of this, the first of three coastels, was a great relief to David, for it meant that he could house all his RAF personnel, amounting to almost a thousand men, and get rid of the tents that had made Stanley airport look like an airfield in Flanders in the First World War.

We naturally felt a little flat after the Prime Minister's visit; but not for long. Apart from the 150th anniversary celebrations to prepare, we had hosts of other visitors in January and February, which were of course not only the best months to visit the Islands but also the best months to get away from Britain. A welcome acquaintance was Jerry Wiggin, who arrived a week after the Prime Minister's departure. Another old acquaintance was Colonel Stephen Love, who had been the Defence Attaché at our embassy in Buenos Aires before the invasion. He came out to organise the forthcoming visit of British next-of-kin. It was a sensitive subject and required careful preparation. We agreed that the last day should be spent in Stanley but, as there would be over 500 visitors, Stephen doubted that the townsfolk could cater adequately for them. His plan was for the military to arrange a buffet lunch in the Town Hall. I strongly resisted, knowing that the Islanders would want to look after such special guests in their own hospitable way. I said that, despite having less than 360 houses, Stanley had not only fed but had also accommodated over 600 men from HMS *Exeter*; they could certainly manage lunch for 500. As a long-stop, Mavis offered to provide lunch for any guests who were not looked after by Islander families; but Stephen remained apprehensive.

One of Jerry Wiggins's requests was to see the *Safe Dominica*. To save time, David provided a Sea King, but unfortunately it became bogged in the soft ground outside the coastel and we had to drive back. I had been bogged many times in a Land Rover, but this was the first time in a helicopter. We had a meeting with councillors, at which the vexed question of the Argentine dead came up. Mr Wiggin explained the unfavourable publicity that Islanders would get if they refused to countenance a visit by Argentine next-of-kin, particularly now that we were arranging a British visit. Councillor John Cheek said that the majority would not object to a visit by *bona fide* next-of-kin, carried out under the auspices of the International Red Cross; but the visit proposed recently by a notorious right-wing Argentine called Destefanis was no more than a publicity gimmick undertaken for political reasons. The general view was that we should ship the Argentine dead over to the mainland for proper burial in their own country. Mr Wiggin pointed out that Britain had offered to do this, but the Argentines had refused. They maintained that the Islands were Argentine territory, so the dead were already buried in their own soil. In truth the Argentines were embarrassed because they did not know, and did not want the public to know, how many men they had really lost.

Shortly after Mr Wiggin's departure, Monsignor Spraggon and I visited the gravediggers at the cemetery and watched them exhuming the Argentine dead. As the Argentine government had refused to accept them back, we had decided to hallow some land near Darwin, which Ted Needham had kindly made available, to be used as the Argentine war cemetery. The macabre task of digging up existing graves (many of them shallow, hurried affairs, some communal and most without coffins) was a specialised job for which professional gravediggers had been recruited from England. In charge of them on the military side was a dashing cavalry officer on David's staff called Jeffrey Cardozo, of the Royal Dragoon Guards. He had no need to join in the actual digging but, when Monsignor and I arrived, there he was in a hole, working alongside his charges and not flinching from any of the unpleasant duties, which included going through the clothes (such as they were, six months afterwards) to try to find some means of identification. Many of the corpses lacked identity tags; indeed, when we were to lay them finally to rest in the Argentine cemetery, the only inscription we could put upon many of their crosses was 'An unknown Argentine soldier'. There were 233 altogether, gathered in from all over the Islands. How many perished or were dumped at sea will never be known. For those we found, however, we gave a proper burial. As Monsignor Spraggon said, 'We looked after the poor beggars a lot better dead than their officers did alive.'

We were shortly to be descended upon by the House of Commons Foreign Affairs and Defence Committees but, before they came, we managed to escape to Carcass Island for three days. I had a despatch to write and the Franks Report to read and Mavis needed a rest. We were delighted to find Senior (the pet night heron) still on the roof of our chalet and as tame and as greedy as ever. Lorraine and Janie McGill met us with the news that the men were over on Grand Jason trying to put out a fire that had been started three weeks ago. How it was started was a mystery, since the island was uninhabited, but the peat had caught and therefore the only way to put it out was by trenching. HMS *Liverpool*'s Lynx brought back four weary fire-fighters at 8.30 that evening: Rob and son Roy, John Cheek and Chris McCallum. The last two were holidaying on Carcass. Rob said that they had been unable to contain the fire as they had no sharp spades. They could not get a Chinook for the next two days, but one appeared on the morning we left, full of Gurkhas (and sharp spades), and Rob and Roy went off to help them to dig trenches to contain the fire. We heard later that they had succeeded. On our way back to Stanley, we spotted another fire near Roy Cove. The whole hillside was burning. We reported it by radio, but a fire-fighting patrol was already on its way. The fire hazard in summer in the Islands was another problem, like closing farm gates, that we had difficulty in getting across to the military. The terrain was so boggy that it seemed unlikely that there would ever be any risk of fire; but the diddle-dee became as dry as tinder in the summer months and one cigarette or stray tracer bullet was enough to set off a major conflagration. If the peat under the diddle-dee also caught, the fire could burn for months.

Back in Stanley, my Saturday morning routine was to walk to the racecourse to see how the preparations were proceeding for the 150th anniversary and then to visit the Brewster housing site next to the racecourse. Jim Brewster was there himself at the time, working all hours and living on site in a mobile home. The original target dates for completion were probably over-optimistic, but the whole venture had been plagued from the start with the most extraordinary bad luck. As no assistance with off-loading or transport could be spared by the military (whose own loads in any event had to have priority in the harbour), Brewster's had to be completely self-contained. Great care was therefore taken in the loading in England, to ensure that the items required first were in a position to be off-loaded first in Stanley. Unfortunately, the ship chosen by the Crown Agents to carry these items, which included a lighter, low-loaders, mobile homes and the workers' hostel, caught fire shortly before sailing, and the second broke down in transit. Everything was reloaded the wrong way round on another ship. This delayed not only the arrival but also the off-loading and took months to sort out. Another major snag was that ODA had assumed that PWD would provide the basic infrastructure, which without the necessary equipment (dumper trucks and JCBs) was simply beyond their capacity.

We had no doubts in Stanley that housing was the key to development. We could not implement Lord Shackleton's proposals without the personnel and we could not get the personnel without the houses. HMG had agreed to provide £31 million for a five-year development programme, but too little had been allocated to housing (the cost of the Brewster houses had come out of rehabilitation funds). For some doctrinal reason, ODA did not consider that housing was 'developmental'. I was to have a running battle over this until my departure in 1985, just as I was to do battle with MOD to keep what houses we had for civilians. Mr Wiggin had mentioned the possibility of members of CBFFI's staff serving longer tours if they could have their families with them. I had welcomed the idea, both for the sake of continuity and because service wives would be an asset to the civilian community; but I balked at the suggestion that they should have eight of our precious Brewster houses. If we were to implement Shackleton, we needed every one – and more besides. I pointed out that, with the vast resources at MOD's disposal, it could have eight houses built before the Brewster houses were anywhere near ready; we could provide the site and buy the houses when headquarters moved to Mount Pleasant. The final outcome of this sometimes acrimonious argument was the usual unsatisfactory compromise: CBFFI's staff got two Brewster houses and two older houses belonging to FIG, which had been damaged in the war and repaired by the military.

Media interest in the Islands was still high and almost every air bridge (as the Hercules flights from Ascension had come to be called) brought in a new wave of journalists or television crews. Every photographer wanted shots of Government House and the red taxi and we did our best to oblige. One of the more heavyweight visitors towards the end of January was the BBC's *Panorama* team, led by Fred Emery, whom I had known in the Far East. The controversy over Lord Shackleton's most radical proposal – subdivision of the absentee-owned farms – was an obvious topic and I explained that, in order to ascertain from Islanders the likely demand for their own farms, FIG had circulated a questionnaire at the beginning of the year, requesting replies by the end of February. Fred asked about the response to date and I gave him the details, emphasising that these were early days and that we should not draw any conclusions until all replies had been received. A week or two later, the FCO took me to task for embarrassing the Secretary of State. It assumed that I had seen the offending programme, although of course we had no live television in the Falklands. Eventually, I received a video of the programme in question and understood Mr Pym's embarrassment. The *Panorama* producer had edited out my remarks about not jumping to conclusions, and Fred Emery, interviewing the Secretary of State, had quoted my figures as if they were the final results of the questionnaire. Mr Pym was naturally nonplussed, whereupon Fred had accused us of a breakdown in communications, though he knew that my report on the questionnaire was not due until the following month. I learnt to be more wary of so-called 'respectable' presenters after that.

The Foreign Affairs Select Committee of the House of Commons arrived on 2 February, to take evidence in Stanley and to pay informal visits to many of the settlements. Under the chairmanship of Sir Anthony Kershaw, the committee consisted of nine members of the House of Commons from all parties and their task was to conduct an examination of the consequences for British foreign policy of the Argentine invasion of the Falkland Islands and their subsequent re-occupation by Britain. The visit got off to a bad start by an unfortunate incident at my welcoming party in Government House which, though minor in itself, was blown out of all proportion by the Press. Three of the Labour members of the Committee, Messrs Frank Hooley, Dennis Canavan and George Foulkes, were outspoken in their criticism of HMG's policy towards the Falklands and professed their belief that colonialism was a mistake and morally reprehensible. While this was a perfectly sustainable argument in general (with which I nevertheless disagreed), senior Islanders present were quick to point out that the Falklands were unique in that they had never had an indigenous population; but Mr Canavan took the argument a stage further by asserting that the Argentines

had the stronger claim to the Islands. This provoked a robust re-
buttal from Betty Miller, who as Betty Felton before she married
was a great-great-grand-daughter of Sergeant-Major Henry Felton
of the Lifeguards, who had come to the Falklands in charge of the
Chelsea Pensioners whom the British government had sent out in
1849. Hearing voices raised, I moved in to placate the combatants
but became embroiled myself when Mr Canavan attacked the
Prime Minister, describing her recent visit as 'an electioneering
gimmick'. I assured him that it was certainly no gimmick for those
present at the time and he then dismissed me as an 'imperialistic
bloody clown'. At this point, Monsignor Spraggon intervened and
I withdrew. Later, I heard voices raised again and saw Harold
Rowlands moving in to calm the Monsignor. On taking his leave
at the end of the party, Harold muttered, 'If he [Canavan] carries
on like that, he'll be lucky to get out of these Islands alive.' It was
a private party, without the Press, but someone who should have
known better spoke about the incident outside and it ended up in
the Press with the Monsignor having raised his fists as well as his
voice to Mr Canavan.

The rest of the visit passed off uneventfully and, apart from one
or two members who had prejudged the issues, the committee departed with a better understanding of Islanders' views. It was in the
process of considering its chairman's draft report when Parliament
was dissolved in May and its successor did not produce the final
report (based on revised terms of reference) until October, 1984.[1]
The report contained some useful and constructive recommendations and, on the crucial issue of sovereignty, was unequivocal: 'It
is clear that, when referring to negotiations on sovereignty, the new
Argentine Government is pursuing a policy essentially no different
from that of its predecessors: that such negotiations, once begun,
must lead eventually and inevitably to the relinquishment of the
United Kingdom's claim to, and administration of, the Falklands'.

Hot on the heels of the Foreign Affairs Committee came the
House of Commons Defence Committee, under the chairmanship
of Sir Timothy Kitson. David was mainly responsible for their
programme, but I helped to brief and entertain them, and gave
formal evidence as I had done with the Foreign Affairs Committee.
The Labour members, the Rt Hon Dr John Gilbert and Mr Dick
Douglas, made a good impression on the Islanders and said nothing
to offend them. As they left the Islands, our guests for the 150th
anniversary celebrations were beginning to arrive. The first two

were Michael Brown and Harry Dempster, of the *Daily Express*. They were official guests in gratitude for their and their paper's support for the Falkland Islanders since before the war. Another guest in this category was John Junor (as he then was), Editor of the *Sunday Express*. Two familiar voices, which had sustained Islanders during the occupation, materialised in the shape of Harold Briley and Peter King of the BBC, and a familiar face, Ted Needham, came as head of Coalite. Supporters from the House of Lords were Baroness Vickers, Lord Shackleton and Lord Buxton, who was accompanied by Maria, Cindy and Annie (almost one of the family) and their youngest daughter, Vicky. Supporters from the House of Commons were Michael Shersby and Eric Ogden, HMG's representative was Mr Timothy Raison, Minister of Overseas Development, and Lord Bishopston and Russell Johnston represented the Labour and Liberal Parties respectively. As Mr Raison wished to combine work with the festivities, he was accompanied by two of his ODA staff. To round off our guest list, HMS *Endurance* steamed into Port Stanley in time for the celebrations. Accommodation was a problem, but our guests were most understanding and made light of the difficult conditions. Bad weather disrupted and delayed the programme, but no item had to be cancelled, although the carnival and the fireworks display (kindly supplied by Ted Needham) were not held until after most of the guests had gone.

The carnival was a huge success. All the ships in Ports Stanley and William participated and produced some ingenious floats. Judging was difficult but eventually we awarded first prize to the *Fort Toronto*, a motor tanker chartered from Canadian Pacific and serving as a base water supply tanker. The crew had one of the most boring (but vital) jobs of all, sitting in Port William waiting for other ships to come to them to fill up with fresh water (making drinking water, incidentally, more expensive than whisky). The carnival provided a welcome diversion. They had constructed a realistic North American fort and dressed up as Redcoats and Red Indians. Dressed down would be more correct for some of the Red Indians, who wore no more than a loincloth, feathers and war-paint. Two hours in the open in Stanley in such garb, even in February, was not the best way to keep warm, despite whooping round the float and flashing tomahawks. After the prize-giving, they were pleased to come into Government House and thaw out with the help of rum generously donated by the Barbados Rum Committee.

Annya Smith was chosen as the Carnival Queen and became

well-known in Britain when Duffy Sheridan's excellent portrait of her appeared on the front page of the *Sunday Times* magazine. But the most popular lady in Stanley that week was Baroness Vickers. She had been determined to come for the 150th anniversary, despite having fallen and broken her hip some months before. The Hercules was not designed to carry eighty-four-year-old ladies with broken hips, but she had disembarked as perky and immaculate as ever. Mavis and I remembered her well from the time that she had stayed with us in Kuching. Then Miss Joan Vickers and a staunch member of the Conservative Party in the House of Commons, she had caused a sensation among the Dyaks by being the first woman they had ever seen with blue hair. For her week in Stanley, she had asked particularly to stay with a true kelper family and Syd and Betty Miller were delighted to oblige. On the last day of the festivities, we heard that an amendment to the Nationality Bill, which she had proposed in the House of Lords, had been passed in the House of Commons. This meant that most Islanders could now claim British citizenship under the new act and it was fitting that I could break the good news to Lady Vickers in the home of two loyal kelpers whose children, without her intervention, would have lost their British nationality.

One of my pleasant duties during the week was to open Everards' brewery and launch Penguin Ale. With commendable initiative, Everards had decided before the end of the war to brew beer in the Falklands. It had been an act of faith at the time, taken without market research or preliminary investigation. Islanders were renowned for their beer-drinking capacity but, even so, there were not enough of them to warrant a brewery all to themselves. Everards hoped that the presence of a large military garrison would make the venture viable. Unfortunately, beer for the troops was supplied by NAAFI, which had exclusive worldwide contracts with another British brewery. Penguin ale could not compete and, sadly, after losing money for two years the Stanley brewery had to close down.

A familiar and much-loved figure missing from the anniversary celebrations was Monsignor Spraggon. He had caught a respiratory infection and was confined to bed. I visited him several times during the week to keep him informed of events, which he was furious to have missed, and Cindy and Annie called in to cheer him up. It was interesting to note how the incidence of chest infections, and coughs and colds in general, had risen amongst Islanders with the influx of

British troops. When I mentioned this to Alison, she said that she was not surprised: most Islanders caught colds when first visiting the UK because they did not have the immunities that we had built up.

There were several exhibitions to mark the 150th anniversary, from philately to handicrafts. Perhaps the one that impressed our guests most was the work of local artists, which included superb portraits by Duffy Sheridan, birds and mammals by Ian Strange and Tony Chater, wild flowers by Sonia Paul and ships by John Smith. For such a small community, the exhibitions displayed an unusual amount of talent. The week's festivities were enriched with performances by the bands of the 1st Battalion, Royal Hampshire Regiment and the Royal Engineers and, after a spectacular free-fall parachute display, ended with a Victory Ball and prize-giving ceremony in the Town Hall. I read out the following messages:

From Her Majesty The Queen:

I have great pleasure in sending you my congratulations on the occasion of the 150th anniversary of continuous British settlement of the Falkland Islands. You have recently been through a terrible experience during which the sympathies of the British people were with you. I hope that we can now look forward to a peaceful and prosperous future for the Falkland Islands. My very best wishes to you all.

ELIZABETH R.

From the Prime Minister:

I have the greatest pleasure in sending you my congratulations and very best wishes on this historic occasion. 1982 brought both tragedy and triumph to the Falkland Islands. Neither you nor we in Britain will ever forget those experiences. Today, we salute a brave and loyal people. We remember with pride the role of the Falkland Islands in British history. We look forward to a future in which you and your children continue to live in Freedom and Justice, in Peace and Security. It is worth working for. We shall strive and succeed together.

MARGARET THATCHER

Several of our guests stayed on to make visits to camp: the Buxtons went to Carcass, New Island and Westpoint and Lord Shackleton and Bob Storey (who had been seconded to Shackleton's team from the Highlands and Islands Development Board) to Hill Cove. We had urgent decisions to make in Executive Council and met on the first working day after the celebrations. We agreed to buy Fox Bay East and Packe's, Port Howard – the third farm to be subdivided – and hammered out the details for the establishment of a Falkland Islands Development Agency, as recommended by Lord Shackleton. We were fortunate that he returned from camp that evening to give councillors his valuable encouragement and advice. The Falkland Islands Development Corporation (as it came to be called) started its long gestation from this day.

I was also glad that Lord Buxton was still with us and had visited Westpoint, because David warned me that the MOD was seriously considering putting a radar station there. I knew that Roddy Napier would be bitterly opposed, for it would be impossible to erect a radar station without disturbing the wildlife, and Roddy cared deeply for his mixed colony of blackbrowed albatrosses and rockhoppers. If, however, David was to advise that it was necessary for the security of the Islands, it would be difficult for me to refuse to sign a compulsory acquisition order. As a keen conservationist, Aubrey naturally took Roddy's point of view. David was sympathetic and finally convinced MOD that there were genuine military as well as conservationist reasons for siting the radar station elsewhere.

Having decided that the last week in February was the latest that we could safely hold the 150th anniversary celebrations, 1 March produced a perfect summer's day, better than any in the previous week. It was Lord Shackleton's and Bob Storey's last day and we had a useful round-up discussion, particularly on the social aspects of living with a large garrison. After eight months' experience, I was more sanguine than Bob, who forecast an increase in local community tensions. Surprisingly, this had not happened and did not happen. I accompanied Lord Shackleton and Bob Storey to the airport to see them off and dashed back for dinner on board HMS *Exeter*, which we were glad to see back in Falklands' waters and with the same Captain, Hugh Balfour. Another most welcome return visitor was Sir Jeremy Moore, who flew in the following day to participate in a BBC documentary about the war. He and David joined us for a farewell dinner for the Buxtons, who had returned from Carcass and were leaving the next day.

Departures and arrivals came thick and fast. A loss to the Islands was Jack Abbott, who had returned intending to stay but decided that, since the Islanders would not accept him as a true kelper, even now, he would settle in England. I tried to explain to him that no one could be a true kelper, no matter what he had done for the Islands or how long he had lived there, unless he was of kelper stock and born there; but Jack left, a sad and disappointed man. The last of our 150th anniversary guests, on the other hand, could not have been happier: Peter King, of *Calling The Falklands*, was delighted with his visit and the warm reception that he had received. The Islands and Islanders had more than lived up to his expectations. Other happy visitors were Angela Herbert, Charles and Tony, who were sailing round the world in their yacht, *Reveller*, to raise money for cancer sufferers. Angela and her husband Bill ran a Cornish inn and Bill had given her leave of absence to go round the world for a good cause. We gave them what fresh vegetables we could and saw the *Reveller* depart as Mavis and I and our new house-guest, Robin Edmonds, flew out to HMS *Cardiff* in a Lynx. Robin was an ex-FCO colleague who had been in charge of Falkland Islands and South American affairs in the seventies. HMS *Cardiff* was due to have a look at Beauchene Island and I could not miss my first opportunity to visit the furthermost island of the archipelago. A seal reserve and wild animal and bird sanctuary, it bore the name of the French navigator, Gouin de Beauchene, who first discovered it in 1701. About 130 miles south of Stanley, it had no safe anchorage, but neither distance nor inaccessibility caused the Lynx any problem; the only difficulty was to find a landing spot without disturbing the birds.

Beauchene must be the supreme place for albatrosses and rockhoppers; I had never seen so many in one spot. This year's fledglings were almost ready to fly and their clumsy antics reminded me of my first flying lessons. They actually had an airstrip on a flattish patch in the middle of the island where, by tacit agreement, neither mollymawk nor rockhopper attempted to build a nest and the few gentoos that wandered up from the shore were quickly shooed away. The inexperienced birds tried their first runs into wind, waddling awkwardly on their over-large feet, wings flapping furiously. Some seemed startled when their feet left the ground; they stopped flapping their wings and came back to earth with a jolt. Others were more adventurous and gained a few feet before overshooting the runway and coming down in a heap of squawking rockhoppers. One or two caught the wind and, after a shaky start, soared off over the cliffs and the sea with supreme confidence. Before long, they would all be away across the oceans.

On one of my trips to the airport to see how the reassembly of the new Islander aircraft was progressing, I was interested to see two Buccaneers on the apron. It could not have escaped Argentine notice that we had the capacity to operate these formidable strike aircraft from Stanley. We also had the occasional Nimrod, which could now carry out long-range maritime reconnaissance from Stanley, ranging as far south as the South Sandwich Islands. Media interest had been aroused in this group because HMS *Endurance* had reported finding the Argentine flag flying once again over Southern Thule. A shore party had found the Union Jack neatly folded at the foot of the flagpole, but no evidence of human occupation. We could give the media no satisfactory explanation. The most likely culprit was the *Almirante Irizar*, but her declared itinerary did not include a trip anywhere near the South Sandwich group.[2]

Media interest revived over an announcement in Buenos Aires that Destefanis had chartered a ship and intended to sail to 'Islas Malvinas' with Argentine next-of-kin. Councillors were adamant that Destefanis should not be allowed to land in the Falkland Islands. After much debate, they agreed to allow a visit for humanitarian reasons (which ruled out Destefanis) under the following conditions: any visit must be organised under the auspices of the International Red Cross; it must be on a neutral ship; only genuine next-of-kin, with names submitted and approved in advance, should be allowed to disembark; no Press should accompany them; no national flags or emblems should be permitted and the visit should be restricted to one day in and out of Choiseul Sound. The FCO sought to modify some of these conditions and signals flew between us. I was inundated with calls from the BBC, ITN and the national dailies, but could say nothing. John Ezard of *The Guardian* happened to be in Stanley at the time and he came to see me with a fairly accurate but damaging story that he had pieced together from various local sources. He was about to file it but had been decent enough to seek my comments first. I took him into my confidence, told him the facts and asked him not to file until after an announcement that the FCO proposed to make in two days' time. He could have gone ahead and achieved a minor scoop, but he appreciated that this would not have been in the best interests of the Islands and, to his credit, did not file.

The Hampshires were coming to the end of their four-month tour and one of the community works that they had undertaken was the redecking of North Arm jetty. Tony and Lyn Blake invited me to open it and Mavis and I jumped at the chance to get out of Stanley. Captain Chris Hoden of No 658 Squadron, Army Air Corps, flew us down in a Scout and picked us up again the next day. There was a sadness in the community hall that afternoon at the impending departure of 'their company' of the Hampshires, who had mixed in well and become part of the settlement. North Arm was not scheduled to retain a military presence and all they could expect in future was the occasional patrol. For the moment, however, they had not only one company of the Hampshires but also a survey party from HMS *Endurance*. We were delighted to find Chris Todhunter in charge. Almost a year ago, he had helped to shred and burn my files. Tony and Lyn were also looking after a lone New Zealand yachtsman. Lyn served us all with upland goose and we switched happily back to camp tempo. If only we could get out of Stanley more often.

On the way back the next day, Chris dropped in at Darwin to refuel and we had smoko with Eileen and Brook Hardcastle. The Development Officer, John Reid, was having difficulty drawing up an inventory of Fox Bay East, (a necessary prerequisite for subdivision) and I wanted to enlist Brook's help. He nobly volunteered and, thanks to his local knowledge and diligence – given, incidentally, in his own time and without fee – we were able to speed up the process. From Darwin we flew to Mount Kent to see the progress on the radar station. For weeks past, we had watched Chinooks flying up the harbour with loads of stones and cement slung underneath, like storks carrying babies. It must have been the most expensive method of transporting building materials in the world; but, given the urgent need to have ground-based early warning radar, it was the only way. The results were striking. Ninety Royal Engineers were living in containers while laying foundations for more permanent structures. Already the giant-sized golf balls to house the radar were taking shape. There was mud everywhere, but we happened to be lucky with the weather: it was dry and sunny, with little wind. One could see by the heavy cables tethering everything down that wind was a major problem. Until they modified the doors to open inwards, many were pulled off their hinges when opened. Despite the harsh conditions, morale was high and the troops were not without their comforts. One enterprising sapper had made himself a sauna, which was in great demand. Touring CSE parties dropped in to give a show in the cramped dining hut. We were told the story of one pretty young girl who declined the food offered because she was a vegetarian: instead, she asked for a fresh salad, to which a burly sergeant-major replied, 'Just come outside with me dearie and pick your own lettuce.'

On the short hop from Mount Kent to Stanley, I was wearing earphones and chatting to Chris when a 'May Day' call came through. It was a Harrier pilot, baling out near Tussac Island, in Port William (he was actually on the downwind leg of Stanley Airport, preparing to land, when his engine flamed out). We did not see him crash but, as we touched down at the triangle, a Sea King landed on the football field and a dripping figure alighted and walked across to the hospital. I was amazed at the speed and efficiency of the RAF's Search and Rescue flight: from May Day call to hospital could not have exceeded ten minutes.

Owing to the large number of visitors, we had been unable to make our annual trip south on HMS *Endurance* during the summer season. We were determined, however, to have one coastal trip before she sailed for home in April. I could not get away in March because, apart from Destefanis, we had the contractors for the new airport. The MOD had put the management of the project in the hands of the Property Services Agency (PSA), whose representatives were Robert Gomme and Dermot Boylan. They brought down teams from interested contractors to inspect the sites before submitting their tenders. We entertained twenty-five of them in Government House and received an excellent briefing from Robert and Dermot. A full PSA team had been established in February to start the detailed design and planning; tenders had been invited and the closing date for submission was May.

As March came to an end, our thoughts naturally turned to events of the previous year. 1 April this year was Good Friday and, after the evening service, Don and I played snooker with two newcomers, Harry Jones from Britten-Norman, who was supervising the reassembly of our Islanders, and Dick Whorlow of the Crown Agents, who was supervising the reconstruction of the Stanley roads. The peaceful atmosphere in the snooker room was a far cry from the warlike preparations of a year ago, although the bullet-holes in the wall and the window-frame were constant reminders of the night that followed. At the weekly briefing at HQBFFI the next morning, I thought how different it might have been if only we had had the intelligence then that we had today.

After the briefing, I walked along to the racecourse, the main buildings of which were now being used by the military as an education centre, and to the Brewster houses. Fifteen were up and in the process of being occupied. Bill Richards had been one of the first to move in. There were no drives, garages, fences or gardens, but Bill had put a notice on his sea of mud which read 'Keep Off The Grass – When It Grows'. Mavis joined me at Dick and Connie's, where she and Tony had spent the night last year, and we had a quiet drink together before lunch. Don said the 'diddle-dee radio' was unusually quiet that day, so we were not alone in our thoughts.

Four days later, we were at last able to go on board HMS *Endurance*, though only for a night. Nick Barker was a hard act to follow but, in Colin MacGregor, the Royal Navy had picked the right man. As soon as we stepped aboard, there was that indefinable atmosphere that goes with a happy ship. Colin had kindly invited Elspeth, my secretary, to accompany us and the crew did everything to make the ladies welcome. It was a dull but calm day and I stood on the bridge, as I had many times before, as we sailed through the Narrows and into Port William. There were sixteen ships anchored there and, off Tussac Island, a small lighter with divers working on the crashed Harrier. We followed the course of our first trip in the *Forrest*, to Salvador. There, Mavis plucked up courage and we flew in by Wasp. We just had time to call on all the families in the settlement before returning to the ship at dusk. After dinner, we watched an excellent film on Ernest Shackleton. An addition to the plaques and pictures on the walls was the Wilkinson Sword of Peace, which the ship had won the previous year.

Next morning we found that we had been joined by HMS *Achilles*. Her Captain, Andrew Ritchie, had been in charge of the naval party on the *Elk* during the war, a roll-on/roll-off cargo vessel requisitioned for the transport of aircraft, arms and ammunition. She was a frequent visitor to San Carlos Water and was probably the most dangerous ship to be on at the time – a bomb into her cargo would have produced spectacular fireworks. Andrew deservedly received the OBE for his efforts; but perhaps his greatest claim to fame was that he had a parrot called Nelson, with whom he shared his cabin. On arrival in Salvador Water, Andrew had hoisted his special parrot flag. Not to be outdone, Colin hoisted a penguin flag. Invited over for morning coffee, Colin and Mavis (I had flown to Rincon Grande) went by Gemini, with Colin flaunting a stuffed penguin sellotaped to his shoulder. Mavis said that Nelson had not known what to make of it.

Our sojourn on *Endurance* was all too brief: I had to fly back to Stanley after lunch to meet the Bishop of Her Majesty's Forces, the Right Reverend Stuart Snell, who had come to dedicate the memorial at San Carlos cemetery in the presence of the next-of-kin. I must confess that the impending visit of the next-of-kin caused me some apprehension. Stephen Love had done a magnificent job in organising it, down to the last detail; but, with so much emotion involved, it could easily go wrong. The *Cunard Countess* was due to sail into San Carlos Water on Saturday, 9 April and, after the service of dedication at the cemetery on the Sunday, parties were to be taken to the individual memorials and flown over the spots in the ocean that had been declared war graves. On Monday there was to be a service on the *Cunard Countess* as she steamed through Falkland Sound on her way to Stanley, and Tuesday was to be spent in Stanley before sailing for Montevideo in the evening.

The Chief of Defence Staff, Field Marshal Sir Edwin Bramall, flew out for the dedication ceremony and we held a dinner party in his honour on the Friday night. During the course of the evening, the Bishop and I discovered that we had been at the same college at Oxford at the same time (1948-50) and played together in the college rugby team. By another strange coincidence, one of the Commonwealth War Graves Commission representatives, Philip Mathew, calculated that he and I must have been on the same RAF short course at Oxford in 1944.

Next morning, we flew over to the *Cunard Countess* in San Carlos Water and Sir Edwin and I welcomed the next-of-kin. I had difficulty in choosing the right words for my address, but I need not have worried: the feeling on board was so warm and friendly, it was as if we were all enveloped in an embrace of caring. This feeling persisted throughout the visit and was particularly noticeable in Stanley, where the townsfolk opened their doors and their hearts and shared the common grief. Indeed, friendships were forged that day that have lasted to this, and I was not surprised to hear afterwards that the next-of-kin had formed a Falklands Families Association on board the *Cunard Countess* on their way back to Montevideo. The Association flourishes and at the time of writing is organising a third trip to the Falklands.

Early Sunday morning brought thick fog to Stanley. Helicopters could not land on the triangle so we had to go by boat to the Camber, where the Sea Kings were based. Ascending vertically in the fog, we broke into brilliant sunshine at 500ft and had a magnificent view of March Ridge and Mount Pleasant, which were perfectly clear. It was almost as if David and I had laid it on for Sir Edwin, to convince him (if convincing were needed) that Mount Pleasant was the better site for the airport.

The weather at San Carlos was reasonable and the Fox Bay stone looked soft and mellow in the sun. Stuart Snell delivered an excellent address and, at the end of the service, a lone piper played a lament during the laying of the wreaths. The florists on board the *Cunard Countess* had brought down a wonderful variety of flowers, which made the most vivid splash of colour ever seen in the Falklands. The memorial had inscribed upon it the names of all those who had no grave but the sea. Designed by the Commonwealth War Graves Commission, it was a fitting tribute to those who died in the service of their country and ensured that their names would live for evermore. Pat Short assured Sir Edwin that, as long as it was his land, the cemetery was in good hands.

On Monday we went on board the *Cunard Countess* for the special service for those lost at sea. The weather was perfect; not a cloud in the sky and the sea a Mediterranean blue. It was not, however, a Mediterranean climate and we wore sweaters and anoraks for the service on the open afterdeck. As we steamed down Falkland Sound, we had as escort HMS *Cardiff*, HMS *Active* and the RFA *Fort Grange*. After the service, as the wreaths bobbed in the wake, the escort vessels put on speed and passed alongside, dipping their flags in salute. It was an unforgettable experience. We flew back to Stanley just in time to receive a telephone call from the Prime Minister, who wanted to know how the visit was going and asked me to pass on her best wishes to the next-of-kin. That evening we had the two Commonwealth War Graves Commission masons, Hanahan and O'Connor, in for drinks and to thank them for their splendid work.

Surprisingly for so late in the year, Tuesday brought another fine day. We kept open house for the next-of-kin and many dropped in for coffee or a drink, but we only had eighteen for lunch, and most of them were officials, journalists, Red Cross or members of the crew. As expected, the Stanley folk welcomed the next-of-kin into their homes and were more than happy to provide lunch. It would be wrong to describe the atmosphere as festive; but it was certainly celebratory, like the feeling after an examination or a successful operation. Several of our guests told me that they felt a sense of relief, as if a great weight had been lifted from their shoulders.

Having seen where their son or husband had perished, they could now accept the finality of it all, and come to terms with it. All who spoke to me considered that the trip had been well worthwhile and, though doubtful before the visit, I was now convinced that it had been a wise decision. Not one of the bereaved expressed to me the view that their loved ones had been lost in vain.

As the *Cunard Countess* steamed out of Port Stanley, David, Mavis and I flew out by Gazelle and landed on board. I passed on the Prime Minister's message over the ship's Tannoy and thanked the Master, Colonel Love and the other officials for organising the visit. We then returned to the triangle, dropped Mavis, picked up Bishop Snell and saluted the *Cunard Countess* in Port William as we went to the airport to see off the Bishop in the Hercules.

The next day dawned cold and bleak, with an ominous wind from the south. We could not have been luckier with the weather for the next-of-kin visit. That afternoon, as David and I flew to the airport to meet his successor, Keith Spacie, it began to snow. The next two days were filled with Executive Council meetings and farewell parties for David. We were all very sad to see him go. In nine hectic months, he had achieved a tremendous amount for his troops and endeared himself to the Islanders. Councillors had been disappointed with MOD for refusing to allow his wife to join him over Christmas, since he had offered to stay longer if the request had been granted. They passed a resolution in Legislative Council deploring the MOD's decision, which said much for the regard in which they held David. Over the months, he had become a personal friend and we had built up a mutual trust and understanding. Nigel Thursby, the OC, No 658 Squadron, Army Air Corps, flew him with Mavis and me from the triangle to the airport, where a guard of honour was mounted by the Irish Rangers, who had just taken over from the Hampshires. A southerly wind was still blowing and it was bitterly cold as David said goodbye to his staff and to councillors before stepping on to the Hercules.

Mavis and I should have been following him in eleven days, but Destefanis was threatening to come and the FCO thought that it would be wiser if I stayed. As Diana was looking forward to having us with her for her twenty-first birthday on 2 May, Destefanis was not the most popular man in the Hunt family. We kept fingers crossed but, in the event, Mavis and Tony left on the 26th as planned and I had to stay on. Before that, however, we were able to celebrate the Queen's Birthday in style on 21 April. The Royal

Navy was represented by detachments from HMS *Cardiff* and HMS *Active*, the Royal Marines produced a contingent, the RAF was strongly represented and the Irish Rangers provided the band and an extremely smart section of infantry. The FIDF paraded in force and most of Stanley town turned out to watch.

The Queen's Birthday this year was special for them because last year they had to celebrate quietly in their own homes, under the noses of the Argentine occupation forces. As we gave three lusty cheers for the Queen, the captured Argentine vessel, the *Tiger Bay*, sailed past the saluting dais and the RAF provided a flypast of a Hercules flanked by a Harrier and a Phantom. Back at Government House, I presented honours to those who were unable to get to Buckingham Palace, and the South Atlantic medal to members of the FIDF. Keith Spacie presented me with mine, which fell off as soon as I went to walk away. This produced some ribald comment when we later repaird to the Drill Hall for the traditional drinks with the FIDF.

Next day, we held a meeting of Legislative Council to pass important Bills on the Falkland Islands Development Corporation and tax exemptions for airport construction workers. Keith Spacie was also sworn in and welcomed by councillors. Several minor amendments had been incorporated into the FIDC Bill and I only hoped that this would not lead to further delay. It was already almost eight months since the Prime Minister had presented Lord Shackleton's report to Parliament and all the interested parties had agreed in principle to the establishment of a development agency; but ODA was making heavy weather of getting it started.

Monsignor Spraggon had planned to go on leave with us and we had agreed to pick him up on the way to the airport. I do not know how it happened, but I did not remember this until Mavis and Tony were boarding the Hercules and the loadmaster said they were one short. Don started to dash back to Stanley, but fortunately Julian had come to Monsignor's rescue and was driving him to the airport in his Land Rover. I incurred the wrath of the RAF in keeping the Hercules waiting; but that was nothing to what Monsignor would have said had I caused him to miss it.

Over the next few days, various reports emanating from Buenos Aires indicated that Destefanis had chartered a vessel (some said with Argentine Government help) and was intending to sail for the Falklands with next-of-kin aboard. Keith Spacie and I discussed the problem of turning him back on the high seas without endangering passengers; it was not going to be easy. A report that his ship had left Buenos Aires came through at about the same time as the welcome news from the FCO that the Cabinet had confirmed the FIG view that Destefanis should not be permitted to land. Whether this influenced the Argentine Government or not we do not know, but on 29 April we heard that it had ordered Destefanis not to proceed with his plan. His ship wallowed in the South Atlantic for several more days until, on 5 May, we received reliable reports that he was heading back to Buenos Aires. He claimed on his return that he had landed on 'Islas Malvinas' and planted an Argentine flag, but his navigation must have been as erroneous as that of the early Spanish explorers who recorded the Falklands hundreds of miles from their correct position. We knew for a fact that he had not even penetrated the 150-mile protection zone.

With Destefanis safely back on the mainland, and thoroughly ridiculed to boot, I could now go on leave. Elspeth was leaving with me and her replacement, Sue Biggins, arrived by sea on the day of our departure. I was struck immediately by her composure and sense of humour and, as I was subsequently to discover, she was as professionally efficient as she was socially pleasant. Knowing the drill on the Hercules, I grabbed one of the forward stretchers and slept most of the way. We had a good tailwind and reached Ascension in ten hours forty minutes. The new Administrator, Ian Thow, took Elspeth and me up to the Residence and I was amazed at how green everything looked. Apparently they had had an unusually heavy downpour, which had temporarily transformed the lunar landscape. After breakfast on the terrace, looking down on a freshly washed Georgetown sparkling in the tropical sun, we drove back to Wideawake airfield past the new RAF camp, which had mushroomed since my last visit, and boarded the VC10 for Brize Norton. Again, we were lucky with the winds and landed after eight hours twenty minutes. Nineteen hours flying time from the Falklands to England – my best to date.

Notes
1. Fifth Report from the Foreign Affairs Committee, Session 1983-84, Falkland Islands.

2. Under the Antarctic Treaty, member states were obliged to circulate their programmes to other signatories.

19

Mount Pleasant: The Beginnings

It was good to be reunited with the family again, but I did not see much of them for the first two weeks, with appointments in the FCO, MOD, ODA and the Cabinet Office. I also spent some time with Adrian Monk, who was finding that being FIG's representative in London was more than a full-time job and warned me that he would not be able to stay for much longer. His health was suffering and he was spending too much time away from Nora and his smallholding in Wales. A possible successor was Alastair Cameron, but he was enjoying working for the FIG in Stanley and I did not know whether he would be willing to be considered for the post. Some councillors might also think that he was too young for such a responsible position. We were fortunate in having his sister, Sukey, in FIGO from its inception. She had worked voluntarily for the Falkland Islands Association during the war, knew her way round Whitehall and, being a Cameron and born in the Islands, she knew the Islanders and they knew her. She was essential for the smooth running of the office and I was delighted when she said that she would be happy to work for her brother if he was appointed.

On one of my visits to FIGO, I was delighted to find Monsignor Spraggon, looking in the best of health. He had forgiven me for forgetting to pick him up in Stanley and, together with Adrian and Sukey, we had a most enjoyable pub lunch in The Elephant and Castle. He was off to Rome for an audience with the Pope and the next time I saw him, towards the end of my leave, we were both at Buckingham Palace to receive our respective honours from the Queen.

Another dear friend who came over from the Falklands when we were on leave was Nanny. She had never been to England before; indeed, the only time she had left the Islands was to go for a holiday to Comodoro Rivadavia. I picked her up in Southampton. She looked at my Lotus a little apprehensively, but gamely folded herself into the front seat. There was a lot of traffic on the Winchester Road – more than she had ever seen in her life

– and she could not understand why we were all driving so fast. It was all utterly strange to her and she looked somewhat ill at ease until, as we passed Odiham, she saw a helicopter coming in to land. 'Ah, a Chinook!,' she said, beaming, 'I feel quite at home.' During her stay, we visited Cheryl Bonner in the Ockenden Venture home in Camberley. Cheryl smiled and her eyes lit up when Nanny spoke to her, but whether she recognised the Falklands' accent or Nanny herself, it was difficult to say. Nanny said that it would have made Doreen and Harry happy to see her so well cared for. After too brief a stay with us, Nanny went off to Ireland, as guest of her old employers, Sir Cosmo and Lady Haskard.

While Britain was being lashed by the media into election fever, we went touring on the continent until it was all over. As expected, the Conservative Party was returned with an increased majority. Mrs Thatcher made some changes to her Cabinet: Sir Geoffrey Howe took over the FCO from Mr Pym and Mr Michael Heseltine became Secretary of State for Defence. Baroness Young became the FCO minister responsible for Falkland Islands affairs, in place of Mr Cranley Onslow, and Mr John Stanley took Mr Jerry Wiggin's place in the MOD. I met them all before I went back and also had a good session with the Prime Minister. An immediate need was to secure the land for the airport. The decision to build at Mount Pleasant had been taken and a consortium consisting of John Laing Construction Limited, Mowlem International Limited and Amey Roadstone Construction Limited (LMA) invited to proceed. FIC were willing to sell the land but negotiations over the price looked as though they might be protracted. I explained that I had the power under Falklands' law to issue a compulsory acquisition order and the contractors could move in a month after my signature. The procedure existed after that date for compensation to be settled between the parties, with an independent arbitrator in the event of failure to agree. It was not, however, the Conservative Party's policy to use compulsory acquisition, save as a last resort, and they settled on a figure that worked out at about £29 an acre. To the Treasury Solicitors who negotiated the land purchase, £29 an acre must have sounded very reasonable, compared with British prices; but as the going rate for agricultural land in the Falklands at the time was from £12 to £14 an acre, it sounded exorbitant to the Islanders.

It was evident from my meeting with RAF officers and civil servants in the MOD that they were treating Mount Pleasant as just another RAF airfield, to which civilians would be allowed access (like Brize Norton), and they were planning accordingly. They even referred to it as RAF Mount Pleasant. I was at pains to point out that, as it would be the Heathrow of the Falklands, an international airport and the *only* means of entry and exit for civilians, it should be called Mount Pleasant Airport. I argued that the RAF would be there as the FIG's welcome guests for as long as a threat existed from Argentina but, if that threat should ever cease to exist, the airport would revert to civilian use and control. Of course the RAF would need secure areas, which would be out of bounds to unauthorised personnel, but civilians should have the right of entry into a terminal building and facilities for meeting and greeting. The plans should also allow for office space for the FIG's Director of Civil Aviation, Immigration, Customs and police officers. It was gratifying to receive the Prime Minister's support for the name of the airport, but it was to be a constant battle to preserve civilians' rights there. After my return to the Islands, I sought to secure the principle by arranging for the Attorney General to take over the title deeds from the FIC and sign them on behalf of the FIG. We then leased the land to the MOD.

Another contentious issue was the future of the BAS base at Grytviken. I came under strong pressure from the FCO to implement the agreement that we had signed before the war, which was made when BAS was facing a ten-per-cent cut and its members provided the only British presence on South Georgia. The picture had changed radically since then, with a military garrison at Grytviken and BAS not only being spared the ten-per-cent cut but also receiving (at the Prime Minister's behest) substantial extra funds. In the circumstances, I saw no reason to run down South Georgia's meagre reserves to finance a scientific base which, on Dick Laws' own admission, was BAS's least important.

ODA was continuing to make slow progress on the Falkland Islands Development Corporation. One of Lord Shackleton's basic recommendations was the creation of the post of Chief Executive, who would not only be responsible for the FIDC but also supervise the FIG departments through the Chief Secretary. We recognised that it would not be easy to find such a man: ideally, he should have experience in colonial administration and development organisations. ODA had employed a firm of 'head-hunters', whose recommended candidate had started a career in the colonial service in Tanganyika (as it was then) and gone into commerce on that country's independence. He was now a senior executive in Booker McConnell, with experience in developing their businesses overseas, but he had no experience of a government development agency. ODA suggested that he should come out to the Islands to see whether he would like the job and whether Islanders would like him. This was an excellent idea and so it happened that David Taylor accompanied us back to Stanley at the end of July, 1983.

Before that, however, we attended an investiture at Buckingham Palace. Those of us who were to be knighted were briefed on how to kneel before the Queen and then I was asked to join the other recipients of honours for services in the South Atlantic, who were due to receive their awards at the end of the ceremony. Monsignor Spraggon and Stuart Booth were the only other civilians from the Falklands. Stuart was receiving his OBE for a lifetime of dedicated public service, first as headmaster of the Stanley Senior School and then for many years as the Islands' librarian and a Justice of the Peace. The others were members of the armed forces who had performed acts of valour during the conflict or had made an outstanding contribution to the success of the Task Force. There was a buzz of excitement as the South Atlantic honours were announced and I felt both proud and humble to be the first of that distinguished band. The Queen bestowed my knighthood with the lightest of accolades and asked solicitously about the welfare of the Islanders. I was happy to be able to reassure her that they were in good heart and recovering from the trauma of occupation. After the investiture, Mavis, Tony and I were entertained to lunch by Baroness Vickers in the House of Lords and, as I took my morning suit back to Moss Bros in the afternoon, I wondered if I should ever get used to being called Sir Rex. It seemed so unreal and I was reminded of Sir Eric Norris's story of the little boy who greeted him quizzically, 'If you're a Knight, where's your shining armour?'

The introduction of a new post between the Civil Commissioner and Chief Secretary was a delicate matter. Throughout the colonies, the Chief Secretary had been traditionally number two to the Governor and acted for him in his absence. During my current leave, for example, Dick Baker was Acting Civil Commissioner. There was no problem with Dick, because he was leaving before the Chief Executive was appointed (in fact, he was already overdue but had selflessly extended his tour until my return); but it would be difficult to explain to his successor that he would be number three in the hierarchy. To ease the transition, I had long urged that the

Chief Executive should be in post before Dick's successor and that, to clarify the new arrangement, the title should be changed from Chief Secretary to Government Secretary. The FCO wished to appoint a Diplomatic Service officer to this post and, on hearing that Bernard Pauncefort (ex-Administrator, Ascension) was available, I asked for him. Before the end of my leave, this was agreed and we arranged to have lunch together, at which I carefully explained the revised hierarchy. To my relief, Bernard expressed himself perfectly content with his position and looked forward to a full tour in the Islands. Unfortunately, due to family commitments, he could not join me until about a month after Dick had gone – a gap we could ill afford. Even so, it was not until early December, 1983, that David Taylor was able to take up his post, by which time Bernard had become accustomed to the chief secretary's office and house and the Islanders had come to regard him as my number two. It said much for the tact and understanding of both that the transition was accomplished without friction and that they subsequently became an efficient and harmonious team.

David's first trip to Stanley was not one of the best. From Brize Norton to Ascension took over ten hours (via Dakar) and a very crowded Hercules took almost fourteen to Stanley. We did have a decent break, however, in Ascension. Ian Thow met us and took us up to the Residence, where we were delighted to find Cindy and Annie, who were spending several months in the island, filming wildlife for *Survival*. David spent a week in the Falklands and liked what he saw. He had reservations however, on two counts: as a bachelor, he was not sure that he would enjoy living in Stanley, and he had no experience of development corporations. I said that the councillors whom he had met had been favourably impressed and that, if he was prepared to take a risk with his first reservation, we were prepared to take a risk with the second. Happily both proved unfounded and David proceeded to enjoy over three years of fruitful and productive work for the Falklands.[1]

One of my first and pleasurable duties after returning was to hand over two Brewster houses to townsfolk who had lost theirs during the war. The recipients' reactions could not have been more diametrically opposed. The first family were so grateful and delighted they could not find the words to express their appreciation. They acknowledged that the house was infinitely superior to the one they had lost and could not believe their good fortune. The second grumbled and moaned about everything: the fence was not strong enough, there was no lagging on the pipes, there was no fire escape, they had wanted a bungalow, not a house, snow would get under the roof – the list was endless. For an exercise in ingratitude, it took some beating. Thank goodness I knew Islanders well enough to realise that this one was untypical. Patrick Watts, who was covering the ceremony for the local radio, switched off his microphone and walked away in disgust. Other Islanders apologised to me for the man's attitude, for which he was well known.

There had been slow but steady progress in Stanley in my absence. All the Brewster houses were complete on Sir Jeremy Moore Avenue and work had started on the remainder on Callaghan Road. The heavy duty circuit of town roads was more than half finished. This work was being carried out by civilian contractors (Fairclough's), with the object of providing a route through town of concrete roads designed to take the heaviest vehicles. Unfortunately, it had come too late for most of the main Stanley roads, which had given up the unequal struggle. The potholes were bigger and the mud thicker than ever before. Work was also in hand on the airport road but, in a mistaken attempt to save money, ODA had specified a spray-and-chip surface (and too thin a coating at that) when what was needed to cope with the heavy traffic was tarmac or concrete. On the airport itself, Fairclough's had completed a new taxiway for the Islanders. The old one had been destroyed by the RAF and the Royal Engineers had undertaken to replace it but, with reduced numbers, they were now hard pressed to meet even the immediate military requirements. Both Islanders were flying, as well as the Beaver, and spirits in FIGAS were high. I flew with Andy Alsop and soon realised why he was so popular with the people in camp. He handled both the Islander and its passengers with consummate skill. Nothing was too much trouble: he carried the luggage, helped people in and out of the aircraft and showed them how to fasten their seat-belts, all with a friendly smile and reassuring banter guaranteed to put the most nervous passenger at ease.

On the military front, Keith Spacie briefed me on recent Argentine incursions into the 150-mile Falkland Islands Protection Zone (FIPZ). There had been two by a Lockheed Electra reconnaissance aircraft, and three by trawlers. We deduced that their object was twofold: to check our reaction time and to manufacture propaganda to use against us at the forthcoming UN debate. Our Phantoms had flown alongside and photographed the Electra, which had not loitered in the FIPZ. Nor had the trawlers.

There was still a strong Royal Navy presence, though most of the ships had changed since I left. On our first ship's visit, to HMS *Birmingham*, we met Keith's wife, Valerie, who had arrived while we were on leave. She was the first service wife to join her husband in the Falklands, shortly to be followed by a few others on CBFFI's staff. In return, of course, accompanied officers served longer tours, which was highly desirable for continuity. Undoubtedly, more would have opted for accompanied tours had we been able to make more houses available, but it was simply not possible. Even when all the Brewster houses were occupied, we should still have a waiting list of over sixty civilians. Many householders were still doubling up or accommodating lodgers. Indeed, the night of our visit to HMS *Birmingham* was the first time that Mavis and I had had Government House to ourselves since before the war. Alastair Cameron, our last house-guest, moved in with Archie Mitchell, the first manager of the Standard Chartered Bank, which had bought Jack Abbott's house.

All too soon it was time for Dick and Connie to leave. They had met us on our first arrival in 1980 and we had been through some stirring times together. Dick was a devoted colonial administrator, a loyal first lieutenant and a good companion. He carried a huge burden in the Secretariat and rarely did less than a 60-hour week. Connie gave him maximum support, helped Mavis with the entertaining and at the same time managed to bring up two charming daughters. They were popular in the Islands and would be sorely missed. It was typical of Dick that he left without fuss. He, Connie, Karen and Helen stood with the rest of the civilians in the cold and wet on the open deck of a harbour work-boat as it took them from the public jetty to the *Uganda* in Port William. They deserved a better send-off.

In my weekly talks with Keith, it soon became apparent that we did not see eye to eye on a number of basic issues. His interpretation of our respective positions under the Order-in-Council was different from mine. This led to difficulties of protocol, which I was prepared to overlook for the sake of good relations: but, more importantly, it led him to pursue a policy of distancing the military from the civilians. He wanted his own hospital, radio studio and police station, and all troops out of Stanley. What David Thorne had called 'a suitable degree of separation' became for Keith complete divorce. His theme was that the civilians should not be allowed to become too dependent upon the military, otherwise they would never stand on their own feet. I could not convince him that Falkland Islanders were the most independent people on earth and were canny enough to benefit from the military while they were there, but resourceful enough to adjust once they had departed. Nor could I convince him that the UK was a more appropriate model for the Falklands than Germany or Cyprus. Indeed, he even followed the example of our military rulers in occupied Germany immediately after the Second World war and forbade his staff to fraternise with mine (needless to say, his order had no effect: my secretary Sue carried on seeing his cook; they are now happily married with two children).

One consequence of Keith's attitude was that senior military visitors came and went without my meeting them. Another was that my military visits, which had been encouraged before, now became curtailed, although of course I continued to attend the weekly briefing at HQBFFI and Keith attended (and made a valuable contribution to) Executive and Legislative Councils. At my first Joint Rehabilitation Committee since returning from leave, I was surprised to find that the only military personnel present were the Deputy Chief of Staff and the Commander, Royal Engineers. In my absence, the committee had been downgraded. It was perhaps time to rename it and to meet less frequently, but in my view a regular meeting of top officials from FIG and officers from BFFI was essential, and I was glad when Keith agreed to its reconstitution as the Joint Liaison Committee. He would not agree, however, to another of my suggestions: namely, that I should accompany him to welcome the troops on board the ships bringing them from Ascension. I considered it my duty, on behalf of the Falkland Islands Government and all Falkland Islanders, not only to welcome the troops on arrival but also to thank them when they left. To my regret, I was unable to do this until Peter de la Billière replaced Keith in June, 1984.

We now had two regular sailings a month to and from Ascension in the *Uganda* and the *St Edmund*. Both were familiar sights in Falkland waters: *Uganda* had been the main hospital ship for the Task Force, and *St Edmund* (now renamed the MV *Keren*) had been one of the two dormitory ships anchored in Port Stanley. With the arrival of the second coastel, the remaining dormitory ship, the *Rangatira*, was able to lift its rusting anchor and sail away. We gave a farewell luncheon for the Captain, Pat Liddell and some of his officers, who had made their home in Stanley harbour for the last fifteen months. They had entered wholeheartedly into the life of the local community and we were sorry to see them go.

The absence of the dormitory ships from the harbour did not, however, relieve the congestion. 'B' slip was the bottleneck and ships were queueing up in Port William, waiting to unload. Everything had to be taken ashore by Mexeflote and, as military supplies and equipment had priority, civilian cargoes had to wait. The Standard Chartered Bank building, for example, arrived in early September but could not be unloaded until the end of October. Although the bulk of the construction equipment for the new airport was to be unloaded at Mare Harbour, it would be two or three years before all military cargoes could be handled there. MOD came up with a brilliant interim solution: the Falklands Intermediate Port and Storage System (FIPASS). This consisted of six large oil-rig barges, four of which had huge warehouses built upon their decks and two provided jetty space. They were securely moored to piles driven deep into the harbour bottom and joined to the shore by a Bailey-type bridge. Unloading facilities included provision for Ro-Ro cargo vessels as well as the more orthodox ships and the depth of water at the jetty head enabled any ship that could get through the Narrows to tie up alongside. Built in Middlesbrough, it was costly – over £20 million – but it saved a tremendous amount of demurrage charges and more than justified the expenditure.

One of Lord Shackleton's recommendations had been the construction of a new all-purpose jetty, allowing the unloading of ships of up to eight metres draught, at an estimated cost of £3½ million. We knew from previous surveys that the only way to provide Stanley with a really satisfactory deep-water jetty was to build it in Port William. As this would mean building an access road to the Camber, the total cost would eat up far more of the £31 million development grant than we could spare. The ODA had commissioned yet another feasibility study on the subject but, apart from that, no progress had been made. The arrival of FIPASS changed our thinking: if FIG could take it over when MOD had finished with it, there would be no need to build another jetty. Battered and damaged and inadequate as our existing jetties were, we should make do with them until we knew the future of FIPASS.[2]

This caused us some embarrassment with the generous government and people of Jersey, who had donated £5 million for 'the recovery and rehabilitation' of the Falklands and were naturally interested to know how their money had been spent. I had argued all along that the £5 million should have been handed over to the FIG so that the elected representatives of the Islanders could decide on a worthy project for it. However, the FCO said that the money (less £250,000 contributed to the Falklands Appeal) had gone into HMG coffers and was part of the £16 million already allocated for rehabilitation; all that was now required was FIG's identification of a suitable project that could be attributed to Jersey. We replied that there was no single project in the rehabilitation programme that could neatly be so ascribed. The FCO then asked us to nominate a project from the £31 million development programme and we chose the jetty because we estimated that the cost would approximate to the Jersey donation. With no new jetty in prospect by the time I left the Islands in 1985, the patient people of Jersey were still waiting to hear how their money had been spent.[3]

Shortly after Jersey had announced its donation to the Falklands, Guernsey followed suit. The States of Guernsey decided initially to donate £250,000 but later,having heard what had happened to the Jersey donation, reduced it to £100,000. In correspondence with the Bailiff, I suggested that he might tie the donation to a specific project and, after further discussion, we agreed on sheltered accommodation for the elderly. In this way, we were able to avoid the confusion and embarrassment that had arisen over the Jersey donation.[4]

The first minister to visit the Islands since the general election was Mr John Stanley, Minister of State for the Armed Forces. Having spoken to him in London, I knew that he was keen to meet as many Islanders as possible; yet we had the greatest difficulty in persuading HQBFFI to accept any civilian input to his programme. Naturally, the main purpose of his visit was to see the troops on the ground and the warships at sea, but he had given himself enough time – a whole week – also to see something of the Islands and Islanders. Eventually, I think we got the right mix and the visit was successful from everyone's point of view. He took after the Prime Minister in his appetite for work, cramming a tremendous amount into seven long days. Mavis found him one of the most agreeable and considerate of guests and his genuine liking for the Falklands came over to the Islanders. Many of them had assumed that he was descended from Lord Stanley, after whom Port Stanley was named, but he explained that there was no such evidence in his family tree. However, he was to forge strong links with the Islands during his term of office, visiting them four times. He was a kindred spirit in his love of wildlife; fortunately he had more time than the Prime Minister and was able to visit New Island, one of the best for penguins, seals and sea-birds.

During his stay, the RAF suffered a tragic loss. Mr Stanley had spent the night on board HMS *Bristol* and I was flying by Islander to join him at San Carlos. It was a lovely day, but there was low cloud over Mount Usborne. We heard on landing that one of the Phantoms had gone straight into it, killing the pilot and navigator instantly. Mr Stanley rearranged his programme to attend the memorial service in Christ Church Cathedral two days later. We had a meeting of Joint Councils that morning so all the councillors were also able to attend. The cathedral was packed, with both servicemen and civilians, who regarded the loss as one of their own family. There was never any complaint about the noise of Phantoms – the 'sound of freedom' was the Islanders' description – and aircrew were always welcome guests in Stanley homes and in camp. The loss of two well-known and experienced flyers, not to mention an expensive aircraft, came as a grim reminder of the continuing price of that freedom. Sadly it was to be brought home to Islanders again a few weeks later, when a low-flying Harrier crashed in Lafonia, killing the pilot.

One item in Mr Stanley's programme was to witness a platoon attack, using live ammunition, on Hornby range. This was a chunk of Chartres farm of between 20,000 to 25,000 acres, which Bill Luxton had offered to BFFI in gratitude to the Task Force at a nominal rent of £1 a year. It was unique in that nowhere else in the world could British warships, aircraft and ground forces exercise jointly with live ammunition.

My most abiding memory of Mr Stanley's first visit was Mount Pleasant. We landed by helicopter in a small paddock next to Mount Pleasant shanty. This was a small outside shepherd's hut, not now occupied on a regular basis but used occasionally by shepherds from Fitzroy when lamb marking or gathering in the area. We were met by the PSA representative, Maurice Chammings, who was to supervise the whole operation in the field from beginning to end. A giant of a man, with a ready smile and a soft Westcountry accent, he was ideal for the job. He showed us on his plans where the main runway was to be and the route of the feeder road from Mare Harbour, then we boarded the helicopter and traced them from the air. It required a huge leap of the imagination to picture that peaceful land a hive of activity, yet already the pioneer workforce was on its way from the UK in the Cunard ship *England*, together with the *Merchant Providence*, which was to fulfil the role of jetty head for the unloading of all the plant, equipment and material needed to build the airport. Everything had to be imported except the stone, which it was hoped would be found in sufficient quantity and quality locally.

The coming of the austral summer saw the return of our regular visitors: the BAS ships *John Biscoe* and *Bransfield*, and the tourist ships the *World Discoverer* and the *Lindblad Explorer*. Captain Aye announced with great sadness that the *World Discoverer* would not be returning to Stanley after the current season. Her new owners had decided that she would be more profitably employed in the Pacific. He did not relish the prospect of presiding over a floating gambling casino and night club, which was what he said his ship would become, and much preferred his present nature-loving passengers to the sort that such activities would attract. Eric Lars Lindblad on the other hand saw an expanding future for adventure tours and had plans to acquire two more ships for operation in the South Atlantic.

As usual, we allowed Government House to be used for a reception for all the *Lindblad Explorer*'s passengers – all, that is, except for one stowaway, who was no other than our old friend Destefanis. Captain Neilsson had warned us that he had discovered Destefanis aboard when they were one day out from the mainland and had readily acceded to our request that he be kept locked in a cabin while in Falkland waters. To assist the captain, Bill Richards had flown to New Island and boarded the *Lindblad Explorer* to ensure that Destefanis did not go ashore with other passengers there or at Carcass or Volunteer Point, which were their other stopping places. On arrival in Port Stanley, Bill had put a police guard on Destefanis's cabin, where it remained until the *Lindblad Explorer* sailed again. On return to Argentina, Destefanis once more claimed that he had landed on Falkland soil and planted the national flag.

Bill Richards' opposite number in the Military Police at this time was Ken Greenland, who liked the Falklands and said that he would be prepared to leave the army and return if there was a job for him. As Bill wished to rejoin the Metropolitan Police some time before his retirement and there was no other Islander sufficiently qualified or experienced to take his place, this seemed an admirable arrangement. In due course, Ken secured his release and returned to Stanley as Chief Police Officer.

The last day of 1983 saw the *Lindblad Explorer* back in Stanley (without Destefanis) for a New Year's Eve party at Government House. One of the passengers on this trip was Mr (now Sir) Jack Hayward, from the Bahamas, where he was known as 'Union Jack' because of his patriotism and the lavish hospitality he gave to visiting British warships. By way of returning his kindness, we were able to arrange a conducted battlefield tour by 'teeny-weeny airways'. Major Peter McQueen picked us up in a Gazelle at the triangle in the morning and we flew first over Mount Kent to San Carlos, where we paid our respects at the cemetery and had smoko with Pat and Isabel Short. From there we flew along 2 Para's route to Goose Green, receiving as we flew a most dramatic and lucid account of the battle from Major McQueen. We landed at Darwin for lunch with Brook and Eileen, who welcomed five extra guests at short notice without the slightest concern, and retraced Colonel H's last steps. After refuelling, we flew over Mount Pleasant (where Keith Spacie was cutting the first turf on the main runway) to Fitzroy and the Welsh Guards' memorial. Finally, we followed the Scots Guards' route to Tumbledown, then over Two Sisters, Longdon and Wireless Ridge before circling Stanley airport, the Canache and the harbour and returning to the triangle. It was a fitting way to end the year, a reminder of the sacrifices made and the hope of things to come. Jack thanked me for a truly memorable day. He had always been a strong supporter of the Falklands, but I did not realise at the time what a great friend and benefactor he was to become in the new year.

Notes

1. Indeed, he was tempted back again in 1988, when his successor left at short notice.

2. The FIG bought FIPASS from the MOD in 1988.

3. A new housing estate, built in 1988-9 from fishing revenues, was named the Jersey Estate in gratitude to the people of Jersey. The new water filtration plant, built as part of the £31 million development programme, was also ascribed to the Jersey donation.

4. Sheltered accommodation for the elderly was built as an adjunct to the new hospital. Part of it was named after Guernsey and the Bailiff attended the opening ceremony in December, 1987.

20

Ice and Fire

We celebrated the formal reopening of the Stanley golf course on New Year's Day, 1984. A few enthusiasts had worked hard to cut the greens and fairways, and smart new flags adorned the holes. The main driving force was an army physical education instructor, Mike Kempson, who spent most of his spare time on the course and managed somehow to produce such unlikely pieces of equipment as a heavy roller and vibrator. For the 'Open', he found a marquee and persuaded some of his friends in the Catering Corps to provide a buffet lunch. The hot sun shone and the cold wind blew on twenty-four competitors – more, I was told, than at any time since 1933. The winner was a young merchant navy crewman from the *Avelona Star*, Paul Mooney, and the field was truly international in that two American passengers from the *Lindblad Explorer* competed. They were thrilled to play on the most southerly golf course in the world.

Our first VIP visitor in the new year was Lady Young, Minister of State in the FCO. In six days she visited eleven settlements and several military units, met councillors and a large cross-section of the Islanders, and saw the progress at Mount Pleasant. Maurice Chammings welcomed us aboard the *Merchant Providence*, which was now firmly secured to the shore and handling a tremendous amount of cargo across its deck. In twelve short weeks, the contractors had built twenty miles of road and their huge earthmovers were attacking the peat and blue clay on the runway site itself. The quartzite quarry on Mount Pleasant and the tillite quarry near March Ridge were working twenty-four hours a day to supply the hundreds of thousands of tonnes of stone needed. The rock was harder than expected and drilling bits had to be replaced more frequently than the planners had anticipated; nevertheless, thanks to the ubiquitous Hercules, they remained on target.

Lady Young was philosophical about the vagaries of the weather and problems with transport. A sudden squall caught us out in the open, looking at rockhoppers and albatrosses on New Island, and we were soaked and battered by the hail and sleet. While waiting for the Bristow helicopter, one of Lady Young's staff found the ground collapsing beneath him and was surprised to see two fat baby penguins scuttling from under his feet. He had inadvertently trodden on a jackass burrow (I did not tell him about the fleas). Bristow's flew us to Fox Bay West, where the tail rotor went unserviceable, so it was back to the bumpy old Land Rover (by courtesy of Shirley Knight) for a half-hour drive to Fox Bay East. The day before, HMS *Yarmouth*'s Wasp had refused to start at a Rapier site overlooking San Carlos Water, but a Gazelle had come to our rescue and taken us to HMS *Apollo* for lunch. On that same trip, we also flew by Sea King and Islander, leaving only the Chinook and the Beaver for the minister to experience.

About 200 people turned up to the public meeting in the Town Hall. Perhaps they were expecting too much after the Prime Minister the previous year, but there was adverse comment afterwards. The general consensus was that the 'Foreign Office' was being faint-hearted again and unnecessarily negative over the fisheries issue, which was a pity, because in Lady Young the Islanders had a good friend and staunch supporter.

Two days after her departure, the Secretary of State for Defence, Mr Michael Heseltine, arrived. He came for a shorter time (three days) but with a bigger posse of Press. His party included his Parliamentary Private Secretary, Mr Keith Hampson, and the Deputy Chief of Air Staff, Air Vice Marshal Sir Peter Harding. His first day was entirely military, ending with dinner on board one of HM warships; but Keith Hampson ducked out of this and asked me to take him on a pub crawl in Stanley, to savour civil/military relations at a lower level. We visited the Globe, the Victory Bar and the Rose, received from many civilians, soldiers, sailors and airmen their candid comments and found none of the animosity that some British newspapers had reported.

On the second day, we started with an early visit to the hospital, where I saw poor Alan Miller for the last time,[1] and then flew from the triangle to Mount Pleasant. I was amazed at the progress in only a week. Mr Heseltine lowered the first ablutions unit into place, like a giant piece of Lego, to mark the beginning of the main contractor's camp. Within three months it had sufficient accommodation to house a thousand men. The units were prefabricated by Wyesplan

Limited and could be assembled in single or double stories. They were planned for use as servicemen's permanent accommodation after the contractors had finished.

From Mount Pleasant we flew to San Carlos, where Mr Heseltine and Sir Peter Harding laid wreaths at the cemetery, called at a Rapier site on the ridge above and then went west to Hill Cove for lunch with Tim and Sally Blake and all the other councillors, who had assembled there for an informal meeting with the Secretary of State. There was also a military presence there, for Tim had agreed to the settlement's use as an adventure training and leisure centre for the troops, as well as one of the main helicopter refuelling bases in West Falkland. After lunch we attempted to get to the radar site on Byron Heights, but failed due to low cloud. There followed a frustrating afternoon, with the cloud beating us wherever we tried to get in. Mr Heseltine, a keen naturalist, wanted to see something of our wildlife and the best spots near to Byron Heights were Westpoint and Carcass. We watched with dismay as, ahead of us, the clouds rolled in and covered both islands. Next on the programme was the radar site on Mount Alice, but here again the clouds beat us to it. Coming back low over Falkland Sound, we were passing Great Island when the Secretary of State espied a gentoo colony. The versatility of the helicopter was once again demonstrated: in less than a couple of minutes we had landed and were striding over to the colony. Frightened jackass bolted for their burrows, but the gentoo held their ground, the young chicks trying to hide under their parents, not realising that they had already outgrown them. Mr Heseltine was delighted, but eager for more. We made for Volunteer Point, but again the clouds beat us. On the way back to Stanley, we dropped down at Berkeley Sound to see a rockhopper colony and landed back at the triangle only minutes before the clouds caught up with us again.

That evening, Mr Heseltine asked for more and I advised that, if he was prepared for a very early start, we were certain of a truly spectacular sight at Beauchene. He jumped at the chance and so it was that, at 4.45 the next morning, I was knocking up our guests. One of Bristow's helicopters took us there in an hour, and Mr Heseltine was not disappointed. If anything, there were even more rockhoppers and albatrosses than on my previous visit. From Beauchene we returned direct to Goose Green in time to fulfil his arranged programme.

After a Press conference at battalion headquarters, which had now moved from Stanley to Goose Green, I was delighted to meet up again with Jeff Cooper, who had been at Cranwell with me in 1945. He had stayed in the RAF, retiring as Air Commodore, and was now the *Daily Telegraph* air correspondent. We flew back to Stanley together, where we held another Press conference, this time on civilian matters. It went very well except for criticism of the cost of and delay in completing the Brewster houses. The Secretary of State travelled home that evening non-stop in a Nimrod maritime reconnaissance aircraft, breaking the record in the process.

The following week was a sad one, with memorial services for Captain Belt and Sergeant Jones of the Army Air Corps, who had been killed when their Gazelle crashed in bad weather; Alan Miller and Dot Cheek, Fred's wife and mother of John and Gerald. We also had the parents of Leading Seaman Mills, who had been tragically killed on board HMS *Fife* in a missile-firing accident. They bore their loss with great fortitude and had nothing but praise for the way in which the Royal Navy had looked after them. Mavis and I flew out to HMS *Fife* a little later in their Lynx. Over Teal Inlet, I noticed that the pilot shut down one engine. Mavis raised her eyebrows and I explained that it was probably because David Barton had complained about low-flying helicopters (he had had to shoot one of his horses when, frightened by a passing aircraft, it had injured itself trying to leap out of the paddock) and the pilot wished to reduce the noise level. In the event, we stayed on one engine until over *Fife*'s helicopter deck, where Mavis was alarmed to see men in white foam suits, fire extinguishers at the ready and every indication of an emergency. We landed safely and the pilot explained that one engine had lost pressure and he had shut it down as a precautionary measure; the activity on deck was the normal drill for an emergency landing.

Our next visitors should have been two Members of the European Parliament, Sir Henry Plumb and Mr Bob Battersby but, at the last minute, Sir Henry could not get away. Mr Battersby proved a lively and entertaining house-guest and, as the European member for Humberside, was interested in our fisheries potential. We arranged a visit for him to one of the Polish ships in Berkeley Sound, after which he reinforced our belief that the sooner we got a 200-mile zone the better.

The time had come for our annual trip to the South on HMS *Endurance*. Sue had been working hard since my return from leave and Colin MacGregor kindly invited her to join us. Leaving David Taylor in charge, we boarded the *Endurance* and sailed out of a virtually empty harbour. We passed only two ships, the *Fort Toronto* (still dispensing fresh water) and the *G A Walker* (base fuel tanker) in Port William and the tug *Irishman* heading into Port Stanley. There were no Commerson's dolphins to escort us through the Narrows but, a little further out, we saw scores of dead penguins – jackass and gentoo – floating in the water. Our report sparked off an investigation, which attributed the cause to captured ordnance being exploded too close to the penguins' feeding grounds. Thereafter, instructions were given to take dangerous cargo further out to sea before exploding or dumping it. The birdlife round and behind the ship was as varied and plentiful as before: the first wanderers joined us less than one day out and storm petrels and pintados appeared a day later. Our first landfall was Elephant Island, after a relatively easy crossing of Drake Passage. The cloud was very low and we did not see Cape Valentine – where Shackleton first landed – until we were within two miles of the shore. The cloud base was too low for flying and the sea too rough to lower a boat, so we could not go ashore. There was no need, however, to set foot on land to see the penguins: there were hundreds of chinstraps porpoising round the ship, like shoals of flying fish. There were also hundreds of pintados swooping on the water like swallows and a few of the lovely dove prions.

Running along the south coast of Elephant Island, we came across a Russian factory ship, with two big stern trawlers tied alongside. The captain spoke good English and we exchanged greetings as we passed. The following morning we arrived at King George Island, steamed past the Polish base, Arctowski, and went ashore by boat at the old British base in Admiralty Bay. We were surprised to find new huts there, belonging to Brazil. Twelve Brazilians welcomed us with cans of 'Antarctica' Brazilian beer. They had inaugurated the base eight days ago and planned to batten it down and go home for the winter, returning to expand it next summer and have a permanent garrison thereafter. Though in civilian clothes, they were all Brazilian Marines. We found the old British hut damp but sound, with a store of groceries that still looked edible. Colin and I walked up the hill to the four crosses marking the graves of FIDS personnel. Tink Bell's had been blown over so we restored it as best we could. He had fallen down a crevasse in 1959. In the same year his colleague, Alan Sharman, had been knocked over by huskies, slid out of control and fallen over a rock cliff. Eric Platt had died of a heart attack in 1948. About the other cross, marked 'Gordon', we could find no details or background. Down on the beach near the British hut, the skeleton of a blue whale, carefully reconstructed and laid out by Commander Cousteau for one of his films, remained recognisable and largely intact.

Returning to the *Endurance*, we found that the wind had dropped to permissible limits for the Wasps to operate and, after a quick change to replace wet clothing, we flew to Arctowski. This was a large, well-established base, staffed by thirteen Poles with one West German and eight Brazilian guests. The Polish team included two attractive women, both working scientists in their own right, though one was also the wife of the Polish krill expert, Professor Edward Kilakowski. They made us most welcome and plied us with vodka and coffee. Lunch included fresh tomatoes, peppers and lettuce grown in their own greenhouse. Back on the ship, the wardroom had a surprise party waiting for Colin, who had not divulged that it was his birthday. Several of the Poles and Brazilians were able to join us and a jolly evening ensued.

Our next landfall was Deception Island, lower down the South Shetland group, but there was a Force 9 gale, even inside the lagoon, and we could not land. The Chilean hut was occupied and two men braved the elements to dip their flag in response to our salute. There was no sign of life at the Argentine base in Fumarole Bay. Colin could find no safe anchorage, so we battled our way through Neptune's Bellows again and out into the open sea. Skirting Brabant, we found refuge the next morning in the lee of Anvers Island and paid a courtesy call on Palmer Station. Hospitable as they always were, I think the Americans would rather we had given them a miss, for they had received eighteen ships' visits in the last two months. The base commander, Phil Calvert, outlined their expansion plans: they had forty-four berths at present (thirty-nine occupied) and would have room for sixty-six in 1985 and ninety in 1986. Their scientific work was mainly in the maritime sciences, but they were also looking at pollutants and their effect on the ozone layer. He said that their Zodiacs were still attacked from time to time by leopard seals – a remark that I could not dismiss wholly from my mind as we went later by the smaller Gemini to an Adelie penguin colony across the bay.

We hoisted anchor about lunchtime and sailed through the Neumayer Channel to Port Lockroy, another abandoned British base. The bay provided a marvellous anchorage, but there was insufficient snow on land for Colin's purpose, which was to stage a Winter Olympics. Accepting that we should have to go further south for snow, we retraced our route through the Neumayer Channel and sailed down the even more spectacular Lemaire Channel. The weather was still bad, with low cloud and sleet, but it was not snowing, so there were no snowball fights this time. We passed superb icebergs and Adelies, crabeater and leopard seals in abundance.

Mavis's birthday, 17 February, found us off Brabant, waiting for the weather to abate before taking mail and supplies to the Joint Services Expedition, which was spending two years on the island, climbing hitherto unscaled peaks and carrying out scientific investigations. Flying commenced in the late morning, but Mavis could not come ashore with us because she had hacked her shin on an iron bulkhead and had difficulty in walking. The expedition's leader, Chris Furse, had pitched his camp on a small saddle surrounded by chinstrap penguins. Indeed, the landing pad was in the middle of a colony. The smell was overpowering, but Chris said that they had become used to it. It seemed, too, that the chinstraps had got used to the camp: they scurried away as we landed, but regrouped and settled down again as soon as the helicopter had gone. The wind was still blowing hard and bitterly cold, so I quickly declared open the Brabant Post Office and we all piled into one of the small bell tents. There was Colin, Sue, me, the ship's photographer, Chris Furse and Ted Atkins, a member of the expedition from RAF Gutersloh and cook for the day. He produced an excellent potmess, made from the supplies we had left in 1981 and washed down with tea and malt whisky. With our combined body heat and two Primuses going, we soon had to peel off anoraks and sweaters. I was surprised at how snug and comfortable the small tent could be, even with six occupants; but this was summer. Chris, Ted and the expedition photographer, Jed Corbett, intended to winter over. Chris handed me three first-day covers franked with the Brabant Post Office chop and addressed to the Prince of Wales, Captain MacGregor and myself. After lunch, we walked through the chinstraps down to the fur seals on the beach. The weather was marginal for flying and we had to beat a somewhat hasty retreat when the Wasps came for us ahead of time; but it had been an unforgettable visit.

We sailed from Brabant Island to the BAS base at Rothera, which was south of the Antarctic Circle, on Adelaide Island. During this passage, the various messes were putting the finishing touches to their toboggans and designing outlandish outfits for the *dressage* competition, which took place on the flight deck before the teams went ashore for the *Endurance* Winter Olympics. There were some ingenious designs and Mavis had difficulty in selecting the winners. Finally the weather cleared and we were able to go ashore by Gemini at about midday. Mt Gaudry (8,490ft) made a magnificent backdrop to the base, which was attractively situated in a sheltered bay on the southeast side of the island. The base commander, John Hall, met us at the quayside and showed us round. It was larger than the other BAS bases because it was used as the jumping-off spot for virtually all the summer field expeditions. Though not so far south as Halley Bay, it was more accessible and, with the Twin Otter aircraft, opened up a large part of Antarctica for detailed investigation. It was also the only BAS base that still had huskies. John introduced us to them after lunch. They were truly magnificent dogs, soft and affectionate with humans but fierce – indeed, murderous – with each other. They were tethered on long leads, just out of reach of their neighbour. Despite the convenience of Snocats and Skidoos, the huskies were still firm favourites among BAS members. They brought a whiff of the old way of life in the frozen wastes.

Activities on the ramp to the left of the base brought a different flavour, rather a mixture of Hampstead Heath and the nursery slopes of a popular ski resort. The Ski MacGee frolics had begun. After an exceptionally mild winter, the snow was soft and sticky and several events had to be cancelled, including the tray race. We could not find a single tray or plastic bag that would slide more than a few yards. Some of the toboggans, however, ran well and finished the course. One ran too well: a couple of BAS men were trying it out after the races were over and it sped out of control into the crowd, knocking over an unfortunate bystander and breaking his leg. There was much mirth among the Senior Rates when they discovered that the poor victim was POMA (medical assistant) Kevin Mitchell, who had earlier reproved them for indulging in reckless games and warned that he would regard any injury as self-inflicted and refuse to treat it. There was sympathy, of course, when the doctor announced that the fracture was complicated and needed specialised treatment.

Thus began one of the most remarkable rescue operations in Antarctic history. Kevin was flown from HMS *Endurance* by Wasp to the BAS skiway, about two miles from Rothera, where a Twin Otter was waiting to take him to the Chilean base of Rodolfo Marsh, on King George Island. Meanwhile, RAF Stanley despatched a Hercules to collect him from Rodolfo Marsh and fly him to Stanley in time to catch the air bridge to Ascension, from where he was transported by VC 10 to Brize Norton and then whisked down to the Royal Navy hospital at Haslam (Portsmouth). The accident occurred on Sunday, 19 February. The travelling arrangements were made on Monday, he left HMS *Endurance* Tuesday morning and was in hospital in Portsmouth by Thursday, 23 February. Less than three days to travel almost 10,000 miles from one of the remotest spots on earth. It was bad luck for Kevin, but comforting for all the naval and BAS personnel down south to know that, in an emergency, they were less than three days from home.

At John Hall's invitation, I spent the Sunday night ashore, in a sleeping bag in his cabin. After the movement of the ship, sleep did not come easily. Next morning, Gary Studd, BAS senior pilot, took Colin and me by Snocat to the skiway, where a Twin Otter stood knee-deep in fresh snow. We cleared away enough to be able to climb aboard and Gary carried out his daily inspection, but the cloud base was too low for flying. This was particularly galling for me, since it was the only opportunity I ever had of flying in a Twin Otter in Antarctica. On our way back to the base, Gary said that his home airfield was Biggin Hill but that the BAS aircraft were serviced and based for the austral winter at Fairoaks, which was the nearest airfield to our home in Sunningdale. It seemed an awfully long way to fly twice a year, but all the options had been considered and BAS had decided that this was the best way of preserving their aircraft. They took the northerly route across the Atlantic, then down through Canada, the USA, Central America and the western seaboard of South America. Normally they had no problems but, immediately after the war with Argentina, someone had tried to sabotage their aircraft in Peru by putting sugar in the fuel tanks. Fortunately, they had spotted the trouble and rectified it in time.

After lunch on the base, I walked round the point, being dive-bombed by skuas and revelling in the marvellous views. Crabeaters, leopard seals and Adelies adorned the scene, but the best was yet to come. That evening, back on board and about three miles out of Rothera, we had our first good sighting of humpback whales.

There were four of these massive beasts, which measure over 50ft in length and weigh at least 60 tonnes, about a hundred yards from the ship, moving leisurely, not breaching but blowing and going down with a flourish of their huge tails, like ducks up-ending themselves on a pond.

In view of the mild winter, Colin decided to try to force The Gullet, a narrow channel to the north of Rothera separating Adelaide Island from Arrowsmith Peninsula on the mainland. The *Endurance* had never managed to do this before. The senior pilot, John Farmar, took me up in one of the Wasps to survey the route. Visibility was good and the scenery breathtaking. There was plenty of pack ice, but it appeared to be loose and we spotted one or two possible leads. On our way back, John put down on an ice floe. The Wasp sank to its axles in the snow and I to my ankles as I jumped out to take a photograph of the helicopter with the 'Red Plum' in the background. Airborne again, we could see three humpback whales in the clear water, gliding along like submarines. I arrived back frozen but exhilarated.

The passage through The Gullet took most of the afternoon. The *Endurance*'s strengthened bows had no trouble pushing the pack ice out of the way, but the unexpected movement startled the penguins and seals basking on the ice. Some fled into the water as soon as we approached, others were more reluctant to move, sliding off the ice at the last moment. For the second time that day I was frozen; but the scenery was too good to miss by going indoors.

We were carrying some of the BAS geologists back with us from Rothera to Stanley. They were most interesting companions and, together with my constant guide, Sir Vivian Fuch's *Of Ice And Men*, provided me with much valuable information. As had been our practice on previous voyages, we entertained members of the wardroom and Senior Rates before dinner every evening at sea and visited each of the Messes on board for morning coffee, or 'Stand Easy' in naval parlance. We were delighted to find in 3 Mess Marine Stan Egan, who had been one of Bill Trollope's section on the night of the invasion.

The next five days were spent surveying Grandidier Channel. We started in a violent blizzard, with snow driving horizontally across the bridge and making life difficult for the officers on watch, who had to dodge several spectacular icebergs. The weather cleared in the afternoon and the two Wasps were busy ferrying surveyors and BAS geologists ashore. We spent the time reading and watching the wildlife, which included another three humpback whales (or perhaps the same ones) and a school of killer whales. In the wardroom, we watched a video of the Prime Minister's visit to the Falkland Islands.

As we were close to Argentine Island, we were able during the survey to fly to the BAS base at Faraday. This was much improved since our visit in 1981, with accommodation for twenty-four, although there were only thirteen in post at the moment. The base commander, 'Mouse' Lewis showed us round and I swore in David Cotton, who was to be the winter base commander, as Magistrate. He and 'Mouse' took us in rubber dinghies to the old British base at Wordie House, named after James Wordie, who had been in the Shackleton expedition and was one of the party stranded on Elephant Island in 1915. He was later Sir Vivian Fuch's tutor at Cambridge and had taken him on his first expedition to East Greenland, in 1929. The simple hut looked as insubstantial as a garden shed, yet many FIDS personnel had wintered there until the new base was built in 1954. On our way to and from Wordie House, we saw Weddell and fur seals as well as the usual crabeaters. Back on board the *Endurance*, we had a magnificent view of two humpback whales as they cruised unconcernedly past not twenty yards away. We looked in awe at their size and majesty. It was most encouraging to see so many humpbacks on this trip – more than had been seen for years.

Next day, Sunday, 26 February, 1984, was the fourth anniversary of our arrival in the Falklands. As I read the lesson at the morning service, I thought back to our first day in the Town Hall and Dick's promise of a tranquil but absorbing way of life. That certainly applied in British Antarctic Territory; but Argentina had shattered the tranquillity of the Falklands and their Dependencies – how long before it happened here? Our hopes were pinned on the Antarctic Treaty, but what if member states could not agree on a minerals regime? This was the bullet which, sooner or later, they would have to bite. Meanwhile, Antarctica's hostile environment was its best defence. Technology, however, had already mastered the wastes of Alaska and it was now possible (so the geologists told me) to drill through a moving ice sheet. In a world of diminishing known natural resources, was it not simply a matter of time before world interest focussed upon Antarctica? Up on deck, admiring the glorious scenery, I prayed that this vast continent, of which we had seen but the tiniest part, would remain as it was today, an international laboratory, unspoilt and unexploited by man.

Two people who agreed wholeheartedly with these sentiments were Jerome and Sally Poncet, whom we visited the next day on their yacht, *Damien II*. Jerome had long been in love with the South Atlantic and Antarctica. He had also been closely associated with BAS since the FIDS at Grytviken had helped him and his companion in 1971 when, after capsizing three times, pitchpoling (stern over bow) on one occasion and remaining upside down for four minutes on another, they had limped into port on a jury rig made from a genoa pole and an inverted stay sail. The FIDS had nursed them back to health, overhauled their engine and helped to repair their boat (*Damien*). Jerome had never forgotten their kindness and, after returning to his native France, acquiring a new boat (*Damien II*) and an Australian wife (Sally), he went back to Grytviken in 1977. After wintering in Marguerite Bay, which was further south than Rothera, they returned to South Georgia in 1979, where Sally gave birth to a son at the deserted whaling station of Leith. Their second child was born more conventionally in Australia and here the four of them now were, at Faraday, living a happy family life on their warm and comfortable yacht in the ice. The children, Dion and Lief, looked in excellent health and were great favourites with the BAS men on the base. Jerome said that they intended to come to Stanley in March and hoped to spend the winter in the Falklands.[2]

The weather going north was even worse than it had been going south. In the teeth of a Force 9 gale, we could only make seven knots. Landing at Deception was out of the question, so we struggled on to King George Island, where Colin braved the elements and went ashore to thank the Chileans for their help with Kevin Mitchell and to collect his stretcher and the medical assistant who had accompanied him. He also called at the Russian base next door, but it was too late and the weather too unreliable to have the Russians and Chileans back on board.

The storm had blown itself out by the time we reached Elephant Island, where we met up with the Brazilian ice patrol vessel, the *Barao de Teffé*. Her captain accepted Colin's invitation to come aboard and flew over in the ship's single Wasp. The Brazilians apparently had no qualms about flying a single-engined helicopter over the sea and ice without any back-up. Captain Paulo Andrea had been Naval Attaché in London from 1981 to 1983 and knew

Nick Barker well. He said that he was on his way to Admiralty Bay to pick up the Brazilians whom we had met. He invited us back to his ship but tactfully mentioned that he had an Argentine officer on board, so I though it diplomatic to let Colin go over on his own. Colin returned loaded down with gifts, having been treated with charm and courtesy by all the officers aboard, including the Argentine.

Drake Passage was surprisingly calm, Mavis was at last able to present SkiMacGee shirts to the winning 'clankies' and the wardroom threw a farewell party for Sue, who had proved as popular aboard as she was in Stanley. One day out from the Falklands, our last wanderer left us and, at Lively Island, we went ashore to lay a wreath on the Royal Marines memorial. Yona and Albert Davis were in good heart, enjoying a family gathering to celebrate their son Nick's engagement to one of the Lee girls from Fitzroy. We did not go direct to Stanley because Colin had to sail round to San Carlos Water to rendezvous with the *Bar Protector*, which had taken over from the *Stena* ships as the off-shore support and repair vessel. As we sailed in, HMS *Liverpool* was sailing out. Other ships at anchor were the *Fort Grange*, HMS *Penelope* and HMS *Alacrity*. It was almost like 1982 again. After grateful thanks to all crew members and sad farewells, we clambered aboard the *Bar Protector*, on whose spacious flight deck a Bristow helicopter was waiting to take us back to Stanley.

There were twenty-six items on the agenda for Executive Council the next day, so ExCo papers were my first priority. That evening, David Britton brought in the new Deputy Chairman of Coalite, Mr Eric Varley, who had been a Cabinet minister in the Labour government. It was his first trip to the Falklands and I invited him and David to join councillors for drinks before lunch the following day. He made a good impression and subsequently became a good friend and supporter of the Islands. Executive Council was a full but satisfying day, finishing after 7pm. There was concern over the FIDC and I determined to send David Taylor and Michael Gaiger to London as soon as possible to sort out various difficulties that had arisen (I saw them off on 13 March).

Most of the councillors had not seen Mount Pleasant since the contractors had started, so before they dispersed we arranged a conducted tour for them. It was a real eye-opener. The scale of work, the size of the plant and the speed of progress were difficult for them to comprehend. Maurice Chammings and the contractor's manager, Wynn Kenrick, showed us round and gave an expert commentary. Councillors' main concern was naturally with damage to fences and tracks. Fitzroy farm had been virtually cut in half, making Ron Binnie's life as manager extremely difficult. But Ron was not the type to let little things like airports get him down and, with patience and goodwill on both sides, Fitzroy somehow managed to survive. Regrettably, relations between the contractors and Kevin Kilmartin at Bluff Cove were not so harmonious, and we all spent a lot of time mending fences, both figuratively and literally.

Bransfield paid her last call of the season and the Stanley Shield was played for by Stanley and *Endurance* – sure signs that winter was not far away. Mavis presented the shield to the Stanley side, who had managed to win it back, on 1 April, the eve of the second anniversary of the Argentine invasion. A few days earlier, we had been reminded of those tragic times when Steve Whitley had brought in Sue's mother, Eileeen Giles, and brother, Peter, to meet us. They had come with a heart-warming proposal: after Sue's death a considerable amount of money had been donated by the people in her home town in Wales; they now wanted to establish a Sue Whitley Trust, with local trustees, to see that the money was spent sensibly on Falkland Islands' children. We quickly organised a meeting and agreed that, as Sue had taught handicrafts at the senior school, the money should be used to encourage that subject. Annual prizes would be awarded, not only for the best handicrafts but also for those pupils who had made the most progress. It was a living and lasting tribute to Sue, who had done so much herself to encourage handicrafts in the Falklands.

A bigger disaster even than the three civilian lives lost in the war was to befall us. On Tuesday, 10 April, 1984, I was awakened at 4.55am by the fire siren. Looking from my bed through the east window, I could see a red glow coming from the direction of the Monsignor's new house. I knew that he was in hospital, having visited him there several times, but Father Monaghan was also living there. I dashed to the window and saw to my horror that it was the hospital. As I hurriedly dressed, Don came in and confirmed that it was the old wing of the King Edward Memorial Hospital. Throwing on an anorak I dashed across the football field to the west entrance (the new wing), where Marvin Clarke and Brian Porter were standing, holding breathing apparatus. They were calling for water. They had tried to get down the corridor towards the old wing, but the heat had driven them back. I dashed round to the front of the hospital and found Rudy, Marvin's father, at the fire engine. I told him that Marvin wanted water and he said he would get the hoses and bowser round as quickly as possible. There were already lots of servicemen present, with their own fire appliances, laying out hoses to the harbour.

When I got back to the west entrance, someone said that all the patients were out of the hospital and safely accounted for, but over in the nurses' block they told me that this was not so – Monsignor was still inside, and Teresa and her baby, and perhaps others. I dashed back to the west entrance and tried to make my way through the smoke to Monsignor's room, but after a few yards I was coughing and spluttering and realised that, without breathing apparatus, it was hopeless. I returned to the door and waited anxiously, feeling utterly frustrated and helpless. Suddenly figures emerged from the smoke wearing breathing apparatus and carrying a body. 'It's Barbara Chick', said one, in a voice which I recognised as Marvin's. 'She's dead, but there are more in there.' They put her down in the entrance and went back into the smoke. I tried to lift her, but she was too heavy for me. Helping hands appeared and we managed to lay her to one side of the main entrance. Apart from a blackened face, she was unharmed and indeed looked quite serene. Out of the gloom for the second time loomed three figures, carrying another body. 'It's the Monsignor', said Marvin, 'He's still alive.' Four of us took him from the firemen and, as we did so, he groaned. It was music to my ears. As we carried him across to the nurses' quarters, his pyjama trousers slipped and I found myself holding him by one leg and a bare bottom. Alison was in the nurses' quarters and quickly put him on oxygen. His face was absolutely black, but he was breathing. As the life-giving oxygen filled his lungs, his eyes opened and he recognised me through the oxygen mask. Kneeling beside him, I said 'Well, Daniel, I never thought I'd hold a Monsignor by the right buttock!' His eyes twinkled and I knew that he was going to be all right.

Alas, Monsignor was the only one that the firemen brought out alive. Len McGill waited in the nurses' block in vain for his wife Teresa (daughter of Tim and Jean Dobbyns) and their first baby, Karen. They should have been out of hospital a few days before, but Teresa had elected to stay a little longer to have a minor operation unconnected with the child-birth. I dashed back to the west entrance and my hopes shot up when one of the firemen emerged carrying a baby's cot. I took it gently from him and looked inside. It was empty. A little later, they brought out Teresa and the baby. Like Barbara they looked unharmed, but had been suffocated by the smoke. We carried Teresa and Barbara up the road to a shed on the corner of St Mary's Walk, which had become a makeshift mortuary. Marvin said that they had found Fred Coleman in the corridor. He had been burnt to death in his wheelchair. They had also found the bodies of Topsie McPhee, the Chief Fire Officer's wife, Mary Smith and Mabel Neilson. That left one unaccounted for: old Gladys Fleuret. As she occupied a flat above the old wing, there was no hope of finding her alive. Eight deaths out of a population of 1,812. It was the biggest disaster in Falkland Islands' history.

Thanks to the combined efforts of the town firemen and the three services, the fire was now under control. While my attention had been on the rescue of patients from the west end of the hospital, others had been rescued through the north windows of the Churchill Wing and the fire-fighters had been concentrating on containing the spread of the fire to the east. It had already engulfed the new military ward recently opened by Valerie Spacie, and threatened private houses to the east. With a strong wind blowing from the west, there had been a risk of its spreading to the rest of the town.

I walked along to Willie Bowles's house and broke the tragic news to Jean Dobbyns, who I knew had been staying there during Teresa's confinement. I promised Jean that I would get news to Tim, who was on their farm, before he heard it over the radio. There was no telephone, but fortunately on my way back to Government House I bumped into Keith Spacie, who readily agreed to send a helicopter to get Tim. In Government House, I called Adrian Monk in London and asked him to inform Barbara Chick's parents in Bristol. Barbara was one of the State Enrolled Nurses recruited by FIGO since the war and I wanted to be sure that her parents knew before they heard it on the BBC. We were fortunate in having a highly respected BBC reporter in Stanley at the time, Robert Fox, who had been with the Task Force in 1982 and received an MBE for his good work. I had seen him at the fire and asked him not to broadcast until the next-of-kin had been informed. He graciously acceded to my request. Patrick Watts also gave no details on the local radio until we had confirmation that all the next-of-kin had been informed. I went on FIBS myself to announce the tragic news, offer condolences to the bereaved and promise a full inquiry. Before that, however, I had to postpone an Executive Council meeting, scheduled for 9am, until the afternoon. Councillors had dutifully turned up on time, to be met by a black and dishevelled chairman, dressed in anorak and wellies. Keith gave me the good news that Tim Dobbyns was on his way into Stanley by helicopter. I collected him from the football field and took him to join Jean at Willie Bowles's house. I then called at the Town Hall, which I had previously authorised for use as a temporary hospital, and was amazed at the transformation. The military medical teams had done a tremendous job in installing beds, rigging up screens, an operating table and all the paraphernalia that go with a modern hospital. It even *smelt* like a hospital. Alison said that the two worst casualties from the fire, Monsignor Spraggon and Lena Davis, were under sedation and in poor shape. Monsignor had not stopped coughing up thick black fluid (he told me later that he was doing so for months afterwards) and Lena had severe burns on her arms.

Alison's main problem, however, was what to do with the old people. We had never had an old people's home in the Falklands, or even sheltered accommodation for the elderly. Several beds in the hospital were always occupied by those who were not terminally ill but just incapable of looking after themselves at home. There was no room for them in the Town Hall. Tim and Sally Blake came up with the answer: they nobly offered the use of their town house, Westlands, which was conveniently situated between the hospital and the Town Hall on Ross Road. I visited the old dears several times in Westlands after that and found them delighted with their new environment. I determined then that the new hospital would incorporate sheltered accommodation for the elderly, close to but separate from the main wards.

Within the next twenty-four hours, messages of sympathy flowed in from all over the world. Both The Queen and the Prime Minister sent their condolences and Jack Hayward signalled from the Bahamas with an immediate donation of £1 million towards the rebuilding of the hospital. We were stunned by his spontaneous and most generous response. I asked councillors if they would like me to launch a hospital appeal, but they thought there had been too many appeals since 1982 and declined. Nevertheless, even without an official appeal, friends and well-wishers sent donations and raised money in all sorts of ways. Mrs Thatcher pledged HMG's full support in the building of a new hospital, so these voluntary contributions went into a special fund to provide extra comforts and amenities for patients.

By a cruel irony, the fire had played into the hands of the advocates of separate civilian and military hospitals. Certainly there was no alternative in the short term. The only building that we could possibly adapt for use as an interim hospital was the accommodation block for the Brewster workers, which would not be large enough to house both civilian and military patients. Keith said that he would convert a series of Portakabins into a military hospital at the Canache, with an intensive care unit which would also be available to civilians. As the military would have more staff and specialist surgeons, this made good sense. The Canache was not too far for Stanley folk to travel and operating facilities in the Brewster block would necessarily be limited. The Brewster workers and PWD did a magnificent job in converting it in record time, and the Royal Engineers exceeded even their previous best efforts in producing a British Military Hospital on the Canache within weeks.

In the meantime, all serious casualties had to be flown to the UK. Alison decided that the Monsignor and Lena would have to go as soon as they were fit enough to travel. Mavis and I visited them regularly in the Town Hall and saw some improvement. Monsignor could hardly speak, but clearly appreciated the whisky we took him (so, incidentally, did Lena, with whom he shared it when Alison was not looking). They left on the same flight ten days after the fire. It was a sad day for us, for we were sure that we should never see either of them again.[3]

Before he left, Monsignor recorded an interview with Patrick Watts, who broadcast it on the night of his departure. In a croaking voice, he described how he awakened to find smoke in his room. He had made for the door but the smoke was even denser in the corridor. He had closed the door and tried to get to the window, but had fallen over the wooden arm of an easy chair, breaking two ribs in the process. He passed out with his face in a narrow layer of air that divided the lighter smoke from the heavier fumes. He was like that when Marvin and Brian found him, and the pain in his ribs as they moved him caused him to cry out. He finished in his own indomitable way, 'The good Lord obviously doesn't want me yet.'

There were many brave deeds that night, but none more so than Barbara Chick's. Barbara was one of two to discover the fire at the east end of the hospital. The other was Lance-Corporal Shorters, who was on duty in the military ward, which was joined to the old wing by a corridor. Together, they raised the alarm and there is no doubt that, had Barbara thought only of her own survival, she would be alive today. Her efforts to save Fred Coleman, Teresa and her baby sadly did not succeed; but they were no less heroic for that, a fact that was eventually recognised by the Queen's Commendation for Brave Conduct in 1985. Eleanor Reid (now Eleanor Peck) was similarly honoured.

The week after the fire was a busy one for funerals. Our Chilean carpenter had to work overtime making coffins and Angus Jaffray needed extra help in the cemetery. The first service was for Topsie McPhee. Pat, as Chief Fire Officer at the time, never recovered from the shock of losing his wife in the fire. Next was a joint service for the four old people, at which the theme of my oration was taken from Donne's famous lines: 'Any person's death diminishes me because I am involved in mankind. Therefore never send to know for whom the bell tolls. It tolls for thee.' Most of the large congregation present had been in the King Edward Memorial Hospital at one time or another, as patients or staff. They all knew the deceased and realised that the same tragedy could have befallen them. I was struck once again by the closeness of this island community; one person's grief was everybody's grief. The same people went to St Mary's Church for the service for Teresa and Karen as had been at Christ Church Cathedral the day before. Father Monaghan conducted the service, with Harry Bagnall present and Monsignor Spraggon listening from the Town Hall just across the road. People joined in from outside the church, undeterred by a fierce hailstorm.

After the service, we were flown by Bristow helicopter to Tim's farm at Riverside Camp for the burial. The FIDF and many others had driven there earlier. Teresa had been a keen member of the FIDF, and her husband Len was Sergeant-Major. He and Tim had chosen a beautiful spot for Teresa's and Karen's final resting place, at the top of a hillside overlooking a grand sweep of the Fitzroy river. It was bitingly cold as we filed past the graveside. A piper from the Royal Scots played a mournful lament and I was reminded of the departure of the *Sir Bedivere* from San Carlos in 1982, with her load of sixty-four coffins for reburial in the UK.

I had promised the Islanders a full and early inquiry into the cause of the fire and was impressed by the speed with which the FCO moved when it heard that I was setting up a commission of local residents. It was clearly desirable to have an independent chairman

430

from outside the Islands if possible and we were extremely fortunate in securing the services of a distinguished Queen's Counsel, Mr David Calcutt. He arrived in Stanley on 23 May and I was relieved when he expressed the view that inquiries into public disasters of this sort should not drag on for months. I administered the oaths to the members of the Commission, Captain Fretwell, RN, Eric Goss (now manager of North Arm) and Jan Cheek, schoolteacher and wife of Councillor John Cheek, and they set a magnificent example by taking evidence from forty-seven witnesses in three days and getting their report published by July. This was a record not surpassed in the UK. Even so, the Commission's findings came too late to correct the misleading speculation by the media that the fire had been caused by an electrical fault.

In proper judicial fashion, the Commission refrained from speculation and stuck to the evidence. It not only ruled out an electrical fault, but also spontaneous combustion. It concluded that the fire was man-made and had started in the mattress store at the east end of the old wing, next to the bathroom. In the absence of concrete evidence, it did not proceed further. One possible explanation was that someone was smoking in or near the mattress store and discarded a match or cigarette end, which ignited the mattresses. As to the identity of such a person, the store was equally convenient to patients or staff from the military and civilian wards. It could even have been a trespasser from outside. While it was conceivable that the fire could have been deliberately started, this seemed unlikely in the absence of a known arsonist or any possible motive.[4]

Rumours that an electrical fault had caused the fire were based upon a report by John Brodrick (then Director of Public Works) shortly after we had agreed to share the KEMH with the military in 1982. He complained that the Royal Engineers had made alterations and additions to the hospital wiring without reference to PWD. He drew attention to the fire risk of overloaded services and utilities on a twenty-seven-bed hospital catering for over fifty. Since then, however, the wiring had been rectified and a new ward constructed to relieve the pressure. The Commission of Inquiry criticised PWD not over the wiring but for its failure to connect the hospital hoses to the water supply and to install fire doors in the corridors of the old wing. Fire doors might have saved some lives and their absence was a grave omission; but there was little point in connecting up the hospital's hoses until major improvements had been made to the town water supply, because the general pressure was too low. The sad truth was that, in the aftermath of war, the already overstretched and understaffed PWD could not cope with all the urgent demands made upon it.

The same was true, to a lesser extent, with *all* FIG departments. This was well illustrated when we gave parties to the medical and fire-fighting staffs to thank them for their efforts during and after the fire. We had twelve civilian medical staff and forty-five military; nine civilian firemen and forty military. Our short-term visitors did not appreciate the shoestring on which the FIG had been run for years. They naturally tended to think along the lines of the latest British safety standards, whereas the Islands were at least fifty years behind and had neither the money nor the people to catch up. Nevertheless, we learnt from the Commission of Inquiry and implemented its recommendations on fire safety as rapidly as we could. In particular, we improved the fire-fighting equipment and organisation and ensured that the temporary hospital in the Brewster block had adequate fire doors, extinguishers and emergency exits. We sent one of the firemen, Marvin Clarke, on a specially tailored course in the UK and he became the Chief Fire Officer on his return. Now equipped with modern apparatus and skilled in the latest techniques, I am confident that this small service would acquit itself as creditably as any comparable force in Britain.

Notes

1. He died of cancer the next day.

2. Jerome subsequently took *Damien II* to the mainland for overhaul, leaving Sally and the children in Stanley. To provide them with accommodation, we employed Sally as cook in Government House. They both decided to stay in the Falklands and have since acquired an interest in Beaver Island.

3. Thank goodness we were wrong: both recovered and returned to Stanley while we were there.

4. Following further investigations, Shorters was tried for arson at the Old Bailey in 1991, and acquitted.

21

A Strangled Colony

Shortly after the Commission had finished its hearings in Stanley, I was summoned to London for talks. The Hercules was unusually cold and I felt sorry for the seven medevacs on the long journey to Ascension. Boarding the VC10 at Wideawake, I was delighted to find that the pilot was Flight Lieutenant Johnston, who had flown us from Montevideo after the Argentine invasion in 1982. He invited me up front for the landing at Brize Norton and I enjoyed yet again the thrill of returning to England's green and pleasant land. My first surprise was when the barmaid in the Gateway Hotel refused to accept Falkland Islands' money. I had become so used to British and Falkland notes being interchangeable on the Islands (they were the same denominations and had equal value) that I had forgotten to bring British currency with me; but the trusting barmaid accepted my promise to pay on the way back in six days' time. Arriving in London on a Sunday, I enjoyed a leisurely stroll through the parks. At one of my old haunts, the Captain's Cabin, I had my second surprise. I was chatting to a convivial soul who had served in the RNVR in the last war. The conversation turned to the recent conflict and he said he had served on the ARA *25 De Mayo*. He explained that the Argentine aircraft carrier had started life as the British 'Colossus' Class HMS *Venerable*, commissioned at the end of 1944, and he had sailed on her from Singapore to Hong Kong with eighteen Seafires aboard. After the war, she had been sold to Italy and the Italians had subsequently sold her to Argentina.

The weekdays were filled with the usual round of talks with the FCO, ODA and MOD. I also had a most interesting visit to Robert Gomme's PSA team at East Croydon and useful discussions with Adrian and Sukey at FIGO. In the evening, I was well looked after by Lords Buxton and Shackleton, Ted Needham and Andrew Palmer, who was now in charge of the Falkland Islands Department in the FCO. He had thoughtfully arranged for me to meet Keith Spacie's successor, Peter de la Billière and, though rushed, it was long enough to see that he would go down well with the Islanders.

I met most of the ministers concerned with the Islands and was pleased to see the Falklands well displayed in Mr John Stanley's office in MOD; he had paintings by Tony Chater, Duffy Sheridan and Ian Strange.

I flew back to Ascension feeling like a mid-summer Santa Claus, loaded with presents from the Buxton family for Cindy and Annie. The new Administrator, Michael Blick, and his wife, Margaret, put me up overnight and got up at 4.45am to deliver me to the airfield for the now-familiar pre-dawn take-off. I always felt sorry for the Administrator and his wife on Ascension because we invariably arrived and departed at the most ungodly hours.

I returned to Stanley just in time to say farewell to the 1st Battalion, The Royal Scots who, under the command of Lieutenant-Colonel Patrick Cardwell Moore, had done an excellent job during their four-month tour and were about to be replaced by the Coldstream Guards, under Lieutenant-Colonel Sir Brian Bartellot. Patrick called in to say goodbye, accompanied by Pipe Major Frame, who presented me with a record of 'The Crags of Tumbledown', composed by his friend, Pipe Major James Riddell of the Scots Guards, and played it on his pipes for us on Government House lawn. As he played, we stood in the pale sunshine, looking at Tumbledown in the distance.

We celebrated Liberation Day, 14 June, 1984, in cold but clear weather: Harry Bagnall conducted the service in the cathedral before we gathered at the Liberation Monument, which was dedicated jointly by Harry and Father Monaghan. Harold Rowlands, who laid the first wreath on behalf of all Falkland Islanders, vowed that they would never forget those who had made the supreme sacrifice for their sake. At last, two years after the end of the conflict, the Falklands had a fitting memorial 'In Memory of Those Who Liberated Us'. We were pleased to have present at the ceremony the Chairman of the Falkland Families Association, Mr Des Keoghane, whose son was one of the casualties from the Welsh Guards.

I did not have an easy time in Executive Council, having returned from London with no substantial progress to report on the hospital, the fisheries zone or the new Constitution. We thanked and said farewell to Keith Spacie, who was attending his last Executive Council meeting. Alastair Cameron was also about to leave to stand in for Adrian Monk in London until a substantive replacement could be found. Peter de la Billière arrived and was sworn in to both Executive and Legislative Councils, which were meeting to debate the Budget. During a particularly cold spell immediately after the Budget session, Harold slipped on ice near his house and broke his leg. It was late at night and there was no one around. He dragged himself along the ground until within earshot of his neighbours (the McGills, from Carcass Island). Exhausted, and with hypothermia setting in, he was beginning to despair when young Roy was awakened by his cries. Thanks to the efforts of the military doctors and their staff, Harold made a full recovery; but it took a long time.

Peter de la Billière invited me to accompany him to welcome the Coldstream Guards and other units on board the SS *Uganda* and this became our regular practice with both the *Uganda* and the MV *Keren* until Mount Pleasant airport was opened. He also asked me to take him round the settlements, which of course I was delighted to do. Henceforth, whenever we could spare the time, we took a helicopter and dropped in to each of the settlements in turn. It took us several months, but eventually we managed to get to almost all. We also called on military units along the way, particularly the lonely Signallers on their remote hilltop sites. One of our first joint responsibilities was the pleasurable one of handing out some well-chosen gifts from the Returned Servicemen's League (RSL) of Australia, which had donated money for the purchase of vehicles for Islanders who had helped British servicemen during the war. There were six Land Rovers, two tractors and three motor cycles. We had had a difficult job selecting the most deserving cases and keeping the awards a surprise, but somehow the chosen recipients had been inveigled into Stanley and their pleasure at receiving spanking new machines was a joy to behold. Claud Molkenbuhr received one of the tractors. He jumped into the seat and, with a big smile and tears rolling down his cheeks, told us that he had never had anything new in his life before.

During the winter months, keeping the hostel children amused was a problem. Despite the addition of Portakabins in the grounds, indoor space was restricted and amenities limited. A great innovation, however, was swimming lessons: the second coastel had a swimming pool on board and the hostel children were allowed to use it every Saturday morning. There was no shortage of voluntary instructors and, for the first time, Falkland Islanders had the opportunity to learn to swim. Another innovation was gymnastics: thanks to some kind PE instructors, young Falkland Islanders learnt how to do back flips, aerial somersaults and other bodily gyrations not accomplished in the Islands before.

The military presence thus benefited the Islanders in many different ways. However, it did not suit everyone. The Bleaneys finally decided to leave and I could not dissuade Alison from tendering her resignation. Their reasons were manifold, but basically it was because Stanley was no longer the Stanley that they had known and loved. I countenanced patience and managed to persuade them not to commit themselves until after Alison had had a decent rest in the UK. I hoped that their links with the Islands and the Islanders would prove so strong that, after a few months away, they would change their minds; but, to my dismay and the Islands' great loss, Alison wrote from home to say that they had decided to make a new life for themselves in Australia. Another great loss to the Islands at about this time was Steve Whitley, who also decided to make a new life for himself and his bride-to-be, Jenny, one of the teachers recruited to the Falklands in 1982.[1]

All too soon, it was time for home leave again. Ever since we had first gone to Uganda in 1952, we had wanted to travel on the SS *Uganda*, which was then one of the two British India (BI) ships plying between Mombasa and the UK. The BI line had a better reputation for comfort and service than the Union-Castle (unkindly called the Union-Cattle) line. Whether one travelled by BI or Union-Castle was purely arbitrary, depending upon sailing times and leave dates. In eleven years in Uganda, we had never been fortunate to hit the right date for the SS *Uganda*. Now, in the South Atlantic, over twenty years later, we had the opportunity and we were not going to miss it. Everything was arranged for us to board on 31 July, 1984, in San Carlos Water for the ten-day voyage to Ascension, when we received notification from MOD that Mr John Stanley was intending to visit again, arriving 27 July. This time, he planned to go down to South Georgia, spending a few days in the Falklands both before and after. I offered to postpone my departure, but he would not hear of it. We could sail on the *Uganda* as planned and our staff would look after him at Government House on his return. He arrived in the late afternoon and we crammed a lot into the next forty-eight hours. First on the programme was Mount Pleasant, where he was delighted with the progress made since his last visit, then North Arm, Fox Bay East (Doctor's Creek), Goose Green, a visit to HM Submarine *Swiftsure*, in San Carlos Water, and a tour of the extensive works on the Canache. He even managed to fit in an appointment with the army dentist to sort out a tooth that had been troubling him. That evening, Bridget de la Billière held a dinner party for all of us at Britannia House. Considering that she had arrived with three children only the day before on the *Uganda*, it was a noble effort. Next morning, he was off to an early start at HQ BFFI, followed by visits to the new coastel, the *Pursuivant*, the British Military Hospital, our own temporary hospital, the Liberation Monument, the Secretariat and back to Government House for a meeting of Joint Councils and lunch with councillors before boarding the ship for South Georgia. Our staff were quite happy to look after the minister and his entourage upon their return; indeed, they told us afterwards how much they had enjoyed having them.

Stepping into the lounge on the SS *Uganda* was like walking into Raffles Hotel, Singapore. There was little evidence of her latest role as a hospital ship, though the First Officer, Paul Dilks, told me that they did not get rid of the smell of burnt flesh for months afterwards. He showed me round the main decks, explaining how the ship had been converted from cruise liner carrying a thousand schoolchildren to a hospital ship with helipad, satellite communications, replenishment-at-sea facilities, operating theatre, wards and mortuary, all in the space of three hectic days in Gibraltar. He was proud of the fact that, of 750 patients treated (150 of them Argentine), only four had died. The worst day had been when the *Sir Galahad* and the *Sir Tristram* were hit: he thought that the stream of helicopters bringing in the wounded would never cease.

Five days north of the Falklands, we changed into Red Sea rig and the next day, the swimming pool was opened. I enjoyed re-reading Conrad's *Lord Jim*, which I had spotted in the ship's library; coincidentally, the first time I had read it was on another troopship, the MV *Devonshire*, on my way to India in 1946. On the tenth morning, we drew alongside the tanker off Ascension and a Wessex landed on the helipad to take us to Wideawake airfield. We had waited a long time to travel on the *Uganda*, but it had been worth it.

Cindy and Annie and the Blicks were waiting at Wideawake to look after us for the next twenty-four hours. We went to the Residency first and then to a huge tern colony just south of the runway, which Cindy had been filming for *Survival*. The flight home was smooth and, within days, we were driving to Germany to see Diana and John, who was on secondment to the 3rd Battalion, the Queen's Regiment, at Fallingbostel. August was a quiet month in Whitehall and we were determined to take a holiday before the inevitable round of meetings. We booked a passage back on the Norland, from Rotterdam to Hull. Driving into the car park on the dockside, we were amazed to see the Falklands' flag fluttering from the mainmast. At the top of the gangway, with a bouquet of roses, was 'Wendy', who had looked after Mavis so well on her return to the Falklands in 1982. We were treated like long lost friends and had a most enjoyable crossing.

My first task back in England was to chair an appointments board to select Adrian's replacement. There were six candidates, but Alastair Cameron was the only kelper. Other things being equal, this had to be the decisive factor. Only Alastair's comparative youth was against him, but the board decided to give him a chance and he responded to the challenge. His presence in London during the introduction of fishing licences was to prove invaluable.

The most pressing problem in my talks with ministers and officials was the hospital. The Prime Minister had announced in the House of Commons that HMG would finance its rebuilding, but I was dismayed to find that there had been virtually no progress since my last visit in June. The project had become bogged down in an interdepartmental wrangle over cost-sharing. There was still a rearguard action in MOD against having a joint hospital at all. There was also opposition by ODA against the quickest solution, which was to offer the contract to one of the consortia constructing the airport and ask PSA to manage it. Both had the expertise and the men on the ground and with a modest expansion could easily have absorbed the extra work. But ODA was inflexible: its proven method was by open tender and independent management consultants and it was not prepared to make an exception.

Other major topics, which by now had become hoary old chestnuts, were the establishment of a fishing zone and off-shore oil exploration. I had already issued one oil prospecting licence to a British company to drill on the Islands, but the FCO frowned upon my issuing any off-shore licences. Although there was little chance of finding oil on-shore, there was considerable interest in off-shore prospects. I wanted to advertise concessionary blocks up to the putative median line, as the Argentines had done before the war (they had in fact advertised blocks extending beyond the median line). The FCO view was that no reputable British oil firm was interested in drilling in the South Atlantic and that advertising

438

blocks would thus be needlessly provocative. On the creation of a fishing zone, Sir Geoffrey Howe said to me that there was no point in declaring something that we could not enforce and that we must attempt to seek a multilateral solution through the FAO. I accepted that, in presenting our case to the world, it would look stronger if we were seen to have tried the multilateral approach first; but we knew that it was bound to fail and, in the meantime, the FIG was losing much-needed revenue and the waters round the Falklands were being overfished. I contested the figures in a Cabinet paper, which had concluded that the cost of enforcement would exceed the revenue from licence fees. I argued that the FIG could police the zone at a fraction of the cost calculated by MOD.

My other main concern was over the new Constitution: we had argued for some time about the future of Executive Council, which councillors wished to retain and the FCO sought to abolish; but it came as a shock to me on this visit to learn that the new Constitution was to be used as an excuse to change the status of the Falkland Islands Dependencies. No longer would they be dependencies of the Falkland Islands, but simply South Georgia and the South Sandwich Islands. There had been no consultation with councillors on this important change and, in the absence of a better explanation, Islanders would be bound to suspect that the FCO was clearing the decks to make it easier for a future British government to get rid of the Falklands, while retaining their old dependencies.

We were due to fly back to the Falklands on Tuesday, 16 October, 1984. One of my last appointments was with the Prime Minister, at 11am on Monday, 15 October. On the Friday before, an IRA bomb exploded in the Grand Hotel, Brighton, narrowly missing Mrs Thatcher and killing some of her closest colleagues. After her lucky escape, I rang her private secretary on the Sunday and said I assumed that my appointment for the following morning was off, only to be told that it was business as usual.

As I entered her room in Number 10, it was obvious that Mrs Thatcher was suffering from a severe cold. Despite this, she listened to my account of progress in the Falklands since her visit as if the welfare of the Islanders was the only topic on her mind. I explained the problem over the rebuilding of the hospital and she agreed that I could not go back empty-handed. She promised that I should have a letter to read out to the Islanders before my departure from Brize Norton at 9 am the following day.

I had intended also to raise with the Prime Minister the

declaration of a fishing zone, off-shore oil concessions and the Constitution, but I had already over-run my allotted time and did not wish to burden her with further problems. I mentioned these to the private secretary on my way out and he assured me that, if I submitted a paper through the FCO, he would see that it reached the Prime Minister.

After a final session with senior colleagues on the change of status of the Dependencies, I arrived back home with half-an-hour to pack and head for Brize Norton. Mavis had wisely decided that we should spend the night at the Gateway Hotel and get up at a reasonable hour the next morning. We were delighted to see that Robin and Jene Pitaluga would be our travelling companions. As always, the RAF looked after us superbly well. We were drinking coffee in the lounge at 8.30 the next morning when Squadron Leader Hobbs of Number 10 Squadron appeared with several golf clubs, trolleys, balls and tees for me to take down as gifts for the Stanley Golf Club. He was followed by a despatch rider with a letter signed by Sir Geoffrey Howe stating that HMG had taken the firm decision that the KEMH should be replaced by a single, joint civilian/military hospital on the same site in Stanley and asking me to assure Islanders that HMG intended that there should now be swift progress.[2]

Head winds caused us to put down at Dakar on the first leg of the journey south. We savoured once more the monsoon drains at the side of the apron until the VC10 was refuelled. At Ascension, Michael and Margaret Blick whisked us away to join their dinner party and have a reasonable night's sleep at the Residence. Take-off the following morning was at the more respectable hour of 8am and we were pleased to find that some concessions had been made to passenger comfort. Cushions had been provided and a Portaloo fitted for the ladies, in addition to the Elsan bucket for the men. The captain of the Hercules, Twig Taylor, and his 30 Squadron crew were to begin a four-month tour in Stanley, where they were to become one of the most popular crews ever to serve in the Falklands, organising trips for old people and school children, showing them all over 'Fat Albert' and giving some of them their first taste of flying.

Thanks to the cushions and the loadmasters' care and attention, our thirteen-hour flight passed quickly and we landed in the cold and wet to a warm reception from Peter and Bridget and all the councillors. Don conducted us through the new buildings on the Canache as we drove into Stanley and Nanny, Mallie and Sue were standing on the doorstep to greet us. 'Welcome home', said Nanny and we felt that it was indeed our homecoming.

Next day, Peter and I accompanied the councillors to Mount Pleasant to see the progress made since their last visit. Despite the austral winter, work had forged ahead. The huge Tristar hangar had taken shape, the 10 megawatt power station was under construction and the main contractors' camp could now accommodate over 2,000 workers. The runway foundations were all but completed and would be ready for asphalting in the forthcoming summer, and a permanent road network of over twenty-five miles on and around the airport was under construction. With such a large work force, there was an urgent need for better postal facilities than one itinerant postman (or, in this case, postwoman). We agreed that, if the contractors could provide the building, FIG would provide the staff. Thus it happened that a fortnight later, we were invited back to perform the opening ceremony of the Mount Pleasant Post Office. Consisting of one Portakabin, it was somewhat smaller than its namesake in London; nevertheless, it served the same purpose. Moreover, first day covers bearing the Mount Pleasant frank soon became collectors' items. After the ceremony, Bill and Enid Bloomfield entertained us to lunch on board the *Merchant Providence*. Bill was the project general manager. He and a few of the top management had accommodation on the ship, driving the six miles to the airport every day. As they all worked incredibly long hours, Enid spent most of the time on her own in a not-too-spacious cabin; but she was self-reliant and resourceful. Bill led by example and it was largely due to him that the whole massive project was completed on time, despite the manifold difficulties encountered.

The months seemed to fly more quickly than ever. We attended a farewell party for the Coldstream Guards in the Town Hall (was it really four months since they arrived?) and welcomed the Greenjackets, under the command of Lieutenant-Colonel Charles Vyvyan; Trafalgar Night, Remembrance Day, Liz Perry's ninety-fourth birthday and Battle Day came and went; Peter and I resumed our trips to camp and to the troops arriving and leaving on the *Uganda* and *Keren*, and visitors continued to stream in. A particularly interesting all-party group of MPs came as guests of the MOD, primarily to visit military units but also to see as much as they could of the Islands and Islanders. The senior statesman of

the group was the Rt Hon Julian Amery, whose Churchillian ora-
tory was much appreciated at a public reception in the Town Hall
and on the local radio.

Another well-known and popular visitor was Chay Blyth who,
with his partner, Eric Dunn, was attempting to break the record
for the trip round the Horn from the eastern seaboard of the USA
to the western. A BBC television crew from Pebble Mill, Birmingham, was covering the voyage and had arrived in Stanley a few days
before. We invited them all to Government House for drinks. Noticing that Chay was limping, I asked the reason and diagnosed from
his reply that he was suffering from gout. Being a fellow-sufferer,
I recognised the symptoms and gave him a few of my pills. After
he had gone, we were joking about the aptness of the name of his
trimaran – *Beefeater II* – when the Pebble Mill producer asked me
kindly not to divulge that Chay had gout in his big toe, since gout
invited ridicule not respect. He intended to let it be known that his
hero was struggling round Cape Horn with a broken toe. We saw
Chay and Eric off and later flew over *Beefeater II* as she sailed out
of Port William. She was a lovely sight, but already looked frail and
small in that huge sea. In the event, Chay soon had more to worry
about than a painful toe. Having rounded Cape Horn, *Beefeater II*
was knocked down by a beam wave and capsized. Chay and Eric
cut their way through the upturned hull and sat on it for seventeen
hours before being rescued.

Official visitors included Gordon Manzie, the PSA's Chief Executive, and David Thomas, who had taken over from John Ure
as the FCO's Assistant Under-Secretary for the Americas. Gordon
enjoyed his visit. He walked the length of Mount Pleasant runway
and was most impressed with the energy and enthusiasm of all the
PSA staff, the consultants and contractors. This was the PSA's
largest project and he was justifiably proud of the achievement to
date. David had a more difficult time. We had received copies of
the FCO's draft Constitution only two weeks before his visit and
it was the main talking point. Councillors were angered by the
revelation that HMG had decided to separate the Dependencies
from the Falkland Islands as long ago as July, 1982, and had neither
consulted nor informed them until now. Tim Blake's Select Committee report on constitutional reform had been submitted to HMG
with Legislative Council's formal approval in August, 1983. It had
not proposed any change in the relationship between the Falkland
Islands and their Dependencies and had assumed that what had

been considered expedient since 1908 would remain expedient today. David would only say that a further change to the new Constitution at this late stage would delay its introduction. Councillors were most unhappy at being treated in this cavalier fashion but had set their minds on having the Constitution in force before the general election in October, 1985. Reluctantly, therefore, they settled for less than they would have wished, with a clause in the Constitution stating that they would be consulted on any proposals concerning South Georgia or the South Sandwich Islands that might affect Falkland Islands' interests.

On the continuation of Executive Council, the abolition of the titles of Civil and Military Commissioners and the restoration of the title of Governor, councillors got their way. Almost as an afterthought, they also managed to have inserted in the preamble to the Constitution a statement recognising the right of self-determination for the people of the Falkland Islands. Although this right was enshrined in the UN Charter, Argentina had always maintained that it did not apply to Falkland Islanders, on the spurious grounds that the Islands were an integral part of the mainland. Councillor Tony Blake raised this question with David Thomas and me late one night when we were staying in his home in Little Chartres. David thought it a reasonable suggestion and promised to do what he could upon his return to the FCO. When the Constitution Order was finally laid before Parliament on 28 March, 1985, it began, 'Whereas all peoples have the right of self-determination . . .' It was an inspired thought of Tony's and future generations of Islanders may live to thank him for it.

David's visit was not all disputation: councillors respected his sincerity and genuine desire to be helpful. They thanked him for the firm stand that he had taken with the Argentines in the abortive Berne talks and acknowledged the commitment to self-determination made by HMG in the United Nations and elsewhere.[3] Nor was his visit all work. At Salvador, for example, he had an early morning ride on one of Robin Pitaluga's horses, while I tried out Robin's latest acquisition, a three-wheeled Honda. We also had a marvellous afternoon observing the wildlife on Carcass and enjoyed an excellent visit to HMS *Berwick*. After six full days, he left with a better understanding of the Islanders and their way of life and, I believe, a more sympathetic attitude towards them.

Although the threat from Argentina under its new civilian government was minimal, Peter had to keep his troops alert and in

443

a high state of readiness. To this end, he held frequent exercises, one of which was to test his forces' reaction to a nuisance raid, to be carried out by a party of Royal Marines. Several days before the exercise was due to start, their commanding officer called on me in great secrecy and asked if I would mind if his men were to kidnap Mavis and me early one morning while we were staying with Tony Pole-Evans on Saunders Island. Unless apprehended on the way, they would take us to Westpoint and drop us off there. I readily agreed to co-operate. The night before, we warned Tony and his daughter, Biffo, which was just as well because Biffo was the first to hear the dogs barking early next morning. Looking out, she discerned figures flitting across the paddock and, as she said, had it been 'for real', she would have had time to raise the alarm on the 'diddle-dee radio'. As it was, she put the kettle on the Rayburn to brew tea for our guests. Mavis and I watched them approaching; it was too much like 2 April, 1982 for comfort. Dressed in combat jackets, with blackened faces and woolly hats, they looked indistinguishable from the Argentine special forces. They were, however, decidedly more friendly. 'The Captain presents his compliments and invites you and your good lady on board for breakfast, Sir.' We walked down to the water's edge, where we donned once-only suits and lifejackets and clambered aboard a hard-bottomed rubber inflatable called a Ribs. As we skimmed past Port Egmont at over twenty knots, I wondered what Commodore Byron would have made of this strange craft. A couple of Commerson's dolphins played in our bow wave, keeping up with us without effort. It was barely light when we drew alongside HMS *Guardian*. She was one of three converted tugs used by the Royal Navy for coastal patrols. Her captain, Lieutenant-Commander Paul Backley was eager to store the Ribs and get moving. Each man knew exactly what to do and we were steaming westwards at full speed before Mavis and I managed to struggle out of our once-onlies. Paul escorted us to the tiny Wardroom for a traditional English breakfast, which after our early morning exertions was most acceptable, and departed for the bridge to prepare for BFFI's reaction.

Biffo's report of our kidnapping was apparently most convincing. For a while, it was treated as authentic and many Islanders were worried until HQ BFFI realised who our kidnappers were and announced that it was merely an exercise. On board HMS *Guardian*, we waited expectantly for the sound of a Phantom or a helicopter, but none came and we had a trouble-free run to Westpoint. Roddy and Lily Napier came on board for a quick drink before taking us ashore. We waved goodbye to our kind kidnappers as they slipped away to prepare for further nefarious deeds in the hours of darkness. Peter assured us on our return to Stanley that, had the *Guardian* been an Argentine vessel, his quick reaction force would have stopped her before she left the FIPZ. Nevertheless, we were glad that it was only an exercise. Incidentally, it showed yet again the value of the Islanders' radio network.

My next adventure was of a different kind. For eighteen months or more, successive RAF commanders had been trying to get authorisation for me to fly in the back seat of a Phantom. Now, at long last, it had come through. Provided that I passed a medical, I could go supersonic and be subjected to manoeuvres up to 5g. To my relief, the RAF doctor passed me as fit. This last hurdle overcome, Wing Commander Martin Widdowson, Officer Commanding No 23 Squadron, arranged for me to be kitted out with bone dome, survival suit, oxygen mask, gloves, boots, knife and layer upon layer of inner clothing. By the time he had strapped me in, I felt like a trussed turkey. In my fighter days, the important thing was to avoid being bounced from behind and, to do this, one needed a free and mobile neck. Now, weighed down by a helmet and strapped tightly into an ejector seat, I could hardly look out of the cockpit sideways, let alone backwards. Martin started up one engine and I was trying to find my way round the instruments when the second engine built up to a crescendo, then suddenly all was quiet. Even the hum in my earphones stopped. Looking up, I saw Martin throwing off his straps, so started to do the same; but I was all thumbs. Martin came to my assistance and had me out and down the ladder in a flash. Flames were licking up from the Phantom's belly. 'Nothing to worry about', said Martin cheerfully as we hurried away. 'Just a starter motor fire – a common fault in Phantoms.'

'Fair enough', I said, 'But how did you know?'

'When you see the groundcrew running, you know it's time to get out - quick!'

In truth, they were probably at more risk than we were, because the aircraft was fully armed and operational, with Sidewinder missiles and live ammunition.

We watched as the fire-fighters brought the fire under control and my heart sank: was I to be denied a trip in a Phantom at the last minute? Martin read my thoughts: 'No problem', he said, 'We have a standby aircraft in the next hangar.' This time, both engines started sweetly and Martin made a most impressive take-off, using after-burners up to 15,000ft. I was amazed at the sheer brute power of the machine: it seemed as easy to go straight up as straight and level or straight down. After burning off some of the fuel, we went down to 200ft and cruised over West Falkland at 450 knots. To show me its acceleration, Martin then switched on the after-burners and we shot up to 600 knots (Mach .9) in no time.

Hurtling over Lafonia at treetop height (if there had been any trees), I was struck by the size of the place – even at 600 knots – and the absence of roads. I remembered flying over the western high-lands of Scotland and, even there, one could not go for many min-utes without coming across a road or track of some sort; but here, all one could see were sheep trails. The title of an article that I had recently read crossed my mind: 'A Strangled Colony'. Written in 1891, it was a protest against 4 ½ million acres being in the hands of twenty-seven 'landgrabbers and monopolists'. I remembered the figure because we now had exactly twenty-seven sub-divisions (all but two owned by Islanders). As we sped north, towards Goose Green and Mount Usborne, I thought, 'Yes, we are still a strangled colony and will remain so until we have roads joining all the farms.' My musing was interrupted by a sudden bumpiness: we had run into a hailstorm. It could not have lasted more than thirty or forty seconds, but it caused some damage, which we were not to know about until we landed. The perspex on the wing navigation lights had been smashed in, also the nose-cone of one of the Sidewinder missiles, and a sheet of aluminium was flapping loosely from the aircraft's fin. It could not have been serious because, after flying through the hailstorm, we went supersonic and also performed a series of aerobatics, during which the aircraft responded normally to the controls. But first we followed the Argentine pilots' line of attack, over Sussex Mountains and down into San Carlos Water, to give the Rapier batteries some practice.

To avoid causing a sonic boom over land, Martin then carried on going north and we went through the sound barrier at 12,000ft. At Mach 1.2, Martin asked me if it was the fastest that I had flown and I could not resist the rejoinder that I had in fact been faster – in Concorde. Returning to Stanley, Martin asked if I should like some aerobatics. I jumped at the chance, having loved aerobatics ever since my instructor had shown me how to loop a Tiger Moth. He started with a few gentle rolls, until I made the mistake of boasting that we used to roll a Spitfire faster. He then did so many so quickly that I lost count and became thoroughly disorientated. He finished a dazzling display with an immaculate loop, roll off the top and what we used to call an upward Charlie, though it probably goes under a more technical name today.

More exciting than any of this, however, were the attacks that we carried out on the radar station on top of Mount Kent. Martin said that the Blowpipe batteries were always eager for practice, and he was happy to oblige. Hugging the valley bottom, after-burners on, we approached the huge golf balls from below. We were actually aiming up at them for a few brief seconds before we were past and hugging the contours down the other side. The negative 'g' was so much that I almost redded out.[4] But, as Martin explained, that was better than having a Blowpipe on our tail. The landing was as spectacular as anything that had gone before. Martin told me to make sure my straps were tight as, wheels and arrester hook down, he approached the runway at 175 knots. We engaged one of the arrester wires at 140 knots and decelerated to a stop in 800ft. Without the restraining straps my face would have smashed into the instrument panel. I was drenched in sweat, but it had been an exhilarating ride and I was full of admiration for today's fighter pilot.

After lunch with Martin and members of his squadron, I called in at the BMH on my way back to town to see the Harrier pilot who had crashed the day before. He had been doing a low-level attack on Stanley airport when a bird had shattered his windscreen, momentarily blinding him. He ejected immediately, landing upside down in the Canache where, luckily for him, some Royal Marines happened to be diving. They fished him out of the water before he could drown. Despite a severely lacerated face and broken collar bone, arm and leg, he was in excellent spirits, sitting up in bed and looking forward to being flown home in the next Hercules.

Christmas 1984 dawned with the first live hook-up between Stanley and London on television. A large crowd had gathered on Government House lawn long before dawn, cold but in festive mood, waiting to participate in the BBC's 'Late, Late Breakfast Show' (though it was very early breakfast for us). The co-ordinator and presenter, Noel Edmonds, presided over the programme from the top of the Post Office Tower in London. It was running late and the cold was beginning to eat into our bones. I felt particularly sorry for a Chief Petty Officer who, to raise money for charity, had agreed to shave his beard off in front of the camera. He had to sit in the open without any head covering, waiting for the cue to have cold water and lather thrown upon his chin and his friends attack it with cut-throat razors. Eventually, his turn came and the beard duly disappeared, by which time he and his colleagues were clearly in need of sustenance. I invited them into GH and opened a special bottle of Pusser's Rum, which had been presented to me the day before by Lieutenant-Commander Clive Waghorn, the leader of the second summer party of the Joint Services Expedition to Brabant Island. To my astonishment, the Chief Petty Officers finished the bottle before marching smartly away, having been, as one of them put it, 'nicely thawed out'.

Another sponsored event on Christmas Day was a run to Goose Green from Stanley. Monsignor Spraggon and I were having a quiet nightcap and chewing the cud over the year's events when at about 1.30am the runners turned up from Goose Green. They were still in track suits, wet, covered in mud and much in need of refreshments, which we duly administered. As Monsignor remarked after they had gone, there was nothing wrong with the young generation when it produced boys like that.

We agreed that progress had been spectacular in 1984. On the military side, all the troops were now housed in coastels or Portakabins; Mulberry Mark 2 (as Monsignor called FIPASS) was operational; two of the three radar stations were complete and a colony-wide communications system had been installed. On the civilian side, over 6,000ft of the main runway was virtually finished; all the contractors' accommodation and most of the main buildings had been erected; over forty miles of road laid and thousands of tons of equipment imported through East Cove. Monsignor now visited Mount Pleasant once a week (as did Harry Bagnall) and held a service in the special chapel that they had built. He was full of praise for the ordinary working man there. Many had come from the north-east of England, a region of high unemployment and where both of us had our origins. How they must have enjoyed his warm Geordie accent! Inevitably, there were one or two rotten apples, who always drew a disproportionate amount of publicity; but the vast majority were hard-working, law-abiding and well-behaved. They deplored as much as we did the introduction of drugs into the Islands, and the culprits were quickly sent packing. As far as we were aware, there was no attempt to market the drugs, nor was there evidence of any interest shown in them by Islanders.

More surprising than serious was the introduction of a new strain of venereal disease. The South American varieties had been present for many years, but doctors identified a South African strain hitherto not found in the Islands. It was surprising because the contractors' work force in theory had no opportunity of contracting the disease on their way out to the Falklands, since they were transported by bus directly from the airport in Capetown to the ship. As Monsignor remarked, they were fast workers in more senses than one.

Remarkable as the contractors' progress had been, nothing was so remarkable as Monsignor's own recovery. I thought on the morning of the fire that I should never have the pleasure of his company again; yet here we were, sitting in front of the peat fire in the small drawing room in Government House on Christmas night, reminiscing and chatting confidently about the future. 'I want to stay until you go', he said, 'and then I'll go.' Sadly, he was to go before me.

Notes

1. We attended their wedding in Cornwall later in the year and, after looking after the Sultan's goats in Oman, Steve bought a farm in Devon, where he now raises a family – and goats.

2. The ODA provided most of the money and was therefore the department in charge of the project, which it ran in its traditional way. As a result, the new hospital was not finished until August, 1987.

3. In an attempt to improve British/Argentine relations, officials had met in Berne but had failed to find a common basis for talks because the Argentines had insisted upon placing sovereignty on top of the agenda, which HMG had made clear beforehand was unacceptable.

4. 'g' is the measure of the force of gravity. Positive 'g' drains the blood from the head, inducing black-out, and negative 'g' forces the blood to the head, inducing red-out.

22

The Dawn of a New Era

New Year's Day, 1985, was another magnificent day for the Stanley 'Open'. We had thirty-eight entrants, including three golfers from the *Lindblad Explorer*: a dentist and a pathologist from America and the Swiss tour director. Once again the Army provided a marquee and the food, organised superbly by Sergeant Mick Morris. In the afternoon, we invited all the *Lindblad Explorer*'s passengers and crew to tea at Government House and, as usual, the newcomers were amazed to find grapes growing so far south and the conservatory a blaze of colour from the summer flowers.

Lord Trefgarne, Minister in the MOD, was our first official guest in the new year. He had only three days on the Island but, in addition to his military programme, he was able to meet councillors and see some FIG departments and the FIDC. On the day he left, we dined on HMS *Minerva*, returning to the jetty to greet an American yacht which had just arrived and was about to tie up for the night. Her skipper told us that his last port of call had been Easter Island, in the Pacific.

We held a short session of Legislative Council in January, to debate the new Constitution and to pass a few Bills that could not await the Budget session. One of them was to exempt more airport contractors from local taxes. The motion on the Constitution was carried, with Harold Rowlands abstaining in protest at the separation of the Dependencies from the Falkland Islands.

The work-force at Mount Pleasant was building up to its peak of over 2,000, and visits from the PSA, contractors and consultants became more frequent. One of the spin-offs from the LMA consortium was the construction in a remarkably short time of girls' and boys' dormitory blocks and alterations to Stanley House. The mobile homes had served us well, but a more permanent construction was necessary. Children, parents and teachers declared themselves well pleased with the final result.

Bill Bloomfield asked me to talk to the work-force about the Falkland Islands and invited Mavis and me to spend the night on the *Merchant Providence*. Although they worked a ten-hour day, there was an excellent attendance at my talk and a genuine interest in the Islands in the questions afterwards. I was pleased to meet two men from my home town, Redcar. They had been unemployed before applying to LMA and were glad of the opportunity to work at Mount Pleasant, not only because it was financially rewarding but also because it was a job worth doing. Like the vast majority of the work force, they were highly motivated by the project and determined to complete it on time. Their attitude to the Islanders was simple: if they wanted to stay British, why the hell shouldn't they? Sentiments, of course, which I fully shared.

An unusual visitor was Bryan Griffiths, a professional golf consultant. He came on his own initiative to investigate the prospects of upgrading the Stanley golf course to attract golfing enthusiasts from overseas. In his view, there were many golfers who would jump at the chance of playing the most southerly golf course in the world if only the proper facilities were provided. The FIDC was encouraging tourists to view the unique wildlife, why not broaden the appeal by offering something equally unique to golfers? Non-golfing councillors were naturally somewhat sceptical, but they agreed to provide Bryan with a photomosaic of the area so that he could redesign the course and produce a brochure with which to seek commercial support.[1]

Although interest in visiting the Falklands was growing, there was no future in a tourist industry – or anything else – unless we could persuade the MOD to lower its proposed air fares. At first it professed to have based its calculations upon the cost of flying from the UK to the Falklands by normal commercial airline. We obtained quotes from a 'normal commercial airline' which were less than half the MOD figures. Not to be outdone, the MOD then moved the goalposts and asserted that its calculations were based upon actual operating costs. We consulted our civilian airline friends again and they produced figures to show that the MOD would make a healthy profit if the aircraft was only a third full. Fortunately, we had the sympathetic ear of Mr John Stanley, reinforced later by the Secretary of State himself, and eventually we reached agreement on a reasonable fare structure. The MOD wished to limit the lowest fare (which was about a third of its original proposal) to Falkland Islanders only, but we managed to extend this to include Islanders' dependants and relatives, expatriates working for FIG and FIDC and officially sponsored business visitors. We also managed to get a reduced rate for tourists. During these protracted negotiations, I often felt that the MOD regarded us as a foreign government rather than a British colony administered by British civil servants, many of whom were paid, like themselves, by British taxpayers.

Although we had problems with MOD, civil/military relations under Peter de la Billière's wise leadership continued to be excellent on the ground. Together, we opened the second water main from the filtration plant to the town supply, which was a good example of co-operation between the Royal Engineers and PWD on a joint effort of benefit to civilians and military alike. At our regular Joint Liaison Committee meetings, we sorted out many problems before they reached the MOD or the FCO, and Peter and I continued to make joint visits to settlements, military units and ships.

Early in February 1985, I accomplished another of my flying ambitions, which was to experience a dogfight between a Hercules and a Phantom. Twig Taylor and his crew took me up one Sunday. I stood in the astrodome at 500ft over Lafonia and waited for the Phantom to attack. This was no 'Fat Albert' today: under Twig's deft hands, it weaved and turned like a fighter. In the long hours of droning between Stanley and Ascension, I had never dreamt that a Hercules could be so agile or responsive to the controls. It was hot in the astrodome and I needed a rubber neck to keep the Phantom in view. I felt the 'g' pushing me down and waves of nausea; but it was intensely exhilarating. I sympathised with the Argentine crews who must have flown like this during the occupation, hugging the ground and weaving in deadly earnest. After the dogfight, we cruised low over Carcass and Westpoint, sitting on the open back door to get some fresh air and waving to Rob and Lorraine and Roddy and Lily as we passed. Back over Port Stanley, we dipped our wings in salute to the *Endurance* and the *Bransfield* and Twig made a perfect landing in a 35-knot crosswind.

Next day, Mavis and I sailed in the *Endurance* on our last trip south. Pat McLaren had taken over from Colin MacGregor, but we recognised many of the crew from the previous year. We ran into a very heavy sea almost immediately after leaving Port William and, against a southerly gale of 50 knots, could only make ten. I felt drowsy and retired to my bunk early but, as usual, the ship's movements had no effect on Mavis. The black-browed albatross were with us the next morning, to be joined by pintados as we approached the Antarctic Convergence; but no wanderers appeared until the third day. Our first port of call was King George Island, in South Shetlands, where Pat and I flew ashore to Rodolfo Marsh, the huge Chilean base. The commander was a Chilean air force officer, who had first served there in 1972 and was now doing a two-year tour, shortly to be joined by his wife and two children. He took us to the hotel, which had seventy beds, and proudly showed us the crest from No 1312 Hercules Detachment, Falkland Islands, which had been presented by the crew who had flown in to collect POMA Mitchell last year. He said that there were several wives on the base, six children, two teachers and two doctors. The only aircraft at the moment were two Bell 212 helicopters and a Twin Otter, but a Hercules made regular flights from the mainland with personnel, mail and supplies.

We walked across the little stream that divided Rodolfo Marsh from the Russian base of Bellingshausen and were surprised to meet several Chinese there, in army uniform. They explained that they were building a base (yet another!) on King George Island, to be called 'The Great Wall of China', and that ten or twelve of them intended to spend the winter there. The Russian base commander, a cheerful soul by the name of Anatole, told us through his English-speaking assistant, Michael, that he had twenty-six on the base, of whom eighteen were scientists. He was sceptical of the scientific input of the Latin Americans and did not expect much from the Chinese. He agreed when we suggested that the biggest problem in King George Island now was disposing of each other's rubbish.

During the night, we sailed round Trinity Peninsula to James Ross Island. We managed to push a little further south than we had with Nick Barker before coming up against the ice shelf in Prince Gustav Channel, where we put down the gangway and went ashore. It was a beautiful, sunny day and the scenery was every bit as spectacular and breathtaking as we remembered it. Most of the crew cavorted on the ice shelf, some kicking a football, two keen golfers driving balls (old ones, we hoped) in the direction of the South Pole, the Senior Rates and Mavis reclining in style in deckchairs under a parasol, and others simply walking or standing about. Against the white backdrop, they looked like figures in a Lowry painting. A few of us scrambled up a small iceberg which appeared to be firmly attached to the ice shelf; but, as more of the crew joined us, our weight must have upset its stability, because a quickly widening gap opened up between us and the permanent ice and we started to drift out towards the open sea. Hoping that the berg would not suddenly turn turtle under our weight, we waved to the duty watch on the *Endurance*, who quickly perceived our plight and sent the *Dudley Docker* to our rescue. It was a harmless little incident and the source of some amusement back on board, but it illustrated

453

again how easily a light-hearted frolic could turn to tragedy in that hostile environment.

Next day, the weather was completely different, with grey, overcast skies and snow in the air. The Wasps recovered the ship's detachment of Royal Marines, who had spent an uncomfortable night bivouacing on James Ross Island, and we retraced our route, almost unrecognisable now, with much more pack ice than we had encountered on our way down. We crashed through it towards the Argentine base of Marambio, passing close to the spot where Nick had shoaled so rapidly in 1981. I flew over Marambio again: there was no aircraft to be seen, but the Argentine icebreaker, the *Almirante Irizar*, was just leaving. We flew low over the ship and gave them a friendly wave, which was reciprocated. Despite the pack ice, Pat managed to manoeuvre the *Endurance* further south down the side of Snow Hill Island than the ship had ever been before. We almost circumnavigated Lockyer Island but, with only 500yd to go, we were stopped by a crazy jumble of pack ice and stranded bergs, heaped up on each other by the wind and absolutely impenetrable.

The weather deteriorated as we sailed for the South Orkney Islands and the BAS base at Signy. We were going across the wind and the swell and I think it was the most uncomfortable night that we had ever had on *Endurance*. I had not realised until now how far she could roll without capsizing. We were heartily glad to pull into the lee of Coronation Island and shelter from the gale, which was gusting up to 90 knots. Flying was out of the question but, with some athletic jumping from the ship to boat to rubber dingy, we managed to get ashore at Signy and pay our respects to the BAS personnel. It was a great pleasure finally to set foot on the base for, as previously related, we were to have called there on our first trip south.[2] The base commander, David Rootes, showed us round and entertained us to lunch. As with all the BAS bases, we were impressed with the high morale, sense of purpose and warm camaraderie. We were delighted to see Ian Lovegrove, whom we had last met at Rothera. He missed the huskies, he said, but otherwise was enjoying his sojourn in the 'Banana Belt'.

Although only just below latitude 60′S, Signy could experience severe weather, with winds up to 100 knots and temperatures down to -40°C. It was ideal for marine, terrestrial and freshwater biological studies of the polar region. BAS had built an excellent two-storey hut, with laboratories on the ground floor and living accommodation above, plus ancillary buildings, water and fuel tanks and a sound jetty. Their nearest neighbours were Argentines, who had a base called Orcadas, on Laurie Island, about eight hours' sailing away. I had not realised how large and scattered the South Orkneys were: we said farewell to Signy at about 10am (just as, incidentally, a German research ship was anchoring there) and steamed along the coastlines of Coronation Island and Laurie Island for most of the day. The sea was roughening up all the time and we had another bad night crossing the Scotia Sea to South Sandwich Islands.

We made landfall at Southern Thule on Mavis's birthday. The weather was marginal for flying so she declined to go ashore. I left her in the good care of the Senior Rates and flew in to look at what was left of the illegal Argentine base. It was all desolation and destruction. The Union Jack hoisted by *Endurance* on her last visit was in tatters. We had brought a new one with which to replace it but, before we could haul it down, we received an urgent recall from the ship. Thick fog was rolling in and there was not a minute to lose. We beat it to the flight deck by a short head. It then descended upon us like a curtain, obliterating everything in sight.

Next morning, it was still foggy, but not so thick and, to everyone's relief, the sea was not so rough. In the night we had crept past Bristol, Montagu, Saunders and Candlemas Islands, which had been discovered by Captain Cook and now we were passing Visokoi, with Leskov out of sight to our port and heading for Zavodovski. These were three islands missed by Cook (he might well have encountered the same sort of fog as we had) and subsequently discovered by the Russian explorer, Bellingshausen, who was said to have named them after three of his lieutenants. But if Zavodovski was a strange sounding name to British ears, its various parts were not only named in English but also most aptly described. The main peak on the island was called Mount Asphyxia and there was Stench Point, Fume Point and Acrid Cove. The foul smell pervading the island was a combination of millions of chinstrap droppings and sulphurous fumes emerging from every little crack and crevice. The volcano was still active, a low cloud sat on the summit and puffs of steam erupted from the crater. As we hovered over it in the Wasp, I thought of Deception and wondered how long it would be before another part of the great Scotia arc had a major eruption. Although there would be no humans at risk on Zavodovski, it would wreak havoc in the largest penguin colony that I had ever seen.

Back on board, we had our first sighting on this trip of humpback whales – eight of them – off the starboard bow. It was reassuring to

see them but sad to think that, in the old days, they and the even
bigger blue and sperm whales were commonplace. In four trips down
south, we had not seen a single blue or sperm whale; but at least
the humpbacks seemed to be making a comeback. And the fur seals
were thriving. We spent half-an-hour walking among the chinstraps
on Zavodovski and in the process came across scores of these lovely
animals, with their baleful eyes and vicious teeth.

We hit very rough seas again heading northwest for South Georgia.
We were pitching now, rather than rolling, and the new motion required a different technique to wedge one's body in the bunk. Two
days' steaming saw us off Annenkov Island, off the southern coast
of South Georgia. It was still too foggy for us to fly so instead, as it
was Chinese New Year, we went down to the laundry to wish Tommy
'Kong Hee Fat Choy'. He had well-wishers coming and going all day.
As the laundry was tiny, and also served as his cabin, he could only
entertain four or five of the ship's company at a time. We returned
his hospitality that evening by entertaining him in our cabin as we
rounded Cape Disappointment, so named by Captain Cook when he
realised that South Georgia was not the beginning of a new continent.
It was a far cry from the Chinese New Years that we had celebrated
in the Far East, with firecrackers, drums, Chinese dragons and noisy
bustling crowds. Like most Chinese we had known, Tommy loved
to gamble. He was always present at the ship's tombolas, casino
nights and horse racing and was the most consistent winner; but his
generosity to the ship's crew on Chinese New Year must have eaten
up most of his year's winnings.

Pat anchored in Royal Bay and, despite winds gusting to 100 knots,
put a party ashore to walk over to St Andrews Bay. We watched
the gusts blowing from the Ross Glacier across the bay towards us,
whipping up the surface of the water and covering the *Dudley Docker*
in spray as she battled towards the shore. The *Endurance* reeled
under the blows as the gusts hit us broadside on. The shore party
was soaked before it landed and, after labouring vainly against the
elements all morning, decided to give up the unequal struggle. They
returned to the ship with difficulty, bedraggled and half-frozen but
gratified at having seen King penguins, gentoos, elephant seals and
reindeer. There was no sign of a break in the weather, so we hauled
up the anchor and sailed round to Grytviken. Cumberland Bay was
as calm as Royal had been rough, though not thirty miles along the
coast. The sea was so placid that Pat decided to do some night diving.

We went ashore the next morning, paid our respects to Shackleton's grave and called on the Greenjackets at Shackleton House. Under the guidance of Sergeant Tug Wilson, a Royal Marine instructor in Arctic warfare, a party of them had recently retraced Shackleton's epic route from King Haakon Bay to Stromness. They were, of course, fit young men, well fed and well equipped. The trek had taken them thirty-three hours. Shackleton and his two companions, Worsley and Crean, had done it in thirty-six, after sixteen days in an open boat on the stormiest seas in the world and five-and-a-half months existing on ice floes.

The next day, I was thrilled to experience a little of what Shackleton and his comrades must have felt when they heard the Stromness hooter and realised that they had reached the end of their incredible journey. We anchored off Stromness and seven of us went ashore to find Shackleton's waterfall. It was windy but dry and sunny and we enjoyed walking up the left side of the valley behind the old whaling station. Out of the wind, it was uncomfortably warm and we were soon stripping off anoraks and sweaters. We reached the top of a low ridge at the head of the valley and, suddenly, there below us was a splendid herd of reindeer. Three handsome stags nearest to us shuffled to their feet and ambled off towards the main group, which consisted of a few more stags and about fifty hinds and fawns. They eyed us warily but did not seem unduly perturbed. It was incredible to think that they were all descended from three stags and four hinds introduced at Husvik in 1925. They looked in excellent condition and the number of fawns indicated a healthy herd, with plenty of grazing available.

Leaving the reindeer in peace, we made our way up a river-bed to a sharper incline which, with a stretch of the imagination, could have been a waterfall in May, but now, at the height of the austral summer, was the merest trickle of water between bluffs of easily negotiable rock. Shackleton described his waterfall as a raging torrent between impassable ice-cliffs, with a twenty-five to thirty foot perpendicular drop. In their desperate state, the three men had gone down the waterfall with the aid of a rope, which they had left dangling over the edge. Soaked in icy water, they had stumbled on down the valley sustained by the sound of the hooter calling the whalers to work. We scrambled easily up the river-bed without even getting our feet wet. At the beginning of the snow-line, we decided to make a traverse across to the gully on our right, to see if we could find a more likely thirty-foot drop as described by Shackleton. The going was reasonable except for soft patches where the ice had thawed under a surface of glaciated slurry. It looked firm enough but walking through it was like wading through treacle. The next gully looked even less likely to have been Shackleton's waterfall and we concluded that our first guess must have been right. Having followed the contour across the head of the valley, we decided to carry on over the saddle and down into Leith. From the top, however, the descent into Leith valley looked long and precipitous and, as time was getting on, we sadly turned back towards the near side of the valley that we had just left. Slipping and slithering down the steep scree, I realised for the first time how arthritic I had become. Hips, knees and ankles turned to jelly and I could not keep up with my fit young companions. Considerately, they reduced their speed to the slowest ship in the convoy and dusk was approaching before we reached the valley bottom. Encouraged by the ice-light on the *Endurance*'s bows, I thought that, if Shackleton and his companions could make that last stretch after all they had been through, I could make it after our short Sunday afternoon stroll.

As we approached the rusty old buildings of the whaling station, two bull elephant seals reared up and gave that distinctive snort that sounds like something between a pig's grunt and a hippo's honk. They would not have been there in Shackleton's day – the whalers would have had them in a boiler. In Shackleton's book, he recounted how the first human being they met on arrival at Stromness was a young boy, who fled at the sight of them. He added that they must indeed have had a fearsome countenance and must also have smelt foul, unwashed as they were and wearing garments that had not been changed for a year. But the stench as we passed the elephant seals was far worse than any odour that could have emanated from Shackleton and his companions. And there was no young boy to flee away from us as we arrived: only a solitary, sleeping King penguin, beak tucked under his flipper. I approached to within three feet before he woke up, shook his beak from side to side and then, raising it to the heavens, gave a mighty yawn. I walked round him and finally staggered onto the wharf. This was the spot at which Shackleton had found the man who 'stuck to his station' and replied to his question as to the whereabouts of the manager, Mr Sorlle.

As the *Stancomb Wills* disembarked the Royal Marines for a night exercise, I asked them, 'Tell me, when was the war over?' They looked at me blankly. Alas, none of them had read Shackleton's book and could not give me Mr Sorlle's reply.[3]

Next morning, we recovered the Royal Marines and were on our way to Rosita Harbour, in the Bay of Isles. Through binoculars I could see a large penguin rookery on the shore near Salisbury Plain, which appeared to be the only suitable site on South Georgia for an airstrip long enough to take a Hercules. Unfortunately, the weather was too rough for flying or for putting a party ashore by boat, so we sailed on to Bird Island, where the wind relented a little and we were able to fly to the BAS hut. Its five occupants were relieved to see us because two of them were due to come back to Stanley with us. One of those remaining, Mark O'Connell, took me to see a wanderer on his nest. His lovely plumage was spoilt with a large red blob, but it certainly made him easy to identify from a distance. Mark said that he and his mate had been coming back to the same nest for ten years, though they often missed a year because it took longer than that to raise a chick. With the winds freshening up again, Pat wisely recalled the helicopters and we left the three who were wintering over to their wanderers and fur seals.

Battering our way through Drake Passage at its worst, I tried to film the waves breaking over the bows from the open deck above the bridge, but the lens kept getting covered with spray, even at that height. On our second day out from Bird Island, the weather eased a little and we were surprised to espy among the white horses a solitary yacht. There was no sign of life and Pat was unable to raise any response on the radio so, with considerable difficulty, the *Dudley Docker* was lowered and a boarding party went across. Before they reached the yacht, however, the radio spluttered into life and the yachtsman identified himself in broken English as Nikolay Djambozr, from Bulgaria, on the yacht *Tangra*, sailing solo from Sydney to the Canaries. He had been asleep when we first tried to call him. He said he was delighted to see us – we were the first ship he had come across for over two months – and he was fine, though short of food. Pat had anticipated this and sent a box of food (and a bottle of whisky) over with the boarding party. The Bulgarian was overjoyed and thanked us profusely on the radio. We wished him bon voyage and resumed our course towards the Falkland Islands. As he disappeared from view, I found myself envying him his solitary, self-contained world. There was something very appealing about having the sea and the sky entirely to oneself for over two months.

A day later, we steamed into Berkeley Sound and another world. Pat decided to do some night-flying and 435 (the same number as our ill-fated St Andrews Bay aircraft) took Mavis and me on the short hop over Mount Low into Stanley. We landed at the triangle to be met by Don with the news that Government House had almost gone up in flames in our absence. Apparently an electric heater at the office end of the building had caught fire. Luckily the wind was not the prevailing westerly and the fire and been contained. Other bad news was that Eric Goss had been thrown during the East Falkland sports and was under intensive care at the BMH. I went along with Monsignor Spraggon to see him the next day: he was still suffering from concussion but thankfully there was no brain damage and he subsequently made a full recovery. Peter and I flew to the *Uganda* in San Carlos Water to welcome the Royal Welsh Fusiliers and a few days later said farewell and thanks to the Royal Greenjackets, who by then were aboard the *Uganda* in Port William. The ship's Master for this trip was Captain Robert Ellingham, who normally commanded the *Canberra*. We entertained him to lunch at Government House and he said what a pleasant change it was from normal cruising. The same evening, Captain Toby Frere invited us on board HMS *Brazen* to meet Prince Andrew (now Duke of York). At the time, the FCO had not told me that he would be opening Mount Pleasant airport. I was of course delighted but a little taken aback when Prince Andrew said that he was at my disposal for twenty-four hours for any public ceremonies – planting trees, kissing babies, etc – that I cared to name. I could not think of anything on the spur of the moment but assured him that we would prepare a full programme. He suggested that I got in touch with Sir Philip Moore at Buckingham Palace. As I was due in London for talks the following week, I called on Sir Philip and met Prince Andrew's private secretary, Wing Commander Adam Wise. We ran through the programme and arranged the timing so that Prince Andrew spent the night before the airport opening at Government House and flew off to rejoin his ship immediately after the opening, thus leaving room for Mr Michael Heseltine and other VIPs who were flying down on the inaugural flight. Mavis and the GH staff would be even busier than they were during the 150th anniversary celebrations.

Apart from the arrangements for the opening of the airport, I had the usual discussions with ministers and officials in Whitehall and took the opportunity to visit Westminster Hospital to thank them for the excellent nurses that they had loaned to us since the conflict. I also called at Bush House to thank the BBC's 'Calling the Falklands' team. Travelling companions back to the Falklands were Alastair Cameron, who had settled down well in the FIGO, and Nicola de la Billière, who was coming out to join her parents for the last time before they left Stanley.

Shortly after my return, Peter and I paid our last visit to the

Uganda to thank the troops who were going home. It was also the last trip down for Captain Denis Scott-Masson, who had first sailed into Falkland waters in command of the *Canberra* in 1982 and had been down many times since. It was a sad occasion, made sadder by the likely prospect that he would be sailing the *Uganda* back to the scrapyard. She had had an honourable career and deserved a better fate. Denis gave a farewell dinner on board and left us with a few mementoes for the Stanley museum.

On Easter Saturday, Mavis and Gene borrowed a 'BV'[4] from the army and went up to Mount Longdon to plant a thousand bulbs of daffodils and crocuses which had been sent out from the UK by the parents of one of the Paratroopers who had fallen in the battle there. To my surprise, they found enough soil on that craggy peak to plant all the bulbs. We could only hope that nature would be kind to them and that they would survive the winter.

The results of the contractors' hard work were beginning to bear fruit. Bill Bloomfield invited Peter and me, with Bridget and Mavis, to open the Stanley – Mount Pleasant road. Working night and day, from both ends, his men were now ready to close the gap. We drove out to the 24km mark, where a bulldozer was waiting on each side. Peter climbed into one and dumped his load from the Mount Pleasant end and I dumped mine from the Stanley end, thus joining the road. It was bitterly cold, but Bill had brought champagne along to celebrate the link-up and we toasted his engineers and work-force from the warmth of our Land Rovers. It was truly a milestone in Falklands history, the first road of any length to be built in the Islands and a dramatic improvement on the old track. It cut the time taken to get to Darwin from five hours to two. The sad part was that it was a temporary surface, designed to last only until HQ BFFI and all military personnel had moved from Stanley to Mount Pleasant. Thereafter, the burden of maintaining and resurfacing the road would fall on an already overstretched PWD.

We were more fortunate with the weather a few days later, for the Queen's Birthday parade. The Royal Welsh Fusiliers were led by their Pioneers, resplendent in white aprons and gleaming axes, followed by detachments from all the armed forces serving on the Islands and finishing up with the FIDF and the Girls' Brigade. We held our customary birthday party afterwards in brilliant sunshine, with the band of the Royal Welsh Fusiliers providing the music. One of the Royal Marines present was Corporal Mick Sellen, who had been in Government House on the night of the invasion. (In fact,

461

he was one of the two defenders who were credited with shooting the three Argentines in the chicken run.)

The first day of May dawned cold and overcast, not an auspicious start to another milestone in Falkland Islands' history. The main runway at Mount Pleasant was completed and the first aircraft was due to land there from the UK that morning. It was the proving flight before the official inaugural flight scheduled for Sunday, 12 May. Interest was naturally intense and many Islanders made their way to Mount Pleasant from both Stanley and Goose Green. I drove the Government House Land Rover, with Mavis, Harold Rowlands and Monsignor Spraggon as passengers. They were amazed that we covered the thirty miles in one hour twenty minutes. Our first sight of the airport came from the top of Fitzroy Ridge. The silhouette of the huge Tristar hangar dominated the skyline and the white concrete of the runway seemed to stretch for miles. As we stood surveying the scene, Norman Parrin rode up with his dogs, driving a flock of sheep to Fitzroy. Norman was well over seventy and had been an outside shepherd for longer than anyone could remember.

'Well, Norman', I said, 'What do you think of it?'

'Not much', replied Norman, turning in his saddle. 'It may take a jumbo, but it won't take a horse – them fellers forgot a corral!' Then, nodding towards the Tristar hangar, he added, 'Must say, though, that's the biggest woolshed I ever seen.'

Fortunately, the cloud base lifted during the morning, though visibility remained poor. Peter had told me that two Phantoms would escort the Tristar in, and it was the black smoke from their jet engines that we first saw, followed by the landing lights of the Tristar. A cheer from the work-force went up as the Tristar's wheels touched the runway, giving off the familiar puffs of burnt rubber and smudging the shiny new surface. The passengers included some civilians, who had turned up at Brize Norton expecting to fly from Ascension on the Hercules and were pleasantly surprised to find that they were travelling the whole way by Tristar. That evening, we entertained the aircrews to drinks in Government House and learnt that they belonged to No 216 Squadron. Their Commanding Officer, Wing Commander Keith Filbey, had flown the aircraft down. I congratulated him on the landing and he said with a smile that it had nothing to do with him: he had let the Tristar land 'hands off' to test the airport's Instrument Landing System. Everything had worked perfectly and he had no hesitation in giving the green light for the inaugural flight.

A week after the proving flight, Prince Andrew's private secretary and detective arrived the old-fashioned way by Hercules. They spent the night with us before going over the route to be followed by HRH and then joining him on HMS *Brazen*. The twenty-four hours during which Prince Andrew was 'at my disposal' began at Blue Beach Cemetery with a short service and wreath-laying. Prince Andrew was still in naval uniform, having flown directly from HMS *Brazen*. He delighted us all by wearing the green beret of the Royal Marines, to which of course he was entitled having successfully completed the Royal Marine Commando course. He also sported a beard and bore a striking resemblance to photographs of his father taken on a visit to the Falklands in 1957, when he, too, wore a beard. After interviews for television on Blue Beach, we flew by Sea King to Fox Bay East to open the Cockwells' woollen mill. Richard had worked wonders in mastering the machinery and putting it together, despite a vital part having been sent from the UK to Pakistan by mistake. Prince Andrew unveiled a plaque to commemorate the occasion and Richard and Grizelda showed him round. They presented him with one of their first Falklands' sweaters, which they hoped he would find useful on cold night watches at sea. Fox Bay East at that time was also home for Fortoser Limited, the firm conducting inshore fishing trials. The staff had been allocated the bunkhouse and it was there that we had lunch, which included fresh crab caught by Fortoser's small trawler, the *Coastal Pioneer*.

From Fox Bay we flew back to Stanley, where Prince Andrew made a quick change into civilian clothes for his next engagement, the unveiling of a plaque at the site of the new hospital. The weather was fine, but cold with a biting wind and the old hospital site was bleak and forlorn, in marked contrast to the high spirits of the medical staff who lined up to welcome HRH. Dr Pearce, the Chief Medical Officer, thanked him for honouring the new hospital by unveiling a plaque, which people would take as an earnest of the British Government's good intent. From now on, everyone believed that the new hospital would be built, and built on the old site.

Prince Andrew elected to walk from the hospital to the new school hostel, along Ross Road and John Street, stopping to chat with passers-by on the way. It was turning dark by the time we reached Stanley House, but that did not dampen the children's enthusiasm. Before cutting the tape and declaring the new dormitory blocks open, he won their undivided attention by saying, 'Now, pin back your lug'oles and listen to me for five minutes.' He won their hearts when he said 'At your age, I hated school as much as you do!' and rose further in their estimation by sticking to his words and stopping after five minutes. During tea and cakes, he made a point of meeting every child and chatted so naturally to them that they answered without the slightest inhibition. They were sorry when I had to take him away for our evening engagements.

First was a reception for over seventy guests, each one of whom he managed to meet in little over an hour. This was followed by a dinner party, which included councillors, senior Falkland Islanders and of course Peter and Bridget. Midnight brought the end to a memorable day, marred only by the fact that it had also been the day of Liz Perry's funeral, which we had been unable to attend. She had died the day before, in her ninety-fifth year.

We breakfasted early the next morning. Don had already left with the red taxi to be at Mount Pleasant airport to meet us and Mavis and I had to leave before HRH, to be there to meet him. Peter and Bridget picked us up and we flew from Stanley airport to Mount Pleasant in an Islander, piloted by Eddie Anderson. It was a great thrill to touch down for the first time on that huge runway. Eddie was proud to be the first Islander and only the second aircraft to land there. We taxied to the small apron next to the control tower and waited for Prince Andrew to arrive in a Sea King. (Our staff told us later that, before leaving Government House, he had gone into the kitchen and thanked them all for looking after him; a touch that they had much appreciated.) We then took him up to the tower to watch the Tristar land. With typical RAF precision, it touched down within a minute of the estimated time of arrival, after a flight of over sixteen hours from Brize Norton, plus an hour's refuelling stop at Ascension.

Leaving Prince Andrew in the tower, we drove across the airport to the main apron to meet our other distinguished guests. The Secretary of State for Defence, Mr Michael Heseltine, was first down the steps, followed by his wife, Anne. As the others came down – some familiar faces like Lords Strathcona, Shackleton and Buxton, some unknown to me – I rehearsed the names in my mind until I was sure that I had the right name for the right face. When Prince Andrew arrived, however, I mixed up Mr Ian Gow and Sir Humphrey Atkins, a blunder for which I hope they have since forgiven me. Apart from that, the ceremony went without a hitch. Despite the poor acoustics in the Tristar hangar, Prince Andrew's speech was extremely well received and there was a great roar when he unveiled the plaque and declared the airport open. Afterwards, he looked round a display of Falkland Islands' products and activities, which had been organised on one side of the huge hangar. This was the brainchild of Mrs Norma Edwards, an Islander married to a naval officer on Peter's staff (she was a Porter before marriage), and a lot of work and effort had gone into the exhibits.

Prince Andrew's time was precious: he had agreed to perform the opening ceremony only on condition that HMS *Brazen*'s programme was not affected in any way. After an arduous tour of duty in Falklands' waters, the ship's crew was looking forward to a long-promised run ashore at Fort Lauderdale, in Florida, on the way home. Indeed, the ship was already steaming in that direction and HRH was due to catch up with her by Sea King. Regretfully, therefore, we had to leave the other guests enjoying the sumptuous lunch prepared by Kelvin Caterers as soon as the consortium chairman, Mr Oliver Whitehead, had spoken and Prince Andrew replied. Don was waiting to drive us across the airport to the control tower, where HRH was to change back into naval uniform and flying kit before boarding the Sea King. We all piled into the taxi: HRH, Adam Wise, Peter and myself in the back and his detective in the front. It was a thrill for Don to fly the Royal Standard from his red taxi. It was also a thrill for Prince Andrew. As we crossed the main runway, he turned to me and said, 'Do you know, this is the first time I've ridden in a London taxi!' Strange, that he had come 8,000 miles from London to do it.

It had been a magical twenty-four hours, during which Prince Andrew had captivated everyone whom he had met. To the intensely loyal Islanders, who already knew his worth as a naval helicopter pilot, he could not have been a better choice to open their lifeline to the mother country.

Returning to the lunch, we found Pat Luxton seething with anger over some disparaging remarks that Mr Foulkes[5] had made about the Falkland Islanders. Apparently, she had thumped the table in indignation, which had made the water jug rattle at one of those unfortunate moments of silence that sometimes descend on public luncheons and dinners. The media naturally made the most of it, one lurid account even having Pat pour the water jug over Mr Foulkes. As she said later, looking back she wished she had.

After inspecting the runway, we were all flown to the Canache by Chinook. Sorting out guests and luggage there was a little chaotic, but eventually we delivered everyone to the right accommodation. The three Ministers of the Crown, Mr Michael Heseltine, Mr Ian Gow and Mr Timothy Renton, were assigned to Government House and

Lords Strathcona and Shackleton to Sulivan House. David Taylor was on home leave at the time but had kindly agreed that his house could be used in his absence.

By 6pm, all our VIPs had been safely accounted for and reunited with their luggage. Some took the opportunity of a short nap before a huge party arranged that night by HQ BFFI at Look-Out Camp. Now that Prince Andrew had departed, I was able to pay full attention to the Secretary of State. To my relief, at 10.30pm he and Anne said that they had had enough and asked to go back to Government House. Don took us in the taxi and, after the Heseltines had retired, I left Mavis in the small drawing room and returned to Look-Out Camp to collect our other two house guests. We must have crossed en route, because they were not there when I arrived. I was about to leave the party for the second time when an army Captain called to me from the bar. His face was familiar, but not his rank. I remembered him as Warrant Officer Ian Wafforne, last seen in Saigon in 1975. One drink led to another and I did not get the early night that I had promised myself.

As a result, I missed breakfast with the Secretary of State the next morning. But he was understanding and we were on time for the Bristow helicopter, which took us on a tour of the military installations. On our return to Stanley, Bridget entertained us to lunch at Britannia House and we then split up into smaller groups. Having failed to get to Volunteer Point on his last visit, Mr Heseltine was determined to see the King penguins this time. We had received Osmund Smith's permission to land a couple of small helicopters near the colony, so Michael and Anne Heseltine went in one Gazelle, together with Air Marshal Sir Peter Harding, while Lord Buxton, Ian Strange and I went in the other. I had expected the pilots to land near the shanty, but they put down between the gentoo colony and the King penguins. Both Michael and Anne Heseltine were keen photographers and managed to get very close to the Kings without disturbing them. Indeed, Anne took one glorious shot of the Secretary of State lying full length in the penguin guano, photographing a handsome adult, while a bunch of inquisitive big brown chicks showed a keen interest in his feet.

As we watched from a distance, George Smith (Osmund's cousin) joined us. He said that he had lit a fire in the shanty and we were welcome to use it if we wished. I thanked him for his trouble, and for coming all the way from Johnson's Harbour to greet us. 'That's nothing', he said nodding towards our guests, 'If them fellers can come 8,000 miles, I can manage ten!' He said that there had been 107 baby Kings born in the past year and that the colony now numbered about 400. It was almost dark when we managed to drag our guests away with (I hoped) some memorable photographs of one of the most fascinating sights in the Falkland Islands.

At the drinks party at Government House that evening, I presented Jack Hayward with a Falklands' 150th Anniversary silver crown as a token of the Islanders' gratitude to him for his prompt and generous donation towards the new hospital. He was deeply touched and said that he would keep it as a cherished heirloom. After the drinks party, we gave a farewell dinner for all the VIPs: three ministers, three Lords, four MPs and Jack Hayward and somehow managed to fit in a farewell drink for one of my staff who was leaving with them on the Tristar the following morning.

As the Secretary of State wished to experience the troops' transport from Stanley to Mount Pleasant, we arranged to drive out to the airport in one of the RAF coaches. There had been some criticism that they were not strong enough for the job, and this appeared to be justified when we broke down. By ill luck, we had become snarled up with another coach's discarded leaf spring. It was not a serious delay, but it illustrated the hazards of using vehicles designed for tarmac on a temporary surface. The Tristar was waiting and, before boarding, the Secretary of State promised to look into the whole structure of air fares, freight charges and landing fees, on which I had expressed my concern over breakfast. He was true to his word, for it was not long before we received more reasonable proposals.

Not all the VIPs left with the Secretary of State. Mr Renton took the opportunity of this, his first visit to the Islands, to stay on for a few days and I accompanied him. We travelled by FIGAS and spent the night with the Cockwells at Fox Bay East, where the minister and I shared a room (and where, apparently, I kept him awake with my snoring). Ian McPhee flew us from there in foul weather, creeping up the coast to Roy Cove, over a gap in the hills to Dunbar, and along the coast again to Carcass. Rob McGill was with us on the aircraft and it speaks wonders for the Land Rover (and Rob's mechanical skills) that his old 1954 model started first time, having been sitting out in the elements at the airstrip for a month. Mr Renton was fascinated by the multitude and variety of wildlife – no one from Mr Ridley onwards had failed to be captivated by Carcass – and as usual the visit was all too short. At Hill Cove we joined Lord Shackleton, who had also stayed on and was spending two days with Tim and Sally

Blake. We lunched together before flying back to Stanley with Eddie Anderson. Lord Shackleton moved into Government House and we held a drinks party for over eighty that evening for Mr Renton to meet more Islanders. As GH staff had taken quite a beating over the last few days, Bridget and Peter kindly offered to have our house-guests to dinner. It was this consideration and co-operation that made our lives much easier and we felt sorry for future governors once the Commander BFFI had moved to Mount Pleasant.

Mr Renton spent two more days with us before taking the uncomfortable ride back to Ascension in a Hercules. He had a most amicable meeting with Joint Councils and finished with an excellent press and radio interview. His private secretary said before they left that it was the best overseas visit he had made with his minister, and councillors told me that here was one 'Foreign Office' minister whom they felt they could trust.

Lord Shackleton stayed on for a few more days and flew home in greater comfort in a British Airways Beoing 747. The RAF was having problems with its Tristar crew training and could not initially provide a regular service, so British Airways was awarded a six-month contract. Lord Shackleton's 747 was the first Jumbo ever seen in the Islands and it caused quite a stir as the pilot made a low pass over Stanley, escorted by two Phantoms. We were standing on the lawn of Government House, with all the staff, waving madly. Mally, one of the maids, had not yet seen Mount Pleasant airport and, thinking of the Islander's grass strips, she gazed at the Jumbo in disbelief. 'How can that land in camp?' she asked.

Before Lord Shackleton left, we had a useful round-up discussion in my office. I always valued his wise counsel and sound advice; his knowledge of the Falklands, the South Atlantic and Antarctica far exceeded my own and it was encouraging to find that his and my way of thinking for the future ran along the same lines. He was heartened to see how far we had gone since 1982 in implementing his 1976 recommendations.

The advent of the Jumbo saw the demise of the troopship. Peter and I went on board the RFA *Sir Geraint* two days after the first BA flight to welcome the last seaborne troops. We had to make the same speeches twice, first to a hundred RAF personnel and then to a similar number of Royal Marines and Army. By this time, we both knew each other's welcoming address almost off by heart; but it was, we were told, generally appreciated by the troops and we wondered how we would get the message across in future to those arriving by air. We could not go out to Mount Pleasant two or three times a week. The answer was a video recording, to be shown in the transit lounge while passengers were waiting for their luggage. We duly made recordings, but whether they were ever shown I do not know.

We had coffee with the Master of the *Sir Geraint*, Captain Robin Green, who had been Master of the ill-fated *Sir Tristram* in 1982. It was appropriate that he should be in command at this time because Sir John Fieldhouse, who was now First Sea Lord, was about to come down with Lady Fieldhouse to attend the dedication ceremony of the RFA memorial at Fitzroy. The *Sir Geraint* was due to anchor on the spot on which Robin had parked the *Sir Tristram* on that fateful day, but in the event the weather was too bad and we had to fly to Fitzroy for the ceremony. The memorial had been erected next to that of the Welsh Guards and was in memory of all members of the Royal Fleet Auxiliary who had lost their lives in the conflict. These included eight Chinese seamen from Hong Kong and, after the wreath-laying, two of their Chinese colleagues stepped forward and scattered beer and food on the ground in front of the memorial to fortify the departed spirits. They carried their offering in an old plastic bag, but performed the simple ceremony with such quiet dignity that there were few dry eyes in the assembled company. After the ceremony, we all flew back to Stanley and had lunch on board the *Sir Geraint*, which was moored alongside FIPASS. That evening, we gave a party for the senior officers and civil servants concerned with the Royal Fleet Auxiliary, including Ken Pritchard, the Director General, Royal Navy Supply and Support; Commodore Gordon Butterworth, the Chief Marine Superintendent; Gordon Wilson, Senior Manager, RFA Services; Robin Green from the *Sir Geraint* and Phil Roberts, who had been Master of the *Sir Galahad* and whom we had first met in 1980 on the RFA *Plumleaf*. I believe it was at this party that someone first raised the suggestion that Mavis and I might like to go home in October in a RFA vessel. We did not realise at the time that we would be travelling on the *Sir Geraint* (though with a different Master).

The *Keren* was in Port Stanley at the same time as the *Sir Geraint* and her departure marked a sad end to the brief resurgence of shipborne travel to and from the Falklands. As the *St Edmund*, she had become a familiar figure in Stanley harbour and had earned the affection of Islanders and many of the troops who had been billeted or had sailed in her. We went aboard for a farewell dinner with her colourful Master, Sandy Kinghorn, whose talent on the concertina and repertoire of nautical songs guaranteed an enjoyable evening.

Like Denis Scott-Masson and many others besides, Sandy had come down to the Falklands during the war, liked the place and the atmosphere and volunteered to come back time and again. It was a popular trip because it was a change from the normal merchant navy routine, whether on cruise ships, ferries or freighters. We were to find that it had the same appeal for BA crews, and for the same reason – it was different. We entertained them in Government House whenever we could, and the FIGAS pilots took them round the settlement strips whenever they had a spare seat in the Islander. The only complaint was that the stewardesses were not allowed to travel down as members of the cabin crew: we were told that the MOD considered the overnight facilities at Ascension inadequate.

With the introduction of direct flights from the UK, the contractors had no further use for the MV *England*, which had carried 9,000 passengers between Capetown and East Cove and steamed more than 150,000 miles since October, 1983. Before her final departure, we went on board at East Cove and had a nostalgic trip round the coast to Stanley. I thanked the Master and crew for their invaluable contribution to the Islands' security and development and expressed the hope that their handsome ship would not follow the *Uganda* to the scrapyard. With the *England*'s departure, there was no passenger ship left in Falklands waters.

Our next sad farewell was to Peter and Bridget. Bridget left in early July and Peter just over a fortnight later. We gave Bridget a farewell dinner and asked her to choose her fellow-guests. It was typical of her that all but three were Islanders. In the relatively short time that she had been in the Falklands, they had made innumerable Islander friends both in Stanley and in camp. Indeed, they had entered so enthusiastically into the way of life that many said they would not be surprised to see them back as farmers after Peter retired from the army. That they would be sadly missed was made clear by councillors in Peter's last Legislative Council meeting. Indeed, their warm and sincere tributes were too much for Peter; he was so overcome that he could not finish his last address to them.

Fortunately for the Islands, the MOD had selected Peter's successor very carefully. It had wisely been decided to rotate the appointment between the three services and Air Vice-Marshal Kip Kemball was an admirable choice as the first Commander from the RAF. He had been one of the first British pilots to fly the Phantom, which was now the Islands' front line of defence, and he came from farming stock. His wife, Val, loved the country life and they both settled in immediately. There was no longer any possibility of confusion over our respective positions because the title 'Military Commissioner' died with Peter's departure and my title was due to revert back to 'Governor' after the general election in October.

Kip carried on Peter's practice of inviting me to accompany him to visit the settlements and, as I was about to begin my farewell visits to all the people in camp, I found his helicopter extremely useful. Before this, however, we received another visit from Mr John Stanley, Minister of State for the Armed Forces. He brought good news on the air fares and we made useful progress on the operating procedures for Mount Pleasant airport and the terms of the lease. At his suggestion, I sent the Attorney-General back to the UK to settle the outstanding points. We held a good meeting of Joint Councils; by now councillors had come to trust Mr Stanley and were pleased that he took such a helpful interest in their affairs. After he had left the meeting, we briefed John Cheek on what he should say to the Committee of Twenty-Four in New York. This had become a sterile but necessary annual chore. Although HMG had decided not to co-operate with the Committee any more, Councillors considered that, as long as the Argentines continued to be represented, they could not allow the Islanders' case to go by default.

Kip and Val, Mavis and I flew with Mr Stanley to Mount Pleasant in a Sea King to see him off and Mavis and I spent the night on the *Merchant Providence* (I was speaking to the work-force again that evening). It was good to see Wynn Kenrick back – he had been in England for the last few months – but we were sorry that Bill and Enid Bloomfield had gone. There was still much to be done in the second phase of construction; indeed, Wynn said that another million tonnes of quartzite would be needed from Mount Pleasant quarry and that more buildings were still to be built than had been built to date. The next morning we watched them sinking piles for the new jetty alongside the *Merchant Providence*, which was due to leave within a few months, and Brian Brown, who had taken over from Maurice Chammings as the PSA's regional director, showed us the works being undertaken by the new consortium, Wimpey-Taylor Woodrow, as well as those under continuation by LMA. The total work-force was now at its highest peak at over 3,000.

Mickey Clarke collected us from the PSA office at Mount Pleasant to drive to Darwin, where we were to stay with Brook and Eileen for the last time. Although the road from Stanley to Mount Pleasant was much improved, the track from Mount Pleasant to Swan Inlet was probably worse than it had ever been, owing to heavy use by contractors' plant and vehicles. The approaches to the L'Antioja Stream were particularly bad and Mickey picked the wrong spot to charge over. As a result, we came to a sudden halt, with the front wheels embedded solidly into the bank and my head bleeding from an argument with the roof. It was only a scratch, but Mickey was most concerned. He was able to reverse without too much trouble and find a gentler crossing, but it delayed us and we came across Brook about half-an-hour out of Darwin on his way to look for us.

Next day, we visited the military camp at the old school site. It was totally dead and deserted. Brook and I wandered through creaking doors and down empty corridors, like the opening scene from *Beau Geste*, until in one room we found two caretakers, civilians from Turner's, the contractors engaged by PSA to maintain the military installations in the Islands. True to form, Brook was making the best of a sad situation (no one wanted the troops to leave): he was negotiating with the Command Secretary to take seventeen of the Portakabins, the kitchen and the power-house in return for cleaning up the site with his own men and not insisting – as he had a right to do – that the army restore it to its previous condition. While he discussed details with the Turner's men, I excused myself and went to pay my last respects to Colonel 'H' and Nick Taylor. The spot where Colonel 'H' had fallen three years ago was slowly disappearing, but I was amazed to find bits and pieces of Argentine accoutrements still lying around the old foxholes. I followed the route of the 2 Paras up to Gorse Ridge and was pleased to find that the gorse was growing again, with fresh green shoots pushing through the black. It was snowing when I reached Nick Taylor's grave, but the snow was not too thick on the ground to see that the grave was well tended. That afternoon, Brook drove us to the Argentine cemetery, which again was in good order, and we had tea in Burntside House with the Morrisons, who would never forget the night that they were stormed by 2 Para, but could now joke about it. In the evening, Goose Green and Darwin threw a farewell party for us in the community hall. Like Peter at his last Legislative Council, I was too overcome to finish my speech.

Next day we set off overland for Fitzroy. The track was worse than at any time I could recall and we were bogged before we had gone far. Fortunately, as we were about to start the laborious task of jacking up the wheels, Brian Porter arrived with a load of youngsters heading for a 'two-nighter' at North Arm. They soon pulled us out and we wished them the best of luck for the rest of their journey.

As it happened, they were to arrive in North Arm before we got to Fitzroy. L'Antioja Stream was our bugbear again. Mickey managed to find a safe crossing, but there was no alternative up the hill on the other side but to go through the only gate in the area, the approach to which had been hideously churned up by a huge Terec, a heavy earthmoving vehicle with gigantic balloon tyres. After one-and-a-half hours, we had to accept that we could not get out under our own steam. Fortunately, Mickey managed to raise the PSA at Mount Pleasant on his 2-metre set, and Brian Brown sent two Land Rovers to our rescue. One of them became bogged in trying to extricate us, but eventually we all rolled into the PSA office, cold and muddy but otherwise unharmed. Brian produced some very welcome coffee and, after warning Ron Binnie that we would be late, we were on our way again. Ron kindly drove down the Fitzroy track to the main road to meet us and we had no further problems. I must confess, however, to feeling very tired at the farewell party that the good people of Fitzroy gave us that night.

The following day was a Saturday, but Mickey was happy to call in at Riverside and Bluff Cove on the way home. Tim Dobbyns came out to the main road to show us a safe route across his wet camp and we followed him back to his new house. All around was evidence of his friendliness with the troops and contractors: two containers, a shearing shed and many smaller items. The military presence in the Islands had certainly benefited Tim. He also had plenty of local friends: Roddy McKay from Port Harriet and Doug Hansen from Stanley were helping him to gather some sheep for slaughter and daughters Kathy and Jeannie, both of whom lived in Stanley, were lending a hand. Jean produced lunch for us all and it was a pleasure to see them so well established. If only Teresa and her baby had survived the hospital fire, their happiness would have been complete.[6]

Mickey Clarke negotiated the wet camp between Riverside and the main road without difficulty, but it was an obstacle course from the road to Bluff Cove. The contractors were working on the drainage ditches beside the road and it took us some time to find a way across. The farm looked like a junk-yard. On our first visit in 1980, I had been intrigued to see a Second World War Bren gun carrier lying there; but now there was a collection of military vehicles, in various stages of disrepair. Kevin had made the most of the auctions organised by the military to sell vehicles that would otherwise have finished up on the scrap-heap or as gunnery targets. His mechanic, Steve, was a wizard at coaxing old wrecks back to life. After tea, Kevin, Steve and a friend who had walked over from Fitzroy decided to come into Stanley with us. They travelled to the main road on Kevin's tractor, which Kevin left for their return journey, and we battled on behind in the Land Rover. Access to the road had been completely cut off by a JCB, which was boring along the roadside like a mole. We had to ask the operator to fill in a Landrover's width so that we could get back onto the road. Unfortunately, he broke a track in the process and we had to finish the job by hand, throwing rocks into the ditch until Mickey could negotiate the gap. 'Now you can see what I've had to put up with for the last two years,' Kevin said. We sympathised and were pleased to hear later that the contractors had made handsome amends by building an access road for him right up to his farm.

We were too late getting back to Stanley to call in at Malcolm Ashworth's new house, which was a little out of town on the Mount Pleasant road, so we called there the next day. With the help of the FIDC, Malcolm had imported a prefabricated kit from a Scottish firm, Clanwood, and constructed it himself. It was an attractive, five-bedroomed, two storey house, finished to a high standard and well insulated against the weather. The surrounding fields were green and lush and Malcolm looked forward to going to the UK and purchasing his dairy herd later in the year. With any luck, his dairy would be supplying milk to Stanley again next season. 'Are you glad you stayed?' I asked. 'I am that', said Malcolm, with a smile. But it had been an uphill struggle; if anyone deserved to succeed, he did.

Over the next two months, I visited all the other settlements. Mavis accompanied me to most of them. With the new sub-divisions, the number of farms had doubled since 1980, from thirty-one to sixty-two. Not all the new owners, however, had moved onto their land, so there were fifty settlements altogether to visit. We used every mode of travel: FIGAS, Bristow, 'teeny-weenies', Land Rover and the three RN patrol vessels, *Protector*, *Guardian* and *Sentinel*. With their Ribs, they could take us into the smallest islands and the shallowest of harbours. The most novel ride I had was on a wooden sled behind a tractor, on George Island. Albert and Sally McLeod had lived there in a temporary shanty for the last fifteen months while building their house, which they completed only three weeks before my arrival. Like the Larsens on Speedwell, they had entered into a share-farming agreement with the FIC. The airstrip was some way from the house and, as it was raining when the Islander landed, Albert met me with the sled. It was a surprisingly comfortable ride, sitting in style in an armchair under a tarpaulin. Sally was yet another Jaffray and sister of one of our maids, Mally. She said she was delighted to have me as her first house-guest.

I was enormously impressed with all the new young farmers. They were working extremely hard, keen on improving their farms, happy in what they were doing and optimistic about the future. When we called on Richard and Toni Donna Stevens, for example, at Port Sussex (one of the San Carlos sub-divisions), they were about to depart with motor cycle, tractor and mobile hut (on a sled) for their far paddock, where they were to spend the next three weeks erecting a fence. One of them would return daily to the farmhouse on the motor cycle to feed the animals. Richard had come out to the Falklands originally as a teacher and had been the Turner children's tutor for a while at Rincon Grande. Toni Donna was Tony and Heather Pettersson's daughter and had given up a comfortable home in Stanley for this pioneering life. They were both loving it and would not have swapped with anyone.

Some of the new farmers were not so young, but they were enthused with the same spirit. On Great Island, for example, Doug and Rose Goodwin had moved in with their son, Neil, to help him to make a success of another share-farming venture with FIC. Doug had worked for most of his life in Stanley, Fitzroy and Horseshoe Bay and was virtually starting from scratch again on this inaccessible island. He was planting tussock grass as hard as he could go, even though it was a perpetual battle against the upland geese. Rose was keeping house under extremely difficult conditions, yet had no regrets on taking the plunge at an age when most people would be thinking of retiring into Stanley.

It was on this trip, on HMS *Guardian*, that we came across nine Polish trawlers, fishing five miles off Cape Meredith, at the extreme south-west tip of West Falkland. We had never seen so many seabirds in one area. There were thousands of black-browed albatrosses, prions and petrels, wheeling and diving behind the trawlers. As they alighted on the sea, it looked as though the ships were laying a paper trail. We kept well clear because John Rainbow, the *Guardian*'s Captain, said that the trawlers' nets extended for quite a long way behind and to the sides. They were steaming up and down a relatively small stretch of water, as if hoovering a carpet. And we had no control over how often they did this, or on the size of the net, or what or how much they caught. Standing on the *Guardian*'s bridge, it seemed obvious that it could be only a matter of time before the stocks would be dangerously depleted.

Our farewell tour of the Islands was not accomplished without incident. We had been staying for the last time with Robin and Jene Pitaluga, at Salvador, and were due to make the short hop across the sound to say goodbye to Diana and Ron Turner. It was very windy, but Robin decided that he could fly us across without difficulty. He took off directly into wind and we were airborne after only twenty yards. He landed across the strip at Rincon Grande in only fifteen yards, which indicated the wind velocity. We pushed the Cessna back to the edge of the strip and he took off again without trouble. He landed safely at Salvador but, without Mavis and me to provide the extra weight, a particularly severe gust caught him as he taxied to the hangar and threw the aircraft over onto its back. Robin was unhurt and had the presence of mind to switch everything off. There was no fire but Robin feared that it might be a write-off.[7] It was a sad way to leave Salvador.

I asked each person I met in every settlement the same question: 'If a future British government decided that it could not afford to keep the Falkland Islands, would you go or would you stay?' Only one person said that he would stay. He was prepared to 'give it a go' under the Argentines for a year, he said, and if he did not like it after that, he and his family would go. But all the rest said that they would not stay in the Islands with an Argentine presence, no matter how diluted or unobtrusive that presence might be. This applied to old and young farmers alike. I thought, for example, that Osmund Smith at his age might not like to give up the family farm and venture out into the unknown (he had never left the Islands); but he was adamant. 'After what the Argies did in '82', he said, 'I couldn't stay here if you let them back.'

I pressed him: 'But they didn't touch you or the farm.'

'That's true,' he said, 'But I still couldn't stay.'

'Well, where would you go?'

'Oh, England or Scotland or New Zealand – anywhere where there's sheep.'

'But what if we refused to offer you compensation or resettlement?'

'If necessary', he said emphatically, 'I'd leave like the Vietnamese boat people.'

That summed up the general view. All those with whom I spoke in Stanley were of the same opinion. Indeed, Harold Rowlands, not renowned for histrionics, said to me that, if we let the 'Argies' back, he could not stay, but nor could he bear to leave.

'Well then', I asked 'What would you do?'

'I'd commit suicide', said Harold. And he meant it.

In discussing the future with Islanders, they all held the view that there could be no compromise, no middle-of-the-road solution over sovereignty. The majority were willing to see Britain and Argentina resuming normal relations, but totally opposed to any discussion on the Islands' sovereignty. They were pleased with, and fully supported, the Prime Minister's stand that sovereignty was not negotiable. If a British government ever agreed to put sovereignty on the agenda, they believed that the Argentines would interpret that as British recognition of their claim and that all we would be discussing thereafter would be the modalities of the transfer of sovereignty from Britain to Argentina. Leaseback was a non-starter. Islanders would never surrender sovereignty. If it were to be imposed upon them, agreements on the length of lease could never be reached and, in any event, Argentines would accept it only as a short-term stepping stone towards full control of the Islands. If the British Government would declare a 200-mile exclusive economic zone (except, of course, to the west, where it would run to the median line), Islanders could look forward to a bright economic future, with certain revenues from fish and probable revenues from oil and gas. It was clear now, they said, that it was not the 'dead hand of the dispute' that was stagnating the economy – as Mr Ridley had told them in 1980 – but the 'dead hand of the Foreign Office'. Lord Shackleton had pointed the way ahead, they had made a good start and shown the Islands to be economically viable, but their full potential could not be realised unless they were allowed to exploit the seas (and seabed) around them.

These views were expressed clearly as the time drew near for the general election. We held our last Executive Council meeting under the old Constitution on 17 September. I thanked them all, particularly Bill Luxton, who had served on Executive Council for longer than anyone else, having been nominated orginally by my predecessor. In the interests of democracy, it was probably right that nominated members should go; but Bill's steadying influence would be missed by the new Council. Bill Goss and Ron Binnie were also stepping down, having intimated that they had no wish to be considered for re-election. Their wise counsel and experienced heads, too, would be missed; but Bill considered that it was time to enjoy his retirement and Ron had found that running Fitzroy and attending to Council business was really too much. I could see that this would become a major problem for all camp councillors in future, with Council business increasing and labour on farms decreasing. Yet we were a long way from having fully paid councillors, like Members of Parliament. There were just not enough leaders in the community to meet the demands of both the private sector and the public service.

After my last Executive Council meeting, I was heartened to see Monsignor Spraggon back that evening, looking fit and well. He had been on extended sick leave at home, but promised to return in time to see me off. Sadly, this was not to be. Ten days later, I had just returned to my office from the weekly briefing at HQBFFI when Father Monaghan came in, so overwrought that he could barely speak. It transpired that Monsignor had died just a few minutes before of a burst aorta. Mavis took Father Monaghan through to the small drawing room while I telephoned the headquarters of the Mill Hill Fathers in London. Thanks to the satellite dish, I got through to the Superior General, Bishop de Wit, immediately. He promised to tell Daniel's family and without a moment's hesitation said that he would come down for the funeral. He caught the first available aircraft and arrived in my office with Daniel's nephew, Edward Spraggon, six days later. A striking figure of a man, 6ft 7in tall, the Superior General spoke excellent English but with a strong Dutch accent and in a deep resonant voice that seemed to come all the way up from his boots. He gave a most moving address at Monsignor's funeral the next day, 3 October, which happened to be Polling Day. He took as his theme the names of HM ships on the hillside across the harbour, which he had seen from the windows of Monsignor's house, and used the name of HMS *Endurance* to illustrate one of Daniel's greatest characteristics. We walked together behind the hearse to the cemetery, where Monsignor had always wanted to be buried. For once the wind was not blowing on that bleak hillside and all was calm and serene, which was doubly welcome because we attended another funeral that afternoon. Poor Doug Goodwin had died suddenly of a heart attack shortly after we had visited him on Great Island. This time the service was in Christ Church Cathedral, but the burial was in the same place – we had only the one cemetery.

Under the new Constitution, the Falkland Islands were divided into two constituencies, Stanley and Camp, each of which returned four elected members. The Stanley election results were announced that evening: John Cheek was the only outgoing candidate to be re-elected and Lewis Clifton, Charles Keenleyside and Norma

Edwards became councillors for the first time, Lewis obtaining a record majority. The four successful camp candidates were Tim and Tony Blake, who were re-elected, and Robin Lee and Eric Goss, who had not stood for election before. The first Legislative Council under the new Constitution was convened for 8 October, for the purpose of electing three of their members to Executive Council. The three elected were Tony Blake, Lewis Clifton and Charles Keenleyside. Immediately afterwards, the officials (myself, the Chief Executive and the Financial Secretary) withdrew and the elected members chose John Cheek and Lewis Clifton to represent them at the forthcoming session of the United Nations. Councillors then joined us at Government House and we opened Simon Winchester's bottle of champagne to celebrate the reversion of my title to Governor. Five days later, we left the Islands.

The night before our departure, the FIG conferred upon me the freedom of Stanley. The ceremony was held in the Town Hall, before a large crowd of friends and colleagues with whom we had shared so many experiences in that same building, from my swearing-in through May Queen and fancy dress balls, darts matches and weddings to General Garcia, military concerts and Margaret Thatcher. It was a signal honour for me to receive the freedom of Stanley, and a gratifying way for us to end almost six years in the Islands.

Next day, Don drove us out of Government House in the red taxi for the last time. A small crowd stopped us at the cattle grid to give Mavis a bunch of daffodils. We were stopped again at Victory Green and again at Stanley House, where the schoolchildren had gathered to present us with an album of their own drawings depicting our departure. The crowds were so dense along Ross Road that from thereon we had to walk. The Girls Brigade were out in strength, smart and bright and perky as ever. Before I inspected the military guard of honour, we walked up the path to Jubilee Villas to say goodbye to Vi Bonner, now badly crippled with arthritis and unable to move beyond her doorstep. The 1st Battalion, Light Infantry, were on parade with their buglers and in their best greens. Next to them were detachments of Gurkha engineers, the RAF and the Royal Marines. As we approached the public jetty, I wondered whether its battered piles would take the weight of all the people who were now standing upon it. We moved slowly down the line shaking hands with Islanders and expatriates, civilians and military, until we reached the jetty-head. There stood a detachment of the FIDF, my diplomatic colleagues and our Government House staff (all except Nanny, who watched from Philomel Hill because she was too upset to come to the jetty). For the first time since the war, we boarded the *Forrest*.

Sailing slowly up the harbour, Nut Goodwin was at the helm, but it was Jack Sollis that I could see. The FIDF fired a seventeen-gun salute as we passed Victory Green and FIGAS showed that they could fly as neat a formation with two Islanders as the RAF did with their Phantoms. Nut took us on a broad sweep of Port Stanley before coming alongside the RFA *Sir Geraint*. We were blessed with calm weather and had no trouble transferring to the larger ship, where the new Master, Jeremy Carew, was waiting to greet us. Preceded by HMS *Protector* and followed by the *Forrest*, we were steaming slowly through the Narrows when two Phantoms appeared from nowhere at mast height, stood on their tails, turned on after-burners and went vertically upwards. The noise made the eardrums vibrate. It was perfect timing and a spectacular way to see us off. I looked for our friendly dolphins, but not surprisingly they were nowhere to be seen. Out in Port William, the primary schoolchildren were assembled on the deck of the *Black Pig* and, as we sailed past, they unfurled a banner giving me the best accolade of all. The appellation 'Ché' is normally reserved for true Islander-born kelpers, meaning 'one of us'. In bold letters, the banner read 'THANKS CHÉ'.

Notes

1. Sadly, there the matter rests. More substantial ventures have kept Bryan Griffiths occupied elsewhere in the world and the brochure has yet to be printed.

2. See page 169.

3. Shackleton had sailed from Britain at the outbreak of the First World War in 1914 and had been out of touch with the outside world for almost two years.

4. A Swedish tracked vehicle used by the army for cross-country terrain.

5. Mr Foulkes was the Labour Party's representative at the opening of the airport.

6. Tragically, Jean Dobbyns died of a heart attack in 1988, leaving Tim on the farm on his own.

7. Robin eventually got it repaired, but not until 1988.

Postscript

Mavis and I returned to the Falkland Islands in 1989 and again in 1990. We found dramatic changes. Most strikingly, Falkland Islands Government revenue had soared from six million to forty-two million pounds a year and the number of farms had increased from sixty-two to eighty-four.

The great leap in government revenue was a direct result of the declaration of a 150-mile fishing zone round the Falkland Islands. Loligo and illex are now words heard as frequently in Stanley as wether or hogget. They are the two species of squid found in Falklands' waters and they have attracted fishing fleets from all over the world. By prudent husbandry, the Islands have always managed to balance their recurrent budget; now, thanks to fishing licence fees, they have been able to undertake an ambitious development programme. Defence costs remain the only burden on the British taxpayer.

The number of farms has increased because more of the larger ones have been split up or have divested themselves of smaller chunks. 1991 saw the final demise of the absentee landlord with the purchase by government of the last of the farms owned by the Falkland Islands Company: North Arm, Goose Green, Walker Creek and Fitzroy. Virtually all the farmland in the Islands is now owned and occupied by Islanders. The government may offer the ex-FIC farms for further subdivision, though present indications are that there would be few takers. The policy of splitting up the larger farms, which has been followed successfully since 1980, has probably satisfied demand for the time being, and the government may prefer to run these farms as they stand, through either a private company established for the purpose or a farming co-operative. There will always be a need for a few large farms because not all kelpers want the responsibility of running their own. The large farms will also remain invaluable training ground for new farmers.

Despite the lowest wool prices for many years, great progress has been made in the subdivisions. Every penny of profit has been ploughed back into the farms and, in almost every case, the size of the wool-clip and the number of sheep have increased.

The increase in the human population has been less dramatic, owing to the chronic shortage of housing; but many houses are now being built and growth is expected to accelerate over the next decade. Nevertheless, more houses will be needed for many years to come, and there will be more jobs to fill than people to fill them.

We were, of course, delighted to see the new hospital (despite its hideous blue roof) and the Sir Jack Hayward sheltered accommodation for the elderly. Already, however, with 4,000 seamen in the vicinity at the height of the season, there is a shortage of beds. We were also glad to see the new swimming baths and the long overdue resurfacing of Stanley roads.

Throughout the Islands, we sensed a feeling of buoyancy and optimism that was absent in 1985. The very presence of Mount Pleasant Airport has created a sense of permanence and security and the wealth from fishing has provided hitherto undreamt-of opportunities, which the kelpers themselves have been quick to seize. Costly mistakes have been made, but they are learning fast; at the same time, they are losing neither their heads nor their roots.

On our last camp trip, overland from Long Island to Stanley, one of the new farmers, Neil Watson, was driving us to the boundary of his farm. As we reached the highest point on the track, we stopped and surveyed the majestic sweep of Berkeley Sound behind us. There were nine trawlers and two reefers riding at anchor. Neil's farm ran from where we stood along the shore towards Green Patch. Nodding in the direction of the ships, Neil said, 'The squid may come and go, but this land will last forever.' Then, stretching out his arms to embrace the farm beneath, he added with a big smile, 'And this is all mine!'

How do we ensure that it remains all his? Above all, we must stand firm on sovereignty. We must never again lead the Argentines to believe that, if they push hard enough, we will give in. Before 1982, the Islanders suffered from the neglect of successive British governments. They caused no trouble, therefore they were ignored. If they were considered at all, it was in the context of British interests in South America, where their very existence was an irritating anachronism. British interests would be best served, thought some, by handing over the Islands to Argentina. It was a wishful step from there to think that this would also be in the Islanders' best interests. Let us not delude ourselves: we shall never persuade them that their best interests lie with Argentina. If we believe in the principle of self-determination, we must accept that the Islanders will never willingly agree to becoming Argentine. If a future British government decides it cannot afford to defend the Falkland Islands, it will have to impose a settlement upon the Islanders and renounce the principle of self-determination. In that event, the sacrifice of British lives in 1982 and British money and effort since will have been in vain.

There is, however, a wider dimension. Sea communications are still of vital importance to the West. The futures of Central America and South Africa are uncertain. South America is volatile. The traditional trade routes through the Panama Canal and round the Cape of Good Hope could be put at risk; but the Cape Horn route is safe as long as the Falklands remain in British hands.

There is also a wider economic dimension. We have already seen what riches have been discovered in the waters around the Falkland Islands. We do not know what riches may await us under the seabed. Nobody has yet drilled for oil, but the indications are promising enough for interest to be shown in further seismic surveys.

The strategic significance of the Islands is even more apparent when one looks south. Interest is awakening in the last great undeveloped continent, Antarctica. Whether mankind decides to exploit it or protect it, Britain has an important role to play, a role that is helped by our having a permanent presence in the South Atlantic. It is therefore in Britain's own interests to continue to hold the Falkland Islands.

R.M.H.
Sunningdale
1992

Abbreviations

APC	Armoured Personnel carrier
ARA	Armada Republica Argentina (Republic of Argentina Navy)
BAS	British Antarctic Survey
BAT	British Antarctic Territory
BBC	British Broadcasting Corporation
BFBS	British Forces Broadcasting Service
BEM	British Empire Medal
BFFI	British Forces Falkland Islands
BMH	British Military Hospital
CB	Order of the Bath (Companion)
CBFFI	Commander, British Forces Falkland Islands.
CMG	Order of St Michael and St George (Companion)
CSE	Combined Services Entertainment
DIY	Do-It-Yourself
DOBOPS	Director, Borneo Operations
DPW	Director of Public Works
DSM	Distinguished Service Medal
EEZ	Exclusive Economic Zone
ENSA	Entertainments National Service Association
ESRO	European Space Research Organisation
FAC	Forward Air Commander
FAO	Food and Agricultural Organisation of the United Nations
FCO	Foreign and Commonwealth Office
FIBS	Falkland Islands Broadcasting Service
FIC	Falkland Islands Company
FIDC	Falkland Islands Development Corporation
FIDF	Falkland Islands Defence Force
FIDS	Falkland Islands Dependencies Survey
FIG	Falkland Islands Government
FIGAS	Falkland Islands Government Air Service
FIGO	Falkland Islands Government Office (London)
FIPASS	Falklands Intermediate Port and Storage System
FIPZ	Falkland Islands Protection Zone
FO	Foreign Office
GH	Government House
HF	High Frequency
HMG	Her Majesty's Government

ABBREVIATIONS

HMS	Her Majesty's Ship
HMSO	Her Majesty's Stationery Office
IRA	Irish Republican Army
ITN	International Television News
JCB	John C. Bamford, the manufacturers of a popular mechanical digger
JRC	Joint Rehabilitation Committee
JSE	Joint Services Expedition
KEMH	King Edward Memorial Hospital, Stanley
KGB	The Russian intelligence service
LADE	Lineas Aereas de Estado
LMA	Laing, Mowlem, Amey Roadstone Corporation
MBE	Order of the British Empire (Member)
MFA	Ministry of Foreign Affairs (Argentina)
MOD	Ministry of Defence
MP	Member of Parliament
NAAFI	Navy, Army and Air Force Institute
NCO	Non-Commissioned Officer
OBE	Order of the British Empire (Officer)
ODA	Overseas Development Administration
POMA	Petty Officer Medical Assistant
PSA	Property Services Agency
PUS	Permanent Under-Secretary
PWD	Public Works Department
RAF	Royal Air Force
RAS	Replenishment At Sea
REME	Royal Electrical and Mechanical Engineers
RFA	Royal Fleet Auxiliary
RMS	Royal Mail Ship
RN	Royal Navy
RNVR	Royal Navy Volunteer Reserve
Ro-Ro	Roll On, Roll Off
RRS	Royal Research Ship
RSL	Returned Servicemens League (of Australia)
R/T	Radio Telephone
SNOFI	Senior Naval Officer, Falkland Islands
SOA	Sheep Owners Association
SRAFOFI	Senior RAF Officer, Falkland Islands
SS	Steam Ship
STUFT	Ships Taken Up From Trade
UKMIS	United Kingdom Mission, New York
VIP	Very Important Person
WRNS	Womens Royal Naval Service
YPF	Yacimientos Petroliferos Fiscales – the Argentine National Oil Corporation

Index

INDEX